O'C

O'CONNELL

The Life of Daniel O'Connell

1775–1847

Oliver MacDonagh

WEIDENFELD AND NICOLSON

London

George Weidenfeld and Nicolson Ltd
91 Clapham High Street, London SW4 7TA

ISBN 0 297 82017 6

Printed and bound in Great Britain by
Butler & Tanner Ltd, Frome and London

Contents

CONTENTS

BOOK II

Preface

This volume brings together my books *The Hereditary Bondsman: Daniel O'Connell 1775–1829* and *The Emancipist: Daniel O'Connell 1830–47*, which described, respectively, the first and second halves of O'Connell's tumultuous career.

Down to the achievement of Catholic Emancipation in 1829, O'Connell was pre-eminently a barrister-agitator, a political outsider who was forced to operate extra-murally. From 1830 on he was a fully professional popular politician – perhaps the first of his line – a leading British as well as Irish liberal, a first-rank member of the House of Commons, and the main sustainer of the whigs in office. Thus the later part of his career was inevitably the more 'public'. It was also the more complex. *The Hereditary Bondsman* was really a simple story of a single supreme achievement. *The Emancipist* tried to describe a lengthier and more arduous ascent, in which the mountaineer could give a name to, but never clearly see, the summit at which he aimed. None the less, it was a single-purposed, closely-integrated life which was being spanned. For all the heterogeneity and variety of their accidents, the substance of O'Connell's character and principles were remarkably invariable. In this respect, the joining of the two parts of a life-long undertaking is peculiarly appropriate.

The combined volume is, like its constituents, essentially biographical. But the nature of the subject and his circumstances take us far beyond the person in himself. The life of O'Connell was, in certain senses, more than one man's life. He was a very extraordinary individual who did many extraordinary things and he underwent a much grander and more varied range of the everyday experiences than most of us. But it is not for this reason that we should regard him as 'larger' than himself. It is rather that he was, in part, the faithful reflector and, in part, the actual shaper, of the emergent Irish nationalist Catholic culture. O'Connell's own history is a vital element in the history of this development. As Sean Ó Faoláin put the point, with magnificent extravagance, 'he was the greatest of all Irish realists who knew that if he could but once

vii

define, he would thereby create. He did define, and he did create. He thought a democracy and it rose. He defined himself, and his people became him.' A Heidelberg horseboy once put it more simply. When a traveller asked him whom he thought O'Connell was, he answered, 'The man who discovered Ireland.'

'Discovery' may seem a word ill-suited to O'Connell, most of whose ideology was derivative and whose career was strewn with abandoned initiatives. Yet he was perhaps the greatest innovator in modern democratic politics, as well as the originator of almost all the basic strategies of modern Anglo-Irish constitutional relations. Faced with the problems (and opportunities) of turning the deeply aggrieved from their endemic violence; of concentrating, and deploying purposefully, the force inherent in their teeming numbers; of turning to his own account the established parliamentary and legal systems; and of exploiting the new levels of literacy and communications, he became, perforce, a tireless political experimenter and gadgeteer. Over decades of trial and error, he worked out new programmes of public affairs, and of mass organization and mobilization, which were to have universal application. Simultaneously, he developed a methodology peculiarly appropriate to colonial counter-attack, in situations where violence was eschewed and the imperialist power a constitutional government. Well might Lecky acknowledge 'the splendour and originality of the genius' which could devise such things. But the very magnitude and permanence of this achievement adds another supra-personal dimension to the biography.

I have provided references for all direct quotations; more general attributions may be found in the Bibliographical Note; and Biographical Notes are also supplied to furnish additional information on individuals.

In the Preface to the original books, I acknowledged but a small portion of the debts I owed to others. My 'creditors' were very numerous: I could thank only the chief among them. Now I reduce the list once more, to the handful whose aid was absolutely indispensable to the enterprise. Accordingly, I acknowledge with the deepest gratitude the help of Professor M. R. O'Connell, whose magisterial new collection of the O'Connell correspondence provided the foundation for my work, of Mrs Pamela Crichton and Mrs Beverly Gallina, who have served me stintlessly through half-a-dozen campaigns of book-making – for writing history, like war, is hell; and of my wife, ever my inspirer.

Canberra, February 1990   O.MacD.

BOOK I

Mise-en-Scène

Most of the old biographies of O'Connell began by depicting 'the O'Connell country'. This more or less coincided with the baronies of Iveragh and South Dunkerron (generally spoken of simply as 'Iveragh' by the O'Connells), the western portion of the main peninsula of Kerry, which runs south-west to the Atlantic from the Kenmare-Killorglin line. There was good reason for such an opening. Iveragh is matchless for its strange variety of weather, seascape, headland, bay, mountain, rock, torrent, lake and valley. O'Connell himself once struggled bravely to convey its 'awful beauty' through the swathes of contemporary prose. In 1838 he wrote to W. S. Landor,

> Would that I had you here . . . I could show you at noontide – when the stern south-wester had blown long and rudely – the mountain waves coming in from the illimitable ocean in majestic succession, expending their gigantic force, and throwing up stupendous masses of foam, against the more gigantic mountain cliffs that fence . . . my native spot . . . or, were you with me amidst the Alpine scenery that surrounds my humble abode, listening to the eternal roar of mountain torrent as it bounds through rocky defiles, I would venture to tell you how I was born within the sound of the everlasting waves . . .
>
> Perhaps, if I could show you the calm and exquisite beauty of these capacious bays and mountain promontories, softened in the pale moonlight which shines this lovely evening, when all which during the day was grand and terrific has become calm and serene in the silent tranquillity of the night – perhaps you would admit that the man who has been so often called a ferocious demagogue, is, in truth, a gentle lover of Nature . . .[1]

It was standard form to present Iveragh as symbolic of O'Connell himself. The storms and calms, thunder and quiet, steep falls and level sands of south-west Kerry were taken to epitomize not only his popular oratory but also the range and changeability of his disposition. Even for his oratory, the symbolism was not especially apt. The equally hackneyed metaphor of O'Connell playing on an audience as on an instrument was closer to the truth. At least, it

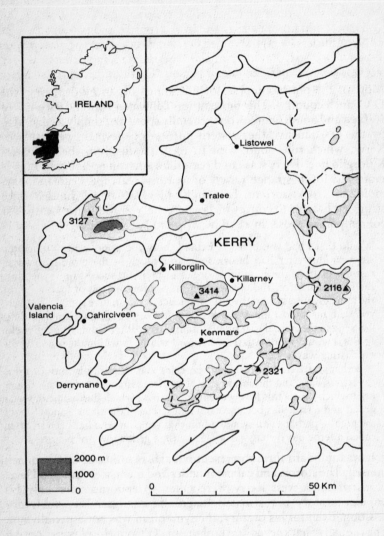

Map 1.   County Kerry

allowed for the orator selecting his own pitch and for the interaction between demagogue and crowd. But to categorize O'Connell as volatile, or swinging between extremes of mood and conduct – and the image of Iveragh was meant to convey just this – was quite misleading. He was an extraordinarily resilient being, but steadfast in his resilience; and his life was singularly purposive and patterned.

None the less Iveragh stamped O'Connell deeply. As he played upon his audience, so it played upon him. This is not to imply that he was an *extraordinarily* impressionable person. Quite an ordinary share of sensitivity was enough. For Iveragh is one of the more memorable settings of the world. Apart from the dreamlike succession of dramatic terrain and ocean vista, it is hauntingly beautiful in light and sound. Cloud, massive, shredded or scattered puffball; skies, low and leaden, washed blue, patching cobalt or milky pale; land, grey, green, dun and chocolate, broken by heather and yellow furze – the shades deepening and lightening almost momentarily – paint the mind. Seas breaking riotously or metronomically, streams in tumult or steady glide, rain stealthy or imperative, and wind and the calls of gulls or solitary curlews provide accompaniment. O'Connell was deeply responsive to this incomparable physical, chromatic and aural whole. His vacations in Iveragh, after he grew to manhood, were literally recreative: they restored his harmony. It was not merely a matter of being in tune again with an extraordinary environment, or of the revivification of a sense of ownership of such natural beauty, but also a sort of ratification of his own identity.

O'Connell himself specifically explained his life of political agitation as a response to his native countryside: 'the loveliness as well as the dreariness of the ocean and Alpine scenes' engendered in him, he claimed, 'a greater ardour to promote the good of man, in his overwhelming admiration of the mighty works of God.'[2] This was far-fetched, even if some wandering connexion between feelings of reverence and feelings of altruism may seem plausible enough.

But there was nothing vague or shallow about O'Connell's rooting himself, psychologically, in Iveragh. In all senses it provided the ground for his absolute assurance about his own identity. The point is important. The romantic type of nationalism which was to challenge O'Connell's formulation – that stemming from the Young Ireland movement of the 1840s – centred upon the question, 'Who am I?' For O'Connell this was never a question; if it were, the answer would have been quite self-evident. Being Irish was merely being himself; and totally assured and at ease in his national identity, he could extend this identity large-heartedly to all the inhabitants of his island. Various elements went into the making of such poise. But first and perhaps even foremost was his sense of fitting into his own land and in particular into his own wild square of Kerry.

O'Connell's intense sense of location was more than topographical. The O'Connells had been a minor but persistent force in their part of Kerry for at least two centuries. As wardens for the MacCarthy Mórs they had enjoyed the hereditary custodianship of a castle. Even after the Cromwellian and Williamite débâcles, they – rarely among Catholic proprietors – retained possession of some land. Aptly enough in the light of O'Connell's career to come, the law's quirks had favoured them in this. They also maintained a profitable French connexion, a trade in priests and soldiers as well as brandy, silks and other luxurious contraband, throughout the eighteenth century. All of this, all their capacity to survive and even to advance as small gentry, depended more or less upon their geography. No part of Ireland was less accessible or freer of state surveillance than mountainous, roadless Iveragh. No strip of coast was more contorted or indented, richer in small coves and beaches, safer from customs and naval vigilance than the run from Kenmare to Carragh (now Waterville). No peninsula in the land was better placed for a traffic with Brittany.

The O'Connells had never been pressed down into mere peasantry because they had recognized and exploited the natural advantages of their environment. 'We have peace in these glens,' said O'Connell's uncle, Maurice (generally known as Hunting Cap), to an antiquarian, Charles Smyth, seeking information on Kerry in 1753, 'and amid their seclusion enjoy a respite from persecution: we can still in these solitudes profess the beloved faith of our fathers . . . but if you make mention of me or mine, these seaside solitudes will no longer yield us an asylum. The *Sassenagh* will scale the mountains of Darrynane, and we too shall be driven out upon the world without house or home.'[3] Isolation was not, however, in itself enough to guarantee security. Even the poor-lands of West Kerry attracted a scatter of planters in the Cromwellian settlement; and this petty Ascendancy was gradually reinforced by conforming Catholics. The eighteenth-century O'Connells (epitomized by Hunting Cap) accommodated themselves effectively to the superior caste. As thoroughly organized and business-like smugglers, they supplied the local Anglican gentry regularly with contraband. This rendered them extremely useful. It even purchased them practical immunity from the law. Moreover, Kerry was too wild and broken a terrain to be easily amenable to anglicization. Something of the old clan system survived, and families like the O'Connells retained considerable power over their immediate followers and dependants. Thus they could participate, even if only upon a Lilliputian scale, in a form of 'indirect rule' which was extremely helpful to the authorities. The order and quiescence which they could instil in their own territory was a tacit *quid pro quo* for their freedom from religious persecution. Finally, both the paucity of the Kerry upper class and their intermarriages led to a strong sense of local solidarity which, to some extent, transcended even the religious boundaries. Prudential conversions to the established church helped to blur the distinction. They could also help more directly. A conforming cousin of Hunting Cap's, Hugh Falvey, saved some of the O'Connell property on several occasions by fictitious or collusive legal actions.

Of course, good relations with the immediate controllers of their destinies had to be paid for by a subservient mien and some political pandering. Maurice O'Connell's reply to the antiquarian Smyth reveals the characteristic Catholic cringe, the characteristic shrinking from the master's eye, of the penal era. To some extent, this was deceptive. As with the speeches of Thady Quirk, the 'faithful steward' in Edgeworth's *Castle Rackrent*, sly self-parody and a not-entirely-concealed resentment may be read into Hunting Cap's words. Irony has always been a defence of the colonized. Certainly, Hunting Cap would never countenance opposition to the Irish Administration. Certainly, he would curry favour with Dublin Castle when he could. But there is abundant evidence of his hidden anger at the systematic abasement of Irish Catholics. He was fully sensitive to the contempt and injustice of the Ascendancy. It was not to Irish Protestants that he looked for relief from his legal disabilities but to British cabinets. He was unquestionably a loyalist but it was to the British, rather than to the Irish, Crown that he was loyal.

Yet covert hostility was only one facet of a complex attitude to the Ascendancy; and down to the 1780s at least, it was of small practical importance. Normally, the Catholic well-to-do of the peninsula lived in a tolerably comfortable little system of limited mutual support, civil relations and cross-favours with their Protestant counterparts. Sectarian suspicion and dislike, and the vaunting of superiority or resentment of inferiority, were generally subordinated to the business of ordinary living. It is important to remember that the locale which produced this special type of relationship cradled O'Connell no less than his uncle, Hunting Cap. O'Connell was reared in much the same

Iveragh as Maurice – but not quite the same, for their boyhoods were separated by almost fifty years, and this made a certain difference. All the traditional elements of the Kerry Catholic's bearing towards the privileged are to be found in O'Connell, too. But their relative weight and emphasis had changed significantly over the half century.

The O'Connells were, then, decidedly favoured by their location at the end of a poor and remote peninsula. The comparative strength, numbers and wealth of better-off Catholics in Iveragh derived largely from the isolation and lack of 'development' of the region. No family did better out of these conditions than the O'Connells. Their survival and even slow advance, economically and socially, after 1700 is testimony of their extraordinary capacity to turn their geographical advantages to good account. The same forces tended to produce in them a curious historical cast of mind. On the one hand, the very fact of survival in their ancient territories engendered a sense of continuity, even of immemorial possession. This naturally reinforced the feeling that they were in their proper or ordained situation in the world. On the other hand, their furtive and precarious hold upon their hereditary lands gave them a degenerative view of history. Inevitably they looked back resentfully to the supposed golden era in which they had been masters in their own place. Moreover, the tenacious O'Connells could remember that they had lost one branch, expelled across the Shannon to co. Clare, and that their collateral, Maurice O'Connell of Caherbarnagh, had died on the roadside on his journey northwards. But the sense of continuity, which stretched back in family annals at least to the Hugh O'Connell commissioned by Edward III in 1337 to reduce his neighbourhood to order, and the sense of discontinuity, located in the cataclysms of 1649 and 1691, could join hands. Each induced the bitterest resentment of the fallen state of the native aristocracy. When at the Clare election of 1828 the tory candidate, Vesey Fitzgerald, spoke *de haut en bas*, though kindly, about his opponent, O'Connell rounded upon him fiercely with 'this man, in my native land – the land of my ancestors – where my forefathers were for centuries the Chieftains of the land, and the friends of her people, makes it a species of kindness that he honours me with his patronage. I treat with disdain and contempt the condescension of such patronage.'[4] This epitomized the O'Connell image of the past. The ferocity sprang from a consciousness of degradation in one's native spot.

CHAPTER 1

Growing Up

1775-93

I

To specify place and time, Daniel O'Connell was born in a
cottage close to Carhen, near Cahirciveen, on 6 August 1775.
Carhen was a farmhouse, moderate in size and abutted by small
farm buildings. But its location, on the banks of an estuary, and facing
low mountains upon the opposite shore, was open, spacious and
dramatic. Carhen and the surrounding land was one of several pieces
of O'Connell property which the family was able to retain by virtue of
leases pre-dating 1691; and as such, it had passed to Morgan, Daniel's
father, one of the older of the twenty-two children of Donal Mór and
Máire ni Duibh O'Connell. Morgan, like his eldest brother, Hunting,
Cap, combined the occupations of grazier, merchant and smuggler.
But his operations were on a much smaller scale, and indeed he often
acted as Hunting Cap's agent or junior partner. Nor did he acquire
extensive new land or set up in manufactures, such as tanning or salt-
making, after Hunting Cap's fashion. Like Hunting Cap, he married
into a Catholic family, of similar rank, fate and fortune to his own. His
wife, Catherine O'Mullane, belonged to a small landowning family in
north-west Cork. But whereas Hunting Cap was childless, Morgan
and Catherine had ten children; and Daniel was the first of the long
line, as well as the eldest boy, of the next generation of O'Connells.
This conjunction was to be crucial in O'Connell's career.

Partly because it was customary in Gaelic society but perhaps also
because of the pressure upon space in a modest middle-class home
where servants and followers were numerous and children arrived
with almost annual regularity, O'Connell was fostered-out in infancy
and did not return to Carhen until he was four years old. His surrogate
mother was the wife of a herdsman on Morgan's own land. The home
of his infancy was meagre, an ill-ventilated mud cabin; his earliest
experience that of a poor country child; his only tongue the Irish

language. The herdsman and his wife were, in his eyes, his parents. When, on a visit to Carhen, his father asked him (in Irish, of course) if he had ever eaten mutton before, O'Connell answered, 'Yes . . . My Dad brought in one of Morgan O'Connell's sheep and killed it.'[1] Yet there is no suggestion that such an early childhood had the traumatic consequences which the present century would predict. O'Connell became deeply attached to his true mother and father. The bond with his foster-parents – to be rewarded, according to the conventions of the day, by subsequent favours and support – remained strong; but this implied no division of loyalty or psychological confusion. So far from resenting his own early exile, O'Connell subjected his two eldest sons, Maurice and Morgan, and some at least of his younger children, to the same experience. It was after all the social norm, from which no one anticipated – and perhaps therefore everyone escaped – injurious results. Nor were such familial devices confined to remote Irish peninsulas or the 1770s or 1800s. Readers of Trollope's *Dr Thorne* will recall that in that most English of counties, Barsetshire, Frank Gresham was fostered out to Mrs Scatchard, and in effect 'bonded' to her, in the 1830s.

It scarcely needs saying that fostering-out in the form and for the length of time that O'Connell experienced gave him a profound knowledge of Irish peasant attitudes, needs, aspirations and forms of thought. It was a later commonplace that he could enter into and play masterfully upon the minds of ordinary Irish people, and especially country people. The social system in which he grew up in Iveragh, and the shared experience of inferiority of all the Catholic classes, would have promoted such powers of divination in any case. But to first realize the world in a herdsman's dwelling, and to see it through the eyes of the herdsman and his family, laid bare the secret life of even the very poor. It was, in many ways, the perfect opening lesson for a demagogue.

When O'Connell returned to Carhen, and still more when he later removed to his uncle's home at Derrynane, he left, to some degree, the Gaelic world. Both Hunting Cap and Morgan had dropped the patronymic 'O'. They called themselves 'Connell'. This was a standard mid-eighteenth-century precaution against easy identification as Catholics. But it was of course only in English that the name was, or ever could be, changed. As the alteration indicates, the male O'Connells had become bi-cultural. Irish was their working language with servants, labourers and tenants. But among themselves they spoke, and wrote, in English only. The contrast with their parents and in particular their mother, Máire ní Duibh, was striking. Through-out Kerry she was celebrated as a Gaelic poet and rhetorician; she never moved from the old ways of life. The sea-change between her and her children's generation was beautifully epitomized by a scene at the death-bed of one of her many sons. She was outraged when her daughter-in-law knelt down to pray in silence by the bedside. Instantly, she broke into a torrent of poetic lamentation in Irish. The women all about took up the funeral keening, in counterpoint, as she extemporized with magnificant abandon.

The process of de-Gaelicization was far from complete in Hunting Cap's generation. He himself exercised the traditional sway over his tenants and followers, even to the romantic detail of a crooked-handled knife, *sgian na coise cuime*, as the symbol of his authortity. When, in 1782, contraband was captured at Derrynane,

> Hunting Cap knew the peasants were furious at the capture, and dreaded mischief, so he besought the officer to let him send with him one of his nephews (the O'Sullivans of Couliagh), as otherwise he could not answer for the people. In Captain Butler's presence he handed the crooked knife to his nephew, bidding him escort the officer to the river-bank at Waterville.
>
> Thus singularly guarded, the representative of law and order set out. In passing through the hamlet of Cahirdaniel they noticed lowering looks and hostile gestures, but a sight of the crooked knife caused the peasants to make way. Some distance beyond the village, Captain Butler begged young O'Sullivan to go back, and struck across the high mountain for his home . . . a mob of angry peasants had skirted the other brow from Cahirdaniel. They fell on the officer, routed his men, and beat him to within an inch of his life.[2]

This glimpse of the ancient Celtic world of spells and tribal fealty is matched by Morgan O'Connell's struggles with the Crelaghs, a band of local cattle thieves. They raided his herds; he and his followers assailed them in the mountains; they in turn attacked and almost killed him in revenge. It could have been a story from the Red Branch cycle before the embellishments of folklore.

Moreover, several of the women of Hunting Cap's generation remained totally unanglicized. As late as 1795, his sister Alice mourned her husband in an outburst of Irish poetry as passionate yet formalized as that even of Máire ní Duibh. Indeed the greatest of all such laments in Irish literature was composed by another of Hunting Cap's sisters, Eileen O'Leary, in 1773. Five years before, Hunting Cap had greeted the news of her elopement with the wild Art O'Leary, who was soon to be outlawed and shot, with: 'I am sorry to Learn that our

Sister Nelly has taken a step contrary to the Will of her Parents, but Love will not know or hear reason.'[3] As Gerard Murphy describes the sequel,

> That document [Hunting Cap's letter] is preserved, for it belongs to the Anglo-Irish side of O'Connell tradition. Nelly's own Gaelic version of the incident would have been lost, however, to history, were it not for the retentive memory of Irish-speaking farmers and cottiers in Cork and Kerry. *Mo ghrá go daingean tu*, she said, as in May 1773, some five years after the elopement, she stood beside her outlawed husband's bloodstained corpse,
>
> > *Mo ghrá go daingean tu!*
> > *Lá dá bhfeaca thu,*
> > *Ag ceann tí 'n mharagaidh,*
> > *Thug mo shúil aire dhoit,*
> > *Thug mo chroí taitneamh doit,*
> > *D'éaluíos om anthir leat,*
> > *I bhfad ó bhaile leat:*
> > *Is dom nárbh atuirseach!**
>
> Already in reading those opening lines do we not feel ourselves transported into a different world? – a world in which Nelly is no longer Anglo-Irish Nelly, but Gaelic Eibhlín Dubh, and in which her husband is no longer 'poor Arthur Leary', whose 'violence and ungovernable temper' were disapproved of by his brother-in-law, but Art, son of Conchúr, son of Céatach, son of Luíseach Ó Laoghaire . . . and terror of the Sasanaigh who killed him . . .[4]

O'Connell grew up, then, in a sort of double dualism. Carhen and Derrynane were islands in a still largely Gaelic sea; and for the most part his elders were either bound by practical necessity or committed instinctively to the traditional culture. This had, however, remarkably little effect upon himself. On 7 December 1796 he wrote in his private journal apropos the *Ossian* controversy, which had happened to engage his attention then, 'the names of Ossian's heroes were familiar to my infancy, and long before I had heard of Macpherson or his translation the characters of the poem[s] were mostly known to me.'[5] It was equally characteristic of O'Connell, first, that he should have known the Ossianic legends from his childhood, secondly, that he should have taken them for granted as one might do nursery rhymes, and thirdly that he should have been led to notice them again only through a British literary dispute. O'Connell was ever at ease with, not

---

* You are my beloved for ever! One day that I saw you, At the market-house gable, My eye perceived you, My heart loved you, I eloped from my father with you, Far from home with you: I never repented it.

to say casual about, his Gaelic heritage. He entered smoothly into not only the language but also the thought-forms and private codes of the Iveragh peasantry whenever he was 'home' in later life. But in the larger matters it was Hunting Cap whom he followed, and not his aunts. In fact, O'Connell represented the next stage on in Gaelic disintegration. He needed to employ Irish less than his father or uncles. The old order was weakening in Kerry, even in his adolescence; and his adult life was to be spent in work and places where English was universal. He was, moreover, a deliberate utilitarian about the native language, where Hunting Cap was simply bent upon the common courses of self-security and advancement. When asked in 1833 whether the use of Irish 'was diminishing among our peasantry', O'Connell answered,

> Yes, and I am sufficiently utilitarian not to regret its gradual abandonment. A diversity of tongues is no benefit; it was first imposed on mankind as a curse, at the building of Babel. It would be of vast advantage to mankind if all the inhabitants of the earth spoke the same language. Therefore, although the Irish language is connected with many recollections that twine around the hearts of Irishmen, yet the superior utility of the English tongue, as the medium of all modern communication, is so great, that I can witness without a sigh the gradual disuse of Irish.[6]

Perhaps this credo is not in itself decisive on O'Connell's attitude to Irish. It was, after all, but a single conversational response. But it certainly matched his general approach in manhood. He did speak in Irish occasionally from the platform, though reports of such speeches are few and far between. But even these excursions were 'sufficiently utilitarian'. He spoke in Irish only where he had to do so in order to be understood. The rarity of such performances in a period when there were still extensive monolingual Irish-speaking regions in itself indicates that the prime sources of his support lay elsewhere. Nor did O'Connell ever show interest in the preservation or revival of the Gaelic language or culture, although enthusiasts, both singly and collectively, were already beginning to promote these causes. The work of Peter O'Connell of Clare on an Irish-English dictionary was shown to O'Connell by Peter's nephew in 1824 'expecting that he would call public attention to it'; O'Connell who (according to Eugene O'Curry) 'had no taste for matters of this kind . . . suddenly dismissed his namesake, telling him that his uncle was an old fool to have spent so much of his life on so useless a work.'[7]

This is not to say that O'Connell had no romantic attachments to the past. But his Golden Age lay not in Ossianic Ireland, or in the pre-

Norman or pre-Tudor Gaelic world, but in the early Christian era, and in particular in the sixth and seventh centuries A.D. It was the Island of Saints and Scholars which inflamed his imagination – according to his own account – from very early days: 'my dreamy boyhood dwelt upon imaginary intercourse with those who are dead of yore, and fed its fond fancies upon the ancient and long-faded glories of that land which preserved literature and Christianity when the rest of now civilized Europe was shrouded in the darkness of godless ignorance.'[8] In 1827 he spoke of pre-invasion Ireland as 'a nation famous for its love of learning, its piety, its heroism',[9] and two years later told Bishop James Doyle, 'Ireland seems to me to be the most proper nursery for missionary priests . . . in my day-dreams I revise the brighter period of Irish history when Erin was the hotbed of saints and Science.'[10] All this was a far cry from the Golden Ages of the Irish Revival movements of later in the nineteenth century, which glorified either the pagan Celts or the traditional peasant culture. O'Connell's vision was in fact outward-looking or even imperialistic, at least in the spiritual sense. It was Irish domination, in terms of monasteries and bishoprics, from Lindisfarne to Malmsbury, from Ghent to Angoulême, as far east as Mecklenburg and Vienna and as far south as Lucca and Taranto, which fired his imagination. It was an empire of high and formal, instead of popular and mythic, learning, and positively Christian, not to say positively Catholic, in purpose.

How are we to explain O'Connell's virtual abandonment of his Gaelic 'birthright'? The basic reason for the decline of Irish and the advance of the English language – the two processes are effectively if not necessarily linked – was the desire to survive in the modern world, or better still to improve one's lot. This is why the proportion of monolingual Gaelic speakers in the Irish population declined from 50 per cent to 0.5 per cent in the course of the nineteenth century. It is also why the Catholic *avant garde*, the gentry, merchants and professional men of whom the O'Connells were archetypal, had led the way in this cultural surrender. In mid- and late-eighteenth-century Ireland, social advancement, and even the emergence from a helot condition, depended largely upon the acquisition and use of English. This was generally the case, but it applied with special force to the upper Catholic classes. Not only had they to traffic constantly in the Anglo-Irish polity, but also their striving for some measure of social parity with the local squirarchy and other elites impelled them to enter, if they could, the Anglo-Irish culture. Class instinct reinforced the instinct for survival. For English was, practically speaking, the sole language of administration, law, politics, commerce, money-making and the towns. It was also, almost universally, the language of literacy and letters.

By 1750 the old connexion between Gaelic culture and the aristocratic way of life had been completely broken. The sophisticated court poet had given way to the peasant poet, and the development of Gaelic as a literary language or as a medium of learning had long since been arrested. Side by side with this interchange and petering out, the Irish language had come to be associated more and more with ignorance, indigence, struggle and distress. Hunting Cap and his brothers were merely anticipating by sixty or seventy years, and at a much higher social level, the nineteenth-century drive of the Catholic masses to rid their children of the language of poverty and sub-ordination and replace it by one more materially advantageous.

It may be significant that in O'Connell's family it was women who preserved the Gaelic tradition longest. At least, there are striking instances of its survival among them for a generation after it had been rejected by the men, who had to deal first and most with the greater world. The women still lived largely in their domestic circles; and they had little or no social intercourse with Protestants. In O'Connell's generation, however, even these vestigial remains of Gaelicism seem to have disappeared. His own sisters appear to have been thoroughly anglicized. Nor is there anything to indicate that his wife, Mary, was even capable of speaking Irish. She lived all her life before marriage in a middle-sized town, Tralee, and though the chances may have been against it, a child could certainly have grown up monolingually English-speaking in such a place in the last two decades of the eighteenth century.

Very broadly, then, O'Connell may be said to have belonged to the third anglicized generation upon the male side and to the second such generation upon the female. Yet, equally important, the process of de-Gaelicization was not complete in him: indeed the first language learnt by his two eldest sons was still Irish. He had no doubts – whatever about sentimental regrets – that Irish would and should disappear as a working language. From boyhood his ambitions were projected into political and professional arenas where it could scarcely have a place. On the other hand, he had been thoroughly immersed in infancy in Gaelic milieux. In certain senses, and to a considerable degree, we might even speak of him as their product. It was not merely a matter of spoken language, of folkloric inheritance and of the web of customary life – important though all three were – but also of idiosyncratic thought patterns and modes of understanding and communication. Yeats once described William Carleton as 'the great novelist of Ireland by right of the most Celtic eyes that ever gazed from under the brow of a storyteller'. How much more truly could the equivalent be said of O'Connell in terms of public affairs. No other Irish politician of the first rank stands on a par with him in intuitive sympathy with the native heart and mind; nor can any match him in being totally and unselfconsciously bi-cultural. Even de Valera's self-vaunted insight into 'the aspirations of the Irish people' was often at odds with more than half of the Irish population, while his Gaelicism could never be more than a conscientious artefact. This is not of course to claim any inherent personal superiority for O'Connell. It was the chances of time and place which rendered him, in the fullest sense, a man of two worlds, moving effortlessly about both Gaelic and post-Gaelic Ireland. But it was of crucial importance that this should have been the case. It gave him ease and security in his Irishness, and presented him with a key to mastery of the masses.

II

While still very young – in which year we do not know but possibly as early as 1780 – O'Connell was, in effect, adopted by his uncle, Hunting Cap. Derrynane Abbey then became his home. It was a real break with Carhen. Although Derrynane was scarcely a dozen miles away according to a straight line drawn upon the map, the journey was very difficult across rugged and mountainous terrain.

Derrynane lay, like Carhen, upon the shore of an estuary. But its water prospect was much grander, its opposing mountains much more distant and its inland surroundings much more enclosed. As if to escape attention, not merely was it hidden by high trees and a steep rise of ground upon the landward side but it also 'resolutely turned its back on sea and sunshine, and looked into a walled courtyard'.[11] The air of secretiveness and even gloom which encompassed Derrynane was apt, for the building had been begun by O'Connell's grandfather in the nadir of Irish Catholic fortunes, the 1720s. But this was accompanied by an air of substance and solidity. Derrynane was not a Big House, after the usual eighteenth-century fashion; it was much too small and undesigned for that. None the less it was remarkable in its own neighbourhood as easily the largest and best finished residence, far superior in scale and pretension to such a farmhouse as Carhen. Moreover, no inwardness of aspect or agglomerative ugliness could substract from the magnificence of the southern vista, embracing verdant strip, bone-clean sands, the ruined monastery of the Canons Regular on a spit, a lacework of tiny coves, bays and promontories, the great sweep of the Kenmare river and the wall of the Slieve Miskish mountains far away. This was to be the main home of O'Connell's boyhood. He had passed rapidly from the lowest to the highest level of Kerry Catholic society, with only a brief interval at Carhen.

When O'Connell moved to Derrynane, Hunting Cap was a childless widower in his early fifties and already a landed and commercial magnate, in a modest way. He was also strongly patriarchal and dynastical in temperament, as well as something of a clan chieftain in the old sense. As eldest son himself, he accepted unquestioningly responsibility for the younger members of his family, and not least for the increasingly numerous children of his brother Morgan. He was probably urged in the same direction by another of his brothers, Daniel, then a colonel in the French Army, who was particularly solicitous for the future of his nephews. All this helps to explain Hunting Cap's evident intention that Morgan's eldest son, Daniel, should be his successor. We do not know the exact terms on which he received the boy into his house. But there seems to have been at least a tacit understanding that O'Connell was Hunting Cap's heir-presumptive – the presumption being, in this case, that he would prove himself grave, prudent, industrious and ambitious enough to be worthy of such a destiny. At any rate, it is clear that O'Connell spent his boyhood proper in his uncle's house and under the shadow of great expectations.

The 'adoption' placed an immense burden upon the boy, even if it also spread great possibilities before him. He was, permanently, on trial; he was totally dependent on a patron; his own easy-going father had been replaced by a hard and implacable foster-parent. He grew up in fear and awe; and the spell of Hunting Cap upon him was not altogether broken for over forty years. Hunting Cap was always dominant and often domineering. But it would be wrong to cast him as a tyrant, still less as an ogre, however much this might be suggested by the subservience and even servility which he commanded. For Hunting Cap's authority was innate, as much the product of strength and depth of character as the consequence of wealth and station. In 1794, his brother Daniel (by now forty-nine years old, a count of France and in rank a major-general) whom he had given, out of simple generosity, 300 guineas in the preceding year, wrote to him in these very deferential terms:

I shall not attempt justifying my having spent so large a sum as 150 guineas in the course of one year, but merely by stating that the accomplishing the object I had in view required I should live in the best company and make a decent, tho' modest, appearance. On that line I have walked those twelve months, and trust you will approve of it. Sincerity, that the greatest comfort of my life will always be to merit your approbation. The part you have ever acted towards me being that of a kind Parent, I consider myself as much bound from duty as I am led from inclination to lay my heart and actions before you on every occasion.[12]

This should place what might seem the nervous obsequiousness of O'Connell's later dealings with Hunting Cap in fair perspective. It also reveals the paradoxical willingness of one who was rightly notorious as a tight-fisted – in fact, positively grasping – accumulator, to part with money. We should never forget that, however sourly, Hunting Cap eventually did meet every account during the long years of O'Connell's education. This expenditure alone cost him well over £1,000.

Hunting Cap determined that O'Connell's education should begin early, and he apparently arranged for him to be tutored locally. According to his own account, O'Connell proved to be both precocious and competitive. At the age of four (he told W. J. O'Neill Daunt much later), 'I learned the alphabet in an hour. I was, in childhood, remarkably quick and persevering. My childish propensity to idleness was overcome by the fear of disgrace: I desired to excel, and could not brook the idea of being inferior to others.'[13] Three stories of his early boyhood are suggestive. Two relate to 1784, when he was nine years old. First, at a dinner-table discussion of current Irish politics Charlemont was generally denounced and Flood generally lauded, but the company was hotly divided on Grattan's recent conduct. O'Connell, naturally silent among the contesting adults, seemed also quite abstracted; but when one of the women asked him suddenly, 'What ails you, Dan? – what are you thinking of?' 'I'll make a stir in the world yet', he answered. Secondly, it was in 1784 that he was given what became the favourite book of his boyhood, Cook's *Voyages*. Much later he recalled the hours spent half-hidden in one of the recessed window seats which flanked the main door of Derrynane, poring over the *Voyages* and tracing their successive references with his finger on the map. 'I used to run away and take my book to the window, ... there I used to sit with my legs crossed, tailor-like, devouring the adventures of Cook.'[14] He had chosen his reading-place to escape the other children and their calls to play. The third – undated

– glimpse of the small boy at Derrynane reports his fascination with the *Dublin Magazine*'s portraits of contemporary celebrities, most of them the leading Irish politicians of the time. One day, O'Connell told his elders, his picture would appear in the illustrious succession. As it happened, he was right: the *Magazine* published his portrait in 1810.

One can build little upon a handful of random recollections. But, for what it is worth, they indicate solitary, autodidactic and escapist strains scarcely discernible in the later O'Connell. They also hint at elements much more familiar in the customary accounts: ambition, the passion for mastery and the prizing of political, and in particular parliamentary, achievement. For this last trait, the early 1780s were extraordinarily exciting. Ireland was in an unprecedented ferment, and this was popularly presented in a simplistic form, in which an imaginative boy could readily participate. The cult of personality and the romanticization of issues had been unleashed. It was an epoch of apparent heroes and villains in Irish politics, and of apparently noble causes and ignoble resistance to national reform. O'Connell's lifelong glorification of the Patriot 'victory' of 1782 and praise of its 'architect', Henry Grattan, may have had their roots in the consequent childish idealization and choice of sides.

But Derrynane must also have taught him something of the practicalities of Irish politics. Hunting Cap would not have taken 1782 or the Patriots at their face value. His primary objective was Catholic liberation, and the slackening of Britain's control over the Irish Parliament might not prove at all conducive to this end. On the other hand, prudence dictated that one stay on terms with the Ascendancy. O'Connell was seven years of age when in 1782 the family's greatest crisis of the century brought this home to all. When Captain Butler was savagely assaulted after the capture of contraband at Derrynane, a warrant was prepared for the arrest of Hunting Cap, of O'Connell's father, Morgan, and of their cousin, Daniel O'Connell of Tarmons, for having instigated the attack. The repentant Butler himself secretly alerted Hunting Cap to what was afoot; and immediately the enlistment of Kerry Protestant friends and connexions to ward off the danger got under way. The real peril was that the defendants would be refused bail. If this happened, the trial would almost certainly take place in Dublin, with the chance of a conviction there upon a capital charge. But by pulling every string to hand and by engaging as leading counsel the brother-in-law of the powerful John Fitzgibbon, Hunting Cap managed to exercise sufficient influence upon the lord chief justice (whose decision it was) to be granted bail, and with it a hearing at the Tralee assizes. Here, with a grand jury composed largely of O'Connell customers, the bills were immediately dismissed and the charged men triumphantly acquitted. But the crisis had lasted many weeks; and even as a child of seven, O'Connell must have sensed the family's alarm and come to understand something of the tactics necessary for Catholic survival in a still dangerous world. Whatever else, the episode certainly made clear the importance of mutuality in Irish life. This was to become – and remain – central in O'Connell's politics.

O'Connell left Derrynane for boarding school in the summer of 1790, when he was little short of fifteen years of age. Catholic schools had only recently been rendered legal; and the one to which O'Connell went at Reddington (or Ballybrassil) on the Great Island in Cork Harbour may even have been the first such post-penal establishment. It was very small, conducted singlehandedly by the Rev. James Harrington, a Jesuit who had been secularized when the order was suppressed. Although the building was a mere converted farmhouse, Reddington gave O'Connell a new experience of beauty in landscape. The house looked south across an immense harbour to the headlands at its mouth. To the right lay other islands and the roadsteads, often thronged with sails. To the left the harbour crept about until the water was lost to sight between the near and far-off woods. Though each looked out upon the trapped Atlantic, its prospect was very different from Derrynane's; level planes of slate-grey, blue or turquoise sea prevailed, and the innumerable slopes and declivities in distant view were green and gentle. But it was just as heart-stirring and haunting in its way.

Much later O'Connell claimed to have been an assiduous and fearful pupil:

> I was the only boy who wasn't beaten at Harrington's school; I owed this to my attention . . . One day I was idle, and my teacher finding me imperfect in my lesson, threatened to beat me. But I shrank from the indignity, exclaiming, 'Oh, don't beat me for one half hour! If I haven't my lesson by that time, beat me *then*!' The teacher granted me the reprieve, and a lesson, rather a difficult one, was thoroughly learned.[15]

But in 1848 James Roche, who knew several of O'Connell's classmates, remarked that 'if not beaten by the master, he was by the scholars for his unsociability, apparent shyness and preference of study or secluded reflection, to play.' O'Connell's schoolfellows, Roche added, had assured him that he was not 'particularly distinguished amongst them for superior capacity, at that early period'.[16] This tends to confirm the fragments of self-portrait which paint O'Connell as a solitary, reading boy, living in a world of models for emulation. But if he really failed to stand out among the handful of pupils at Harrington's, either the remainder were extraordinarily able boys or he was to leap forward suddenly in his fifteenth year. For when he left the Academy for school in France, he was immediately recognized there as a boy of quite exceptional talent, whose grounding in classics was remarkable.

III

Despite the establishment of regular Catholic schools in Ireland in the 1780s, O'Connell was always destined to finish his secondary education in France. For decades this had been the pattern for boys of his class, and his own uncle, General O'Connell, had long been a prime arranger of the French education of boys from Cork and Kerry. Although Harrington himself was an unusually able man, his single-handed Academy, with a mere dozen pupils, could not compare in quality with the great English Catholic schools upon the Continent.

Evidently it had been decided that O'Connell's brother, Maurice, a year younger than himself, should accompany him to school in France. This would explain why Hunting Cap did not apply to the General to arrange for the boys' education until 21 May 1789, when Daniel was already almost fourteen years of age – the normal age of commencement was thirteen. Four weeks later, the General replied recommending St Omer as the most suitable college but also proposing that the boys enter in the autumn of 1790 rather than 1789. 'Maurice [O'Connell] of Tarmons', he wrote, 'proposes, I believe, to spend next Summer in Ireland, and you can charge him with the care of the two Boys as far as St Omers, where I shall previously make it my business to ensure their admittance.'[17] Hunting Cap concurred, and the boys continued at Harrington's for the period 1789–90.

The General had expressed no concern about the state of France when he wrote in June 1789. Seven months later, however, he was thoroughly alarmed, and advised Hunting Cap strongly not to send the boys abroad 'until tranquillity be more solidly established': not merely did disorder threaten France, but her troubles were likely to spill over into the Austrian Netherlands, where the other major English Catholic colleges were located. 'I shall let you know', the General continued, 'in the month of April or May [1791] my fixed sentiment in the Matter, and if things shu'd not bear a prospect of peace, I would be very much at a loss to point out a proper place to send them to . . . You see, Dear Brother, that it's no easy matter to determine a proper place to send two Children without a Governor.'[18] Again Hunting Cap acquiesced, and the boys remained at Harrington's for yet another year, 1790–1. In fact, the General did not wait until the spring of 1791 to make his final determination but wrote again on 2 September 1790, this time so despairing of what had once been 'the finest country in Europe' as to tell his brother that all plans for a Continental education should be abandoned. 'I think you must lay aside all thoughts of sending our young Nephews over. I know no place either in France or the Low Countries where you can safely send 'em.'[19]

But Hunting Cap was not to be deflected from his purpose. Despite the General's decisive advice, despite the rapidly growing instability of France and its neighbours, despite the disruption of the Irish network of mutual assistance on the Continent, he dispatched the boys at last to the English College at Liège in August 1791. Apparently, the decision was a sudden one. Certainly, the rector at Liège was not forewarned nor was the general (whose position as a French royalist officer close to the Court was in any event becoming desperate) involved in the arrangements. Why was Liège abruptly substituted for St Omer? Possibly because Hunting Cap hoped that, located as it was in an independent and neutral prince-bishopric, the College might escape the coming conflict. It is hard to find any reason beyond his own iron determination for Hunting Cap's decision to send the boys abroad at all at such a stage. But O'Connell was now sixteen years of age: it would soon be too late – if it were not too late already – for him to enter any secondary school.

In fact, O'Connell and his brother *were* rejected as beyond the age for entry when they presented themselves at Liège; and the rector posted them on to Holy Trinity in Louvain (a preparatory college for Louvain University). There they awaited orders from Derrynane to tell them what they should do next. The boys' letters to Hunting Cap never mentioned – let alone complained of – either their difficulties or their fears. He was not the sort of man to whom one confessed weakness. But their experience must have been frightening. Daniel, just sixteen years of age, had been packed off, probably in a hurry and without much funds to spare, to an unknown country, whose language he could not have spoken well, to hosts who had no forewarning of his arrival, and with a younger and still more ignorant boy in tow. At a time when even moderately prudent foreigners were streaming out of France and the Low Countries, the young O'Connells had been pitched there for a two- or three-year sojourn. Only two casual recollections of the journey survive. Forty years later, O'Connell told his son John that his first experience of England was a ducking in the surf as he disembarked from the Irish brig at Dover, and that his first national challenge – by a Frenchman who abused him for England's iniquities on the diligence from Ostend to Liège – was met with this reply, 'Sir, England is not my country. Censure her as much as you please, you cannot offend me. I am an Irishman, and my countrymen have as little reason to love England as yours have – perhaps less.'[20] No anxieties or trepidation were recalled. But boys upon such an adventure at such a time could not possibly have escaped them.

Although the boys had to wait six weeks in Louvain before Hunting Cap's answer reached them, they were fortunate in their enforced staging post. Louvain was an ancient university city, with innumerable Irish connexions. Maurice later told his uncle that they had been received with much kindness at the houses of both the Irish Franciscans and the Irish Dominicans. They did not study at Holy Trinity, where the courses were too advanced, but (again according to Maurice) 'attended the University schools . . . and had recourse to the library of the Dominicans'.[21] We may take this with several grains of salt. Hunting Cap would have been enraged at the thought of their enjoying weeks of idleness on the Continent at his expense. But in fact there was little that they could or would feel inclined to do but sight-see and lark about. On 19 October 1791, Hunting Cap's orders arrived at last. They were to go immediately to St Omer. Thus all the delays and diversions ended with their entering more than two years late the college for which they had been originally intended.

St Omer, founded in the late sixteenth century by the great English Jesuit, Robert Parsons, but since 1762 in the hands of the English secular clergy, epitomized three traditions – Counter-Reformation Catholicism, Renaissance educational theory, and aristocratic and gentry recusancy. Neither O'Connell nor his brother ever adverted to the first in their correspondence: piety was not the sort of subject one discussed with Hunting Cap. For that matter, neither ever wrote a word about people, whether masters, boys, servants or St Omerians, or about the place in which they lived, the college with its three heroic centuries, the charming town or the tamed countryside of Artois.

The second tradition, that of Renaissance pedagogy, was a different

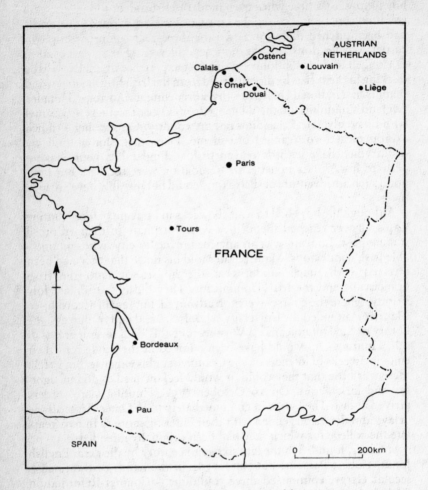

Map 2. O'Connell's continental locations

story. As a school, St Omer remained faithful to its sixteenth-century origin. The basic curriculum consisted primarily of Greek and Latin, and secondarily of English and French (which the boys were obliged to speak); arithmetic and geography were the minor subjects. The gentlemanly accomplishments, which embraced dancing, fencing, music and drawing but also included 'mathematics', were optional.

The aim of such an educational system might not be immediately apparent today. It was – following Cicero's and Quintilian's texts on oratory – designed to produce the complete public man, whose eloquence was based on sound learning and a thorough grasp of the techniques of exposition and persuasion. In practice, the syllabus included declamation, dialectic and dramatic performance; and its climax was the regular study of rhetoric and philosophy. All in all, it was well-tailored for O'Connell's subsequent careers of lawyer, demagogue and tribune. Whether or not St Omer did much to train him directly for these trades, it certainly provided him with a vision and defence of the ideal, and a body of supporting metaphors and images.

O'Connell succeeded at once at St Omer. Three months after his arrival, he reported to Hunting Cap,

> In this college are taught the Latin and Greek authors, French, English and geography, besides lessons. given during recreation hours in music, dancing, fencing and drawing. I have not yet inquired about rhetoric but will do it (please God) as soon as I receive an answer from my uncle [General O'Connell]. We have composed for the second time since I came here. I got second in Latin, Greek and English, and eleventh in French; before the places are read out there is a scene or two of play acted on a small stage, which is in the college, by one of the first four schools (each in its turn); these they call orations, and of them there are eight in the year. Of consequence we compose eight times; there is a whole play acted in the month of August.[22]

He soon advanced to work in which the oratorical element was still more to the front, 'Mignot's harangues, Cicero and Caesar . . . Caesar is given us chiefly to turn into Greek; our Greek authors are Demosthenes, Homer and Xenophon's Anabasis; our French one is Dagaso's speeches.'[23] But well before this elevation, the president of St Omer had marked him out as an extraordinary boy. Soon after the O'Connells reached the college, Hunting Cap had asked the president, Dr Stapylton, for a candid opinion of his nephews, apparently adding the observation that such candour was not ordinarily to be had from headmasters. Stapylton, an English gentleman, administered a delicate rebuke to the rough inquirer, before going on to make a most remarkable prediction.

> You desire to have my candid opinion respecting your nephews and you very properly remark that no habit can be worse than that of the instructors of youth who seek to gratify the parents of those under their care by ascribing to them talents and qualities which they do not really

possess. You add that, being only the uncle of these young men, you can afford to hear the real truth respecting their abilities and deficiencies. It is not my habit to disguise the precise truth in reply to such inquiries as yours; you shall therefore have my opinion with perfect candour.

I begin with the younger, Maurice. His manner and demeanour are quite satisfactory. He is gentlemanly in his conduct and much loved by his fellow-students. He is not deficient in abilities, but he is idle and fond of amusement. I do not think he will answer for any laborious profession, but I will answer for it, he will never be guilty of anything discreditable – at least, such is my firm belief.

With respect to the elder, Daniel, I have but one sentence to write about him, and that is, that I never was so much mistaken in my life as I shall be unless he be destined to make a remarkable figure in society.[24]

Though based upon less than three months' acquaintance, Stapylton's analysis of Maurice's character was masterly. Yet he says nothing of Daniel's except possibly by implication. We can, I think, infer that he thought O'Connell to be ambitious, able and assiduous. We cannot fairly infer that he thought him lacking in Maurice's more attractive qualities, such as gaiety and being 'much loved by his fellow-students'. But the president's 'one sentence' does seem to carry something of that air.

It is difficult to gain any impression of O'Connell's own reactions to St Omer: his letters to Hunting Cap are altogether formal and even stylized. But one wistful observation, 'I had no place to retire to from whence I might write to you',[25] may reflect a boarding-school boy's hopeless longing for solitude. Again, each of O'Connell's letters from St Omer, even the first, dated 3 February 1792, pointed out that the college did not provide the highest range of studies: rhetoric, logic and philosophy. This does not necessarily mean that he himself was pressing to be sent where they might be pursued, for his uncle, the General, had long been an advocate of these subjects for the boys. None the less, O'Connell's persistency seems to provide some *prima facie* evidence of his determination to excel. At any rate, it carried the day. Soon after O'Connell wrote for a second time to Hunting Cap about 'the college of Douai' where the higher syllabus could be followed, although 'French is paid no great attention to there, nay almost totally neglected',[26] an instruction arrived from Derrynane that the boys were to remove there immediately from St Omer.

The departure for Douai, some seventy-five miles inland from St Omer, was as uncomfortably precipitate as each of the boys' earlier journeyings. Leaving St Omer at 5 a.m. on the morning of 20 August 1792, they reached Douai on the same evening: it was no light affair to travel such a distance by diligence. Hunting Cap had simply given the boys their marching orders, leaving them to solve their many difficulties for themselves. They had to borrow their coach money from Stapylton, and further monies from the rector of Douai and from an Irish pupil there, as soon as they reached their destination. For Douai, an ecclesiastical seminary as well as a secondary school, was much more austere than St Omer. 'At St Omer's', wrote O'Connell on 14 September 1792, 'everything was done for the boys, here the boys are obliged to do everything themselves.'[27] Not until they arrived did the O'Connells discover that the pupils were obliged to supply their own furniture. Their first night was spent in a room containing only beds, and they had to borrow several guineas next day to buy mirrors, candlesticks, basins, chairs, desks, cupboards, powdering-tables, knives and forks and similar equipment. Meanwhile, his first stark night at Douai had left O'Connell with 'fits of ague',[28] and he soon departed for the infirmary. Another unpleasant surprise was the meagre servings at dinner. Most boys – those on scholarships excepted – received additional helpings, called 'seconds', at a cost of £3–4 per annum. In this case, O'Connell plucked up enough courage to ask Hunting Cap to pay the extra fee. 'We would be much obliged to you for leave to get them [seconds], but this as you please. I hope, my dear Uncle, that you will not think me troublesome in saying so much on those heads.'[29]

Moreover, Hunting Cap had failed to consider the rhythm of the school year. At Douai the rhetoric and philosophy courses began at Whitsuntide, so that O'Connell had almost a term's leeway to make up. We have no idea how he fared: in fact, all that we can discover about his career at Douai derives from the school account which tells us little more than that he bought a violin, took violin lessons and much frequented the school infirmary. Everything was overshadowed, anyhow, by the growing political crisis. The September massacres of 1792 rightly plunged the college into fear soon after the boys' arrival; and the move to Douai had brought them almost to the war-zone as the Austrians advanced into northern France. The battle of Jemappes was fought so close to Douai on 6 November 1792 that the boys could hear the distant roar of the cannon; and soon afterwards, when they were on a school walk, a waggoner of Dumouriez's army so frightened them by shouting, 'Voilà les jeunes jesuites, les capucins, les récolets!', that they ran headlong back all the way to the college.

It was soon clear that Douai's status as 'the English College' would not preserve it much longer from revolutionary depredation; by the beginning of 1793, those boys who had their parents' permission were being allowed to go home. The O'Connells were in their usual predicament of needing Hunting Cap's sanction for every action, with a six- to eight-week interval between the dispatch of a letter and the receipt of a reply. On 4 January 1793 Maurice sent a panic-stricken appeal to Derrynane. Already, he wrote, they were in danger of being cut off in Douai, where the local revolutionaries were increasingly menacing. 'From above 206 [pupils] . . . there are now not 90, and these decreasing every day.' If Daniel and he should be forced to leave suddenly, 'we will go to London, write immediately, and having been supplied with money by the procurator or Mr Kirwan, will wait until we hear from you.'[30] Their uncle, the General, who had fled France in September 1792, was in London already.

For once the boys had to act on their own initiative, or possibly they were driven to act by the college president. On 21 January 1793, they left by coach for Calais – a two-day journey – in such haste that most of their clothing, to say nothing of their other belongings, was abandoned, to the ultimate benefit of the French Republic. The journey from Douai to Calais was dangerous enough. Louis XVI was guillotined in Paris on the day they left, the war with Great Britain only ten days off. The O'Connells were certainly treated as if they were English, as well as clericalist and reactionary. The carriage was surrounded by republicans and butted by soldiers' rifles in the towns, and the passengers denounced as 'young priests' and 'little aristocrats',[31] despite the tricolour cockades the boys wore in their hats as protective colouring. When they were safe at last upon the packet boat at Calais, they threw the cockades defiantly into the water, to the fury of French fishermen alongside.

> Then two Irishmen joined them on board, full of excitement, as they were just come from Paris. They had even been present at the execution, and they soon produced a handkerchief, horribly stained with red, which they had bribed one of the National Guard to steep for them in the blood of Louis XVI. A passenger asked them how they could have brought themselves to face such a revolting scene. 'For the love of the cause,' was their reply. The two Irishmen were the brothers Sheares . . . afterwards to be executed for complicity in organising the rebellion of 1798.[32]

The whole scene was deeply symbolic. The Sheares and O'Connell stood for opposite Irish reactions to insurrectionary violence. O'Connell was always to separate himself from bloodshed, revolutionary disorder and conspiracy. The experiences of his last months in France had even driven him temporarily onto the right wing.

IV

O'Connell has left us with few contemporary and still less later impressions of his seventeen months in the Austrian Netherlands and France. We can certainly list much that he experienced. The landscape of Brabant, Flanders and Artois, flat, mild, tidily pieced and untouched by oceans, contrasted altogether with his boyhood world. He who had never lived in towns was placed in turn in Liège, Louvain, St Omer and Douai. Each was an ancient provincial centre, redolent of the sixteenth century, with intricately patterned forms of urban and ecclesiastical life. He spent his time abroad in large, regimented institutions, cheek by jowl with many other boys, and speaking an unfamiliar language on most occasions; all this was new. We cannot tell what he made of these strange surroundings and circumstances, apart from one hint that he sighed for solitude and another, that his happiest days on the Continent were the few spent at a country house owned by the college near St Omer.

We are still more in the dark about O'Connell's religious formation. This is curious. After all, his seventeen continental months were spent in great bastions of the English – and in the case of Louvain, also the Irish – Counter-Reformation. Each had its roll of honour, scholars and martyrs. Each had a special ethos of piety, developed over many generations. Yet O'Connell recorded nothing whatever under either head. We cannot assume from his silence that they left no stamp upon him. Eighteenth-century schoolboys rarely wrote about such things, and Hunting Cap himself would have expected a decent reticence. Still, there is nothing in O'Connell's later life to suggest that he was marked significantly by his exposure to the traditions of seminarian gallantry or the simple, severe spirituality of the English colleges. For that matter there is nothing to suggest that he made even one English friend at either St Omer or Douai.

But there is some evidence on O'Connell's reaction to the political turmoil by which he was surrounded in 1791–3. What a chance, to have seen one critical phase of the Revolution at close range! He had reached Ostend soon after Louis XVI's abortive flight to Varennes; he left Calais two days after his execution. In between, O'Connell had breathed the air and felt the interior life of the ancien regime, even while it was being steadily weakened, and crushed in parts, by the revolutionaries. In between, France had gone to war, and Catholicism become aligned with the opposition to the new order. Moreover, in the five months of O'Connell's sojourn at Douai, Anglo-French relations had worsened rapidly. His surroundings, teaching and companions all impelled him towards the counter-revolutionary camp. It is true that O'Connell's mildly Francophile upbringing, and his boyish espousal of 'Grattanism' in Irish politics, told a little the other way. But this was easily outweighed by the grim realities of violence, social upheaval, republicanism and irreligion which pressed upon him in the Netherlands and France – especially as these were mediated by the reactions of the communities in which he lived, and the alarms of his royalist uncle, the General. He said later that when he left France in 1793 he was 'half a Tory'.[33] This was probably a considerable underestimation: 'three-quarters of a reactionary' might have been closer to the mark.

O'Connell was soon to undergo a political sea-change. By 1795 he might fairly be described as radical. Yet his experiences at St Omer and Douai had placed permanent limits upon his radicalism. He had discovered what it meant to be deeply frightened, both as a person and as a member of a group. He had learnt that revolutions can quickly gather an irresistible momentum, and slip beyond rational control and predictable direction. He had come to loathe mob rule and the unleashing of the irrational in politics. Above all, in his last six months in France he had heard almost daily of great carnage, by the guillotine and in war, and this left him with a lasting hatred of bloodshed, as almost the ultimate evil in affairs. It also left him with a lasting dislike of France and a lasting suspicion of French models. All these legacies of his continental schooldays certainly circumscribed and gave peculiar directions to his radicalism.

Yet the most important single effect of O'Connell's French education may well have been the reinforcement of his ambition to be a public man. As we have seen, the educational programme of St Omer and Douai was specifically designed to produce leaders, statesmen and orators – polished men of action, but of constitutional action only. The fundamental metaphor employed by the ancients, from whom this concept of education derived, was that of the vestibule. There the young, by mimic contention and disputation, prepared themselves for the real theatre, the great auditorium of affairs. There, as Cato put it, 'those who are preparing for what is done in the forum, as in the field of battle, may alike learn and previously try their power, by practising in sport.' To this end, boys should also be trained as easy-mannered and accomplished gentlemen. Thus when Stapylton predicted that O'Connell would cut 'a remarkable figure in society' he had a particular type of success in mind – the political. That O'Connell himself was deeply impressed by this teaching is evident from several of his later reflections. An excellent example is the self-programme which he outlined for Hunting Cap's benefit nearly three years after he had fled from Douai.

> I have now two objects to pursue. The one, the attainment of knowledge; the other, the acquisition of all those qualities which constitute the polite gentleman. I am convinced that the former, besides the immediate pleasure which it yields, is calculated to raise me to honours, rank, and fortune: and I know that the latter serves as a general passport or first recommendation. And as for the motives of ambition which you suggest, I assure you no man can possess more of it than I do. I have indeed a glowing and (if I may use the expression) an enthusiastic ambition which converts every toil into a pleasure and every study into an amusement ... Indeed as for my knowledge in the professional line that cannot be discovered for some years to come. But I have time in the interim to prepare myself to appear with greater *éclat* on the grand theatre of the world.[34]

O'Connell's sixteen months in the English Colleges, dedicated to the ideals of Renaissance education, may have only confirmed and explicated his innate tendencies and boyish dreams. But this they certainly did, in providing him with an elaborated programme and a justificatory philosophy for what he proposed to do. By chance, the opportunity for an Irish Catholic boy to become in time 'a public figure' had suddenly opened up while he was still 'composing' for his 'orations' at St Omer. On 18 April 1792 Sir Hercules Langrishe's Act (32 Geo. III c. 21) enabling Catholics to practise as lawyers, and even as junior counsel at the Irish Bar, had received the royal assent.

CHAPTER 2

London

1793–6

I

So far as was practicable, O'Connell and his brother Maurice took up again in England the life of Douai from which they were forced to flee. They had not expected to stay in London. At first, they were meant to return to Kerry with cousins who were also refugees from France. But their uncle, the General, who had now fixed himself in London as the most promising place for finding new military employment, intervened and persuaded Hunting Cap that the boys should continue their education there under his own eye. A fellow Hiberno-French emigré, Chevalier Fagan, accepted them into his 'academy', a sort of crammer's school which was run from Fagan's house in the Strand. The boys saw him periodically for the supervision of their work and the allotment of new tasks and reading; and O'Connell later boarded with him for a time. Their syllabus was little changed by the translation from Douai. On 3 June 1793 O'Connell reported to Hunting Cap,

> We study at present Rhetoric and logic. For the Rhetoric we read and get by heart Cicero's orations, Orationes Collectae, Bossuet's funeral orations and Boileau's art of poetry. The two last are French authors. In Logic we get by heart the Douai College dictates, not being able to find any other book on that subject in this town, I mean any valuable work for there are treatises on logic in English but none with theses, at least, that we could find. Besides, the Douai College dictates are good. We write themes very often . . . [1]

Fagan also groomed the boys in the gentlemanly arts, setting them, as O'Connell wrote, 'a kind of exercise to go through every day for about 20 minutes or half an hour' to improve their 'carriage'.[2]

O'Connell and Maurice had left France so precipitately as to carry with them little more than the clothes in which they stood up: 'we had every single article of wearing apparel to buy.'[3] Probably it was the

General who first doled out Hunting Cap's money to them; but by July 1793 Fagan was acting as their banker. They overspent and were soon in Hunting Cap's black books for some unauthorized expenditure. Having already twice apologized profusely for their foolish and ungrateful conduct, O'Connell abased himself yet again in writing to Hunting Cap on 1 July:

> You have seen by it [a second letter of apology] only a part of that sorrow which I was not able to express as I wished. No one can be more convinced than I am of the justice of your anger against us. You have done everything for us, and we have shown no advantage from it. I shall not, my dear Uncle, take up your time in making promises. That would be childish. I shall only beg of you to be assured of my regret and to reckon on the future.[4]

Maurice fell into much worse trouble later in the year. There are no clues as to the nature of the scrape, but it was serious enough for Hunting Cap to bring his education to a close and recall him to Kerry to put him to some lowly occupation. O'Connell courageously protested, telling Hunting Cap that Maurice had been reared 'with the idea that he should never be necessitated to earn his own bread', and that being forced into 'business, I mean [a] mechanic one' would probably drive him to despair and thence to ruin.[5] Maurice was spared eventually – at least to the extent of his being purchased a commission in the army. It was doubtless the General's pleas rather than O'Connell's which carried the day with Hunting Cap. But it was true testimony of fraternal love that O'Connell, at the age of eighteen, should have braved Hunting Cap's anger for his brother's sake. It was also an augury of his future at the bar, for his long letter was a skilful piece of advocacy, down to its emotional peroration. 'But what do I say? No, I hope he will never be guilty of such a complicated piece of ingratitude as to offend again. Do then, my dear Uncle, forgive this once more. Add this to the many favours you have hitherto loaded us with.'[6] Meanwhile O'Connell's own schooldays were coming to an end. Fagan closed his academy suddenly in October 1793. Costs had risen and the number of pupils had fallen off: O'Connell was one of only two 'constant boarders' by that stage. But, as Fagan told him, he suffered very little from the closure. He was practically at the end of his course in logic – rhetoric had presumably been completed earlier in the year – so that the only substantial change in his circumstances was the welcome one of removing from Fagan's to other lodgings.

Hunting Cap had decided some time before (possibly when Langrishe's Act was passed) that O'Connell should read for the bar. He now determined that he should be entered at the Temple in time for the next law term. But after more than two years abroad the boy was homesick, as well as faced with the imminent loss of his brother Maurice who had been his companion during all his exile. This drove him to present an elaborate plea to Hunting Cap to be allowed to read law instead at the newly constituted King's Inns in Dublin. Again, the artistry of his argument was striking. Having distanced himself from those to whom London offered advantages, 'giddy and thoughtless young men who come there to spend money, not to study', and taken the precaution of securing both Fagan's and the General's 'approbation' (for what is not clear), O'Connell proceeded to draw up a balance sheet showing how much less he could live on in Dublin than in London. He could not deny that the common law of England and Ireland was essentially the same; but he made the most of the solitary significant difference in the respective legal systems, the laws of place. He also attempted to turn his own youth to account and to play effectively upon his uncle's *amour propre*.

> As for the other class how am I to discern the honest man from the designing villain? The experiment would be dangerous in the highest degree for my youth and inexperience. But in Dublin your known credit and character would be the means of introducing me into the acquaintance of some of the most eminent lawyers in the Kingdom; who would not only assist me in forming the plan of my studies, but likewise be of service to me when engaged in the profession.[7]

Hunting Cap was unmoved. But although O'Connell had probably spent several days in composing his petition, it was not altogether wasted time. He had made another remarkable trial in advocacy.

On 19 January 1794 O'Connell enrolled at Lincoln's Inn: he had had to change his allegiance when it had turned out that the Temple was still closed to Catholics by its requirement that members take the sacrament. So began a lonely year in London. Neither lectures nor examinations were available to, let alone mandatory for, bar students. Eating thirty-six dinners in one's Inn and occasional attendance at the court of King's Bench during term constituted the entire formal education of a barrister. The best contemporary apprenticeship for the bar was to devil with a celebrated counsel. But this, at a cost of at least £100 per annum, was beyond O'Connell's reach. All that remained was the steady, untutored reading of textbooks in his dingy lodging room off the Strand, scraping acquaintance with fellow-students if he could, and joining a circulation library. Professional reading began, inevitably, with the four volumes of Blackstone's *Commentaries*: this headed a long list of legal works which he compiled in the hope that his uncle would purchase them for him in Cork. But from the 30,000 volumes of the circulating library which he joined, he set out to 'relax' his mind 'with the study of History and the Belles Lettres, objects absolutely necessary for every person who has occasion to speak in public, as they enlarge the ideas, and afford that strength and solidity of speech which are requisite for every public speaker.'[8]

He appears to have had few if any London friends, at any rate during 1794. The two or three acquaintances whom he mentions in this year were Irish youths. He was poor. There is no reason to doubt his statement of 11 March 1794, 'I have not gone to one single place of entertainment since I came to London', nor the truth of his wistful observation, 'I am perhaps the only law student in London without a Watch.'[9] Three months later he had to try to justify to Hunting Cap an appeal to his own father for some money. He pleaded that, through inexperience and inattention, he had failed to anticipate fully his daily needs. Meanwhile his health was poor. A 'weakness of nerves' from which he suffered in the spring of 1794 suggests perhaps some psycho-somatic disorder or adolescent crisis. In summer he fell seriously ill of 'ague' and 'slow nervous fever'. After he had recovered – despite the heroic remedies of 'a bottle of port per day during the first ten or twelve days of my sickness' and 'a blister applied to my side' which rendered him unconscious from pain – he told Hunting Cap, ' I was attended by a country man of ours, a Dr Pendergast who having already made a fortune by his profession, behaved very genteely to me as he gave me the four last visits without a fee. Notwithstanding this you may be convinced my illness has cost a round sum of money . . . your former kindness induces me to hope that you will be good enough to make it up in my next half-term's allowance.'[10] The General warmly backed O'Connell's plea. The malady, he told Hunting Cap on 21 August 1794, had inevitably proved expensive, the cost of medical fees and drugs in England being 'enormous': 'It is, however, a great Comfort that he [Daniel] is perfectly recovered, having been severely attacked.'[11] This was a characteristic intervention. The General invariably supported O'Connell's requests for more money during his London years. Early in 1794 he had assured his brother that O'Connell could not possibly live in even 'the most modest gentility' in London under £120 per annum.[12] A year later he revised this to £130–140 at the very least. 'Every article has risen in price very considerably, and in the line he lives in a certain appearance must be kept up. You know as well as I do that professional Abilities, however transcendant, require to be supported by genteel Manners and gentlemanly Education. Mixing in good company is the only way of acquiring them.'[13] Equally important, his London uncle vouched for O'Connell's rectitude and gratitude to his Derrynane uncle: he 'will show himself worthy of your unequalled favours, which he entertains the deepest sence[sic] of'.[14] Hard as O'Connell's path as a student may have been, it would have been much stonier without an indefatigable and respected intercessor.

II

Before the close of 1794, O'Connell's political and religious opinions had begun to change direction. Almost certainly, a crucial event was the trial of Thomas Hardy for high treason, which O'Connell attended between 28 October and 5 November 1794. Hardy, secretary of the London Corresponding Society, was a foremost radical of the day, and from the beginning his prosecution was a trial of strength between the forces of repression and libertarianism, conducted amid great publicity and excitement and charged with political passion. The defence, led by Erskine, called upon leading liberals like R. B. Sheridan and Philip Francis as witnesses to such good effect that the case proved an immense triumph for the reformers. When the jury returned a verdict of 'not guilty', Hardy was drawn through the streets of central London by the crowd; and later the whig Earl Stanhope presided over a grand celebratory dinner. Not only had the contest been protracted and dramatic, but it had also taken the shapes of David against Goliath and of freedom against suppression. It was not likely that a twenty-year-old student would have hesitated long in choosing sides. Moreover, some time in 1794 O'Connell had joined the Cogers, a London debating club of artisans, journalists and self-improvers, in which radicals and freethinkers predominated. If he had become a member early in the year, some of the ground for the political turnabout which followed his attendance at the Hardy trial had probably been tilled already.

We do not know how rapidly O'Connell's radicalism developed. It had certainly gone far by the close of 1795 when he began to compose his journal. Two items entered under 30 December of that year record his uncle Daniel's railing at him for his 'folly in being a democrat',[15] and an American girl's gibe that 'in fifty years I [O'Connell] would doubt whether I was a man or a cabbage-stump, so much was I inclined to scepticism'.[16] This democratic and philosophical 'conversion' may have been only recently completed. Certainly, O'Connell had undergone two significant radicalizing experiences in the three weeks or so preceding these entries. First, he had read William Godwin's *Political Justice*: probably no other book affected him so profoundly. Secondly, he had moved his lodgings from a cul-de-sac off Coventry St to Mrs Rigby's *pension* at Chiswick, a nest of the avant garde and *esprits forts*.

O'Connell had failed to win Hunting Cap's permission to return to Kerry for the long vacation in either 1793 or 1794, but he at last succeeded in 1795: it was by then almost four years since he had seen his family or homeland. When he returned to London in October 1795 he found that his rent had been raised to a guinea and a half per week ('so much has the price of provisions increased'[17]), and accordingly he was ordered by Hunting Cap to find a cheaper place out of town, at any rate for vacations. This explains his move to Chiswick at the end of the Michaelmas law term of 1795; and doubtless Mrs Rigby's establishment was chosen because his solitary friend among law students, R. N. Bennett, stayed there. On 10 December 1795 he described his translation to Hunting Cap with his customary guile:

> The society in the house is mixed – I mean composed of men and women all of whom are people of rank and knowledge of the world; so that their conversation and manners are perfectly well adapted to rub off the rust of scholastic education. Nor is there any danger of riot or dissipation as they are all advanced in life; another student of law and I being the only young persons in the house. This young man is my most intimate acquaintance . . . His name is Bennett. He is an Irish young man of good family, connections and fortune. He is prudent and strictly economical. He has good sense, ability and application. I knew him before my journey to Ireland. It was before that period our friendship commenced. So that on the whole I spend my time here not only very pleasantly but I hope very usefully. [18]

No doubt Hunting Cap was not completely taken in. But he would surely have been astonished had he read O'Connell's private 'sketch' of his new landlady. Mrs Rigby, O'Connell noted in his journal, was endowed with 'a strong mind, a clear comprehension, and a tenacious memory', fluency in French and Italian, a fair knowledge of Latin and excellent knowledge of history, literature, heraldry, drama and the stage.[19] She was

> a most violent and inveterate democrat, as well as a deist. Her own misfortunes make [her] peevish on these subjects. But, with all her information, she has not a grain of common prudence. The servants neglect

their business, plunder and cheat her ... while she should be exerting herself to procure another house she is talking of Beaumont and Fletcher's plays, descanting on Paine's *Age of Reason*, or arguing on the politics of the day ... In her attachment for cats she becomes foolish and absurd. But she has a greater failing than any yet mentioned. It is a fondness for liquor. She gets drunk sometimes and would in all probability do it oftener were she unrestrained by the fear of her lodgers forsaking the house. She is at all times familiar, but when heated with drinking she is rude in her familiarities.[20]

Such was the mistress of the raffish, bohemian and free-thinking household in which O'Connell was to spend his remaining year and five months in London.

O'Connell's new home was in a tranquil setting. The large house fronted the Thames, with Barnes to be seen on one side of the opposite shore and the Margrave of Ansbach's mansion upon the other. Chiswick Eyot, replete with the reeds and osiers so lovingly described in many a Victorian idyll of the suburban Thames, lay directly across from the hall door. The lodgers' rooms, O'Connell noted, were spacious and isolated apartments, as if each were living in a separate house.

His life at Chiswick, however, by no means mirrored the Arcadian surroundings. Even before he went to live at Mrs Rigby's, he and other young men had been involved in a semi-drunken fracas there in which a servant had been struck and a constable called to separate the combatants. In his first month or so at Mrs Rigby's, he was served with a writ for non-payment of debt, and all but took the disastrous step of signing a *post obit* for £1,200 for a man whom he thought might become a bankrupt. He also attracted the amorous attentions of a young married woman; he was by now a tall, splendidly proportioned youth, strikingly handsome in the blue-eyed, black-haired Kerry style. This 'fine young woman ... seemed to be partial to me, and I endeavoured to improve this partiality. She is a most debauched woman. She pretended before we parted to have taken a great liking to me. Nay, she acted the part of an *inamorata*.'[21] He was moreover bound over to keep the peace in consequence of a dispute with Douglas Thompson, the son of a local porter brewer, over the favours of another young woman. When O'Connell had called on Thompson to issue a challenge for a duel, Thompson struck him repeatedly with a stick: 'I seized him, and though I had a heavy cane in my hand I did not return the blow.'[22] When O'Connell later sent his friend Bennett with a more formal challenge, Thompson's father had him arrested. The upshot was O'Connell being hauled before a magistrate with his uncle Daniel having to act as his bondsman. The General gave O'Connell a rare dressing down, abusing his new politics equally with his behaviour. He 'railed at me for not having returned the blow', O'Connell wrote resentfully, but would have been angrier still had O'Connell been so ungentlemanlike as to fight 'with cudgels like common porters, etc., etc.'.[23] Despite the berating, Uncle Daniel had treated O'Connell with his usual generosity, for not a word of this or of the earlier scrape was passed on to Derrynane.

None of these were perhaps very wild oats for a nineteen-year-old boy, loose in London for almost two years already, to have sown. But they were considerably wilder for O'Connell than they would have been for others of his age. The shadow of Hunting Cap lay always across his path. This was partially counteracted by his great good fortune in having the General's unwavering support, in advocacy as well as silence, according to occasion. When, for example, Hunting Cap was enraged at what he took to be O'Connell's negligence in arranging for being entered on the books of King's Inns, Dublin, it was his London uncle who pleaded, 'Dan's Letter to Mr Franks came to Dublin at a time when he was absent, therefore the Disappointment, or rather the Delay, cannot be imputed to our Dan, because he could not forsee the circumstance. I hope you have before now received his letter, which I forwarded you from here, and I beseech you to relieve him from the anxiety he feels least [sic] he might have incurred your displeasure.'[24] But there was also a strong streak of caution in O'Connell himself even in his 'wildest' day. He reproached himself deeply for falling into debt and almost falling into ruin by signing another's *post-obit*. 'I remark a great deal of neglect, or at least a certain dilatoriness of disposition, which seems a constitutional failing of mine',[25] he wrote of the first. As to the second, 'the chance of this [the *post-obit*] transaction coming to my uncle's knowledge would (had I been concerned in it) be a source of continual anxiety and apprehension.'[26] He was far from sure that he would have responded to the young wife's advances had there been an opportunity for the affair to develop. Indeed he speaks of marriage at this time with deep respect as the event which constitutes the source of 'unmixed sorrow' or of 'pure happiness'.[27] Even the frustrated duel was a matter of moralizing and self-analysis. He had not returned Thompson's blow (O'Connell decided) because Thompson was smaller and weaker, because O'Connell might have killed him, and because he remembered his earlier fisticuffs and 'its consequent expenses, troubles and inconveniences . . . having no witnesses, I was afraid of the law'. On the credit side, he was delighted to discover that he had courage enough to challenge another to a duel, although this left him with a new fear of 'precipitation in plunging myself in future quarrels'. Again, while duelling was a vice, 'yet there is a certain charm in the independence which it bestows on a man'. Interestingly, in the light of events a quarter of a century away, O'Connell wound up his laborious examen with the announcement of his decision never to fight a duel again 'from the time I become *independent* of the world'.[28]

Whatever about duelling, there is a certain charm in O'Connell's youthful sententiousness. True, no gleam of wit or gaiety relieves the leaden periods of his journal – here the contrast with Wolfe Tone's sparkling self-notes could not be more complete. Not only did O'Connell sometimes sink to the owlishness of a solemn schoolboy, but also he was as bent on self-improvement as Samuel Smiles. In fact, his prime reason for keeping a journal was to eradicate his 'faults', the most obdurate of which continued for years to be over-sleeping in the mornings! None the less, O'Connell's earnest, pedantic wrestling with experience should touch the heart of anyone who can recapture the frets and fears of adolescence. The struggle to impose order upon his matters for decision, and even the laborious moral balance-sheets and numbered pros and cons for actions done, are in the end impressive. No less, if rather less pleasantly, so are the shrewdness and calculated self-interest underlying certain of his decisions. Towards the end of 1795, for instance, he noted, 'I have entirely lost this day owing to my being in town. I believe it will be better for me [to] attend the Society [of Cogers] no longer. It is true I there acquire a great fluency of speech, but the loss of time and money which my attendance occasions makes me conceive it preferable to go there no more.'[29] O'Connell certainly took seriously the furnishing of his mind according to the Ciceronian specifications he had received at Douai. When at home at Chiswick he read and noted his reading 'almost continually'. Characteristic was his entry for 19 January 1796:

> I read this day 110 pages of Gibbon [*Decline and Fall*], Vol.4, thirty-two pages of Godwin, and thirty-three pages of Para [*Physique Experimentale*]. I read likewise part of the treatise on aerology in Hall's *Encyclopaedia*.
> I read but five pages of 'E.N.P.' [Espinasse's *Nisi Prius*].[30]

As this indicates, apart from his legal work (normally a much larger portion of the whole than on 19 January), O'Connell read extensively in history, political philosophy and natural sciences. His fluency in

French much increased of course his potential range. But he also read poetry spasmodically (eighty-five pages of 'Ossian's *Poems*' and two hundred and thirty-four of Pindar's in one evening) as well as belles-lettres, Shakespeare and the Bible. Johnson, Blair, Voltaire and Rousseau were among the crop of one short season. He worried repeatedly about the poverty of his style, his failure to arrange 'a united train of ideas', and his incapacity to express himself aright or say exactly what he meant. 'This defect has, I believe, two sources, the one an inherent shallowness of conception, the other frequent interruption. The first can be remedied one [*sic*] by the attainment of a more enlarged stock of ideas; the latter, being only a bad custom, may be laid aside with the assistance of care.'[31] He devoted much time to Gibbon's *Decline and Fall* not only for its intrinsic excellence as history, but also as the supreme stylistic model.

O'Connell, then, saw himself as both an apprentice studying the work of masters and an accumulator of a store of reference and allusion against his eventual appearance on the world's stage. But he was not always on parade. He confessed to reading novels and 'trifling productions of the day unworthy of my notice'. [32] These he generally regarded as lost time, to record which would be merely to waste more time still. But he made two exceptions: Mackenzie's *The Man of Feeling* and Godwin's *Caleb Williams* were discussed at length. The choice is significant. Each novel was foremost in its genre in the late eighteenth century. They glorified, respectively, the cults of sensibility and rational improvement. As always in such cases, it is difficult to say whether the deep impression which these two novels made upon O'Connell derived from his own predisposition. But certainly he carried their doctrines forward into his future, as, say, his courtships and his dauntless advocacy of humane causes will richly testify. Perhaps the hero of his own projected novel (which may have been begun as early as February 1796) would have attempted to intertwine the strains. According to his sketched plot, an illegitimate son of George III was to have been taken as a child from his mother, Hannah Lightfoot, sent to school at Douai, and thence taken to the West Indies. 'He was to be a soldier of fortune – to take a part in the American war – and to come back finally to England, imbued with republican principles.'[33] It is difficult to guess at the intended fate of O'Connell's hero, for nothing of the novel has survived. But he was surely fulfilling many of his creator's day-dreams – parentage, presumably, apart!

But the staple, if not always the bulk, of O'Connell's reading at

Chiswick was law. He had to determine for himself even which books to buy and study, with no further outside assistance than the occasional offhand advice from Irish barristers whom Hunting Cap had importuned for help. It was a dreary and often repellent grind. Of Coke's *Institutes*, for instance, O'Connell wrote that 'were it not for the happy absurdities with which they abound, the pedantry of style, the obscurity of matter, and the loathsome tediousness of trifling would create unsurmountable disgust.'[34] Blackstone's *Commentaries* alone were endurable, Blackstone being both clear in style and attractive in exposition. Espinasse's *Nisi Prius* (a collection of recent judgments) was, conversely, the most odious of all. O'Connell found the 'artificial' distinctions of the judiciary sickening and 'the iniquity of punishing ignorance' a shock. Doubly was ignorance punished in the courts. To the inevitable unfamiliarity with law which brought down many of its lay victims was to be added the still more appalling lack of knowledge of many of the special pleaders. 'The omission of a word in a declaration is sufficient to set aside the best-founded judgment. And this case is peculiarly cruel, as the individual who suffers is innocent of the mistake or neglect which proved fatal to his interests.'[35]

Perhaps the most striking expression of O'Connell's hostility at this time to the operating principles of the profession for which he was preparing followed an attendance at the Old Bailey on 14 January 1796.

Two highwaymen were tried and found guilty. Now, if these unfortunate individuals are hanged, will one more virtue be infused into the bosom of any individual? Will one crime less be committed than would be had they escaped? Certainly not. The experience of ages has shown the inefficacy of punishment. The reasoning of the speculatist shows its immorality. Yet men continue to inflict punishment on their fellow-beings. Driven to despair by the wants of nature and the contempt of his acquaintance, the man whose most strenuous efforts are insufficient to procure him subsistence takes the road and forcibly deprives the luxurious or the unfeeling of a portion of their superfluities. The sacred rights of property, thus violated, devote the head of the *unwilling* spoliator to destruction. And this is what we are thought to call justice. O, Justice, what horrors are committed in thy name![36]

Doubtless this was written under the influence of reading Godwin, who was opposed to all punishment – with a final flourish perhaps from Mme Roland. But it also accorded with O'Connell's earlier, as well as his later, disposition. For although he was to become a finished lawyer, in every technical respect, he remained strangely at odds with his calling in certain of its fundamental contemporary assumptions. One was the punitive system of the day, in either its vengeful or its deterrent aspect. It was fortunate for him that on the criminal side he was almost invariably a defending counsel. Not only by nature but also by abiding inclination was he cast in the role of a Bayard of the courts.

Until the publication of his journal more than a century after its composition, the accepted picture of O'Connell's tertiary study was that of a sedulous, uncritical reader of legal texts, and of nothing else beyond Gibbon and the Bible. This as we have seen was quite mistaken. In fact he tried systematically to garner knowledge, taste and modes of judgment from every field within his touch. At the same time, he set about mastering law as if it were the language of the enemy.

III

Perhaps the most important elements in O'Connell's intellectual development in London, which lay hidden before the publication of his journal, were the sources of his political ideas and his lengthy period of religious scepticism. Fortunately the two months in which he kept up his journal at Chiswick appear to coincide with the critical stage in each of these unfoldings.

Godwin's *Political Justice* was O'Connell's crucial piece of reading at this time. Its essential theme was human perfectibility. By means of reason, man is bound eventually to attain intellectual amd moral perfection and complete control of both his own nature and the external world: in the end all government and every external restraint would fall away as otiose. Meanwhile, many existing institutions should be abolished: marriage, organized religion, private property, contract, monarchy, the peerage and various other apparent immutabilities. All this was little more than the outer limits of one form of contemporary radicalism. Where Godwin really struck home with O'Connell was, first, in his total opposition to violence and revolution as bound to hold back the long march of rational progress – 'Revolutions . . . suspend the wholsome [*sic*] advancement of science, and confound the process of nature and reason'[37] – and secondly, his conviction that the key to every beneficial change lay in the enlistment of public opinion. 'All government is founded in opinion . . . Make men wise, and . . . you make them free.'[38] O'Connell's entire political structure was to rest, ultimately speaking, on these two simple propositions. He himself was overwhelmed by Godwin's argument. Godwin's 'work cannot be too highly praised', he wrote upon turning the last page. 'All mankind are indebted to the author. The cause of despotism never met a more formidable adversary. He goes to the root of every evil that now plagues man and degrades him almost beneath the savage beast. He shows the source whence all the misfortunes of mankind flow. That source he demonstrates to be political government.'[39]

Fittingly, perhaps, O'Connell interleaved his reading of *Political Justice* with his reading of Mary Wollstonecraft's *A Vindication of the Rights of Woman*: she was very shortly to become Godwin's mistress, and then wife. O'Connell regarded the *Vindication* as opening 'the road to truth by clearing away prejudice'. It was not a prejudice that he had shared: 'that mind has no sex, and that women are unjustly enslaved, are opinions I have long entertained.' How precisely, and to what degree, women should exercise political power remained puzzles to him. But Godwin had at least provided a general principle for judgment 'by proving that government to be best which laid fewest restraints upon private judgment. Surely the judgment of the one sex ought to be as unshackled as that of the other.'[40] This too was a significant conclusion for O'Connell. He was not to become a female suffragist or emancipationist; the first half of the nineteenth century was not a kind climate for such beings. From his later conduct we can, perhaps, even infer an acceptance of the prevailing ideology of 'separate spheres'. But, in general terms, laying the fewest possible restraints upon private judgments of every kind epitomized and interlinked O'Connell's reformism across the spectrum.

Paine's *Age of Reason* appears to have been as telling for O'Connell's religious doubt as was *Political Justice* for his social faith. As with his move to radicalism, his drift towards scepticism appears to have been a gradual development from late 1794 to late 1795. In the summer of 1794 he still regarded proximity to a Catholic chapel for Sunday mass as a significant factor in selecting a resort. But a year and a half later he justified his distaste for making a journal entry by his feeling oppressed 'by the same sensations which I used to feel when, formerly, I intended on a day to go to confession'[41] – with the seeming implication that he had for some time given up this practice. *The Age of Reason* was a powerful deist tract, anti-dogmatic, anti-ecclesiastical, anti-revelationary and anti-Christian, except in so far as Christ himself was saluted as a notable philanthropist. O'Connell, who may well have borrowed it from his redoubtable landlady, did not read it in isolation from similar tracts. During the same period he studied, for example, Voltaire's ironic assault upon Catholicism, 'Zapata's' *Questions*, as well as *Recueil Nécessaire*, an anthology of freethinking authors. Doubtless his simultaneous perusal of *Decline and Fall* (which he was of course to re-read later) speeded up the inroads on his inherited religion. But it was *The Age of Reason* which really confirmed O'Connell's unconversion. 'This work gave me a great deal of pleasure', he recorded on 13 January 1796, when he had completed the first volume. 'In treating of the Christian system he [Paine] is clear and concise. He has presented many things to my sight in a point of view in which I never before beheld them.'[42] Six days later O'Connell wrote of the second volume,

> This part has given me more satisfaction than the former. It has put the foundation of the religious question of the Christians in a point of view in which a judgement is easily formed on its solidity. I now have no doubts on this head. I may certainly be mistaken. But I am not wilfuly mistaken, if the expression has any meaning. My mistakes I refer to the mercy of that Being who is wise by excellence. To the God of nature do I turn my heart; to the meditation of His works I turn my thoughts.[43]

Scepticism, however, was not to be embraced completely without nervous *arrières pensées*. As O'Connell himself confessed, 'The prejudices of childhood and youth at times frighten and shake the firmness of my soul.'[44] In short, he asked, was he taking a terrible false step? What if after all Catholicism turned out to be the truth? He tried to console himself with the thought that the benign Deity would never punish error, if honest. 'He will not punish for the unbiassed conviction of the soul. To affirm the contrary would, in my apprehension, be to calumniate.'[45] His attempt to exorcize the past and secure himself against every possibility eventually took this shape:

> These fears, these doubts, perhaps imply a libel on the First Cause, the Great Spirit who created the planetary systems that roll around. It is impossible that He whose justice is *perfect* should punish with eternal torments the belief which is founded on conviction. It appears impossible because the conviction of the mind does not depend on us. We cannot prevent, we cannot change, the belief that our souls form on the perceptions of the senses. Again, these perceptions are not in our power. We receive impressions from the surrounding objects notwithstanding all our efforts to the contrary. It would in fact be as absurd and criminal to say that the Great Spirit would punish me for not believing that it is *now* noon

as to affirm that He would inflict tortures for not believing another proposition the belief of which is equally impossible.[46]

We can never speak with certainty, or perhaps even confidence, of another's spiritual condition. But the evidence to hand does seem to indicate that O'Connell 'lost his faith' during 1794–5, and committed himself deliberately to another, Paineite deism, early in 1796. In doing so he did not, however, rid himself of doubts. Rather he exchanged doubts that Christianity might not be true for doubts (or at least extra-rational fears) that it might be, after all.

IV

O'Connell made the last London entry in his journal on 18 February 1796. Possibly this was because his departure for Ireland (though still almost three months distant) was settled on about that date. New regulations had been issued for the Irish bar. These required the keeping of nine terms at the King's Inns, as well as satisfying the requirements of a London Inn. In order to meet both conditions and yet be called to the bar in Dublin in time to go on the summer circuit of 1798, O'Connell would have to begin attendance at the King's Inns by mid-May 1796. So it was arranged. As things turned out, he had also to change from Lincoln's to Gray's Inn for his last London term so that all this could be fitted in. Hence what he himself described as his 'threefold apprenticeship to the law',[47] though in fact the triple apprenticeship meant little more than experiencing three different sorts of dinners.

The new regulations meant heavy additional calls upon Hunting Cap's purse – even the formal transfer to Gray's Inn cost £11 – and he was already angry at what he divined to be O'Connell's folly and extravagance during his last months in London. O'Connell bent himself to counteract this impression. On 26 February he wrote from Chiswick,

> Had I to do with anyone else but you I should deem it politic to mention the different articles at different periods that in the division the bulk of the aggregate may be lost sight of. But with you all low cunning would be as base as it would be useless. Your liberality takes away the will as your penetration does the means of deceit.

Fees at Lincoln's Inn	£22. 4.0
Transfer to Gray's Inn if necessary	£11. 0.0
Travelling charges	£12.12.0

Analysis of Travelling charges

Carriage to Holyhead	£5. 0.0
Luggage *as at coming*	£2. 2.0
To guards and coachmen	15.
Passage to Dublin	10.6
Victuals on the road – suppose	£1. 3.0
	£9.10.6

The overplus is £3. 1. 6 in case of no delay whatever at Holyhead but as there is a possibility of delay the impropriety of travelling with only the exact sum necessary for the speediest journey is self-evident.[48]

O'Connell was probably disingenuous. Clearly he expected Hunting Cap to be flattered when he described him as too perspicacious to be cheated; but his words read unpleasantly like a confidence man's opening gambit. Not all O'Connell's justifications of his accounts sound even plausible. He explained the purchase of several pairs of black silk stockings, for example, as prudent because they were cheaper in London and proper because they were *de rigueur* in his future profession. It is certain that he left England in debt; and he later bemoaned his extravagance at Chiswick. 'Indeed, I knew not what it is to be economical in London. I spent foolishly what I bitterly regretted since.'[49]

His spending and his debt were comparatively trivial in amount. They loomed large for O'Connell only because Hunting Cap was his sole resource. From past experience he knew that asking for or accepting money from his father would bring down his uncle's wrath upon him. This explains, if it does not altogether excuse, O'Connell's unctuous pleading and pathetic concealments. His extraordinary dependence on his patron and that patron's automatic parsimony and suspicion nurtured in him some unattractive qualities – bombast, cajolery and deceit – though they also gave him some ultimately useful practice in the art of persuasion and finesse.

Although Hunting Cap would never have recognized, let alone admitted, it, he had received good value for the money spent on O'Connell's London education. Despite his continual dissatisfaction with his own progress, O'Connell succeeded in teaching himself a great deal, as well as learning something from his surroundings. Few bar students of the day would have known as much law as he by the age of twenty-one, and fewer still could have matched him in wider fields; and he had trained himself earnestly in speaking at the Cogers, and in dialectic with his fellow-boarders at Mrs Rigby's. He was industrious to the end of his London days. Even he allowed that he had augmented his hoard of knowledge in 1796. True, he added that his 'acquaintance with the law has not been much, if at all, improved'.[50] But this was surely too gloomy an account, given his steady legal reading.

His recreational life in London is only rarely and fleetingly revealed; but one guesses that it was both inextensive and comparatively innocent. Most of the few companions mentioned in the journal were Irish (Kerry cousins in all but two cases), and his worst misconduct little more than a night's overdrinking and a consequent brawl or scuffle. He recorded nothing which suggests debauchery. Much inclined to priggishness in self-judgment, he none the less noted privately on 31 December 1796, 'During this year there has been no action of mine which ought to bring regret to my conscience or shame to my cheek.'[51] Overall, O'Connell did not greatly exaggerate when, shortly before he left London, he gave Hunting Cap a résumé of his achievements and his hopes:

> I hope to be pretty well master of the subject [law] before I have an opportunity of putting myself forward to public notice. If I can come forward at first with any thing like tolerable *eclat*, there will be an hundred to one in my favour. Though I am extremely anxious to become a greater lawyer, law makes little more than the principal part of my study. I read with attention history, rhetoric, philosophy, and sometimes poetry. While I apply myself to the English language, I endeavour to unite purity of diction to the harmony and arrangement of phraseology . . . And as my life will be a chain of study and application until I appear on the great stage of the world, I will endeavour to appear there with brilliancy and solidity.[52]

It is perhaps significant that, as usual, O'Connell's master metaphors were those of the actor and the stage. Only once does he refer to play-going in his London journal. But other evidence suggests that this was by no means his only visit to the theatre; and we must keep in mind that not only did he record selectively while he kept the journal, but also that he only kept it for only three of the forty months of his London sojourn. The single theatrical entry is however filled with interest, for O'Connell, then only twenty years of age, concentrated his dramatic analysis on rhetoric and elocution. Contrary to the current orthodoxy that John Kemble was a master of rhythm and declamation, O'Connell found him deficient in both. His lines (in Nathaniel Lee's *Alexander the Great*) were, O'Connell noted, poor in matter but with 'a smooth flow of numbers in them pleasing to the ear'. To render them palatable, he continued, 'they should receive from the speaker this the only beauty they possess. Now Kemble, on the contrary, pronounces them as if they consisted of a number of disjointed half-sentences.' Kemble's sister, Mrs Siddons, was by contrast the complete speaker of dramatic lines. 'The strength and modulation of her voice render any character doubly interesting in her hands. With our modern actors it is no small difficulty to understand the dialogue of a tragedy. But Mrs Siddons has the faculty of making herself clearly understood in every part.'[53] O'Connell contemptuously dismissed the performance of a third Kemble, Charles, as impudence without merit – this despite, or possibly because of, Charles Kemble's having been his schoolfellow at Douai. Even so severe a judgment may not have been astray, for the younger Kemble had only recently taken to the stage. O'Connell was well aware that his estimates challenged the contemporary orthodoxy at several points. But whatever the rights of the matter, they certainly revealed an acute and independent intelligence. It is also noteworthy that where O'Connell moved beyond comment upon declamation, it was fire and force which he most admired in acting, and affectation which he excoriated. All in all, even Hunting Cap might not have been dissatisfied had he known what O'Connell had made of his night at Drury Lane. In proper Ciceronian fashion, he had rendered it an exercise for his future work and painfully elaborated his own conception of the forensic art. It is true that London had also transformed, or at least helped to transform, O'Connell into an extreme political radical and a religious sceptic. It is hard to guess which development would have been more abhorrent to Hunting Cap, had he known of the march of his nephew's mind. But he could scarcely have withheld approval altogether from O'Connell's earnest intellectual endeavour, however unfortunate its immediate fruits.

O'Connell had arrived in London a schoolboy of seventeen accustomed to following instructions and set texts and measuring his achievement in terms of the mastery of appointed tasks. He departed a young man of nearly twenty-one accustomed, painfully, to formulating his own judgments, with a heterogeneous accumulation of knowledge and ideas and the main principles of his political philosophy already chosen. Some schoolboy features were still clearly discernible in the bar student of ten terms' standing, in particular unremitting application and ambition. Curiously, there is no indication, apart from the mollificatory transmission of a little London political gossip to Hunting Cap from time to time, that O'Connell took any interest in the parliamentary proceedings at Westminster while he lived in England. This contrasts strikingly with both his earlier and his later enthusiasm for the debates of the Irish House of Commons at College Green. None the less, there is no mistaking the thread of a more or less deliberate political apprenticeship running through O'Connell's adolescence and early manhood from his Douai to his Chiswick days.

CHAPTER 3

Dublin

1796–1800

I

O'Connell reached Dublin on 12 May 1796, just in time to keep the Trinity term at King's Inns. Hunting Cap, whose influence with various Dublin lawyers had helped to speed up his enrolment, had evidently expressed displeasure with his later London career, for, as soon as he reached Ireland, O'Connell promised amendment now that he had 'as it were arrived at a new stage of my life'.[1] As an earnest of his repentance, he even sought Hunting Cap's approval of the route which he proposed to take on his way to Kerry for the long vacation – to Cork, thence to his MacCartie relatives in the north-west of that county, thence to Carhen and finally to Derrynane. We may take it that this itinerary was sanctioned and successfully fulfilled; but the upshot was not so happy. Some time after he returned to Dublin in October 1796, O'Connell noted that he had quite fallen out of favour with his uncle, who had begun to treat him with suspicion. The explanation is probably to be found in his summer visit to Derrynane. After his departure, Hunting Cap wrote savagely to O'Connell's mother,

> Your son left this ten days ago, and took with him my favourite horse. Had it not been for that, I might have dispensed with his company. He is, I am told, employed in visiting the seats of hares at Keelrelig, the earths of foxes at Tarmons, the caves of otters at Bolus, and the celebration of Miss Burke's wedding at Direen – useful avocations, laudable pursuits, for a nominal student of the law! The many indications he has given of a liberal mind in the expenditure of money has left a vacuum in my purse as well as an impression on my mind not easily eradicated.[2]

O'Connell was to fall into further trouble immediately. On 22 December 1796 a French invasion fleet reached Bantry Bay, and when it departed six days later without having been able to land its troops, it was believed to be bound for some disembarkation point on the Ulster coast. Dublin was therefore in a fever of apprehension for the first week or two of 1797 as well as the last days of 1796; and in the excitement, O'Connell followed the lead of most lawyers and law students and enrolled in the Volunteers on 2 January. Hunting Cap may well have forbidden any such step already. At any rate, it was practically certain that he would disapprove. Yet O'Connell enlisted a day before he asked Hunting Cap's permission to do so. 'I have this day', he noted, on 3 January, 'written to my uncle to get leave – that is in fact money – to enter into this [the Lawyers' Artillery] corps.'[3] He pleaded to Hunting Cap that he was the only young lawyer who had not joined a corps; that it was generally believed that those who refrained would be 'marked by government' as politically disaffected; that if he held back he would be disgraced in his profession and obliged to leave Dublin; and that the Lawyers' Artillery (he said that he *wished* to join it, not that he had already done so) was, with its lace-free uniform, 'the best regulated and least expensive' corps, costing no more than £20 to enter. 'I need not add', O'Connell concluded mendaciously, 'that your decision will be religiously obeyed . . . the whole of my conduct rests with you.'[4] In a later letter, he appears to have added the argument that the lord chancellor, Fitzgibbon, would prohibit his being called to the bar if he failed to enrol in a volunteer company. Hunting Cap's reply has not survived, but it is clear from later correspondence that he angrily rejected O'Connell's application. Worse still, he refused to credit most of O'Connell's assertions. He did not believe for a moment that the government would 'mark down' those who did not join a corps or that the chancellor could determine single-handedly what was properly a matter for the Benchers as a whole. O'Connell's 'threat' to abandon Dublin incensed him most of all.

The situation was potentially disastrous. Hunting Cap had been not only deeply alienated but also deceived. Yet for O'Connell to try to leave the corps now, with his enrolment still undetected by Hunting Cap, presented opposite perils. To disengage himself might be disgraceful, and word of the ensuing stir might well make its way to Derrynane. When on 16 January 1796 O'Connell received Hunting Cap's answer to his initial letter, he was cast into such despair as to write of suicide.

Good God, what a strange world we live in! How stale, flat, and unprofitable are to me its uses! Would I was quietly in my grave! But what is there to prevent me from going to rest? Unreal mockeries, womanish fears, hence! Do not shake the firmness of my soul. ETERNAL BEING, in whose presence all things exist, look to the wretch who addresses Thee.

Direct as it has been ordered by Thee. Rule as Thy wisdom pleases. But let not the phantoms of disordered imaginations disturb him who reposes on Thee with confidence.[5]

Perhaps so Hamletish a declaration of *possible* intent should not be taken seriously; it smacks of posturing. Yet O'Connell added in his journal on the same day, apropos an unidentifiable 'Eliza' with whom he had recently fallen in love, 'There must, assuredly there must, be an exquisite pleasure in madness. Would I was mad! Then, Eliza, I would rave of thee; then should I forget my uncle's tyranny, the coldness and unfeelingness of his heart, my own aberrations.'[6] A day later, he noted that his mind was now more calm. 'Study has restored it to tranquillity.'[7] None the less the crisis was real. Attitudinizing about suicide on paper is no guarantee that the attitudinizer will stop at that.

At least the crisis was not protracted. A second letter from Hunting Cap, received only a week after the first, granted O'Connell permission to enrol, albeit with 'almost as [great] harshness as he last week refused to permit me'.[8] Hunting Cap's continuing resentment was shown by his refusal to supply money for a uniform, telling O'Connell to apply to his father instead. There are no clues to explain Hunting Cap's change of mind. The best presumption would seem to be that, as often before, he had been forced to accept that, in preparing O'Connell for a profession, he was also committed to the adoption of that profession's practices and standards. O'Connell may have exaggerated, but there could be no gainsaying the plain facts that bar students were expected to enlist during the current emergency, and that they would lose face with their peers and elders should they fail to do so.

More fundamentally, the surface appearance of things – that is, the unilateral domination of O'Connell by his uncle – may not have truly represented the balance of power between the parties. Hunting Cap had already invested too much in O'Connell to foreclose recklessly. Whatever the outward-seeming relationship, Hunting Cap's commitment to O'Connell's career – in terms of money, vanity, sense of lineage, vicarious ambition and even perhaps affection – had in reality rendered him vulnerable. Doubtless there were still limits to this endurance, and there was still some level of offence at which he would cast O'Connell off. But the limits and level were surely being extended and raised steadily as O'Connell's career advanced. O'Connell may even have sensed this himself, at least subconsciously. In his reply of 23–4 January 1797 to Hunting Cap's churlish submission (of which reply O'Connell insouciantly observed, 'I am well satisfied with my letter to my uncle, but that is no proof that he will be so'[9]), he argued each point raised in anger or disbelief by Hunting Cap pertinaciously. He also carried sarcasm to the very border of insolence – or so his words would seem to read today:

> You had been so long in the habit of treating me as a child that I forgot that I was expressing with too much warmth the danger I was in of being looked upon by the men who are to be my companions and fellow labourers through life, as a coward or a scoundrel, or as both. That I now see my error can be of service only to prevent me from relapsing into a similar error. But of that indeed there can be little danger while I have so good a monitor as your last letter before my eyes. No. Despicable as any possible conjunction of circumstances may make me, dispirited and wretched, I will only shrink into myself; nor dare to raise my eyes so high again.[10]

Hunting Cap may not have caught the note of irony in this fulsome obeisance (though it almost echoed his own in reply to the antiquarian Smyth many years before), but, privy to O'Connell's journal, we cannot fail to detect the underlying hostility which it expressed.

The episode was significant in marking, as it were, a coming-of-age in O'Connell's relations with his patron. Not only had he won the bout but he had even persisted in his defence after victory. Moreoever he soon set about conciliation. By flattery and attentions, he won his way back into Hunting Cap's good graces well before his legal education was complete. We might also note that the episode prefigures, in lineaments if not in outcome, a much more important later happening, O'Connell's secret marriage in defiance of Hunting Cap's plans. Possibly O'Connell over-relied on the lessons of history in supposing, then, that the coup of January 1797 could simply be repeated.

II

Professionally speaking, O'Connell's eagerness to enlist in a Volunteer Corps was quite comprehensible. But in any event his temperament would have driven him strongly in the same direction. He fell in love immediately with the colour and self-important bustle of gentlemanly soldiering: the smart uniforms of scarlet faced with blue, parades before the *ton* in Phoenix Park, all the happy business of cannon-loading and the guns, and excited manoeuvring. His journal regularly deplored the consequent neglect of study. But there can be no doubt that he enjoyed what was in effect a form of holiday – perhaps even the correction of an imbalance stemming from his long and lonely labours. 'Certain it is', he noted on 23 February 1797, 'that I should have read and written much more if I did not enter into any corps. Yet the recollection of having been in one will hereafter be pleasant. It will be still more pleasant to be always able to say, "I was a volunteer".'[11] But politically O'Connell's move was curious, to say the least. The immediate cause of the wave of volunteering in Dublin in late 1796, after O'Connell had returned from his long vacation at Derrynane, was, first, the threat and then the materialization of a French expeditionary army. But the purpose of a French invasion was to join forces with the potentially revolutionary movement in Ireland, the United Irishmen and possibly also the Catholic agrarian conspiracies. Thus volunteer corps such as the Lawyers' Artillery were automatically aligned with the causes of authoritarian control and repression. In the event of armed conflict they would rapidly become an integral element of the state's machinery of defence. How then did O'Connell square his enlistment with his Godwinite radical beliefs, not to mention his Godwinite pacifism?

He was certainly dismayed by the news of the arrival of a French fleet at Bantry Bay. His immediate reaction on 29 December 1796 took the form of:

> Liberty is in my bosom less a principle than a passion. But I know that the victories of the French would be attended with bad consequences. The Irish people are not yet sufficiently enlightened to be able to bear the sun of freedom. Freedom would soon dwindle into licentiousness. They would rob; they would murder. The altar of liberty totters when it is cemented only with blood, when it is supported only with carcases.[12]

Over the next four months – until 1 May 1797 when the journal entries end in mid-sentence with the next pages torn out, probably to avoid some form of incrimination – O'Connell returned several times to the subject of revolution. Two notes struck in his initial reaction of 29 December to the news from Bantry Bay – distrust of the French and fear of the masses in Ireland – were repeated shortly after, with the firm conclusion, 'A revolution would not produce the happiness of the Irish nation.'[13] He soon constructed a corollary of his position: 'Of real patriotism moderation is the chief mark.'[14] By this O'Connell meant that demagoguery and violence were as inimical to political liberty as oligarchy and repression. After a Sunday walk with Bennett and another friend on 22 January 1797, he noted:

> We talked some pure, because moderate, democracy. Hail, Liberty! How cheering is thy name! How happy should mankind be if thou wast

universally diffused! Strange it might appear that thou shouldst be hateful to any. But thou are calumniated, as thou art disgraced by the nominal advocates. The interested, those who grow fat on the miseries of mankind, the tyrant, and the demagogue condemn thee. The one raises his voice aloud and is heard in the public places to declaim against thee; the other more effectually damns thee by his support.[15]

For all these fine words, he worried increasingly whether self-interest lay at the bottom of his passion for 'moderation'. By the end of March 1797, there were indications that he was drifting towards bolder courses, as Dublin Castle adopted ever more brutal suppressive measures, and gave the Orange Society its head, more or less, in debasing Catholics. On 25 March O'Connell 'trembled' as he asked himself whether his own likely fate coloured his 'desire or dread of a revolution'.[16] Six days later he followed this up with another Hamlet-like soliloquy – the romantic-dramatic strain in him was still evidently running strong:

> It is impossible for any young man at the present day to guess with probable success at the mode in which his existence will terminate. This opinion has been in my mind these two days past. I have in consequence been accustoming myself to consider death without shrinking. Much yet remains to be done before I can familiarise myself with the idea . . .
>
> I must avoid disclosing my political sentiments so frequently as I do at present. It would be a devilish unpleasant thing to get *caged*! Nonsense! *Liberality* can never become dangerous.[17]

It seems likely that the mood of O'Connell's last sentence took over temporarily as 1797 proceeded, and that he was led a fair way down the path of 'immoderation'; the torn-out pages would suggest as much. We also have O'Connell's own testimony that his closest friend, Bennett, was 'an adjunct to the Directory of United Irishmen' and that he himself actually joined the movement – probably under Bennett's influence – later in the year. He recalled, moreover, attending about this time a meeting of radical lawyers, at which the United Irish leader, John Sheares, was present, adding, 'It was fortunate for me that I could not then participate in the proceedings. I felt warmly – and a young Catholic student stepping prominently forth in opposition to the Government would have been in all probability hanged.'[18] It seems clear then, that O'Connell moved into the penumbra of Irish revolution and conspiracy in 1797. This is not surprising given the government's gross provocations throughout that year to Catholics, liberals and even merely chivalric or decent-thinking men. It was to be a common enough experience in Ireland over almost the next two centuries that moderates should be driven temporarily to the left by bouts of official brutality. But it seems equally clear that the outer edge of the United Irish movement and the left-wing of the Irish bar represented the full extent of O'Connell's deviation from 'moderation', and that in his case the tide receded rapidly from its high-water mark. We can be tolerably certain that this fairly summarizes the history of his political opinions in 1796–8. But it still leaves us with the original question – how to explain his enthusiastic service in the 'para-forces' of the crown?

There is no indication that this question ever concerned or even occurred to O'Connell himself. Almost side by side in his journal he recorded, on the one hand, his delight in corps drill and on the other the increasing chances of his ending on the wrong side of a revolution. Beyond reasons of pride, prudence and even companionship, enlistment was, in O'Connell's eyes, equated with 'Volunteering'; and the Volunteers of the early 1780s, formed to repel invasion but soon to be turned into an instrument for winning Ireland's 'constitutional liberty', were for him a heroic (and perhaps also an imitable) body. In fact, the original Volunteers had soon moved on in various directions. Some corps became nurseries of radicalism, and even here and there of violent revolution; others ended, virtually en bloc, as Orange lodges. These extremities emblemize the complexities of Irish political choices and destinations during 1780–1800. Ultimately the basic Irish pattern of Protestant Ascendancy and Catholic disaffection reasserted itself overall. But in between there were several phases of flux and change, and not a few individuals deviated, temporarily or permanently, from their hereditary alignments – sometimes, it would seem, with quite small chances determining their final points of arrival.

O'Connell was certainly in the midst of such a phase in 1797. We must be careful not to impose retrospective rigidities, the logic of a later century, upon him. His own political position was by now a tolerably settled one; but such a position in such a place at such a time was bound to be more or less ambiguous. Where the contrary winds of the day might blow him could not be foretold. This is not to remove our question altogether. Whatever the pressures, he had voluntarily joined a force under the direction of Dublin Castle while yet a political radical and formally a member of a proclaimed organization. None the less, the ideological turmoil and confusion of the later 1790s in Ireland surely clears him of any suspicion of double-dealing or cold calculation. The essence of it all would seem to be that he was, from the first to last, a young man of the centre struggling to find his place on a spectrum of ever – and quickly – changing length and range. This is confirmed by another line of journal entries which coincided with and in effect overrode his gloomy speculations upon revolution.

III

O'Connell's ambition did not diminish as he came to manhood or even – a still more effective puncturer of pretension, perhaps – to Dublin. If anything, it grew in purposiveness and precision. True, he occasionally doubted whether he could 'estimate' his talents accurately; he feared, when low in spirits, that he would never rise above mediocrity. But sometimes '– and this indeed happens most frequently – I am led away by vanity and ambition to imagine that I shall cut a great figure on the theatre of the world . . . Distant prospects rise unbidden to my sight. They are not unwelcome to my heart.'[19] Often the prospects were distant in the sense of being unspecifically 'patriotic', though also astonishingly large for a student who had just reached his majority. 'I will endeavour to give liberty to my country',[20] ran one such solemn resolution. In another he gravely dedicated his 'public life' to 'the good of my country'.[21] But by the beginning of 1797 his ambition was also taking on a much more definite form. He commenced to delineate his future in terms of a parliamentary career. On the face of it, this was extraordinary. Less than two years before, on 5 May 1795, the Irish House of Commons had rejected a bill to admit Catholics to membership by a majority of more than three to one; and currently the British government was set upon a course of Catholic repression. Yet on 28 January 1797 O'Connell noted, 'I have been this day thinking on the plan to be pursued *when I come into Parliament.*'[22] Four weeks later he attended a Commons debate on the defence of Ireland, and, struck by the mediocrity of the major speech, exclaimed. 'I too will be a member. Young as I am, unacquainted with the ways of the world, I should not even now appear contemptible.'[23]

Moreover, O'Connell was already considering the party and the parliamentary line to which he should attach himself. It was out of the question that he should be a government member. Support of a repressive, corrupt and oligarchic regime was anathema. But though he might rocket into fame 'by becoming a violent oppositionist', this also would run athwart his essential purpose in entering politics, 'to serve my country'.[24] As before, a line of 'moderation', which would eschew both the venal and coercive and the mob-pandering and reckless parties, was O'Connell's choice. In contemporary Irish parliamentary terms, this would probably have placed him in or close to Grattan's camp, as an 'advanced' whig.

But there was also a prophetic strain of nineteenth-century radicalism in O'Connell's early speculations on his coming political career. Concurrently, he was reading *The Jockey Club*, a merciless indictment of royal and aristocratic corruption in England, much in the vein of John Wade's later *Black Book*; and this may explain his self-dedication to the task of eliminating one specific source of 'the misery of man' from government. 'Oppression harasses his [man's] faculties. Privilege confined by *accident* insults his understanding. His industry is consumed to support the follies and vices of men who help him not.'[25] Albeit in idealistic and generalized form, O'Connell was marking out already a political and parliamentary position not dissimilar to that actually adopted by him at Westminster in the 1830s. There were of course to be important changes. When he came to Parliament at last, it was a British not an Irish House of Commons that he entered, and this very fact constituted his overriding grievance. Otherwise, however, the O'Connell of 1837 was anticipated to a remarkable degree in the O'Connell of forty years before. Economical and administrative reform, and war upon almost every form of civil discrimination – all handled 'moderately' or pragmatically of course – linked the naive aspirant and the hardened parliamentary performer. For in 1797 his hitherto inchoate ambition had begun to take definite shape, his career to have a clear direction; the gears, so to say, were starting to engage. Yet in all probability this was the very year in which he associated himself, formally at least, with the United Irishmen.

As with the puzzle of his enlistment in a corps, the explanation of this seeming dualism probably lies in the turmoil and fluidity of contemporary Irish politics. If anything could have projected O'Connell in the direction of armed resistance, it would have been the course of brutal repression and virulent no-popery on which the Irish government was embarking. But no provocation could have driven him deeply, let alone permanently, into the camp of revolutionary conspiracy. He found disorder and unrest abhorrent; the sudden or violent disruption of the social fabric represented the supreme danger. His French experience had driven these lessons home. In short, his leftward lurches of 1797–8 were quite uncharacteristic, though also perhaps inevitable in the circumstances. It was not these but the focusing of his ambition upon constitutional reform through parliamentary methods which lay along the true trajectory of his life.

IV

Throughout all the excitements, O'Connell continued his humdrum student life, although inevitably with differences from London. Dublin, where he was to dwell for most of the remainder of his life, was not a large city; its population was then little above 200,000. But 'O'Connell's Dublin' was in effect still smaller. If one stood in the centre of College Green and drew a circle of about a mile in radius, one would cover the area in which practically his entire life in the capital was lived out. This circle contained rookeries of the utmost squalor, but it also embraced the main glories of the Georgian city and its principal institutional ornaments. It was the opulent and noble thoroughfares which O'Connell generally trod. Perhaps his familiar townscape reinforced his socio-political choices. Certainly, when he spoke – as he often did – of Ireland's poor, it was invariably to agrarian rather than urban impoverishment that he referred; and when he spoke – as again he often did – of Ireland's regeneration it was the native capture of Dublin Castle and College Green, and equal treatment in the Four Courts, University, Banks and Exchanges, Corporation Chamber and Mansion House, which he had in sight.

His first Dublin lodgings – with a Mrs Jones for almost eighteen months, and then with one Regan, a fruiterer 'by appointment' to Dublin Castle – were a far cry from the Chiswick *ménage*. He set down the Joneses immediately as 'a most pleasant family', while Regan, as we shall see, was to interpose paternally to save him from himself. It is possible that the 'sweet Eliza' with whom he was infatuated early in 1797 was a Jones daughter. This might account for both the apparent frequency of his encounters with her and the silence of his worship. 'Sweet Eliza', he rhapsodized in his journal on 28 January, 'let me again offer up to you the tribute of my silent wishes. Now by myself, in the lonesomeness of my heart I reflect on thee with satisfaction and delight.'[26] It might also explain his sudden departure later for Mr Regan's. 'I left Mrs Jones's this day [13 January 1798]. Some other time I will descant on my reasons. My heart is now sick.'[27]

In contrast to his later London days, O'Connell's early Dublin life was spent in the heart of the city, mostly within a radius of half a mile or so of Dublin Castle. His lodgings were much less important to him than his room had been at Chiswick. He spent four days a week, and did the bulk of his reading, at the Dublin Library in Eustace Street; he had expended two guineas ('a great sum of money for me'[28]) to join the Library soon after he had settled in the capital. 'My life', he noted on 10 December 1796, 'though it is not in any degree insipid, is monotonous and unchequered. I spend the greater part of the day in the library. In the perusal of a favourite author I feel not the time slip away. Was the library to remain open till one o'clock, I am sure I should frequently be there at that hour. As it shuts at ten, I am forced very reluctantly to leave it at that hour.'[29] There were other excursions about the city, with the Artillery Corps, of course, but also to listen to speeches from the gallery of the House of Commons, to eat dinners in the Inns, to join in moots and debates at Trinity College (although he was not an undergraduate) and to sup at nights in taverns. So far as it goes, the fragmentary evidence of the journal suggests a much fuller and more varied life than he had led in London. Curiously, almost all the companions whom O'Connell mentions in the 1796–7 Dublin entries were young Irish Protestants, several of them members of Kerry gentry families. Two of these figures appear in a strangely boyish passage, in which O'Connell, while cloaking himself in mystery, daydreams of later friendships.

> I like [Ralph] Marshall very much, as everybody must who knows his character. He *knows* me not; yet he wishes to be acquainted with my heart, my disposition. I will not hurry his knowledge of it. Let time unfold by degrees that which it would not be easy to show at once. A man, I believe, meets with many difficulties in playing even his own character. I am anxious for the friendship of Marshall and Bland. I think we will make a valuable triumvirate. I can here indulge what elsewhere would be deemed vanity.[30]

In fact, Marshall did become O'Connell's friend. Like Bennett, he was an advanced liberal, but probably more congenial to O'Connell politically in being both an anti-revolutionist and a Francophobe.

Young Kerry gentlemen were not O'Connell's only links with the Anglo-Irish Ascendancy. In compliment to Hunting Cap, various lawyers with whom he had dealt over the years extended invitations to his nephew. Amongst these were the Frankses, the Rices and the Days, the last two of whom belonged to Kerry county families into the bargain. O'Connell was immediately – but not too grievously – oppressed by a sense of inferiority. After dining with 'the three Rices' (one of whom, Dominick, was to sign the memorial for his call to the bar) on 4 January 1797, he noted, 'Stephen Rice seems to me to possess more information than any man in whose company I have ever been. How different, how decisively superior, is his knowledge to mine! He made me creep into my ignorance. Yet I am at times apt to be vain of what little I know . . . He is by no means obtrusive in his learning.'[31]

Seven weeks later he dined with Robert Day, another barrister, who was to become a circuit judge in the following year, with much the same effect. 'I wish', he wrote on returning home, 'I had that smoothness which society bestows on its frequenters.'[32] Later still, he even called upon Lord Kenmare, a Kerry magnate, at Hunting Cap's indirect suggestion.

It may seem strange that O'Connell, a twenty-one-year-old Catholic student, should have been able to breach at least the outer circle of the Ascendancy, and that so many of his Dublin associations were with Anglicans. It was not however truly surprising. Hunting Cap was rich and influential, and O'Connell himself destined to become a barrister. The Irish bar was still almost exclusively Protestant; O'Connell belonged to the very first wave of Catholic aspirants. But if the profession *had* to include Catholics (and not a few of its members were former Catholics who had conformed to enable them to practise), it was only sensible to include them also in its social traffic. Moreover, this was still 1797, before the outbreak of the Wexford rising and the re-embitterment of Protestant-Catholic relations which followed in its wake. Further still, O'Connell was especially favoured by his own cleverness and charm. But even if readily explicable, his movement into the outskirts of Protestant society is of considerable interest. It shows the possibilities of Irish Protestant and Catholic intersection in the late eighteenth century, even in the inner sanctuary of the home. More particularly, it made clear that Catholics at the Irish bar would be treated more or less as equals in personal and communal relations by the incumbent Protestant brethren. The mess at least would never be divided. It also signalled in advance something of the later variety and complexity of O'Connell's intercourse with Irish Protestants. The inherent contradictions in this intercourse were still mercifully hidden from the great 'non-sectarian'.

Although it is proper to stress O'Connell's religious affiliation as of crucial social and political significance, he continued to be a Catholic in name and form rather than materially. Apparently he attended Sunday mass in Dublin, perhaps even regularly. There is even evidence to suggest that he may have toyed with the idea of attempting to recover his lost faith. On 13 December 1796 he reported the receipt of a letter from his cousin Henry Baldwin, 'advising me to go to confession to Mr Beattie [probably the celebrated Fr Betagh], a Jesuit, etc., etc.'.[33] But Sabbath churchgoing was then a general observance for the respectable; and when Baldwin proposed a confessor for O'Connell, he may have been acting entirely on his own initiative.

Certainly, there is nothing in the journal to suggest that O'Connell ever visited the priest. On the other hand, there is abundant confirmation of O'Connell's continuance in deism punctuated by scepticism. 'Virtue' and 'Philosophy' were frequently apostrophized. Established churches were anathemized: 'Oh, Religion, how much have mankind suffered to [sic] thee . . . Christianity has had her millions of victims. The great Moore [sic] fell beneath her axe.'[34] A friend's death led to gloomy reflections on the dissolution of 'the particles that composed his frame';[35] thoughts of ghosts to the brave conclusion, 'Philosophy teaches me there can be none.'[36] Overall O'Connell appears to have adhered steadily to Godwinite philanthropy, albeit with some nervous self-reassurances should Catholicism turn out, after all, to have been the truth. 'I would, and I trust I will, serve man', he wrote on 7 January 1797,

> . . . I will endeavour to increase the portion of the knowledge and virtue of mankind. Oh, ETERNAL BEING, Thou seest the purity of my heart, the sincerity of my promises. Should I appear before your august tribunal after having performed them, shall not I be entitled to call for my reward? Will the omission of a superstitious action, will the disbelief of an unreasonable dogma, that day rise in judgement against me? Oh, God, how hast Thou been calumniated![37]

Despite his jeremiads on the time taken up by the Lawyers' Artillery and other dissipations, O'Connell's general reading remained extraordinarily extensive. During the two months from mid-December 1796 to mid-February 1797, for example, he not only re-read Gibbon, Godwin, Buffon and other favourites of his Chiswick days but also broke new ground in several directions. Irish antiquity, through Grose and Ledwich and the *Transactions of the Royal Irish Academy*, was one such fresh field; English history, through Henry and Whitaker (*History of Manchester*), another; diplomacy, through Bolingbroke, Condorcet, John Adams and Baron d'Holbach, a third. O'Connell covered not only more chemistry along his accustomed lines but also Cassini on astronomy. He read Barthelemy on ancient Greece, Colquhoun on the policing of London and even a little metaphysics. Johnson became an absorbing subject. Having worked carefully through Boswell's *Life*, he proceeded to Johnson's *Poems of London*, *Vanity of Human Wishes*, *Lives of the Poets* and *Rambler* essays. This listing, though not exhaustive, is surely sufficient to establish the seriousness, persistence and depth of O'Connell's preparation for the greater world.

We know little about O'Connell's law studies after he removed to Dublin. He no longer mentioned his legal reading in his journal, beyond bemoaning the inroads made upon his working time by the calls of the artillery. Eventually, he made a major resolution to amend his ways. 'I misspent my time during the summer', he wrote on 13 January 1798, 'and have done very little better since my return to town [in November 1797]. I am now to take up the study of the law with all the ardour which my situation requires.'[38] Doubtless, as usual, he exaggerated his own shortcomings. Two of the scanty journal references to what he actually did in Dublin suggest as much. On 29 December 1796 he noted, after a law students' test at Trinity College, 'I knew the part of Blackstone in which we were examined, I may safely say, better than any individual';[39] and on 25 January 1797 he recorded his attendance at a technically interesting writ of error case at King's Bench.

O'Connell's stern resolution of 13 January 1798 probably sprang from the imminence of his call to the bar, which might, all going well, take place in the next law term. Hunting Cap was agreeable to his being called then, provided that no 'rub or obstruction could be thrown in the way to impede';[40] he raised no 'rub' himself to meeting the formidable bills which admission to the bar entailed. But O'Connell did fear another sort of obstruction: 'such is the complexion of affairs', he had added on 13 January, 'that it must appear extremely doubtful whether I shall be called to the bar.'[41] In part, O'Connell had in mind the 'odium against the Catholics', which, he told Hunting Cap on 1 March 1798, 'is becoming every day more inveterate. The Chancellor [Fitzgibbon] seems hardly disposed to leave them the privileges which they enjoy at present.'[42] Fitzgibbon was also hellbent against sedition amongst the student body. He had already secured the postponement *sine die* of the call of a politically radical law student, and he was shortly to conduct a purge of Trinity College resulting in the expulsion of nineteen undergraduates who were members or supposed to be members of the United Irishmen. Thus O'Connell felt doubly vulnerable.

He may have been even more vulnerable than he thought. On 7 March 1798, Francis Higgins, the government's principal secret agent, reported to Dublin Castle that O'Connell had covertly received a despatch from one of the leading revolutionaries-in-exile, Napper Tandy. 'Connell holds a commission from France (a Colonel's). He was to be called to the Bar here to please a very rich old uncle, but he is one of the most abominable and bloodthirsty republicans I ever heard of. The place of rendezvous is the Public Library in Eustace Street, where a private room is devoted to the leaders of the United Irish Society'.[43] This was of course a farrago – but by no means total nonsense. Higgins had confused O'Connell with his *emigré* uncle, and stated precisely the opposite of the truth in describing O'Connell as 'bloodthirsty' or, in the French sense at least, a 'republican'. None the less it was undeniable that O'Connell had flirted with United Irishmen in the preceding year, or that the Dublin Library was the United Irish haunt. Young men were to be hanged – let alone denied entry to a profession – on no more damning evidence than this during 1798 and 1799.

There are moreover certain indications that O'Connell moved radical-wards again in the early spring of 1798. He entered nothing in his journal between 13 January and 31 December 1798; but in a posthumous memoir his son John described a dinner party held 'about March 1798' by O'Connell's intimate friend, Murray, a cheese merchant, at which O'Connell, flown with wine, talked politics indiscreetly. He was subsequently warned by his landlord, Regan, whose work rendered him au fait with the gossip of Dublin Castle, against committing himself publicly. In later years, Murray's son, Peter, recalled another fateful evening at his father's house:

> I well remember O'Connell one night at my father's house, during the spring of 1798, so carried away by the political excitement of the day and by the ardour of his innate patriotism, calling for a prayer-book to swear in some zealous young men as United Irishmen at a meeting of the body in a neighbouring street. Councillor — was there, and offered to accompany O'Connell on his perilous mission. My father, though an Irishman of advanced liberal views and strong patriotism, was not a United Irishman, and endeavoured without effect to deter his young and gifted friend from the rash course in which he seemed embarked. Dublin was in an extremely disturbed state, and the outburst of a bloody insurrection seemed hourly imminent. My father resolved to exert to the uttermost the influence which it was well known he possessed over his young friend. He made him accompany him to the canal bridge at Leeson Street, and, after an earnest conversation, succeeded in persuading the future Liberator to step into a turf boat that was then leaving Dublin. That night my father's house was searched by Major Sirr, accompanied by the Attorneys' Corps of Yeomanry, who pillaged it to their heart's content. There can be no doubt that private information of O'Connell's tendencies and haunts had been communicated to the Government.[44]

It is difficult to evaluate this statement. Though highly circumstantial, it was made long after O'Connell's death and may well have been a second-hand reminiscence. Certainly, if O'Connell did leave Dublin in the spring of 1798, it cannot have been for long; and it seems quite out of character with O'Connell of the *Journal* to try to embroil others in a perilous conspiracy. On the other hand, the Castle's witch-hunt in Dublin in March and April, not least among the student population, might have produced a desperate reaction – especially in a moment of pot-valour; and the very vehemence of O'Connell's later denunciations of conspiracy, as the natural begetter of informers, betrayal and ruin, might well have sprung from a sense that he himself had narrowly escaped the trap.

Whatever the degree of his political entanglement, however, O'Connell kept his eye fixed upon his call to the bar. Hunting Cap was applied to long in advance for money for the call, as well as help in securing the necessary memorials of support from practising senior counsel. Evidently pleased that the first staging-post in O'Connell's career was now in sight, Hunting Cap responded with unusual benignity, in addition to his invariable efficiency and despatch. He could not resist playing Polonius for a while; the role was both congenial and practically demanded by the occasion. 'One maxim you should always keep in view, which is, that it is, by much, more decent and reputable to advance gradually and as circumstances will prudently admit, in expense, than to set out ostentatiously and soon be obliged to recede and retrench.'[45] But platitudes broke no bones. O'Connell was now provided with all he needed for his admission, and despite Fitzgibbon's hostility to Catholics and pursuit of the disaffected, and even Higgins's delation of him on 7 March, he safely attained the rank of barrister in the earliest possible law term, Easter 1798.

Within five days of O'Connell's admission the United Irish rebellion, which was also a massive agrarian and sectarian revolt, broke out in Wexford. For a time Dublin itself seemed threatened, and almost a month passed before the final decisive defeat of the insurgents at Vinegar Hill, near Enniscorthy, on 21 June. Meanwhile, legal work was disrupted for the remainder of the term. O'Connell must have left for Kerry soon after the courts were suspended, for land communication with the interior was still cut off when he departed: 'so eighteen of us sailed for Cork in a potato boat, bound for Courtmasherry [*sic*]'. Disembarking at the Cove of Cork, 'after a capital passage of thirty-six hours', he proceeded overland to Carhen.[46] Before the summer assizes (much delayed) commenced, O'Connell fell gravely ill. 'I did not go to it [the summer circuit], as I was confined to my uncle's house by a violent fever, of which I was near to perish.'[47] Possibly his malady was rheumatic fever; at any rate, it was brought on by sleeping in wet clothes and accompanied by bouts of delirium. It lasted for several weeks; for long his life was in danger. 'During my illness', O'Connell later recalled, 'I used to quote from the tragedy of Douglas these lines:

> *Unknown I die; no tongue shall speak of me;*
> *Some noble spirits, judging by themselves,*
> *May yet conjecture what I might have proved;*
> *And think life only wanting to my fame.'* [48]

How revealing was this choice of verse! There is no reason to suppose that O'Connell's memory played him false; but even if it did, even if he picked these lines not upon his sick-bed but retroactively, how very suggestive his selection still would be.

It was November 1798 before O'Connell returned to Dublin and his 'practice'. This last had yielded him but a single guinea since his call to the bar six months before. Yet his involuntary idleness of the summer is not to be set down as an unmitigated misfortune. Possibly – though he himself would doubtless have been amazed at such a thought – he needed a long respite from strain and striving. Certainly, he gained from his remove from the storm-centre of Irish politics; Kerry was quite untouched by the insurrection or its bloody aftermath. Not only did he escape all governmental attention in the inquisitory months which followed the collapse at Vinegar Hill but also he could watch the development of Irish revolution at a philosophic distance, and learn from it two lessons which he was to prize throughout his life. One was the danger and the debauchery of conspiracy. The post-rebellion trials furnished much painful evidence of cowardice and treachery, of spies, informers and *agents provocateurs*. The other was a deep distrust of (as well as pity for) the masses, once they were unloosed from 'rational' control. 'I dined today with Bennett', he wrote in his journal on 2 January 1799. 'We talked much of the late unhappy rebellion. A great deal of innocent blood was shed on the occasion. Good God! what a brute man becomes when ignorant and oppressed! Oh, Liberty, what horrors are perpetrated in thy name! May every virtuous revolutionist remember the horrors of Wexford!'[49] No less interesting however is the opening of the sentence which preceded this particular entry in the journal: 'I finished my notes of *Fee Tail* out of *Coke on Littleton* today.' Two days later, he added, 'In the course of another year I shall be a tolerably good lawyer. My present method of studying the common and statute law I believe to be the best. When I have proceeded in it for some time, I will commence equity on the same plan.'[50] The industrious apprentice was clearly back on course. As with Sieyès' celebrated estimate of his achievement in the French Revolution, O'Connell could say of 1798, 'J'ai vécu'.[51]

V

O'Connell had been called to the bar on 19 May 1798, and earned his first guinea five days later for drawing up a declaration on a promissory note. But practically speaking his legal career did not commence until the following February. The law year had been much disturbed in 1798, and in any event, as we have seen, O'Connell's illness prevented his going on circuit. In 1799, however, he made a brave beginning at the bar, earning twenty-three guineas from sixteen fees. Ten of these fees came from the attorney who had given him his first brief in 1798, James Connor of Tralee. Connor may have acted from old friendship. He was a remote connection of O'Connell by marriage; but a very distant link could scarcely have been counted for much in the almost infinitely intersected society of middle-class Kerry. At any rate, Connor was soon rewarded for his early patronage for O'Connell proved himself, almost immediately, to be a quite extraordinary junior.

The bulk of O'Connell's earliest work at the bar was more or less mechanical, drawing up declarations, composing petitions for compensation from the local rates for cattle houghed, and the like. But he was briefed as junior by Connor in a case of some magnitude – possibly concerning a challenge to a duel – at the Tralee summer assizes of 1799. It was then the Irish practice for senior and junior counsel to cross-examine witnesses in turn, but also for inexperienced juniors to waive their 'right' to cross-examine if the cross-examination looked like being more than merely formal. But O'Connell, although still only twenty-three years old and in his first few months of effective practice, refused to pass up his chance of glory. As he later described it,

There was one of the witnesses of the other party whose cross-examination was thrown upon *me* by the opposite counsel. I did not do, as I have seen fifty young counsel do; namely, hand the cross-examination over to my senior. I thought it due to myself to attempt it, hit or miss; and I cross-examined him right well. I remember he stated that he had *his share* of a pint of whisky; whereupon I asked him *whether his share was not all except the pewter?* He confessed that it was: and the oddity of my mode of putting the question was very successful, and created a general and hearty laugh. Jerry Keller [a leading counsel on the Munster circuit] repeated the encouragement Robert Hickson had already bestowed upon my activity, in the very same words: 'You'll *do*, young gentleman! You'll do'.[52]

Despite possible high-colouring by its hero, the episode points to several of the courtroom qualities for which O'Connell was later to be celebrated. First, his controlled audacity: here it manifested itself merely – though in the circumstances also strikingly – in taking a considerable risk in the hope of leaping into a local reputation. But it was soon to operate more grandly. O'Connell was to become remarkable for the boldness with which (having calculated carefully beforehand) he struck out his strategic legal line, and also for his indomitable resistance to, and even contemptuous counter-attacks upon, bullying or exorbitant judges. Secondly, his Tralee performance illustrates his speed of response and flexibility in cross-examination. Finally, it exhibits already a strength for which he was to be often and justly celebrated – his capacity to read the minds of ordinary Irish people. In this instance, he understood immediately the shadowy balance between fear of the legal and spiritual consequences of perjury and the desire to avoid the admission of fatal evidence. The consequent word-play, unschooled but cunning casuistry, and blithe differentiation of the *suggestio falsi* from the false – these were characteristic features of a mental world that he could enter and move about in with consummate ease.

Jerry Keller proved a good prophet. O'Connell '*did*', and '*did*' very quickly, at the bar. In his second year proper in practice his gross earnings exceeded £400, and although he earned a little less in 1801, the decline was temporary. By his thirtieth year, 1805, his fees brought in over £1000, and from then on he climbed rapidly through £2000, £3000 and £3500 per annum. In short, O'Connell was prodigiously successful as a junior counsel. Monetary translations between the centuries are notoriously difficult and dubious; but it would be safe to say that his annual income must have exceeded £100,000, in modern terms, within ten years of his being called. Let us not slide over this achievement easily. Even had he been a Protestant, a tory and a judge's son or nephew, all together, such an early climb would have been accounted a marvel. R. L. Sheil, who shortly followed O'Connell to the bar, wrote of the contemporary profession as he found it: 'There is at the Irish Bar a much larger quantity of affliction than is generally known . . . The struggle between poverty and gentility, which the ostentatious publicity of the profession in Ireland has produced, has, I believe, broken many hearts.'[53] Most were doomed never 'to attain to station . . . to live for years in hope, and to feel the proverbial sickness of the heart arising from its procrastination.'[54] Sheil described the typical beginning of even the most eminent career: 'For some years he remains unemployed: at last gets a brief, creeps into the partialities of a solicitor, and sets up a bag and a wife together.'[55] This should make clear the extraordinariness of O'Connell's initial achievement.

Success of this kind at the bar implied immense labours. Most of O'Connell's fees were small sums, down even to one or two guineas; and much of his work continued to be mechanical and tedious, eating

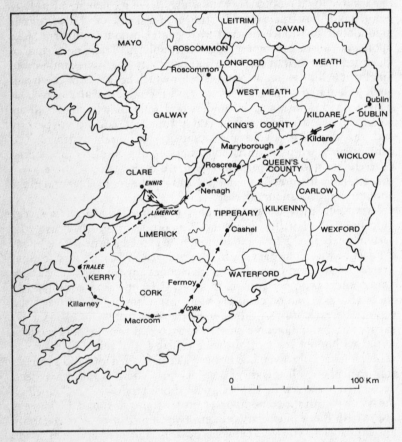

Map 3. The Munster circuit

68

the hours without compensating stimulation. Extraordinary physical strength, concentration and elasticity of disposition were demanded by such a life, all the more so as it was seasonally peripatetic. Each late spring and each high summer, the young O'Connell undertook by mailcoach, carriage or horse the laborious five- or six-week circuit of Ennis, Limerick, Tralee and Cork. With various deviations, the mere time spent on roads and tracks during a circuit probably accounted for six or seven full days. A great deal of this journeying would have been on execrable surfaces or over rain- and windswept high terrain. Parts of the route, especially north of Tralee and south-west to Macroom, were very difficult: 'if anything were capable of destroying my natural vivacity', wrote O'Connell in 1806, 'it would be those infernal mountains and roads.'[56] A stretch near Kilworth was sometimes brigand-ridden during his early circuit years.

O'Connell's descriptions of parts of two of these journeys survive. One summer morning, almost certainly in 1799, he left Carhen at 4 a.m. and reached Tralee, some fifty miles away, soon after midday.

> I then rode on, and got to Tarbert about five in the afternoon – full sixty miles, Irish, [over ninety statute miles] from Carhen. There wasn't one book to be had at the inn. I had no acquaintance in the town; and I felt my spirits low enough at the prospect of a long, stupid evening. But I was relieved, by the sudden appearance of Ralph Marshall, an old friend of mine, who came to the inn to dress for a ball that took place in Tarbert that night. He asked me to accompany him to the ball. 'Why,' said I, 'I have ridden sixty miles'. 'Oh, you don't seem in the least tired,' said he, 'so come along'. Accordingly I went, and sat up until two o'clock in the morning, dancing. I arose next day at half-past eight, and rode to the Limerick assizes.[57]

Two years later, while crossing the mountains from Killarney to Kenmare en route for the Cork assizes, he brooded upon the passage of the Act of Union:

> my heart was heavy at the loss that Ireland had sustained, and the day was wild and gloomy. That desert district, too, was congenial to impressions of solemnity and sadness. There was not a human habitation to be seen for many miles; black, giant clouds sailed slowly through the sky, and rested on the tops of the huge mountains: my soul felt dreary, and I had many wild and *Ossianic* inspirations as I traversed the bleak solitudes.[58]

These contrasting vignettes enable us to feel, as it were, a little of the texture of O'Connell's circuitry under our hands. But it would probably be misleading to use light and shade in equal proportions in any sketch of his first years as a working barrister. Toil, gloom and struggle there certainly were. But the predominant impression given off by the evidence – scanty though it be – is of O'Connell's delight in his young powers and in the variety and colour of his experiences and companionship. In 'chambers' (which meant, in Dublin, the Law Library and one's home study), O'Connell was succeeding; and for all its discomforts, circuit life was bustling and exciting – at any rate, for a confident junior growing rapidly, twice-yearly, in reputation. Admittedly, much of the material from which one's sense of the fun, glamour and camaraderie of the Munster Bar at the turn of the eighteenth century derives, consists of reminiscenses; and these are notoriously selective. Even if it was larger than life, however, it was a real life which was being twopenny-coloured. The world of dashing chaises and sudden briefs, of ramshackle inns and clarety bar messes, of challenges, and even duels, and contesting wits, of judicial ogres and oddities and 'characters' to fill each courtroom role, had a basis in actuality. (Even the blackly-comic story of O'Connell's being challenged to a duel by a hostile witness, who withdrew the challenge on recalling that O'Connel's was one of the three lives on which his lease depended, but offered to repeat it if O'Connell would insure his life, may well have been substantially true.) Such a world was the young O'Connell's oyster. Tall, handsome, quick, dextrous, brilliant and assured, he could exult in it and exploit it, in more or less equal parts.

CHAPTER 4

Love and Money

1800–15

I

O'Connell entered into a secret engagement with Mary O'Connell late in 1800, probably when he was in Tralee for the second assizes of that year. He was then twenty-five years old, she three years younger. He may have known her long, since she was a distant cousin. But his intimacy with her was new, and probably arose from her being sister-in-law to his friend and chief professional support at the time, James Connor of Tralee. O'Connell fell in love, if not absolutely at first sight, at any rate on first seeing Mary with fresh eyes. He acted with corresponding dispatch. As he recalled almost forty years later, 'I said to her, "Are you engaged, Miss O'Connell?" – She answered, "I am not." "Then," said I "will you engage yourself to me?" – "I will," was her reply. – And I said I would devote my life to make her happy. She deserved that I should – she gave me thirty-four years of the purest happiness that man ever enjoyed.'[1]

Mary O'Connell was one of eight children, whose father, Thomas O'Connell, a Tralee physician, had died fifteen years before. She was consequently penniless; and it was this which led O'Connell to insist upon the strictest secrecy in their engagement. It was all too likely that Hunting Cap would disinherit him, and perhaps even break with him entirely, if he discovered that he meant to marry a dowerless girl. 'You know as well as I do', O'Connell wrote to Mary on 28 November 1800, in what was probably his first letter to his future wife, 'how much *we* have at stake in keeping the business secret. I have certainly more at stake than ever I had before or I really believe if I fail at present I shall ever have again. Secrecy is therefore a favour I earnestly beg of you.'[2] It was also the case that Mary's brothers, taking their religion from their father, were Protestants, and impecunious ones at that.

Mary was quite willing to flout convention. A concealed engagement was highly improper, but scarcely less so was the illicit correspondence in which she was now to be employed for eighteen months. O'Connell may, as he said, have loathed the subterfuges and lies which such a correspondence demanded. But he was always a capable intriguer. He induced another, much closer, cousin, also named Daniel O'Connell but generally known as Splinter, to act as receiver of his letters from Dublin to Mary in Tralee. Whenever Splinter, another attorney, was in Dublin on business, *he* addressed O'Connell's letters directly to Mary. This led to difficulties when Splinter was not where he was needed: 'he is not to be found. He is very inconsiderate',[3] O'Connell once complained. It also produced a potentially dangerous situation when in June 1801 Mary's brother, Rick, identified Splinter's handwriting on a cover addressed to Mary. So furious was he at her impropriety in corresponding with the young attorney, that at one point a challenge to Splinter was impending. Rick's bellicosity probably owed something to Splinter's being a notoriously bad match. This crisis led to a temporary suspension of the correspondence. Later, when James Connor was admitted to the secret, he was used in Splinter's place, again with unhappy results. When Connor's wife Betsey saw a cover addressed to Mary in his handwriting, she assumed that he was suffering from a grave illness which he wished to conceal from her! Betsey too had to be told of the engagement, much against O'Connell's wishes.

There were also misunderstandings between the engaged couple. O'Connell was curiously insensitive to women's feelings – at any rate, at this particular time and to a woman of lower social standing than himself. There were distinct elements of Frank Churchill's conduct to Jane Fairfax in his behaviour. When in Kerry in the late spring of 1801, he deliberately fostered the idea that there was an 'understanding' between Mary and another local barrister in order to divert suspicion from himself. 'You are probably indebted to me', he wrote to Mary on 28 April, 'for all the jokes you suffer about Peter Hussey.'[4] O'Connell also forced clothes and finery upon her. At first, Mary resisted. She felt a 'delicacy', she told him, about being given articles which she had asked him to buy for her in Dublin. Behind this there doubtless lay some resentment of his Cophetua-like indulgence; Mary was acutely sensitive about her poverty. But she did enjoy Tralee's envy of her new veil; and in the end O'Connell's persistent argument that she was already effectively, though not legally, his wife, wore her down. By the close of 1801 he was writing of the kerchief and the '*few* pairs of white stockings' which he had purchased for her, and of her 'loose coat' in the tailor's hands.[5]

On the other hand, Mary rebelled mildly, once or twice, against the constraints of O'Connell's secrecy and the consequences of his finesse. The most serious quarrel of the betrothal arose from her writing to him in mock-formal terms, in January 1802, because his letters had fallen off. Angry and fearful, O'Connell misunderstood Mary's tactic and offered (or perhaps we should say threatened indirectly) to end the relationship should she maintain her caprice. His lapse in correspondence, he told her indignantly, had been for prudential reasons. There had been no safe conduit for letters at the time. Full of his own virtue in restraining his pen and in plotting laboriously for concealment, he was furious at what he regarded as Mary's petty and wanton revenge. She was mistaken, he wrote,

> I did not laugh at your former letter to me. Indeed, its producing a comical effect on me would be directly contrary to every impression I entertain of you. I trust and am pretty confident that this experiment will suffice and that you will not in future sport with the feelings which you know are too sensitive to bear being played on. How could you, my only darling, treat me so coldly on so slight an occasion for you had not insisted that I should write to you by every post . . . Judge then how mortified I felt at finding so small an offence – shall I call it an offence? – put every idea of tenderness out of your bosom . . . I beg of you, my love, humbly but as a favour which I think my respectful regard for you merits, that you will consider seriously before you treat me with such coldness. Indeed, indeed, I am unable to bear it.[6]

Mary learnt her lesson. Quizzing and pique were to be the male's preserve.

Despite this, the attachment, passionate from the start on either side, grew rapidly in depth. Mary could express her love the more effectively, at least in correspondence. In yielding to O'Connell's claims to provide for her as if they were already married, she wrote, simply,

> Let me then hope you are satisfied I do consider you as my husband, as my dearest and only love. Indeed, Dan, you are dearer to me than I can express. I have told you before and I will now tell it to you again that you are the only man I could ever love or wish myself united with . . . I am indeed very well convinced of my darling's love, and trust he is also convinced of mine for him.[7]

Mary had, as O'Connell himself observed twenty years later, 'a clear and distinct mind'.[8] By contrast, he could not avoid inflation.

> In disposition and in heart she ['my little woman'] is all excellence, in

temper all sweetness, in person all that painting can express or youthful poets fancy when they love. To tell you how much I love my little woman would be to express that of which no image can be formed. Think how much you love me and then add ten hundred thousand times as much . . .[9]

But the fact that one could write straightforwardly, and the other only through a zig-zag of rhetorical postures, does not mean that their emotional commitments were unequal; the future was to show that O'Connell was Mary's peer in love.

No wedding date or plan is mentioned in the pre-marital correspondence, which stretches from November 1800 to May 1802. Presumably Hunting Cap was to be bearded before a date could be set, but O'Connell feared to hazard such a step. Meanwhile, their meetings alone must have been few and hurried, as well as covert. From the start, O'Connell had counted much on a projected visit to Dublin by Mary. 'I anxiously hope you will come up to town after Christmas with Mrs Connor', he wrote in his initial letter of 28 November 1800. 'Here I would have many more opportunities of seeing and conversing with you than in that prying, curious, *busy* town of Tralee.'[10] Presumably, it was hoped that this would afford them the chance of settling their future. But a year and a half were to pass before the visit could be managed. In the end, it did need the help of James and Betsey Connor (whom O'Connell had tried again to use, to get Mary to Derrynane, in August 1801) to bring the lovers together for a considerable time. Mary accompanied the Connors to Dublin, at last, on 12 May 1802.

It is most unlikely that a wedding in Dublin was planned beforehand. Neither O'Connell's nor Mary's letters suggest, in any way, that this was in contemplation before she left Tralee. But on 24 July, a day or two before the Connors had to return to Kerry, a private marriage did take place in the Connors' Dublin lodgings. How the celebrant, a local parish priest, was persuaded to act in such secrecy, it is impossible to say. Nor do we know why O'Connell left his own family entirely in the dark; none of them as yet had heard anything of even the betrothal, although it was by now quite widely known among Mary's close relations. Possibly O'Connell reasoned that – Hunting Cap perhaps apart – the best course was the boldest, that of presenting them later on with a fait accompli. But the most probable explanation is that the decision to marry was a very sudden one, taken in the light of the imminent separation. There are times when, all in a flash, waiting can become unendurable, and prudence crumble.

74

II

The public deception continued long after the wedding had taken place. Mary returned to Tralee with the Connors within two days of her marriage, lived with them there for a few weeks, and then, with her mother, took new lodgings. It was two months before she next saw O'Connell when he visited Tralee in the course of his annual Kerry vacation. All this time, and indeed throughout the remainder of 1802, she lived as a single girl. O'Connell himself addressed her, on the cover of her letters, as 'Miss Maria O'Connell'. Even when, in September, he told his sister Ellen in confidence of '*our secret*', it was the 'attachment' only that he revealed and not the marriage.[11] By the beginning of November however O'Connell knew that his wife was pregnant; the period of possible concealment was now limited. He set the time of disclosure for his Christmas visit to his relations. On 30 December 1802, O'Connell wrote to Mary from his father's home, Carhen,

> I am just going to Derrynane. I will remain there nine days, then three here – one in Killorglin on business and the following I shall embrace the best, most amiable and most beloved little woman in the world. I wish to God *my story* was told to the old Gentleman [Hunting Cap]. I shall feel devilish awkward. But I am full of hope and know no reason to be otherwise. If contrary to my sanguine expectations I should find my uncle desperate in not *permitting me to marry without a fortune*, I will not go further but you and your mother shall (if I get hers and your consent) come to Dublin on your way to join Maurice [Mary's brother]. But this is a scheme which I am determined not to want although I mention it. For I will not quit my uncle until I tell him of our marriage. At all events do not expect to hear from me till you see me as I shall like to be the bearer of my own good news.[12]

O'Connell's optimism, if ever genuine, was short-lived. In the event, his courage failed him and he did not dare to tell Hunting Cap of his marriage, face to face. Instead, on returning to Dublin at the end of January 1803, he left a letter of confession with his brother, John, to be handed to Hunting Cap at a propitious moment.

The result was disastrous. Hunting Cap, in 'a most violent flood of tears', was 'grieved and exasperated' beyond expectation. 'I never witnessed', wrote John, 'such a struggle as was exhibited by him between affection and displeasure.' Displeasure carried the day. He ceased to regard or treat O'Connell as his heir; relations between the two became merely formal. O'Connell fared far better with his own family. His father, John reported, disapproved of the marriage only in so far as it would injure him in the estimation of his uncle. 'At any moment you please, he is satisfied to receive Mary at Carhen. You may easily suppose she will meet with every attention from the rest of the family.'[13]

Hunting Cap's anger was to have been expected. He had, characteristically, planned an advantageous match for O'Connell, and had one such actually in train. Now his will was permanently thwarted. It was not the Protestant strain – the fruit of a comparatively recent conformity – in Mary's family which he found offensive, but rather their poverty and social decline. He had spent half a century securing himself and his relatives from both. O'Connell quite failed to understand how deeply he had wounded Hunting Cap; successful manoeuvres such as that which secured his membership of the Lawyers' Artillery may have rendered him carelessly confident. At first, he looked to a further letter, which he had 'written with feeling and I think with some degree of talent',[14] to coax his uncle out of his resentment. Two months later he still airily asserted that 'what remains of his displeasure will be apt to vanish when we come to converse soberly'.[15] By the end of 1803, however, Hunting Cap had brought home to him the intensity of his resentment by knotting the purse strings absolutely. It was now O'Connell's turn to try to allay his wounded pride. He professed himself surprised and 'almost ashamed' that he had reigned so long as his uncle's favourite. 'He could not but perceive that in every action my mind scorned the narrow bounds of his.'[16]

O'Connell's immediate family however proved altogether compliant. At first sight this is surprising. Marrying both money and social equals or superiors was a family article of faith – marriage for sentimental preference anathema. In November 1802, his parents had compelled his sister Ellen 'to give up that foolish attachment' to her cousin, Splinter. 'Sure it would have been hard', wrote his mother, still ignorant of O'Connell's own secret marriage, 'that my ever dear Ellen should refuse to act as each of her sisters did, who gave up early prepossessions to gratify me who they well know had their interests only at heart.'[17] Yet O'Connell's breach of this marriage code was never openly condemned – a testimony to his commanding position within his own family. John did not exaggerate when he wrote that his father's displeasure was vicarious not personal, for Morgan's treatment of Mary appears to have been consistently affectionate and kind. There are many indications that Catherine O'Connell resented her son's marriage and his bride, not only immediately but also for several years after the disclosure. But this was no extraordinary reaction for a mother in such a situation; and Catherine certainly did not spare herself in helping the young couple in the first years of their marriage.

The marriage's 'external relations' were however a secondary affair; its interior proved sound. O'Connell's passion grew. Often he expressed it in terms at once cloying and bombastic. 'Sweet Mary, I rave of you! I think only of you! I sigh for you, I weep for you! I almost pray to you!'[18] But a professional rhetorician and advocate is perhaps bound to stumble in the language of the heart. Moreover, his letters to Mary were in the strictest sense private communications, and as he himself once observed,

> Love, I conceive that an indifferent person would smile at a *husband's* writing thus to his wife after being married even so long as we are; but I should be truly ashamed if any person felt more fondness, or passion or did or suffered more for the object of illicit and criminal love than I would cheerfully do for my Mary. And yet I see men endure every hardship for the obtaining the possession of women whose persons alone can be desirable.[19]

A crisis came suddenly upon them at the end of January 1803, after O'Connell had returned to Dublin, leaving Mary in her lodgings in Tralee under her mother's charge. It was from her mother that he learnt that Mary had fallen so ill in pregnancy that her life was in danger. On 1 February he wrote frantically, trying to convey 'an idea of the black agony that harrows up my soul of souls'.

> If you were well I care not for uncle, relatives, or fortune. I would accept poverty, tortures and death to give you either happiness or even a single proof of the unceasing and consuming passion which devours whilst it consumes this anguished heart of mine . . .
>
> Mary, sweet, sweet Mary, I cannot, indeed, I cannot live without you. You are my life, my comfort. If I were a religionist I should spend every moment in praying for you – and this miserable philosophy which I have taken up and been proud of – in the room of religion, affords me now no consolation in my misery. How much truth do not I now feel in the assertion that man is a creature more of the heart than the reason. Sweet, dearest darling, write to me as soon as you can but do not hurry yourself until you are quite recovered, for you must indeed, my own Mary, you must recover. I have the insolence [*sic*] madness to say it must not be otherwise, or if it be, depend on soon meeting your husband, if a spirit so pure as yours will elsewhere consort with such a vile being as mine.[20]

Mary recovered quickly, O'Connell's letter actually crossing one of hers written from her sick-bed on 3 February. His anxieties for her were fully matched by her fears that he would break down under his

uncle's displeasure which 'will I know give you more real sorrow than
the loss of his fortune'.

> I beg and entreat of you then, my heart's dearest treasure, to take care of
> yourself and not give way to unavailing grief. I know from experience how
> injurious it is to the health. Consider, darling, if you do make yourself
> unhappy you will make one whose existence depends on yours the most
> miserable of beings.[21]

The O'Connells' reciprocal misery was succeeded by reciprocal joy as
each learnt of the other's recovery from real or supposed distress.
Happy letters of relief soon flowed in either direction. But one great
difficulty, probably an ill-consequence of the rupture with Hunting
Cap, remained. O'Connell had been searching for a house (presumably to rent, and not to buy) in Dublin. This quest was now
abandoned. His prospects had been dimmed and his usual recourse in
extremities – further support from Hunting Cap – would certainly not
be forthcoming. It was clear that Mary would have to remain in
lodgings in Tralee until her baby was born. Some time before the birth
took place on 27 June 1803, however, O'Connell's parents must have
agreed to take in the mother and newborn child as soon as practicable
after the confinement.

Although the house at Carhen was comparatively modest in scale,
the elder O'Connells provided a home for Mary and her children for
most of the two and a quarter years which followed the birth of her
first child, Maurice. When she went to Tralee for the birth of her
second son, Morgan, in October 1804, Maurice remained in the care
of his grandparents at Carhen. For the next year, they were virtually
his parents, and apparently so regarded by Maurice himself. 'Our
sweet Maurice is perfectly well', wrote Mary to O'Connell soon after
her reunion with her elder son. 'He is much attached to me though he
sometimes calls me a bitch and desires me to go to Tralee to Dada
Dan.'[22]

Mary had not found it easy to regain her niche at Carhen after her
second accouchement at Tralee. On 9 November 1804, ten days after
Morgan's birth, she sounded out her husband in Dublin,

> Tell me, darling, did you write to your father requesting he would permit
> his namesake [Morgan] to stay at Carhen until after Christmas? If you did
> not, I wish you would on receipt of this without mentioning that I had
> wrote or spoke to you on the subject, and do not omit mentioning if your
> mother has no objection to it. Perhaps it would be better for you [to] write
> to herself about [it]. In my opinion it would. The two nurses and the
> children could sleep in my room very well.[23]

A week later, she followed this up, rather despondently. 'You did not tell me if you wrote to your mother. What I would give to have her keep my little darling [Morgan] at Carhen while I remained there, but I fear I have no chance.'[24] It is clear from the December 1804 correspondence between O'Connell and his wife that they expected to achieve the removal to Carhen before Christmas. But, for whatever reason, this fell through and Mary's return was delayed until mid-April 1805, by which time some seven months had probably elapsed since she had seen her elder child. Evidently the interval – or Mary's first period of residence with her parents-in-law – had created soreness on either side. On 16 April 1805, upon her eventual return to Carhen, she wrote to O'Connell:

> I arrived here late yesterday evening and was met by James [O'Connell's youngest brother] at Filemore who told me he had come at the instance of his father and mother to request I would go down to Carhen. To gratify you, my heart, I agreed to do so. Your father came to the gate to meet me and welcomed me in the kindest manner. Your mother was out walking but soon came in and received me rather stiffly. However, I don't mind that as she is coming off of it this day. I found our darling Maurice much improved. He talks a great deal but all in Irish. He is already taken with me and calls me Mama Mary. He is very fond of your picture since morning, kisses it and calls it Dan.[25]

But such jarring was after all a natural concomitant of the awkward situation in which all the O'Connells – Daniel himself perhaps excepted – were placed by his improvident match. For the first three years of her marriage, Mary had mostly to live apart from her husband, either with his parents or in lodgings in a provincial town. Catherine O'Connell had to provide for O'Connell's family, or part of it, for over two years, and to care for the children on her own on two occasions in mid-1805 when Mary visited Dublin. As Mary herself acknowledged, it was very hard for old people to look after infants for considerable periods at a stretch.

Meanwhile, from July 1802 to July 1805 O'Connell had endured a solitary life in Dublin lodgings or circuit inns for at least three-quarters of each year. He often expressed a longing for Mary and his children. 'Darling,' he wrote towards the end of 1803, 'I doat of you with an affection which absence only increases – and which renders the air I breathe poison until I shall have clasped to my breast at least *the thoughts* of my beloved . . . Tell me how my sweet boy gets on. My darling infant, how I doat of him because he is yours.' [26] However effusive or even foolish the expression, the feeling was real enough.

The steady rain of O'Connell's letters and his scarcely-to-be-credited exertions to join Mary in almost every interstice of his pressing professional life were proof of this. Equally, he was an anxious, eager, boastful father. On one of the very rare occasions on which the children were in his sole charge, he told his wife,

> I have not seen Morgan yet [he was being wet-nursed on Valentia Island] but am just going in to him. He is, however, I am informed, the sweetest and finest creature imaginable. Your son Maurice is as like you as two eggs – and has all that sauciness of temper and disposition. He is a wonderful favourite and the most affectionate little villain in the world. His temper is certainly hasty but he is never for one moment sulky or sullen and I already perceive that there would be little difficulty in bringing him into proper discipline.[27]

It was doubtless the accumulated strain of protracted separations which induced O'Connell, at last, to set up his own household in Dublin. His purchase of no. 1 Westland Row in mid-1805 was financially imprudent. On the other hand, by the time his wife and children moved there in November 1805, he had been a married man without a home for well over three years and his third child was shortly to be born. Much more provident husbands than O'Connell might have taken this leap long before.

Doubtless Mary had suffered much more than he from the delay. Countless humiliations and embarrassments – as well as a great deal of tedium – must have flown from her enforced residence with her husband's parents, especially in the long months of his absences. But the senior O'Connells also had much to bear, and O'Connell's father and two at least of his sisters, Ellen and Kitty, seem to have given Mary constant comfort and affection. In fact O'Connell's extraordinary marriage was more striking for the comparative amity and decent restraints on all sides than for the occasional brushes and the underlying resentments and domestic wounds. Correspondingly, O'Connell's own magnanimity was quite as remarkable as the family's acknowledgement of his continued leadership or its corporate capacity to absorb the blow. Even his brother John's elevation, at the end of 1803, to the station of Hunting Cap's heir-presumptive, in the place of Daniel, did little to weaken the ties of affection and cross-support between the brothers. John seems to have striven honestly to maintain Daniel in Hunting Cap's favour. Reciprocally, Daniel and Mary attached no blame to John when he replaced O'Connell – in part at least – in his uncle's will. Mary privately execrated the 'old sinner' for his treatment of her husband, but John altogether escaped her condemnation. Again, when two years later O'Connell's father re-wrote his will and passed over some of the estate intended for him to his youngest brother, James, and O'Connell quarrelled with the new beneficiary, Mary wrote:

> It grieves me, my darling, that you should have any difference with any of your family, more particularly as I feel myself unintentionally the cause of your present quarrel with James. Don't refuse me this request, my own darling, and consider that you have every prospect of making a fortune independently of the dirty trifle taken from you and left to James, and consider also, heart, that you have a wife who doats of you and who would equally be as fond of you were you in poverty as in affluence. I know I need say no more to you on this subject. Write to me on receipt and let me know if you will gratify me. Indeed I am sure you will. [28]

O'Connell did so immediately. The family, and O'Connell's headship of the entire concern, had triumphed again, much to his own ultimate advantage, as James was loyally, however querulously, to support him in many a crisis over the next two decades and a half.

Even Hunting Cap was partly reconciled to O'Connell in the end. Evidently O'Connell took the initiative early in 1805, passing on information to his uncle which would be useful to him in both his proprietorial and his smuggling roles. Gradually, they slipped back into their old business relationship, with O'Connell helping Hunting Cap with trifles of legal work or counsel, though still formally addressing him as 'Sir'. A year later they met in Tralee when O'Connell was on his spring circuit. 'As to the meeting with my uncle', he told Mary on 31 March 1806, 'nothing could be pleasanter to me. He told me of the hereditary property being mine and gave me most distinctly to understand that he intended all the rest for me. He told Robin Hickson that he had forgiven me and I felt it completely.'[29] As usual O'Connell was over-sanguine. But the restored cordiality deepened steadily until by 1809 Hunting Cap was settling property on O'Connell, while Mary was a-flutter over the purchase of a new bed for his visit to their home in Dublin. Mary attributed the change in Hunting Cap partly to family feeling but also to pride in O'Connell's rising fame. A characteristic comment was that of 11 October 1810: 'Surely your uncle is the kindest of men but, my heart, independent of his affections for you, he feels quite proud of you. The *noise* which you make here and the esteem in which you are held must flatter him greatly.'[30] Mary's judgment of people was always shrewd.

III

The O'Connells' regular married life began with their removal to Dublin towards the end of 1805. By then their third child, Ellen, had been born. Four others followed soon: Kate in March 1807, Edward in July 1808, Betsey in February 1810 and John in December 1810. Edward died when he was one year old, but all the rest flourished; and within ten years of their marriage, the O'Connells had a family of six, ranging from eight years downwards. During this time their life settled to a pattern. O'Connell was on circuit for almost a quarter of each year, five to six weeks or even longer in March–May and again in July–September. He was also from home at other times, generally for a week or two, for special assizes, arbitration or as legal officer at parliamentary elections. Posterity is the gainer, as the bulk of the letters passing between O'Connell and his wife from 1805 onwards derived from these absences. But the absences forced Mary to serve as family manager and decision-maker for considerable periods of time. This was markedly the case after 1809 when the O'Connells moved upwards socially in Dublin by purchasing no. 30 Merrion Square. Mary had to negotiate and supervise extensions to their new home, manage a larger household and act, to some extent, as O'Connell's banker and man-of-business, in ever more complicated financial circumstances, while he was away.

Moreover, her place in Dublin society was now more demanding and her children required much more attention once they commenced school. On hearing of one particular dinner invitation while he was on circuit, O'Connell wrote (with remarkable marital tact) to Mary, 'I hope you went to Mrs Blaquiere and that you were pleasant there. But, my heart, I have a strange notion floating in my mind that she is not precisely the kind of woman I should be anxious to have you intimate with.'[31] On another occasion, Mary told O'Connell of her distress at having to chastise her five-year-old daughter.

> My poor Nell, such a scene as I had with her yesterday. You may suppose how bold she must have been when I was obliged to beat her with a rod, all occasioned by fear and terror of going to school. The day before, Mrs Bishop [the proprietoress, a sister of Mary Wollstonecraft] beat and punished her for not having her hymn, and doubled her task for yesterday in consequence of which the poor infant made every resistance to going to school. You would hardly believe what a complete battle she had not to go.
>
> She never ceased crying from the time she got up in the morning and entreating of me not to send her any more to Mrs Bishop's, but when I

would not listen to her she threw herself on the stairs and I assure you it was a difficult matter to take her up. However, she was at length forced to school.[32]

O'Connell warmly applauded Mary's resolution, 'I am greatly obliged to you for your firmness with my poor Nell. If you had given up the point she would have conquered you for life.'[33] It was easy to be an armchair disciplinarian 160 miles away, but again hard for Mary to have to act alone.

She was often fearful or fretful when O'Connell was away, especially when – though it was rarely the case – several days elapsed between his letters. Her special terror was that he would be forced to a duel, either on his own account or through his belligerent brother, John. 'All I dread', she once wrote, typically, 'is that John (who I know is very hasty) may try to be avenged on Mr S[egerson]. and thereby involve you but for my sake, darling, . . . do not think it worth your while to take notice of anything he says or does for he is beneath your notice.'[34] These fears were far from groundless. O'Connell had apparently come quite close to having to fight the same Segerson on two occasions already. Pistols were a common resort of the quarrelsome Kerry gentry and the Munster bar; and eventually O'Connell was indeed embroiled. One reason for Mary's dislike of his taking in Kerry, and in particular 'going into Iveragh', when he was on circuit or vacation was that, in the early years at least, these were most likely places for challenges. Another was the difficulty of extricating O'Connell from Kerry once he had reintegrated himself into beloved kinship networks and sporting life. Mary's letters were often punctuated with little jibes of the kind dispatched by her to, respectively, Derrynane and Tralee on 29 September and 1 October 1812, 'Perhaps, love, you were *induced* to remain for the pattern [festival] of this day', and 'I have at length the satisfaction to hear you are arrived in Tralee and have fixed your departure from thence on Monday next . . . let nothing induce you to put it off any longer.'[35]

But the most important reason of all for Mary's fear of Kerry was O'Connell's propensity to spend heavily and to incur fresh obligations there. O'Connell was not only the crown prince – or even already reigning king – of his own family, but also embedded in countless other connexions of blood, dependency or friendship. He found it extremely difficult – not that he ever really tried – to deny applications for loans of money, and, still more, to deny applications to act as guarantor for the loans of others, these being conveniently distant and hypothetical obligations. Conversely, he found it fatally easy to borrow small sums and incur other debts. Mary was soon painfully aware of the danger of these Kerry entanglements. When, in the spring of 1809, she was in such straits in Dublin as to write, '*I want money, love*',[36] he had to excuse the paucity of his remittance with – 'I had several debts to pay in Kerry.'[37] This was a harbinger of the crisis which was almost to engulf O'Connell, once and for all, in 1815.

A further though minor difficulty which O'Connell's Kerry perambulations threw up for Mary was the promised hospitality which he cast about. Invitations to stay or to dine or to use his horses when in Dublin were scattered far and wide. Perhaps Mary did not much wish him to be sparing in this particular regard. But it certainly bore hard upon her. On several occasions she complained to O'Connell of the extreme awkwardness of her finding (or even having!) reasons for putting off the relations whom he had asked to stay at Merrion Square. As to his horses, she wrote sharply on 15 January 1809 when his cousin Connell was taking up O'Connell's preferred loan,

> William [the O'Connell manservant] will not nor cannot attend to the mare and, if every person who wishes for it is to get it, you must hire a groom to convenience them . . . if you wish Mr O'Connell should get her, his servant must make her up when he brings her home every day, for John [the O'Connell coachman] cannot attend me if he is to attend him.[38]

O'Connell had worries of his own arising from his long absences. Sometimes his first letters from circuit spoke of his black depression or his agitation at the tearful parting or his concern for Mary's apprehensions. He also left behind him an ever more precarious financial house of cards. Dublin outgoings and receipts were invariably in a delicate balance, depending on Mary and various other agents delaying payments until he could send back enough of his bar earnings to meet the bills. None the less, even Mary realized that circuit work, with its clamour, dash and triumphs, was her husband's breath of life. 'I ought not, darling,' she wrote in 1810, 'regret so much your going circuit, for in general the change and bustle of it is of use to you . . . and then, heart, the pleasure you have in looking forward to the time you will be with your *little woman* and your babes again makes up to you in a great measure for being away from them.'[39] This was fair comment. And apart from the exhilaration of the court-room combat and the crowding clients, O'Connell usually enjoyed, and even exulted in, the pull of home as each circuit drew to its weary close. As he himself once put it, when handing over his final brief to a fellow-counsel in order to save a day, he was riotously joyful as a schoolboy on the eve of term's breaking-up. Moreover, in the early years at least, he rejoiced in reporting to Mary, assize town by assize town, the mounting total of his earnings. These were a measure of both the demand for his services and his success in fulfilling the role of family hunter and gatherer. Not least (as he once said) were the thoughts of his 'sweet bedfellow'[40] as the time for their reunion drew near.

IV

The greatest shadow over O'Connell's marriage, down to 1829 at any rate, was money. In the last analysis, it was lack of money which drove him to conceal his betrothal, to marry in secret and to board his wife and children with his parents for most of the second and third years of his married life. From 1805 onwards it was the magnitude of his expenditure rather than the meagreness of his income which caused the trouble. The upshot was however much the same. In the immortal words of Mr Micawber (whom O'Connell came to resemble strikingly in certain ways), 'Annual income twenty pounds, annual expenditure twenty pounds ought and six, result misery. The blossom is blighted, the leaf is withered, the God of day goes down upon the dreary scene, and – in short you are for ever floored.'[41] Of what avail was it for O'Connell to multiply his income rapidly and enormously if the ought-and-sixes grew just as fast?

In the year in which he became engaged, 1800, O'Connell earned about £420 at the bar. To some extent, this figure was misleading as £175, two-fifths of the whole, derived from a single extraordinarily protracted case, *Segerson* v. *Butler*, at Tralee. His next year's total, £387, should not therefore be taken as marking a real decline in business; this is confirmed by the 1802 earnings, £522. Hunting Cap may well have supplemented O'Connell's income in these early years, as it was not to be expected that a barrister should support himself initially; he could certainly not have lived off his fees in 1798 or 1799. If this is so, perhaps £150–200 annually should be added to these figures. Most likely, Hunting Cap simply continued the allowance made to O'Connell as a student, which was probably within this range. Conversely, O'Connell had inescapable professional expenses, Law Library fees, books, copying, travel, mess charges and accommodation in the assizes towns. At a guess – and it is nothing more – these outgoings would have counterbalanced, at the very least, Hunting Cap's hypothetical allowance. Thus, at the apex of our airy pyramid of surmise we are left with a net income of something like

£500 for O'Connell, in the year of his marriage, 1802. Had the 1800s
been a classificatory decade this would have placed him, at the age of
twenty-seven, in, say, the B1 or possibly even A2 rank of incomes; he
would not have been subject, we should remember, to any form of
direct taxation. None the less, he was probably in debt already.
Marriage certainly increased his outgoings without any compensating
accession of capital. But in 1802–3 Mary lived substantially the same
life as she had done as a single girl, and over the next two years she and
her children were largely supported by O'Connell's parents. The
wedded state, therefore, added less immediately to O'Connell's
expenditure than would ordinarily have been the case, although it led
undoubtedly to the loss of his uncle's allowance from 1803 on, if this
were still being maintained.

In 1805, however, O'Connell was pushed onto a much higher level
of spending when he bought a house in Dublin and set up the usual
middle-class domestic establishment. Professor M. R. O'Connell
believes that 'O'Connell said goodbye to solvency when he purchased
No. 1 Westland Row'.[42] Certainly he was forced to borrow substantially – and, he hoped, secretly. To one friend he wrote – it is
possible that similar letters were sent to others – 'The purchase of my
house and the first expenses of getting into it have made it extremely
desirable to me to get the use of £200 for a year, but it is still much more
necessary for me that no third person should know that I wanted or
got the money.'[43] In 1805 O'Connell earned £841 in fees and in 1806
£1,077, which probably meant net incomes of about £600 and £800,
respectively. Though these were considerable sums, they were clearly
insufficient for his altered circumstances. There were several signals of
financial difficulties in 1806. In April O'Connell evidently borrowed
(or received as a gift) £50 from his father, and both Ralph Marshall and
an unidentified 'Zeb Mac' in Kerry lent him further sums. Zeb Mac's
£100 went towards staving off a sheriff's execution upon the property
of his old confederate, Splinter. All this time, O'Connell, with amazing
buoyancy, spoke to his wife only of his increasing income. 'Darling',
he wrote from Cork on 15 April 1806, 'I have made a little fortune
here – and have I believe laid the foundation for a *much greater*.'[44]
From the summer circuit he reported that he had done extraordinarily
well at Ennis, that Limerick had proved 'a *spendid* assizes', that he had
had his full share of the meagre business at Tralee and that Cork,
where he was 'one of the foremost in briefs and bustle', had provided
'an *immense* deal to do'.[45] Characteristically, not only did he set up his
wife and children in Tralee for a long vacation in the summer, but he

also insisted on Mary's engaging a carriage to go sea-bathing. 'The only reason that can operate to prevent you is the expense and if we could not afford that I confess I would applaud your prudence in avoiding it. But, sweet love, I can well, very well afford it.'[46]

O'Connell continued in this exultant strain in 1807. Early in the spring circuit he wrote, 'Ennis was very well'. From Limerick came a 'spare fifty guineas' with expressions of delight in the prospect of giving his wife 'every convenience' and later every 'comfortable luxury': 'I doat of you, my sweet Mary, and nothing can give me such pleasure as seeing you in affluence.'[47] Cork was as usual the crown of all. 'I am really getting a load of money', he reported from there on 26 March 1807,

> At this rate you shall soon have not only carriages but a country house. It is an infinite pleasure to me to succeed thus as it enables me to give my sweetest little woman all the luxuries of life. We loved each other, darling, when we were poor, and as we were really so, it was almost our only consolation to love each other. And now that we are becoming rich it is the chief sweetener of life.[48]

It may be difficult for the more provident portion of humanity to understand how a man, who was almost certainly sinking deeper into debt year by year, could write persistently in such a strain. But, *experto crede*, there is another sort of person who can empathize with O'Connell all too readily. He will immediately recognize the illusory glow generated by sudden cash inflows. It was very easy for O'Connell, dazzled by a flood of coin and notes at the assizes, to forget the distant, daily drain of a household of wife and children, housekeeper and five or six servants in Dublin. Again, it was only to be expected that he should draw a wildly rising income curve upon his imaginary graph of the future. He really *was* succeeding prodigiously. In 1806 not only had he earned well over £1,000 at the bar, but he had also entered the highly profitable field of special engagements. The £2,000 per annum barrier was to be broken in 1807, and the £3,000 barrier within four years. The trouble was that the counter curve – that of expenditure and monetary obligation – was gradually drawing ahead. But what man of O'Connell's temperament ever projected the two lines with an equal hand?

Finally, we must bear in mind the likely effects upon O'Connell's outlook of his partial reconciliation with Hunting Cap in 1806. He was actually guaranteed no more than the eventual reversion of the hereditary O'Connell lands. But as we have seen he leapt to the conclusion that this was merely the first step towards total restoration as his uncle's heir. We must also remember that Hunting Cap was seventy-eight years old in 1806, and had already suffered at least one serious illness. O'Connell must have assumed that a fortune lay more or less close to hand. Why count the pennies or withhold subscriptions or displease friends petitioning for loans or guarantees when so massive an accession of wealth as to render each individual item negligible was just around the corner?

Mary was not entirely ignorant of the true situation. When in 1806 a Kerry kinsman, Mountain Mahony, unexpectedly repaid O'Connell a loan of £100, she wrote lightheartedly, 'I wish all those who owe you money would *surprise* you as he has done', and added, her husband being on circuit, 'Remember, darling, I expect you will bring a great *purse* home with you.'[49] By 1808 she was deeply involved in, and therefore privy in part to, O'Connell's affairs. His letter of 2 April from Limerick is a comparatively simple example of the dealings in which she was to be henceforth embroiled.

> You have enclosed a bill for £115.10.7 out of which you will have two large payments to make, the one of £70 – a bill of mine to Hickson, the woollen draper, which will be due the 14th of April and other of £26 and some shillings which will be due a few days after. This second bill I gave McKenna for his work in the house . . .
>
> There is also a note or bill of mine out for £50 which you are not to pay, darling, unless you get money for that purpose from a Mr Clarke, an attorney. You may in the event of its not being sent to you, I mean the money, by Mr Clarke allow it to be protested [i.e. dishonoured]. I am not one bit uneasy about it.[50]

She was already apprehensive, as a letter from her to O'Connell which probably crossed his of 2 April 1808 makes very clear: 'should you, my darling, not send me up the money as you earn it, you will be *tempted* to distribute it when you go to Kerry. It is there all the claims are on you, putting *Splinter first of all*.'[51]

Things worsened in 1809. On the face of it, this may seem very strange. Not only did O'Connell's bar earnings exceed £2,700 in that year but he also received £750 from Hunting Cap to buy land in Iveragh and inherited the bulk of his father's property when he died in May. In fact, it may well have been the improvement in income and prospects which led O'Connell to take the fateful step of moving from Westland Row to the nearby but much more fashionable Merrion Square in September. If O'Connell was still within hailing distance of solvency after buying his first house, he was certainly far removed from it by the purchase of his second, and the consequent elevation of his family and himself to the most expensive reaches of Dublin professional life. Mary realized this fully. Late in the month, she wrote to him, desperately,

> For God's sake, darling love, let me entreat of you to give up this house in the Square if it is in your power as I see no other way for you to get out of difficulties. If you borrow this money [one thousand guineas] for Ruxton how will you pay it back? In short, love, I scarce know what I write I am so unhappy about this business.[52]

None the less the purchase of no. 30 Merrion Square went ahead.

Mary's worst fear however was that O'Connell would ruin himself by going security for friends and relations, and she apparently wrung from him a solemn undertaking to abandon this practice, or at least to indulge it only if she were fully informed. A much shrewder head than Mary's, Hunting Cap's, also saw this as the chief source of danger. When in 1811 Hunting Cap heard rumours that O'Connell was about to become guarantor for a large sum for John Primrose, a friend and kinsman whose son was later to become O'Connell's steward, he warned him of the consequences with the utmost portentousness:

> I can scarcely express to you the uneasiness I feel since this matter has occurred to me, well knowing as I before mentioned the softness and facility of your disposition and with what ease designing men may draw you into their measures, when in fact and in truth acceding to such a proposal from Primrose must have the effect of inevitably ruining you beyond redemption. I therefore again and again most earnestly caution you against it and further add that no feeble or temporizing excuses will have any sort of weight with me, and that your neglecting to comply with what I not only so earnestly beseech and request but what I absolutely and decidedly command, will create a breach between us never to be healed, and decidedly determine me during the period of my existence never to exchange a word with you. It distresses me indeed to think that it is necessary to write to you in such strong terms when a bare intimation of my will ought . . . be sufficient . . .[53]

Mary and Hunting Cap were proved right in March 1815, when James O'Leary, a Killarney merchant, went bankrupt. O'Connell, who had gone security for him was liable for £8,000. Mary learnt of the disaster not from her husband but from his brother, James. She wrote so fiercely to O'Connell for the breaking of his promise to her that he destroyed her letter. 'I wept over it for two hours this morning', he replied on 13 March 1815,

When once suspicion enters the human mind, there is an end of all comfort and security. It is, I see, in vain to make any protestations to you. You are, I see, irrecoverably unhappy. I blame, indeed I do, my brother James for instilling this poison into your mind . . .

Darling believe me, do believe me, you have no cause for your misery. Did I ever deceive you?[54]

Mary's anger could not stand when she found O'Connell so 'exquisitely miserable'. More admirably than accurately, she assured him that it was not in his nature to deceive her – in fact, she was probably still unaware of the magnitude or certainty of the disaster – and went on to entreat him to trust in her love for him and 'forget what is past'.[55]

No such forgiveness would be had from Hunting Cap: he had specifically warned O'Connell long before against dealings with O'Leary. As we shall see, when at last the news of the bankruptcy became widely known, every effort had to be made to conceal O'Connell's involvement from his uncle. The ultimate disaster of being unmasked and repudiated by Hunting Cap was avoided. But short of that O'Connell came quite close to ruin. For an Irish working barrister his income was by now enormous, probably between £6,000 and £7,000 in 1815: property which he had inherited from his father or been given already by Hunting Cap between 1809 and 1811 produced net about £2,000 per annum. Yet by the end of 1815 his debts cannot have been less than £15,000, and were probably much more. It required a sustained effort by his family to save him from bankruptcy. James arranged the necessary loans and pledged himself as guarantor, although he believed that he too would be removed from Hunting Cap's will if word of the transactions came to his uncle's ears. General O'Connell advanced a large sum later to reduce the horrific outflow of interest. Mary not only forgave her husband fully but joined him – perhaps, led him – in battling through the crisis. He had no doubt, he told her on 21 March 1816, that 'we will work over the difficulties into which my most absurd credulity involved me. Dearest sweetest, how I *ought* to love you for the manner in which you have met those difficulties.'[56]

There is a certain charm in O'Connell's lightness of spirit and indomitability, not to add in the unbreakable loyalty of both his inner and his outer families. But this should not lead us to forget that O'Connell had wantonly brought his troubles on his own and others' heads, with a trail of subterfuge and concealment, of broken promises and unmet obligations, and of reckless disregard for his brother's interest, in order to indulge the 'softness and facility' of his disposition. *O felix culpa*, however, so far as his marriage was concerned. It appears to have emerged all the stronger and warmer for his pardoned delinquency. Like Captain Wentworth in *Persuasion* he had to brook – and who would brook it more easily? – being happier than he deserved.

CHAPTER 5

Public Lives

1800–13

I

O'Connell had entered public life, dramatically, on 13 January 1800. Earlier, the Irish bar had resolved against the proposed Union of Great Britain and Ireland by an overwhelming majority; among other things, the members believed that it would cost them a great deal of their business. As both a very young and newly called barrister and a Catholic, O'Connell was a mere silent supporter of that course. But all the more did he resent the argument of the Castle faction at the bar that the Irish Catholics en bloc favoured the amalgamation of the two kingdoms. It was probably this which drove him to take a leading part in organizing a Catholic meeting at the Royal Exchange in Dublin in January 1800 to repudiate 'so horrible a calumny'. The Catholic resolutions, which he introduced and largely composed, were milder than those carried by the Irish bar. This was a caution well justified by the event, for the town major, Sirr, appeared at the commencement, examined the agenda and only reluctantly accepted it as anodyne, before he would allow the meeting to proceed. O'Connell was foremost in checking panic in the crowd when the military drew up in front of the Exchange, and also in the preliminary parleys with the major. It was an extraordinary initiative for a young man of twenty-four years to take, all the more so as it implied a further defiance of Hunting Cap. The Castle faction had been substantially right in claiming that the Union had the backing of the Irish Catholics, for the bishops believed that the British government was committed to full Emancipation in return for their support. Hunting Cap himself, and another of O'Connell's uncles and his brother, John, were among those working up a pro-Union campaign in Kerry. Thus O'Connell's stand was even more daring than it publicly appeared.

Essentially, O'Connell argued that Catholic interests should be subordinated to 'Irish'. He even denied that there *was* any special

Catholic interest. 'The enlightened mind of the Catholics', he told the meeting, 'had taught them the impolicy, the illiberality, and the injustice of separating themselves on any occasion from the rest of the people of Ireland. The Catholics had therefore resolved, and they had wisely resolved, never more to appear before the public as a distinct and separate body.' Of course, the fact that they were accused of having a distinctive sectarian policy on the Union had compelled them to come forward 'as a distinct body'. But they did so 'for the last time' and only to repudiate the foul charge that they 'were ready to sell their country for a price, or, what was still more depraved, to abandon it on account of the unfortunate animosities which the wretched temper of the times had produced'. Even in his first public speech, O'Connell used extravagance for purposes of emphasis; 'let every man who feels with me proclaim', his climax ran,

> that if the alternative were offered him of union, or the re-enactment of the penal code in all its pristine horrors, that he would prefer without hesitation the latter, as the lesser and more sufferable evil; that he would rather confide in the justice of his brethren, the Protestants of Ireland, who have already liberated him, than lay his country at the feet of foreigners. (This sentiment was met with much and marked approbation).[1]

The condemnatory resolutions – which in fact sound rather tame after such a flight – passed unopposed, and would have passed presently into oblivion had they not occasioned O'Connell's first declaration of political faith. Broadly speaking, his claim to have adhered to this faith throughout his life was justified.

When Hunting Cap expostulated on O'Connell's performance at the Royal Exchange – it was widely reported in the newspapers – he took the traditional line of Irish Catholics of substance, that the Protestant Ascendancy was their true enemy, and the British government their only agent of their relief.[2] Nothing could make clearer the nature of O'Connell's departure. He had taken colour – permanently – from the peculiar epoch in which he had grown up. The fifteen years 1778–93 were marked by a train of concessions to the Irish Catholics; it was natural for the young O'Connell to regard the penal code as both anachronistic and in a steady process of dissolution. The same years were also marked by various apparent triumphs for Irish liberalism, vis-à-vis both Great Britain and the rule of caste at home. Again, it was natural for the young O'Connell to take these at their face value, and also as heralds of a new harmony of sects and classes. The idealizations of the growing boy crystallized into lasting certitudes. On 14 April 1843 O'Connell wrote that when Irish Protestants combined 'to make our beloved fatherland a nation again ... the utmost cordiality will prevail, as in 1782, between all Irishmen and we will be able to make the mighty change [repeal of the Act of Union] with perfect safety to person and property, and to the continuance of the connection between the two countries'.[3] Seriously meant, this gives us a measure of the indestructibility of O'Connell's early visions.

In immediate terms, O'Connell's stand at the Royal Exchange was an isolated episode. True, the subsequent enforcement of the Union enraged him. Later he recalled his feelings on 1 January 1801 when he heard the bells of St Patrick's Cathedral pealing out in joy at the surrender: 'My blood boiled, and I vowed, on that morning, that the foul dishonour should not last, if *I* could ever put an end to it.'[4] But there was nothing to be done. Ireland lay inert in the aftermath of the Union; even the Catholic question fell away once Pitt was forced out of office because of his promise to press it upon the united Parliament. O'Connell had only abhorrence for Robert Emmet's Dublin insur-rection of 1803, the solitary demonstration of resistance to British rule in Ireland in the first post-Union years. Emmet, he wrote on 28 August of that year, 'merits and will suffer the severest punishment. For my part I think pity would be almost thrown away upon the contriver of the affair of the 23rd of July. A man who could cooly prepare so much bloodshed, so many murders – and such horrors of every kind has ceased to be an object of compassion.'[5] His wife did nothing to mitigate O'Connell's deep-set anti-revolutionism. Although he had remained a serving member of the Lawyers' Artillery, regularly called upon for guard and patrol duty in Dublin, he evidently decided to join the Kerry yeomanry as well, in the alarm which followed Emmet's rising. 'I am quite delighted', Mary told him on 18 November 1803,

that you should enroll yourself in Sir Edward Denny's corps though, if it could be helped, I had rather you were not in any. However, it is a great consolation to me, should the French land, not to have you obliged to remain in Dublin. Kerry will be the last place they come to and the yeomanry, I trust in God, will be able to keep down the common people. *They are the* only [one word missing] I dread in this part of the world.[6]

Perhaps O'Connell had indoctrinated his wife with his original fears of both revolution and the masses. If so, the pupil was all too ready to turn teacher. This way or that, they seem to have reinforced each other in these particular forms of reaction.

Pitt's restoration as prime minister in May 1804 revived Catholic hopes in Ireland. The Catholic Board, which had been put down in the general welter of repression in the preceding year, now reconstituted itself as the Catholic Committee. In either form it was a far from radical body, being dominated by noblemen and landed proprietors. The most able member, the veteran John Keogh, belonged to the Dublin merchant class which had been prominent in the Board in former years; but his participation was by now intermittent. A new group, the Catholic barristers, were however beginning to push their way forward. Of these much the ablest was O'Connell; but he was not the most senior, nor had he, apparently, taken any part in Catholic politics before the new Committee met on 16 November 1804. Neither his earlier abstention nor his participation on 16 November should cause surprise. Each is readily explicable in terms of his profession and his marriage. Down to 1804 these naturally absorbed his mind and energies, all the more so as the Irish politics of 1801–3 were at once dangerous and torpid. But by the end of 1804 his earnings at the bar had risen to almost £800, and his second son was born. On both counts he found himself suddenly face to face with the practical penalties of being a Catholic in his own land. Were he not excluded from the inner bar by his religion, he could have looked forward to taking silk soon, and to a glorious professional career ending in the mastership of the rolls or the chief baronship of the exchequer, at the very least. Correspondingly he was bitter that his sons were starting their race of life already shackled by their religion. In his first reported speech to the Committee he presented himself as an epitome of Catholic disabilities. He was not only a young man artificially prevented from rising in his profession, but also the father of children doomed to the same fate: 'It was the liberties of those children the present petition sought – would they postpone for an hour that sacred blessing?'[7]

O'Connell pushed himself to the front so vigorously on the Catholic Committee that he was appointed to both the standing committee of twenty-five, and the small sub-committee charged with drafting the parliamentary petition. He was delighted to rub shoulders with the peers and baronets who graced the first, and proud of his responsibilities on the second. 'Dearest', he wrote to Mary on 4 December 1804,

I am very busy at present in framing the Catholic petition. The fate of millions perhaps depends on my poor pen – at least so in my enthusiasm I say to myself and *to you* – But to you, *you alone*. There are five appointed for *this* purpose. We must have the petition ready on Sunday. Until then believe me that I shall sleep little. Heart, my *law* business goes on right well.[8]

Constantly, he assured Mary that his professional work was not suffering because of his labours for the Committee. But unknown to her he was prepared to sacrifice his career, to a limited extent at least, in the pursuit of new glory. On 19 December he proposed himself to Denys Scully (an older Catholic barrister and the acknowledged master of the Catholic question) as an appropriate person to go 'to London on the business of the petition'.[9] O'Connell was prepared to be reimbursed his expenses but nothing more. Professionally, the journey to London would truly be 'both inconvenient and injurious', he told Scully, 'nor should I upon any terms consent to *be paid*. The fact is that even in my humble situation at the Bar no money could repay me for the loss *consequent* to absence during term.'[10] In the event, a large party, including Scully and another barrister, accompanied the petition, but O'Connell – presumably because he was still comparatively unknown and undistinguished – was not selected. He had not done badly in his first Catholic venture. His was the seventeenth name on the petition, and he acted, in effect, as the Dublin political manager of the petition-bearers while they negotiated in London. A certain measure of wounded vanity, however, may be detected in the would-be facetious opening of his letter to Scully on 19 March 1805, reporting on the Dublin end of things.

High and Mighty!

For certainly the great Rustifusti or the greater Miamouchi was a mere dandle compared with the representative of four million, five hundred thousand of the creatures in Ireland styled *men*. Out of the excess of your dignity your recollection has been thrown away and you have not a thought *to throw away* upon your former acquaintance.[11]

Whether O'Connell's volunteering to go to London is to be explained by vanity or ambition or a sense of his own superiority, it was certainly an act of familial irresponsibility. His wife and children were still without a home, and he was soon to be forced further into debt in order to buy even a comparatively modest house. Yet, quite unprompted, he had offered to forgo a quarter or more of his year's earnings so that he could cut a public figure in the metropolis. Domestically speaking it was an ominous political debut.

II

The Irish Catholic 'initiative' of 1804–5 failed dismally. Pitt not only refused to act on behalf of the deputation but even told them roundly that he would now oppose any measure of Catholic relief. The dismayed delegates found his rival Charles James Fox perfectly agreeable to stepping into Pitt's discarded shoes. But on 14 May 1805 Fox's motion for a Relief Bill was rejected in the House of Commons by a majority of three to one. The Catholic Committee had been routed; but in one sense the débâcle represented a triumph for O'Connell. He was easily the foremost in its ranks in opposing the Act of Union, and the Catholic case for support of the Union had always rested upon Pitt's promise to carry Emancipation and the assumption that the British Parliament would prove more tolerant of Catholic claims than had its Irish counterpart. Pitt's defection and Westminster's contemptuous rejection of the Committee's petition swept away the old pro-Union case. O'Connell had proved the better prophet. But in 1805 he still lacked the standing to mount a challenge to the ruling junta on the Committee, backed – as it was generally believed they were – by the Irish episcopate. Moreover, the dominant 'cautious party' was given a fresh lease when Pitt died and the 'Ministry of All the Talents' came to office in February 1806. Fox, who was now in government, had assured them that he would press their claims, even if he could not do so immediately with the struggle against Napoleon at its crisis. Despite O'Connell's dissatisfaction, the Committee agreed that their illustrious 'friend' should be placed under no pressure for the present. But Fox fell ill in July 1806 and died two months later, without ever having raised the Catholic question since attaining office.

The division within the Committee sharpened. Keogh and his aristocratic allies desired only to entrust their cause to the discretion of their surviving well-wishers in the ministry. But O'Connell had no faith in well-wishing and no taste for patrician restraint. At the aggregate meeting of 17 February 1807, in anticipation of the coming parliamentary session, his fiery oratory produced a majority in favour of petitioning for Emancipation once again. He was aided by the accident of Keogh's absence from the meeting and his own tactical skill in drawing into light the hereditary servility which really underlay the aristocratic plea for dignity of bearing. He also repeated his denunciation of the Act of Union as the immediate cause of the continued degradation of the Irish Catholics. Keogh, warmly supported by the nobility and squires, was furious at the passage of O'Connell's aggressive motion. O'Connell's charge, that Keogh would prefer a measure to fail than that it should be carried by another leader, may not have been wide of the mark. At any rate, Keogh procured a second aggregate meeting at which his authority and numbers carried the day, and O'Connell's motion in favour of petitioning was rescinded. None the less, O'Connell had made progress. At least he had forced himself to the forefront of both the 'forward' element and what might be termed the 'barristers' faction' in the Committee.

The battle was refought in 1808, the Ministry of All the Talents having meanwhile fallen. Petitioning was again proposed at the aggregate meeting of 19 January, only to be met with a contrary amendment grounded on the Keoghite argument that a petition would 'only expose us to the mockery and insult of men in power; to division, rejection and defeat'.[12] At this point O'Connell intervened, acknowledging that Catholic division was deplorable, but arguing that even division was preferable to the loss of self-respect. He refused to be cowed by the British mighty, in earnest of which he treated them to a round of fishwife's abuse. Irish Catholics, he said, 'had little to fear from the barren petulance of the ex-advocate, Perceval, or the frothy declamations of the poetaster, Canning – they might meet with equal contempt the upstart pride of the Jenkinsons [Lord Liverpool], and with more than contempt the pompous inanity of that Lord Castlereagh.'[13] The effect on the meeting was electrifying. It may puzzle us to understand why such rhetoric was accounted admirable, or why O'Connell descended to such vapid and vulgar personalities or jogtrot, over-laden cadences. They were henceforth to constitute one of his characteristic styles, particularly before a popular audience. The answer would seem to be, in part, that we cannot see the look and gesture, or hear the voice, which apparently transformed these banalities; in part, that telling oratory is the creature of its own time; and in part, as O'Connell himself frequently confessed, that lapses into Billingsgate were a fault which he could never overcome. But it is probably also true that such language was calculated to reduce his political enemies to a level with Catholics, Irish or any other category of inferior beings; that it was designed to counteract the instinctive cringe of the oppressed, and to force the proud and disdainful to engage with them upon equal terms. At any rate, O'Connell's coarse eloquence certainly helped him to achieve his object on 19 January 1808. Keogh, who arrived late for the meeting, proffered no reply, and his supporters withdrew their amendment and allowed O'Connell's motion in favour of a petition to pass unchallenged. In the battle of the young and old bull seals, O'Connell had triumphed comparatively quickly. 'From that day', as Dunlop puts it, though with some exaggeration, 'he and not Keogh was the leader of the Catholics.'[14]

When the motions in favour of Catholic relief arising from the petition came before Parliament in May 1808, they were heavily defeated in both Houses. However, the proposers in the Commons, the whig leader George Ponsonby and the veteran Henry Grattan, were confident that a compromise could be reached. Accordingly, they offered the British government, on behalf of the Irish Catholic hierarchy, at least a negative veto on all Irish episcopal appointments. Their speeches also disclosed the fact that in 1799 the ten Irish archbishops and bishops who constituted the trustees of Maynooth had tendered Pitt just such a veto, as well as acceptance of state payment of the Irish clergy, in return for Emancipation. Now the fat was in the fire. It was true that Bishop Milner, vicar-apostolic of the Midland District and the English agent of the Irish bishops, had not had time to consult his principals before coming to the agreement with Ponsonby and Grattan which had led them to make their offer. It was also true that Milner's concessions fell far short of warranting Ponsonby's final assurance to the House of Commons that 'the appointment [of every Irish bishop] should finally rest with the King'.[15] None the less, Milner, who had reason to expect considerable Irish episcopal support, had placed no specific limitation upon the practical use of the veto. As to the Maynooth trustees' 'surrender' of 1799, this was indisputable, though hitherto no hint of it had reached the Irish public.

O'Connell, who had been quite as much in the dark as the laity in general, was outraged by these disclosures. Arguing that any form of veto would render the bishops, in time, so many puppets of a government dedicated to the retention of both the Protestant and British Ascendancy in Ireland, he set about organizing and deploying a popular furore. This was done mainly through the press, which was fortunately provided with a vent when Milner visited Ireland in the following August. As Milner himself described his reception,

> It is a fact that all the newspapers, particularly the *Dublin Evening Herald*, and also the *Irish Magazine*, are full of abuse against Lord Fingall and his friends Dr Troy [Archbishop of Dublin], Dr Moylan [Bishop of Cork] and myself, as having pledged ourselves and the body to acknowledge the royal Ecclesiastic supremacy by giving the nomination of Prelates to the Crown.

Not only the many-headed mob have taken the alarm, but also most of the inferior clergy, and a great portion of the Bishops; in short they are to meet about it on the 14th September.[16]

O'Connell spoke of Milner's visit as a 'vetoistical mission'. Whether or not this was justified, his description of the outcome – that the Irish people 'rejected the mission and the missionary'[17] – was undeniable. More to the point, the Irish bishops followed substantially the same course as 'the Irish people'. To some extent, the members of the hierarchy, denied the Emancipation which had been tacitly promised in 1799, must have shared O'Connell's anger at their treatment at the hands of British politicians. But doubtless they were also moved by the excited, even threatening, lay agitation. The National Synod which had been hastily convened in Dublin in September 1808 condemned, by the overwhelming majority of twenty-three to three, every form of interference by the crown in appointments or other matters of government of the Irish church. Even the three recalcitrants would haved voted for the resolution had 'at present' been added to its wording.

Obviously this marked a further advance in O'Connell's influence in Irish affairs, especially in demonstrating his willingness and capacity to call in popular forces to help pressurize his domestic opponents. But the price was division in the Catholic movement. Although this was not fully apparent for another four years, the foundation for a 'vetoistical' party within the Catholic Committee had been laid. In itself, the anti-O'Connell faction, comprising the small aristocratic element with a few old Keoghites and some of the more malleable lawyers, did not look formidable. But it had episcopal sympathizers, if not outright supporters. Troy and Moylan, for example, while subscribing in 1810, like all the rest, to sixteen resolutions reaffirming the Irish episcopate's hostility to the veto, were always prone to compromise on the issue. Moreover, the English Catholic Board, dominated by noblemen and squires, was decidedly vetoist in inclination, as well as influential at both Westminster and Rome. Thus, although insignificant in terms of numbers, O'Connell's Irish lay opponents were far from negligible as a force. Over the next fourteen years, they were to constitute his 'running sore'.

There was however one significant, though hidden, change preceding this particular conflict which should be noted. Mary O'Connell's letter of 21 March 1809 to her husband makes its nature clear:

I hope, darling, you did not eat meat on Friday or Saturday since you left this and surely I need not beg you to abstain from meat next [Holy] week. You can't be at a loss for fish in Cork. And Good Friday the *judges* will go to prayers and certainly you can then *spare time* to go. At all events I hope you will hear prayers on Easter Sunday. You see, heart, how good I want you to be. I do, darling, because I doat of you. I would wish you to be attentive to your religion and thankful to God for all his blessings and favours to both of us. I often with delight, darling, heard you say you were the happiest of men and I say with truth I am the happiest of women. In gratitude to the Almighty then we should at least attend to the duties of our religion and, darling, I can't tell you what real happiness it gives me to have you this sometime back say your prayers and attend Mass so regularly, not to say anything of your observance of the days of abstinence. I will, heart, say no more on this subject until we meet.[18]

All this suggests that comparatively, though not very, recently, O'Connell (who had unquestionably still been a deist in 1803) had returned to the practice of Catholicism. It also suggests that it was under pressure from Mary that he first began to move in this direction, and that as yet he was 'infervent' if not precisely 'lukewarm'. But fervour would come; and meanwhile it was certainly something that a Catholic leader should have again become, apparently, a believing Catholic.

III

O'Connell's success at home in 1808 was directly related to the failure of Emancipation in Parliament. Not only were the Catholic claims decisively rejected yet again, but also leading parliamentary 'friends' had been embarrassed by the public wrangles over what Milner had really conceded or could properly concede. The final Irish rejection of the veto was an open rebuff to Ponsonby, Grattan and the whigs in general. Worse still perhaps, it was impossible for them really to comprehend the Catholic objection to the veto, since parliamentary supremacy over the Church and ultimate lay control of the clergy were fundamental presuppositions in the Anglican tradition. In these circumstances, there seemed no prospect of success for another petition or campaign after the 1805–8 pattern, and no move was made during the 1809 session. Indeed, Keogh would claim to have been vindicated in his earlier opposition to petitioning on the ground that it led only to humiliating rebuffs in both houses and internal discord. O'Connell may have stood at the head of the Irish Catholic movement from 1808 on, but it was a stationary and covertly divided column which he led.

It is not surprising then that he turned joyfully in another political direction when an opening unexpectedly appeared – all the more so as it brought the matter back to what he regarded as first principles. Although a Protestant redoubt, the Dublin mercantile interests had never been reconciled to the Act of Union. The commerce, trades and petty industry which the Corporation represented had suffered heavily from the disappearance of the Irish Parliament and its complex of social appendages; and after a decade's experience, they had convinced themselves that the Union spelt the ruin of business. Accordingly, on 20 July 1810 the Corporation resolved that only the restoration of the Irish Parliament could halt the city's decay. A consequent aggregate meeting on 18 September (to which Catholic as well as Protestant freeholders were invited) determined to petition for Repeal. O'Connell, who had of course thrown himself into the movement from the moment that it spread itself beyond the guilds, was one of the nine selected to draw up the parliamentary petition.

Later in the aggregate meeting O'Connell produced the second of his now-celebrated rhetorical set pieces. Essentially, it repeated his original anti-Union speech of 13 January 1800, although the range of the appeal was wider and its force much increased by many bitter words upon the faithlessness of British politicians as revealed by their collective conduct since 1801. 'What sympathy can we in our sufferings, expect from those men? . . . What are they to Ireland, or Ireland to them?' As before – indeed as always – O'Connell explained Irish subjection in terms of Irish disunion, 'which the enemies of Ireland have created, and continued, and seek to perpetuate amongst ourselves, by telling us of, and separating us into wretched sections and miserable subdivisions.' Conversely, combination was strength.

The Protestant alone could not expect to liberate his country – the Roman Catholic alone could not do it – neither could the Presbyterian – but amalgamate the three into the Irishman, and the Union is repealed. Learn discretion from your enemies – they have crushed your country by fomenting religious discord – serve her by abandoning it for ever . . . I require no equivalent from you – whatever course you shall take, my mind is fixed – I trample under foot the Catholic claims, if they can interfere with the Repeal; I abandon all wish for emancipation, if it delays that Repeal. Nay, were Mr Perceval, to-morrow, to offer me the Repeal of the Union, upon the terms of re-enacting the entire penal code, I declare it from my heart, and in the presence of my God, that I would most cheerfully embrace his offer. Let us then, my beloved countrymen, sacrifice our wicked and groundless animosities on the altar of our country . . . – let us rally round the standard of Old Ireland, and we shall easily procure that greatest of political blessings, an Irish King, an Irish House of Lords, and an Irish House of Commons.[19]

O'Connell was received with acclaim though his audience was largely Protestant and Orange in composition. Immediately, he became a public figure in the capital in a larger sense than domination in the Catholic Committee. It was evidently this speech which he had in mind when, in later life, he recalled seeing his portrait in a Dublin shop window after a meeting in 1810 'at which I had attracted public notice . . . [I] said to myself with a smile, "Here are my boyish dreams of glory realized".'[20] But for all its early sparkle this political stream soon ended in the sands. Though noisy, the mercantile discontent was neither deep nor lasting; and the 'wretched sections and miserable subdivisions' of religious hatred rapidly reasserted their normal supremacy over political fraternity. There are indications that Dublin Castle had stirred itself to restore this particular form of Irish normalcy, and also not a few which suggest that O'Connell was now well on the way to becoming a marked man in its dossiers.

Although the interdenominational anti-Unionism of 1810 proved a political cul-de-sac – to be closed off almost as soon as entered – O'Connell's fierce espousal of the cause is worth some consideration. In the first place, it reiterated his concept of Irish nationality as essentially locational, to be determined solely by Irish birth or residence. These dwarfed every difference of class, interest, culture, language or even religion. It was significant that in his original anti-Union speech of 1800 O'Connell had deliberately thrown into antithesis 'Catholics' and 'country' and 'sect' and 'people', as well as proclaiming, in the name of his co-religionists, that even the humiliation and deprivations of the penal code were preferable to political subordination to Great Britain. Rhetoric could be stretched no farther to drive home the notion that Irish nationality was both an affair of place and superior in its claims to any other form of self-identity. There remained the difficulty that considerable bodies of Irish Protestants and Irish Catholics alike had favoured the Union in 1800. Worse still – the Dublin Corporation notwithstanding – there could be no doubt that by 1810 the Union was supported vehemently by the great majority of the Church of Ireland and the Presbyterian communions.

How was the British allegiance of so many Irishmen to be

explained? O'Connell's answer – his second principle, in effect – was – by Britain's steady practice of divide and conquer, in particular, by her 'artificial' fomenting of religious discord. It is important to note that thus far O'Connell's position was identical with that of another founding father of Irish nationalism, Theobald Wolfe Tone. Of course, Tone and O'Connell stand at the heads of opposed traditions, the violent and the non-violent movements. But both put the same gloss on the idealistic Grattanism of their youth. Both argued or assumed that Ireland was indivisible politically and inherently a sovereign nation; that sectarian distinctions (and *a fortiori* any lesser principles of segregation) were irrelevant to national identity and equality; and that Irish subjection to Great Britain was the fruit of Britain's determination to bribe, divide and confuse sufficient natives to keep the entire island under her ultimate control.

There was however a third element in O'Connell's apologia of 18 September 1810 which has had no counterpart in the revolutionary camp. His speech marks one extremity in what was to prove a life-long tactical oscillation. The poles of O'Connell's practical politics were, on the one hand, attempts to collaborate with British whigs, liberals or radicals and, on the other, attempts to make common cause with Irish (generally Orange to tory) Protestants, in order to achieve an end. Movement between these poles, in response to some particular discouragement or defeat, or the exhaustion of some earlier initiative, constituted a basic pattern over O'Connell's entire career. The effort to capitalize upon Dublin Corporation's anti-Unionist fling of 1810, following the parliamentary débâcles of 1808, is the first clear manifestation of the phenomenon.

Finally, another characteristic constituent of O'Connell's grammar of politics was introduced in his peroration. The final words of his speech of 18 September apostrophized 'an Irish King, an Irish House of Lords and an Irish House of Commons' as the 'greatest of political blessings'.[21] This and similar phraseology served two important purposes. To the utmost practicable extent, they secured his flank against charges of revolutionism: 'King, Lords and Commons' was the most solemn incantation of all in the liturgy of the high and dry constitutionalists. They also suggested that his programme was moderate, to the point of being, literally speaking, reactionary. After all, he proposed repeal of the Act of Union in terms of a return to the condition of 1800. This *restorative* emphasis masked – perhaps even from himself – the essential radicalism of his objectives. For he could not have meant what he appeared to mean, a simple turning back of the hands of the constitutional clock. To no one was the narrow, rigged, corrupt and externally manipulated Irish parliamentary system of 1782–1800 more of an anathema.

As if in response to the 'law of oscillation', new hopes of an advance at Westminster sprang up almost as soon as the old hopes of collaboration with the Dublin Protestant merchants were quenched. George III's 'madness' returned in November 1810; a regency bill was introduced in the Commons on 20 December. The Catholic Committee in Dublin took it that the Prince of Wales, an old friend of Fox and Sheridan and widely assumed to share their political liberalism, would prove a *deus ex machina* for Emancipation. O'Connell led the field in organizing a royal address. But in doing so he ran foul of the conservative faction on the Committee. First, they were both shocked and frightened by the scurrilous abuse of the prime minister, Perceval, with which O'Connell inter-wove his laudation of the Prince. Where O'Connell sought to flaunt his defiance of, and break the spell cast by the British political class, the Catholic conservatives sought to appease it and to demonstrate their parity as gentlemen. Their motion to forbid reports of the meeting because of O'Connell's provocative language was, however, defeated. Secondly, the conservatives feared O'Connell's increasing power within the movement. In the spring of 1810 he had acted for several weeks as secretary of the Committee while its permanent secretary, Edward Hay, was conducting Catholic business in London, and later in the year he organized a national testimonial to Hay to reward him for his services to the cause. These opened up for him connections with London politicians, the Irish hierarchy and above all the network of prominent Catholics scattered across the counties. *A la* Stalin and Khrushchev in later days, control of communications through the general secretary-ship meant a further access to power! O'Connell was also resented as the leader of a supposed barristers' party in the Committee. At a meeting early in January 1811 Lord Ffrench, himself a truculent boor, accused the lawyers of self-seeking – they 'ought to be suspected, having more to expect than any other description of Catholic' – and announced his intention to 'put [them] down'.[22]

Having been steadily worsted on the Committee, Ffrench proposed that its decisions be referred to aggregate – open, public – meetings for ratification. He failed to see the irony of a gentry appeal to the populace against the influence of the professional class. Nothing could have better suited O'Connell's book. He also was disenchanted with the Committee – but for its timorousness and obeisance to respect-

ability. The more popular (and perhaps we should add, vulgar) the
agitation, the greater his own leverage and the leverage of the
movement generally. The primary obstacle to 'going public' was the
Convention Act of 1793 which had been designed to prevent Irish
Catholics from forming a representative body. O'Connell hoped to
steer a safe way amongst its provisions by issuing a general invitation
to the Catholics of Ireland to appoint 'managers' of the Catholic
petition in each county. When a number of these 'managers' turned up
at the Committee meeting of 2 February 1811, at which the petition
was being drawn up, the Ffrench–Keogh party bitterly opposed their
attendance as opening the way to prosecution under the Convention
Act. O'Connell beat off this internal attack with the argument that
since the Committee itself was not a representative body its attenders
could not be, legally speaking, representatives. But the Irish chief
secretary, Wellesley-Pole, responded almost immediately by issuing on
12 February 1811 a circular to all sheriffs and magistrates instructing
them to proceed immediately, under the Convention Act, against any
person involved in appointing representatives to the Committee.

Before the month was out, magistrates broke into and attempted to
disperse an ordinary meeting of the Catholic Committee. Ffrench and
his opponents joined ranks. Advised by O'Connell and other
barristers, Ffrench refused to leave the chair unless charged with a
specific offence or forcibly removed. The legal battle was finally
transferred to a conference to be held at the Castle itself. It never took
place; for the time being O'Connell was triumphant. Aggregate
meetings, with the ostensible purpose of preparing petitions, were held
in March and July 1811 without governmental intervention. At both
O'Connell, as lawyer, dictated the tactics and tone: caution and
attempted conciliation were the order of the day. None the less
O'Connell had been emboldened by his success in February, and at the
aggregate meeting of 9 July he strongly supported a resolution to add
to the Committee not only all Catholic peers, baronets and prelates
but also ten persons chosen by the Catholics of each county, and five
from each Dublin parish. That he understood the risk involved is clear
from his offering himself as a parish candidate ready to give bail so
that the legal issue could be determined. One wonders what Hunting
Cap made of the newspaper reports of this particular piece of heroics!
He had written a few months before, 'Nor would reason or experience
in any degree bear him [O'Connell] out in the vain expectation that he
could resume with any prospect of success a profession which he had
once, though partially, withdrawn from or relinquished.'[23]

On 30 July 1811 the Irish Administration responded to the second challenge with a proclamation, under the Convention Act, declaring illegal the appointment of county or parish representatives. The indictment of a number of people concerned in these elections (but not of O'Connell or any other leading member of the Catholic Committee) followed swiftly, although the magistrates bungled the next step – attempting to disperse the subsequent meeting of the Committee – by arriving in force after its conclusion. The first trial, that of Dr Edward Sheridan, was held on 21–2 November. Although he could not of course lead in the case, O'Connell designed the defence upon the construction to be placed on a single word in the Convention Act, 'pretence'. The chief justice summed up heavily, but vainly, against such a line of argument; the jury found for Sheridan. Now the battle was really joined. Foolishly, the Committee counter-prosecuted the chief justice for illegal arrest, and suffered its first defeat of the year; and when it assembled for its next meeting on 23 December, it found a police magistrate, Hare, already in possession of the hall. There followed one of the great set-pieces of early-nineteenth-century agitation, with O'Connell dictating the Committee's moves stage by stage.

When Hare demanded to know the purpose of the meeting, the chairman, Lord Fingall, replied obliquely with a tangential formula of O'Connell's devising. When Hare took this to be an admission that the meeting was one of the Catholic Committee, as defined by its own resolution of 9 July 1811, O'Connell insisted that this could be only a private and not a judicial opinion. When Hare none the less declared the assembly to be illegal, O'Connell advised submission, under protest, to what was now a magisterial action, but also that the chairman await formal arrest so as to provide the basis for a future law suit. When Hare used token force to remove Fingall, another peer, Lord Netterville, and, on his being deposed in turn, Lord Ffrench, were voted into the chair. Next, the Committee transferred itself to a private house, where the magistrate followed them and a further imbroglio transpired. In the end, the meeting was transformed into a 'gathering of private individuals', and Hare declared that Fingall and Netterville had not been arrested after all!

Despite the vein of farce running through all the proceedings and the absurdity of their conclusion, the interplay was significant. First, it signalled the Irish government's absolute determination to check any expansion of the Catholic movement either socially or geographically; it was acting on the secret instructions of the Catholics' supposed friend, the Prince Regent. Secondly, although Hare's intervention was not wholly successful, he had so disrupted and threatened the future activity of the Committee that O'Connell decided on 29 December that it should be replaced by a new 'Catholic Board', designated as a mere petitioning body. Moreover, despite the acquittal of Sheridan on 22 November, Dublin Castle persisted with its prosecutions, and on 3 February 1812 secured a verdict against another of the offenders, Kirwan. On the other hand, O'Connell was well aware that, ju-jitsu like, the very force of his opponents' charge could be turned to his own account, if handled cunningly. Both the uproar and the government's insolent and secure exorbitance on 23 December 1811 provided tinder for future agitation. O'Connell ensured that the episode was exploited for publicity, making it in turn the subject of meetings of protest not only in the capital but also in the provinces, in particular in the circuit towns and cities. The success of any individual move or counter-move in the new game of cat-and-mouse mattered comparatively little as against maintaining, and if possible raising, the level of political excitement.

O'Connell was now well into his apprenticeship as agitator. It was he who had been primarily responsible for the changes in form and emphasis of the Catholic movement during 1811. Basically, he had set out to widen, render national and, to a limited degree, popularize the campaign. The Convention Act of 1793 made it almost certain that such moves would precipitate a legal and constitutional conflict. This he welcomed both from professional and natural inclination and because it placed the direction of the campaign in his own hands. From February 1811 onwards even the aristocratic leaders in the Committee acted almost as his chessmen in the game of common and statute law which he was playing with his Castle counterparts.

We might also note that it was during 1811 that politics began seriously to compete with his profession for O'Connell's time. Some thirty years later, he replied bitterly to the Earl of Shrewsbury's charge that he was greedy in accepting the public's financial support:

At a period when my minutes counted by the guinea, when my emoluments were limited only by the extent of my physical and waking powers, when my meals were shortened to the narrowest span, and my sleep restricted to the earliest hours before dawn – at that period, and for more than twenty years, there was no day that I did not devote from one to two hours, often much more, to the working out of the Catholic cause . . . For four years I bore the entire expenses of Catholic agitation, without receiving the contributions of others to a greater amount than £74 in the whole. Who shall repay me for the years of my buoyant youth and cheerful manhood? Who shall repay me for the lost opportunities of acquiring professional celebrity, or for the wealth which such distinctions would ensure?[24]

There were to be fluctuations in the extent of his political commitments. In certain phases, 1816–17 for instance, no expenditure of energy or talent could set or keep a serious agitation in motion. But in general, O'Connell understated, if anything, his outpouring of time, money and physical, nervous and mental energy in the public cause in the decades 1811–30. Already in 1811 the pattern was being set in which, 'Busy all day long, either on circuit or in the law-courts, he could still find time to arrange meetings, draw up resolutions, make speeches and in short direct the whole business of the Catholics.'[25] The student who could not rise in the mornings had by now reduced his sleep to six hours a night, now rose at 5 a.m., toiled as a lawyer for nine hours or more, and then took up his other career again each afternoon. It had become a life of Hercules and Sisyphus in one.

IV

By the opening of 1812, the Catholic Committee had been effectively stifled; there is no evidence that O'Connell ever contemplated putting his assertions of the illegality of its suppression to the test. But some cards still remained in Irish Catholic hands. Foremost was the war with France, now entering perhaps its most critical year of all. For a variety of reasons, ranging from the international influence of the Papacy to the high proportion of Irish Catholics among recruits to both the army and navy, this was the factor which had impelled successive British governments since 1793 to toy with Emancipation. Secondly, the Catholic question had begun to divide British politicians deeply and, still more significant, cross-factionally. Cabinet building, the management of the Commons and the quality of the war administration all suffered from the consequences of this extraneous source of contention, with corresponding incentives to end it by some final settlement. Thirdly, and most immediately, there remained the traditional English 'rights' of petition and assembly to be exploited, and these O'Connell continued to exploit in the early months of 1812. County or other aggregate meetings were held during the spring assizes, with O'Connell to the forefront in Ennis, Limerick and Tralee; their business spread rapidly from protests against Hare's conduct to denunciations of 'That grave of Irish prosperity, the Legislative Union'.[26] Meanwhile the new Catholic Board, despite its self-imposed limitations, conducted itself in substantially the same fashion as the Committee had done, with meetings reported in the press and a deputation sent to London for the parliamentary session. In all this, O'Connell was the master figure; already the cult of personality was manifest. At the Limerick meeting of 24 July he told the enthusiastic crowd:

> I feel it my duty as a 'Professed Agitator' to address this meeting; it is merely the exercise of my office of Agitation . . . If the Emancipation Bill passes, next Sessions, as it is likely to do; and that no other candidate offers, I myself will bring your present member to the poll. I probably will have little chance of success; but I will have the satisfaction of shewing this City and the County, what the freeborn mind might achieve, if it were properly seconded. [*Here the Applause became so great, as to prevent the Speaker for some minutes, from proceeding.*][27]

After Kirwan's conviction on 3 February 1812, the Irish government did nothing to check the Catholic movement for several months. A serious effort was being made in London to resolve the Catholic question once and for all; it was no time for further stirring of the hornet's nest. When at last Canning showed his hand it was to give notice on 6 May that he would move in the Commons for 'the consideration of such securities as might be necessary to fence the Established Church' in the event of Emancipation.[28] Simultaneously, it was rumoured that the prime minister, Perceval, was attempting to reach a settlement with the Irish Catholic hierarchy behind the backs of the Catholic Board, and at successive meetings of the Board on 12 and 16 May O'Connell denounced this 'insidious' move and expressed his conviction that 'no such proposition had been made'. As Professor M. R. O'Connell suggests, however, 'O'Connell's denunciation on 12 May may well have been mere kite-flying in order to discover whether there was any truth in . . . [the] information.'[29]

In between these meetings of the Board news had reached Dublin of Perceval's assassination on 11 May. Immediately hopes had risen that the reconstituted government would prove more favourable to the Catholic claims, and O'Connell held off calling an aggregate meeting in Dublin until he saw how things would shape themselves. It was soon apparent that they would shape themselves badly. The illusion that the Prince Regent was the Catholics' friend, awaiting only opportunity or political encouragement to liberate them, was rapidly destroyed by his refusal to grant a personal interview to the delegates of the Irish Catholic Board, and his ready acceptance of a new ministry constructed by Lord Liverpool upon the familiar anti-Catholic lines.

Catholic anger expressed itself in the subsequently notorious 'witchery' resolutions passed at the Dublin aggregate meeting of 18 June – the witchery being that of the Prince's current mistress, Lady Hertford.

> We learn with deep disappointment and anguish, how cruelly the promised boon of Catholic freedom has been intercepted by the fatal witchery of an unworthy secret influence, hostile to our fairest hopes, spurning alike the sanctions of public and private virtue, the demands of personal gratitude, and the sacred obligations of plighted honour. To this impure source we trace, but too distinctly, our afflicted hopes and protracted servitude, the arrogant invasion of the undoubted right of petitioning, the acrimony of illegal state prosecutions, the surrender of Ireland to prolonged oppression . . .[30]

The ringing phrases were Denys Scully's but it was O'Connell who, boldly and savagely, applied them directly to the Prince. The disclosures had transformed him into an absolute intransigent, much to the fright and chagrin of the cautious party in the Board.

The formation of the new government, however, worked for as well as against the Catholic interest. The fact that such able tories as Canning and Wellesley had been prevented from joining a tory administration, at a time of supreme national crisis, solely because the Catholic question remained unsettled, had its effect upon high political opinion. The ground was ready for an attempt to remove the question once for all from British politics by some agreed solution, to be worked out essentially by the various contestants at Westminster. Accordingly, when Canning proposed on 22 June 1812 that the issue of Catholic disabilities should be tackled at last in the next parliamentary session, the Commons supported him by the overwhelming majority of 235 to 106.

O'Connell, unlike many, perhaps most, members of the Irish Board, reacted with uncompromising hostility. At an aggregate meeting on 2 July he called upon Irish Catholics to redouble instead of relaxing their agitation. They should settle for nothing less than unqualified Emancipation; the cry for 'securities' to allay Protestant fears was an insult to free men and in itself a sort of confirmation of Catholic servility. Borrowing a Grattanite slogan of the early 1780s, O'Connell ran 'Simple Repeal' up the masthead. This presaged a fundamental cleavage in the Board; but during the summer of 1812 there was no public repudiation of O'Connell's call for intransigence, although he repeated it at every aggregate meeting on the assize circuit. Did he really mean to reject all adulterated forms of Catholic relief? Or was his primary purpose to build up Catholic bargaining power against the moment of eventual compromise, or to popularize the movement, or to out-manoeuvre his opponents in the Board, or generally to extend the practice of agitation, the habit of defiance and the sight of his co-religionists bearing themselves as equals? We lack the evidence to make a choice of motive, but he himself would doubtless have liked us to select the last. Perhaps it was in earnest of this passion for equality that he sought to drag down in ridicule the new Irish chief secretary, Robert Peel, appointed on 4 August 1812 at the age of twenty-four. Instantly, O'Connell employed the obvious derogation, 'Orange' Peel.

Nine months were to pass, however, before the two engaged closely in combat. It took Peel time to establish his domination over the permanent officials at the Castle and to form an alliance with its most effective member, William Saurin, the attorney-general; it took the lucky accident of the near-simultaneous departure of the viceroy and a permanent under-secretary in May 1813, to clear his way to over-riding power. Meanwhile, the Catholic cause had at least held its ground. O'Connell's fortunes had been mixed in the autumn of 1812. The opportunity of demonstrating Irish Catholic electoral strength in the general election of October was neither well-seen nor well-seized: pro-Catholic borough seats were actually lost in Cork and Newry. Worse still, in the course of the subsequent recriminations, the Catholic Board, despite O'Connell's earnest protest, carried a motion on 28 November condemning and repudiating those Catholics who had failed to support the Emancipationist candidates. 'One would suppose', O'Connell told the meeting, 'that Ireland was not sufficiently divided and distracted already, but that division and dissension in the Catholic Board could be afforded in addition.'[31] Later, summoning all his influence, he managed to have the condemnatory resolution rescinded, but by then the charges of cowardice and self-serving had worked their poison on personal relations.

On the other hand, the lost and unwon Irish seats seemed scarcely to matter when the new House of Commons assembled at the beginning of 1813. Grattan's resolution in favour of Catholic relief was carried by a majority of forty; his motion in committee on 1 March, that all Catholic disabilities be removed, subject only to 'securities' to guarantee the Protestant establishment, passed still more easily and the bill derived from this motion was read for the first time on 30 April. The 'securities' prescribed in the bill consisted essentially of an oath of allegiance to be taken by all Catholics, lay and clerical alike, swearing to uphold the Protestant succession, Protestant property and the established church, and to reject the episcopal nomination of any candidate whose loyalty and 'tranquil disposition' was in doubt. All this was in the eighteenth-century style. Substantially the same oath had been freely sworn by Irish Catholics of the preceding generation; in practice, it constituted little more than a ritual of abasement.

The very symbolism of subservience, revived in Grattan's bill, may explain the ferocity of O'Connell's opposition to the new measure when it was considered *in camera* by the Catholic Board on 1 May 1813. But although most supported his condemnation of the bill, several members were prepared to close with Grattan's 'offer'. O'Connell countered these by 'leaking' an account of the proceedings to the newspapers; he wished to rally popular support to intimidate the compromisers. When challenged at the next Board meeting, he agreed to allow a statement to be sent forth that the Board had come to no determination on the bill. He had already achieved his objective, the silencing, temporarily at least, of his opponents. At the same time, O'Connell sought to guard his other flank by threatening the bishops obliquely. While he noisily proclaimed his belief that the clerical order might be trusted to safeguard its own independence, he also made it clear that he would resist it strongly should the last relic of national pride and honour, an unmanaged Church, be tarnished by episcopal compromise. Whether or not influenced by this warning, the Irish hierarchy publicly condemned the ecclesiastical clauses of Grattan's bill in the strongest terms on 29 May. In fact, the bishops' action was unnecessary; two nights before, the House of Commons had so emasculated the bill that its supporters withdrew it as now worthless. O'Connell was fortunate that this news had not reached Dublin until after the bishops met, for their resolution practically enlisted them in his ranks in the current struggle.

His sense of triumph was unbounded. At the next Board meeting, he lauded the prelates to the skies for saving the Irish people from the perpetuation of their 'degradation'. Cleverly, he capitalized upon this line of argument by using the bill's proposal that there should be a governmental commission to control Irish episcopal appointments as a means of denigrating its likely members – as to whom, incidentally, his guesses were remarkably accurate. The chief victim of his invective was 'Orange' Peel, 'a raw youth squeezed out of the workings of I know not what factory in England, and sent over to Ireland before he had got rid of the foppery of perfumed handkerchiefs and thin shoes, upon the simple ground that, having vindicated the murderous Walcheren expedition, he was thought to be a lad ready to vindicate anything and everything'.[32] Such vituperation could scarcely have been quite without design. But O'Connell may have been carried along by the tide of his own thoughts, by his smarting under the vision of the perpetual 'degradation' just avoided, as he strove to force down a brutally disdainful caste to the common level.

The price of gross abuse was the making of personal enemies in politics: we may plausibly date Peel's lifelong aversion to O'Connell from this occasion, just as we may date the Prince Regent's from O'Connell's elaboration of the 'witchery' resolutions. A further cost was the tearing apart of the Irish Catholic movement. O'Connell's motion of gratitude to the hierarchy was bitterly resisted at the Catholic Board meeting of 29 May 1813. Twenty members opposed it, and they and their friends seceded permanently from the Board after they had been defeated. Henceforth there was an Irish 'vetoist' party in schism from the O'Connell-dominated majority. The division was not quite on the lines of social class, still less of generation, and not quite as marked in the provincial cities as in the capital. Certainly, the 'vetoists' comprised, by and large, the Irish Catholics of the highest social rank. But they also included a number from the professional and mercantile classes and, especially important, some of the ablest men of the rising generation, such as Richard Lalor Sheil and Thomas Wyse, and some of the most ambitious of the young Catholic barristers, such as Nicholas Ball and Stephen Woulfe. This was in part a matter of self-interest. But the perennially attractive political argument that substantial gains might be made for only the cost of insubstantial guarantees of good behaviour could also be deployed. As one critic put the point, the anti-vetoists, like the Gregorian calendarists, 'found out an evil which did nobody any harm, and provided a remedy which did nobody any good'.[33] The critic himself went on to suggest that the leading vetoists saw government influence over the Irish clergy as a remedy which might do *them* a little good. They feared, he wrote, O'Connell's efforts to build up a clerical caste. '[The] aristocracy would not forget the humble origin of most of the priests . . . This was never mentioned in the whole *veto* controversy, but it was really the point at issue. The aristocracy sought the *veto*, because they hoped that the government would use its influence to preserve the prelacy at least "*unvulgarized*".'[34]

At any rate, it was clear that O'Connell could no longer rely on the aristocratic and professionally-pushing factions even to form a common front in emergencies. He signalized as much by summoning a public meeting at Fishamble Street theatre on 15 June 1813 at which he specifically adopted the principle of popular agitation. This marked a radical departure. Making a virtue of necessity, O'Connell pointed to the benefit of the postponement of full Emancipation – a mere delay, of course, for nothing was more certain than its eventual passage. The interval of frustrated hope would inevitably breed agitators, and agitators were bound to accustom 'the popular mind' to consider public issues, to awaken it to a knowledge of its wrongs and to lead it into the passions and machinations of politics. Once aroused and directed, 'the people' would prove irresistible in the end. But the condition precedent of their success was to eschew all violence or even illegality and to rely exclusively upon 'the repetition of your consti- tutional demands by petition, and still more by the pressure of circumstances and the great progress of events'. In the most solemn words, O'Connell warned his audience that should any crime or illegality in the movement bring down upon them a renewed reign of terror, he himself would be found in the ranks of the suppressors. 'There would not be so heavy a heart; but there would not be a more ready hand to sustain the constitution against every enemy.'[35]

This very curious declaration set out the philosophy of political action which was to govern O'Connell's entire agitatory career. The philosophy was complete already, even if the machinery of imple- mentation remained to be invented. It represented a specific repudi- ation of the revolutionary tradition, just as it also repudiated directly the republican objective. O'Connell confined political action to the limits of the British constitution, and the goal of all such action to a full, fair and equal place within that constitution. It was an extra- ordinary doctrine and recipe for a demogogue to offer the masses whom he intended to 'create'. But, albeit inert and hidden for at least a decade, it contained the dynamite which would eventually blow apart the old Protestant Ascendancy in Ireland.

There remains the question, why did O'Connell adopt the role of absolute intransigent during 1812–13? In many ways it was out of character. By temperament he was averse to extreme positions, by training a settler out of court in doubtful issues. Moreover, he himself probably stood to gain more from Grattan's original bill, in terms of eventual status and income alike, than anyone in the vetoist cliques. The answer is, partly, that current and future compromise in the bill would be mainly at the expense of the Irish Catholic Church's autonomy, and O'Connell was sincere in regarding this – vis-à-vis Great Britain at least – as integral to Irish independence. Secondly, he still rated the French threat to Britain as powerful enough to force her to come to a satisfactory accommodation with Irish Catholicism, if only the Irish Catholics pressed hard. But, most important of all perhaps, he judged it unlikely that the House of Commons of 1813, with Liverpool's anti-Catholic ministry in office and the Prince Regent the ultimate determinant, would yield anything of substance unless intimidated by Irish agitation or disorder. A half or a quarter measure now, drawing off most of the lay Catholics on the make, might render it impossible to mount another major offensive for many years. O'Connell's political judgment was probably correct at every point.

CHAPTER 6

Championing

1813–15

I

During 1813, O'Connell began to manifest a new style, suited to a wider and more popular audience. He had already become a daily public spectacle in Dublin's streets, known to and watched with awe by multitudes. A perceptive observer later described his half-hour morning walk from Merrion Square to Arran Quay:

> When breakfast was over, his burly form excited attention, as he moved towards the Four Courts, at a pace which compelled panting attorneys to toil after him in vain. His umbrella shouldered like a pike, was his invariable companion; the military step which he had acquired in the yeomanry, strangely blended with the trot characteristic of an active sportsman on the mountains of Kerry, gave him the appearance of a Highland chieftain – a similarity increased, when his celebrity as an agitator began to ensure him a 'tail' of admiring followers whenever he appeared in public.[1]

In a comparatively small city, politics could become personalized in a specific and physical as well as a large and metaphorical sense.

With his violent direct assaults upon the Regent and Peel, O'Connell had, to some extent, assumed the role of gladiator engaging enemies in personal combat. This development reached its apotheosis in the Magee trial of 26–7 July 1813. On 3 June, John Magee, the Protestant proprietor of the main pro-Catholic newspaper, the *Dublin Evening Post*, was arrested on a charge of publishing a libel on the lately departed viceroy, the Duke of Richmond. The arrest was part of a deliberate campaign, by Peel, to destroy or intimidate the opposition press. Already two other pro-Catholic publishers, Cox and Fitzpatrick, had been gaoled. But Magee was much the most important victim of the new Castle offensive, and O'Connell decided to turn the consequent publicity to account by rendering the trial, in effect, a political tournament. There was of course a full array of counsel on either side, but he was to dominate the defendant's, just as the attorney-general, Saurin, a narrow, bitter but upright and competent Protestant zealot and Ascendancy man, was to dominate the prosecution.

O'Connell and Saurin had clashed already in Fitzpatrick's case, when O'Connell electrified the court by demanding that both the attorney-general and a judge, Norbury, be summoned as witnesses – Saurin's and Norbury's conduct in a recent capital case being a leading item in Fitzpatrick's 'libel'. Saurin had been breathtaken by the measure of O'Connell's insolence in attempting to arraign the entire administration of justice, and to reduce two of its ornaments to the level of mere cross-examinees. 'Were they', he exclaimed, 'to convert the trial of a person charged with libel, into a trial of his Majesty's Government?'[2] This described precisely O'Connell's objectives in the Magee affair. When he rose to address the court at the outset of the trial's second day, it was to hold 'the law' (and the whole governmental system) up to ridicule and scorn. He began with Saurin's opening indictment:

> That which yesterday excited my anger, now appears to me to be an object of pity; and that which then roused my indignation, now only moves to *contempt* . . .
>
> It was a discourse in which you could not discover either order, or method, or eloquence; it contained very little logic, and no poetry at all; violent and virulent, it was a confused and disjointed tissue of bigotry, amalgamated with congenial vulgarity. He accused my client of using Billingsgate and he accused him of it in language suited exclusively for that meridian . . .
>
> I cannot repress my astonishment, how Mr Attorney-General could have *preserved* this dialect in its native purity; he has been now for nearly thirty years in the class of polished society; he has, for some years, mixed amongst the highest orders in the state; he has had the honour to belong for thirty years to the first profession in the world – to the only profession, with the single exception, perhaps, of the military, to which a high-minded gentleman could condescend to belong – the Irish bar. To that bar, at which he has seen and heard a Burgh and a Duquery; at which he must have listened to a Burston, a Ponsonby, and a Curran; to a bar which still contains a Plunket, a Ball, and despite of politics, I will add, a Bushe. With this galaxy of glory, flinging their light around him, how can he alone have remained in darkness? . . . Devoid of taste and of genius, how can he have had memory enough to preserve this original vulgarity? He is, indeed, an object of compassion . . .[3]

These lacerating words were directed at two audiences. The first was the ruling powers – the chief justice and his companion judges on the bench, and the chief secretary Peel, the Irish chancellor of the exchequer, the Irish commander-in-chief and all the lesser potentates of Dublin Castle ranged beneath it. They sat stunned by the onslaught, in a stupor of disbelief that a papist junior counsel should charge the first officer of the Irish Government, in open court, with congenital and irremediable vulgarity. The second audience, on the rear benches and in the gallery, was but a token of the shadowy masses whom O'Connell was addressing from afar, the Irish Catholic millions whom he was telling not to crouch, not to admit inferiority, not to fear. The public humilation of Saurin was meant to be a demonstration lesson, so to say, for raw pupils on their first day at school. Far into his address, O'Connell was checked at last by the chief justice. Under a very transparent disguise, he had just spoken of Saurin as 'an infamous and profligate *liar!*' for charging the Catholic Board with sedition.

CHIEF JUSTICE: What, Mr O'Connell, can this have to do with the question which the jury are to try?
MR O'CONNELL: You heard the Attorney-General traduce and calumniate us – you heard him with patience and with temper – listen now to our vindication![4]

There were no further interruptions.

The alleged 'libel' was based on a sentence in the *Evening Post* ending, 'but truly . . . they [the people of Ireland] must find themselves at a loss to discover any striking feature in his Grace's [Richmond's] administration, that makes it superior to the worst of his predecessors'[5]: the review had described earlier viceroys in such terms as 'the profligate, unprincipled Westmorland', 'the cold-hearted and cruel Camden' and 'the artful and treacherous Cornwallis'. O'Connell first tackled the charge by attempting to justify these descriptions of Richmond's predecessors, and he had no difficulty in producing similar condemnations by their various British political enemies. As for Richmond himself, O'Connell distinguished the honourable private individual from the public man guilty of all the customary sorts of Irish misgovernment. Together, these lines of defence enabled O'Connell to survey, systematically and scarifyingly, the entire course of British management of Ireland over the preceding quarter of a century. Again the Bench and the 'quality' in court sat amazed under the attack, their world suddenly turned upside down, their ears hearing audacity beyond belief. Peel epitomized their reaction when he later declared that if Magee had published a gross libel, O'Connell was uttering one even more atrocious – and doing so with impunity.

But such an Ascendancy form of judgment was undercut completely by O'Connell's second, concurrent defence tactic. This was his 'honest and conscientious opinion . . . that in the discussion of *public subjects*, and of the administration of *public men*, *truth* is a duty and not *a crime*'.[6] Flat or facile though this may read in the late twentieth century, it was the simple, almost the sole issue in mid-1813. Today Magee's diatribe might disgust as vulgar, inflated or wild, but only in a deeply totalitarian state would it so much as occur to an official that it constituted a seditious or defamatory statement. Unerringly, O'Connell traced the British coercion of his time to its source – the Star Chamber mentality, which had lived on in those eighteenth-century English and early-nineteenth-century Irish courts, where 'Servility at the Bar, and profligacy on the Bench, have not been wanting to aid every construction unfavourable to freedom, and at length it is taken as granted and as clear law, that truth or falsehood are quite immaterial, circumstances constituting no part of either guilt or innocence.'[7] As this indicates, the libel action against Magee was – in our terms – a mere mechanism of political censorship, with cruel penalties being imposed retrospectively for breaches of an unspecified and unpromulgated code.

O'Connell threaded his libel defence with further assaults upon the current Irish Administration, and in particular Saurin. He mocked the packed Protestant jury as 'suppressors of vice and Bible distributers' (a reference to the repressive and proselytizing societies to which most of them belonged), demanding of them, 'Are you sincere, or are you, to use your own phraseology, whitewashed tombs – painted charnel-houses? Be ye hypocrites?'[8] He assailed Peel directly as the briber of the newspapers in Dublin Castle's pay. 'Would I could see the man', he exclaimed, staring Peel in the face, 'who pays this proclamation money and these pensions . . . I would ask him whether . . . this be the legitimate use of the public purse.'[9] But it was Saurin above all whom O'Connell continued to hound down. Because of his Huguenot ancestry, he was depicted as a carpet-bagger, a 'bigoted and intemperate stranger', filled with '*French* insolence, than which there is nothing so permanent – even transplanted, it exhibits itself to the third and fourth generation.'[10] In 'putting an imaginary case' (*à la* Mr Jaggers), O'Connell heaped scorn upon Saurin's 'church-wardening piety' and 'maidenly decorum of manners'; but also pictured him, bigotted, prejudiced, pompous, vain and loaded with the booty of the attorney-generalship, using, once raised to the Bench, 'that character for SANCTITY which has served to promote him, as a sword, to hew down the struggling liberties of his country'.[11] The climax of this terrible rending was probably O'Connell's rehearsal of Saurin's political career before the Union.

> The charge of being a Jacobin, was at that time made against the present Attorney-General – him, plain William Saurin – in the very terms, and with just as much truth as he now applies it to my client. His reply shall serve for that of Mr Magee; I take it from the anti-Union of the 22nd March, 1800.
>
> > 'To the charge of Jacobin, Mr Saurin said he knew not what it meant, as applied to him, *except it was an opposition to the will of the British minister.*'
>
> So says Mr Magee; but, gentlemen, my eye lights upon another passage of Mr Saurin's, in the same speech from which I have quoted the above. It was in these words:-
>
> > 'Mr Saurin admitted, that debates might sometimes produce *agitations*, but that was the PRICE *necessarily paid for liberty.*'
>
> Oh, how I thank this good Jew for the word. Yes, agitation is, as Mr Saurin well remarked, the price necessarily paid for liberty. We have paid the price, gentlemen, and the honest man refuses to give us the goods. (*Much laughing.*)

In the end O'Connell implied a charge of selling principles for profit, when he asked, 'But, gentlemen, is the Attorney-General at liberty to change the nature of things with his own official and professional prospects?'[12]

O'Connell's address concluded with a brilliant sustained appeal-by-role-reversal. He asked the jury to suppose themselves inhabitants of a Portugal, four-fifths Protestant in composition and ruled, through a viceroy, by a repressive foreign Catholic power:

> your native land shall be to you the country of strangers; you shall be aliens in the soil that gave you birth, and whilst every foreigner may, in the land of your forefathers, attain rank, station, emolument, honours, you alone shall be excluded . . .
>
> Only think, gentlemen, of the scandalous injustice of punishing you because you are Protestants. With what scorn – with what contempt – do you not listen to the stale pretences – to the miserable excuses by which, under the name of state reasons and political arguments, your exclusion and degradation are sought to be justified![13]

He proceeded to outline, in acerbic detail, the full course of Richmond's administration – all in the form of a Catholic viceroy's oppression of Protestant Portugal. At last he reached the stage matching that at which the genuinely Irish Protestant Magee had published his 'libel' upon Richmond's rule.

> But if at such a moment some ardent and enthusiastic Papist [in 'Portugal'], regardless of his interests, and roused by the crimes that were thus committed against you, should describe, in measured, and cautious, and cold language, scenes of oppression and iniquity . . . if this liberal Papist, for this, were dragged to the Inquisition, as for a crime, and menaced with a dungeon for years, good and gracious God! how would you revolt at and abominate the men who could consign him to that dungeon! . . . What pity would you not feel for the advocate who heavily, and without hope, laboured in his defence![14]

The final words challenged the jurors on their home ground, 'earnest', fundamentalist, evangelical religion. O'Connell demanded that they show whether they were sincere believers, whether with 'all this zeal – with all this piety', there was a single conscience among the twelve, or a single soul which felt terror at violating the sacred oath. If he had 'alarmed religion . . . in one breast amongst you, Mr Magee is safe . . . but if there is none – if you be slaves and hypocrites, he will await your verdict, and despise it.'[15]

O'Connell failed to 'alarm religion' in, or otherwise disturb, a single juror-breast. Magee was quickly declared guilty, although his sentencing was postponed until the next law term. O'Connell was generally condemned at the time for sacrificing his client's interest to his own political ends, and by and large posterity has endorsed this verdict. But such a judgment seems superficial. It was morally certain that the carefully culled ultra-Protestant jury would find against Magee whatever conventional line of defence was chosen. O'Connell's bold and wonderfully executed strategy – to try to bring home to even one juror an understanding of his proper function or of the plain brute oppression which the so-called Irish Government merely masked, or to awaken a scruple or qualm in a single juror's conscience – may well have represented the sole hope of securing a hung jury, if not acquittal. An acute contemporary, who was by no means an uncritical admirer of O'Connell, adjudged that he 'did not neglect any material point in his client's defence; and even if he had confined himself strictly to his duties as an advocate, the issue would still have been the same'.[16]

Nevertheless it is true that Magee's fate was a secondary consideration. O'Connell used the trial first and foremost to assert, in a more public and telling form than had ever been available to him before, that Catholics were fully the equals, rank for rank, of their Protestant counterparts. For once, he could, literally, confront his enemies; they were bound to their seats in court, bound to hear him in silence, by the weight of their own mores and self-regard. For once it was they who were on the triangle, and for four and a half hours O'Connell lashed them with irony and scorn. On only one occasion had the court attempted to wrest the scourge from O'Connell; and it had been almost contemptuously swept back. The address, magnificently structured and endlessly fertile in invention and allusion, was probably O'Connell's master forensic display. It also marked a new stage of Catholic pretension, even arrogance.

O'Connell's speech was reported extensively in the Irish newspapers, Magee's *Evening Post* reprinting it in full. It was also issued immediately as a pamphlet, as well as translated into French and Spanish – though not Portuguese! All this of course multiplied O'Connell's offence in Castle eyes. But (to anticipate Mr Gladstone) the resources of 'civilization' were not exhausted. On 10 August, 1813, Peel wrote to Lord Desart, 'I hope the Chief Justice [Downes] will not allow the Court to be again insulted and made the vehicle of treason, but that he will . . . interrupt his [O'Connell's] harangue by committing him to Newgate for contempt of court.'[17] No doubt this message was conveyed to Downes; already the government had told him that O'Connell's performance at Magee's trial had disgraced his court. It was not surprising therefore that when Magee came up for sentencing on 27 November 1813, Saurin, himself still smarting from the trouncing he had received on 27 July, should have presented O'Connell's advocacy and Magee's publication of his address in full as an aggravation of the original crime. 'For I do say', declared Saurin of O'Connell's 'blustering and bravadoing' performance, 'such an outrage on public decency has not occurred in the memory of man.'[18] When the attorney-general went on to imply that O'Connell had participated in Magee's criminality, O'Connell replied that Saurin had done well to store up his resentment for four months so that he could express it in the safety of the courtroom: otherwise he would have received the chastisement he deserved. Downes and his brother judges were aghast; two, Daly and Osborne, threatened O'Connell with immediate committal for a criminal offence. But he stood his ground until Saurin was induced to withdraw any imputation that O'Connell had participated in Magee's crime. Then, flushed with victory, O'Connell went on – under the thin veil of a vision of the future – to depict Saurin as 'some creature – narrow-minded, mean, calumnious, of inveterate bigotry, and dastard disposition', and their Lordships as interrupting and threatening defence counsel 'lest he should wipe off the disgrace of his adversary'.[19] The Bench sat silent now.

Although O'Connell seemed to have won yet another round, he had in fact overreached himself. His renewed violence and insolence towards the Bench so frightened Magee that he suddenly threw him over in the hope of a lighter sentence. Wallace, another advocate, announced that Mr O'Connell was dismissed and disavowed as Magee's counsel; he urged that the defendant should not suffer for O'Connell's 'abuse of the forensic robe'.[20] This did not save Magee from a sentence of two years' imprisonment as well as a fine of £500 and the threat of further retribution should he ever resume his radical political journalism. But O'Connell also suffered grievously. He was deeply humiliated by being thrown over by his client, and widely spoken of as incompetent or self-seeking in his conduct of the defence. Hunting Cap, whom he dared not offend again, was gravely displeased by the contretemps. 'I have therefore', he warned O'Connell on 14 December 1813,

> most earnestly to request, and will even add to insist, that you will in future conduct yourself with calmness, temperance and moderation towards him [Saurin], and that you will not suffer yourself to be hurried by hate or violence of passions to use any language unbecoming the calm and intelligent barrister or the judicious and well-bred gentleman, or that may tend to expose you to the reprehension . . . of the court.[21]

In addition, the Catholic cause had been further injured by the crushing of its supporting press (what editor would dare to step into the breach left by the *Evening Post*?) and by the desertions from O'Connell's camp within the movement. His dwindling band of political friends tried to stem the adverse tide by suscribing a thousand guineas to present him with a service of plate in recognition of his indominability and matchless powers. In making the presentation John Finlay, a fellow barrister and member of the Catholic Board, depicted him as a sort of latter-day Cuchulainn, striving to hold back single-handed the government's onslaughts upon the independence of press and bar. Finlay concluded with a gloss upon some lines from Scott's *Marmion*:

> *Let him but stand in spite of power,*
> *A watchman on the lonely tower*
> *His thrilling trump will rouse the land*
> *When fraud or danger is at hand*
> *By him, as by the beacon light,*
> *The pilot must keep course aright.*[22]

As 1813 drew to a close, neither his trump nor his light was much regarded. It was true enough, however, that he still stood in spite of power.

II

Not altogether coincidentally, the weakening of O'Connell's position during 1813 was paralleled by Napoleon's decline. By the beginning of 1814 all Bonaparte's gains since the first Italian campaign of 1797 had been dissipated; the French had been practically driven back to the lines of the Rhine and the Pyrenees, and the fear of defeat, and even the sense of being engaged in a life-or-death struggle had been lifted at last from Britain. Nor was it altogether a coincidence that Rome's decision on an appeal from the English Catholic Board against the Irish Catholic bishops' condemnation of the veto in 1808, which had been meandering for years about the channels of the curia, should have been declared early in 1814 (16 February) or that it should have met substantially the desires of the British government. The Roman rescript recommended acceptance of the veto on the ground that the British crown desired it only for reasons of public security, and not at all to wean Irish Catholics from their religion, which was, moreover, 'friendly to public authority, gives stability to thrones, and makes subjects obedient, faithful, and emulous of their country's welfare'.[23]

This rescript produced consternation in the Irish laity, apart from the still small though growing faction of vetoists; O'Connell was appalled. Some comfort was eventually derived from the fact that it had been signed by Mgr Quarantotti, the vice-prefect (Dublin was soon to translate this as 'a mere understrapper') of Propaganda. It was argued that the document was 'non-pontifical' because Pius VII, at that time Napoleon's prisoner, had not seen the rescript before its despatch. O'Connell did not however commit the cause wholly to casuistry, but set about organizing a series of fiery protest meetings, both open and at the Catholic Board, at which he threw down the gauntlet in the plainest language. At one he roundly declared, 'I would as soon receive my politics from Constantinople as from Rome.'[24] It is interesting to note that, as with the Union in 1800, O'Connell took – and maintained – his stand upon a simple liberal principle: any Roman intervention would constitute an invasion of civil liberty, and better that Irish Catholics should remain forever without Emancipation than that they should purchase it at such a price. Meanwhile, he had placed pressure, whether necessarily or not, upon the Irish hierarchy, and their private meeting on 27 May 1814 issued in a unanimous decision to reject the veto in any form. Daniel Murray, co-adjutor Archbishop of Dublin since 1809, was dispatched to Rome 'to inform his Holiness of the real state and interests of the Roman Catholic Church in Ireland'.[25] These turbulent and defiant reactions were so successful that the Quarantotti rescript was withdrawn for re-examination by the pope and Propaganda.

At best this represented a successful holding action, and simultaneously O'Connell was undergoing a further humiliation because of the unfortunate Magee. Peel insisted that Magee be subjected to a second prosecution. On 10 August 1813 the *Dublin Evening Post* had published resolutions passed at a public meeting in Kilkenny congratulating O'Connell on his address of 27 July 1813 as 'calculated to control the partialities of the Bench, to shame and stigmatise the bigotry of a selected jury, and to rebuke into native insignificance the vain and vulgar law officer'. In pressing for this to be punished, Peel had no particular animus against Magee. 'I shall be disappointed', he wrote almost immediately after the Kilkenny meeting, 'if we cannot strike at higher game than the printer. I hope those who presided at their [the resolutions'] birth may have the manliness to avow themselves as the authors.'[26] Doubtless he had the chairman of the Kilkenny meeting, Major George Bryan, a wealthy and active O'Connellite, and Denys Scully, the author of the resolutions, in his sights. But another Magee trial would also further counteract O'Connell's original triumph of 27 July. Re-engaged by Magee, O'Connell would not dare to repeat the 'insolence' which had led Magee to repudiate him on 27 November. In fact Dublin Castle was in an even stronger position here than Peel could realize, for, before the second Magee trial came on, Hunting Cap specifically enjoined O'Connell: 'I have not only to entreat, but decidedly to insist, that on your part they [the coming exchanges with Saurin] will be carried on with calmness, discretion and decency, and that you will not in any degree glance at anything that has passed between you on former occasions or animadvert with severity or strained conclusion on what may fall from him.'[27]

At the second trial, held on 23 February 1814, O'Connell did indeed comport himself with 'calmness, discretion and decency' – in itself a sort of admission of defeat. As to the rest, Bryan refused to accept any responsibility for the Kilkenny resolutions; Scully failed to take the stand; and poor Magee ended with a further six months' imprisonment and a further £1000 fine. But even the 'escape' of Bryan and Scully turned out to be another victory for the Administration. Magee made it clear that he felt betrayed by the Catholic Board. As the solicitor-general put it, 'the Catholic Board entered into partnership with the traverser, but left the jail part of the concern exclusively to him'.[28] Bryan was widely condemned by Catholics, even among the membership of the Catholic Board, for pusillanimity. Yet O'Connell – as befitted a political boss demonstrating loyalty to the loyal and also anxious to retain a very wealthy and influential supporter – championed Bryan warmly. In an attempted pre-emptive strike, he moved at the commencement of the next Board meeting that Bryan take the chair. A rival Catholic demagogue from Belfast, the journalist-barrister John Lawless, countered with a motion strongly deploring Bryan's behaviour. For the first time, O'Connell found himself in conflict with the 'democratic' section of his movement; he was even hissed and shouted down when he attempted a defence of Bryan. He at once tacked masterfully, throwing himself upon the mercy of the crowd. 'These cries convince me that in some instances I have fallen into error. I do not consider myself infallible, and this I know, that my countrymen will impute my mistakes not to any dereliction of principle, not to the errors of my heart, but of my judgement. [Great and prolonged applause.][29] In the end O'Connell secured a resolution which merely reproved Bryan for an error of judgment while praising him personally as 'pure, independent, honourable, and efficient'.[30] At the same time the Board resolved to make good to Magee his pecuniary losses. In this fashion, O'Connell escaped from the second Magee affair as best he could. He had probably minimized the damage to himself; but even the minimum damage was considerable.

On 22 March 1814 Mary O'Connell wrote to her husband, then on circuit at Tralee:

> As to politics I am indeed a very bad judge but I much fear there is little 'chance for Emancipation. Every *thing* seems to be against it and surely, while the Catholics continue to disagree among themselves, what can they expect? The Convention Act will be carried and, what I consider worse, the veto. I hear there is to be a great meeting of the Board on Saturday relative to a letter from Lord Donoughmore. His Lordship, like all the other *seeming friends* to the cause, wishes to give it up.[31]

Mary was in fact a very shrewd rather than a very bad judge. No new 'Convention Act' eventuated because Peel and Saurin finally concluded that the Catholic Board could be suppressed without one, and the veto continued to hang fire. But otherwise her comments and prophecies were justified. They amply indicate the third field in which O'Connell was embattled in the first six months of 1814: internal Catholic policies. The Quarantotti rescript embarrassed the Board profoundly in its annual parliamentary offensive, for it provided a ready pretext for its 'spokesmen', Grattan and Lord Donoughmore, to refuse all directions, or even so-called 'suggestions', as to the presentation of the petitions. In fact Grattan merely tabled the petition in his charge, with a bald announcement that he would introduce neither bill nor motion in 1814. Donoughmore rebuffed the Board with equal insolence.

To try to find some counter to this latest blow, O'Connell summoned a meeting of the Board for 3 June 1814. So demoralized and divided were the members, however, that even an hour after the advertised time, the attendance was still seven short of a quorum. At this point, the Castle delivered the *coup de grâce* when its messenger entered the room and handed O'Connell a proclamation suppressing the Catholic Board, under the provisions of the 1793 Convention Act, as a body which assembled only 'under pretence of presenting petitions to Parliament on behalf of the Catholics of Ireland'.[32] O'Connell immediately denied the legality of this action, and announced – by then it was quite safe to do so! – that the meeting would proceed if a quorum materialized. None the less, when what remained of the Board gathered a few days later it did so in O'Connell's own drawing room and under agreement not to name itself the 'Catholic Board' any longer or to agitate further except by way of aggregate meetings. In short, Peel and Saurin had achieved the last of their objectives. Already they had effectively emasculated the pro-Catholic press, largely offset O'Connell's humiliation of the Irish Bench and Administration ten months before, and capitalized upon the schism in the Irish Catholic movement which the veto had rendered deep and open. Now they had destroyed even its basic organization.

O'Connell's spirits can scarcely have been raised by a jobation received from his Uncle Daniel in Paris, hard on the heels of the Board's suppression. 'I cannot refrain myself', wrote the Count on 16 June 1814,

> from congratulating you on the fair opportunity the late proclamation affords you of bidding farewell to the late Catholic council or committee of Dublin, as well as to all your political pursuits, and to confine yourself in future solely to the practice of your profession . . . It has always been my

steady opinion that the only effectual way to attain that desirable end [Emancipation] can only consist in gaining the good will and confidence of government and of those of the Established Church by a prudent, peaceable and loyal deportment, and that tumultuous assemblies or meetings of what denomination soever, intemperate speeches and hasty resolutions are better calculated to defeat than to promote that object . . . allow me, my dear nephew, most earnestly to entreat you to submit and conform your conduct to the letter and spirit of the Lord Lieutenant's late proclamation, and to listen to no proposal nor suggestion that could tend to elude or counteract the intent or scope of it. Let me add that to pursue a different course would be folly in the extreme and only expose you to a rigorous and, I must say, a merited prosecution.[33]

But O'Connell's wife was made of much sterner stuff; in this period her influence was always thrown against, rather than for, more cautious courses. When in September 1814 the Cork Catholics meekly accepted some contemptuous responses from Grattan and Donoughmore but resolved none the less to commit their parliamentary petitions to them once again, Mary wrote fierily, 'Did you ever read such an insulting letter as Lord Donoughmore's? What little spirit the Catholics of Cork show in leaving their petitions in his hands.'[34] O'Connell, who had himself, at an earlier stage, spoken in Cork in favour of just such a course, now held his heroic place in Mary's eyes by answering, 'The letter of Lord Donoughmore was excessively impertinent and insolent and the *submission* of the people of Cork seems to me to prove they are fit to be slaves. I am very, very sorry I was not at the meeting. I never would have consented to have put that presumptuous peer in charge of the petition. I can scarce tell you how angry I felt at his letter.'[35] This was mere private and, practically, meaningless indigation. But for O'Connell to work himself up in such a fashion, and before his wife, may have had its own uses for him in so bleak a season.

III

Towards the end of 1814 rumours began to spread in Ireland that the papacy had agreed to yield the veto to the British government in return for the restoration of the Papal States, the future of Italy being then under negotiation at the Congress of Vienna. Simultaneously, the Irish vetoist and anti-vetoist factions were faced with the problems of whether, in whose name, through whom, and for what, to petition in the approaching parliamentary session. On 10 January 1815, Lord Fingall summoned a private meeting of the leading Catholics of each group in his house. For this the rising (indeed the only) vetoist star, the brilliant young dramatist-barrister Richard Lalor Sheil, had prepared a draft petition. It was elegantly composed but also – in O'Connell's view – servile and compromising. O'Connell's powerful opposition secured its rejection together with the formation of a committee (he himself being a member) to frame an alternative petition. This in turn failed to produce agreement on anything more than that some petition or other should be presented.

O'Connell now proceeded to raise the stakes alarmingly *vis-à-vis* both Rome and Westminster. At an aggregate meeting which he organized at Clarendon St Church in Dublin on 24 January 1815, he proclaimed his absolute and undying opposition to the veto. 'Let our determination never to assent reach Rome . . . [and] should it fail I am still determined to resist. I am sincerely a Catholic but I am not a Papist.' He went on to repudiate in advance the Pope's power to bind the consciences of Irish Catholicism in any particular whatsoever without the Irish bishops' assent. He felt, he said, that he could count on the Irish episcopate; but if

> the present clergy shall descend from the high station they hold to become the vile slaves of the clerks of the Castle – a thing I believe impossible – but should it occur, I warn them in time to look to their masters for support, for the people will despise them too much to contribute (*Great applause*). The people would imitate their forefathers. They would communicate only with some holy priest who never bowed to the Dagon of power, and the Castle clergy would preach to still thinner numbers than attend in Munster or Connaught the reverend gentlemen of the present established Church.[36]

This was Gallicanism with a vengeance, except that it now rested on popular instead of monarchical power; and that it was not altogether a rhetorical ploy in a game of political pressures is indicated by O'Connell's private references to relying upon the regular clergy should the seculars fail. In a later letter to the Knight of Kerry, for example, he declared:

> if they enact restrictions, the effect will be worse than the present state of affairs. The *Crown Priests* will be despised and deserted by the people, who will be amply supplied with enthusiastic anti-anglican friars from the Continent. There is a tendency *already* to substitute friars for any priests who are supposed to favour the Veto. It is very marked in Dublin, and they know little of Ireland who supposed that they could *abolish friars* by law.[37]

Certainly, the friars appear to have constituted a species of ecclesiastical left wing at this particular stage. It may be significant that the church in which O'Connell spoke belonged to the Carmelite order; and that the Carmelite prior, William L'Estrange, was a fervent admirer of O'Connell and, by the standards of the day, an advanced nationalist.

O'Connell's dramatic oration from the altar steps of Clarendon St Church marked a new level of lay assertion and defiance in Ireland. It also scandalized the staid and delighted the masses, and put the greatest possible weight upon the Irish bishops to fall into line. But it had no effect upon the politicians at Westminster. Grattan announced that he would promote the Catholic cause in 1815 only on his own terms, that is, qualified concessions with, in all probability, a veto. This was angrily rejected by O'Connell at the next private Catholic meeting on 15 February; and he and his faction immediately set about framing a petition which would express, and finding a member who would introduce, their demand for simple and total Emancipation. For the immediate purpose, O'Connell established his first, short-lived, 'Catholic Association'; it was essentially a front organization for the petition, and in drawing it up O'Connell avoided, with elephantine care, any structural element that might draw it within the ambit of the Convention Act. All this labour bore little fruit. Not until 23 April 1815 did he find a compliant member of the Commons in the Irish whig, Sir Henry Parnell – his 'own' M.P., the Knight of Kerry, had tactfully evaded him on the ground of his relative insignificance as a politican. When on 18 May Parnell sought to introduce several resolutions embodying the Catholic claims (according to the O'Connellite version), the first met such disapproval from the House that he withdrew it and abandoned the remainder. Even his motion, twelve days later, that the House go into committee to consider the claims, was resoundingly defeated by a majority of 81. Worse still, the Knight told O'Connell, 'were we to go to a vote on unqualified relief, we should not divide with fifteen'.[38] O'Connell was then reduced to urging on Parnell and the Knight a ludicrous proposal for squaring the Anglo-Irish political circle – the concession of unqualified relief to be followed by the imposition of 'securities'!

He had been sustained throughout the spring of 1815 by the joyous news of Bonaparte's return from Elba and resumption of the French throne. On first hearing of the escape on 17 March he wrote to Mary, 'and then, love, the public news – the public news!! I can scarce draw my breath. Good God, how I die with impatience for the next packet.'[39] She reciprocated, 'I am told that he [James Sugrue, a kinsman and later agent of O'Connell] is in great spirits since the *good news* came.'[40] When Bonaparte was opposed, O'Connell reassured her, 'Do not be uneasy about the Allies. They will only tend to consolidate the great man's power if they attempt to attack him. His popularity with the French people is the most glorious and extraordinary of his achievements.'[41] In all this, O'Connell saw England's difficulty as the Irish Catholics' opportunity; and he did what he could to frighten the parliamentarians accordingly. 'The fall of prices has beggared the peasantry and ruined the farmers', he told Parnell on 13 June 1815. 'The restoration of Buonaparte has given a new direction to their hopes and wishes.'[42] Correspondingly, the outcome and aftermath of Waterloo cast him into utter – though being O'Connell, only temporary – political despair. 'I am horribly out of spirits', he wrote to Mary from Ennis on 12 July. 'There is all the bad news confirmed even beyond our fears and liberty for ever crushed in France.'[43]

Meanwhile the news was bad again on the final, Roman front. Long preceded by the usual accurate rumours in Dublin, the new rescript from Propaganda, published in May 1815, realized almost, if not quite, the worst fears of the majority of Irish Catholics. It was found that, although the Quarantotti concessions had been modified in several respects, the papacy was quite prepared to submit the names of candidates for vacant sees to the crown for approval. Of the various forms of allowing the temporal power to influence episcopal appointments, this was perhaps the least obnoxious; Rome already allowed it freely in its dealings with other Protestant states. None the less it represented an inverted veto, and was as such anathema to O'Connell. Much now depended on the reaction of the Irish hierarchy. Whether because of O'Connell's earlier intimidatory campaign or from native inclination, they fortunately swung round to the most outspoken support of their flocks. At a National Synod held on 23–4 August 1815, the bishops resolved unanimously that they should 'at all times, and under all circumstances, deprecate and oppose, in every canonical and constitutional way, any such interference . . . [It] must essentially injure, and may eventually subvert the Roman Catholic religion in this country.' They added that Murray, who had presented their 'very energetic memorial' at Rome in the preceding year, was far more 'competent to inform his Holiness of the real state and interests of the Roman Catholic Church in Ireland, than any other whom he is said to have consulted'.[44] The episcopal declaration was greeted rapturously at a mass meeting organized by O'Connell five days later, and he carried, with acclamation, a series of still more violent resolutions against any attempt by the papacy to exercise temporal power in Ireland, which '[we] would, if necessary, resist at the peril of our lives'.[45] He followed this up by a 'remonstrance', to be taken hotfoot to Rome by a contumacious friar, Rev. Richard Hayes, O.F.M., protesting 'against the interference of your Holiness, or any other foreign prelate, state, or potentate, in the control of our temporal conduct, or in the arrangement of our political concerns'.[46] Defiance could go no further. In due course the pope curtly replied that he merely followed the Holy See's invariable rule of appointing none to bishoprics whose loyalty was suspect or who were otherwise displeasing to the Powers concerned; and Hayes himself was destined to undergo a very knotty time in Rome, ending in his forcible deportation from the Papal States. But perhaps the worst damage of all, from O'Connell's standpoint, was that both the parliamentary shufflers and the vetoist cliques could now claim, without challenge, the support of the ultimate ecclesiastical authority.

IV

The supreme form of championship was single combat, at the risk of life, on behalf of one's adherents; this also fell to O'Connell's lot in 1815. For the preceding twenty years he had lived in duelling times and circles, and had inevitably come close to an actual engagement on several occasions. He had even invited one in 1800 or 1801 when he had struck his cousin, John Sigerson, with a cane in open court after Sigerson, whose cause he was opposing, had sprung up from his chair to abuse O'Connell. On 13 August 1813 he was on the very brink of fighting. Again the origin of the quarrel was a 'scene' in court. During a case at Limerick assizes O'Connell had shouted 'That's a lie, Maurice' at the opposing counsel – a friend – Magrath. Magrath had responded by hurling a volume of statutes at O'Connell's head and kicking O'Connell's shins, the upshot being a challenge from O'Connell and a meeting next day at Limerick's *place de duel*, the Windmill Fields. The contest was one of prominent Catholic barristers, surrounded by other prominent Catholic barristers, merchants, squireens and attornies, and one of these, N. P. Leader, interposed, just before the firing, with the '*very dextrous proposition*' that O'Connell should declare that 'he was about to fight a man against whom he entertained no enmity'.[47] His friends and second prevailed upon O'Connell to make the declaration, upon which Magrath and he were 'reconciled', without exchanging shots.

Even at the time O'Connell was unhappy at his own conduct. 'I have now, my dear Dan', wrote his second, Nicholas Purcell O'Gorman, a few days later, 'to request you will give yourself no uneasiness on this topic. You were advised by some of the bravest and most skilful men on those subjects in existence'.[48] In Protestant quarters however he was soon spoken of as a poltroon. 'I do not know', Peel told his intimate, J. W. Croker, 'a finer subject for speculation than one which now presents itself; namely: given, a kick upon the posteriors of O'Connell by a brother counsel at Limerick, and an acquiescence in the said kick on the part of O'Connell, to determine the effect which will be produced in the Catholic Board.'[49] Nor was it only his enemies who felt that O'Connell had failed in courage. Even his own brother-in-law, Rick O'Connell, confessed later that 'the unfavourable impression that remained fixed on my mind and which I could not divest myself of, relative to the manner in which your affair with Mr Magrath was patched up by that miserable meddler in Catholic affairs [Leader], gave me the most serious uneasiness'.[50] The episode threw a heavy shadow over O'Connell as a public man. True, his baiting of Saurin and his near-open invitation to the attorney-general to challenge him during the course of the Magee trials of 1814 could be construed as reckless bellicosity. But many construed it otherwise, simply writing Saurin off as the greater coward of the two, and O'Connell's brave words as a safe exercise in bombast.

Between them, the Magrath and Saurin by-plays probably go far to explain the D'Esterre duel of 1 February 1815. On the one hand, it was expected that O'Connell would not fight; on the other, Saurin's humiliation needed to be avenged. Ten days before the duel O'Connell had described the Dublin Corporation – then petitioning against Emancipation – as 'beggarly'. Ironically, it was this (for O'Connell) mildest of abusive epithets which produced the fatal challenge. By a further irony the challenge came from one of the few pro-Emancipationist Dublin Protestants and the only member of the Common Council of Dublin Corporation to have opposed the anti-Catholic petition. John D'Esterre, a provision merchant and naval contractor on the brink of bankruptcy, chose to interpret O'Connell's word as having a personal application. He was also currently a candidate for the lucrative office of city sheriff and may have hoped to ensure his election by stepping forth as the Orange champion against O'Connell.

D'Esterre was certainly no coward, being celebrated for his physical courage. He was both a deadly marksman and the hero of one of the more dramatic incidents of the Nore mutiny of 1797, when, with the noose about his neck and bound hand and foot, he was given a last chance by the mutineers to join them but replied, 'No, never! Hang away and be damned! God save the King.'[51] Thus the probable explanation of his hesitant course of conduct before the duel is not that he was frightened, but that he never expected to have to fight O'Connell, assuming instead that O'Connell would eventually eat humble pie and he himself emerge with all the éclat of the paladin who had exposed the braggart. But O'Connell responded effectively to D'Esterre's first call for an explanation by refusing either to confirm or to repudiate the newspaper account of his words, or to answer any further letter. A second letter from D'Esterre was returned unopened, and a third greeted by a message expressing O'Connell's astonishment that he had not 'heard from' D'Esterre in the usual fashion – if indeed he were really serious in his protestations. By now four days had passed since D'Esterre first wrote; all Dublin was a-buzz with the exchange; and, unfortunately for D'Esterre, he and O'Connell had been transformed into symbols of the Protestant-Catholic conflict, and forced to move about with bodies of supporters. On 31 January 1815, D'Esterre, manouevred by events into the role of Orange bravo, proceeded to the Four Courts with a horse-whip to chastise O'Connell; his accompanying party included Saurin's son, and Alderman Bradley King, formerly lord mayor. As O'Connell described the outcome:

> The ruffian appeared in the Hall [of the Four Courts] for a moment with a whip. The instant I heard it I left the King's Bench and he disappeared. He paraded the quay with his whip. R[ichard] O'Gorman [N. P. O'Gorman's brother] met him, asked him did he want me, for that I told him I would fight him (D'Esterre) in three minutes whenever he chose; that he had but to send me a message and that he should be instantly met. He (D'Esterre) said the message ought to come *from me*, at which O'Gorman laughed. The fellow then took post at Briscoe and Dicksons [drapers] in College Green. I came there with my friend, Major MacNamara, but the delinquent had fled . . .
>
> The crowd accumulated so fast that I took refuge in Exchequer Street, where Judge Day followed me and bound me to keep the peace on *my honour*. Was there ever such a scene?[52]

Despite the 'impeccability' of his behaviour up to now, O'Connell had begun to lose reputation. His old adversary in the Magee trials, Lord Norbury, who was said to 'have shot himself up to the bench', had laid down the rule for the Irish bar that 'the first report of a duel should be that of the pistols';[53] and the D'Esterre affair was quickly degenerating from high drama to low farce. So when next day Sir Edward Stanley, barrack-master at Dublin Castle, called upon O'Connell on D'Esterre's behalf and attempted to settle the matter with 'explanations', O'Connell refused to hear a word and directed him peremptorily to Major MacNamara. In turn, MacNamara, a noted duellist and fire-eating petty country gentleman in the best Lever tradition, also declined to enter into 'explanations', leaving Stanley with nothing to deliver but – at last – the challenge. This was accepted with alarming alacrity, MacNamara insisting on a meeting within three hours.

In fact, D'Esterre was late in arriving at the appointed field, just across the border of co. Kildare and some thirteen miles from the city; and the duel did not take place until 4.40 p.m. By this time the light had begun to fail, despite the white covering of snow upon the ground. When the handkerchief fell, D'Esterre missed but O'Connell's shot hit hip and stomach. It was not realized then that D'Esterre had been fatally wounded. Indeed, Stanley and MacNamara shook hands upon the fact that the duel had ended without loss of life. Stanley had particular reason for his relief. Earlier he had been apprehensive that the expected outcome – O'Connell's death – would endanger D'Esterre and his whole entourage. The long delay had multiplied the number of O'Connell's supporters on the scene, including hundreds of local peasantry. In fact, O'Connell's returning carriage passed a party of dragoons which had been despatched from Dublin to maintain order upon a false report that D'Esterre had killed his man. Whatever the sentiments of the combatants, their respective publics insisted on regarding the contest as a deadly tournament of orange and green.

O'Connell did not regard himself as yet out of difficulty by any means. Fearing Castle vengeance, he went into hiding in Denys Scully's house on the evening of the fight, also warning his wife, 'If any suspicious person should come do not send *here* at all.'[54] He was moreover apprehensive of the ecclesiastical reaction: duelling, condemned as a grave sin by the Council of Trent, was sternly prohibited by the Irish bishops. But O'Connell's concern proved needless on both accounts. Immediately after D'Esterre's death on 3 February, Stanley reassured him: 'Lest your professional avocations should be interrupted by an apprehension of any proceeding being in contemplation in consequence of the late melancholy event, I have the honour to inform you that there is not the most distant intention of any prosecution whatever on the part of the family or friends of the late Mr D'Esterre.'[55] Meanwhile O'Connell's brother, James, who had 'supported' him at the duel, set out to propitiate Archbishop Murray. This passed off with equal ease. Murray is reputed to have greeted James with, 'Heaven be praised! Ireland is safe!'[56] Even if Murray's words were actually less grandiloquent, the report is morally true in stressing both the blind eye which the Church turned towards O'Connell's offence and the fact that Murray, like most other churchmen and the entire laity, looked upon O'Connell as the 'Catholic' and 'national' champion.

This last was of course the popular attitude in Dublin, and the night of the duel, 1 February, was accordingly celebrated with bonfires in the city, though the rejoicing was also said to have been decently muted out of feeling for the fallen D'Esterre. O'Connell's social peers certainly made their approval plain. Scores of cards were left next day at his house in Merrion Square. Perhaps the most pleasing tribute came from Rick O'Connell's unschooled pen:

> I was decidedly aware, whenever it came to the point and when you were fairly committed and left to your own judgment and with such a friend as Mr McNamara, that you would have conducted yourself with that steadiness, carriage and coolness which are the true and leading characteristics of an O'Connell . . . You have laid low the champion of intolerance and the beggarly Corporation of Dublin, to use your own words, who selected the unfortunate D'Esterre as the man, the only man, they could prevail upon of that highly respectable body to put down the troublesome Counsellor O'Connell.[57]

Initially O'Connell felt quite justified. On 6 February he wrote to Major Bryan, 'The affair was forced on . . . I could not have acted otherwise and I am therefore free from self-reproach . . . *Those are*, my dear friend, the consequences of labouring for the country';[58] while he told Mary, 'however to be regretted, [it] will purchase years of safety'.[59] But he was soon overtaken by remorse, as well. Characteristically, this took dramatic, even theatrical, forms. Already half-sunk in debt, he offered to share his income with D'Esterre's widow and orphaned children! He was said thereafter to have raised his hat each time he passed D'Esterre's house on Bachelor's Walk on his way to and from the courts, and to have worn a black glove on his duelling hand whenever he received Communion. But this was simply – or rather complexly – O'Connell's style; he was temperamentally incapable of the plain or unobtrusive. Extravagance was far from insincerity. O'Connell's heart was extraordinarily soft, his disposition extraordinarily sentimental, and his conscience, in the narrowest Catholic sense, increasingly merciless in its judgments upon himself. Meanwhile, his common life went on. Even the sententious pater-familias rapidly regained the shoes of the desperate, fugitive husband. Within a month of D'Esterre's death, he was writing – from co. Kildare! – to Mary, 'Kate's breath this morning smelt most terribly of worms. Darling, see what can be done for her.'[60]

V

As with innumerable other early-nineteenth-century affairs of honour (including D'Esterre's), O'Connell's next duel sprang from ludicrous blunderings and misunderstandings. It would probably never even have reached the stage of challenges had not Peel and O'Connell been designated as champions by their respective factions. On 30 May 1815 Peel had told the House of Commons that O'Connell's Association would not merely present itself as dissatisfied but also pose as an aggrieved party if granted anything less than its full demands. From newspaper accounts of the speech, O'Connell took this to be a charge of dishonesty against himself. He interpreted it thus before a Catholic meeting of 4 July 1815 in Dublin, adding that Peel would not abuse him to his face, 'personal prudence [being] a quality in which he [Peel] was said to be not at all deficient'.[61] This having passed unchallenged, O'Connell took the further step, at another Catholic meeting on 29 August, of accusing Peel of sheltering behind parliamentary privilege in impugning his honour; and he called upon the police reporter to place his remark on record.

Now Peel acted. With the approval and encouragement of the lord lieutenant, he sent his friend, Sir Charles Saxton, a former Irish under-secretary, to tell O'Connell that he was ready to avow publicly whatever he had said in Parliament. Saxton could have brought the matter to a rapid close when he saw O'Connell on 1 September. For so far from regarding the message as an affront, O'Connell proceeded to expiate on Peel's 'handsome and gentlemanlike' conduct until Saxton interrupted with a virtual demand that O'Connell challenge the chief secretary immediately. It is evident that the Castle party thought that O'Connell might be driven into a humiliating retreat. The lord lieutenant described O'Connell's speech as 'an attempt at intimi-dation, but O'Connell mistook his man';[62] William Gregory, Saxton's successor as under-secretary, added that O'Connell, though he killed D'Esterre, 'remains the same man who was kicked by Magrath'.[63] In fact, O'Connell had expected to fight from the moment that Saxton left him. Forced into a corner by Sir Charles, he had nominated a 'Protestant country gentleman', George Lidwill, to serve as his 'friend'. 'Do just as you please', he told his prospective second,

> I only think the county of Kildare ought to be the place. I care not where there. Everything will be ready expeditiously. My family would be less alarmed if we postpone it till morning; but do just as you please.[64]

On meeting Saxton, Lidwill told him that the challenge, if any, should come from Peel, as the aggrieved party. In the interview it also emerged that Peel had in fact not imputed dishonourable behaviour to O'Connell in his speech of 30 May, and Lidwill duly expressed regrets for O'Connell's mistaken reaction.

There is no doubt the entire business should have ended then. At least at second hand, Peel had made it clear that he had not intended to offend and O'Connell had apologised for his error. But Saxton – whether in pique at O'Connell's supposed escape or in the hope of forcing on a contest after all – at once published a sententious 'statement' of the affair. Lidwill claimed that Saxton had misrepresented him as well as O'Connell, and proceeded to challenge Saxton on his own account. For his part, O'Connell replied with an angry public letter accusing Peel of 'a paltry trick' and of 'ultimately [preferring] a paper war'.[65] Now it may have been *he* who calculated that his opponent would not fight; the opening sentence of his note on the evening on which his letter was published seems to indicate some surprise: 'Peel has sent me a *challenge*'.[66] None the less, he set out to find another 'friend' (Saxton and Lidwill being now, in all senses, otherwise engaged), and apparently found the Knight of Kerry acquiescent. But before the Knight could make arrangements with Peel's new second, Colonel Samuel Browne, deputy quartermaster-general at the Castle, O'Connell was immobilized by his wife's intervention.

Mary O'Connell had probably known nothing of the quarrel before Saxton and O'Connell appeared in print. But within a few hours of the publication of O'Connell's letter in the Dublin evening papers of 4 September she acted decisively. After O'Connell had set arrangements for the duel in train and gone to bed – probably about 10 p.m. – she sent covertly for the sheriff to place her husband under arrest. This proved to be a form of house arrest, for next morning he asked the Knight to call on him at his home where he was being confined. Later he received there a humiliating message from Colonel Browne who found 'himself under the painful necessity of reminding Mr O'Connell of the letter which he delivered yesterday from Mr Peel and of the impropriety of any delay in a case of so much delicacy'.[67] Already O'Connell was suffering from the disparity in treatment which was to injure him throughout the business. Peel was given ample forewarning of the sheriff's visit to him, and was able to remove himself at leisure to a comfortable hiding place. While his valour was being extolled by the Castle clique, pasquinades on O'Connell's use of his wife to secure him from combat were beginning to be circulated.

Meanwhile O'Connell was driven into a tangle of subterfuge which was meant to end in a meeting with Peel in Ostend as soon as both men could make their way to Belgium. For Peel the change in plan presented no difficulty. 'It is much better', he told Gregory, 'to go to Ostend than to be, in any event, knocked on the head in the country of Kildare, which "ought" to be the place, in Mr O'Connell's opinion.'[68] For O'Connell, however, even the first stage of the journey involved escorting Mary and the children into Kerry for a supposed family vacation and then doubling back secretly to Waterford (under the pretence of an urgent, unexpected case in Cork) to catch the cross-channel packet.

These tortuous manoeuvres took time and Peel was already in Calais (practising his marksmanship, according to the O'Connellites) before O'Connell even took ship for Wales. Dublin gossip was well abreast, if not ahead, of events. The Castle press openly (and jubilantly) reported the progress of Peel and Saxton and their respective seconds across England on their way to France. Far otherwise with O'Connell. It took him a week to reach Waterford by way of Killarney, where he at last succeeded in breaking away from the unsuspecting Mary, and to arrange that his new second, R. N. Bennett, meet him at the embarkation point. O'Connell elaborated his plan to join Bennett with even more than characteristic deviousness, by means of 'my letter to [Eneas] MacDonnell [which] . . . contained a letter for Sugrue . . . Bennett's letter was enclosed in Sugrue's'![69] The cloak-and-daggerism probably derived from O'Connell's fear that Mary would learn of the Ostend arrangement. It was both extraordinary and most fortunate for his reputation that she failed to do so. As Lidwill pointed out after it was all over,

> It was very lucky she never suspected anything as, besides her uneasiness, she might have attempted to have you bound over which, coming from any of *your* friends, would destroy [you] for ever and encourage the enemy to do that which he otherwise would not, to send you a message.[70]

Apparently, O'Connell did not expect to be apprehended as he journeyed from Milford Haven to Dover, although he was surprised when, on disembarking at Milford on 14 September 1815, '*our names* were carefully inquired into ... What was this done for? No matter.'[71] In fact the British government had determined that he and Lidwill should be stopped. Constables and Bow Street runners were stationed at Dover and Ramsgate and some even sent ahead to Calais. As things fell out, these particular precautions proved unnecessary. Both men were arrested in London, O'Connell as he was boarding a chaise for Dover on 18 September. There is little doubt that the arrests were arranged by the Home Office; and Conant, the chief magistrate at Bow Street, made it clear that the government meant business by warning O'Connell that, if he killed Peel in a duel, he would be rigorously prosecuted *in England* and assuredly executed, if convicted. '*They* have got their wicked will of us', O'Connell wrote bitterly to Scully. 'Our hands are tied behind our backs and they have full liberty to abuse us. What a glorious opportunity have they not deprived me of – living or dying – but regret is vain and would console our enemies.'[72]

He had counted on victory over Peel. 'It is perhaps absurd', he had written on his way through Cheltenham, 'but I cannot bring myself even to doubt success.' His own fate apart, however, 'the real value to poor Ireland is the contest itself. There never was such a battle. Waterloo was nothing to it.'[73] In Irish imaginations it truly had assumed the proportions of a meeting of Bonaparte and Wellington without their armies. As the O'Connellite *Dublin Chronicle*, for example, put it,

> Who does not see that the entire quarrel is that of public men? English placemen on one side, the favourites of Ireland on the other, patrons of Orangemen against the advocates of religious freedom, the hirelings of an iron rule seeking the lives of the champions of Ireland, and indeed for the second time the life of Mr O'Connell ... Mr Peel, Colonel Brown, Sir Charles Saxton and a Mr Dickenson ... all Englishmen, all placemen, all feeding upon Irish salaries, lodged in Irish mansions ... are the four champions of the Castle.
>
> Can it be believed for a moment that a mere personal difference, a private quarrel, can have arisen between such persons and Mr Lidwill, Mr O'Connell, and their friends? The one class belonging to the relentless foes of Ireland, the other to her ardent and resolute protectors. What can have brought into conflict such men but the cause of Ireland alone?[74]

Peel was also, to some extent, the tool or instrument of his party. He was no friend to duelling. When he had wished to laud the late prime minister, Perceval, to the skies, he had said of him that no consideration would have induced him to fight. Some of the English advice which Peel received was very different from the Castle's urging. Two of his evangelical friends condemned his challenge as an outright sin, one adding that to fight was 'arrant cowardice to man, contempt of God and hardy defiance which can receive no mercy.'[75] Peel's brother-in-law, William Cockburn, argued that O'Connell had been within his rights up to the point where he had spoken of 'a paltry trick' and of Peel's preferring 'a paper war'. But, he went on, such 'immaterial trumpery expressions ... used too in the heat of the moment' were not worth fighting over, and 'the slightest apology, the most simple explanation' by O'Connell should be seized upon to bring the deplorable business to a close.[76] But by then Peel, as much as O'Connell, was locked into Irish paladinhood. It was, however, much easier to play the role of government paladin than that of people. Notwithstanding the Home Office's preventive measures, 'our adversaries', as O'Connell complained, 'advertised themselves at every stage, and were allowed to go on unimpeded. This is called "*activity*".'[77] O'Connell was made to cut a rather hangdog figure in London, while Peel was proving his 'manhood' costlessly in Calais. In the battle of public images, which the affair largely represented, official manoeuvres ensured that Peel would take the palm.

After O'Connell's being bound over, the projected duel had to be abandoned once and for all, and the protagonists wound their way gradually back to Ireland. On reaching Dublin, O'Connell wrote to Mary in Killarney,

My darling Heart,
...I left London on Monday [25 September 1815] and posted to Shrewsbury, and travelled thence in the day-coach to Holyhead. We reached the Head on Thursday at one o'clock, and sailed at three. The night came to blow tremendously and the packet was crowded to excess. Not a berth could be had for love or money. I lay on the cabin floor as sick as a dog, with three gentlemen's legs on my breast and stomach, and the sea water dripping in on my knees and feet. I was never so completely punished ...[78]

O'Connell's penitence, real or assumed, is curious. His wife's stance, to be inferred from her actions and his concealments alike, seems to present no difficulties for the interpreter. She loved O'Connell deeply; the eldest of her six children was barely twelve years old; the family lived extravagantly and was at that stage head over heels in debt;

financial and social ruin was certain if O'Connell died. By no means least, she knew that duelling was a mortal sin and one for which, practically by definition, there was no opportunity for repentance if one fell to the opponent's shot. Why should Mary stop at anything to prevent her husband hazarding his life and soul within nine months of the last blessed escape? Perhaps a real gentlewoman would have feigned ignorance or at least refrained from public intervention in a men's matter of such apparent importance. But Mary had not been bred a real gentlewoman. She was merely clear-headed and afraid.

But O'Connell neither would nor could elude the gentlemanly code. Reduced to the individual level, his political *raison d'être* was to establish his absolute equality with Protestants of the same 'class'. Nothing would have been more wounding socially than rejection as too 'low' to be challenged or to have one's challenge taken seriously. The Cato Street conspirator, Thistlewood, turned to assassination only after the home secretary, Lord Sidmouth, refused to fight him 'honourably', thereby placing him in the blackguardly classes. The clear corollary of admission to the circle of gentility was obedience to the laws of honour. Correspondingly, O'Connell's leadership of the Catholic movement demanded that he prove his courage and defiance in the most elemental fashion, by personal combat on behalf of the cause which he was held to epitomize. So far, all is self-evident. But gentlemen were also meant to keep all knowledge of affairs of honour from their womenfolk, or at the very least to see to it that the women maintained a decent show of ignorance. That women should seek to control them was beyond all bounds. Mary had broken the sacred code and exposed O'Connell to ridicule and shame.

Yet it was O'Connell who excused himself to Mary, not she to him. How is this to be explained? Partly, perhaps, by O'Connell's own moral unease. His attempts to make atonement to D'Esterre's family suggest that, while he could exonerate himself completely when his conscience held open court, he could never argue away the fact that he had killed; the black glove worn on his fatal hand was a symbol of guilt, even if 'guiltless' guilt. Secondly, although there is no evidence that such was the case, it would have been quite in character for O'Connell to have promised Mary to eschew duelling forever, in the excited aftermath of the D'Esterre affair. No one was more accessible to remorse or softened feeling, nor was there ever a readier promiser than he. Last but far from least, Mary was used to moral domination in their mutual relationship. She was the perpetual forgiver; it was she who took up and held the strong positions. This is not to say that she would have thought, for a moment, in such adversary terms, still less that she was ruler of the marriage. Indeed the very language of conflict and mastery is most malapropos in so interpenetrant a union. None the less fifteen years as the virtual pronouncer of judgment on such ethical questions as arose between them had rendered her confident in decision. Conversely, O'Connell was habituated to surface acquiescence and covert circumvention. When, emboldened by fright and love, she did not hesitate to place the saving of his life above the saving of his 'honour', it was much more likely that he would follow his accustomed course and deceive her rather than round upon her. This was their particular way. Perhaps Tolstoy was wrong in proclaiming that happy families are all the same. Instead, they seem to rest upon a myriad of almost imperceptible accommodations. In this case, even the public world of championship seems to have failed when it clashed with the private world of intimate marital balance.

CHAPTER 7

Entr'acte

1816

I

During 1816, O'Connell reached the age of forty, a sort of meridian of life. Let us attempt to cast a balance sheet-cum-profit and loss account for him in this particular year.

How did he stand in politics? Since 1813 he had decidedly lost ground. First, the general climate of affairs had worsened. From the late autumn of 1813, the defeat of France seemed certain, and accordingly the British need to conciliate Irish Catholics diminished, if not disappeared. The Hundred Days of 1815 was too short and hectic a span to produce even a temporary change in this disposition. Its conclusion, at Waterloo, confirmed the government in its new-found disinclination to concede; Protestant toryism was firmly in the saddle once again. Moreover, peace precipitated an agricultural depression. As Robert Owen put it, on the day the war ended the great customer of all the producers simply went off the market. The consequent distress emasculated the politics of rights and principle in Ireland. On the one hand, support for the abstract justice of Emancipation fell off, even in the towns; not one Catholic in ten thousand would either earn or eat more if it were granted in the morning. On the other, constitutional agitation withered in the face of fresh outbursts of agrarian violence.

Rome had also played a part recently in dimming the prospects of full Emancipation. O'Connell's remarkable achievement in mobilizing both popular and episcopal resistance to – and even virtual defiance of – the Papal rescript of February 1815 had been partially offset within a year. As we have seen, Pius VII dismissed the Irish remonstrance against the modified form of veto which he had sanctioned, pointing out that it conformed to common practice in the Church's treatment of Protestant powers; the Hayes mission itself was treated contemptuously. It was all too evident moreover that the Papacy was set on conciliating Britain to the utmost possible extent during the phase of post-war settlements and restoration. The pope's final and formal rejection of the remonstrance on 1 February 1816 consolidated the vetoist party in Ireland and deepened the gulf between them and the O'Connellites. Antagonistic petitions were presented to Parliament by the two factions later in the spring. At a meeting at Lord Trimleston's house on 13 February the vetoists resolved to accept 'qualified' Emancipation, and Grattan assured the House of Commons that they would cheerfully agree to 'securities'. O'Connell's Association, which still demanded full Emancipation, used Sir Henry Parnell as spokesman. Parnell was no firebrand; he advised O'Connell to reason rather than demand in his petition: 'The former course would obtain converts but the latter never will, though it will certainly give new life to your enemies.'[1] O'Connell had the dark satisfaction of seeing his rivals' hopes – he could scarcely have held any for the success of his own petition – dashed when on 15 May 1816 the Commons by a majority of 31 refused even to consider the Catholic question. So much for Roman and genteel Irish conciliation!

The growing sense of futility in Irish Catholic ranks increased rather than diminished internal conflict. Not only in Dublin but also in Cork and other cities, the vetoists and O'Connellites challenged each other openly. In even so small a place as Skibbereen, rows broke out in the Catholic chapel on 17 and 22 March as signatures were sought for the rival parliamentary petitions, with the parish priest denouncing the vetoists violently and being violently denounced in turn. 'What a shocking scene has taken place in Skibbereen Chapel', wrote Mary O'Connell on 2 April. 'I think Mr Sandy Tim [Alexander O'Driscoll, a leading Cork vetoist] has no great cause to be proud of himself. I could forgive him anything but attacking the clergyman in the house of God. I fear the Veto will do more mischief.'[2] Almost alone among the liberal Catholic leaders, O'Connell struggled on to restrict the mischief. During the spring circuit, he secured strongly anti-vetoist resolutions from aggregate meetings at Limerick and Cork, and he maintained some semblance of a central organization from his own pocket. But his enemies discounted what they called meaningless huzzas at popular assemblies, and the decline of his Association in the capital was signalled by its removal from Capel St to a still cheaper and meaner room in Crow St.

Characteristically, O'Connell found another tack to follow before the year was out. The spread throughout England during 1816 of Hampden Clubs dedicated to the extreme of parliamentary reform set O'Connell upon his first venture in making common cause with British radicals. His adoption of Hampdenism was understandable. The unreformed House of Commons had proved a persistent stumbling block to even partial Emancipation, and O'Connell had never wavered from his faith in full and free political representation. But the agitation for parliamentary reform in 1816, especially in this 'root and branch' version, carried overtones of religious scepticism, moral licence and social instability. It was besides an essentially British movement. For these reasons there was considerable danger that it would repel not merely 'respectable' Irish Catholicism (generally vetoist in sympathy at this particular juncture) but also clerical and popular Irish Catholicism into the bargain. None the less O'Connell took the first step safely at an aggregate meeting held in Cork on 6 September 1816 at the end of the summer assizes. There he secured a resolution attributing the succession of Catholic failures to the corruption and inequity of the parliamentary system, and urging 'our fellow subjects of every religious persuasion, to leave no constitutional means untried in order to procure a full, free, and frequent election of Real Representatives of the people of these Nations in the Commons' House [of] Parliament'.[3] When, however, the equivalent aggregate meeting took place in Dublin three months later, the parliamentary reform issue proved so divisive that O'Connell refrained from moving his intended resolution in its favour. By this stage his efforts had attracted the attention and approval of such well-known radicals as Major Cartwright and John Hancock, and he persisted for a month or two with moves to stir up an Irish reform agitation. But the Catholic public was unresponsive; the movement – if it deserved such a name – petered out early in 1817.

O'Connell's political fortunes between 1811 and 1815 had generally conformed to a pattern of remarkable advances followed by considerable losses of ground. He had attained the leadership of a heterogeneous Catholic agitation and rendered it a comparatively well-organized and effective pressure group, which also embraced many lower-middle and upper-working-class Catholics in the larger towns. Yet by 1816 he stood at the head of only one wing of an ailing movement, and his 'organization' was both penniless (or, more exactly, heavily indebted because it had been saddled with the unpaid costs of earlier Catholic petitions) and practically dependent for survival on his exertions as an individual.

O'Connell had also built up a vigorous, metropolitan pro-Catholic press to support the Catholic Committee. But this too had been punished and bullied almost out of existence by the successful prosecutions of Cox, Fitzpatrick and Magee in 1813–14. In 1816 the Irish Government stamped just as hard upon a smouldering ember when it arraigned the *Cork Mercantile Chronicle* for reporting a speech of O'Connell of the previous year in which he had criticized the administration of justice in Ireland. In the libel action heard on 18 May 1816, Saurin accused O'Connell of inciting rebellion, while O'Connell denounced him as an incompetent. It was a pale shadow of the Magee affair, but O'Connell suffered defeat once more; the unfortunate printer was fined £300 and sentenced to two years' imprisonment. O'Connell's plea for clemency because his client was both old and poor was cursorily dismissed. The case diminished further the éclat which he had won by his original excoriation of the attorney-general and the entire Irish legal apparatus on 27 July 1813. Not only was another sympathetic newspaper silenced but also Saurin had ridden through O'Connell's abuse once more to carry off the verdict. Even O'Connell's triumph in the D'Esterre duel had been offset by the dismal – and, worse, in parts comic – failure of his attempt to meet Peel later in the year. The effects of this débâcle lasted into 1816: it was widely expected that he and Peel would face each other when the original alarms had died away, and his reputation was certainly not enhanced as the months passed by eventlessly.

Peel's arrival in Ireland as chief secretary had proved the turning point in O'Connell's early political career. Peel had given direction and determination to the Castle's counter-attack during the later war years. It is true that Bonaparte's decline and, ultimately, defeat had provided the new chief secretary with favourable conditions, and also that he had gained from the British government's skilful exploitation of the Papacy's vulnerability in a phase of European reconstruction. But, having chosen Saurin for his leading acolyte, he had seized his chances to divide the Irish Catholic body deeply; to destroy the major Catholic organization, without even needing, in the end, a new form of the Convention Act; and to weaken O'Connell's standing as the Catholic hero.

Yet O'Connell's original achievements could not be altogether effaced. He had demonstrated more clearly than any predecessor the power of Catholic combination and discovered already some of the potentialities of a Catholic mass movement. On the crucial veto issue, he had won over to his side almost the entire Irish episcopate; this support he never really lost, despite some temporary shuffling later on. His defiance and abasement of the Irish Administration even for one glorious day had destroyed the assumption that it was, and must always be, effortlessly superior; he had forced it onto level ground and into dirty war in order to circumvent himself.

For the contest between O'Connell and the Castle was no fair fight. The Government could, in large measure, extend the offence of 'libel' as it wished, and count upon its packed juries for favourable verdicts and its subservient judges for favourable rulings and court management. It could afford to run its own press and force opposition newspapers out of business – at any rate, out of the business of criticizing its members or activities. It could even use its executive powers to enable its chief secretary to cut a fine public figure, and ensure that O'Connell would cut a sorry one. But the inequity of such a use of official force could be neither entirely concealed nor sustained forever. '*Ní h-é lá na gaoithe lá na scolb*' – the windy day is not the thatcher's day, runs a Gaelic proverb. It all depended on whether O'Connell would remain in the thatching business until the adverse gale abated. He did: herein lies the significance of his lonely persistence, against all the odds, throughout 1816 and the following hopeless years.

II

O'Connell may well have had more at stake in the Catholic question, materially speaking, than any other person in the United Kingdom. By 1816 he stood head and shoulders above any other junior at the Irish Bar. Had his religion not barred the way, he would have taken silk long before that year. Although many before and since have found that they lost instead of gaining money by being called to the inner bar, O'Connell, with transcendant abilities and national fame, was surely justified in his conviction that he would both augment his income and halve his work were he a King's Counsel. As it was, his professional life was more or less a treadmill. Nearly a quarter of a century later, even the bitterly inimical *Dublin University Magazine* admitted the reasonableness of his grievance:

> If O'Connell appears regardless of truth and justice in his persecutions of the Protestants, let them recollect what must have been the feelings naturally excited in his soul by the laws to which he was subjected in the earlier part of his life. With talents which he must have felt sufficient to raise him to eminence in his profession, or to enable him to act an important part in the grand theatre of politics, he found himself precluded by our Protestant institutions from all hope of attaining the rank and honours which are the legitimate rewards of success in his profession, and

condemned to pass his life in the drudgery of a stuff-gown lawyer . . . Even those who may be disposed to defend those restrictions as necessary for the protection of our Protestant institutions, will at least admit that they were not calculated to excite any kind of feeling towards those institutions in the breasts of those who suffered from them.[4]

During the spring circuit of 1816 even the indomitable O'Connell owned to arriving at his first stage, Nenagh, very weary as well as very late, only to be lodged 'there in a wretched cold room'. A few days later he 'left it [Limerick] at five in the [Monday] morning and did not get here [Tralee] till near nine [p.m.], very much fatigued, having *worked* at my trade till past twelve on Sunday night, and of course . . . slept very little'.[5] At Cork 'Judge Mayne sat so early and Judge Day so late that there was not a moment left for me to breathe in'.[6] During the summer assizes of 1816 he spent over ten hours daily (from before 9 a.m. till after 7 p.m.) in court at Cork, and the spring assizes, with both judges 'miserably slow',[7] would have been quite as bad. Yet with the spring circuit of 1816 coinciding with Lent, which he observed most strictly, he was without food during all his time in court, sometimes until as late as ten o'clock at night. Even Mary urged him to relax his extraordinary mortification while he was on circuit: 'Wednesday, Friday and Saturday would be quite sufficient for you to fast from breakfast.'[8] But he ignored her counsel. O'Connell never complained of hardships – a most endearing, as well as very rare quality in a husband. Fasting, he told Mary repeatedly, 'agrees perfectly with me in every respect'. 'Sweetest love', he wrote from Limerick, 'I am as well, notwithstanding my fasting, as any man in Ireland.'[9] After his long journey to his 'wretched cold room' in Nenagh, 'instead of finding myself the worse for it I am considerably better, indeed quite rid of the cold in my head of which every symptom has vanished'.[10] But for all this brave front, it was beyond human nature that he should not often have felt his stuff gown to cling to him like a hair shirt, if not indeed a very shirt of Nessus.

O'Connell earned considerably more on circuit than any other counsel, including his seniors, at the Munster Bar. 'My business', as he assured Mary on 13 March 1816, 'is far beyond that of any other barrister. I am quite and without any rival at the head of this circuit. I am not drawing upon my vanity in telling you so. I am saying just what is the simple truth.'[11] He was briefed in every 'record' (civil action) in Ennis, and in all but one in both the city and county suits at Limerick. It took him more than a fortnight to work off his briefs in Cork, and after that he had to turn to his '*chamber business*' there, and return to

Limerick for more. None the less it was a lean circuit. From Limerick O'Connell had already reported it as 'bad' for business; from Tralee he wrote, 'Only *two* records . . . so that for the first time since I was called to the Bar I have had [? but one] record brief.'[12] Litigation was as depressed as any other gainful activity in Ireland in 1816. As Mary observed, 'In truth I believe the people had not money *even* for law';[13] O'Connell himself bemoaned the change in the times on 18 March. Desperate for money in 1816, he engaged himself heavily in the less remunerative criminal work. Perhaps his 'chamber business' in Cork and Limerick is another indication of his straits, although it was probably true, as his wife argued, that he would have earned as much at his desk in Dublin as at Cork. One way or another it was grinding labour for small rewards that year.

Much of it was also distasteful. Many of the criminal briefs were for capital offences, usually the product of agrarian violence. O'Connell's feelings about such cases may be gauged from his note to his daughter, Ellen, from Tralee on 1 April, 'I am . . . a little out of spirits as this was a very bloody assizes . . . seven men capitally convicted and I really believe they will all be executed.'[14] Conversely, when he defended successfully in Cork in August, he exulted, 'I am, dearest, in the gayest spirits. I will suffocate my Nell for her darling letter. I am just out of court after a *great* acquittal and as soon as I dine I will go to the play.'[15] Verdicts for the crown in these cases cast him into gloom; even pending 'capital' briefs rendered him apprehensive. For counsel were not distanced from the ultimate consequences of adverse verdicts in the Ireland of 1816. The convicted were often hanged within a day or two, and generally before the legal train had moved on to the next assizes. The drudgery of the stuff gown was not the worst experience of a circuit.

Bitterest of all perhaps was O'Connell's sense that he was systematically belittled. He was good-humouredly contemptuous of the circuit judges. 'We have hourly the most ludicrous scenes with Judge Mayne', he told Mary on 13 March. 'He is *an animal*, easily managed, and he and I agree perfectly and I have the pleasure of laughing at him by the hour.'[16] It seems true that he and Mayne dealt well together. Later in the year Mayne took much trouble to facilitate an effort by O'Connell to win a reprieve for a client condemned to almost immediate execution. But O'Connell believed himself to be incomparably superior as a lawyer not merely to Mayne but also to the great majority of the judiciary. He also felt himself to be at least the equal of the leading Irish silks. He dismissed the great Curran, who was to have led him in a major defamation action, *Bruce* v. *Grady*, heard at Limerick on 7–9 August 1816, as 'a wavering inconsistent fellow!';[17] and he adjudged the statement of the case in this action by the almost equally renowned silk, Goold, as 'an excellent speech . . . but very tedious'. As a junior in this case his role was limited to the opening address for the defence; but he had no doubt that his was the triumph of the affair: 'It was *my* best speech I think and the entire Bar think so too.'[18]

Thus the toil was doubly irksome. When every possible penny had to be grasped, juniors' work included much dull routine and many mechanical legal operations. Yet O'Connell had to bear a senior's responsibility in significant political cases (such as those arising from the Skibbereen Catholic fracas or the *Cork Mercantile Chronicle* 'libel') and celebrated civil suits (such as *Bruce* v. *Grady*) without a senior's rewards or a senior's increase in profitable reputation. Miltonic allusions may ill-fit an overworked, stout, middle-aged barrister. But just as O'Connell, in his political nadir of 1816, suggests *maligré lui* Lucifer's

> *What though the field be lost?*
> *All is not lost; th' unconquerable will . . .*
> *And courage never to submit or yield:*
> *And what is else not to be overcome?*,

so, too, his diurnal course on circuit may suggest even Samson's

> *Eyeless in Gaza, at the mill with slaves.*

III

The prime cause of O'Connell's money-hunt of 1816 was the O'Leary bankruptcy, gazetted at last on 13 February. The most important thing of all was to keep knowledge of O'Connell's involvement in the crash from Hunting Cap. O'Connell's brother James reassured him on 4 January: 'I think it is now almost impossible he can hear it.'[19] One of his Kerry cousins, Myles McSwiney, reported on 16 February after a meeting with Hunting Cap that he had no suspicion of O'Connell's entanglement. Next day James wrote more fully from Derrynane:

He repeatedly asked me if you were engaged for him for any sum. I assured him you were not. Indeed, he was at first so earnest and particular in his inquiries that I feared some person had made him acquainted with the facts, but on my *solemnly* assuring him you would not lose a guinea by the fellow as you never became security for him to any amount, he seemed quite satisfied and says that you possibly may loan something to this blackguard but that he himself told you last year O'Leary would unquestionably snap from the expensive manner in which he lived. I, of course, allow him to take what merit he pleases for his friendly caution.

You have a right to feel much obliged to Ellen [his sister] for her exertions in preventing my uncle from hearing this unfortunate business. She had two confidential men stationed, one at the upper gate and the other at the strand, to caution every person who was coming to Derrynane not to mention this business. This, I assure you, was a very necessary caution as every individual in this country knows every circumstance connected with O'Leary's failure. I now hope we have little to fear but we must still keep a sharp look out.[20]

James had lied to Hunting Cap already. To explain the delay in his visit to Derrynane – caused in fact by the O'Leary business – he had invented a bout of illness. He was well aware of the danger he was running for his brother's sake: 'should this affair come to the knowledge of my Uncle Maurice I am convinced he will never give me a guinea.'[21]

The most immediate problem however was to raise enough money to cover O'Connell's new liabilities. James having failed to negotiate a loan of £4000 from their uncle Daniel, O'Connell was driven to borrow most of that sum from his banker-agent, John Hickson, at the beginning of the year. While acknowledging that O'Connell was entirely at Hickson's mercy, James deplored both Hickson's 'very *unfair and usurious* terms' and O'Connell's 'too sanguine disposition [which] makes you calculate on some ideal *good* that may never occur'.[22] James determined that somehow or other a less exacting creditor must be substituted for Hickson before 1816 was out. Meanwhile, much more money was required, and on 16 January O'Connell went to Cork to 'work [?for] funds enough to keep myself above water'.[23] Funds enough to keep O'Connell above water would have been funds indeed! But at least he secured another very considerable sum, although at the expense of James who had to join him as guarantor. Poor James was painfully aware that he had put his small patrimony in hazard. 'You will have this *precious deed* [signed by himself] by Thursday morning', he informed O'Connell savagely on 22 January 1816,

and I sincerely hope it will be the means of saving you from *destruction*, whatever my fate may be, but now *that the die is cast* I can with truth say that I am, by being made a party to this business, exquisitely miserable as I am no longer master of my own time or of the very limited property I inherited in right of my father . . . I was well aware when I affixed my name to this accursed deed that in all human probability my prospects in life were for ever blasted. I again repeat, whatever my sufferings may be, I will never be guilty of the folly of blaming any person as, alas, alas, I am too well aware of the consequences . . . I now conclude this, to me, most disagreeable subject by saying you have involved me in the ruin you have been so long preparing for your amiable wife and interesting family.[24]

But these were only two, though probably the largest, of the fresh obligations which O'Connell incurred or sought. Within a fortnight of receiving James's guarantee, he employed his friend Bennett to arrange a further loan of £2000. The terms were onerous; in addition to interest, '£2,200 [was] payable within two months after my uncle's death or in four years, whichever shall first happen.'[25] Even that leading signal of nineteenth-century ruin, the *post-obit*, had made its appearance. Still the pressure continued, and even Mary took a hand. 'I called to see Mrs O'Sullivan', she wrote on 26 March,

and, in the course of our conversation, she told me her niece, Mary Coppinger, had at present a £1,000 to put at interst. *It* immediately occurred to me that you may wish to get it, and Mrs O'S joined me in opinion that Mrs Coppinger would give it. What would you think of writing to her on the subject without mentioning her aunt's name but, except you want the money very much, darling, I should prefer your not taking it. Interest money to you must be so heavy just now.[26]

Income was problem enough without interest and capital repayments. James, who was then acting as O'Connell's principal agent for his Kerry lands, bemoaned on 17 February 1816 the 'wretched state of this country with respect to money'; he would not be able to collect enough for O'Connell to pay even the head rents falling due. 'What is to become of us if the times do not improve! I have had recourse to the harshest methods to try and extort some payments from your tenants for the last week, all the pounds of the country filled with their cows but all to no purpose.'[27] On 31 May Myles McSwiney, who also acted for O'Connell and would soon take over the major role, told him that he could get in no rents; he could not even pay an old woman's jointure which O'Connell owed locally. O'Connell himself had the same story to tell when he visited Iveragh in September. 'The rents are coming very slowly', he wrote to Mary, 'and between the fall of prices and the dreadful weather there is nothing but rain and wretchedness.'[28]

All this threw a greater burden on O'Connell's bar earnings. But despite his utmost exertions these remained depressed. The summer circuit appears to have been still worse than the spring. That

O'Connell failed to report to Mary his takings in some of the assize towns, a rare occurrence, probably told its own story. 'I hope, heart', she wrote to him from Dublin on 21 August, 'you will be more fortunate in Cork than you have been in Tralee. You did not tell me what you made at Ennis and Limerick. I don't suppose (excepting your first assizes in Tralee) you ever got so trifling a sum as you did this time [thirty-four guineas] but if the business was there you would get it.'[29] Mary had good reason to be anxious. At different stages during the circuits she had to press O'Connell for money to pay the governess's, the nurse's and the housekeeper's wages; in the last case, ten days elapsed before she received the long-overdue ten guineas. On one occasion Mary and Hickson were in dispute over £30: each had received one half of every banknote. 'From your letter', Mary wrote on 8 April, 'he understood the money was for him, but surely, darling, you very plainly told me to send to Hickson for the remaining halves of *these* you sent me.'[30] Evidently Hickson won the tussle of the half-notes, for five days later came a cry from Mary, 'No letter from you this day, which is indeed a very great disappointment as I have not one farthing of money and Saturday with me is always *pay* day.'[31]

The last resort in these straits was personal and family economy. O'Connell was profuse in resolutions and even in self-congratulations. In his first spring circuit letter from Ennis he assured his wife, 'Darling, I am become one of the most attentive fellows living, taking most excellent care of my money',[32] and following this up from Limerick with, 'Darling, I am become really an economist.'[33] Mary reciprocated with equal professions of virtue, 'I have kept a regular account of every shilling I received and of every penny I laid out since you left home with the strictest economy . . . not a penny was laid out that could in any way be avoided.'[34] But the O'Connells were not the stuff of which financial martyrs are made. Mary's 'strictest economy' ran at over £16 per week (more than twenty times a contemporary labourer's wage) on ordinary household expenses; simultaneously, she reported to O'Connell that she could get only two dozen bottles of white wine and half-a-dozen bottles of port from his usual supplier and asked where she should purchase a further dozen and a half of port 'as it will be necessary, love [?to have] it in before your return'.[35]

Characteristic was her approach to buying a new piano. 'I would rather, darling,' she told O'Connell on 4 April, 'you would at once say to me buy or don't buy it, for I feel delicate in putting you to any expense at present, though, as I before told you, I think we ought to trespass a little for the advantage of our children.'[36] The sly wife could not have doubted for a moment that such a husband as O'Connell would respond by '*commanding*' an immediate purchase.[37] In the event he was lucky in that Mary failed to find a desirable instrument on her first foray. For his part, he pressed her irresistibly to accept a staying guest in order to oblige a useful friend, and James wrote apropos his autumn vacation of 1816 'your *own personal expenses*, which I know from what occurred when last you were in Iveragh, are to a man circumstanced as you are, ruinously heavy'.[38] It was a true marriage of untrue minds, blossoming from moral sleight of hand. O'Connell never ceased to thank her for the generosity with which she forgave his former folly, and Mary never ceased to shift the blame from his to other shoulders, in particular the iniquitous O'Leary's. 'My dearest Love', she wrote to him on 9 August,

> Dumas [a Kerry attorney] told me there was not a greater buck in Bond Street than Mr James O'Leary, dashing away at his usual rate and most elegantly dressed, at the opera and theatres every night, and living at one of the most expensive taverns in London. This is the way, darling, he is spending your eight thousand pounds. My God, what a horrid perjured fellow he is. Surely, heart, you will never think of signing his certificate. Believe me, you owe to your own character not to do so and I ask you as a favour not to sign it.[39]

Antiphonally, O'Connell replied, 'I promise you, darling, not to sign O'Leary's certificate. I only despise myself heartily for allowing so contemptible a scoundrel to impose on me.'[40]

None the less reality could not be altogether kept at bay. When the piano campaign re-opened in August, O'Connell was compelled to respond – and there could have been no greater measure of his financial desperation – 'Tell my sweet Nell that she shall have the piano as speedily as I can possibly get it for her but, love, the fact is that I have still near £1,700 of guarantees or bills of that scoundrel O'Leary outstanding and I want every shilling which I can put together to avoid being obliged to have my bills protested, and myself sued.' Although the pill was sweetened with, 'Nobody can be more prudent that you are, *that* is quite certain',[41] the fact remained that O'Connell was forced to confess to Mary (probably for the first time in their married life) that he could not afford a family good. Early in 1817 James thrust upon O'Connell a list of debts, as known by him at the end of 1816, with the comment, 'My dearest fellow, what do you mean by saying that in two years the far greater part of your debts will be discharged? Surely, when you speak in this way, you are not aware of the magnitude of them.' James's list, a compilation pitiful in the host of small sums owed to relatives, clients and friends, and including £130 'due of you to Maurice, my uncle's clerk' and £3000 'Due of you in Iveragh to common men in *all at least*', totalled nearly £19,000,[42] and James recognized that there were probably many other debts and outstanding obligations of which he had been told nothing. It is all too easy to cast O'Connell as the glorious skimming bird and James as the croaking raven. But, if only thoughtlessly, O'Connell was a heartless man with others' money. What did he care about the security of 'Widow Connor of Killarney', or of his uncle's clerk, or of the common men of Iveragh who had been flattered into doing a favour for the local Sun King? When James told him, after signing the fatal deed on 22 January 1816, 'by the contents of your letters you seem to think I have the egregious folly to suppose I am doing a mere act of courtesy',[43] his scorn for O'Connell's vacuous and convenient optimism was all too well deserved. But it was long since such barbs had penetrated the time-toughened hide.

O'Connell and his wife were never more loving towards or deeply in accord with one another than in 1816. Evidently the crises of the autumn and winter of 1815, the Peel duel and the O'Leary failure, ending in penitence and resolutions of amendment on O'Connell's part, and the exercise of the sweet power of absolution on Mary's, had brought them closer. O'Connell's first letter in 1816 lauded her as 'the greatest blessing that ever man had';[44] at the close of the summer circuit, he wrote, 'darling, I owe you my deepest debt of gratitude for the manner in which you have borne the privations which my absurd credulity has compelled you to endure.'[45] Mary reciprocated with still more warmth and expressions of trust than usual; implicitly and explicitly she told him that he was – in her eyes – faultless for all his faults. She had become pregnant again in the preceding November; she was also probably responding to O'Connell's new religious fervour which may well have dated from about the same time.

The effect of this last change was apparent from the beginning of 1816. On 13 January O'Connell wrote to Mary from Tralee, 'Tell [Rev.] Mr L'Estrange [he had become O'Connell's spiritual director], darling, that I long to be back with him. I promise you, love, I feel myself beyond any comparison happier in *this* change which, with the grace of God, I hope will prove complete. Pray for me, darling, fervently and often.'[46] The note of extraordinary piety was un-precedented, the implication that of a Methodist-like conversion. In fact that very word was used by either O'Connell's wife or his eldest son to describe the spiritual transformation. Maurice, wrote Mary on

11 April 1816, 'had many questions to ask about you, thanked God with his hands clasped for your *conversion*'.[47] Since O'Connell had returned to Catholic belief and practice by 1809, and possibly even for some years before then, the reference is probably to the replacement of conventional by 'vital' religion: the evangelical sea-change of the soul was by no means confined to Evangelicals in 1815. L'Estrange was almost certainly the instrument, but the trigger may well have been O'Connell's latest and greatest financial trouble and the consequent confession to Mary of his broken promises. 'We will be ourselves a great deal the better for it',[48] he told her on 13 January apropos O'Leary's bankruptcy; from Limerick he wrote two months later, 'We shall be, I hope we are, the happiest and the better for *this* event. As to the happier, that alone relates to you for better, sweetheart, you could not be';[49] and there are other comments apparently connecting his reformation to his near-disaster. His near-duel with Peel, however, may also have contributed something to his change of heart.

That O'Connell's 'conversion' was a family as well as his own affair is made clear by Mary's letter of 26 March 1816.

> You have indeed, my darling, a great deal of merit for your attention at present to your religious duties, and it is a delightful reflection to me that amidst all your bustle and business you continue a pattern of piety to all of us. I had yesterday the happiness of being at Communion and as my *health* will now permit me to be more regular than I have been this time back, I shall with the assistance of God try to follow your example. God be thanked, darling, the times are changed. You are now the better *Christian*. My girls are to pay [Rev.] Mr Walsh a visit this week and, as for our darling boys, I need have no fears that their religion will be neglected.[50]

Mary's own religious practice intensified; on the eve of her confinement she attended no less than three Sunday masses; and L'Estrange became her regular visitor. Maurice's fervour was perhaps less attractive, though due allowance must be made for twelve-year-old piety. He prayed God that he would fulfil his promise to his father to study harder, adding 'I think a lecture from Mr L'Estrange would do him [his younger brother, Morgan] a great deal of good.'[51] O'Connell's resolutions of amendment probably included a determination to give his children more time, attention and (though he had always been a loving father) affection. In 1816 he added to his circuit labours a warm correspondence with each of his elder sons and elder daughters; they of course eagerly competed for his letters and open praise. When Morgan fell ill O'Connell reproached himself for his habitual severity in dealing with his rather idle, though winning, second son: 'I felt as if I had treated the poor fellow badly and my grief was embittered by a very painful sensation like remorse.' He sent a message through Maurice that he 'doated' upon Morgan 'with the tenderest affection'. Morgan, he added, 'has every promise of being a delightful fellow . . . I intend to be more punctual in writing to you and your brother than I have been. Tell my Morgan so.'[52] It was however difficult to remain forever in such a state of parental grace. When O'Connell heard the results of the summer examinations at the boys' school, a new Jesuit foundation, Clongowes Wood, he could not altogether repress the stirrings of vicarious ambition. 'I must own', he told Maurice, 'I felt a passing shade of disappointment that you are not higher in your class. I am very willing to believe that it was not your fault, and do not blame you; and yet, my child, I consider *you could* have worked out a better place. However, be assured I say this without one particle of anything like anger. Will you make an effort to gratify me next time?'[53] Next came Morgan's turn. 'The truth is that if you took it into your red head you could easily be head of the class . . . but a little laziness and a little carelessness combine to keep you down . . . Do, my sweet Morgan, take the trouble.'[54] Neither could O'Connell maintain the volume of children's correspondence. He was reproached by Mary on 17 October: 'He [Maurice] complains as Morgan *does* of your not writing to him since you went to the country.'[55] Five weeks later O'Connell had to apologize to Morgan for a broken promise to visit him at school: 'Professional hurry makes me forget those things, but your mother does not love you better or more tenderly than I do.'[56] The way of paternal perfection was very hard.

The old Adam was not to be put down altogether even in O'Connell's dealings with his wife. The beginning of September found him still winding up the business of the summer assizes at Cork, and he apparently considered going directly to Kerry for his annual vacation without returning to his wife, who had been delivered of her seventh child in Dublin only nine days before. At any rate he told her that neither his mother's illness nor his friend Butler's marriage settlement was really so urgent that he could not 'afford to run to see you' for a few days, 'but . . . only for a few days'.[57] Mary replied with justified asperity:

Had you gone to Kerry without coming to see me and my boys, I should be most highly *offended* with you. Your mother is not in that dangerous state that you should hurry off to her, and James Butler having lived so long a bachelor, the delay of a week cannot add much to his *age* . . . As to your being back from Iveragh until November I have not a hope nor do I expect it. I own I would rather you did not spend much of your time in *that* country. A fortnight to amuse you is all I should *allow* and a week to spend entirely with your uncle.[58]

Iveragh of course brought on the old Adam by leaps and bounds. James's later comments make it clear that O'Connell spent and borrowed in his customary reckless way during his autumn vacation of 1816. O'Connell also wrote angrily to Mary from Kerry when she failed to forward business (probably money) papers because she was uncertain of his whereabouts or time of return to Dublin. 'This nasty letter from Carhen has dispirited me', she replied on 17 October. 'It is the first *serious* letter I ever got from you and I exactly feel like a *spoiled child*.'[59] But it would be wrong to suppose that the occasional exchange of hot words between O'Connell and his wife, or even his pecuniary relapses in Kerry, amounted to more than a ruffling of the marital surface: they could not dwell forever at the high altitude of fervid reconciliation. While O'Connell was still in Iveragh, Mary's love for him passed a sterner test than squabbles over his absence or her neglect of business. She received a series of anonymous letters in Dublin denigrating her husband, and apparently accusing him of unmet obligations and other misbehaviour. Her sole concern was that he should be comforted and supported. 'I am quite displeased that you should for a moment suffer the slightest uneasiness on *this* subject. Believe me, my *own* Dan, when I assure you that the machinations of *our anonymous friend* has [sic] not lessened my confidence in you. I should indeed be most ungrateful for your tenderness and affection if I allowed myself to fret or felt less happy than I did before the receipt of those contemptible scrolls.'[60] This struck the true note of their marriage, after fourteen years.

O'Connell ended 1816 with a significant political past but seemingly no political future, somewhat tarnished as hero in the public eye, trapped as a labouring junior counsel, monstrously indebted with no real prospect of relief beyond his precarious expectations from Hunting Cap, and pressed as well as blessed by teeming family affections. But though forty, defeated, burdened and hemmed in, he was still never to be repressed. 'Darling', he wrote to Mary from Derrynane on 26 September, 'I will be at Carhen on Saturday and we are to have great racing at the pattern. All my schoolboy feelings are alive again and I am as merry as ever I was.'[61] This too was an authentic voice.

CHAPTER 8

Ploughing Sands

1817–22

I

'**B**y no kind of means', wrote O'Connell's son, John, of the post-war years, 'by no manner of exertion, and he *did* look about for means, and *did* use a thousand exertions, could he arouse the Catholics to action, or even to a defensive position.'[1] Between 1815 and 1823 O'Connell's political exertions were ever varying and ever futile – at first sight a kaleidoscope of failures. But we must not forget that this was how he learned his trade and tested his later instruments and courses.

In mid-1817 he formally wound up his first Catholic Association – it was a pronouncement that life was extinct rather than a mercy-killing – and called an aggregate meeting in Dublin on 3 July to try to reconstitute the movement. The meeting agreed that 'individuals who belonged to the late Catholic Board and Association', and such others as they admitted to their ranks, should come together to draw up a petition for unqualified Emancipation.[2] The new group, generally known as the reorganized Catholic Board, met for the first time on 12 July 1817. Initially, O'Connell was fortunate in finding a piece of ready-made business for the revived body. Rev. Richard Hayes, O.F.M., who had taken the Catholic remonstrance against the veto proposals to Rome two years before, was on the point of being expelled from the Holy See, and O'Connell proposed that the Board draft a 'Letter of Complaint' to His Holiness. Even this produced much wrangling – Nicholas Mahon and his nephews, Nicholas and Richard O'Gorman, opposed the move – but a watered-down version of the letter was accepted at a later meeting. There was however much more to be squeezed out of the business than a futile epistle to the pope. O'Connell saw to it that the new Board sent one circular to all the Irish bishops, and a second to the clergy generally, expressing alarm at Hayes's ill-treatment. The first circular struck the note of chauvinism, pretending to outrage that Ireland should still fall within the sphere of Propaganda 'as if this were a mere missionary country without a national church'. The second raised the spectre of covert British influence at the Curia. Both seized the opportunity to rehearse the anti-vetoist case and to pressurize the clergy once again. The bishops were urged to see to it that the pope guaranteed them 'Domestic Nomination' to the episcopate and thus 'confirm[ed] the Irish Church in her National Independence'.[3]

In part, O'Connell was really worried lest the bishops weaken in their resistance to the veto. Archbishop Murray had already expressed anger at a violently political sermon delivered at the Carmelite Clarendon St Chapel (the meeting-place for the Dublin aggregates) by L'Estrange on 9 March 1817. O'Connell soon came to suspect that Archbishop Troy, whom he regarded as a truckler to Dublin Castle, had won over his coadjutor to his side. The joint reply from Troy and Murray to the reorganized Board's episcopal circular seemed to suggest that they might compromise on the veto issue; at any rate, they had responded coldly to the anti-vetoists. O'Connell wrote excitedly to Edward Hay, the secretary to the new Board, on 27 July,

> I perceive 'the pliant Trojan' [O'Connell's habitual nickname for Troy] has got Dr Murray's support for the Veto. Their publication of their letter to you was intended to intimidate other bishops from that zealous opposition to the Veto which the people look for and the times require . . . I am, I own, greatly shocked at the part Dr Murray is taking. I had the highest opinion of him and the greatest respect for him. But I see he wishes, with Dr Troy's see, to inherit the patronage of the Catholic Church of Ireland. Oh! it is melancholy to think of his falling off – he who compared the Vetoists to Judas. As to Dr Troy, better could not be expected from him. His traffic at the Castle is long notorious. But the sneer at the Board and the suppressed anger of those prelates would be ludicrous if the subject were not too important and vital. Are they angry because we urge not the *name* but the reality of Domestic Nomination? Alas, the fact is, that is just the cause of their ill temper and the source of their attack upon us.

O'Connell instructed Hay to publish immediately the other bishops' replies 'reprobatory of the Veto and favourable to Domestic Nomination', and this was done during August 1817. He also used aggregate meetings to demonstrate popular support and revived in oblique form his old threat that the people would repudiate vetoist priests and bishops: 'The Methodists were never in so fair a way of making converts.'[4] But by the end of the summer this rather factitious storm in a teacup had been altogether stilled. Whatever Troy's and Murray's

original intentions they had been pulled back into the ranks of a
solidly anti-vetoist episcopate. But the victory left the new Board
practically bereft of business. On 26 September O'Connell spoke of
Ireland as 'most wretched – fever – poverty – party spirit and *want of
animation*'.[5] The only other excitement of the year was the miserable
one of O'Connell's being challenged to a duel for his abuse of a
member of a leading Ascendancy family, J. F. Leslie, at the meeting of
4 December 1817; the affair was finally patched up by O'Connell
conceding that he had spoken of Leslie, not as an individual, but as a
public man. Thereafter the new Board ceased to meet; it decided not
even to petition Parliament during the spring and early summer
session of 1818. O'Connell himself pronounced the requiem on 21
December of the same year: 'The Board is defunct . . . There are many
debts due – there is a great indisposition to *organize*.'[6]

The ill-starred new Catholic Board did not exhaust O'Connell's
efforts to agitate during 1817–18. In the first half of 1817, he took up
the issue of proselytism at the Dublin House of Industry, and was
condemned by the Castle press for dragging the name of the lord
lieutenant into the row. He also denounced Orange supremacism at
one public meeting and Anglican pretensions to a monopoly of loyalty
to the crown at another. By the second half of 1818, however, his
emphasis had changed from the politics of sectarianism to the politics
of ecumenism: in between he had striven to conjoin the Catholic cause
and that of moderate parliamentary reform. Ceaselessly, backwards
and forwards, he probed for some weakness in the government's front
which a new agitation might exploit. Meanwhile, he struggled to bring
into being again, and then support, a sympathetic press. In 1817 he
indemnified the official guarantor of Eneas MacDonnell's pro-
Emancipation newspaper, the *Dublin Chronicle*, and on 24 August
1818 assured Michael Staunton, his new ally as editor of the
Freeman's Journal, 'I have been and am exerting myself to get your
paper into the clubs here [co. Kerry]. You are now the *longe et facile
primus* of the Irish press.'[7] But it was all uphill and ill-rewarded work.

The humiliations, pettinesses and generally derided endeavours of
1816–18 were all the more galling because O'Connell, no prophet in
his own land, discovered himself to be remarkably prophetical in
London. In the early summer of 1817 Mary was sent to Clifton, near
Bristol, to recover her lost health. Having installed her there,
O'Connell spent a week in London, his first visit (apart from the Peel
episode) since his student days. He was lionized in a mild though
thoroughly flattering degree. As soon as he arrived, Charles Butler, the

foremost English Catholic commoner, waited upon him and introduced him to the Duke of Norfolk, Sir John Throckmorton and all the
'great men' of the English Board; he also met leading parliamentary
liberals although he missed Brougham, 'the very first man in England',
who was then ill. On 4 June 1817 the prominent 'Anglo-Irish lawyer'
Anthony Blake

> splendidly entertained [me] . . . at his house with a large party of English
> Catholics of the first rank. And the next day Lord Fingall and I were
> entertained in a similar party at the Thatched House Tavern in St James
> Street – with that name it is one of the first taverns in the world. Our feast
> was turtle – turbot, champagne, etc. On Thursday I . . . paid and received
> many visits. I could not tell you the lords and commoners to whom I was
> introduced nor the attention I met with.[8]

It was a bitter, as well as sweet, experience. In every meeting and
conversation O'Connell felt conscious of his superiority to the host of
'men of high names' who feted him. 'Darling', he told Mary on 10
June,

> do not smile at my vanity, but your credulity with respect to anything in my
> favour will easily make you believe that I felt how cruel the Penal Laws are
> which exclude me from a fair trial with men whom *I look on* as so much my
> inferiors . . .
> I saw the English Bar, darling, in its strength and be assured, heart, they
> are just nothing to the Irish Bar. I felt *that* easily and strongly. I spent almost
> the entire day on Friday in the King's Bench . . .[9]

The resentment of his debased station was political no less than
personal. On his next visit to Mary in September 1817 he wrote from
Clifton, 'I have seen nothing here but stupid loyal slavish English, who
for a rise of one per cent in the funds would truck a republic for the
government of slaves.'[10] To be systematically degraded by such people
was hardly endurable.

II

In O'Connell, however, hope was always tinder-dry; at any spark it
blazed. On 2 November 1818 he wrote excitedly to Owen O'Conor
(The O'Conor Don) of Balanagare, a country gentleman of ancient
Catholic family, 'I have just heard from a credible person in London
that Emancipation is certain. *I believe it.*'[11] It was enough to galvanize
O'Connell once again. O'Conor, respected, honourable and sensible,
was his principal ally in the new campaign; O'Connell summoned him

up from co. Roscommon repeatedly. But he also had hopes of a rapprochement with Lord Fingall (and through him with the aristocratic faction of Catholics) and of making common cause with the Irish whigs and in particular with their most eminent personage, the Duke of Leinster. Fingall, as he told O'Conor on 21 December 1818, proved immovable. None the less, O'Connell was 'decidedly for petitioning. If I petition alone, I *will* petition.'[12] He cast one of his favourite flies over O'Conor by asking *him* to lay out a course of action, assuring him that he would fall in gratefully with whatever O'Conor might propose. But meanwhile he had hit on a device of his own. He would compose a public letter to the Catholics of Ireland for publication on the opening day of the new year: in fact, this turned out to be the first of O'Connell's celebrated New Year letters to his supposed national flock – pronouncements *urbi et orbi* so to say.

Of course, O'Connell did not really wait upon O'Conor's inspiration. While not despairing altogether of Fingall, he set about organizing an Irish Protestant lobby for Emancipation. Eventually, he managed to persuade eight sympathetic peers, headed by the Duke of Leinster, and four M.P.'s, headed by Henry Grattan, to requisition the lord mayor of Dublin (Thomas McKenny, another sympathizer) for a Protestant meeting to petition for Catholic relief. Despite Castle opposition, the meeting held on 11 February 1819 was successful, securing a wide and respectable Protestant support for a petition. O'Connell was exultant. 'Are you not delighted', he wrote to O'Conor that evening, 'that you did not stay in the country and plead, as you might, business &c &c?'[13] It was certainly a triumph for O'Connell, now forced to operate without any organization of his own, and with still very feeble press support. He had not got as close to Grattan, the great embodiment of '1782', as he now desired. To Grattan's memory of O'Connell's coarse repudiation of him in 1815 had been added that of being hooted by a mob of O'Connell's Dublin sympathizers in the general election of 1818. Still, by the beginning of 1819 the two were on civil terms at least; even this was a partial triumph.

But a price would ultimately be exacted for such a move to the right in Catholic politics. Publicly, Eneas MacDonnell pointed out that O'Connell's address of 1 January 1819 had omitted all reference to the veto, and that O'Connell had earlier alleged popular apathy and episcopal division on the subject. The veteran Presbyterian radical, William Drennan, who was organizing pro-Emancipation meetings in Belfast, assumed that O'Connell would beat some retreat upon this vital issue, though on balance he granted him both prudence and probity. 'I see', he told O'Connell on 30 January 1819,

> the whole matter is settled. The Veto in operation already. Well, you must balance the *much* you may receive against the *comparatively* little you lose. The Catholic *regium donum* will follow the Presbyterian *regium donum*, but the love of laymen for liberty will overcome and quench the ecclesiastical proneness to prostration. Take what you *can* get and trust to the future, nor cast away your civil rights in compliment to those who degrade the dignity and sanctity of the latter . . .
>
> *You* will always act the honest part, not the poor spirited and aspiring character of the day. I would not condescend to compliment you or anyone without grounds, but I sincerely think you possess many of the character-istics of Charles Fox, his manly spirit, his openness and candour, his ability and perhaps a little of his gullibility, the weak part of an otherwise impregnable stronghold of honesty and honour. I was going to say to you, as I would have said to him, oddly as it may sound, 'Beware of the goodness of your heart. Your paper, which blinked the Veto, called for an answer and got it. Eneas fought with Achilles. Your reply has vindicated your consistency and politically accounted for your omission.' . . . It is a ticklish station but with moral integrity that disdains the juggling and *leger-de-main* of speculating politicians, your object will be obtained and your name be recorded in History.[14]

Clearly O'Connell was prepared, early in 1819, to compromise, to some extent, upon the veto issue in order to secure a Relief Act immediately; he may well have hoped – insofar as he planned ahead at all – that 'Domestic Nomination' would prove nebulous enough to accommodate the various conflicting interests. But the issue did not come to the test at once. Grattan's motion of 3 May 1819 for a committee to inquire into the laws affecting Catholics was defeated – although, cheeringly, by only two votes.

O'Connell was certainly not dismayed by this result. Attributing their failure to the lateness with which the question had been brought on in the Commons, he told O'Conor soon after the defeat that they must 'recommence operations' much earlier than usual, and if possible before Parliament sat again in the first week in November 1819. 'We have been materially injured by the late period in which the question has always come on.' He also called on O'Conor to help immediately in 'perfecting' the reunion of the Irish Catholic forces.[15] Correspond-ingly, he was careful to continue to cultivate the whigs, English no less than Irish. When in August 1819 Edward Hay (now estranged from O'Connell) 'leaked' to the *Dublin Evening Post* (also estranged by now) the 'information' that the notorious witchery resolutions of 1812 had been inspired by the English whigs, and in particular by

George Ponsonby, O'Connell quickly issued a public denial to save his English allies from embarrassment.

He even cut short his sacred Kerry vacation to make an early start in the new season's agitation. On 21 October 1819 he wrote to O'Conor from Dublin:

> I intend instantly to set the cause in motion. This great experiment is worth making. I think you will let me have your assistance. I write by this post to Lord Fingall. I am strongly prompted by our friends in Parliament. I wish to God you could come up *at once* to help me. If we *show out* before the Regent's speech is prepared, perhaps we may be remembered in it. If you agree with me that this time requires a sacrifice, you will come up. My own opinion is that we will be emancipated *now or never*.
>
> I came to town only yesterday, and already I have many irons in the fire to raise the blaze which should lead us to victory. I want you much, and the cause wants you more.[16]

At this stage O'Connell argued that another failure of Emancipation would render the argument for parliamentary reform irrefutable and demonstrate 'a disposition to make use of bigotry as an instrument to perpetuate the divisions, dissensions and consequent degradation and oppression of Ireland'.[17] He did not however develop this into a distinct threat to turn to Reform or Repeal, if disappointed. On the contrary, he instructed his 'countrymen' in his encyclical of October 1819:

> You will be told that you should despise emancipation as a minor and unworthy consideration, and join the almost universal cry of reform. Do not be carried away by any such incitement . . . we have a previous duty to perform; a favourable opportunity now presents itself to add to the general stock of liberty, by obtaining our emancipation; and the man would, in my judgment, be a false patriot, who, for the chance of uncertain reform, would fling away the present most propitious moment to realize a most important and almost certain advantage.[18]

Moreover, he continued to court the Irish Protestants and whigs. Early in November 1819 he strove to revive their interest in the cause through the device of a subscription for McKenny 'for his virtuous and independent conduct in calling and presiding at the Meeting of the Protestant Friends of Roman Catholic freedom . . . in Febuary last'.[19] In fact, probably for lack of support, the advertised dinner had to be postponed and it was almost six months before it eventually took place early in May 1820. In the interval, O'Connell fell into further difficulties when he rashly declared that the Duke of Leinster and

Lords Fingall and Cloncurry would act with him in resigning from the Kildare Place Society (the semi-state body entrusted with promoting national elementary education) because it permitted the proselytizing of the Catholic children. But he apparently made plausible explanations to, and in due course peace with, his aristocratic patrons. In the end, Grattan departed for Westminster on 20 May 1820 – even later in the session than usual, for all O'Connell's original aspirations. He was armed with a bundle of petitions from Irish Protestants and Catholics alike, and accompanied by even higher hopes than in 1819.

The expedition could not have ended more unfortunately. Grattan fell ill when he arrived in London and died on 4 June. O'Connell apostrophized the dead hero with 'I should exhaust the dictionary three times told, ere I could enumerate [his] virtues';[20] perhaps he half-meant this at least, for much later, speaking privately, he placed Grattan second only to himself among Irish statesmen. The demise brought discord and delay. The choice of a substitute spokesman divided the Irish Catholic deputation which accompanied Grattan. In the end – surprisingly – William Plunket, who had told the deputation that 'securities' or conditions upon Catholic relief were both just and necessary, was preferred (by a casting vote) to the much less accommodating Knight of Kerry, O'Connell's particular friend. When the news reached Dublin, O'Connell denounced the deputation furiously. But though sinister in its implications for the future, the decision had no bearing on the present. By now the session was so far advanced that the government could play out time upon the Catholic claims; the petitions were never presented. Thus by a mixture of ill-luck and ill-management 'the best opportunity', as O'Connell put it, 'I have ever known of pressing emancipation on the ministry, [has] been thrown away and lost for ever'.[21] Worse still, the Irish Catholics had been rent asunder once again and, from the anti-vetoist standpoint, the choice of Plunket had sold all possible passes in advance. The conciliatory strategy which O'Connell had followed for more than twenty months was now in ruins.

III

The travails of the past year had however been partially offset by an agreeable political distraction. The apparent revival of liberalism abroad during 1819–20 had fired O'Connell's ardour. In March 1820 he was overjoyed to learn that Ferdinand VII of Spain had been forced to restore the constitution of 1812.

I am in great spirits. The complete revolution in Spain is so auspicious a circumstance that I hail it as the first of a series of events useful to human liberty and human happiness. Until *the last* papers I was not without my fears of a failure, but now my mind is quite at ease and I enjoy this revolution as all the scoundrels of society enjoyed the battle of Waterloo.[22]

But it was the revolt of the Spanish colonies in South America which seemed to him most apropos the Irish plight. At a dinner which he organized in Dublin on 19 July 1819 to celebrate South American freedom, he came into close relation with John Devereux, who was currently raising an Irish Legion to fight with Bolivar in Venezuela. Devereux, for long a political exile in the United States for his part in the 1798 rebellion, was a vain and unscrupulous adventurer. But O'Connell, completely taken in, 'stood by him even after charges had been made, probably with much truth, that he had organized the Irish Legion for his own financial benefit'.[23]

Devereux's grant of a commission to one of O'Connell's nephews was followed by his making out another, seemingly on his own initiative, for O'Connell's son Morgan, still only fourteen years of age. 'I shall name [him] as on my staff', he told O'Connell on 3 August 1819, 'although it may be no other than a mere compliment yet it will serve to record that affection and respect for you – and for virtues and merits which I feel too strongly to express by words.'[24] O'Connell was now fairly caught. Morgan, with boyish vanity, seized upon Devereux's 'document' and subscribed himself in a letter to his father of 27 August, 'Captain, 1st Regt. of Fusiliers and Aide-de-camp to General D'Evereux, Irish Legion.'[25] In fact, disaster befell the first contingent of the Legion when it landed on the island of Margarita in August 1819; news of its ill-fate reached Dublin months later; and demands for an inquiry into Devereux's conduct – he was widely blamed – followed fast. But the effect on O'Connell was merely to turn him into Devereux's foremost partisan. First, Morgan clung to his commission and hopes of a South American adventure, and therefore to his faith in Devereux, and this predisposed a fond father to take an indulgent view of Morgan's patron. Next, O'Connell had been charmed and flattered by the General 'and mingling his mighty cause with his kindly self I became and in the worst of times continued and am his friend'. Most important of all, O'Connell argued, was the cause itself. 'One more land of liberty is a conquest over despotism and over legitimacy which they cannot afford.'[26] The whole enterprise also touched chords of romance and ambition in the Catholic middle class, not least in O'Connell himself. In one light, it seemed a renewal of the

'Flight of the Wild Geese' in which from the 1690s onwards young Irish Catholics, deprived and depressed at home, sought fame and fortune in the Continental armies of the *ancien régime*. In another, it seemed to renew the age of the conquistadores (though now under liberal banners), for lavish land grants and honours in the freed colonies seemed assured. We must always paint in this glowing foreground if we are fully to account for the intensity of the Irish enthusiasm, however shortlived, for the bizarre undertaking.

For O'Connell there was the additional attraction that Bolivar seemed his political mirror image, half way across the globe. He made no such claim publicly, of course. A letter which he gave Morgan to deliver to Bolivar opened with stately deference,

> Illustrious Sir,
>   A stranger and unknown, I take the liberty of addressing you. I am encouraged to do so by my respect for your high character and by my attachment to that sacred cause which your talents, valour and virtue have gloriously sustained – I mean the cause of Liberty and national independence.
>   Hitherto I have been able to bestow only good wishes upon that noble cause. But now I have a son able to wield a sword in its defence, and I send him, Illustrious Sir, to admire and profit by your example . . .[27]

But it would have come as no surprise to learn from Morgan, after he had arrived at Margarita on 12 June 1820, that praise was heaped upon 'the Irish liberator' in the welcoming after-dinner speeches in the mess. O'Connell was toasted 'as "the most enlightened, the most independent, and the most patriotic man, not only in Great Britain, but in all Europe". This was drunk with great acclamations, and Col. Low's son, standing up on his chair shouted: "Viva el Councellor O'Connell" .'[28] Bolivar himself was respectful of O'Connell's fame, though he turned it neatly to account by postponing the addition of Morgan to his staff because 'I have numberless hardships to go through which I would not bring him into for the character of his father is well known to me.'[29]

It was accepted in Venezuela that the Irish Legion depended largely for its expansion on O'Connell's reputation and vociferous support. Certainly, he was heavily engaged in defending and justifying its projector in Dublin during the early months of 1820; in addition to his own writings and speeches in Devereux's favour and his efforts to secure him a favourable press, he acted as his lawyer and probably – of all things! – his 'banker' at certain stages. But by the time of Morgan's arrival at Margarita, things had gone badly awry with the expeditionary force. The initial contingent of approximately 1000 had mutinied and, for the most part, been shipped out of trouble to Jamaica. Four months later, on 4 October 1820, a letter from Admiral Brion, Bolivar's naval commander, condemning the remainder, was published in the Dublin newspapers. Brion described Devereux's newly arrived forces as banditti, and declared that Bolivar's troops at Baranquilla had refused to receive them. Dogged loyalty still held O'Connell back from abandoning Devereux and the Legion; but the venture was now hopelessly discredited, and he was reduced to consoling Mary on 13 October 1820 with, 'Make your mind easy about my darling Morgan. His share of the evils which befell the Irish Legion are small indeed. He has means to supply his wants and can return when he pleases.'[30] Morgan did return safely at the very end of 1821, although only after he had undergone attacks of ague and fever, two shipwrecks and successive rescues by, first, a long-lost illegitimate O'Connell cousin who was soon to be murdered by an Italian boatswain and die in Morgan's arms, next, an Irish naval officer who had lost his commission for refusing to take the prescribed anti-Catholic oaths and now sailed under Danish colours, and finally an Irish lieutenant R.N. commanding the sloop *Raleigh* who landed him eventually at Chatham. Characteristically, O'Connell cast a roseate wash over Morgan's entire madcap adventure. 'His trip to South America', he wrote on 5 January 1822, 'has done him nothing but good as it would otherwise have been difficult to tame him down to the sobriety of business.' Without having so much as seen him for more than eighteen months, he was none the less assured that Morgan was now 'very prudent in money matters'![31] By this stage the affair of the Irish Legion was receding into memory, apart from occasional scandalous allegations about and counter-charges from Devereux. O'Connell had certainly not enhanced his reputation in Dublin Catholic circles by his persistent credulity or even his obstinate loyalty to his protégé. Yet there was more to it all than a trivial exhibition of ill-judgment. Bolivar remained an ideal for O'Connell all his life, neither was it a coincidence that he came to bear with pride the title invented originally for Bolivar – 'The Liberator'.

From one distraction to another: just as the Devereux business was entering its darkest phase, O'Connell found another welcome political diversion. Upon returning from his Iveragh vacation at the end of October 1820, he conceived the notion that he should be instated as Queen Caroline's Irish attorney-general. Despite the inherent implausibility, it was no mad dream. The Queen's affair was now at its hottest pitch of excitement and agitation; O'Connell's sympathies (liberal and Irish alike) had of course been with her and against her husband from the start; and the whig lawyers Brougham and Thomas Denman had been appointed, respectively, her attorney- and solicitor-general earlier in 1820. Although such appointments to a royal consort traditionally carried with them admission to the inner bar, it is not clear whether O'Connell had any such hope in pressing his own case. The statutory prohibition on Roman Catholics taking silk still stood. He said that his appointment as the Queen's Irish attorney-general 'would be of great use to my clients [in] that I should not be flung into the back row'[32] – an indeterminate aspiration. But he may well have felt that the commotion which would follow his nomination might precipitate a crisis ending in the removal of the bar on Catholics. O'Connell himself told Lord Cloncurry on 16 November 1820 that 'my leading motive in looking for this office is to annoy some of the greatest scoundrels in society and, of course, the bitterest enemies of Ireland.'[33] Whether or not this really was his leading motive, there could be no doubt that such an elevation would infuriate every tory – not to add a considerable majority of the whigs – in the United Kingdom.

Seized with his extraordinary scheme, O'Connell dispatched letters in all directions to concert a campaign for his own appointment. He emphasized, as was essential, that in his view the 'Penal Laws do not exclude a Catholic from being Attorney-General to the Queen.'[34] Through Cloncurry, he tried to ensure the patronage of the Duke of Leinster; through Thomas Spring-Rice, the newly elected whig member for Limerick city, he sought an entrée to Brougham, the Queen's principal legal adviser. From Alexander Wood, an Irish journalist working on the London *Traveller*, he obtained an analysis of the power structure of Caroline's court; Wood advised him to enlist Sir Henry Parnell's aid, to gain introductions to the influential Earl Grey and Lord Darnley and, above all, to try to 'move through' Alderman Wood as well as Brougham 'for when two great orbs spin in the same direction, there is, you know, an eclipse of one!'[35]

At first it seemed as if O'Connell's *coup de main* would carry the day. On 24 November 1820 his former pupil, John Bric, wrote triumphantly from London on the strength of a chain of reports said to have the ultimate authority of Alderman Wood, 'My dear Sir, You are the attorney-general of Ireland for Her Majesty.'[36] Two days later O'Connell described himself as 'Her Majesty's Attorney-General' in replying formally to an invitation from Cloncurry.[37] Doubtless he was also responsible for the news item appearing in a Dublin newspaper, *Carrick's Morning Post*, on 27 November under the headline, 'APPOINTMENT OF HER MAJESTY'S ATTORNEY-GENERAL FOR IRELAND'.

But it was Brougham who held the key to the situation, and he fell at once into the role of the archetypical 'slippery whig' with whom one could neither disagree nor cooperate. His sympathy with O'Connell's objective was boundless, his courtesy unfailing, his tone respectful almost to the point of deference – but there were always difficulties. Brougham first asked O'Connell to seek a precedent for the appointment of consort's legal officer – of whatever religion – in Ireland, and to suggest a Protestant who might be his partner. Later he begged O'Connell to state a case on which Denman and he might give an opinion. O'Connell could find no precedent (he fairly pointed to the deplorable state of Irish public records) but argued vigorously that the only possibly prohibitory legislation referred solely to male consorts. He relied however upon his own professional judgment and the strategy of transferring the onus to the crown by compelling them to challenge his appointment – 'without allowing a thought of the expense of the contest coming from any other person than myself'. As he put it in a letter to Brougham of 15 December 1820,

> My opinion is that I should be entitled to a *mandamus*. A barrister in this country is not a mere creature of courtesy as in England but is called to the Bar by force of a Statute of the reign of Henry VIII and, having that legal capacity, I consider that I should, by her Majesty's appointment, be enabled by a *mandamus* to compel the Chancellor to admit me. I may be wrong but, if so, I am wrong very *premeditatedly*. I may be sneered at for giving myself a wrong opinion though, whether right or wrong, I fancy I do at present give as many – probably more opinions – to others than any Irish barrister. I cannot except one.[38]

It was not easy to counter O'Connell's proposal that he be appointed forthwith, thus forcing the government, if it so determined, to try to disallow the move. At worst, as Bric pointed out, 'their refusal to ratify your appointment, that is, to swear you into office would furnish an excellent topic for invective'.[39] But despite a case stated and 'further letters' from O'Connell, Brougham succeeded in delaying a definitive reply until 8 May 1821 when he told O'Connell that Denman and he did not consider 'the right in question . . . sufficiently established . . . to authorize us to give our advice to H.M. in favour of trying it.'[40] Well before then, however, it was clear that Brougham was opposed. In fact, such a realization probably explains the bitter hostility to

working with the current British parliamentarians which, unexpectedly, O'Connell expressed in his annual address to the Irish people on
1 January 1821.

IV

The address of 1821 constituted a complete turnabout. It recommended that the issue of Emancipation be shelved entirely in favour of
that of parliamentary reform. O'Connell now spurned the yearly farce
and humiliation of a rejected or burked Catholic petition and told his
co-religionists no longer to

> . . . *kneel before their masters doors,*
> *And hawk their wrongs, as beggars do their sores.*[41]

His further plans were vague to the point of vapidity. They consisted
essentially in an appeal to all Irishmen – the by-now hallowed
'Catholic, Protestant and Dissenter' – to stand by their common
nationality and strike for their common constitutional rights as a
nation, without regard to their particular preferences as to modes of
political reform. As a programme this was absurd; but the challenge to
the right wing of Irish Catholics, and especially to the vetoists, was
unmistakeable. Sheil took up the gauntlet on their behalf with a savage
'Answer to Mr O'Connell's Address' which cast doubts upon
O'Connell's sincerity as either Emancipationist or patriot. The war
between the Irish Catholic factions had broken out once more, and
O'Connell responded with a bitter lampoon of Sheil's literary
pretensions, ending by imploring him 'with all the earnestness of the
plainest prose, to refrain from his sneering sarcasms, directed against
. . . the long-suffering and very wretched people of Ireland'.[42] Only
with the greatest difficulty was Sheil persuaded against inflicting the
final blow on the Irish cause by calling O'Connell out.

O'Connell was awkwardly placed when on 7 March 1821 Plunket
introduced bills amounting to Emancipation with 'securities' in the
Commons. The bills had the warm support of the English Catholic
body as a whole, as well as that of the Irish vetoists, and the omens
were good for a parliamentary majority, at least in the lower house.
But O'Connell did not hesitate to denounce Plunket and his proposals
violently. From Limerick, where he was on circuit, he issued a public
letter condemning the measures as 'more *strictly*, *literally*, and
emphatically a *penal* and *persecuting bill* than any or all the statutes
passed in the darkest and most bigoted periods';[43] he made much play

of the danger to even the secrets of the confessional which the supervisory board proposed by Plunket presented. He also arranged meetings of protest in the assize cities, stirred the local Catholic clergy (who would be subjected to an abjuring oath under the new order) to indignation, and worked upon his parliamentary friends to oppose Plunket. 'If the Bill [Plunket's two proposals had by now been consolidated into one] passes in its present shape', he told the Knight of Kerry on 8 April 1821, 'it will tend to exasperate and render matters worse in point of popular tranquillity.'[44] None the less, he remained nervous. Six days later, he confessed to Mary, 'I wish with all my heart that the present rascally Catholic Bill was flung out. While I am travelling on Monday [16 April] morning the rascals will be debating.'[45] He might have guessed, however, that the upper house would muster sufficient 'rascals' to defeat Emancipation, however qualified. Although the combined measure passed the House of Commons, the Lords finally rejected it by 159 votes to 120 on 17 April. O'Connell rejoiced that a disastrous compromise, which might have covered over, without destroying, the essential evil for a generation, had been averted, and no less at the discomfiture of his domestic enemies. 'Even the Vetoists', he wrote, 'must admit that *securities* do no good because we are kicked out as unceremoniously with them as without them.' None the less, it left the Irish Catholics of all sorts stranded and virtually hopeless. As he put it to O'Conor on 23 April 1821, 'What is to be done now? That is the question.'[46]

To the thoroughgoing opportunist, however, almost anything can provide an opportunity. The forthcoming coronation of George IV on 19 July 1821 and his promised visit to Ireland in the following month (the first by a reigning English monarch since Richard II's expedition of 1399) might not seem promising material for a revival of Irish Catholic politics. But O'Connell determined to turn them to account. At first, he intended to combine with a loyal address a fresh statement upon Emancipation. But O'Conor, on whose respectability and standing he relied for the successful requisitioning of a general Catholic meeting, insisted that the business be confined to the address, lest 'we shall be again split into parties and consequently weakened'.[47] This course was rendered more palatable to O'Connell by an overture on 10 July 1821 from the (mainly Orange) corporation of Dublin asking that Protestant-Catholic hostility be set aside for the king's visit and that George IV be received by all under the common denomination of loyal Irishmen. Nothing could have fitted better the volte face which O'Connell had announced in his public pronouncement of the previous 1 January. He also maintained in later years that he was serving the cause of Emancipation as well as Ireland's national interest by his extreme conciliatoriness – not to say, servility – before, during and immediately after the king's descent upon the country.

> This was the most critical period of my political life, and that in which I had the good fortune to be most successful. If I have any merit for the success of the Catholic cause, it is principally to be found in the mode in which I neutralised the most untoward events and converted the most sinister appearances and circumstances into the utmost extent of practical usefulness to the cause of which I was the manager . . . I was able to convert the King's visit to Ireland from being a source of weakness and discomfiture to the Catholics into a future claim for practical relief and political equalisation.[48]

Undoubtedly, O'Connell came to believe this strange claim in retrospect. But there is little evidence that his thoughts ran upon these lines at the time. In fact, he and Sheil pursued their ill-tempered rivalry throughout the whole affair.

No one could have exceeded O'Connell in forbearance when, against the spirit of the entente, members of the corporation offered various Orange provocations. Dublin Catholics were entertained by the piquant spectacle of O'Connell preaching restraint – successfully in the end – to Sheil and his fellow-vetoists. O'Connell was also foremost in public obeisance to the king, as with the extravagance of his welcome. 'In sorrow and bitterness', he orated, 'I have for the last fifteen years laboured for my unhappy country. But this bright day has realised all my fond expectations. It is said of St Patrick that he banished venomous reptiles from our isle, but his Majesty has performed a greater moral miracle. The announcement of his approach has allayed the dissensions of centuries.'[49] During the royal sojourn, O'Connell presented himself loyally to George IV, and, as he was departing, held out to him a laurel crown 'intended with all humility to be replaced by one of Emeralds'.[50] O'Connell also added his name to the subscription list for the erection of a palace to commemorate the king's visit (in the end the money sufficed only to build a bridge), and founded a 'Loyal Union, or Royal George Club' to perpetuate the 'affectionate gratitude towards his Majesty King George the Fourth (whom God preserve,) which now animates every Irish bosom'.[51] The club (curiously similar in detail to O'Connell's later Order of Liberators!) was to meet and dine regularly together and to wear a species of uniform made from cloth of Irish manufacture. He was also reported to boast that a new fur cap he wore was a present from the king. Nicholas Mahon derided this supposed piece of flunkyism soon afterwards in Cork, but O'Connell claimed to have turned the tables on his persistent critic. 'I had great fun at the county meeting. You never saw or heard of anything that took better than my hit at Mahon in reply to his attack on my cap. I concluded by saying "I would call my cap the cap of unanimity, but then the cap would not fit Mr Mahon".'[52]

Both then and later O'Connell preferred a political defence of his season of obsequiousness. He was ever loyal to the crown, as King or Queen of Ireland; and as loyalism (with claims to exclusive rights therein) was the Irish Protestant's stock-in-trade, it behoved the Irish Catholic to express his fidelity in the most unmistakable terms. O'Connell also distinguished between the office and person of the head of state; it was to the crowned monarch, not George himself, that he proclaimed his undying attachment. Moreover, the prime objective of an Irish statesman should be able to find common ground for Irish Catholics and Protestants, and where better to do so than in their joint allegiance to the king?

Despite the thin rationality of all this, a fawning and courtier-like O'Connell presented a pitiful change of front. As reported, with some malicious exaggeration, by the London press, his conduct during the royal visit aroused disgust and contempt among liberals in England. Tom Moore was appalled by the 'bad servile style in which Paddy has received him [George IV] – Mr O'Connell pre-eminent in blarney and inconsistency'.[53] Byron lashed him in verse:

> . . . O'Connell, proclaim
> His accomplishments! His !!! and thy country convince
> Half an age's contempt was an error of fame . . .
>
> Shout, drink, feast, and flatter! Oh! Erin, how low
> Wert thou sunk by misfortune and tyranny, till
> Thy welcome of tyrants has plunged thee below
> The depth of thy deep in a deeper gulf still.[54]

To the very close of 1821 O'Connell struggled to retain the illusion that the royal foray into Irish affairs was, as George IV declared, the harbinger of the end of faction, and the prelude to Catholic equality. In his annual address at the beginning of the year, O'Connell had called for the sinking of Irish sectarian differences and the display of a united Irish manliness of comportment in the face of Britain's contemptuous neglect of their common country. It was ironic that this should have ended in Catholic abasement before both Orange supremacism and the throne.

V

During 1822 O'Connell's new-found conciliatoriness and loyalism took on another form. In December 1821 the Marquess of Wellesley, a supporter of the Catholic claims, became Irish lord lieutenant, though this was deliberately balanced by the appointment of the ultra-tory Henry Goulburn as chief secretary. As a sort of counter-compensation, Wellesley replaced Saurin (much to Saurin's fury – in anger he refused both an English peerage and the chief justiceship of King's Bench) by Plunket as Irish attorney-general. O'Connell took all this to mean the inauguration of an era of non-factional government in Ireland; and as Wellesley was specifically the crown's alter ego it was easy to transfer the hopes and deference of the later months of 1821 to the viceroy. In moving the address of welcome at a general Catholic meeting on 7 January 1822, O'Connell proclaimed him to be the 'representative, not only of the person, but also of the kindly disposition of our beloved Sovereign'.[55]

At the same time O'Connell decided to test the water on whether or not he should make a fresh bid for Emancipation. He announced that after consulting Plunket (Plunket had probably done no more than listen politely) he had framed a scheme of Domestic Nomination which he believed would give the state reasonable securities while not infringing on the essential liberty of the Irish Catholic Church. But he would not, he added, force the issue if it were to revive the bitter division of the veto controversy or if others felt that it endangered ecclesiastical independence. This uncharacteristically tentative proposal did not bode well for further action; and although a Dublin aggregate meeting of 13 February 1822 resolved in favour of petitioning again, this never happened. Later in the spring, O'Connell attributed his restraint to the wave of agrarian outrages currently ravaging cos. Limerick, Kerry and Cork: these had already brought down upon Ireland a grievously repressive Insurrection Act as well as the suspension of Habeas Corpus. For O'Connell to launch an agitation, however 'constitutional', at such a stage might well have been paraded by the malignant as colluding with rural terrorism. Nothing could be further from O'Connell's intention; but it was reasonable for him, from past experience, to fear even so gross a misrepresentation.

But the decisive reason for O'Connell's failure to act was probably Plunket's blank refusal to raise the Catholic question during 1822. On 4 April O'Connell pleaded with him that the mere advertisement, in the debate, of the loyalty of the priests in the present disturbances would more than compensate for the defeat of a motion in favour of Emancipation.

> The Catholic clergy of the second order are unanimous in wishing for it because they are convinced that at this moment every man in the House must admit the zeal and energy the Catholic clergy have evinced during the present disturbances. This testimony you will cheerfully bear. This testimony Mr Goulburn, our mortal enemy, and even Mr Peel *must* now admit to be true . . . These will at all events be precious advantages – to have admitted in Parliament *the innocence* of the Catholic religion as any part of *the immediate* cause of the troubles now raging and also to have praised and *admired* by all parties the exertions and loyalty of the Catholic clergy.[56]

In the name of parliamentary tactics, Plunket vigorously resisted the re-airing of the Catholic question, and indeed the notion that the Catholic question should form the matter for a regular pitched battle in the Commons every session.

> It would not only lose its interest but its friends who, though willing to expose themselves to some unpleasant differences with their constituents (I mean the English Members for counties and open places) in order to carry, or essentially to advance the measure, will not submit to be annually dragged forward merely for discussion. In addition to this there are many persons on the ministerial side of the House who have been amongst the steadiest and most efficient friends of the Roman Catholics who may feel themselves placed in a situation of some awkwardness if in consequence of a determination to bring it on every session, the question should become liable to be considered as one of attack and embarrassment.[57]

With O'Connell still committed to the policy of supporting the crown's representative in Ireland, in the hope of even-handed government at last from Dublin Castle, Plunket's outright opposition was bound to be decisive.

But despite the initial triumph of Saurin's humiliation, O'Connell had by now good reason to doubt the even-handedness of Wellesley's rule. The lord lieutenant had early disabused Irish Catholics of any idea that he might act to support their claims: he had come, he told them in reply to one address, to 'administer the laws, not to alter them'.[58] He had proceeded to recommend an Insurrection Act – which, as an agitator, O'Connell disliked, however much, as a landowner, he might acquiesce in its necessity – and the suspension of Habeas Corpus – which, as a common lawyer, O'Connell instinctively repudiated. Then Plunket had stamped upon any discussion of the

Catholic grievances in the Commons. By 1 July 1822 O'Connell had reached the point of writing satirically to Plunket, apropos of a gross misuse of their legal offices for political ends by Saurin and Norbury which had just been discovered accidentally,

> I am not so foolish or so uncandid as to assert that the case of a Protestant who conspires to injure the Catholics' case can in the present temper of Society in these countries, and under the present system, with at least one half the administration in both decided enemies of Catholic rights and liberties − I am not, I say, so foolish and uncandid as to assert that under such a system the crimes of Catholics and Protestants against each other should be weighed in the same scales of gold; neither theory nor practice warrant me to say so.[59]

O'Connell decided to put Wellesley to the proof. On 11 July he addressed a public letter to the lord lieutenant asking that he 'administer' (that is, enforce) the law next day by prohibiting the traditional Orange celebration of 'the Twelfth' in Dublin: 'it is a direct provocation to tumult.'[60] Wellesley attempted to compromise. He would not enjoin, but pleaded with the Orange leaders to forgo their marches. The appeal was contemptuously dismissed.

Wellesley had failed the test. But where was O'Connell to go from there? Fortunately, since this was a question to which there was no ready answer, he was engrossed for the remainder of the summer and most of the autumn of 1822 by domestic matters; most of September and October were spent with his family, then 'in exile' in France. Still more fortunately, just after his return to Dublin, his remonstrance of 11 July to Wellesley was crowned with a belated success. The lord lieutenant prohibited the secondary Orange celebration of 4 November (to commemorate William III's birth date) and enforced his prohibition by a military guard about William's statue. It was the Orange Society's first public rebuff since its formation, the first official rejection of the implicit Orange assumption of supremacy − with corresponding outrage on the one side and triumph upon the other. Orange demonstrations of increasing virulence against Wellesley followed, culminating in a riot in the Theatre Royal on 14 December 1822 (perhaps the play, She Stoops to Conquer, was ironically appropriate!) in which the lord lieutenant's box was pelted by Orange hooligans with fruit, an empty quart bottle and the timber of a watchman's rattle.

Nothing could have suited O'Connell better in his role of true-blue constitutionalist. He led the way in virtuous Catholic indignation at the Orange lèse-majesté, and could make common cause upon the issue not only with liberal Protestants but even with the moderate Irish tories. A 'mixed' aggregate held in Dublin on 20 December to express sympathy with Wellesley and abhorrence of the 'outrage' was addressed by peers and members of the Commons, knights and barristers, Protestants and Catholics, indifferently. 'There never was such a meeting in Ireland', O'Connell reported. 'The Exchange was crowded to the greatest excess. I was the only person who made himself heard throughout. There was the greatest unanimity and good feeling, and the Orange faction were branded with deserved reprobation. Not a human being to defend the miscreants or to say one word in their favour.' Next day he wrote to Mary, 'You may imagine what a curious revolution it is in Dublin when the Catholics are admitted to be the only genuine loyalists. For the first time has this truth reached the Castle.'[61] On Christmas Eve he crowned it all when, as a member of the sympathizing 'Committee of 21' and in court dress, he waited upon the lord lieutenant in St Patrick's Hall.

All this may have been magnificent but it was certainly not war for an agitator. There were of course profound psychological satisfactions in even the temporary disgrace of his hereditary enemies and his own entry into viceregal favour. But the course of Emancipation had not been and was not being advanced an inch. Instead the old whig-liberal confidence trick was being played upon the Catholics once again. Thomas Wyse's sombre judgement upon the 'experiment' of 1821–2 seems irrefutable:

> It was then, if ever since the first formation of their committees, that the Catholics had attained that perfect state of 'temperance and moderation', which has been so frequently recommended to them by friend and enemy. Nothing contributed to break it for two entire years: neither petition, nor remonstrance, nor speech, nor assembly of any note, was heard of. The entire body seemed to have relapsed into their ancient sluggishness, and to have surrendered their cause to the arbitration of blind chance, or the choice and convenience of their enemies. It was a wretched and successless policy.[62]

The Christmas Eve levee-ing at Dublin Castle was the apogee of O'Connell's 'purple' or romantic phase: in one form or another it had endured since he had taken up the cause of Spanish American liberation in July 1819. The other O'Connell, the cold political calculator, would however very soon re-emerge. Within a very few days, possibly even on Christmas Day itself, he was to project the new Catholic Association. Ultimately, this would spell the doom not only of the *ancien régime* in Ireland but also of historic toryism in Great Britain.

CHAPTER 9

Reaping Whirlwinds

1817–27

I

Mary O'Connell fell into ill-health in the late spring of 1817. The cause is unknown. It might have been some bronchial or pulmonary weakness; there were numerous, though vague, references to her coughs and chest troubles over the years. Alternatively, she might have been paying the penalty for the stresses of 1815 and 1816 and many pregnancies; she had borne nine children, seven of them surviving, already, and was thirty-seven years of age when confined with the youngest, Daniel, only six months before. There was no hint of a collapse of health in her letters to O'Connell while he was on circuit in March and April 1817. She wrote of the usual things – their children, Dublin prices, her pride in the reports of his successes – and was solicitous only for him. On 9 April she laid her 'positive *commands* upon you not to go in a *steam*boat while in Cork. I read this morning [of] a melancholy accident which occurred in England.'[1] Two days later she wrote again to Cork,

> I wish to God you could contrive to get out of court for a quarter of an hour during the middle of the day to take a bowl of soup or a snack of some kind. Surely, though you may not be able to spare time to go to a tavern, could not James [his servant] get anything you wished for from the Bar mess at your lodgings, which is merely a *step* from the Court-house? Do, my love, try to accomplish *this* for really I am quite unhappy to have you fasting from an early hour in the morning until nine or ten o'clock at night. I wish I was with you to make you take care of yourself. I am quite sure there is not another barrister on your circuit would go through half the fatigue you do without taking necessary nourishment.[2]

O'Connell replied in a joking, untroubled strain, 'You order me at once out of steamboats and into cook shops. Now the fact is that I like steamboats much and hate cook shops excessively. So darling, darling, sweetest love, let us compromise our quarrel and have neither the one nor the other.'[3] But upon his return to Dublin, in late April 1817, he discovered that Mary was in serious distress and on 7 May he asked his brother James to sound Hunting Cap 'with respect to getting a few hundreds to pay the expense' of Mary's taking the waters at Clifton and also about lodging the boys with him at Derrynane.[4] It seems clear that Mary had hidden her illness from O'Connell while he was on circuit. He wrote to her a little later, 'You *never deceived* me save about your health and it now, I may say, corrodes my soul to think that you may still imagine you were doing me a kindness by concealing from me the exact state of your health.'[5]

Despite Hunting Cap's deafness to James's '*strong hints*' as to the 'few hundreds' (he was, however, willing to receive the boys at Derrynane), O'Connell took Mary to Clifton immediately. It was a characteristic O'Connell exercise. Mary was accompanied by Miss Gaghran, the governess, a maidservant and her five youngest children, and no sooner was she installed in lodgings than she set off to sample the delights of marketing in Bristol – it was her first experience of another country. 'Really', she told O'Connell on 12 June, 'the exertion I am obliged to make here is of infinite use to me. The quiet, still life I lead at home cannot be conducive to my health.'[6] Correspondingly, O'Connell and she had considered her moving to the south of France for the remainder of 1817. But in this scheme her health and the 'finishing' of her children may have been intermingled, for she now told him, 'If I continue to improve in health as I have since I came here, a journey to France will be unnecessary until the time arrives when it will be an advantage to my boys and girls to spend some time in France. Then, darling, you will be on the Bench and a *little* more your own master than you are at present.'[7]

Two months later the French excursion seemed likely to come about. Mary's health worsened again and her Clifton doctor recommended removal to Toulon or its neighbourhood – he was decidedly against Toulouse! Apparently this advice was accepted; on 11 August 1817 Mary spoke of her '*banishment* (if I may call it so)' as fixed, and canvassed such details as whether or not to take the family carriage to France.[8] But when O'Connell joined her at Clifton in late September, he found that 'Mary is daily recovering and has not, the doctor assures me, one single consumptive symptom.' France was no longer necessary; instead, the family would 'settle for the winter in a warm part of Devonshire'.[9] Whether they ever got farther south than Bath, where they re-established themselves during October, is unknown. So also is the date of their return to Ireland, although it must have been before 3 March 1818, when O'Connell wrote to Mary in Dublin from his first station on circuit, 'I am dying with anxiety to hear from you. I left you with a cough and such weather was never invented as we have had since.'[10]

No matter how he reasoned as to the necessity of Mary's absence, O'Connell could not, he had written on first leaving her in Clifton, shake off 'the sensation of loneliness'.[11] It certainly was, as she replied, 'a new thing to you to be at home without your family';[12] even the elder boys were now at boarding school. In his isolation, his irritated fancy went the length of jealousy of a remote connection, Lieutenant John O'Connell, whom Mary had met in Bristol. 'Laugh at me, darling', he wrote on 24 June 1817,

it is what I deserve for being unhappy without any cause. Yet it will perhaps surprise you more when I tell you the absurdity of my reason. It was that in one of your letters you said he was very *respectful* and in another *very kind*. Now what train of thought was it that could put the word *respectful*? How could it be necessary to think of that! Thus, my own darling Mary, did I torture myself asking foolish questions – and then your consulting me about asking him to dine. Darling heart, you see what a very silly and foolish fellow your husband is, and indeed I am quite ashamed of my folly but could not get cured of it completely without thus exposing it to you.[13]

He threw himself into work – or rather work in unprecedented quantities was thrown at him, quite apart from the arrears which had built up while he was settling his wife in Clifton; these placed 'such a load on me as I certainly never before sustained.'[14] His debts goaded him forward; he claimed that he was getting through the O'Leary bills 'constantly and fast',[15] characteristically asserting that he would be so free of obligations by the following spring that '*even you* [Mary] could not be alarmed'.[16] Although the establishment of a second household in England must have greatly swelled the outgoings, O'Connell may actually have gained financially from his lonely state and the consequent accretions of time for professional labour.

There were perhaps some small compensations for the lamentable division of the family. O'Connell paid at least two, and more likely three, visits to England during 1817; and although these did nothing to raise his opinion of the English and positively enflamed his resentment of his own exclusion from Parliament, they also introduced him to a considerable number of leading public men and useful go-betweens. On quite another tack, his long separation from Mary called forth her most serene and happy tributes to him ever, as husband and father, and possibly as lover too. On 14 July 1817 she wrote from Clifton,

in existence, I don't think there is such a husband and father as you are and always have been. Indeed, I think it quite impossible there could, and if the truest and tenderest affection can repay you, believe me that I feel and bear *it* for you. In truth, my own Dan, I am always at a loss for words to convey to you how I love and doat of you. Many and many a time I exclaim to myself, 'What a happy creature am I! How grateful should I be to Providence for bestowing on me such a husband!' and so indeed I am.[17]

A week later, she added,

you can have no idea how constantly you are the subject of mine and my children's conversation . . . In your children's opinion and in mine there is not such another man in the world as you are. When a handsome man, a good husband or a good father are mentioned, Ellen and Kate look with such anxiety for my answer to their question, 'Mamma, sure he is not half so handsome or so good as my father?' My reply is just what they wish, and it speaks the real sentiments of my heart.[18]

O'Connell's confidence that he would work through his debts quickly proved quite unjustified. The spring of 1818 brought not the release from bondage which he had anticipated but fresh embarrassments. On 12 March 1818 Mary reported to him on circuit that 'a good many bank notices' had arrived; on 18 May he importuned a cousin who had delayed the repayment of £300, exclaiming that he was 'very grievously pressed for money this day . . . it is the actual want of the money makes me thus urge you.'[19] Like Mr Sowerby in *Framley Parsonage*, 'When he wanted to raise the wind, everything was so important; haste and superhuman efforts, and men running to and fro with blank acceptances in their hands, could alone stave off the crack of doom.'[20] A little over a year later O'Connell applied to his uncle, the General, in Paris to be relieved of interest payments on a borrowed £3600; he had already persuaded his brother James to lend him £800 from a trust which the General had set up for the young O'Connells; and he was soon to wangle £1700 from James and his other brother John from their interest in these moneys. The General, as he told O'Connell in strictest confidence, had stripped himself of all but £750 of his annual income in order to provide for his nephews' younger sons (including O'Connell's children). It was these savings which O'Connell was now attempting – with some success – to bleed. In a letter of 30 July 1819, written in French so that Mary could not read it, the General refused to forgo the interest on his £3600 because this would, to some extent, defeat the purpose of his own abnegation. But he offered to share with O'Connell 'the income [£750 p.a.] which I have reserved for myself if your situation demands the help of your friends'[21] – provided that O'Connell too made sacrifices. He might have spared his ink. Neither the £3600 nor any future interest on it was ever paid; and a plan which the poor General drew up for O'Connell's financial redemption made it all too clear that he had no notion of the magnitude of his nephew's debts. In desperate straits, O'Connell seems to have lost any lingering scruples over the despoiling of his own relations, from honourable elderly uncles down to babes-in-arms. Yet none ever broke with him, whatever the provocation: they wept, but they gave.

By this time O'Connell was beginning to be faced with the problem of his elder sons' careers. Two years before, on 3 August 1817, the headmaster of Clongowes Wood College, their boarding school, assessed the boys in terms remarkably similar to those employed by Dr Stapylton in relation to O'Connell and his brother at St Omer twenty-five years before:

> Of Maurice I have everything good to say. His improvement in classical knowledge has been very considerable. If *you* and we can form him to steady habits of application, we shall get him to do anything. God has given him very ample talents. Exertion and cultivation will make him a solid and conspicuous scholar. Of Morgan I cannot say so much. Less talented, he wants application which alone could supply for the deficiency. His dispositions are good; generous, bold and independent. If he had industry he would be no inconsiderable character.[22]

Unfortunately for himself perhaps, Maurice seemed tailor-made to follow in his father's footsteps, as lawyer and public man. But Morgan, like his dead uncle Maurice, seemed fit only for the army – that is, within the range of gentlemanly occupations. When however O'Connell applied to the General in 1819 to put Morgan 'into the French service' he was brusquely refused: this course, the General responded, was 'neither practical nor desirable';[23] he added (a hopeless recipe) that Morgan needed at least four or five years of close application to military studies if he wished to make the army his career. By now, O'Connell was well into the next stage of family concern: how on earth to settle seven children in the world.

II

The staple of O'Connell's income remained the bar. His professional earnings probably exceeded £5000 per annum in the decade and a half 1816–29. True, his fee book suggests a lower figure. But the returns recorded there may well have excluded such highly profitable but peripherally legal work as elections and arbitrations. This would account for such a discrepancy as that presented in 1827 when his fee book registered his income at £4868 for the year but he himself observed on 4 December that 'my [legal] income is now a fine one, upwards of £7,000 a year'.[24] However careless his money dealings may have been, his money calculations were generally meticulous. Except in the management of his own affairs, he was a first-rate man of business.

Such prodigious earnings demanded prodigious labour. By 1822 O'Connell was working a sixteen- or seventeen-hour day, punctuated only by meals and his walk to and from the Four Courts. On 14 May of that year, he told Mary, then in France, 'My trade goes on flourishingly. All the rest of the Bar are complaining but I never was doing so much. In your absence I have nothing to take up a moment of my time but law. I rise at half after four, breakfast at a ¼ after eight, dine at a quarter after five and go to bed between nine and ten.'[25] He had 'an alarm clock fixed between four and half after four';[26] he had also installed a shower bath which completed the awakening. Nor could he have generated his great volume of business — it must never be forgotten that he could still charge only junior's fees — if he had confined himself to his own circuit or circles. Increasingly, he accepted invitations to go 'special' on other circuits; and when a major case, with corresponding rewards, drew him to Galway, Wexford, Sligo or Armagh, he usually took additional local briefs to 'top and tail' his visit. It was of course also politically valuable to spread his knowledge of and influence in fresh fields. Correspondingly, he had to attract Protestant, including many politically hostile Protestant, clients in order to earn so largely. The bulk of the remunerative civil briefs, in commercial, trust, succession, land title and crim. con. suits, derived from the Ascendancy, those with the lion's share of the nation's property, wealth and leisure. Once O'Connell's reputation was established, Irish Protestants seem to have had no hesitation in employing him in such cases. He was of course practically excluded from crown, corporation and specifically 'Orange' business; but otherwise his professional capability was taken to outweigh his offensive or dangerous public conduct. When Peel, in his celebrated reply to a denigrator of O'Connell as a 'low, broguing fellow', declared that there was no one whom he would prefer as counsel in a case in which he had heavy interest, he was probably repeating an opinion common in the class which he supported during his Irish days.

Twenty years' unremitting practice of the law had also shaped O'Connell's mental habits and forensic patterns. It is hardly too much to say that it gives the key to his style of politics. Obviously, the capacities to work closely for long hours, to 'get up' subjects (or rather as much of them as the case demanded) at great speed, to decide instaneously which line of action to adopt and to marshal the appropriate words and arguments as if by second nature, constituted a politician's no less than a barrister's stock in trade. At a deeper level, the lawyer's ineluctable concern with the correctness of forms and formulae, with legal effects rather than moral stances or satisfactions, was already engrained in O'Connell's politics. So also was the advocate's extravagance in framing claims combined with moderation in settling for returns; opening pleas were tactical devices and by no means irreducible demands. Similarly, O'Connell's was a 'verdict mentality', so to say. In one special sense, his politics were passive. He was inured to adverse or otherwise unpleasing decisions being handed down by an exterior authority; only momentarily would these depress or irritate him. There were always other cases, other means. This strange amalgam of acquiesence and resilience, of cutting losses and planning their recoupment – the professional's carapace hardened by the years of practice – was the very stamp of his political behaviour.

O'Connell had also been a landed proprietor since 1809. It was not a role which brought him much satisfaction or reward at first. Perforce, he was an absentee; he was also soon overtaken by agrarian hard times. After 1815 agricultural prices, and *pari passu* rents, fell and remained depressed. His Uncle Daniel was probably close to the mark when he wrote to O'Connell in 1819, 'The income from your lands which was more than £2,000 has presumably fallen to £1,500',[27] and there was worse to come in the immediately succeeding seasons. Moreover, O'Connell seems to have regarded the returns from rents almost as a species of pin money. A great deal of it was earmarked to pay small pensions to former servants or dependants, or the interest on the numerous small debts which he ran up in Kerry. 'Your income by lands', his brother James told him in 1822, the blackest year of all, 'is so cut up by interest of money, annuities to poor relations and to fosterers that, in the best of times, you have but little *to actually touch*.'[28]

O'Connell was a 'traditional' Irish landlord, easy-going, negligent and unimproving. He certainly set his economic rationalism aside when it came to his own fields and tenants. Instead, he followed, if only from habit or as the line of least resistance, a latter-day form of the old clan system, whereby the maintenance of customary positions within the whole complex was placed well ahead of the maximization of profits for anyone. The local repute and responsibility of the O'Connells, as Catholic semi-gentry for several generations, deepened the tribal-feudal character of the relationship with the tenantry. In this regard, as in many others, O'Connell's stance and outlook strikingly resembled Walter Scott's. Typically, O'Connell selected friends or relatives to act as his land agents. His first steward proper, his cousin Myles McSwiney, was amiable but inefficient. He also 'borrowed' heavily from the collected rents, and O'Connell was very lucky to recoup the arrears of several years in 1820 and 1821 when McSwiney received the dubious windfalls of a part in a local road contract and a share in a smuggled cargo of tobacco. Ever the candid friend, James told O'Connell, 'You are yourself much to blame [for McSwiney's poor stewardship] in not having devoted a few hours once a year when you came to Iveragh to look into your affairs.'[29] It was also typical of O'Connell to have delayed the collection of rents in 1820 by his negligence in dealing with requests to set the level of abatements, and to have left it to his brother to announce the change himself when he decided that James should replace McSwiney in 1821. In this last case, however, James rebelled, writing to O'Connell on 19 April 1821, 'I perceive you never said a word to him about your taking your affairs out of his hands, and, until you call on him *either by letter or otherwise* to hand me over his books, I cannot think of calling for them. Did I do so, the entire odium of removing him would be thrown on me which you must admit is not fair or reasonable.'[30]

The 1821 harvest and low prices of 1819–21 brought falling rents and eventually agrarian disturbances in their train. It was James who bore the brunt of O'Connell's proprietorial difficulties. There is no direct evidence on O'Connell's reaction to the sudden spread of 'swearing in' and secret societies (indifferently referred to as White-boys and Rockites at the time) in Iveragh towards the end of 1821. But we can confidently infer his wholehearted opposition from his proposal of January 1822 to set up a yeomanry corps of his own to maintain order in the barony. Hunting Cap opposed his nephew's scheme as both unnecessary and likely 'to protect and cover the smuggling of tobacco . . . a circumstance which speedily would be represented to Government and would of course bring a blemish on you'.[31] James agreed, adding scornfully, 'who in the name of God were *to compose it?*'[32] James did however ask O'Connell to procure 'a military party' to pacify the district: '*every peasant in the Barony of Iveragh is a Whiteboy*', he told him on 18 January 1822. '*Those nightly legislators* profess great respect for the O'Connell family [but] I hope soon to be able to *prove* to some of the leaders by lodging them in Tralee jail, how well I wish them.'[33]

O'Connell neglected even to reply to this appeal, and James indignantly complained that he seemed 'quite indifferent' to the risk which James ran in taking up residence in the centre of his brother's property and assisting in putting down the foremost of the 'atrocious blood-thirsty rabble who have combined against everything that is respectable in the country'. James even 'calculate[d] on the probability' of assassination. This may have been no more than a characteristic gloomy and irritable flourish, for in the same breath he preened himself upon his achievement in stamping out 'the *mania of Whiteboyism*' in Iveragh.[34] In fact, despite the rhetoric of stern repression which he employed, James adopted, successfully, a conciliatory policy, offering a general amnesty through 'the Chapels' in return for the abandonment of conspiracies, and expressing his private relief at the escape of some of those whom he had set out to apprehend.

Had O'Connell, by default at least, abandoned James to his fate in Kerry? He had certainly failed to provide even moral support. But he might well have claimed, in mitigation, such a lifelong knowledge of the neighbourhood and its inhabitants (James often specified particular farmers, labourers and their sons in his reports) as to feel no real alarm. He cannot be acquitted of farming out his work and responsibilities as a landlord, and giving only the light of a genial presence on rare occasions in return for rents. But, even with James as agent, he and his tenantry were far from being in the sort of adversary or confrontationist relationship prescribed by the new political economy. Doubtless, he was not in the least surprised at the ultimate accommodation of abatement on either side, acquiescence in arrears of rent and further huckstering as to what the distressed smallholders really could afford to pay. While one form of Irish landlordism headed for guerilla war in 1822, another, exemplified by the O'Connells, generated violence of words and postures rather than blood or change.

III

By the spring of 1822 O'Connell's affairs were in so desperate a state that his home in Dublin was broken up in an effort to economize seriously at last. Initially, he hoped to rent his house in Merrion Square for at least £365 per annum, as well as sell off his carriage and horses; the letting failed, but at least the establishment was reduced. It may well have been 'the dreadful fall in the times' (as he termed the drying up of rents) which proved the last straw and precipitated O'Connell's decision, for as early as 11 March 1822 he sent instructions to Mary to bargain for her passage and those of her five youngest children and servants to Bordeaux. Possibly the result dismayed him, as he consulted James a little later about their moving to Tralee instead. James's reply was both sour and trenchant.

> Whether you will better your situation much by taking J[ames] Connor's house and fixing yourself in Tralee where *you must keep an open house for all your family*, I will not attempt to decide but I trust you have made your entire family acquainted with your real situation. If they and you are serious in wishing to conform yourselves to your embarrassed circumstances, the South of France would in my opinion be the place to fix them. However of this ye are the best judges.[35]

Even O'Connell seems to have resented candour of this exceptional degree, and a temporary coolness sprang up between the brothers. James was replaced, as O'Connell's agent, by John Primrose, junior, and for a time sneered at as closefisted in O'Connell's correspondence with his wife.

In the end, however, the O'Connells did opt for removal to the south of France, and the hire of a small vessel to take the entire company direct from Dublin to Bordeaux. Meanwhile, O'Connell was 'hoarding gold' to frank the expedition, and pointing to silver linings which few but he could have discerned. He assured Mary that they would be 'splendidly independent' if, as now seemed 'highly likely', they could clear their debts altogether before the 'old gentleman' died.[36] He admitted to his daughter Kate that their parting was 'a cruel thing', but added immediately that 'We must in these dreadful times practise economy', and that she and her sisters would gain immeasurable polish during their exile. 'I expect to join you', he concluded, 'in the vintage which is the gayest time of the year, and I flatter myself that the time will not be the less gay for the arrival of your father.'[37]

Before Mary departed for the Continent, however, the strain of money-raising and of the impending separation told suddenly upon O'Connell. The financial tight-rope which he had left Mary to walk in Dublin became ever more dangerous; on 2 or 3 April 1822 she paid a bill to Hickson earlier than he had intended, with disastrous consequences for his self-devised credit 'system'; he despatched (his own later terms) a 'cruel and ferocious letter ... a barbarous one unbecoming a gentleman or a Christian'[38] and then, horror-struck, followed it immediately with a plea for mercy. Mary proved unresentful, and O'Connell poured forth his relief and gratitude. 'If you had a mind, my darling heart's love,' he wrote on 8 April, 'to wring your husband's very soul you would not have done it more effectually than by writing the sweet, gentle, uncomplaining letter I got from you last night ... I find that my own darling thinks she was wrong merely because her husband unjustly accused her.' We can gauge the near-hopelessness of his pecuniary entanglements (as well as of Mary's difficulties as financial agent) by the conclusion of this letter of penitence.

I perceive by a letter I got last night from James Sugrue that Dr Wilson's bill lies over unpaid. Let it be so, darling, for a few days longer. You have therefore got from me in half-notes between you and James Sugrue £200 and he has got £100 from Roger [O'Connell's clerk] so that, as you gave him the other £50, you will have only to add £12.10.0 to it. Then, giving your mother £15 you will still have £172.10.0 in hands. Take out of that £42.10.0 for house expenses, it will leave you £130 out of which you will, before this reaches you, pay tomorrow £40 – Eyre's bill – and the day you get this £50 Higgins' bill and you will have £40 towards meeting the bills due on Thursday. I believe my letter of yesterday was erroneous in supposing that Eyre's £40 would not be due until Wednesday. I hope this error will not occasion a protest, as in the list I sent I marked down a £40 bill as due the 9th. I will, please God, send you a banker's bill for at least £200. The bills which are to be paid are 9th £40 to Eyre, 10th £50 to Higgins, 11th, £58 *with interest* to Mr Mahon – same day, 11th, £138.10.0 to Dr Wilson, a *fresh* bill not the one already due, 15th £69.19.0 to Roose, 25th £75 Clongowes Wood payable, I think, to Elliot, 28th £50 to Cooper.[39]

On 2 May 1822 Mary, six of her seven children (Morgan accompanied them as protector) and two maidservants sailed from Dublin for Bordeaux. O'Connell was grief-stricken as he moved about the empty house; even the remaining servants had departed, although he partly reconstituted the establishment later on. In his remorse, he cried out, 'My love, do you not now reproach that loose and profligate waste of money to many and many an ungrateful and undeserving object which makes it necessary for us to separate. No, my love, you do not reproach it but my own heart does, and the misery I now endure is nothing but the punishment I deserve.' As the days passed without word from Bordeaux, he began to fear a shipwreck. 'What a vile wretch [I am]!', he exclaimed on 18 May. 'It was for my own follies and idle gratifications that I made it necessary to separate from you and my children.'[40] Three weeks passed before he heard of their safe arrival, and a fortnight more before Mary could try to still his self-accusations. 'My own, own Dan, do not fret . . .', she wrote from Bordeaux,

> You are, heart, much more religious than your Mary and from the moment it was deemed necessary for me to come with my family to France, I put on the resolution to bear it like a Christian. Do not, my own love, make me unhappy by those reproaches you cast upon yourself . . . You never deserved any from me. You have been the best and most beloved of husbands and you will continue such to the last hour of my life.[41]

It was true, as his next letter showed, that O'Connell had become more 'religious' than the remainder of his family. Whether his piety had been growing since 1816 or (more likely) developed further with his troubles, he might fairly have been described as a *devôt* by 1822. He had subjected himself to a regular spiritual director, Rev. Patrick Coleman, whose charming spiritual principle '*beaucoup de piété, beaucoup de gaieté*'[42] he tried to fulfil by being quiet, cheerful and conscientious in adversity. But he also 'practised' his Catholicism with unusual rigour. Persistently, he urged weekly, or at least monthly, communion upon Mary and his elder children when they were abroad; incessantly he fretted over Maurice's negligent attitude towards the sacraments. A long-range battle between him and his wife over his unremitting Lenten fasts ended only when he told her bluntly,

> you say I gratify you in everything else, and are you not therefore bound in common *honesty* to admit I would have great pleasure to gratify in that particular also if I had not that which you will pardon me for calling a higher duty, namely, my obedience to the Church? . . . surely, dearest, I have a *command* to fast if I am able to do it . . .[43]

He was warm in supporting the Catholic cause in current theological controversy and eager in pressing the case for miracles, supposedly flowing from the intercession of the pious Prince Hohenlohe, in 1823. Although he never ceased to revile them as despots, he even found merit in the French Bourbons' support of religion:

With such a people [as the French] nothing will do but the strong government of the Bourbons, and while the Bourbon government is repressing their political tendency to crime they are also fortunately and, I hope providentially, engaged in the restoration of that pure Catholic worship which alone contained genuine Christianity. The churches will soon be all filled with zealous and active clergy . . .[44]

The voluminous correspondence between O'Connell and his wife during 1822–4 also lifts the curtain on his literary taste in middle life. His circuit letters over many years make it clear that he kept up well with the current quarterlies and monthly magazines, as well as the virtually mandatory law reports and daily papers. But, in the early 1820s at least, Scott's novels were his leading pleasure. Fortunately, they were being published with amazing frequency. O'Connell snapped each up as it appeared, and even his iron regime fell to pieces until he had read it all; he stayed up all one night to finish *Peveril of the Peak*, at 4.45 a.m. Scott struck many chords – sentimental, romantic, costume-historical – in O'Connell; besides he was, to contemporaries, the absolute master of the adventure story. O'Connell also read Byron extensively, even if he agreed with the public at large that his current poetic dramas were a failure. But Moore was his chief delight. 'Tell Ellen', he wrote on 27 December 1822, 'that Moore's *Loves of the Angels* is come out . . . It is short, a mere trifle for such a poet, but exquisitely sweet and not stained with a single indelicate thought . . . In spite of the *Edinburgh Review* Moore is the very prince of poets.' In this case, however, O'Connell had been softened by Moore's description of a separated wife and husband which seemed to him to presage love's renewal.

> All this they bear but not the less
> Have moments rich in happiness
> Blest meetings after many a day
> Of widowhood past far away
> When the loved fair again is seen.[45]

The first nine months of the O'Connells' sojourn on the Continent created no tension between Mary and O'Connell. He was however uneasy when they settled initially at Pau, which he supposed, correctly, would prove dry and dusty in the summer; and when he joined his family there on 18 September 1822, he arranged their removal to Tours, where considerable colonies of English and Irish economic refugees, like themselves, resided and where competent masters for the children could be had. Three weeks in Pau were quite enough to revive O'Connell's Francophobia – 'My opinion of France and Frenchmen is not raised by a near inspection.'[46] This animus even increased in violence after his return to Ireland. 'Oh how I hate France', he wrote from Dublin on 6 March 1823, 'I hate it in all moods and tenses, past, present and to come.'[47] Part of his distaste derived from the fact that France was comparatively distant and inaccessible: already it was almost five months since he had last seen his family. He now wished them to remove to the south of England – Exeter was the tentative choice of place – which he could visit more cheaply and more often. 'I am all alive to having you so much nearer me', he went on, 'I was even thinking of getting a furnished house in Kerry, but certainly Devonshire is much better. It is warm and genial too in winter and it would be a seasoning of you on your way home.'[48]

Initially O'Connell planned to meet Mary's party in Paris in August 1823, spend two or three weeks sightseeing there (earlier he had sketched in a possible Italian tour – so much for the Continent as a desperate measure of economy!) and finally lead everyone to Exeter. But when France intervened militarily in Spain, and war with Britain seemed a possibility, he took alarm and pressed for an earlier and more precipitate departure. By the beginning of May 1823 he had – with the utmost difficulty – gathered enough money for the journeys, fixed Paris for the rendezvous about the 20th of that month, rearranged his case-list and even booked his passage on the packet.

It was at this stage that things began to awry between O'Connell and his wife. Mary refused to uproot herself abruptly, and, while still maintaining his ritualistic obeisance to her better judgment, O'Connell responded with a quite uncharacteristic display of malice and self-pity. His reply of 22/3 May 1823 included a reference to a woman whose 'husband should perceive by a thousand little attentions and those manners which sweeten life that his wife was rendered the better woman by embracing a better religion [Catholicism]', and concluded, 'I wish my girls to read more books than you do, sweetest.'[49] Mary was acutely sensitive to criticism, especially of her social origins and education, and a long absence, among the emigrés, had rendered her more peremptory, more ambitious for her children and perhaps also more extravagant. As early as 20 April 1823 she had rejected a proposal from O'Connell, doubtless designed to reduce fresh expenditure, in this decisive, not to say uncivil, manner: 'Now, love, to answer you on the subject of Morgan's becoming an attorney. I totally and entirely disapprove of it. It is a profession I never wished for any son of mine.'[50] She got her way: Morgan was soon launched (through the General's influence) upon the expensive career of Austrian cavalry officer. As was to be expected with her current disposition, Mary fiercely resented O'Connell's letter of 22/3 May. Her reply has not survived, but we can guess its tenor from his complaint of its 'air of coldness and . . . vexation'. He affected surprise that Mary was 'angry with me about what I said of my girls' reading as if I had meant to offend . . . Forgive me, darling, I will avoid such topics in future. How bitterly do I regret that I placed myself in a situation to be compelled to separate from my family.'[51]

Not that he had many honeyed words for the remainder of his family about this time. His sole companion, Maurice, was a daily irritation, as both vacuous and idle. John (his erstwhile *great great* favourite) 'I perceive by your letter, is turning out badly . . . I work fifteen or sixteen hours out of the 24. I . . . only ask him to work 5 or 6.'[52] 'Even my Kate I am sometimes jealous of. My Betsey never loved her father much and I scolded my Nell so much about growing fat that I suppose she resents it.'[53] 'I wish Kate would write to me but no, love, leave them all in that respect to themselves.' The truth was probably, as he said himself, that he needed pity: 'so long separated from all my heart holds dear . . . I feel that weariness of the heart which the Swiss experience when they think of their fond home.'[54] Mary was merciful. Her letter of 12 June told him that he was in want of '*petting*'; and at that he melted. It was not the end of hurtful exchanges. Mary continued to see slights – generally of a social nature – in various later comments or proposals; and she was to fall into an acute fit of jealousy of Miss Gaghran, the girls' former governess whom she had always disliked, before the year ended. None the less, the worst was over; and on 13 July 1823 the old absurdly joyous, irresponsible and elastic O'Connell reappeared when he wrote of their impending reunion,

> I am excessively anxious that my own girls should see Paris thoroughly. I will, please God, spend three weeks there with you, myself. We will visit Versailles, St Cloud, etc. In short I will endeavour to make you all as happy as I possibly can. I anticipate with pleasure the joy of being with you to see that proud but filthy capital.[55]

The late spring and early summer of 1823 probably marked the nadir of the marriage. Perhaps menopausal depression was in part to blame; Mary was in her forty-fifth year and O'Connell in his forty-eighth. But beyond that each was grievously harassed and hardened by lonely cares. After six months apart, their traffic had begun to lose the smoothness of its flow, to miss or distort its customary signals. It seems to have been the prospect of coming together once again, however briefly, which suddenly cleared the paths.

IV

O'Connell found it unexpectedly difficult to join Mary in Paris. During 1822 he had regularly reported to her his success in reducing the load of bills and bonds, and called on her for reciprocal economy. But he was ominously silent about money for most of 1823. In fact, the year probably marked the nadir of his pecuniary as well as his marital affairs. At the beginning of September 1823 he still apparently needed £2000 cash to pay for his own journey to and the removal of his family from Paris and their re-establishment in England, and his sole hope, James, could be induced to join him in a new bond only to the extent of £1500. James had been 'shocked to perceive the state of embarrassment you are in'[56] – imprisonment for debt and the consequent interruption of his practice were looming on the horizon – and was correspondingly caustic about 'the plan of economy adopted by you with respect to your family . . . In the course of a few months they move from Dublin to Pau, from that to Tours, now they are in the most expensive part of Paris and will wind up by fixing their residence in England, the dearest country in Europe to live in.'[57] None the less, O'Connell continued to pursue James for the additional £500, for on 11 September 1823 James wrote again, 'I this evening received your voluminous letter of the 9th inst. and now, for *the third and last time, most solemnly declare* I will not give you the small sum I have in the Funds.' James was unusually gentle with O'Connell, naming him 'ever . . . a most affectionate brother' of whom his family had every reason to be proud, and acknowledging that nothing 'but the greatest distress' would have induced him to persist in his supplication. But he pointed out that the security which O'Connell offered was illusory and that there had never been a 'case of a man who [had] ruined and dissipated his own and his children's property, having too scrupulous a regard' for another's.[58]

Still O'Connell kept up his appeal, and five days later James capitulated with bitter self-reproach. 'I will join you', he wrote on 16 September,

> in another bond for the remaining £500 but I have on my knees bound myself by an oath, during the rest of my life never again to join you in bill, bond or note . . . and, further, I have solemnly sworn on my knees never to give you in any one year during my life any sum of money exceeding twenty

pounds. This oath I have taken without any evasion, equivocation or mental reservation.[59]

With this, O'Connell flung aside all cares. 'I have the happiness to tell you', he wrote gaily to Mary from Cork next day, 'that I have made satisfactory arrangements which will permit me to leave this either this evening or tomorrow morning at farthest before day. My heart is light and my spirits revived . . . Darling, all is well.'[60] It was almost enough to make one fall in love with ruin.

During October 1823 O'Connell settled his family in Southampton, not Exeter, probably to enable Maurice, who had joined Mary and was now entered at the Temple, to eat his dinners with comparative ease. For a time after her husband's return to Dublin, Mary thought that she was pregnant, and O'Connell expressed 'most painful disappointment' when he learned on 30 November that this was not so. Extraordinary as it may seem in a man almost sinking beneath the weight of a numerous and most costly family, the disappointment appears to have been heartfelt. More than once over the past five years, he had grieved that Mary was not expecting another child. Money was of course a more grievous worry than ever after his latest expedition. His rents were being paid again and in four weeks in November he earned an unprecedented £760. But his debts were still immense – '*at least* twenty thousand pounds', James estimated on 19 November. Maurice, already extravagant, especially in his tailor's bills, would henceforth cost even more; and a running battle between Denys Scully and O'Connell during the remainder of 1823 for the repayment of even half of the £2000 which O'Connell had borrowed in 1815 upon the faithful promise that it would be refunded within six months may be amusing for the ingenuity of O'Connell's evasions, but must – or at any rate should – also have been extremely wearing and embarrassing for the contestants. The rector of Clongowes attempted a similar, though more polite, dunning of O'Connell on account of the fees, not of O'Connell's own sons, but of two boys whose father had befriended Morgan in Columbia, and whose school charges O'Connell had grandly, impulsively, taken on himself to pay! His letters to Mary in Southampton were however more concerned with spiritual than financial anxieties – with, for example, injunctions to guard her daughters against 'mixed' marriages and to ensure that all received communion together on Christmas Day.

O'Connell's visit to his family for the New Year proved all too successful. Ardent exchanges followed between Mary and himself, and his children were showered with all his former language of extravagant affection. But this made the fresh parting on 15 January 1824 seem all the more painful and his daily round in Dublin all the more solitary and cheerless. 'How monotonous my life is', he wrote on 27 January,

> The history of one day is the story of all. I rose today at soon after five. I worked till a quarter after eight by the town [clock]. Then breakfast . . . Working then till a quarter before eleven. Then to court. There until near four . . . At four on my way home call at Milliken's [stationers], read the morning papers *for nothing*, then home. Strip off my *day dress*, put on night-shirt, morning gown, *old* wig and so work until a quarter after five by the town. Then dine. In my study again before half after six . . . and so work till this hour, half after nine. Thus in one day you have the history of the entire.[61]

Within a few days his resolution broke and he suddenly proposed that Mary and the children should settle in Killarney, where at least he could visit them more often and without additional travelling costs or the loss of professional income. He had evidently toyed with some such idea in the preceding November, for James had told him that quartering his family at Derrynane was out of the question: Hunting Cap was much too enfeebled to bear noise or bustle.

Mary found 'many objections' to the new scheme. First, 'the chiefest bar', her health would not stand the Kerry climate; Dublin was the only place in Ireland where she could be well 'for a long period'. Secondly, the girls would suffer if they were thrust, impoverished, into the society of an Irish country town; 'they should not appear in Ireland until they can do so as your daughters ought.' Next, 'there would be little saving . . . There would be an eternal *relay* of *cousins*.' Finally, O'Connell had 'a respectability to keep up . . . The world is unkind, and *they* would delight to think your embarrassments were such as to oblige you to send your family to live separate from you in the same Kingdom with you, whereas the delicacy of my health and the necessity of having Maurice in England for a few years is a sufficient reason for our living here.'[62] O'Connell bowed to this powerful reasoning, but meanwhile James had given his *nihil obstat* to a fresh plan, the return of the family to *Dublin*; and Mary (who had since been ravaged by her recollection of 'the melancholy strain' of O'Connell's letter of May 1823 'on the subject of my *then* objecting to quit' Tours)[63] now changed her mind and joyfully agreed to join O'Connell in their home once more. Dislike of England where as 'an Irish Catholic' she felt often snubbed or patronized may have helped to tilt the balance. But the basic reasons for her turnabout were the futility of their current mode of retrenchment and the prospect of an end at last to 'the bitterness of separation'.[64] Some sense of virtue was kept alive by her resolve to dismiss her housekeeper, reduce her establishment to four servants and forgo horses and a carriage upon her return.

It was now O'Connell's turn to waver and consider Mary's spending a further fifteen months or so in England (this time at Windsor) in the name of complete financial recovery. But his 'prudence' was of the crumbling kind, and even he must occasionally have realized that the debtless state would always be a mirage for the O'Connells. His first reaction to his wife's decision proved to be the lasting one: 'never was blooming bride so welcome to her husband's arms as my own own Mary [will be] to mine.'[65] So in May 1824 the entire entourage returned to the home which they had left two years before. O'Connell would probably have been better off had they simply stayed at home, and the economies adopted in 1824 could have been made quite as easily in 1822. But it had ever been the O'Connells' way to live dramatically; they would not have been comfortable walking except on stilts.

V

Hunting Cap had never ceased to be a factor in O'Connell's calculations. On 24 January 1823 he confessed to Mary that he had always counted on 'Uncle Maurice's succession as the means of paying off, and I went in debt on that speculation';[66] earlier he had prayed to be delivered from the 'great sin' of 'look[ing] to his death as a desirable event'.[67] The end came at last on 10 February 1825, with Hunting Cap enduring his long final illness with his customary dignity and fortitude, even composing his own epitaph 'least [sic] it be too fulsome'. Significantly, the epitaph declared that 'the chief ambition of his long and Prosperous life was to elevate an Ancient Family from unmerited and Unjust Oppression'.[68] His nephew might well have liked to appropriate these words for his own tombstone later on.

Apart from his landed property, Hunting Cap left £52,000 in cash, mortgages, overdue rents and other assets; and after some £6000 of rent arrears have been 'forgiven' at James's suggestion, each of the three brothers among whom the personalty had been equally divided received about £15,000. The land bequeathed to O'Connell (mostly as a life interest) raised his total rental income to £4000 per annum. Had he been the sole or principal heir, as Hunting Cap had originally intended, he would have been some £20–30,000 better off in cash, with the probable addition of more rental property. None the less he was very well endowed, and General O'Connell was at first confident that, having received over £20,000 recently from his two uncles and with an income of almost £10,000 a year (his profession averaging £6000 net), his nephew could not only clear his debts entirely but also put by 'with ease' £5000 annually for his children's benefit.

O'Connell also felt an initial surge of affluence. Immediately after the funeral, he set off for London to support a parliamentary bid for Emancipation, and remained there for three and a half months at a cost of 'upwards of £3000' in expenses and lost legal fees. (Just as the accident of O'Connell's solitary state in Dublin during 1823 and 1824 had enabled him to concentrate upon his supreme political work, the building of the Catholic Association, so the accident of Hunting Cap's death at that particular juncture enabled him to gain priceless direct political experience of Westminster and Whitehall.) In the teeth of James's warnings, he set about greatly enlarging and altering Derrynane which he had also inherited, thus releasing a fresh torrent of expenditure. He fixed his daughter Ellen's dowry at £5000, spread money about on charities and even bought a Kerry hooker to carry fish and other local produce by sea to his home in Dublin.

The first sign that he had overstretched himself appeared on his return from London. Towards the end of a letter which opened in his best reformed-Scrooge style – 'Let everything be snug and warm [at Derrynane] . . . I should delight to spend my Christmas there in old Iveragh festivity. Give us as many bedrooms as you can and, above all things, an excellent barrack room' – he asked, 'Have you made any sales of my stock or have the tenants sold any? I want money very, very much.'[69] Although the brothers made their final settlement of Hunting Cap's estate on 27 August 1825, this was followed by still more clamorous demands on Primrose; O'Connell even told him, on 29 October, to threaten tenants who were grossly in arrears with the non-renewal of their leases. Meanwhile, Mary had been left behind at Derrynane after the summer vacation of 1825 partly to act as quasi-overseer of building, but mostly as a measure of economy. 'Nobody need have a cold at Derrynane', her husband now informed her, 'unless *they* earn it for themselves.' He made it clear to her that they were deep in financial trouble once again. 'I am quite sick of being in debt', he wrote on 1 November, 'if I had but one or two years of strict economy I would be entirely out of debt and be able to pay Kate's fortune *on demand* . . . Only *help* me, darling, to get out of debt and then you will, as you always did, command every shilling I have in the world.'[70] The reference to Kate's dowry touched a tender spot. Mary had, as she owned on 4 December 1825, 'that feeling about me (it is pride I believe) . . . [that] I brought you no *fortune*';[71] she was, correspondingly, both proud of Ellen's £5000 and jealous of the precedent for her second daughter's sake. Mary was no romantic when it came to her daughters' marriages. 'Ellen has a good deal of good sense', she had written while betrothal negotiations were being conducted on her behalf earlier in the year, 'and though she likes Mr [Christopher] F[itz-Simon, whom she married soon after], should anything occur to put a stop to the business, she would be quite satisfied to accede to your wishes and mine.'[72] With such a maternal disposition, Mary was deeply concerned lest Kate's marriage-chances should be injured by O'Connell's renewed impecuniosity. 'You married Ellen at nineteen', she told him on 2 December 1825, 'and *why* should you not marry Kate at least as early? I am [?sorry] you were not able to reserve *her* fortune for I feel quite sure you will be soon called upon.'[73] Doubtless this concern explains Mary's willingness to be immured in Derrynane for half the year; in urging economy, O'Connell repeatedly dangled before her the carrot of accumulating Kate's dowry. Meanwhile the fending off of Scully even still continued: on 2 November 1825 O'Connell proposed a final series of five monthly notes to clear the balance of their 'account'!

Now that the *deus ex machina* of his inheritance from Hunting Cap had come and gone, he was more dependent than ever upon keeping up his professional earnings. This became difficult after 1824 as his political standing and commitments grew rapidly – to say nothing of the donations, subscriptions and free services expected of him as a leading public man. In fact, according to his fee book (this, as has been said, almost certainly excluded some of his legal earnings), his average annual income at the bar fell from £5286 in 1822–4 to £4850 in 1826–8. But the maintenance of so high an annual average in the second triennium – and the amount was rising significantly again year by year from 1825 to 1828 – probably represented a considerable increase in 'real productivity', for the time and energy which O'Connell could devote to law had been much reduced.

In the mid- and late-1820s he was at the zenith of his powers, with as much business and as high fees on offer as any junior counsel could possibly manage or command. The mature O'Connell was no ᵔpert of the courts – except when the bold dash seemed the safest tactic – but a painstaking and longheaded strategist. D. O. Madden, who was far from favourably disposed, reckoned that in an era when the Munster circuit was thronged with brilliant counsel,

> O'Connell ranked first among the first. His qualities as a professional have never, perhaps, been sufficiently noticed. Caution in conducting a case was his most prominent characteristic. He affected to be careless, but a more wary advocate never stood in a Court of Justice. Perhaps no great advocate ever had the same relish for the legal profession. O'Connell hunted down a case with the gusto of a Kerry fox-hunter in pursuit of Reynard.[74]

Another appraiser of the contemporary bar, J. R. O'Flanagan, considered his supreme quality to be 'oblivion of himself . . . he forgot everything around him, and thought only of bringing off his client victorious. No lust for oratorical display ever tempted him to make a speech dangerous to the party by whom he was retained . . . He was *par excellence* the safest advocate ever trusted with a case.'[75] O'Flanagan went on to compare him in terms of intellect, oratory and legal knowledge with all the other foremost barristers of his day, English as well as Irish, and while he judged some one of them to be his superior in each particular quality, he believed that none could match O'Connell in terms of their effective combination. But this was a precarious form of supremacy, when it came to income. As James kept reminding O'Connell in the 1820s, were he to die, or even to fall ill or suffer an accident or be arrested for debt, the flow of money would cease instantly, with his family left virtually resourceless. Even O'Connell eventually worried about some such catastrophe. He had reason to. On 5 May 1822, the 'father' of the Munster bar, the hero of scores of stories of mess wit and courtroom repartee, Jerry Keller, died suddenly, and penniless. 'He has left his family in dire distress . . .', O'Connell told Mary. 'I hope and trust the Bar will do something for them. I stirred the matter as much as I could this day in the Hall [of the Four Courts]. His children are real objects of compassion.'[76]

Perhaps, after all, happy families really are all the same in one particular sense – that their 'pattern' remains constant. From the start O'Connell intended the renovation of Derrynane to lead to domestic economizing. If Mary and the children still with her lived quietly, out of Dublin, for half the year, the savings should be considerable. Thus O'Connell wrote on 18 March 1826, 'All our buildings [at Derrynane] are going on gaily . . . I hope I will be able to prevail on my daughters to come down very, very early next summer. It would be a great object to me to get rid of £1000 of my debts during the next two terms.'[77] But the venture proved as counter-productive as the family's residence overseas. In the autumn of 1826 O'Connell, in reply to a request for money from Ellen's husband (presumably an instalment of her dowry was overdue), pleaded the building costs as a reason for his inability to comply. A year later he confessed to Mary, 'I laid out a foolish deal of money at Derrynane to practise the economy which we are now suffering under.'[78]

Suffering they certainly were. As before, O'Connell was driven to the ultimate desperate device of trying to get his hands upon his children's money. This time James refused to give him access to a new trust which the General had set up in 1823 for the benefit of O'Connell's younger sons. It would be, James declared, 'a breach of the most solemn promise I made our uncle'.[79] As in 1822–4, O'Connell repeatedly execrated his own folly and extravagance which were leading once more to prolonged – though much lesser – separations from Mary while she rusticated in Kerry. 'Sweetest love', he wrote to her from Dublin on 4 December 1827, when she was in her sixth consecutive month at Derrynane, 'I am most anxious to be with you and yet my affairs are so deranged that I do not know what to do.'[80] Four days later, he unwittingly summed up much of the dark side of their marriage in a passage which, for its pursuit of the will-o'-the-wisp, solvency, could have been penned (mutatis mutandis) any time over the past twenty years.

> How bitterly do I regret that I was not sooner more vigilant and attentive. There is in fact but one resource and that is strict and unremitting economy . . . I have borrowed much money since I came up [to Dublin in October] and so cleared my way for the present, and I am now labouring to make provision for the money so borrowed. What I want is to keep *all* my income for that purpose. One or, at the utmost, two years of my present economy would clear off all my debts and accumulate Kate's fortune. My duty would *then* be performed because all the rest would be easy. But, darling, why should I tease you with these croakings and yet into what bosom should I pour my sorrows but yours? To whom should I look for comfort, consolation and assistance but to you?[81]

But if their difficulties seemed perpetual, so did their solace. In 1825, in his fiftieth year, O'Connell told Mary, 'when you do condescend to write to me in terms of love you cannot imagine what *a drink of honey* these tender expressions are to me . . . but I have come to a time of life when it is not [?possible] that I should have a woman's love'.[82] She replied simply, as usual. 'Oh Dan, it is impossible for me to give you the smallest notion how beloved you are by me. Why should you speak of your age. . . ? I am for a woman much older.'[83]

CHAPTER 10

Four Years of Irish History

1823–6

I

Looking back from the heights of 1829, Sheil recalled Ireland on the eve of the formation of the Catholic Association in a passage of baroque magnificence:

> I do not exaggerate when I say that the Catholic question was nearly forgotten. No angry resolutions issued from public bodies; the monster abuses of the Church Establishment, the frightful evils of political monopoly, the hideous anomaly in the whole structure of our civil institutions, the unnatural ascendancy of a handful of men over an immense and powerful population . . . were gradually dropping out of the national memory . . . it was a degrading and unwholesome tranquillity. We sat down like galley-slaves in a calm. A general stagnation diffused itself over the national feelings. The public pulse had stopped, the circulation of all generous sentiment had been arrested, and the country was palsied to the heart.[1]

The background to the formation of the Association was almost two decades of near-fruitless exertion and manoeuvring by O'Connell. Between 1805 and 1808 he had struggled to the forefront of the Catholic movement and to induce it to petition and agitate. It had then been riven by class conflict, the veto issue, and the tactical choice of ingratiating itself by passivity or creating formidable pressure by agitation. By 1820 it was again practically at a standstill. In the following year, a new ploy, appeal to the crown coupled with conciliation of the Orange faction, was adopted; by 1822 it was apparent that this too had failed. George IV remained an opponent of concession, and the Irish tories had treated conciliation as a confession of weakness and determined to employ the discriminatory system more ruthlessly than ever. But Orange triumphalism proved in fact the chief precipitant of the Association. The secondary causes of its formation were the effects of time in diminishing the asperities of the veto controversies, and the disorders and renewed Whiteboyism of 1822 which had signalled the danger of loss of control over the peasant masses by both the clergy and the professional men.

At the beginning of January 1823 the long-alienated O'Connell and Sheil were reconciled at a dinner party at Glencullen, co. Wicklow. Whether as effect or cause of the reconciliation, they determined on a renewal of the Catholic movement. Not that their enthusiasm was equal: Sheil doubted whether the time was ripe and, like the other guests, discounted one part of O'Connell's proposal – that as well as full membership of the new society at one guinea per annum, there should be a category of associate members at a subscription of a penny a month. None the less Sheil joined O'Connell in appealing to the leading Catholics for support in the new venture. Some sixty responded in eating their way to cordiality at the initiating dinner at Dempsey's Tavern in Dublin on 25 April 1823; and two weeks later, after endorsement by an aggregate meeting, the Irish Catholic Association was formally instituted, with 'all such legal and constitutional measures as may be most useful to obtain Catholic emancipation' as its particular programme.[2]

The meaning of this programme was the first battleground within the Association. About one-quarter of the original membership was supplied by the nobility and gentry and they wished to limit discussion to the general question of Emancipation, and activity to preparing an annual petition for relief, after the old fashion. But O'Connell's initial purpose was to constitute a Catholic protective organization. As he told the aggregate meeting, the experiment in conciliation of 1821 had not only failed but was also proving dangerous. The masses would not remain passive under an Orange oppression which was virtually unopposed. Already disaffection and disorder were rife, evictions increasing and an additional police force and sectarian yeomanry brought into being. Without a Catholic body, how were the peasantry to be restrained from insurrection or warned against or protected from those who were goading them into crime? As a corollary, O'Connell aimed at raising the consciousness of the Catholic masses by ranging over the entire body of their grievances, and then using their rising and compacted anger as a lever. He had no intention of working immediately for Emancipation. Instead, he insisted that the Association's business should be actual abuses and inequities which would not admit of delay until the day of liberation dawned. In earnest of this, the first issue which he raised at the first regular meeting of the new body, on 20 May 1823, was the appointment of a Catholic chaplain to Newgate prison in Dublin.

The upper-class Catholics, led by Lord Killeen and Sir Edward Bellew, who chaired the early meetings, were rapidly worsted. By June 1823 they had, without exception, ceased to attend Association meetings, and left the field to the lawyers and other professionals and businessmen. This did not mean that O'Connell's policy of enflaming the peasantry was henceforward unopposed. Timid or factious bourgeois members continued to resist extensions of the area of business. Twice at least they attempted to remove the tithe question from the Association's programme. On 19 June 1823 Eneas MacDonnell, often a thorn in O'Connell's side, opposed a protest against Orange processions. Hugh O'Connor, the most persistent advocate of the narrow view of the Association's concerns, condemned the divergences 'from the sole purpose for which it was instituted – Catholic emancipation . . . extraneous topics, and vituperative personalities . . . have done some injury to the Catholic question.'[3] O'Connell, however, was indomitable. Within a month of its foundation, he congratulated the Association on the decline in agrarian crime which it had already occasioned, and thereafter threw himself into work which he himself, practically single-handed, found for it to do, and practically single-handed did. He used every possible occasion to extend the Association's range of agitation, and crushed, none too scrupulously, every attempt at limitation. His majority was secure; and he could always count upon the important support of Sheil. On 15 November 1823 the matter was finally decided in his favour when he secured a resolution that the Association had been formed to watch over Catholic interests and to redress Catholic grievances in general.

In the same month Goulburn, the Irish chief secretary, reported to Peel, now home secretary, that the Association's proceedings were tedious rather than dangerous, and that it would probably die soon of inanition. On the surface, this seemed indisputable. It is unlikely that the total membership exceeded 120 during the first year. No less than six times during 1823, meetings had to be abandoned for lack of a quorum of ten, and on other occasions a tenth member arrived only in the nick of time. Moreover, despite the plethora of committees and apparent press of business, almost everything rested upon a single pair of shoulders. For the rest, the handful of active members served as a stage army relying on the multiplication of their roles to give the illusion of a considerable body.

But the appearance of weakness was misleading. Peel himself realized as much when he observed in April 1824 that 'the insignificance of the members' was more than counter-balanced by the publicity which the Association had received from the beginning. Governmental control of the press had not been maintained, and four of the six most widely circulating newspapers in the country were in its pocket. F. W. Conway, editor of the *Dublin Evening Post*, and M. Staunton, editor of the *Morning Register* and *Weekly Register*, were close allies of O'Connell, as well as deeply involved in the Association; and although the *Freeman's Journal* was hostile to O'Connell himself, it warmly supported the Association. This meant that the media of Catholic Ireland saturated the country with the Association's propaganda. Meetings were reported in a degree of detail which no twentieth-century newspaper would attempt to match. There is abundant evidence that the effective circulation of the newspapers, even in 1823, was far greater than their sales would suggest. As they were passed about and read aloud, their circles of influence widened continually. There is also abundant evidence that the peasantry bowed down before the printed word: type on paper was treated as in itself authoritative. Thus the voices of the dozen barristers and journalists haranguing each other in a little room over Coyne's bookshop in Capel St, Dublin, on Saturday afternoons – above all, the voice of voices, O'Connell's – were magnified a thousandfold by the press, primarily by the nationalist newspapers, but also by broadsheet and pamphlet. Even the government newspapers contributed to the éclat of the Association, reporting its proceedings almost as completely as its rivals. Peel deplored the subsidization of organs which merely advertised O'Connell. But although their readers might receive news of O'Connell's doings with fear, anger or contempt, they had to know about them.

A second reason for the wildly disproportionate national impact of the Association's handful of members in 1823 was the multiplication and noisy canvassing of 'grievances'. Orangeism and Catholic burials provide two early examples of O'Connell's technique of turning a trivial occasion to great account. On 19 June 1823 the Association agreed to petition the lord lieutenant to forbid the traditional Orange procession of 12 July. The petition was rejected; but the procedural wrangles which preceded it and the denunciatory oratory which it unleashed publicized the Orange phenomenon as never before. This launched O'Connell into the set-piece ridicule of the Orange Order with which he was to delight the Catholic masses in later years, as well as a series of legal actions assailing Orange 'oppressions' and pretensions.

Similarly, the refusal in September 1823 by the sexton of St Kevin's churchyard, Dublin – like all cemeteries then, it was in Protestant hands – to turn the usual blind eye to a Catholic priest reciting the *De profoundis* over the grave of a parishioner was brilliantly exploited by O'Connell. Over the next eight months he used the burial issue to prodigious effect. Committees reported on the relevant statutes and common law and pursued the acquisition of a special Catholic burial site in Dublin. Several priests, and in particular Dr Murray, were drawn into the ferment. Somewhat bathetically, this particular phase of the agitation ended when the Association acknowledged that 'As a matter of fact, prayers have constantly been read at Catholic burials.'[4] But by then tens of thousands of Irish Catholics had been brought to recognize another of the badges of their inferiority. Moreover in O'Connell's hands the grievance had spread like a stain. As he expressed it, the Catholics of Dublin were being taxed £20,000 per annum by the Church of Ireland for the right of burial within the city. It was fruitlessly, though bitterly, that the Anglican Archbishop complained that he and his brethren were being 'held up to public contempt and execration by a set of popish priests'.[5] One grievance led smoothly into another and before the year was out the original burial question had proliferated into Association resolutions against tithes, church rates and Protestant Proselytism. Just as the processions of 12 July had been developed into a campaign against the entire system of caste domination, so the momentary bigotry of the sexton was developed into a campaign against the entire system of Anglican discrimination.

Thus beneath the apparent failure to make headway in 1823, the groundwork for a mass movement was being laid. Through the newspapers the Association served more and more as a national sounding board, and through O'Connell's exploitation of Catholic 'grievances' large bodies of people were being quickly politicized. Latterly, the priests also were being entangled. On two seemingly opposite counts, the fewness of the active members and the great and growing extent of their potential public, O'Connell believed that the time had come to popularize the Association according to his original vision.

II

O'Connell's penny-a-month plan represented the second stage in the development of the Catholic agitation. Neither the idea of a Catholic

'Rent' nor the idea of widespread minute subscriptions was new. As O'Connell himself acknowledged, Lord Kenmare had proposed, as early as 1784, levying a 'rent' of £1 per annum on every Catholic parish to build up a campaign fund for Emancipation; and both the English Methodists and the London radicals had attempted to organize regular penny subscriptions by the poor in the 1790s. The very mechanics of O'Connell's scheme in 1824 had been largely anticipated in a suggestion of William Parnell to Denys Scully several years before. But O'Connell brought a fresh energy, practicality and purpose to the projects. In his hands they actually worked.

O'Connell saw his Rent as the transformer of sentimental support into real commitment. Hundreds, and ultimately thousands, of ordinary middle- and lower-middle-class people would be drawn into the bustle and business of collection, while each poor subscriber of the weekly farthing would feel that he had a stake and a sort of proprietorship in the vast national movement. This may even have been his primary objective. It was in fact through the Association's committee for the increase of membership that he first launched his proposal on 4 February 1824. But the acquisition of capital was far from unimportant in either his or the Association's eyes. O'Connell aimed at £50,000 per annum (one penny per month from the heads of Catholic households was the basis of his calculation). His projected division of expenditure reveals his desire to pursue the objectives of 1823 upon a much grander scale. The bulk, £30,000, was to be spent on legal aid for Catholics – in particular, in cases involving 'Orange' magistrates – and the support of the 'liberal' press. The balance was to be devoted, in equal parts, to the education of the Catholic poor; the provision of priests for the American 'mission'; church and school building; and parliamentary expenses, mainly for petitions. Thus, broadly speaking, two-thirds of the effort was to be directed to mutual defence and propaganda, and the remainder to strengthening of what we would now call the Catholic 'infrastructure'. Thus O'Connell's basic strategy was still defensive, although a future aggressive campaign was none the less possible. As the original resolution for the adoption of the Rent put it, 'there is no rational prospect for emancipation, unless the Catholic Association shall be enabled to adopt more vigorous and effectual measures than have been heretofore pursued by the Catholic people.'[6] There was of course no conflict between the embroiling of the many and the filling of the war chest. But they were sufficiently distinct for O'Connell to insist upon a separate committee for each end.

It was only with the utmost difficulty that O'Connell persuaded the Association to adopt the Rent. On its first proposal, he was met with the argument that they needed to re-involve grandees like Lord Fingall rather than recruit a horde of 'houseless, starving wretches'.[7] Sheil's backing helped him to secure agreement in principle in the end; but so tepid was the support in general that the critical meeting of 4 February failed to muster a quorum at the start, and O'Connell had to send his clerk down to the bookshop beneath where they were meeting in order to snare some unwary, browsing priests who, bewildered, made up the necessary number. The subsequent organizational work of March–October 1824 fell largely upon O'Connell himself. First, he tackled the towns. Urban committees appointed collectors for various districts (or 'walks'), and remitted the money regularly through their secretaries to the central Association. Contiguous rural parishes were next drawn in, and then more remote parishes where practicable. None of this was easy. Even Dublin and Cork proved difficult to organize initially; half the Cork Rent had to be devoted to local charities to enhance its appeal. Laymen could usually be found to initiate and sustain the work in the cities, but hardly ever in the countryside. Here the Church was all-important. Curiously, O'Connell had given the priests no significant role in the beginning. But he very soon changed this. Collections had to be taken at church doors to tap those without dwellings of their own: the armies of servants in the capital were a leading case. Priests had to be called on for advice on who should be appointed as inspectors. Where – as was normally the case outside the towns – no Rent committee existed, the parish priest became perforce the channel for subscriptions. O'Connell had however long foreseen some such need: as the French traveller de Beaumont later put it, 'he judges Ireland too well not to know that nothing can be done except by the influence of Catholicism.'[8] Similarly, he knew that Catholicism could be 'operated' only through the Church. Hence he had moved at a comparatively early stage, on 16 June 1823, that priests should be attracted to the Association by the waiving of subscriptions in their case. This had been strongly opposed, not least by Sheil who had supported a contrary motion, that the clergy be admitted only as 'observers', on the ground that O'Connell's proposal would lead to clerical domination of the movement. O'Connell had however triumphed by 'a large majority'.[9] It was a symbolic victory of first importance.

So far as harnessing the Church to the Rent in 1824 went, the critical precedent was the adhesion of Bishop James Doyle of Kildare and

Leighlin to the Rent scheme and his supplying the Association with a list of the priests in his diocese; very few priests would have ventured into the work without episcopal approval. Murray and other prelates soon followed the lead of Doyle. O'Connell capitalized upon this at once. As early as Sunday, 7 March 1824 he travelled to Navan 'and [? spent] the day with the bishop [of Meath], a very fine old gentleman of the age of 86, and met a large party of his clergy. I made a harangue to the people in the Chapel and set the penny a month subscription agoing. It will succeed.'[10] To this clerical offensive we should add the evangelical work on the Munster and Leinster circuits in the late summer of 1824, as O'Connell, Sheil and the other Catholic members of the bar set about inspiriting and instructing the assize towns and their hinterlands, one by one. Through it all, O'Connell was supreme, in organization, in management, in administrative invention, in incessant toil. Well might the Catholic aggregate meeting of 2 December 1824, looking back upon the preceding nine months, resolve 'that we are peculiarly indebted to that honest, eloquent, and dauntless man, for his sagacity in devising the Catholic Rent, and his skill, judgment, and perseverance in carrying that important measure into effect'.[11]

As it extended itself across the country, the Association also altered its character. The local branches began to hire rooms, hold weekly meetings and discuss political issues, just like the parent body. Politicization became both general and systematic. Secondly, a chain of communication and command developed quickly. By October 1824 hundreds of thousands were within the control – or at least subject to the direct influence – of O'Connell's committees. Thirdly, the Catholics in the various localities were advancing in self-confidence and self-management. Gradually some branches began to assume the functions of tribunals – arbitrating disputes, challenging the magistracy and formulating and publicizing grievances. Most important of all, the movement had thrown up a national leader. Before March 1824 O'Connell had been merely much the best-known of a group of well-known agitators. Now he towered over the remainder. His extraordinary national dominance, which was to last until his death, 23 years later, had been suddenly achieved; all at once he was rewarded for nearly two decades of dreary labour. At the same time, the Irish Catholic movement had taken one particular shape at last, centred about an individual hero and commander.

Down to the end of September 1824, the Rent yielded compara-tively little. Then the labours of six months bore fruit. In the last quarter of the year the weekly average leaped to £600, with that sum frequently exceeded. As N. P. O'Gorman, praising 'that wonder-working man, Daniel O'Connell', reported, the last week of November yielded £1032 as against £8 in the first week of February.[12] The weekly average of the first ten weeks of 1825 was higher still, although some of this augmentation must be attributed to appeals for extraordinary subscriptions before the Association was legally suppressed and collections would have to cease. In all, almost £20,000 was raised during the year that the Rent was open, more than nine-tenths of it in the last five months. These vast sums – vast, that is, in the circumstance of the case – were themselves a cause of Catholic exultation. As, at first, each month, then each fortnight and finally almost every week a receipt for £1000 invested in 3 per cents was produced at the Corn Exchange, where the meetings now took place, a sense of power coursed through the proceedings.

Less than one quarter of the Rent collected in 1824–5 was actually spent. Administrative costs were low, mainly for hiring halls and the printing and broadcast of reports and collectors' books. The principal charge was legal expenses, counsels' fees for prosecuting Orangemen or defending Catholics, although these were sometimes waived by Association members. The Rent also furnished £500 for schoolbooks for the Catholic poor, and an uncertain amount – probably very small – for press propaganda. In July 1824 O'Connell proposed that a considerable sum be applied 'towards establishing a [pro-] Catholic paper in London';[13] but when such a paper, the *Morning Register*, was established, he offered no subvention. Doubtless the very excitement generated by the Rent's progress provided sufficient publicity, free of charge.

Thus the money raised proved an even more secondary objective than O'Connell had originally thought. What mattered was the mobilization of Irish Catholicism. If Rent was collected in only half the parishes of Ireland – and this is a low estimate for early 1825 – as many as 30,000 people might have been involved in the business. Local committees varied greatly in size, but in some cases exceeded fifty persons. The number of contributors (women were appealed to as well as men) may eventually have reached half a million, for collections were pressed very hard once the organization took deep root. The priests had taken up the Rent with zeal. By the end of 1824, they were generally the driving force outside the cities. On 24 January 1825, Vesey Fitzgerald, the sitting member for the constituency, told Peel that every parish in co. Clare had been organized: 'in the few instances where the priest has been either cautious or reluctant, a coadjutor of a more daring . . . spirit is sent to take the management out of his hands.'[14] A similar report from co. Limerick spoke of the Rent as being entirely directed by the clergy, whose influence over the people was thereby rapidly increasing. Clearly, the Church had been enlisted with a vengeance. Equally clearly, the process of Rent-gathering was quite as significant as the gathered Rent. As early as November 1824, Peel recognized this when he noted that although the money itself might not be dangerous, 'the organization by means of which it is raised may be very formidable'.[15]

It is difficult to guess how the Rent would have developed if it had not been halted suddenly by the suppression of the Association. So far it had been only triumph; so far the Rent had been virtually its own end. No one, from O'Connell downwards, was apparently concerned that the money was simply mounting, and practically unharnessed to the Association's stated aims. Meanwhile it had at least served the movement's first principle of being: it had embodied agitation.

III

The third phase of the Catholic movement began with the gathering resistance of the interests threatened by the Association. By November 1824, the Irish tories were pressing for arms to defend themselves, and Wellington was prophesying armed conflict. Goulburn, while dismissing civil war or insurrection as chimerical, none the less feared that some trivial collision might set off a general explosion in the existing state of popular excitement. Wellesley, the lord lieutenant, struck out upon a new line, even-handed suppression. In December he determined on the prosecution of both O'Connell and Sir Harcourt Lees, an Ulster Orange leader, for seditious language. Both prosecutions failed ignominiously, and O'Connell rose to dizzier heights of popularity in the event. But the action signalled that the government now felt itself threatened by the Association.

When Peel first considered counter-measures, in a letter to Goulburn of 6 November 1824, he presented the choices as three – to trust to dissension among the leaders, or the inherent folly of the enterprise, to break up the Association; to watch for the false step which would enable a successful prosecution to be brought; and to suppress the body by legislation. Wellesley had evidently been following the second course when O'Connell was charged for a speech at the Association on 16 December, in which he had proclaimed that if

Ireland 'were driven mad by persecution, he wished that a new Bolivar may be found'.[16] Of the three, Peel clearly preferred suppression and this was the course fixed on by the British government at the beginning of 1825. But it was suppression of all Irish associations, and not merely the Catholic which was proposed. It was doubtless true, as Brougham observed, that 'it will be only a nominal equity . . . the Catholic Association will be strongly put down with one hand, while the Orange Association will receive only a gentle tap with the other'.[17] None the less, it was of symbolic significance that the principle of impartiality towards the Irish 'factions' was to be enshrined in legislation. With Wellesley's equality in prosecutions, this marked an open retreat from the automatic identification of British and Irish tory interests.

In introducing the suppression bill Goulburn emphasized the danger of a universal body, controlled by O'Connell and his like, 'men of disappointed ambition and considerable talents'. He tried to tarnish the Association by saying that its membership included those 'familiar with the traitors of old times – Tone, Russell, and Emmett' and to diminish its authority by accusing the Catholic nobility and gentry of cowardice and the priests of being mere automata. Worst of all, the 'Association condescended most strictly to imitate . . . [the] forms [of Parliament]. They appointed their committees of grievances – of education also and of finance. They had almost copied verbatim the sessional orders of that House.'[18] Peel spoke of the frightful ease with which such a vast and co-ordinated piece of machinery might be 'converted into a political engine'.[19] Canning supported the suppression upon the ground that the Association was supplanting both government and House of Commons. This was the favourite and most telling argument in the Commons debates. Nothing was said of the fear of Irish Catholic power which was the true reason for the suppression.

The bill passed rapidly and with very large majorities through both houses of Parliament and came into force at the end of March 1825. But long before then it was apparent that a high price might have to be paid for the success. When the bill was announced in early February, the Association determined to send a deputation to Westminster to plead its cause at the bar of the Commons. It was only with great reluctance that O'Connell consented to be a member; he would miss most, if not all, of the spring circuit; it might (as in fact it did) cost him more than £2000.

The ostensible object of the expedition failed at once; the House of

Commons refused to grant a hearing to the delegation. But both houses conceded select committees to consider the general condition of Ireland, and these gave O'Connell an opportunity to assess and allay the opposition. On 25 February 1825, he was examined by the Commons committee on the state of the Irish peasantry and system of land tenure. His competence, clarity and moderation impressed all members. He was also proving successful as an English agitator. His first major speech, of three hours duration to the English Catholics at Freemasons' Tavern on 26 February, was a triumph. 'I have succeeded, love', he told his wife. 'I was sincerely afraid of a failure . . . but . . . I had the meeting as cheering and as enthusiastic as ever a Dublin aggregate could be.'[20] This was confirmed by Sheil, who heard the speech:

> Mr O'Connell appeared to me extremely solicitous about the impression which he should produce, and prepared and arranged his topics with unusual care. In public meetings in Ireland, he is so confident in his powers, that he gives himself little trouble in the selection of his materials, and generally trusts to his emotions for his harangues. He is on that account occasionally desultory and irregular. But there is no man more capable of lucid exposition, when he previously deliberates upon the order in which he should array the topics upon which he intends to dwell . . . [W]hen he advanced into the general consideration of the grievances under which the great body of the people are doomed to labour – when he painted the insolence of the dominant faction – when he shewed the effects of the penal code brought to his own door – he seized with an absolute dominion upon the sympathies of his acclaiming auditors, and poured the full tide of his own emotions into their hearts. [21]

Meanwhile, he was lionized at whig dinners and receptions. 'We had four Dukes . . .', he wrote of a dinner given by Brougham for the deputation on 27 February. 'I was placed between the Dukes of Devonshire and Leinster, and opposite to the Duke of Suffolk . . . I was again most flattered.'[22] At the Duke of Norfolk's dinner in O'Connell's honour on 6 March, four dukes, four earls, six other peers and two baronets sat down to table with him: 'I was placed between the Duke of Devonshire and Earl Grey.'[23] Of the following night's dinner, he reported to Mary,

> You like to be thought the wife of *a great man*. And now to feed that wish I tell you I dined yesterday with Mr Frederick and Lady Barbara Ponsonby in St James Square . . . We had *only* one duke – of Norfolk – only two earls, Grey and Bessborough, but then we had a Marquis of Lansdowne, the senior peer sitting in Parliament being, I believe, the 35th Baron of

Lixnaw, Sir Francis Burdett and the Knight of Kerry were there . . . Only think that earls are now become so familiar to me that I left out Earls Fitzwilliam and Sefton.[24]

Meanwhile, O'Connell had measured the leading British politicians, and concluded that he himself was superior in calibre to most, and equal to any. 'Darling, they think themselves great men', he wrote home, 'but the foolish pride of your husband would readily make him enter into a contest with them. I have not the least fear of being *looked down on* in Parliament.'[25] Perhaps it was all this agreeable encouragement which induced him to press Burdett, a leading radical, to introduce a motion favouring the Catholic claims, although it is also possible that he had determined to try again for Emancipation before joining the deputation. At any rate, when Burdett did seek leave to introduce a bill on 28 February, it was granted by the respectable majority of thirteen.

It was clear that the Association had suddenly brought Emancipation to the brink of success. To some extent, the Commons vote may have represented a feeling that the proposed suppression implied a *quid pro quo*. But primarily the shift in opinion was caused by fear. The Association might be put down. But it had already demonstrated the power of popular organization, and this might surely be repeated in some other – and perhaps even more subversive – form if the Irish Catholics were constantly frustrated. The most important anti-Catholics were coming to believe that the game was up. Liverpool considered that even if the Lords rejected relief it would be by so small a margin that the next bill would be irresistible, and he wished to resign office to avoid involvement in what he regarded as the inevitable surrender. Peel, on the same reasoning, tried to resign at once, and was persuaded only with difficulty to hold back his resignation until Liverpool's was delivered. There are indications that Wellington was prepared to replace Liverpool as prime minister with the intention of presiding over the concession. Even George IV appears initially to have regarded Emancipation as inevitable. If those at the heart of British politics should have so underestimated the remaining strength of the resistance to relief, O'Connell can scarcely be blamed for his grosser miscalculation.

On the strength of the success of the Commons motion of 28 February, O'Connell collaborated fully with Burdett and Plunket throughout the second week of March in drawing up a Catholic relief bill, together with 'securities' to meet all 'reasonable' Protestant fears. The 'securities' – state payment of the Irish Catholic clergy and the disenfranchisement of the Irish 40s. freehold voters – were to constitute the 'wings' by the aid of which Emancipation itself would be borne through both houses. Clearly O'Connell had concluded that the time had come to cash in these two political assets. In his evidence before the Commons committee, he had decidedly favoured the disenfranchisement of the 40s. freeholders. Despite considerable evidence to the contrary in recent Irish elections, he regarded these as votes in the landlords' pockets. In his evidence before the Lords, he had favoured, though more tentatively and conditionally, state payment of the clergy. After all, Maynooth, which was state supported, had been producing priests for thirty years, and the current complaints were not of their subservience but of their disloyalty to the British government; and even Doyle, the most indomitable of the Irish hierarchy, did not seem absolutely opposed. According to Lord Colchester, Doyle had told the Lords' committee that he was 'unwilling to receive any State provision; rejecting it absolutely unless equality of civil rights were given to the Roman Catholic laity; and even then would accept such provision only as permanently annexed to each benefice or dignity.'[26] At the same time, O'Connell's uneasiness with this 'security' seems evident from the manner in which he disclosed the proposed concession to his wife: 'A provision will be made for our Clergy which, by the by, will be so much the better for the friars as it will leave almost all the individual donations *free*.'[27]

O'Connell does not appear to have anticipated sensible difficulty in carrying Irish Catholic opinion with him on the 'wings'. He informed the chairman of the Association of these in a letter of 7 March 1825, without in any way dissociating himself from either. When this letter found its way to the press, opposition was expressed at once. But this was swallowed up in the larger commotion which followed Jack Lawless's public letter of 15 March denouncing the deputation's treason – 'a furious tirade', O'Connell called it, 'calculated to do extreme mischief here and to raise a flame in Ireland'.[28] Lawless, in his role of *vox populi*, had followed the deputation to London to watch for backsliding – and not in vain. O'Connell was accused of 'selling the people for a silk gown' and succumbing to the flattery and attention of the aristocracy: 'the Circean cup of their hospitality' had drugged and debauched him, and he had surrendered the 40s. freeholders for his own advancement.[29] This was a dangerously plausible account of the recent transactions. England, to use Sheil's phrase, operated as a sedative on O'Connell. 'His deputation to England', Sheil continued playfully, 'produced an almost immediate effect upon him. As we advanced, the din of popular assemblies became more faint; the voice of the multitude was scarcely heard in the distance, and at last died away. He seemed half English at Shrewsbury, and was nearly Saxonized when we entered the murky magnificence of Warwick-shire.'[30] O'Connell himself joked with his wife about being 'lost by *flattery*',[31] but doubtless the rain of dukes had some effect. Certainly, he was soon sucked into the Westminster game of factional manoeuvres. None the less he boldly repelled Lawless' onslaught with a public letter of defence, and in early April 1825 returned temporarily to Dublin where he addressed a large aggregate meeting. The 'wings' were not so much as mentioned, and O'Connell repaired to London once again with the negative security that Lawless and his other enemies had not dared to denounce him before a popular audience.

The flank had been temporarily secured and the main battle seemed to be going well. The relief bill passed the Commons with a final majority of twenty-seven; the securities, eventually embodied as separate bills to smooth the path of relief, followed with majorities of almost fifty. Meanwhile, however, the Duke of York, heir to the throne, had taken the lead in organizing resistance in the Lords. In a speech on 25 April he declared that, like his father, he regarded the coronation oath as an insuperable obstacle to granting the royal consent to Emancipation. O'Connell erred in dismissing this as empty gasconade, for the speech emboldened other peers to hold out against concession. It is true that Liverpool still believed that the question would have to be compromised; and although he now took a stronger anti-Catholic stand in public than he had ever done before, it was to prepare the way for his own resignation. But at the critical division in the Lords, on 18 May, Liverpool's stance was largely responsible for the bill's rejection by a decisive forty-eight votes. The government and Liverpool's prime ministership were unexpectedly saved; Catholic relief had been routed. Moreover, Canning after minatory gestures soon made it clear that he would not leave the ministry; the 'open system' (whereby politicians agreed to differ on the issue of Emancipation when it came to holding posts in government) would continue to sap all pro-Catholic efforts in Parliament.

O'Connell, who had long been exultantly confident, was furious, believing that he had been sold. He immediately announced his intention of renewing agitation and reconstituting the Association, and returned to Dublin to resecure his base. Despite his worthless 'surrender' of the 'wings' and the suddenness and ignominy of his defeat, he had comparatively little difficulty in confirming his leadership. His journey from Howth, where he landed, to Dublin was an unbroken ovation; and when a week later, at the aggregate meeting of 8 June, Lawless attempted to impugn the deputation's conduct in London, he was shouted down and forced to withdraw his motion of condemnation. Later Lawless organized a closed meeting of the Bridge St parish, where his main strength lay, to secure some public condemnation of O'Connell's conduct. But O'Connell would not allow even this petty threat to his mastery to go unchallenged. With a body of supporters he forced his way into the meeting, and despite constant interruptions managed to rout the fomenters of 'discord'. But to do so he had to confess openly that his former support of the 'wings' was mistaken, and to claim the backing of Doyle and Murray for his former acquiescence in state payment. At the Bridge St meeting he also asserted that he had received votes of thanks from almost every county in Ireland; and this was probably true. As he went on circuit during August and September he was hailed as a conqueror by vast crowds in each assize town, as well as in Galway and Wexford where he had special retainers. Significantly, the Cork address declared that 'his purity of intention and devotion to the interests of the Irish Catholics continue unimpeached in the public estimation'.[32] The medal struck in honour of his work for the Catholics of Ireland portrayed, in Roman imperial fashion, his bust upon the obverse side and a half-laurel wreath (the other half being shamrocks!) upon the reverse.

It was now clear that O'Connell had ridden successfully over the Lawless challenge, that his campaign of 1825 was estimated a national triumph and that he had risen to an unprecedented height in leadership. Probably, his position would have been secure even if he had made no extraordinary exertions after the débâcle of 18 May. But he had counter-attacked, first, by challenging Lawless at once on each of the three occasions on which he had attempted to arouse opinion against him; secondly, by disclaiming the 'wings' quickly and without reservation; and thirdly, by making good his promise to reconstitute the Association substantially. He was not yet out of the wood. He had, as he himself put it, 'smashed the Bridge St gang';[33] but in doing so he had offended Doyle, who denied that he had ever sanctioned state payment of the clergy. O'Connell was both wounded and astonished. He had taken Doyle's support for granted, and (very reasonably) regarded Doyle's evidence before the Lords' committee as endorsing a circumscribed form of state payment in return for Emancipation. But Doyle could not be treated like Jack Lawless, and O'Connell bowed before the storm. He had not, however, understood Doyle's line of reasoning; and when he unluckily referred to the matter again at a public meeting in October, Doyle replied angrily that he had told the other bishops in London that he would resign his see rather than accept a salary from the crown, 'for if my hand were to be stained with Government money, it should never grasp a crozier, or a mitre ever afterwards be fitted to my brow'.[34] This rhetoric was not perhaps incompatible with acquiescing in state payment for the clergy generally, for Doyle had also declared that he would cause no dissension if the remainder of the episcopate was in favour of the concession. But O'Connell now understood his danger, and made no effort to chop logic with a bishop. Instead, Canossa – he humbly asked for a reconciliation. Doyle was critically important as the boldest and most intelligent and radical of the episcopate.

Meanwhile, O'Connell had set the New Catholic Association afoot in July 1825, defining its objectives in terms of the subjects specifically exempted from the operation of the Suppression Act – religious worship, charity, education and agriculture, and 'such other purposes as are not prohibited by the said statute of the 6th George 4th chap 4'.[35] This permitted engagement in almost every field in which the first Association had worked, from supporting a liberal press to combating arbitrary ejectments. In fact, the very limitations imposed by Geo. IV c.4 led O'Connell to propose effective new activities, for example the compilation of a religious census which promised the double advantage of establishing the paucity of the Irish Protestants and training 'assessors' in resource calculation and local and national organization. The Association could no longer run a direct campaign for Emancipation; petition-work would *ipso facto* render it an illegal body. Henceforth petitioning had to be managed at aggregate meetings and the fourteen-day limitation upon 'aggregates' induced O'Connell to propose the holding of simultaneous petitioning meetings in every county in Ireland. Here again the Suppression Act, ironically, produced a new and more effective mode of agitation; simultaneous county meetings would demonstrate Catholic strength and coherence dramatically. The remaining threat to the Association's work was the prohibition upon the collection and distribution of subscriptions. O'Connell countered this, well before the Act came into force, by vesting the money in a single individual, Lord Killeen, who became, in practice though not in law, the trustee for the balance of the Old Rent.

In all these ways, O'Connell recovered rapidly from the 'downfall' of May 1825. Superficially, his political losses were very grievous. The Association was suppressed, the Rent suspended, his willingness to yield on matters of great principle revealed, his extraordinary tractability disclosed to his British enemies, and a store of ammunition against his own integrity handed to his Irish ones. But he fought back superbly. As he had promised, he restored both the Association and the Rent in other forms, and reorganized the agitation for Emancipation. In the second half of 1825 the Association proper concentrated upon the 'defensive' or preparatory role defined at the outset in 1823 – but with several new objectives and techniques. These implied a return to steady political education, enrollment, and radicalization. Formally separate was the Emancipation campaign, the first major step in which was taken at Limerick on 24 October when a new system of provincial aggregates, to rehearse grievances and prepare parliamentary petitions, was inaugurated.

Meanwhile, he had boldly recanted his 'errors', crushed or conciliated (according to circumstances) his Irish opponents and processed the country as Victor in order to confirm and solidify his further elevation above the ranks of all other agitators. The instinct of the adulatory masses who responded uncritically to this presentation of himself was not mistaken. The near-triumph of March had been O'Connell's own doing. 'You cannot think', he had written to his wife on the 7th, 'how everybody says that it is *I* who am carrying emancipation',[36] and 'everybody' was right. Correspondingly, despite the Lords' vote of 18 May, he had, overall, won a critical Catholic victory. To have been baulked only by peers and against all expert expectation was surely to render success ultimately certain. O'Connell had many seasons of apparently greater triumph, but considering all the odds and turns of fortune against which he had to struggle, 1825 was probably his finest year of all.

IV

It was however low water for O'Connell and the Association during the first five months of 1826. As planned, the wave of aggregate meetings of late 1825 reached its climax in a fourteen-day session in Dublin in January 1826. But O'Connell feared to press the resultant petition for Emancipation hard lest, with a general election imminent, anti-Catholic sentiment in Britain might be enflamed. Otherwise, the leading event was a dinner held in February to honour liberal Protestant supporters. O'Connell attached great importance to the accompanying parade and oratory of good-will. But we can hardly follow him in this. In fact, his parliamentary 'friends' fobbed off the

Association's efforts to have the Catholic question raised at all during the Parliament's final session. They even persuaded O'Connell that it would be unwise to raise debates on such petitions as they did present. These in themselves indicate the Association's dispirited condition. One prayed that the Treaty of Limerick of 1691 be adhered to; another, that state funds be diverted to Catholic education. Even O'Connell could hardly have supposed that the slightest attention would be paid to either.

Attacks upon O'Connell's leadership were moreover renewed in the Association. Lawless persisted with motions condemning, obliquely, his acceptance of the 'wings' in 1825; on 11 February 1826, a rising young radical, James O'Gorman Mahon, assailed him roundly for condemning the anti-clerical measures of the Spanish Cortes; and two days later, the *Freeman's Journal* denounced 'that violent and vulgar abuse which he [O'Connell] has so long been notorious for pouring out upon every person whom he cannot wheedle or bend to his purposes ... his most slavish sycophants must admit him to be, inconsistent, ungrateful, capricious, vindictive.' We should not perhaps attach much weight to all these challenges. Dublin was not Ireland: O'Connell continued to be received with all the customary deference and adulation at provincial meetings. He could besides still dominate in Dublin whenever he chose to exert himself. But he forwent several of the Dublin meetings on account, he said, of professional business; one at least he attended in wig and gown. At another, a mere handful of hostile members carried some damaging resolutions in his absence. It was all, however, symptomatic of low morale and lack of direction rather than a breakdown of his power. In so far as O'Connell possessed a strategy in the first half of 1826, it was only to petition once more, through aggregate meetings, for a relief bill, after the general election in mid-year had produced a new House of Commons. He never guessed that the election itself would provide a dramatic change in fortune.

To a degree, the critical innovation of the Association in 1826 was both accidental and independent of the official organization. It began with an affront to Catholics in Waterford, a county dominated by the Beresfords, an Ascendancy family remarkable for its resistance to all Catholic claims and for the extent of the patronage at its disposal. Coincidentally Waterford was the home of a Catholic mercantile dynasty, the Wyses, whose latest representative, Thomas, junior, was a young man of extraordinary sophistication and cool judgment, in terms of the circle of agitators among whom he found himself. He was foremost in the long planning of a riposte to the Beresfords. Rev. J. Sheehan of Ballybricken, one of the first and shrewdest of the new breed of political priests and, in effect, O'Connell's agent for Waterford, was also critically important. But it was largely Wyse who devised and managed the systematic Waterford programme of 1825–6.

The objective of the campaign was to wrest one of the county seats from Lord George Beresford. To find a good opponent proved unexpectedly easy. Villiers Stuart, a young liberal landowner and pledged Emancipationist, was so eager to stand as to hasten back from the Tyrol for the contest. But the quality of the candidate was comparatively unimportant. It was the revolutionary methods of Wyse and Sheehan which really counted. A general committee was set up in the city with a subordinate committee in every barony and local agents in each parish. Priests were committee members *ex officio*. Weekly, the local agents and parish priests reported to the baronial committees which reported in turn to the centre, from which they received instructions which were passed down along the same line to the localities. Everyone concerned kept a register of the voters in his district. These, when forwarded to the central committee shortly before the election, predicted correctly the choice of practically every voter in the county.

Of course the purpose of all this work was not mere enumeration – though this was certainly important – but rather to induce the great body of the enfranchised, the 40s., freeholders, to defy the directions of their landlords. The organization used three wedges to split the ruling bond of proprietor and freeholder. First, the Beresfords were presented as historically the very centre-piece of the exclusive Ascendancy system and the most resolute Irish opponents of Catholicism. Secondly, it was reiterated that electors who took both the Beresford shillings (Beresford was attempting wholesale bribery) and the obligatory oath that they had not been bribed were guilty of the mortal sin of perjury. Finally, since many proprietors threated to evict every freeholder who supported Stuart, a local fund, collecting both money and alternative holdings, was set up to provide for the prospective victims of landlord revenge. These themes were repeated in chapel after chapel, Sunday by Sunday, for at least two months before the election; and meetings harangued by peripatetic agitators as well as the local priests enlisted the force of community pressure upon the side of defiance. Families were made to feel the shame of 'demean[ing] themselves before all the county'.[37]

But moving and sustaining bodies was just as important as fixing minds. The carriage of voters to the city, where polling took place; their maintenance there for several days; and discipline, sobriety and direction at the booths, required extraordinary planning. The preparatory network readily provided the requisite machinery, and the central committee used the tradesmen of the city as a sort of police force within Waterford itself. The result stunned contemporaries. Stuart was leading Beresford by 1357 votes to 527 when Beresford called off the contest. At that point Stuart had still several hundred votes in reserve, so that the true Emancipationist majority easily exceeded three to one. Even the Beresford tenants had supported Stuart.

At almost the twelfth hour, a few other counties attempted to imitate Waterford, in general with remarkable success. Louth, Westmeath, Monaghan and Armagh were won by a sudden mobilization-in-revolt of the Catholic freeholders. In some respects, Louth was an even more striking victory than Waterford. Only ten days before the election, a candidate of little name, fame, money or connexions, who refused moreover to pay a penny towards his own expenses, announced himself. Conjuring up the aid of the Association and its lawyers and agitators, and of the Archbishop of Armagh and his priests, he trounced the anti-Emancipation candidates whose families had had the constituency to themselves for half a century. None the less, the Waterford contest was the really significant phenomenon. It was the inspiration of all the rest; it alone was thoroughly planned and systematically executed; it alone was unmarred by violence and disorder, and marked by perfect discipline; and, numerically speaking, it was much the clearest demonstration of the political potential of the 'revolt'.

O'Connell had played a leading part in the Waterford triumph, spending several days before the poll electioneering throughout the county, and several more as Stuart's counsel in Waterford once voting had begun. On the second day of the campaign, he wrote from Stuart's house to his wife:

> We breakfasted at Kilmacthomas, a town belonging to the Beresfords but the people belong to us. They came out to meet us with green boughs and such shouting you can have no idea of. I harangued them from the window of the inn, and we had a good deal of laughing at the bloody Beresfords. Judge what the popular feeling must be when in this, a Beresford town, every man their tenant, we had such a reception. A few miles farther on we found a chapel with the congregation assembled before mass. The Priest

made me come out and I addressed his flock, being my second speech. The freeholders here were the tenants of a Mr Palliser, who is on the adverse interest, but almost all of them will vote for us ... We had a most tremendous meeting here [Dungarvan]; we harangued the people from a platform erected by the walls of a new chapel. I never could form a notion of the great effect of popular declamation before yesterday. The clergy of the town most zealously assisted us. We have, I believe, completely triumphed ...[38]

Everywhere, O'Connell was received even more rapturously than Stuart and the remainder of the entourage. He served as the epitome of defiance and success. Yet his function in Waterford was essentially confirmative. He may have been the foremost harvester; but others, in particular Wyse and Sheehan, had done the work.

For despite the precedents of the general election of 1818 when the 40s. freeholders, mobilized by the priests, had wrested three counties from anti-Emancipation candidates, and the co. Dublin by-election of 1823 when he himself led a similar successful challenge, O'Connell, like the rest of the leadership, had failed altogether to appreciate the weapon that lay to hand in 1826. He did not even bother to register the vote for which he himself was qualified in Waterford. Six months before the election he still asserted in public that the 40s. freehold vote impeded the Catholic cause. When O'Connell was convinced, after only three days' electioneering, that Waterford would be won, he blamed his earlier faintheartedness on bad local advice. 'I took my former opinions from timid persons here.'[39] This is implausible. As early as February 1826, optimistic reports from Waterford were discussed by the Association in Dublin; and Sheehan, O'Connell's own 'man' in Waterford, had supported Stuart's candidature enthusiastically from the start. The truth is, probably, that O'Connell and Sheil simply failed to think out beforehand the possibilities and implications of the new experiment. Metropolitan bickering and manoeuvres always absorbed too much attention in Dublin; and the 40s. freeholders naturally, if altogether illogically, suffered in reputation from having been once thrown over.

All this changed of course with the dramatic events of the general election. Sheil, who had played in Louth the equivalent of O'Connell's part in Waterford, perceived their significance immediately.

A simultaneous and universal revolt against the aristocracy has taken place, – Ireland has been to a certain extent revolutionised. How has this come to pass? How has this extraordinary change in the public mind been effected? ... I do not exaggerate, when I say, that we behold in the events which are passing around us, the results of the Catholic Association.[40]

O'Connell '*read his recantation*' as he himself put it, at the first meeting of the Association to be held after the elections closed. Hitherto he had supported the 40s. freeholders 'for the sake of preserving unanimity' but his 'private judgement' was otherwise.[41] Now they had so completely proved him wrong that he proposed a motion (which passed unanimously, of course), pledging the Association ever to reject Emancipation if it were coupled with their disfranchisement.

This was excellent so far as it went. Unity of heart as well as word had been restored; a treasury of political power had been, almost accidently, stumbled on; an animating programme – to organize the Catholic freeholders in all the other Irish counties – presented itself ready-made. There could be no doubt that almost the entire Irish county representation could be won. The Mr Palliser whose tenants O'Connell had poached wrote, bemusedly, towards the close of polling in Waterford,

> men who in the year 1798 with exemplary loyalty assisted me to keep Rebellion out of these parishes, and in the last year resisted to a man the payment of the Catholic Rent, although called upon by the priests from the altar to contribute, have been now compelled to bow to this Popish Inquisition . . . none but my five Protestant tenants have been polled out of this large estate, and Lord Doneraile who has upwards of an hundred, has not been able to bring to the poll more than his seven Protestant tenants . . . all the remainder have polled against him, as have even Lord Waterford's own tenants.[42]

All this was readily repeatable over most of Ireland.

But there were also difficulties. First, seven years might elapse before the next general election. An agitation which might not come to a head until 1833 could scarcely be white-hot. Secondly, the retaliation of many landlords upon their upsurgent tenants provoked fresh discord in the Catholic movement. There was of course no disagreement that the tenants threatened with eviction (by distress for rent arrears) should be supported. They had, as O'Connell declared, 'made great sacrifices, and it was right they should be protected and indemnified';[43] it was also only prudent. Nor was the extent of the problem ever clear. Reports from the rebellious constituencies were confused, and accusations of landlord vengeance sometimes found to be baseless; and though there can be little doubt that the proprietors concerted counter-action in some places, its precise character cannot be determined. None the less, the threat was unquestionably grave.

Almost £10,000 had to be expended over the next six months in tenant 'protection'.

Where such a sum was to come from was the issue which divided the Association. O'Connell got his blow in first by proposing on 7 July 1826 a New Catholic Rent for the specific purpose of supporting threatened freeholders, with 'the overplus of the fund ... appropriated to the purposes of education'. Significantly, he had already talked over the proposal with several priests, and he meant the Church to serve as the main engine of money-raising: 'in eight and forty hours after the plan was announced, the Catholic Clergy would go the rounds of their respective parishes'.[44] Collections began promptly, but with modest results: the weekly average was £100 at first, although some of the money raised in the embattled counties appears to have been distributed directly instead of forwarded to Dublin. The trouble was that cries for the immediate dispatch of quite large amounts, £300 or £400, began to go up from Monaghan, Westmeath and elsewhere, as particular landlords suddenly moved against their freeholders. In fact, the demands never did exceed what the New Rent and the county protection associations could provide. But throughout the autumn they seemed ever on the verge of outstripping these particular resources. Naturally, people looked to the balance of the Old Rent (over £13,000), left behind after the original Catholic Association had been suppressed in 1825, to meet the likely deficiencies. This proved to be the field of battle.

O'Connell strenuously opposed drawing upon the Old Rent on behalf of the 40s. freeholders. He argued that it was illegal to use it for such a purpose, and was probably sincere in this opinion. But – more important – he was also convinced that Rent was the most effective means of recreating and galvanizing a mass movement, and that the clergy would throw themselves wholeheartedly into a campaign for this particular purpose. Nor did he wish the 'sacred fund' of the Old Rent to be dissipated. It was still needed for his original purposes of opposing Orangeism in the courts, press propaganda and education.

It was not to be expected that O'Connell's apparent coolness towards the victims of 'the grand revolt' would pass unchallenged. As early as 14 August 1826, his loyal supporter Edward Dwyer, secretary of the Association since 1825, warned him:

> the greatest surprise is ... felt at the withholding such assistance to the persecuted 40/- freeholders as we have in our power to give. They say, 'Why not devote a portion of that fund collected from the poor, for their relief now in the day of their distress?' I must candidly give my opinion that

there is much of justice in the expectation for, without such aid, numbers of poor creatures, particularly in Monaghan where persecution rages to a great degree, must be ruined and sent to beggary.[45]

Dwyer concluded by proposing that £300–400 of the Old Rent fund be lent immediately 'to support the suffering patriots'. O'Connell strongly resisted. 'The old rent fund', he replied,

has more than enough of demands on it . . . The interest is applied to the purposes 'as far as it goes' for which that rent was originally collected, and the principal remains a sacred fund to be applied in the same manner when an emergency shall require. Drawing from that fund, even if it were competent to do so, would only relax the efforts of the real friends of the 40s freeholders. Besides, the money drawn could not be replaced without . . . making the new rent illegal.[46]

Not content with this broadside, O'Connell procured a series of unanimous resolutions from the current Munster provincial meeting in favour of maintaining the Old Rent intact. Further, he angled for clerical support by promising that the 'sacred fund' should be entirely devoted to Catholic education once the demands of the Emancipation campaign were over.

But churchmen were not easily led on this special issue. On 30 July, Bishop Coppinger of Cloyne struck the note of boundless clerical sympathy for the freeholders which was to mark the remainder of 1826. 'These poor men', he wrote, 'who generously risked and sacrificed their all, rather than vote against the dictates of their conscience, have an imperious claim upon . . . their catholic fellow-countrymen.'[47] Several priests advanced their own savings to stave off imminent ejectments; others travelled to Dublin to make the case for immediate aid more forcefully before the Association itself. From this it was a short step to priests intervening in debates and even moving resolutions, fierily. One priest from Monaghan, Bogue, supported a proposed raid upon the Old Rent with:

It was surely very easy for men at a distance from the scene of distress to reason coolly on sufferings which they did not witness; but he who had seen what the forty-shilling freeholders were enduring, must feel more warmly and more acutely. It had been well said, that this fund was created by the forty-shilling freeholders; and they did not come there as beggars to solicit alms; – they did not come there to supplicate a pittance, but to demand a right.[48]

A few days later another Monaghan priest, McCusker, 'commented . . . passage by passage, in the most severe terms' on a defence of

O'Connell's policy by Fr Sheehan, concluding with a motion that 'a letter strongly condemnatory of the principle contained in the letter of Mr Sheehan, should be addressed to that Rev. Gentleman'.[49]

In these circumstances, it was not difficult for the factious opposition to O'Connell, led by Lawless and a contumacious young barrister, Dowell O'Reilly, to challenge his direction at the centre. John Bric, his principal spokesman in Dublin, was ineffectual; and even Sheil, whose efforts to prevent public division in the Association were probably candid, admitted to some disagreement with O'Connell. Even O'Connell's trump card, his professional opinion on legality, was called in question. Some junior counsel dared to proffer a contrary view of the consequences of borrowing from the Old Rent; and on 4 September an editorial in the *Freeman's Journal* ended: 'Experience has proved that his [O'Connell's] opinion is not always infallible, when he mixes politics with law.' O'Connell could do no more than protest when, in his absence, the Association resolved to draw upon the Old Rent – though only when other resources had failed – to save the endangered freeholders.

Undoubtedly he had lost a skirmish; and the movement was temporarily distracted from its ends. Yet all this was comparatively insignificant. It was quite overshadowed – if we take the long view – by three general consequences of the election. First, the Association's power to break the connexion of landlord and tenant had been clearly demonstrated. This had been manifested so far only on a narrow front, but how might it not be expanded and multiplied? Such a consideration was to be ultimately decisive in producing Wellington's 'surrender'. On 12 September 1828, he was to tell Peel privately, 'I confess that what has moved me has been the Monaghan, the Louth, the Waterford and the Clare elections. I see clearly that we have to suffer here all the consequences of a practical democratic reform in Parliament, if we do not . . . remedy the evils.'[50] Secondly, the priests had been engaged far more intimately and vigorously than ever before in the Association's campaigns. The cause of the 40s. freeholders struck the right chord in the clergy, whose political 'education' thenceforth leapt forward, much to O'Connell's later benefit. Finally, the New Rent raised quite respectable amounts, over £6000 by the end of 1826. But more important to O'Connell than money were the opportunities which it afforded to re-assert his national leadership. 'Individual subscriptions', he had written at its launching, 'can never be sufficient. It requires a national effort: it requires the revival of the Catholic Rent. Once before at my voice that fund was created. Once before all Ireland became responsive to the call of patriotism . . . The Catholic people of Ireland are a nation. They should have something in the nature of a national treasury.'[51]

In fact, O'Connell had never been alarmed by the variegated opposition of July–October 1826, which was indeed made possible only by his own protracted absence from the capital. Whatever its occasional disadvantages, an eagerly implicated clergy was of critical importance in the agitation; and the Lawlesses and O'Reillys were soon cut down to their proper size when O'Connell returned to Dublin and resumed regular attendance at the Association's meetings. Moreover, the Old Rent was never needed to rescue the 40s. freeholders; this allowed the division in the Association to remain at the level of polite disagreement. Meanwhile, the drive led by O'Connell to gather in New Rent not only reinvigorated priests and people, but also brought other activities, especially the Catholic Census, back to life. O'Connell was always careful to conjoin the New Rent campaign with Catholic education, Catholic enumeration and similar projects which had been near moribund in the first half of 1826.

Thus the year ended with the movement thoroughly revived, a new electoral strategy and a variety of schemes for maintaining or increasing the momentum of agitation. O'Connell was fortunate that things had fallen out so well at home. For in the parliamentary arena the Catholic cause lost ground in 1826. Although the anti-popery cry and organizations had failed the highest expectations of their supporters in the general election in Great Britain, they had done enough to tilt the balance of votes in the House of Commons. This explains O'Connell's slowness in getting the Catholic question raised again in Parliament, despite his pre-general election threats. At the same time, the surge of new power which he felt in Ireland rendered him impatient with the customary whig counsels of restraint and self-effacement. On 31 December 1826 he replied to the Knight of Kerry's latest appeal, 'I am grown weary of being temperate, moderate and conciliatory to no one useful purpose and without having obtained one single advantage . . . No . . . *temperateness*, *moderation* and *conciliation* are suited only to perpetuate our degradation . . . if we want to succeed, we must call things by their proper names – speak out boldly, let it be called intemperately, and rouse in Ireland a spirit of *action*.'[52] Four years of Irish history had transformed O'Connell's bearing as well as the political temper and nature of his country.

CHAPTER 11

The First Hurrah

1827–8

I

Two themes dominated in O'Connell's politics during 1827: the deployment of the New Catholic Association's power within the House of Commons itself and the effort to augment that power throughout the country. The themes were of course interconnected, with the second steadily feeding the first.

The ultra-Protestant party in Great Britain was suddenly weakened by the death of the Duke of York, the heir-presumptive, on 5 January 1827, and the failure of the health of Liverpool, the prime minister, who suffered an incapacitating and ultimately fatal stroke on 15 February. These turns of fortune seemed to O'Connell to present opportunities to apply pressure *within* Parliament itself. The new heir-presumptive, the Duke of Clarence, might prove sympathetic or at least neutral towards the Catholic cause; at any rate, he could scarcely equal his dead brother in virulent ultra-Protestantism. On 15 January 1827 O'Connell asked his friend Bennett, then in London, to make it known to Clarence's entourage that the Irish Catholics

> are disposed to be the most attached people in the world. In plain English the Duke can command Ireland heart, hand and soul if he pleases . . . if possible learn *the wishes* of that party without committing any of them. They *shall* be obeyed. All I want is '*the map of the land*'. I want only the compass, I think I can steer by it.[1]

This was in the best eighteenth-century tradition of an opposition faction attempting to attach itself to the 'reversionary interest', the heir who might bring it to power or influence when he in turn succeeded to the throne. Conversely, O'Connell also sought to use his electoral power to sway Parliament itself, and this anticipated various later British devices whereby the politically deprived exercised leverage upon the politically privileged. Again on 15 January, he practically instructed the Knight of Kerry to join the pro-Catholic whig magnate, the Marquess of Lansdowne, if – as then seemed likely – he entered a reconstructed cabinet. Lansdowne, O'Connell promised, 'would bring with him into office all the support which the Catholics of Ireland ... could give to any administration'.[2] A week after Liverpool's stroke, he wrote to the Knight excitedly,

> We are here in great affright at the idea of the Duke of Wellington being made Prime Minister. If so, all the horrors of actual massacre threaten us. That villain has neither heart nor head. It is impossible to describe the execration with which his name is received amongst us. Could you suggest any act of the Catholic body which might facilitate the views of the Opposition at this moment? And, in particular, could we do anything to forward or support the Marquis of Lansdowne? ... We could have Catholic county meetings, addresses to the King, petitions to parliament or anything else that public bodies may do, if you deemed it useful.[3]

O'Connell set out a clear order of preference for a new ministry. The Catholics' first choice would be a purely whig cabinet; their second, a 'mixed' cabinet (including if need be, some of the present 'Protestant' ministers); and their third, the current cabinet headed by Canning. On 23 February, he ordered Eneas MacDonnell in London to communicate these priorities to specified Irish county members, Daly and Martin (Galway), Prittie and Hely-Hutchinson (Tipperary), Bernard and Lord Oxmantown (King's), Lloyd (Limerick), Hare (Kerry) and Vesey Fitzgerald (Clare), and also to every other Irish county member who, like these, had been supporters of Liverpool's administration. As the accredited 'agent to the Catholics of Ireland', MacDonnell was to tell as many of the members as he could find immediately that

> the Catholics will deem every man *an actual enemy* who does not support Canning against Peel, Eldon and Liverpool. You can go farther and pledge yourself that the men who at this crisis decline to support the Catholic against the no-popery part of the cabinet will meet with decided opposition at every ensuing election. In short it strikes me that you should now take a decided part with *all* our Irish members – [one word illegible] to rally them all if you can for a new cabinet, failing that to a partially new cabinet, failing that to a decidedly Canning administration. James Daly and Vesey Fitzgerald are both Peelers. If you can get *at* these gentlemen, assure them that we will organize an immediate opposition to them in their own counties unless they take a decided part with Mr Canning in any ministerial struggle now going forward. *You may pledge yourself* to have these sentiments re-echoed by public meetings and carried into practical effect.[4]

O'Connell also enjoined MacDonnell to demand an early debate in the

Commons upon the Catholic claims. From long experience of the evasions of 'friends', he rehearsed all the deprecatory arguments in favour of delay with which MacDonnell would certainly be greeted, and to which he must close his ears as if to the blandishments of the siren.

> When they tell you what *will be* if you postpone, reply with the old adage, *What will be, shall be.* Use my name if it be of the least value either here or in England as the author of this advice. Terrify *our* ministerial friends into an abandonment of Peel, etc., and *insist on* an immediate discussion.[5]

This was a remarkable attempt to manipulate conduct in the House of Commons from outside the system. O'Connell's menaces were directed solely at Irish county members who seemed likely to support Wellington for the premiership. The reason is obvious. The Association had shown in the general election of the preceding summer that it had the capacity to seat or unseat the great majority of the Irish county members. Unfortunately for O'Connell his threat was far from immediate; the new Parliament was only eight months old. None the less, no erring county member could discount it safely. Thus the ultimatum could conceivably turn about twenty to thirty votes in the House of Commons, a most significant outcome when divisions were often very close. To put it in general terms, O'Connell was working out, in a first, rudimentary and vicarious form, the idea of an independent Irish faction at Westminster, deriving its power from controlled agitation at home and the struggles of British politicians for office. Faintly, the Parnellite decade, the 1880s, was foreshadowed.

As things fell out, both the objects of O'Connell's lobbying were achieved, although it is impossible to decide what part the lobbying itself played in producing this result. An early debate on the Catholic claims took place when Burdett introduced a motion in favour of Emancipation on 5 March 1827, and on 10 April Canning became prime minister at last. O'Connell was furious at the outcome of Burdett's motion, a defeat by 276 votes to 272. In his '*malignity*' (as he himself half-seriously termed it), he called a Catholic meeting in Ennis, where he was on circuit, on 11 March, at which every Irish member who supported the government was declared anathema and plans were drawn up so to organize through a Liberal Club in co. Clare that only obedient candidates would be returned at the next election. The meeting also determined to petition not only for Emancipation once again but also – *in terrorem* – for both Repeal and parliamentary reform. Correspondingly, O'Connell lashed out at the tame reaction of the Association in Dublin to the news of Burdett's defeat. 'There is a want of spirit and of energy, a crouching beneath defeat which both surprise and afflict me', he told the Association's secretary, Dwyer. 'The resolutions of the separate meeting were puling and weeping but suggesting nothing. There was no manly *rebound*.'[6] The chairman of the Dublin meeting, Sir Thomas Esmonde, had even tried to suppress a letter from O'Connell to the Association because of its 'warmth' of tone and advocacy of Repeal, but Lawless had forced his hand by threatening to read the letter himself should the secretary fail to do so. 'Alas', wrote O'Connell, 'how little do the fault-finders know the species of material with which I have to deal, the kind of persons who eternally clog every movement and who would prefer breaking my head to smashing the pates of 500 Orangemen.' Such men were 'sure to be at the side of *power* and *authority*'.[7]

But O'Connell was soon subject to steady counter-pressure from the whigs (the Knight of Kerry being, as usual, the principal conduit) to stay his hand lest Canning lose the premiership through his association with Irish turbulence. Once Canning was appointed, O'Connell fell completely into line. His earlier burst of indignation and renewed defiance, which may have been in part factitious, ceased as abruptly as it had commenced. On 14 April 1827, O'Connell expressed his hope that the new prime minister would form a 'liberal' ministry. Four days later he announced the postponement of an aggregate meeting, which was to launch a fresh agitation for Emancipation, upon the ground that 'discussion might take place that might be disagreeable to some of their sincere [parliamentary] friends'.[8] With good reason, Mac-Donnell protested from London,

> it was a most grievous error to have stopped your proceedings for a moment in deference to the party manoeuvrings here, and I greatly fear that you will have reason to think so very soon . . . Go on, even now, and determination will mitigate the evil, an evil, be assured of it, that never would have occurred, if you had not evinced vacillation in your Dublin proceedings.[9]

But O'Connell's political tantrum of March was now over; he was back on course, committed to working strictly within the Westminster ambit once again.

Down to Canning's death on 8 August 1827, O'Connell never wavered in supporting the new administration. This may seem strange, for it disappointed him continually. He could scarcely have expected the condition-precedent of the Association's endorsement of

14 April, that Canning form a wholly 'liberal' government, to be honoured. As the Knight pointed out on 23 April, the king's 'voice' alone meant that 'an entirely favourable ministry ... is *totally impossible*'.[10] O'Connell certainly expected wholesale changes in the membership of the Irish, and to a lesser extent the British, administration. Here he was almost uniformly rebuffed, every specific proposal which he made being summarily rejected. Eldon resigned the British lord chancellorship in pique, and John Doherty (later to become O'Connell's *bête noire* but at this stage apparently a 'liberal') was appointed Irish attorney-general; but otherwise the no-popery phalanxes were undisturbed. Worst of all perhaps, not only did the ultra-Protestants remain entrenched in the executive layer in Dublin Castle, but Lord Manners was retained as Irish chancellor despite a widespread expectation that he would be replaced by Plunket.

Manners continued a rampant Orange partisan: 'He is certainly without disguise', O'Connell told the Knight bitterly, 'and even the shallowness of his own understanding makes him the more dangerous because of the open countenance he gives to every species of "illiberality".'[11] With Manners' encouragement, the Orange party reasserted its dominance of Dublin Corporation. He also barred the way to O'Connell's darling hope that he be granted a patent of precedence by the new government, and cost O'Connell much chancery business because clients believed that Manners would find against him wherever possible. Worst of all, the 'liberals' in the government used Manners to excuse their own inaction. On 9 June 1827 Bennett told O'Connell that Brougham had answered charges of indifference to the Catholic interest with ' "*Oh, Lord Manners is playing the devil.*" He sent me to Lamb [the pro-Catholic Irish chief secretary] who ... said, "Lord M. is watching every opportunity to embarrass us." "*Tell Mr O'C. I must for a time be worse than Peel* but when we can, we will do all the good we can. Beg of him to have confidence, though we cannot do much, or worse men will come." '[12] O'Connell expounded furiously on the 'exceeding' fortune of the Orange faction. 'They generally have such secretaries as Peel and Goulburn but when they have a more liberal secretary, *his candour* to our enemies makes him a more useful patron to the Orangists than a decided no-popery man could be.'[13] None the less, O'Connell made no move to distance himself from Canning's administration, despite the fact that even such moderates as Bishop Doyle and Sheil were complaining that the Catholic cause fared worse under its false friends than under its open enemies.

How is the constancy of O'Connell's adherence to Canning's regime to be explained? First, in 1827, as always, his antipathy to the tribe of Eldon, Wellington and Peel was so inveterate that reason and calculation simply flew out the window when it was a question of excluding them from office. In a letter of 24 December 1827 O'Connell supplied his more positive strategy. Emancipation was not to be looked for immediately; in appointing Canning, George IV had forbidden him even to raise the question. But O'Connell hoped to prepare for its successful canvass in 1828 by gradually building up liberal Protestant support in Ireland (and to some extent in Britain also). This hope was based upon his expectation that a species of spoils system would operate upon Canning's and Lansdowne's accession to power: a redistribution of places, honours and privileges would be the surest way to attract influential new support for the Catholic claims. O'Connell looked for one specific reward on his own account, the patent of precedence at the bar which would provide some compensation for his being still prohibited from taking silk. He pursued this objective, which would enhance his standing, and doubtless also his income, quite as tenaciously as he had done the Queen's Irish attorney-generalship in 1820. 'I am everyday made to feel more and more', he told Spring-Rice on 29 November 1827, 'the injustice which is done to me and my clients by the promotion of my juniors to the inner bar and the neglect to give me what I think my *due* precedency.'[14]

O'Connell was extremely loth to abandon such a congery of hopes, all the more so when the alternative seemed to be more and worse tories in office and another stretch of bawling, brawling, sterile opposition. Throughout the four months of Canning's premiership, he awaited, more or less patiently, the gradual liberalization of both men and measures; and he mourned Canning's death as if he had already shown himself to be Ireland's saviour. 'Mr Canning is dead', he told Mary on 9 August 1827. 'There is another blow to wretched Ireland. No man can become of vital importance to her but he is immediately snatched off.'[15] Nor did O'Connell reject Canning's liberal tory successor, Goderich, out of hand. True, he complained to Bennett on 26 September that the new ministry had shown 'no one symptom' of acting 'honestly by Ireland'. Their conduct 'convince[s] me that they are determined to give us good words as long as these can delude, but their acts, *their acts*, are unequivocal . . . The Orange faction unchecked . . . Gregory in full power at the Castle. The Trenches in full pay and patronage at the Custom House . . . The Hills and the

Blackers and the other *Evening Mail* patrons as strong and influential as ever.'[16] But Gregory and the Trenches, Hills and Blackers had all come through Canning's reign unscathed. In fact, Goderich's accession did not worsen O'Connell's situation materially. On the contrary, not only did he now ask more confidently for minor official favours but also on 24 October Goderich replaced Manners at last by Hart, the English vice-chancellor. Hart proved worth waiting for. He was an able equity lawyer and, as the Knight reported to O'Connell, 'though 74 he is in great mental vigour and, as I saw him picking up a Picci in Regent Street, the other day, I presume also in other vigour, and he is a most agreeable gentleman'.[17] Within five weeks O'Connell exulted, 'The system of favouritism has already disappeared.'[18] His chancery briefs had multiplied, and he was emboldened to ask Spring-Rice, obliquely, to bring the question of his precedency before Hart. When however Spring-Rice appeared to reply evasively, O'Connell unloosed all the pent-up irritation of the year:

> It is indeed well that the individual character of Sir Anthony Hart serves to mitigate that system of exclusion which is almost as effectually in action now as ever it was. We have a little also of the grace of hypocrisy to mitigate that system but beyond these advantages – such as they are! – the change of administration has not reached this country for any one useful purpose. Our enemies were at all events sincere, and they deserved respect on that account.[19]

Significantly, this quarrel was soon mended, and within a few days Spring-Rice had written to Hart pleading O'Connell's case. It is equally significant that O'Connell's ultimate failure to obtain his patent of precedence did not move him from his course of qualified support of the administration. He still placed his hopes in making common cause with Irish Protestant liberals and even with unwary members of 'the Orange party'. After reaffirming his faith that such a strategy would undermine the remaining English resistance to the Catholic claims, he assured Mary on 1 December 1827, 'Darling, I really do expect Emancipation this sessions'.[20]

II

At no stage during 1827 did O'Connell play the suppliant or the inferior in his dealings with the whigs, nor did he expect them to yield more than he could force them to. The relationship was a liaison of convenience. The whigs needed Irish 'tranquillity' to strengthen their hand in claiming a part of government. O'Connell looked for, and to a limited degree obtained, a mitigation of Orangeism in the Irish administration and a larger share in the places and douceurs for his political clients and friends. In the longer run, he banked upon the informal alliance slowly bringing home to the British public that concessions to the Catholics, and especially the final concession of Emancipation, was the only means of rendering Ireland governable. For such a policy to succeed, he needed to be demonstrably strong at home; and the Association was the index of his strength. Hence the deaf ear which he turned to the whig pleas of April 1827 that he do Canning's new administration the 'infinite service . . . [of] bringing, at least for the present, the Association to a close'.[21] Hence also his tireless efforts, both before and after Canning was appointed, to widen and deepen the Association's hold upon Irish popular opinion.

On 2 January 1827 O'Connell called upon Doyle (and other sympathetic bishops) for aid in two of the Association's current campaigns, the 'Education Census' and the collection of the New Catholic Rent. Both had especial clerical appeal, the first as that section of the general Catholic census which would reveal the extent of Protestant proselytizing of the young, the second because the priests (rival 'proprietors', as it were) always responded fiercely to landlord retaliation upon the 40s. freeholders. O'Connell approached Doyle most gingerly, pleading 'an honest conviction of the paramount utility of these measures to our religion and country', and the certainty 'that the persecution of the 40s. freeholders has recommenced, and that we are much pressed for relief by persons who suffer persecution for not sending their children to proselytizing schools.'[22] But it was also true that the Rent and census were O'Connell's own particular prescriptions for vivifying and co-ordinating the Association. O'Connell appended a list of the priests in Doyle's diocese who had already sent in census returns; only six had done so, most with forms incomplete. This shows two points of interest – O'Connell's minute knowledge of and detailed work upon Catholic organization even in (to him) relatively unfamiliar parts of Ireland, and the comparative failure of the census device at this stage, except where, as in Waterford and Lismore, the bishop insisted on complete clerical compliance with O'Connell's direction.

The Rent remained O'Connell's foremost organizational concern throughout 1827. Even when on circuit, he regularly returned his own monthly subscription, often with other sums which he had gathered locally and a hortatory address to be read to the Association in Dublin. A typical accompanying letter, sent from Cork on 5 April, argued that the continuance and permanence of the Catholic Rent can be secured only by giving the example of unabated perseverance in the payment of small sums month after month. In fact the people who are both zealous and honest are everywhere ready to pay. If there could be found individuals of the more wealthy class to take the trouble of acting as collectors.

There is nothing our enemies dread so much as the extension and permanence of the Catholic Rent.[23]

Dissatisfied with the Rent returns, O'Connell carried a resolution at the Association meeting of 17 July calling upon each parish priest to establish an effective system of collection in his area. To maximize the appeal, denominational education and voter-protection were again placed in the forefront of the Rent's objectives. But the 'reform' of July proved ineffective – only once did the weekly Rent exceed £100 during 1827 – and at the close of the year O'Connell devised a new 'churchwarden' system. Each parish was to appoint two church-wardens, one by the nomination of the priests, the other elected by the parishioners. On the churchwardens was placed all the local work of the Association – the selection and oversight of the Rent collectors; the completion of the census returns; the furnishing of reports on proselytizing, evictions, the disposition of the district landlords and the local impositions of the Established Church; and the maintenance of electoral registers. The plan succeeded immediately, if not (in the nature of things) universally. In its very first week of operation the Rent rose to £604, and the other deficiencies began quickly to be supplied. But this was only half the story. The regular communication between the wardens and the central body was of equal importance to O'Connell. As the wardens drew other parishioners of standing into the work, Peel rightly discerned 'some scheme of general organisation of the Roman Catholic population' in the venture.[24] Moreover, by securing the appointment of his son Maurice as co-ordinating Secretary of Churchwardens, O'Connell kept the organization under his direct control.

O'Connell had been careful to leave considerable power in the priests' hands. He agreed with Sheil, 'Our great object should be to bring the priests into efficient and *systematic* action.'[25] Privately, O'Connell was not much disturbed by the successes of Protestant evangelization in the remoter regions. 'They are buying wretches in every direction', he told Mary on 22 March 1827, 'who are a disgrace to them and no loss to the church they desert.'[26] But he appears to have been truly worried by the Evangelicals' educational drive. At any rate, this really touched the clerical nerve and was in consequence maintained as a leading item in the Association's business. Character-istically, O'Connell was not content with denunciation but moved on to designing a Catholic counter-system. His efforts culminated in the Association's grant of £1500 on 19 December 1827 towards the establishment of a model school in Dublin 'on such a plan as to be capable of extending scientific education to the poorer classes of Ireland as suggested in the late letter of the Rt Rev. Dr Doyle':[27] pleasing Doyle was a useful bonus. *Pari passu*, and in keeping another favourite grievance of the clergy, Catholic burials, on the boil, O'Connell progressed beyond mere abuse (though again he main-tained this briskly) during 1827. He welcomed L'Estrange's proposal to the Association on 15 September that Catholics enclose their own burial grounds, reiterated his opinion that there was 'no legal obstacle whatever' to such a course, and on 27 October committed the Association to supporting the purchase of land for cemeteries. Again, ecclesiastical and political interests were being intermeshed.

But service to the Church did not always march in step with forbearance towards Canning's and Goderich's ministries. Here Doyle was O'Connell's most dangerous critic. On 8 June 1827, he complained bitterly that O'Connell's ministerial friends had done nothing to oppose either the renewal of state grants to proselytizing educational societies or two recent bills which rendered more secure the stipends of the ministers of the Church of Ireland at the expense of the Irish Catholic population. He had always doubted, he wrote,

> whether it were not better for the Irish Catholics to see Canning and the Grenvilles forced to join the Whigs in opposition, rather than to see the Whigs playing second fiddle to Canning, and both truckling to the Court and the Bishops; but as all are not as patient as I am in politics, nor all so averse to the building of buttresses to the oligarchy and the Church by accepting of Emancipation on Canning's principles, I have known how to be silent and to hold my own opinions without interfering with those of others but I am confident that the public would expect of you that you should do everything in your power, now that the Catholic Association is silent, to save us from being swallowed alive by a cormorant Church without being able to emit a cry.[28]

Humiliated yet perhaps not altogether displeased to possess such a lever, O'Connell forwarded Doyle's letter to the Knight for communi-cation to 'our friends in the Cabinet', with the comment, 'It is not pleasant to be reproached with all that has not *been done* for this country.'[29] On 30 September Sheil also expressed his disquietude on the effects of O'Connell's policy upon the Church and Association:

We should not hide from ourselves, the public mind is beginning to cool. The reason is, I think, this: when Peel and Dawson and our decided antagonists were in office, the Catholics were exposed to perpetual affronts which kept their indignation alive. The priests, especially, were held in constant ferment. But now that Lord Lansdowne is in, we say to each other, 'what a pity that our good friends in the Cabinet cannot do us any service!' and, convinced that they cannot, we 'take the will for the deed'.[30]

Sheil urged that the priests be roused by a more vigorous use of the burials issue; earlier he had proposed at the Association that the bishops compose and enjoin the recitation of a prayer 'that God would turn the heart of his Majesty's ministry'.[31] This last may have shown small knowledge of episcopal sensibilities, but it certainly indicated Sheil's alarm at what he saw as the growing political torpor of the clergy. Such sharp words from men of Doyle's and Sheil's standing help to explain O'Connell's greater concentration, during the second half of 1827, upon the work most likely to draw in the Church.

As virtually the solitary advocate of accommodating the 'liberal' administrations of the year, O'Connell had to bestir himself repeatedly to maintain his dominance in the Association. He resisted every proposal put forward by a potential rival. At the start of 1827, he opposed, initially, the first form of Wyse's detailed programmes for a pyramidical national political organization under the title of 'Liberal Clubs'. On 19 January, MacDonnell proposed from London that the Association propagandize overseas and especially on the continent, and also the setting up of a 'statistical committee' to gather data on the income and conduct of the clergy of the Church of Ireland; O'Connell ignored both suggestions. On 12 March James Dwyer, secretary of the newly-founded Hibernian Bank, pressed for a standing committee of the Association to provide continuity of meetings; O'Connell condemned the scheme as at once illegal and tending to introduce 'secret management into Catholic affairs'.[32] At the Association meeting of 21 July Lawless (in O'Connell's absence) pronounced the existing system of Rent collection 'Barren and unproductive'[33] and carried a resolution in favour of a simultaneous Sunday collection in all parishes to provide a defence fund for the 40s. freeholders; three days later O'Connell called an extraordinary meeting which rescinded Lawless's resolution. Sheil's proposal at a Catholic meeting on 22 September to set up a central committee to correspond with all the Irish parochial clergy was never heard of thereafter.

O'Connell was especially ruthless in crushing Lawless's challenge on the Rent. There seems no reason to doubt Lawless's charge that

O'Connell packed the extraordinary meeting of 24 July to ensure a majority. Certainly, in addressing the meeting, he depicted Lawless as coercing the priests and attempting also to use their bishops to coerce them, and he decried the practice of 'collecting at the chapel doors'.[34] When Lawless announced that he would raise the question again at the next ordinary meeting of the Association on 4 August, O'Connell (from circuit) addressed an artful letter to the meeting combining an assertion of his directional authority ('no person *can* know more of the details of the collection of the Catholic Rent than I do'), a 'most earnest entreaty' to his 'friend Mr Lawless' to think better of his proposal, and a shameless playing of the clerical card:

> Besides being, in my humble judgement, quite ungenerous to interfere with the ordinary resources of the clergy and of charity, it would also, in my humble opinion, be very ungrateful.
>
> The Catholic clergy have individually contributed to our funds. Poor as they are they have not only almost universally contributed to these funds but they have actually contributed as much as, if not (and this is my recollection) much more than, the wealthy classes of the Catholic laity. Would it therefore not be cruel of us to obtrude in any way between the Catholic clergy and these, their almost only resources! . . . the more ready they are to make such a sacrifice the more scrupulous should we be not to resort to the indelicate and unfeeling plan of interrupting any part of their small income.[35]

Vainly did Lawless protest that his plan allowed for the priests' withdrawing their normal 'offerings' before transmitting the balance to the Association. O'Connell had beaten him from the field; his motion was abandoned.

In fact, O'Connell later incorporated most of the proposals made by others during 1827 in his own schemes. His 'County Clubs' plan was 'patently imitative'[36] of Wyse's Liberal Clubs. The collection of data on the income and bearing of the Established Church in the various localities was eventually added to the parish returns. The church-warden system was from the start centrally co-ordinated, and the wardens themselves were instructed to attend the masses on the first Sunday of every month (to be named 'Rent Sunday') to collect subscriptions at the chapel doors! All this makes clear O'Connell's absolute determination to maintain his supremacy within the organization. Its power and efficiency as a political weapon were all-important in 1827; but so too was maintaining his grip – and his alone – upon the hilt.

A much larger, subterranean challenge to O'Connell's leadership, and indeed to the very nature of the movement which he had created, may however have been developing during the year. Wyse certainly believed so; and while Sheil may have been the foremost observer and delineator of the immediate in the Association, Wyse was incomparably his superior in discerning the large and gradual movement of events: in the 1820s, at least, he may be spoken of without absurdity as an Irish de Tocqueville. Wyse traced the origin of the change to a New York meeting in 1825 in support of the Association at which separatist, radical and republican resolutions, composed by the former United Irishman, William McNevin, were unanimously adopted. 'The Friends of Ireland', embodied at this meeting, spread gradually through North and South America, often under the lead of old '98 men and generally attracting those who 'had brought with them the burning sense of accumulated injury – the liveliest desire of retaliation – a deep and solid detestation of the very name – of the very thought, of England'.[37] By 1829 a formidable confederation committed to furnishing aid in Ireland's struggle against her 'oppressors' was on the point of being launched in Washington.

Not immediately, but certainly during 1827, Wyse believed, this development began to affect Ireland. Wyse did not mean that a specific party had been formed; but

> an identity of reasoning, and an identity of feeling . . . has been gradually growing up . . . This identity, by an attentive observer, may be traced through many of their public speeches; but a much better proof of its existence may be found in the frankness and fervour of familiar conversation. Amongst the inhabitants of the large commercial towns, particularly amongst the tradesmen, amongst the younger members of the bar, and even of the church, its principles are to be met with in full vigour.[38]

Wyse saw in this the formative stage of a struggle for control of the Association (and thereby of the Catholic 'nation') in which the violent faction would ultimately triumph over O'Connell.

> O'Connell, who had set out with exciting, was in the latter period of the struggle frequently obliged to moderate, and to allay. This moderation was not the effect of a change in the man, but it was the effect of a change in the men around him. The interposition for a time would doubtless have been regarded. Past services, great experience, habitual command, and numerous adherents, bound by personal as well as public ties, would have, for a long period, assured to him the full enjoyment of his ancient supremacy. But it is not to be concealed, that that supremacy would soon have declined, without an entire acquiescence in the more vehement propositions of his competitors . . . The opposition to their measures

would have furnished grounds for impeachment before the multitude, with whom such men, from the very nature of their principles, would soon have become the favourites; or, had he allowed himself to make the base compromise of principle to popularity, they would have gained by the accession of his name and influence the strongest support to their own cause. Any man who has observed the late proceedings of the Catholic Association, with impartiality, cannot have avoided perceiving that such a contest *had actually commenced* . . .[39]

This was of course speculation, and Wyse, like many intelligent contemporaries, tended to read the future in terms of the recent French Revolutionary past. None the less it is true that the Association, even at home, drew in a remarkable number of former United Irishmen, in much the same fashion as the Land League was later to prove a magnet for ex-Fenians. It is also true that Wyse's account prefigured, most arrestingly, many of the features of the Parnellite era, down even to the significance of American money in extending the agitation and the possibility of depositing such funds in Paris in O'Connell's name, to render them inviolable by the British government. Finally, it is true that some among the younger agitators had begun to speak – if only *sotto voce* – of O'Connell, now in his fifties and having lived almost half his life in the preceding century, as *passé*. All in all, Wyse had probably glimpsed a real potentiality – that is, if Emancipation had continued much longer to be the Cheshire cat which always dissolved as one drew near. O'Connell was no historical seer; but as a superb political animal he would have understood instinctively these consequences of hope too long deferred. Perhaps he really was seeing the 'Wolf' he had so often cried when he wrote to Bennett on 26 September 1827, 'If it [Emancipation] is not carried soon, these countries will certainly separate. I see the growing materials of separation . . . the disastrous struggle will be delayed by us who *now* possess influence, but come it will.'[40]

III

To turn the coin over, and look at 1827 in British political terms, Liverpool's stroke in February had placed the Catholic issue at the centre of the power struggle for the succession. Peel bid on the strength of the anti-Catholic feeling in the Commons, Canning on the pro-Catholic sentiment there. It was soon clear that neither Peel nor Wellington could form a wholly anti-Catholic Ministry. Conversely, the defeat of Burdett's motion in favour of the Catholic claims on 5

March, though smaller than generally expected, was none the less critical in weakening Canning's hand in dealing with George IV. He could not now hope to form a pro-Catholic ministry; so the 'open system', long disastrous for Emancipation, would remain. Although references to his sacrifices for the Catholic cause had been for years part of Canning's stock in trade, his career since 1822 had shown abundantly that office was his overriding aim, provided it came in the face-saving form of the 'open system'. In forming his ministry, he even drew over a large number of the whigs, headed by Lansdowne and Brougham, into support of shelving the Catholic issue *pro tem*; he also bowed to George IV's demand that the Irish Administration remain substantially anti-Catholic. Thus the formation of a government in which three-quarters of ministers were pro-Catholics was in reality of small advantage to O'Connell.

How things would have developed had Canning lived it is difficult to say. Although, immediately, the whigs had been emasculated as a pro-Catholic force by the involvement of many of them in the 'open system', their large number in the coalition might have built up at last irresistible pressure to make some compromise on the Catholic question a government measure. Meanwhile, Dublin Castle might be gradually 'de-Orangeized'. These long-term developments were evidently what O'Connell had in mind when he told the Irish people, on Canning's death, that 'the blessings which under his administration we hoped so soon to enjoy in reality, have now suddenly been hurried from us, and show like a dim and distant vision.'[41] Goderich lacked the master's reputation and charisma, and appeared to accentuate the anti-Catholic bias of the Irish Government by appointing Lord Anglesey (then supposed to be an anti-Catholic) to succeed Wellesley as lord lieutenant. It was not however these deficiencies which finally determined O'Connell to recommence agitation upon the fullest scale, but rather the rapid distintegration of the ministry itself towards the close of 1827.

O'Connell's recommitment to agitation was wholehearted. In January 1828 a massive fourteen-day meeting was held in Dublin to organize petitions for the forthcoming parliamentary session; the churchwarden system was instituted, with immediate effect; Wyse's new *Political Catechism*, designed to politicize the masses systematically, and his Liberal Club proposals were approved; and on Sunday 13 January, simultaneous meetings were held in nearly 1600 of the 2500 parishes in Ireland. Even more than the churchwarden system, Wyse's schemes constituted a most ambitious plan of slow but ever-intensifying political education and development, to relate Irish popular organization upon a national scale to House of Commons politics. But the simultaneous meetings were to act as a sudden blow. This national show of strength had been inspired by the Suppression Act of 1825 and rendered a concrete proposition by Sheil two years later. The actual chain of meetings of 13 January 1828, coinciding as they did with Sunday masses and supplied as they were with ready-made petitions, may have constituted a rudimentary form of concerted action. None the less, a total attendance of one and a half million persons (as calculated by the *Dublin Evening Post*) was an impressive demonstration of both Catholic force and the Association's organizational capacity. O'Connell had rightly discerned the potentialities of massing vast numbers at a single direction when he wrote to Doyle on 29 December 1827, 'The combination of national action – all Catholic Ireland acting as one man – must necessarily have a powerful effect on the minds of the ministry and of the entire British nation. A people who can be thus brought to act together and by one impulse are too powerful to be neglected and too formidable to be long opposed.'[42]

The replacement of Goderich by Wellington on 22 January 1828, and Peel's return to the Home Office four days later, at once enflamed and seemed to justify the new offensive: in angry reaction, the Association, with O'Connell's concurrence, passed the fateful resolution that every pro-ministerial parliamentary candidate for an Irish constituency would henceforth be opposed. O'Connell failed to recognize that the new prime minister was the most likely of all British politicians to bow to the type of pressure demonstrated by the simultaneous meetings of 13 January. As early as 1825, Wellington had come to the conclusion that, sooner or later, the Catholic question would have to be compromised. The capacity to summon forth more than a million persons at will was a powerful argument, to such a mind as his, against allowing such forces to be built up further. It certainly fits this view of the matter that in his first three months of office Wellington should have been exploring, confidentially, possible compromise solutions. Similarly, his agreement in April 1828 to the repeal of the Test and Corporation Acts, which had discriminated against nonconformists, was so clear a precedent for the removal of Catholic disabilities as to suggest a 'dry run' for Emancipation. At the same time, Wellington had been careful to keep on terms with the ultra-tories, as best he might. This became at once more critical and more difficult when the now annual motion for Catholic relief was carried in the Commons on 12 May 1828 by a majority of six.

Meanwhile O'Connell adhered unwaveringly to the whigs in opposition. 'Lord Lansdowne has gone out of office not only with honour unsullied but with character exalted', he told the Knight on 27 February 1828. 'His *whole party* certainly deserve the public confidence and amply justify that confidence.'[43] But he was not so besotted a partisan as to miss the significance of Wellington's decision to repeal the Test and Corporation Acts. Immediately he proposed, at the Association meeting of 1 May, that the January resolution to oppose every ministerial parliamentary candidate be rescinded. For once, O'Connell failed. That this was an index of the growing power of the radicals within the organization is confirmed by O'Connell's letter of 27 May 1828 to his friend Bennett, superscribed *'Most Confidential'*. The nature of O'Connell's secret negotiations through his trusted intermediary may be obscure, but the need to conceal the degree of his 'moderation' is crystal clear.

> See B[rougham] as speedily as possible. *I confide* much in your discretion. Should *we* be able here to do anything, which indeed is not now probable, you may take a *pledge* for me but recollect the Catholics must press forward. The manner and matter of the pressure may be regulated . . .
>
> See Blount, the English Catholic Secretary, from me and tell him that the 'Securities' will produce an immediate rupture between the English and Irish Catholics . . . Tell him I *must* lead in that war. Eneas, the pious Eneas, is raving on the subject. Jack Lawless is mad with delight at a good row. [Stephen] Coppinger [a 'progressive' in the Association] grins a ghastly smile at the prospect of a good quarrel with the English Catholics. See Blount privately. Tell him I would not *write this* because I only wish you to speak it.[44]

Although British and Irish politics, and Wellington's and O'Connell's manoeuvrings, were pursuing largely independent courses, they touched electrically now and then. It was the imminent return of the tories to office which had determined O'Connell to return to the path of remorseless agitation, and Wellington's appointment which had led the Association to resolve that every pro-ministerial candidate should be opposed. Conversely, it was Wellington's decision to rid himself of the most 'liberal' members of his cabinet – probably to prepare the way for a Catholic compromise – which forced the hand of the Association. Vesey Fitzgerald, one of the sitting members for co. Clare, succeeded as president of the board of trade, and was thereby compelled to seek re-election. With the public commitment to oppose every ministerialist still intact, O'Connell was most awkwardly placed. Fitzgerald was a consistent pro-Catholic and lavish distributor of official favours about the county, his father a popular landlord and a former Grattanite. Fitzgerald would be backed moreover by the entire weight of the landed property of Clare, now that the nobility and gentry had learnt by the experiences of 1826 that the political 'rights' of their order, as such, might be at stake.

The critical difficulty for the Association when it met on 14 June 1828, only seventeen days before polling, was to find a candidate quickly – or at all. It was however the forward element which dominated at the meeting and, with whatever misgivings, O'Connell acquiesced in the eventual decision to challenge Fitzgerald at the polls. He agreed moreover to draft the address to the Clare Liberal Club and to descend upon the county, with his principal lieutenants, for the actual days of the election. A subsequent emergency meeting of the Association voted £5000, as a first instalment, for electoral expenses. Thus O'Connell found himself, in effect, presiding over machinery, already in motion, to fight a county election à la Waterford in 1826 without a contestant to which that machinery could be attached. Yet seven more days passed before two of the Association's Clare members, Thomas Steele, a quixotic (or perhaps Sancho Panza-ish) Protestant squireen, and the Barry Lyndonesque James O'Gorman Mahon arrived in Ennis to invite Major MacNamara to stand. MacNamara, a minor Clare landlord and O'Connell's close friend, was the only practicable candidate; no other proprietor in the county could be supposed even to consider standing against his order.

As feared, the Association's delegates found MacNamara unwilling to stand against Fitzgerald because of family favours received; the young William Smith O'Brien, another though more remote possibility as a candidate, was apparently in the same position. Steele's and Mahon's rapid traverse of the chapels of Cratloe, Sixmilebridge, Newmarket-on-Fergus and Ennis on Sunday 22 June left them in no doubt that the priests and the 40s. freeholders were ready to obey the Association blindly. On the other hand, the tenants would not openly oppose their landlords and risk terrible reprisal unless 'they were certain of a contest'.[45] Mahon posted back to Dublin with these mixed but essentially dismal tidings on the evening of the 23rd. Before the next day was out, however, all was transformed by O'Connell declaring himself a candidate.

IV

Success has many fathers, and the line of those with some credit for the idea of a Catholic presenting himself as a parliamentary candidate runs from John Keogh, who had pressed its advantages many years before, through a liberal Protestant, Alderman Roose, to P. V. Fitzpatrick (son of the bookseller, Hugh Fitzpatrick), who actually proposed it to O'Connell on 24 June 1828. Fitzpatrick found O'Connell loth to stand; he had neither money nor the wish to throw up his profession – or even to lose the business of the current law term. He may also have been doubtful of success, and conscious of the dreadful consequences of defeat for both his own and the entire movement's public standing. But Fitzpatrick overbore him, promising to gather in all the necessary funds himself – as indeed he did. (Unwittingly, Fitzpatrick had taken the first step towards becoming O'Connell's financial and general 'manager' for life!) That very evening O'Connell concocted his electoral address to meet the next day's newspapers. Significantly he struck out on a strongly sectarian line at once.

> The oath at present required by law is, 'That the sacrifice of the Mass and the Invocation of the blessed Virgin Mary and other Saints, as now practised in the Church of Rome, are impious and idolatrous'. Of course, I never will stain my soul with such an oath; I leave that to my honourable opponent, Mr Vesey Fitzgerald. He has often taken that horrible oath; he is ready to take it again, and asks your votes to enable him so to swear. I would rather be torn limb from limb than take it.

The address went on to present the choice as one 'between the sworn libeller of the Catholic faith and one who has devoted his early life to your cause, who has consumed his manhood in a struggle for your liberties.'[46] Clearly, the classes were despaired of, and all O'Connell's energies directed to prising the peasant vote from the proprietors by the lever of religion.

The contest instantly became a new 'trial by combat'. The lay Catholic commitment may be gauged from Fitzpatrick's gathering £100 from each of sixteen Dublin Catholics within twenty-four hours of O'Connell's announcement as well as from the succession of mass demonstrations as O'Connell travelled from Dublin to Ennis from the afternoon of 28 June to the early morning of the 30th. It was, however, the involvement of the priests which mattered most. Doyle, to whom O'Connell first and most desperately appealed, recognized this instantly, and called for total support for O'Connell (with a tribute to the devotion of 'your time, your talents, your fortune, and your life' to the 'sacred cause') in a public letter.[47] At the other end of the ecclesiastical spectrum, Rev. Thomas Maguire, an ordinary country priest but the best-known religious controversialist of the day, hastened immediately from Leitrim to Clare. The Irish government had fondly hoped that the Church would divide upon the candidature. 'O'Connell', reported Anglesey, the new lord lieutenant, 'finds himself so much opposed by some of the most respectable of the Bishops, and by many of the lower clergy also, that he is quite wild.'[48] This was to misread the situation. O'Connell could count upon a clerical closing of ranks behind him as 'Catholic champion'. Even the cautious primate, Archbishop Patrick Curtis, had told him only a month before that he would trust O'Connell's judgment rather than his own in Catholic politics. In the event, almost the entire priesthood of the constituency campaigned for O'Connell, most of them in Ennis itself, the county town. Only one parish priest (duly execrated and humiliated) worked in Fitzgerald's interest. This was probably the decisive factor in O'Connell's victory. Sheil provided an epitome of the clerical influence in describing his own electioneering in the chapel at Corofin on the Sunday before the poll. The parish priest, John Murphy ('rather a study' for the enthusiast MacBriar in *Old Mortality*, tall, pale, emaciated, his face 'long, sunken and cadaverous, but . . . illuminated by eyes blazing with all the fire of genius') threw off his vestments after mass and called upon his people in Irish to sacrifice themselves for O'Connell, their faith and their fatherland.

It was a most extraordinary and powerful display of the externals of eloquence . . . his intonations were soft, pathetic, denunciatory, and conjuring, according as his theme varied, and as he had recourse to different expedients to influence the people – shouts of laughter attended his description of a miserable Catholic who should prove recreant to the great cause, by making a sacrifice of his country to his landlord.

The close of his speech was peculiarly effective. He became inflamed by the power of his emotions, and while he raised himself into the loftiest attitude to which he could ascend, he laid one hand on the altar, and shook the other in the spirit of almost prophetic admonition, and as his eyes blazed and seemed to start from his forehead, thick drops fell down his face, and his voice rolled through lips livid with passion and covered with foam. It is almost unnecessary to say that such an appeal was irresistible. The multitude burst into shouts of acclamation, and would have been ready to mount a battery roaring with cannon at his command. Two days after the results were felt at the hustings; and while Sir Edward O'Brien stood aghast, Father Murphy marched into Ennis at the head of his tenantry, and polled them to a man in favour of Daniel O'Connell.[49]

Ennis, wrote Thackerary a little later, 'stands up on the [River]

Fergus, a busy, little, narrow-streeted, foreign-looking town, approached by half a mile of thatched cots'.[50] It comprised a tangle of gloomy thoroughfares and lanes knotted about the marketplace and the cramped courthouse square. The square, with the tops of several tributary streets running into it from crazy angles, constituted the auditorium of the election. But the stage itself shifted, according to scene, from the courthouse steps to the green-bedecked balcony of O'Connell's lodgings, on the right-hand side. Successively, one or other focused the attention of the surging peasantry. Many of these camped on the watermeadows of the Fergus; but when they returned daily to their playhouse, the compression originally signalled by their convergence from all directions along the hilly roads of Clare was powerfully magnified. In its way, this was symbolic of the event: Bonaparte had shown contemporaries that to mass and concentrate one's numbers at the enemy's weakest point was the key to victory. Doubtless the monochromatic 'set', with grey skies and limestone walls and buildings generally prevailing, threw the drama which was being enacted into a higher relief.

O'Connell himself, with endless variety of tone and mood, played the by-election as theatre from the beginning. When preceded on nomination day by Vesey Fitzgerald's tears as he spoke of his father lying close to death, and by an attack from Francis Gore, a Clare proprietor and unsuccessful counsel, for his 'betrayal' of the 40s. freeholders in 1826, he burst out in response,

> And am I now to be subjected to the taunts of a briefless barrister, and a bigot without business? Of what use is my success to me? I have wept over my lot in private – for, unlike some people, I never shed my tears in public – and should I not deplore the cruel fate which places the Gores and other Protestants above me in my native land?

When Edward Hickman, a considerable Clare landlord and notorious duellist, publicly threatened to shoot O'Connell if he canvassed his tenants, O'Connell turned the encounter into profitable ridicule by lauding Hickman but adding,

> but he hasn't told you one thing – sure boys, he's the greatest playactor in the world. And, sure you all know what a playactor can do. He can pretend to be what he isn't at all. Now that is what Mr Ned Hickman is about. He's well aware that every one of you is determined to vote for me, but he wants to keep square with Mr Vesey FitzGerald, and that's what makes him play off the farce.[51]

On 5 July when O'Connell's lead in votes was already overwhelming,

he joked with the crowd in proto-Kiltartanese, 'Arrah, bhoys, where's
Vasy Vijarld at all, at all? . . . sind the bell about for him. Here's the cry
for yez:-

> Stholen or sthrayed,
> Losht or mishlaid,
> The President of the Boord of Thrade!'[52]

The 40s. freeholders and their accompanying crowds often responded
as a sort of collective stage personage. When, for example, Mr
Vandeleur's tenants, about one hundred strong, marching in from
Kilrush behind their landlord's carriage, reached Ennis square, and
O'Connell rushed forward on the platform 'and lifted up his arm'[53],
the contingent deserted Vandeleur en bloc. When a priest announced
that a 40s. freeholder who had voted against O'Connell had just
dropped dead, the crowded square fell into breathless silence, and the
entire body of people knelt in unison.

But popular and participating drama was only one of the theatrical
levels at which O'Connell worked. He was also well aware that
distant, sophisticated audiences were following the play, at various
days' remove, in Dublin, London and even Paris and Vienna. He had
himself declared on 21 June that the fate of Emancipation hung upon
the Clare election, and this was the general view among the politically
educated abroad as well as in Ireland and Great Britain; hence the
eagerness and amplitude with which the fortunes of each day's polling
in Ennis were reported. For the benefit of this 'export trade', so to
speak, O'Connell counteracted his populism by exemplary conduct in
his business with the electoral officers – the sheriff was astonished by
his invariable courtesy and moderation – and strove to appease, and in
effect apologize to, Fitzgerald and the other denigrated Clare gentry
whenever he could safely do so. The play however really rested upon
its stage management. The 3000 county voters were accompanied by
perhaps ten times that number of supporters, friends, relations, wives
and children. The mere housing, feeding and ordering of such throngs,
and the enforcement of the two 'general orders' of the campaign – no
drinking and no physical disturbance – demanded direction and
discipline in a very high degree. The county Liberal Club had helped to
prepare the way. But it was little more than three months since it had
been inaugurated or at least invigorated by O'Connell, so that in
Ennis, in contrast to Waterford in 1826, it was the priests (there were
about 150 of them in the town) who bore the burden of working out
and executing the logistics of polling week. They were of course also

crucial in building up and maintaining pressure upon the 40s. freeholders. Murphy of Corofin wrested away the body of voters led by the solitary pro-Fitzgerald priest, Coffey, at the very vestibule of the election booth with the cry, 'Men, are ye going to betray your God and your country?' Fitzgerald's own tenants seemed to hang in the balance until suddenly debauched (except for a handful) by Fr Tom Maguire's stentorian appeal:

> You have heard the tones of the tempter and charmer, whose confederates have through all ages joined the descendants of the Dane, the Norman, and the Saxon, in burning your churches, in levelling your altars, in slaughtering your clergy, in stamping out your religion. Let every renegade to his God and his country follow Vesey FitzGerald, and every true Catholic Irishman follow me.[54]

By the end of the third day of polling, O'Connell was almost 1000 votes ahead. But it was important to him that the margin should be overwhelming, and when the poll closed he led by 2057 to 982. He had secured 67 per cent of the votes cast; it would have been 70 per cent had not 300 of his votes been disallowed upon the technicality of a printer's error in the oath which they had sworn. Fitzgerald's agent moved to have O'Connell's return declared invalid on the ground that he would never subscribe to the parliamentary oaths abjuring Roman Catholicism. But the assessor ruled that all this must await his appearance at the bar of the House of Commons; meanwhile, he had been duly elected 'as knight to represent' co. Clare. O'Connell's response was modest and conciliatory. He beseeched the landlords of the county not to avenge themselves upon the wretched 40s. freeholders, and assured them that he went to Parliament only to support retrenchment and 'the maintenance of every man's civil and religious rights and to prevent revolution'.[55] Similarly, he attempted to conciliate the British government upon his return to Dublin, 'Wellington and Peel, if you be true to old England, for I love and cherish her . . . all shall be forgotten, pardoned and forgiven upon giving us Emancipation, unconditional, unqualified, free, and unshackled.'[56]

Much the best-remembered comment upon the Clare election is Fitzgerald's 'I have polled all the gentry . . . to a man [but] . . . All the great interests broke down and the desertion has been universal. Such a scene as we have had! Such a tremendous prospect as opens before us!'[57] Even Peel, to whom this was written on the night on which the polling closed, was driven to a rare flight of imagination: 'We were watching the movements of tens of thousands of disciplined fanatics, abstaining from every excess and every indulgence, and concentrating every passion and feeling on one single object; with hundreds of police and soldiers, half of whom were Roman Catholics . . . is it consistent with common prudence and common sense to repeat such scenes and to incur such risks of contagion?'[58] Fitzgerald was depicting the ultimate and Peel the immediate consequences of O'Connell's example. The historic link of property and power had suffered a second blow, still heavier than the first in 1826. But O'Connell's election did even more – it put the government into checkmate. As he himself put it at the Association meeting of 10 July 1828, 'What is to be done with Ireland? What is to be done with the Catholics? One of two things. They must either crush us or conciliate us. There is no going on as we are.'[59] This was fundamentally correct, as was O'Connell's implication that the government would have eventually to choose the second course. Even if it banked upon O'Connell being sincere in anathemizing violence – and he was still sufficient of an unknown quantity in British politics for this to appear a very considerable risk – the cabinet could not bank upon the movement remaining under his control, or discount the danger of successive intensifications of hostile pressure such as that produced in Ennis. It would not be easy to coerce George IV and the ultra-tories into conceding the substance of Emancipation. But how much more formidable, and perilous, would it be to attempt to coerce the forces of Catholic Ireland, as now concentrated by and in the Association.

In making his assessment of 10 July, O'Connell counted upon Wellington's extreme reluctance to use armed force in civil crises, although this by no means precluded him from encouraging doubts about the reliability of the military in Ireland. In fact, immediately upon his return from the election, he publicly sent 'this whisper' to Wellington's ear, 'Three hundred soldiers threw up their caps for me since I left Ennis.'[60] O'Connell could also count upon Wellington's extreme reluctance either to resign from office – which would lead almost certainly to a whig-dominated ministry – or to call a general election – which would lead almost certainly to the loss of control of many other Irish county seats by the landed interest. O'Connell did however take one considerable risk. He made no attempt to claim his seat in the House of Commons before the current session ended on 28 July. This had the obvious advantage of maintaining pressure upon the government in Ireland. But it also meant that Wellington and Peel were given at least six months' breathing space before Parliament reassembled. In the interval, O'Connell would have to keep up the highest pitch of agitation without having any immediate or specific objective. He would have to hold back violence despite the rapid development of an Irish Protestant backlash which would in turn provoke Catholic anger. He would have to beat off the radical challenges to his leadership and management which a lengthy period of apparent inaction or regression might invite. Events were to establish the gravity of all these dangers. None the less he gambled upon his own power of domination. After almost two decades of clambering and slithering, he had at last attained the top of the greasy pole. The question was, could he stay there in balance long enough to seize the prize?

But beyond all political courses and calculations, O'Connell had triumphed as a man. He felt it fully: the moment the polls had closed he dashed off letters reporting his return (including, according to the *Limerick Chronicle*, four to Wellington, Peel, Goulburn and Eldon, respectively!) franked by himself as Member of Parliament. 'The cover [franked 'D.O'C.'] of this will announce to you a cheering fact',[61] he wrote to one Dublin supporter. All Catholic Ireland exulted too. Even before the result was announced in the capital, Dwyer, the Association secretary, felicitated him excitedly,

My dear Sir,
   I have no doubt but that I am right in attaching these delightful consonants [M.P.] to your name. What an era? I never expected to have such a pleasure during the natural period of *my* life. You can have no idea of the enthusiastic feeling which prevades every rank in the city on this momentous crisis. Our receipt of rent this week exceeds two thousand pounds.[62]

O'Connell had prudently decreed that the celebration of victory should be as orderly and muted as the contest. But the Association insisted upon at least a welcoming procession of '*chariots* and *infantry*' to escort him into Dublin from four miles outside the city: 'a *proclamation* goes forth tomorrow [6 July] calling upon the people *not* to illuminate but they shall be gratified with a procession.'[63] So it was to be – cavalcades, multitudes, banners, bands, wands, green boughs and leafy wreaths – all along the slow, crowd-broken way from Clare: these were perhaps the sweetest days of all. As he left Ennis on 7 July 1828, O'Connell was enthroned upon a triumphal car. Lettered in gold about its sides, it bore his own cherished epigraph of the quarter-century's struggle,

> Hereditary bondsmen! know ye not,
> Who would be free themselves must strike the blow?

CHAPTER 12

The Famous Victory,

1828–9

I

'Hard pounding', Wellington's prescription for Waterloo, was called for once again after the Clare election. If Waterford had convinced him that Emancipation must come, Clare had convinced him that it must come quickly; and on 1 August 1828 he presented a memorandum to George IV proposing the removal of most Catholic disabilities, together with suppression of the Association and the disenfranchisement of the 40s. freeholders. Peel, the king, Lyndhurst (the lord chancellor), the remainder of the cabinet and a sufficient number of reactionary peers and influential ultra-tories had now to be battered into acceptance of the inevitable. Peel needed no persuasion that the substance of the Catholic claims had now to be conceded, but a steady barrage of appeals to his sense of duty was required to induce him to remain a member of the government which would eventually conduct the Protestant surrender. In due course, Peel's submission brought Lyndhurst's in its train, which made it very likely that the other members of the ministry would fall domino-like into concurrence when their time came to look the realities in the face. George IV and the Protestant intransigents however would have to be manoeuvred as well as bullied to their doom, and Wellington's attempts simultaneously to buy time, calm their fears, conceal his own intentions and counter bellicosity all round led him into utterances too opaque for even the appellation 'Delphic'. His labours multiplied when on 14 August 1828 the Brunswick Constitution Club of Ireland was founded, in imitation of the Association's Liberal Clubs but with the purpose of fighting *à outrance* for 'the integrity of our Protestant Constitution'.[1] They spread rapidly throughout the country and across to Britain.

Meanwhile, O'Connell, like the remainder of the public and in fact all except a handful at the centre of government, was wholly ignorant of the ministerial developments of August and remained so for several months; in effect, George IV's refusal to make any commitment whatsoever muzzled Wellington for the remainder of 1828. During September the situation in Ireland grew very dangerous. O'Connell and his executive were faced with the problem of maintaining the momentum of the movement without affording the government an opportunity to institute a prosecution or their followers an opportunity to slip the leash. O'Connell's direct response was twofold. First, the Irish Protestant counter-movement was met with the rhetoric of 'loyal' violence. 'Would to God', he exclaimed at the large provincial meeting at Clonmel on 25 August, 'that our excellent Viceroy Lord Anglesey would but only give me a commission, and *if* those men of blood should attempt to attack the property and persons of his Majesty's loyal subjects, with a hundred thousand of my brave Tipperary boys, I would soon drive them into the sea before me.'[2] Secondly, O'Connell sanctioned a proposal of Lawless's to try to extend the organization and activities of the Association to the Ulster counties – at least to those border counties with large Catholic populations: this had the double advantage of diverting the troublesome 'Honest Jack' and, possibly, tapping new veins of moral force and money. Both devices proved ill-judged, although it is difficult to suggest better alternatives or to accept that the Association could safely have lapsed into masterly inactivity after Ennis. O'Connell's 'brave Tipperary boys' answered his braggadocio by a series of demonstrations and processions which soon reached the point of burning a police barracks. Meanwhile, Lawless's 'invasion' of Ulster at the head of a mass of Catholic peasants was confronted at the first sizeable town beyond the 'border', Ballybay, by several thousand Orangemen determined to repel him by force. He prudently but humiliatingly retreated. As Wyse later wrote, 'Ballybay might have been entered, but a rebellion that very night would have commenced in Ireland'.[3]

O'Connell had left for Derrynane before these moments of danger occurred, and Sheil had to intervene immediately. On 25 September the Association resolved, at Sheil's instigation, against the holding of any further processions or demonstrations (simultaneously blaming the government's inaction for their occurrence) and called upon O'Connell desperately for help. He answered with an authoritative address to the same effect. This was published in the nick of time, on 30 September, a day before the Irish executive proclaimed all political assemblages. The Association had learned its lesson, and devoted the winter of 1828–9 to restraining the actions of their followers. Anglesey had read the situation correctly when he reported on 8 September: 'I calculate upon a quiet winter in acts, but not in language . . . the Catholics are persuaded that the Brunswickers will bring on collision if they can, with the view of committing the government against them. This is what the leaders will endeavour to avoid.'[4] In this they were greatly helped by the fact that Anglesey himself had been completely converted to Emancipation, as both irresistible and the solvent for Irish discontents, by O'Connell's victory at Ennis. 'Lord Anglesey is gone mad', Wellington observed. 'He is bit by a mad Papist; or instigated by the love of popularity.'[5] At any rate, he demonstrated a steady sympathy with O'Connell's cause during the remainder of 1828, most dramatically of all when he refused to prosecute Steele and O'Gorman Mahon for their part in a demonstration in November and even left them intact in their magistracies. This indicated to the Orange faction that the lord lieutenant had gone over to the enemy (and nothing better suited O'Connell's book in calming and cheering his own supporters) and Wellington's failure to remove him (he feared the Irish Catholic reaction) seemed to show a calamitous weakness in the anti-Catholic defences, even at the centre.

At a deeper level of response, O'Connell was governed, in the latter half of 1828, by what he read as the lessons of 1825. He would concede nothing but depend upon the weight of Catholic pressure forcing the issue on its own. In 1825, he told his friend Pierce Mahony (now a parliamentary agent in London), he should have 'kept up that salutary apprehension' of Irish disorder which would have brought Liverpool to his knees,

> but, instead of *that*, I listened in an evil hour to the suggestions of Mr Plunket, etc., who said that if we conceded 'the Wings' by way of security, we should certainly carry the bill . . . I procured for this purpose public tranquillity. The Ministry saw that I had appeased the storm, they considered that the danger was passed and the House of Lords scouted our Emancipation bill. Nay, Peel . . . actually taunted me with having betrayed popular rights in order to attain the objects of my personal ambition.
>
> I was deceived once but I should indeed be more than insane, I should be indeed 'a knave or a fool' if [I] were to be deceived in the same way again.
>
> We shall never be emancipated but as we were relieved in 1778, 1782 and 1793, that is, when it becomes *necessary* for the English Government to do something for Ireland.[6]

O'Connell's first objective was therefore to 'control' (his own word) as many Irish M.P.'s as possible. 'If I had fifty county members obliged to attend constantly and to vote against every ministerial measure', he wrote to Mahony, he would soon be bought off by the grant of Emancipation. In earnest of this, he saw to it that the first Association meeting after the Clare election reaffirmed the policy of opposing all pro-ministerial candidates at the polls. He also approved and adopted an elaborated form of Wyse's Liberal Clubs proposal. During the second half of 1828 clubs were set up (sometimes, as in the case of Sligo, by O'Connell directly) in a dozen Irish counties, and earlier foundations were reorganized and fitted into the rapidly developing confederation. By the beginning of 1829, the majority of Irish counties belonged to the network (there were Liberal Clubs even in two of the Ulster counties, Monaghan and Down, though, strangely, none in Kerry), and several of the cities and larger towns ran clubs separately. This set the scene for national political action upon a most formidable scale. It was also intended to cement middle-class command of the popular movement. The subscription to the county clubs was high, 30s. per annum, and the membership of the constituent parish clubs restricted to 'the principal gentry, clergy, churchwardens, and such of the respectable farmers as can read'.[7] O'Connell tried to ensure that even his rank and file would be free of troublemakers. The only supporters whose assistance he would accept, he told the parish priest of Cashel during the Tipperary disorders of September, 'are the *good, honest, religious* men . . . The men I want to contribute to that sacred fund [the Catholic Rent] and to help me to keep the country quiet and to put down Orange oppression are the steady men who are good sons, good brothers, good husbands.'[8] His summoning of provincial meetings of the Association in three of the four provinces during the autumn of 1828 – hitherto such meetings had been occasional and unconnected – is also explicable in terms of his anxiety to canalize, and keep in mastery, the enthusiasm of the masses. The province was the largest unit into which the Association could be broken. By the same token, the provincial meeting was the loudest crowd-hailer and the best medium of popular pageantry at O'Connell's disposal at this time.

Meanwhile, O'Connell never ceased to foster his regular and basic organizational instrument, the Catholic Rent, and its accompanying apparatus. Here he prospered. In addition to the very large sums subscribed to finance the contest in Clare, the Rent brought in nearly £23,000 during 1828 (mostly from 1 July onwards) as against less than £3000 for 1827. Part cause and part effect of this marvellous success, the churchwarden system grew steadily more settled and expansive.

Of special significance in the long months of suspended crisis was the development, through the wardens' work, of parish Reading Rooms (supplied with free newspapers by the Association) and local arbitration or adjudication of disputes over property or easements and personal or factional conflict. Respectively, these signalled a deeper level of systematic indoctrination and the further spread of both the idea and practice of 'alternative government'. Overall, O'Connell's moves may be categorized as a sort of controlled and contingent alienation of the Catholic body from the state. Their vital purpose however was to keep the agitation both fiery and subject to decisive direction from the top.

O'Connell had however also to look to the day when he might be transformed into a professional politician. This was made clear to him on the morrow of the Clare election; letters appealing for or confidently claiming his countenance began to flood in from British agitators and interest groups. In fact, even before the polling closed, the London radicals, headed by Henry Hunt, announced their determination to 'convey' him to Westminster to take his seat with a procession of '50,000' or '60,000'. On 11 July 1828, the Irish liberal peer, Rossmore, begged him to keep his distance from the radicals. All his friends in London, Rossmore wrote, agreed that the time was inopportune for O'Connell to declare himself even a Reformer: 'they think it injures the cause greatly *here at present* and prevents them from being of the use they otherwise could.'[9] O'Connell rejected Rossmore's specific plea that he make no commitment to Reform at a dinner to be held in his honour by the Louth Liberal Club on 14 July. Instead he declared that 'I am now, I ever shall be, a Radical Reformer.'[10] A few days earlier, O'Connell persuaded the Catholic Association to require pledges in future from all candidates for election not only to oppose Wellington's ministry but also to support the cause of parliamentary reform and the repeal of a recent statute which he regarded as particularly obnoxious: the Subletting Act. Diffidently, even deferentially, another liberal Irish peer, Duncannon (heir to the Earl of Bessborough), urged the unwisdom of these additional obligations upon O'Connell:

I think . . . the mixing any other matter with it weakens the first pledge and gives a loophole to those who may be inclined by this means to avoid the whole. It appears to me you have now brought the Catholic question to that point that it must be successful unless it is marred by some unfortunate and unexpected circumstance . . . [Wellington] sees a determination in Ireland to be represented only by those who will oppose him or any other minister that does not make the Catholic question a *sine qua non*. No minister can look on such a state of things with indifference, but you will pardon me when I say that in my opinion, if he was called on to name the means of relieving himself from some of the difficulty, he could not devise a more likely one to meet his wishes than raising in his opponents' ranks a question like Parliamentary Reform.[11]

But again O'Connell closed his ears to the moderating advice of his parliamentary 'friends'.

None the less, he dealt cautiously with the radicals. He believed that their influence, though a useful support, was limited; later he came to doubt where even their large numbers or agitating experience were of any value. 'He [Hunt] has got *no following*', he wrote on 11 March 1829,

> I was until now convinced that the Radicals were in some power – they are *not*; they are numerous but they have no leaders, no system, no confidence in either Henry Hunt or William Cobbett – not the least – not the least.
>
> This is the case with the reformers generally; they are powerless by reason of the people who considered themselves leaders but who are despicable both from their characters and their vile jealousies and ill temper.[12]

In any event, apart from parliamentary reform (in which, in or out of the House of Commons, O'Connell would always have a vital interest) the only constituent of the radical programme which, in the autumn of 1828, he looked forward to promoting in Parliament was the rationalization of the law. 'Law Reform is now my grand object', he told Staunton on 22 September,

> Everybody should help to get rid of the present most vexatious, expensive, cabalistic and unintelligible system of law proceedings ... I do not exaggerate when I say that no man since the days of 'the Sainted Alfred' was ever half as useful as I shall be if I can abolish the present nefarious and abominable system and introduce a code of Common Sense both in its mode of proceeding and in its rules and enactments.[13]

For more than a year, this was to remain the foremost element of O'Connell's radicalism.

Moreover the political alliance dearest to O'Connell's heart was still one with the Irish Protestant liberals. Common nationality had claims even against common radical principle. After the formation of the Brunswick Clubs, such an alliance seemed all the more desirable, as a counterpoise. 'In the meantime, what are *our* friends doing?', he demanded of Lord Cloncurry on 4 September 1828, 'Alas! nothing.

They, the Orangeists, have their peers coming forward with alacrity, openly and with ostentation . . . We have scarcely any symptom of sympathy from the higher order of Protestants.'[14] Three weeks later he again wrote bitterly to Cloncurry of 'the deep conviction the Catholics now entertain that they are either opposed or deserted by the Irish Protestants . . . Protestant assistance will be given us [only] when the difficulties are over.'[15] None the less O'Connell maintained his pressure upon susceptible Irish Protestants throughout the autumn of 1828. He was also careful to avoid sectarian provocation. When for example the Association was asked on 6 November to endorse 'exclusive dealing' (refusing to do business with Orangemen or 'Brunswickers'), he crushed the proposal fiercely, demanding 'an advertisement in the newspapers, calling on all persons who have been persecuted and aggrieved by this heartless practice to come forward.'[16] At last he succeeded. In December the Duke of Leinster was induced to head a specifically Protestant movement to support full Emancipation. A meeting held in Dublin on 20 January 1829, attended by eleven Irish peers and correspondingly larger numbers of baronets, knights and landed gentlemen, resolved that the Duke, supported by a considerable body of Irish noblemen and M.P.s, should proceed to London to present a pro-Emancipation petition personally to the king.

Wyse considered this development to have been critically important in converting a sufficient body of English opinion to the idea that Emancipation might be safely granted. But O'Connell regarded a liberal Protestant auxiliary as useful but in no way essential for the immediate purpose: 'we are doing so well', he calculated on 4 September 1828, 'that we can afford, after all, to go on without being encumbered with other aid.'[17] With the future in sight, however, he was eager to forge whatever links he could with the liberal Ascendancy so that (in Wyse's phrase) the 'quarrel, instead of being Catholic and Protestant, was likely to become Irish and English'.[18] The formation, hard on the heels of the Rotunda meeting, of the Friends of Civil and Religious Liberty and the projection of a supra-confessional Irish Association soon after gave hopes that such links might indeed be forged. There were still too many obstacles in the way of a common political front. Ostensibly, both the Catholic Association and the Friends were bound for self-destruction: the achievement of Emancipation, now very likely, was their *raison d'être*. Organizationally, the bodies worked on very different, in fact often contradictory, principles. The Association's commitment to Repeal and opposition to the Subletting Act and similar land legislation repelled almost all Irish whigs; even the degree of parliamentary reform which O'Connell demanded was abhorrent. None the less O'Connell had produced junctions and collaborations from less promising materials in the past, and there was never a more sanguine or ingenious politician. But whatever his parliamentary prospects or ambitions, he had yet to force an entry into the arena. By now the time had come for him to make the attempt, in accordance with his earlier determination, to win admission to the Commons on the first day of the new parliamentary session. On 6 February 1829 he embarked at Dublin for Holyhead, attended by a train of 'courtiers' like a prince of old.

II

Since August 1828 Wellington had been immobilized by George IV's refusal even to discuss Emancipation; he had no means of forcing him to terms until a decision would be inescapable, that is, when the speech from the throne was being prepared in January 1829. An attempt to persuade the king, in a memorandum of 18 November 1828, that any further resistance to Catholic Relief was futile, failed utterly. This may explain Wellington's letter of 11 December to the Catholic primate, Curtis, promising (according to one reading) eventual relief, which in turn set off an extraordinary *pas de trois* between these two and the lord lieutenant. By the time the flurry of correspondence and breaches of 'confidentiality' at last died away, Anglesey had been recalled. He had demonstrated a steady sympathy with O'Connell's cause during the last five months of 1828, most dramatically of all when he had refused to prosecute Steele and O'Gorman Mahon. The Steele–O'Gorman Mahon affair was in fact the major charge in Wellington's indictment. But no one doubted that it was the general tenor rather than any particular manifestation of Anglesey's conciliatory treatment of the Catholics which had produced his downfall. The parallel with Fitzwilliam's recall as lord lieutenant in 1795, which had marked a sudden turnabout in British policy and raised the curtain upon decades of rejection, seemed alarmingly close.

O'Connell responded to Anglesey's dismissal not only by presiding over a species of national mourning but also by enlarging his agitatory armoury. On 13 January 1829 (the day of Anglesey's departure) he instituted an inspectoral system in the Association. A national inspector was to visit each county successively and appoint five local county inspectors who would in turn ensure that each parish was 'worked' by churchwardens and that Association policy was enforced there. Significantly, the local inspectors were given the additional duty of monitoring and helping to suppress the agrarian secret societies in their districts. O'Connell followed this up by a circular letter to the Irish Catholic bishops calling on each to support a further drive for the collection of the Rent in his diocese. These additional turns of the screw were never really tested, but O'Connell was clearly aiming at further increases in centralization, political arousal and campaign funds.

When at the beginning of February 1829, however, the news reached Dublin that Emancipation would be substantially ceded, the bar 'party' within the Association began to press for the suspension of agitation lest the king or ministry be given a pretext for withdrawing Catholic relief. 'Nothing can so well become us as "mild behaviour and humility"', when the least intimations of national pacification are held out', Sheil told the Association on 3 February.[19] He also set about lobbying the bishops for support for his proposal that the Association be immediately dissolved. Possibly O'Connell was attempting to counter this when he wrote to Doyle on 4 February that 'the blessing you bestowed' upon the Clare contest was now being realized, and when he added, 'If I get into the House, Catholic education will have an unremitting and sincere advocate.'[20] Even after he had had perforce to leave the Irish field of battle, O'Connell continued the struggle against the appeasers. On 8 February he sent forth a public letter from Shrewsbury (on his way to London) urging that the Association remain in being at least until Emancipation had been enacted. But the 'Orange Papists', as L'Estrange called them, proved too powerful when O'Connell was away from Dublin; on 12 February Sheil, claiming the endorsement of 22 of the 26 Catholic bishops, carried his resolution that the Association disband itself forthwith.

Upon reaching London on 9 February O'Connell found that two of his recent commitments were likely to prove embarrassing. First, in an address to the freeholders of Clare on 28 January he had promised to attempt to take his seat in the Commons at the opening of the parliamentary session. But he was persuaded to postpone such a 'provocation'. This exposed him to the radical Hunt's rebuke of 17 March,

> the course of seclusion which you have been advised to adopt since you have arrived in London, together with your not having even attempted to take your seat in the House of Commons as you had promised, and as the public had a right to expect that you would have done, . . . are the most

powerful causes of the criminal apathy of which you so justly complain, and I am quite sure that the above alluded to want of action on your part, has been, and still is, the sole cause of the torpor and indifference of the London Reformers . . .[21]

Secondly, in his Shrewsbury letter of 8 February 1829 O'Connell had called upon the Association 'to reject any bill of emancipation, no matter how extensive if accompanied by any such interference' with the elective franchise.[22] But on 3 March he came under heavy pressure from Brougham to acquiesce in the expected government bill to disenfranchise the 40s. freeholders. 'He spoke to me a great deal on the freehold wing', O'Connell wrote to Mary that evening,

> He wanted to get some countenance from me for the Whigs supporting that wing. I need not tell you that he totally failed. They *trapped* me before. They cannot possibly succeed in that way a second time. Besides, darling, I really am too much indebted to the 40s freeholders. You do not think I could ever turn my back on the poor fellows in Clare. I argued with Brougham in the strongest terms on the subject and showed him how useless it would be to call it a measure of concession, if they were at the same time to destroy the rights of the people at large. Brougham left me, perhaps dissatisfied but certainly without any encouragement from me, decidely the reverse.[23]

He even suspected foul play. His election for Clare had just been challenged (unsuccessfully, as things turned out) on the ground of undue influence on the part of the Catholic clergy, and Brougham's visit immediately preceded the striking of the parliamentary committee to try the petition. 'It was *curious*', O'Connell told Dwyer, 'that Brougham should come to me the very day – the morning of the day – on which my committee was and is to be formed . . . just the day when it is most likely that I should wish to be in favour with the men who might form that committee.'[24] Although O'Connell rapidly came round to the 'opinion [that] the £10 [franchise] will really give more power to the Catholics',[25] he did not abandon the 40s. freeholders immediately. In a public address issued on 7 March 1829 he still called for 'decided, determined, energetic, but constitutional opposition' to their disenfranchisement;[26] and at a meeting of Irish Catholics held in London on the same day, he beat down the 'trimmers' – among them N. P. O'Gorman, Eneas MacDonnell and Pierce Mahony – on the issue of petitioning in favour of the doomed electors. But though the meeting also called on the whigs 'to resist the Disenfranchisement Bill at all hazards', O'Connell had to report sadly on 11 March that 'Brougham and all the party gave in. The Opposition, to a man, will vote for it.'[27] O'Connell probably expressed his true feelings when he bemoaned the whig tergiversation to Dwyer as 'cruel – very cruel';[28] but from now on he virtually threw up the cause of the 40s. freeholders as hopeless. His pledge to reject Emancipation, if accompanied by their disenfranchisement, dropped out of sight in the euphoria of the larger triumph.

Why did O'Connell, who had stood on the right wing of the Association throughout 1828, stand on the left wing – to the left even of Lawless who had supported the immediate dissolution of the Association – during the early spring of 1829? First, he believed that Emancipation would not be safe until George IV was actually forced to put pen to the paper of a successful bill; therefore, no weapon should be laid down before this happened. Next, the 'betrayal' of 1825 had left an ineffaceable mark upon him; he was determined to be neither gulled nor opened up to charges of self-interested opportunism a second time. Last – and perhaps not least – Mary was intensely interested in the outcome, and his political conscience was 'informed' by her surveillance. The characteristic note of his reports to her from England was struck in the very first with, 'I will not hesitate to take a decided and honest part. That, sweetest, *you* will readily allow.'[29]

But all this lay in the shadow of the coming Emancipation. Though common report had it that the ministry's concessions would be large and unqualified, O'Connell could not be easy until the government had committed itself in public. On the expected eve of the announcement of its intentions he wrote nervously to Mary,

> I cannot write politics this day because, my own darling, there is a tremulous anxiety about me for tomorrow. Tomorrow is the awful day, *big with the fate of Cato and of Rome*. You see, love, how poetic I am grown. The fact is that as the crisis approaches on which we *must* know everything, one cannot bring one's mind to do otherwise than merely wish that the time of certainty were come . . .[30]

But all was well. On 6 March 1829 he wrote again, exultantly, 'Great and glorious triumph as far as the Emancipation bill goes – no Veto – no payment of clergy – no ecclesiastical arrangements.' As to the obnoxious clauses, he would 'drive a coach and six' through that aiming 'to prevent the *extension* of the Jesuits and other monastic orders', while a prohibition upon Catholic bishops using territorial titles for their sees was dismissed as 'absurd and childish'.[31] This was fair judgment. Apart from the reservation of a handful of the chief offices of state, the ministerial bill granted Emancipation unalloyed: 'I always said', O'Connell boasted to Dwyer, 'that when they came to emancipate they would not care a bulrush about those vetoistical arrangements which so many paltry Catholics from time to time pressed on me as being useful to Emancipation.'[32] He proved correct in advising the regular clergy – his 'fee' being 'one moment of recollection of me occasionally at the pure and Holy sacrifice'[33] – that they had nothing to fear from the bill because only the attorney-general could act under it against them, and he could procure no testimony as every potential witness would incriminate himself if he gave evidence. Correspondingly, it was only the bishop himself who could be prosecuted in the matter of ecclesiastical titles.

O'Connell remained both delighted and fearful while the bill wound its way through the Commons and Lords. From Dublin, where he returned briefly towards the end of March, he plied his current parliamentary intermediary, Mahony, with appeasing information and assurances that the Catholics were prepared to 'offer' the people to the government. If in addition to Catholic relief a grant for public works were forthcoming, he wrote on 28 March, 'The people will be taken out of *our* hands by Emancipation as we took them from Capt. Rock by *our* agitation'. He also offered to abandon the attempt to take his seat before the Emancipation bill was enacted – in the event he made none – if such a step might endanger the measure. 'This may be an impeachment to my head', he told Mahony, 'but literally my heart overrules me. Thus the language of silly novels steals into politics. I will be sturdy enough on all other points but on this I have, I own it, a woman's weakness.'[34] But there may have been more to it than 'woman's weakness'. Postponement might not only ease the passage of the bill through Parliament but also so place the ministry in his debt that they would submit quietly to his entering the Commons after the Relief Act had done away with the offensive oaths. Mahony later claimed that members of the government, during the Easter recess of 1829, had assured him that the government as such would not oppose O'Connell's attempt to take his seat under the new legislation.

On 11 April 1829 O'Connell was able to tell Mary from London that the bill had passed the Lords. 'It will receive the Royal assent on Monday [13 April] and thus the ascendancy and proud superiority which your neighbours had over you will be at an end the day you receive this letter', he added significantly. It is touching as well as a measure of his pent-up anxiety that he should have specified for her in advance '*the minute*' of liberation – '*about* 20 minutes after four by the Dublin clocks'.[35] In the same vein, his letter to Dwyer of 14 April was superscribed 'The first day of freedom!' To Dwyer he wrote, 'It [the Relief Act] is one of the greatest triumphs recorded in history – a bloodless revolution more extensive in its operation than any other political change that could take place. I say *political* to contrast it with *social* changes which might break to pieces the framework of society.'[36] To Mary he had already written, 'And it was your husband contributed *most* . . . Was it not, sweetest?'[37] Even cruel posterity could not quarrel with either asseveration.

III

Some months after the passage of the Catholic Relief Act, O'Connell, in arranging with Isaac Goldsmid to serve as parliamentary spokesman for Jewish Emancipation, set out the lessons he had learned from more that two decades of campaigning. 'Allow me at once to commence my office of your advocate', he wrote on 11 September 1829,

> and to begin by giving you advice. It is: not to postpone your claim of right beyond the second day of the ensuing session. Do not listen to those over cautious persons who may recommend postponement. Believe an agitator of some experience that nothing was ever obtained by delay – at least in politics – you must to a certain extent force your claims on the parliament. You cannot be worse, recollect, even by a failure and you ought to be better by the experiment . . .
>
> You must I repeat *force* your question on the Parliament. You ought not to confide in English liberality. It is a plant not genial to the British soil. It must be *forced*. It requires a *hot-bed*. The English were always persecutors. Before the so styled reformation the English tortured the Jews and strung up in scores the Lollards. After that reformation they still roasted the Jews and hung the Papists. In Mary's day the English with their usual cruelty retaliated the tortures on the Protestants. After her short reign there were near two centuries of the most barbarous and unrelenting cruelty exercised towards the Catholics . . . The Jews too suffered in the same way. I once more repeat. Do not confide in any liberality but that which you will yourself rouse into action and *compel* into operation.[38]

This expressed O'Connell's now-settled conviction that force – albeit moral, agitatory, intimidatory force – was the only father of concession in British politics. Yet it also made clear his wish to work inside, and with the grain of, that system, wherever possible. His belief in the English penchant for persecution was not accompanied by personal rancour or national righteousness; it was simply (as he saw it) a fact of public life.

Perhaps the key to O'Connell's extraordinary political equipoise was this largemindedness. In crushing challenges to his leadership, he might be merciless or unscrupulous. But, after all, his principal political business was to lead; and he never sought more than to force a challenger back to what he regarded as his proper station of subordination. He forgave personal slights freely, quickly and unconditionally. Several followed hard on the heels of Emancipation. He was blackballed when on 12 May 1829 he allowed his name to go forward for election to the Cisalpine Club, the association of the English Catholic elite. Members of that elite raced shamelessly and successfully to beat him to the honour of becoming the first Catholic M.P. since penal days. The Speaker of the Commons, Charles Manners-Sutton, a nephew of his old adversary Lord Manners, malignly (as he believed) refused him admission to the House under the new Relief Act. Peel and other leading tories surreptitiously and treacherously (as he believed) directed ministerial supporters to back the Speaker in the subsequent debate. Bitterest of all, when in October 1829 the first body of Catholic counsel in Ireland was admitted to the inner bar, O'Connell was excluded from the list, which was moreover composed almost entirely of his juniors in years and fame. Even his chief rival Sheil was soon added to the number. No insult could have cut deeper. Since 1808 O'Connell had been driven to exertion by resentment of both the injustice and the financial implications of the prohibition on his taking silk. Yet in reporting his rebuff by the Cisalpine Club to Dwyer on 14 May 1829 he 'heartily [forgave] them all', merely adding 'But it was a strange thing of them to do; it was a comical "testimonial" of my services in emancipating them.'[39] Anticipating Manners-Sutton's enmity, he observed 'I am a good deal indifferent on the matter. I know that I have demonstrated my right, and that it will be understood and felt in Ireland.'[40] On the debate upon his claim to admission to the Commons, he observed, with rueful humour, 'I should still have had a chance of success but for the conduct of Sir James Scarlett, who made a very strong and argumentative speech in my favour and concluded by declaring that he would vote against me. This, of course, was a decisive blow. But the Attorney-Generalship is vacant, and poor Sir James is a man.'[41] He never inveigled against Sheil or any other of the newly admitted Catholic silks, but bore the blow to his pride and hopes in silence.

O'Connell's magnanimity was something more than the practised politician's useful phlegm and calculated provisionality of alliances and enmities. It was rooted in the ductility of his character. The defect of this quality, in politics no less than financial dealings, was what Hunting Cap had once condemned as 'the softness and facility of your disposition'.[42] This led O'Connell into over-responsiveness to his company, audience, surroundings or immediate circumstances. On balance however his 'charity' was a political advantage – given of course the northern star-like fixity of his ultimate goals. It rendered him perpetually resilient, flexible, fertile in device and ready for accommodation within the grand circle of the negotiable.

The passage of the Catholic Relief Act provides a classic instance of his elasticity. The Irish 40s. freeholders and his own chance of immediate entry into the House of Commons were finally jettisoned in the name of the greater good, though O'Connell was partly compensated by being released from the dual dangers of dependence on a vulnerable electoral force and of incurring the horrific – literally ruinous – penalties attached to illegal entry into Parliament. He made no attempt to combat the punitive clauses of the Act. The fact that he considered them inoperable was enough. O'Connell used the same philosophy in politics as in law, for him the verdict was *the* thing; and just as Wellington and Peel had added the humiliating provisions to their bill in order to ease the sufferings of the ultra-Protestants, so O'Connell acquiesced in the odious clauses in order to assuage the cabinet's unspent resentment of its defeat. Again, for a variety of prudential reasons, not least among them the conciliation of the government, O'Connell forbade exuberant celebration of the achievement of Emancipation. For this, he was prepared even to anger Mary, although his attempt to mitigate his offence was also characteristic of his method. 'I was sorry we differed about the illumination', he wrote to her from London on 15 April 1829,

> but my great reason for being anxious about the prevention of that measure was least you or my girls should be insulted by an infuriate banditti. I should be glad and yet sorry that Maurice was at home. With these mixed feelings, which to a certain extent were applicable to many other families besides my own, I did strongly recommend them [the Catholics of Dublin] not to illuminate. It would be I thought the mere personal gratification of a triumph which might be considered insulting just at the moment when, having got a real and substantial advantage, we want no feathers but, darling, why do I *now* annoy about my opinions? If I were in Dublin I would probably have given up my opinion to yours. At all events, darling, we would not have quarrelled about it.[43]

Correspondingly, O'Connell greeted the Relief Act as the complete accomplishment of his objectives. Yet it was notorious that the 'relief' was limited to the dismantling of barriers to entering certain public offices and professional ranks. *Ipso facto*, it directly concerned only the bourgeoisie and upper orders. Even for them it merely unlocked doors: forcing entries was quite another matter.

How then are we to explain O'Connell's paeans of triumph in 1829? His own initial responses to the final passage of the bill provide some answers. As we have seen, he wrote at once to Mary that she could now stand as an equal with Irish Protestants, and to Dwyer that he had achieved a political, while avoiding a social, revolution. Soon afterwards, on 1 May 1829, he told James Sugrue that when admitted to the House of Commons (he then expected that this would happen within a week), 'I intend to take an *immediate* active part in the proceedings. I need not say to you how impatient I am to be useful.'[44]

The first answer concerned feelings. O'Connell argued – to use the language of a later analogy – that one must begin by thinking of oneself as a man rather than a coloured man; next, one should try to *behave* as if this assertion were in fact the truth; finally, one strove to force the supremacists into acknowledging its reality – insofar at least as a reforming statute could alter attitudes, or even conduct. To O'Connell the Relief Act signified the formal end not only of the 'Catholic crouch' in Ireland but also of the ethos of deference and quietism in which he had grown up. Even the formidable Hunting Cap had known his place under Protestant domination; even the gallant General Daniel had advised his nephew as late as 1819 to 'Put less effort into Emancipation . . . nothing can advance by even a day the time marked out by Providence.'[45] This was of course partly explicable in terms of difference in generation. But no one had done more than O'Connell to deepen – one might even say, create – that particular generation gap, and his own younger brothers were much closer in outlook to their uncles than to himself. Moreover, the intangible benefits of Emancipation – self-esteem, a sense of power and triumph, and similar psychological satisfactions – were by no means unimportant in O'Connell's eyes, and these could be enjoyed, existentially or vicariously, by hundreds of thousands of Irish Catholics who had gained nothing else. Among these satisfactions we should number the colour and busyness, the dash and spirit, which the new political culture of the 1820s had brought to multitudes of hard, barren lives and wretched places. The fifteen-acre tenant who had marched twenty miles in his contingent to the polls, the Ballybricken butcher who had patrolled Waterford with his white wand of authority during election week, the curate who had preached up the

Rent, the collector at the chapel gate, the shopboy who built a speakers' platform upon barrels, the clerk who broadcast weekly to the illiterates from the columns of the *Morning Register*, would never forget that there had once been heady days.

'We were probably the most conservative-minded revolutionaries that ever put through a successful revolution', Kevin O'Higgins concluded at the end of the Anglo-Irish conflict of 1916–21.[46] He should have excepted O'Connell whose second cause of pride in the achievement of Emancipation – as set out in his letter to Dwyer of 14 April 1829 – was its shoring up of the existing social structure. New Left historians have no need to search about for evidence of O'Connell's adherence to the established class system. Not only did he not disguise, he openly avowed his fear and hatred of social disturbance and disorder. When he spoke of the Relief Act as accomplishing a political revolution, he meant that one great chain of legal discrimination had been struck off the body politic; when he gloried in the event, it was because (in one of his own favourite phrases) not a single drop of human blood had been shed in its accomplishment. In all this, there should be nothing to surprise us. O'Connell belonged to one well-known and well-marked camp in each of the great antitheses of contemporary radicalism. He was a respectable, a rationalistic and a moral-force radical, as against his blackguard, millenarian and violent 'comrades' of the left. All of them however would have shared his view that Emancipation was a political advance, however some might have deplored its social ineffectuality. And all of them would also have shared his basic premise, that the case for Emancipation rested upon indefeasible individual right and the absolute *civil* equality of every person – or at any rate every adult male.

O'Connell's third reason for exultation when the Relief Bill passed was not general but particular – that it opened the way for his self-realization. His letter to Sugrue of 1 May 1829 made clear his eagerness to begin a parliamentary career at once. The painfully successful agitator of fifty-three years of age was no different from the boy of nine or ten who had dreamt of emulating Flood and Grattan, or the youth of seventeen solemnly rehearsing for the day on which he would enter the grand theatre of the world, or the young man of twenty-one who debated methodically with himself as to which faction he would join when he attained at last the Irish House of Commons. If the term 'born politician' has not been debased by over-use, it may surely be applied to him. His manoeuvres of July 1828–

April 1829 show the hand of the master at every twist and turn; but his manoeuvres of 1808–9 had been scarcely less skilful. Though O'Connell was a political auto-didact, he had little to teach himself, and that little was grounded surely in his intelligent analysis of every past experience. The agony of a suppressed natural function (to steal words from Shaw) was almost over. He had spent forty years too long in Cicero's vestibule, but now, finally, the Relief Act had released him for the auditorium. Even joy in the evening was joy.

IV

We do not know when, or even whether specifically, O'Connell decided to abandon law for membership of the House of Commons. A London counsel might combine the two careers while he awaited judicial office or a solicitor- or attorney-generalship. But this was impracticable for an Irish barrister, let alone one who would also purport to lead a national party; in themselves, parliamentary sessions would have eaten up more than half the law terms. Thus while O'Connell probably still intended to practise in the interstices of politics, he also knew that his future work and income as a lawyer would be both relatively small and intermittent. It may well be that he never chose deliberately to change careers. Once he had been induced to contest co. Clare – and significantly his resistance to doing so was grounded in his straitened circumstances and the temporary interruption of his practice – there was really no turning back. Nor was he called upon to alter the pattern of his life immediately. Because he did not attempt to take his seat during 1828, he could pursue his profession in the ordinary way throughout the remainder of the year.

When however he left Dublin for London on 3 February 1829, he also, practically speaking, left the Irish bar behind him, once for all. It was his clear intention to enter the House of Commons and adopt a parliamentary career as soon as possible. At some time during the preceeding seven months he must have considered how he and his family were to be supported without the great majority of his legal earnings, and with the added burden of several months of residence in London every year. Yet the first surviving indication of a possible solution only comes in a letter of 10 February 1829 from his friend Cornelius MacLoghlin, who wrote, 'Let me know how things will go on as in the event of your taking your seat, I have a proposition to make that will tend to your future ease and comfort and enable you to devote your entire time to your country.'[47] This was evidently the first step towards the setting up of the O'Connell testimonial on 25 March, for MacLoghlin was one of the seven treasurers 'of the very first mercantile rank' (the brewer Arthur Guinness and the banker David La Touche were others) of the subscription fund. O'Connell showed no compunction in becoming, in effect, a national pensioner, although once the testimonial was turned into an annual O'Connell Tribute, this was to expose him to unceasing gibes as 'the big beggarman'. On the contrary, he followed the progress of the testimonial anxiously, reporting news of promised subscriptions in detail to Mary. In turn, Dwyer and others reported news to him. 'In fact', O'Connell wrote to John Primrose in Kerry on 25 April, 'the thing would be splendid if there were persons capable of conducting it. Every parish should be collected by itself. It was the single shillings that swelled the Catholic Rent. But this is not for me to say and therefore you will of course use the strictest silence as to *my* saying so.'[48] O'Connell's fears of mismanagement of the subscription drive were groundless. The testimonial amounted finally to almost £30,000, well over half the total of Rent raised during the years 1824–9. As ever, O'Connell was worried about immediate needs and blithe about the distant future. He had told Primrose on 25 April, when his expectations were still modest,

> Whatever money is collected in Kerry [in fact, £1500 had been collected there already] should be sent up and lodged in the Hibernian Bank to my credit as rapidly as possible. I think it is likely that the subscription will be sufficient to get me quite out of debt and to pay my daughters' fortunes. If it does so much, I shall be quite content.[49]

Correspondingly, he had written to Mary soon after the testimonial was publicly announced, 'Now if the subscription goes on well, darling, I will have you here [London], please God, early in May.'[50]

This makes clear the intermingling (not to say, confusion) of private and public money which was to characterize O'Connell's finances for the remainder of his life, and also his pressing family needs. Six of his children were now adults, and finding careers or husbands for them had become an urgent business. Kate and Betsey were still unmarried and dowries of £5000 would be their expected portions if they were to remain in the higher professional or lower gentry ranks. Part of Ellen's dowry – she had married into this rank in 1825 – was still outstanding. Morgan was proving expensive: neither his careless, happy disposition nor his life as an Austrian cavalry officer made for economy. On 7 July 1829 he acknowledged receipt of £100, as the first instalment of a sum needed to rescue him from some scrape, adding,

Be assured, my dear father, that this is the last time I will make any such extravagant demand . . . I will however endeavour to prove to you by my future conduct of the change operated in me and of my firm unalterable resolution not again to involve myself in such a predicament. These are not empty words. Time will prove the truth of them.[51]

Ensuring that Maurice (who became twenty-six on 23 June 1829) married well was, however, the O'Connells' most desperate concern. On 6 March 1829 O'Connell reported to Mary a dinner held in his honour by 'rich Jews in the City' with the (perhaps wistfully) jocular comment, 'Perhaps Maurice could pick up a £50,000 amongst them.'[52] A month later he told her that Maurice was 'disposed to make us all happy. It would crown *all* if he were to fix himself *now* well.'[53] The search for a good match for Maurice was however far from a mere matter of general encouragement or unlocated aspiration. O'Connell's letter of 15 April from London makes it clear that Mary was expected to engage in the Dublin marriage mart on her son's behalf: 'Darling heart's love, how I wish to hear about Maurice and Miss Redington or Miss O'Brien! Speak to him yourself about Miss O'Shea. I really think it is to say the least of it *unkind* to bring her to his neighbourhood. Is it a trap?'[54] Did it ever cross O'Connell's or his wife's minds that they were playing a part not unlike that which Hunting Cap had unsuccessfully essayed in 1802? At any rate, their fate as marriage brokers resembled his, just as Maurice's fate as a lover resembled theirs, for he too was to wed secretly and 'unsuitably' in the end.

The warmth of feeling in the family was quite restored. While Maurice was with him in London, O'Connell delighted Mary repeatedly with reports of his social and political success. As he wrote on 5 March 1829,

Maurice is in perfect good health and spirits and goes to all the parties he is asked to. There are many. A lady told me he was the handsomest man of the deputation. I told her his mother was of the same opinion and I added that he was very like his mother. I was so proud to be able to say so. He will go with me into the City and indeed everywhere else where I am asked to dine.[55]

Similarly, he commented antiphonally on reports of his children's doings at home. After learning, apparently, that his youngest son, Daniel, had recovered from illness, and that Kate and Betsey had been presented at Dublin Castle, he replied, on 13 April,

Darling love, how my heart is at ease about our sweet Danny. Give him my tender love and a sweet kiss for his *fado*. Tell my girls how sorry I am that I did not see them in their Court dresses. I wish I had been present when my Betsey was kissed by the Duke. She must have blushed pretty deeply as much [from] indignation as anything else.[56]

O'Connell seems to have set the tone of family intercourse. Certainly, his daughters wrote to him with equal warmth. Kate, for example, followed his departure from London of 3 February 1829 with a solicitous letter about outside travelling on his coach. 'Many a cold and wet mile', she went on, 'I travelled that way with my dearest father when I used to be obliged to ask if it was still raining, he kept his Catty so covered up from all the rain and wind.'[57]

But Mary remained the heart of all. She was ill during the spring of 1829, possibly the beginning of her long decline in health. Kate wrote to O'Connell on her behalf in February, and Fr L'Estrange said mass for her at home. Whether or not O'Connell's suggestion that she might join him in London for the final weeks of the current parliamentary session was seriously meant, she did not in fact live there for over two years. Possibly O'Connell guessed that this would be so. At any rate, he told her on 10 February, 'Your state of health is my great and foremost source of anxiety.' In the same letter he called her still 'my consolation and my solace'.[58] So she truly was. She remained the sole vent for much of his inner political plans and ambitions, the recipient of his private worries over money, slights or corpulence, the confidant of his Lenten penances. The intimate traffic of almost thirty years continued in its daily course. When in late August 1829 Kate had again to take up her mother's pen, O'Connell answered, 'This day I am *afflicted, afflicted* . . . because you were too ill to write yourself. My own, own Mary does not at all understand how I love her.'[59] Perhaps he felt again a premonitory tremor, an early intimation of the death of love.

But nothing – dubious income, exigent children or ailing wife – could now hold O'Connell back from total commitment to a parliamentary career. His first thought was to save as much as possible of his political base at home. The moment 10 Geo.IV c.1, suppressing the Catholic Association, was enacted, on 5 March 1829, he sent word to Ireland that the Liberal Clubs should not be dissolved: they had escaped, in his opinion, the prohibitions of the law. Six days later he set out for Dwyer his scheme for preserving at least the skeleton of the old Irish Catholic organization:

as the law stands, the Finance Committee of the Association can receive no more money [but] ... the Catholic rooms should be kept up by a subscription of from five to ten shillings by each individual, to pay current expenses of newspapers, coals, candles, clerks, &c.

It will serve as a nucleus for talking over Catholic and Irish affairs. Call it the Catholic Reading-rooms. A few months will enable us to do better, but in the meantime a rallying point of this kind is wanting and a reading-room is just the very best you can have.

Let me press the necessity of having such an establishment and put my name and my sons', Maurice, Morgan, John and Dan, as original subscribers. Let us attempt to keep it on foot for some months at least if we can get but ten subscribers. There is no danger of the Lying Act affecting us.[60]

The new vestigial association took its name, discreetly, from its Dublin meeting place, '12 Burgh Quay'. O'Connell's prime objective however was to enter the Commons immediately. As he told Mary on 11 April, 'I *am determined* to spend this sessions in parliament. It would never *do* for the people to have me out of it. I will fight the battle of Ireland and of Catholicity there better than anywhere else save in a Parliament in College Green.'[61] When on 18 May 1829 the Commons finally rejected O'Connell as member for Clare, he arranged to 'have a borough ready for the rest of the sessions',[62] while awaiting re-election for the county. He told Mary on 21 May that he expected to take his seat within a week. He was careful to guard himself from her reproaches for either abandoning principle or squandering their money.

Darling, you of course know me too well to suppose that I would barter any one of my principles for the world's wealth. No, love, I go in for the borough, as I did for Clare, perfectly my own master. Of course you have not the least uneasiness on that head. It will give me a station and rank in addressing the people of Clare and give weight and importance to my exertions in that county. I want too to bring before the country my parliamentary capacities. I want to show of what use I could be to Catholic charities and other Catholic purposes. Do not therefore, my darling heart, be in the least degree mortified at my taking advantage of a free borough for the rest of this sessions. Depend upon it that it can serve only to make me more respected by the public. You will I repeat be greatly pleased with my address to the people of Clare. It would have amused you to have heard the paltry squaling [squealing?] of the voices of the other speakers after me in the House of Commons.[63]

It might have been an English pocket borough which O'Connell so confidently expected. Certainly the Irish pocket borough, Tralee, for which he was in negotiation with its owner, Sir Edward Denny, was far from 'free'; the asking price was reported as £3000. In any event, O'Connell failed to secure a temporary seat, and had to await the second Clare by-election which had been set to commence on 30 July. For a time O'Connell had reason to fear a contest. He was unlikely to lose – a careful canvass had shown him to be clearly ahead even under the revised register of voters – but the costs would be heavy and his testimonial fund perhaps correspondingly diminished. Characteristically, however, he was more concerned with the political than with the financial consequences of being unopposed. 'If I succeed in Clare, especially after a contest', he told Mahony on 4 June,

> it will rouse a fresh spirit in all the counties in Ireland. The only danger is that there shall not be a contest for in that case the usual torpidity will follow, recent exertions there being no adequate stimulant to keep up excitement. But a contest in Clare would rouse all the dormant passions and give an energy to opposition which would not be easily appeased.[64]

Yet this was the very moment when O'Connell was seriously tempted to accept an invitation from his old tory enemies, the Beresfords, to act as counsel for Lord George in a forthcoming by-election in co. Waterford; the fee would have been at least £600. O'Connell was careful to condition that 'there is to be no expectation that I will do anything beyond my professional duty; that is, there is to be *no sale* by me nor any purchase by them of my political exertions'.[65] But the world at large would scarcely have drawn this nice distinction, and O'Connell was fortunate that, in the end, he heeded Dublin advice to resist the monetarily attractive but politically dangerous temptation. How strangely divided can a man's courses be! Simultaneously, O'Connell was ready to sacrifice money for political advantage in co. Clare, and to toy for several days with what would surely have turned out to be the sacrifice of political reputation for money in co. Waterford.

Despite various alarms O'Connell was returned unopposed for co. Clare on 30 July 1829. It was too late for him to take his seat before Parliament would reassemble in the following November. But at least it was certain that he had finally won through. Where would he now move politically? An unknown ocean lay ahead: Cortez-like, 'He star'd at the Pacific'. In his address of 25 May to the electors of Clare (mocked as the 'Address of the Hundred Promises'), he pledged himself to work for a host of Irish local government and tax reforms, an increase in Irish parliamentary representation, the restoration of the 40s. freehold franchise, an Irish poor law, the repeal of the

Subletting Act and measures against absentee proprietors. To Mahony he wrote on 4 June, 'I am most thoroughly convinced that nothing but "the Repeal of the Union" can permanently serve her [Ireland's] interests.'[66] Upon his election, he assured Bentham, 'I avowed myself on the hustings this day to be a "Benthamite", and explained the leading principles of your disciples – the "greatest happiness principle" – our sect *will* prosper . . . You have now one Member of Parliament *your own*.'[67] Soon after, in proposing a scheme for Catholic glebes and parochial houses, he told Doyle:

> Since my return for Clare I have begun to write a species of circular to the Catholic prelates tendering my parliamentary services . . . I have long been of opinion that Catholic interests would never be effectually served in parliament until they were represented by a Catholic man of business, sincere at least in his religious professions.
>
> The present state of the Catholic Church in Ireland demands, I humbly conceive, great attention. Things cannot possibly remain as they are. I do not forsee anything of a retrograde nature, and therefore I look solely to her advance . . . you will smile perhaps mournfully at my enthusiasm and look upon it as but a source of barren speculation but recollect that enthusiasm is the *only* parent of great success.[68]

Behind the apparent infinity of the directions which he might take lay the same simple dream that had driven him on since childhood. During the long vacation of 1814 he had held a grand picnic for a group of friends on an island in one of the Killarney lakes. On 22 May 1829 he recalled that day and 'the speech I made on giving the memory of Washington'. His conclusion had been much cheered. 'Did it not convey this idea? "He found his native land a pitiful province of England. He left her – Oh Glorious destiny! – an independent and mighty nation".'[69] Whether we move backwards or forwards in time, the frame was ever the same. What was stamped on the beginning boy of 1783 was still stamped upon the bruised and soiled politician of 1829. The old vision of becoming his country's Washington continued to hold him in its thrall. There would never be escape from his own inherent ardour, or the hereditary bondage of his ancestry, time or place.

BOOK II

CHAPTER 13

A Sort of Plateau

1830

I

At the beginning of 1830, O'Connell was well into his fifty-fifth year, his wife, Mary, being three years younger. He was still remarkably handsome – in the Kerry style – and tall, powerful and heavy. He had long worried about his burliness, and striven against it by undereating. But, as usual, Mary reassured him. 'As you are well, darling', she wrote on 1 March 1830,

> I care little for your *increasing* size, the more particularly as you always exaggerate your size. *It* can't at all events be unwholesome. It does not proceed from inactive or sedentary habits. You are neither an epicure nor a hard drinker. Indeed if you were . . . large and a gormandizer, I should then be unhappy about you. [But you] have the best of constitutions and may God continue it to you is my constant prayer.[1]

Certainly, he had the best of constitutions. He was seventy years old before he showed the first sign of failing. Apart from mention of some mysterious malaise in mid-1832, the sole surviving reference to his being doctored in the entire decade of the 1830s is an order for 'a box of the seasickness pills' to be sent to him *'at once . . . to Dublin'*,[2] before he faced again the Irish Sea. Meanwhile he worked the same cruelly long hours, often fourteen or fifteen in a day, as he had done since early manhood. It was also true, and perhaps pertinent to his capacity for torrential labours, that he drank only moderately. For eighteen months in 1840–1 he even became a total abstainer under the banner of Fr Mathew; but he did so only to meet a challenge to practise what he preached, and doubtless the practice became tedious with time. Although the entertainment at his home in co. Kerry, Derrynane, where he kept more or less open house throughout the autumns, was wildly generous, it stopped well short of flowing drink. For even O'Connell's holidays were layered with work.

During his long vacations at Derrynane, in addition to his evening hours of reading, account casting and letter-writing, the morning hours of hare-hunting were interspersed with business. He dispensed seigneurial justice, and caught up with the great world's happenings, on the run. As W. T. Fagan described it.

> He delighted in playing the Irish Tanist amongst his dependents. He was Judge, Jury and Executive in all their disputes . . . and like the Court of Law in England in former days, his Court moved about wherever he went. Often, on the top of some mountain crag, while the hounds were at fault, would he sit on one of nature's rude imperishable benches to hear and determine the disputes . . .
>
> His mountain sports never turned him from his absorbing pursuit of POLITICS. He was in the habit of proceeding on his hunting expeditions early in the morning and on foot; wearing thick *brogues* and bearing a substantial *wattle* in the hand. Breakfast was taken out, and at the usual hour, in some convenient spot, it was laid out *al fresco*. Then the post-boy arrived with letters and newspapers. No editor ever had so many at his command or ever read them with more attention . . . letters were read and opened and thrown down. Newspapers were read and flung aside; and when the repast was over, the huntsman's horn was sounded, and the fine pack of beagles summoned to their day's work.[3]

This was his joyous time; it was the loss of the days on the mountains with his dogs that he grieved for most when he was held back in, or torn away to, his parliamentary or agitatory duty. It was in part an exultation in bodily well-being and the physical challenge, but still more a form of reconsummation of his union with his native landscape. Nowhere could he satisfy his abiding sense of place as fully as on the foot-hunt along the uplands behind Derrynane. Half-way about the compass, as one looked around, towered higher mountains, jagged in outline or lost, across a line, in mist or rain. Southward lay the vast stretch of Kenmare Bay, with its broken near-coast and dreaming or tortured sea, and in the distance, the dark mass of the opposing ranges in west Cork. Love of country was O'Connell's political stock in trade and deepest passion. It was a love of Ireland's earth and skies no less than a constitutional idealization, and the epicentre of its physical expression was the match-less stretch of territory about Derrynane.

His wife, though also born and bred in Kerry, was far from sharing this enthusiasm. For her, Kerry carried memories of an impoverished childhood in the 'prying, curious *busy*' county town, Tralee.[4] It also symbolized a provincialism which she wished her own children, and in particular her daughters, to escape. Moreover, all through her married life, it had drawn her husband away from her for much longer than she would have sanctioned were his movements really under her command. He kept being caught – a most willing fly – in the webs of relations, connexions, clients, flatterers and friends spun all about the county in the years of his boyhood and during his three decades of practice at the Munster bar. Mary still chafed, and remonstrated occasionally at the resultant absences; but she knew that the lures of Kerry could never be altogether overcome. Worst of all for her was being immured in Derrynane in winter. As a counter, she had for years pleaded her 'delicacy' in a wet, wild climate: she was, she insinuated, healthier in almost any other place, and in particular in the cities, Dublin and London. Conversely, O'Connell tried to undermine her resistance to the place, as in writing to her from Tralee on 13 March 1832,

> I wish to God we were together, darling, and that Derrynane agreed with you as well as London. But I hope, darling, that you will come back so stout as to be able to *run about*. I am getting a road from the end of the kennel road to the chapel which will greatly extend your usual drive and thus give you a little *circuit* of your own. I will take care to have a good car horse for you, love.[5]

There is little to suggest that she lived much 'in society' in either of the capitals. In 1830 she forwent even accompanying the O'Connell family party to that great event in the Dublin calendar, the 'Patrick's Ball' on 17 March, with the easy comment, 'Going out by day and going out by night are very different to those who are apt to take cold as I am'.[6] We do not know how she spent her months in London whenever she joined O'Connell for the parliamentary sessions. But certainly she entertained and was entertained there little, if at all. None the less, whether in her home in Dublin, 40 Merrion Square, or in London lodgings, she liked urban life. It offered modest luxury; it had style; it might open the door to good matches for her unmarried daughters. When in March 1830 she was about to join O'Connell in London for the first time she wrote,

> My dearest Love,
> ... If you think that lodgings will answer, why not take them? Perhaps those you have might answer with some additional rooms. Of all things let the rooms be large and airy. They must consist of three best sleeping rooms with one for James [O'Connell's manservant] and his wife and a servant man's apartment. Richard [O'Connell's coachman] is very anxious I should send him and the horses by the *steamer* from this to London. We must have him and the horses at expense in Ireland and be obliged to have job horses and coachmen in London which, from what I can learn, will [be]

dreadfully expensive . . . Perhaps if James would be on the look out he may be able to get a small house on reasonable terms with coachhouse and stable for the time we may be in London. All this I leave to your consideration . . . my wish is to be as saving as possible both here and elsewhere but I am anxious to make a good appearance in London for the sake of our girls. It might be of great advantage to them.[7]

Despite their covert tug-of-war over where and at what level to live, O'Connell and Mary were still, as they had always been, in fundamental unison and harmony. Their love-match of 1802 had never worn thin. After almost thirty years of time's abrasions, its lineaments still showed out clearly in the rubbed brass. On 24 July 1830 Mary wrote to her husband,

This is the eight-and-twentieth anniversary of our wedding day – the day of the week too – which to me was the commencement of a happiness that through your fault [never] was and never will be decreased. I have been the happiest of women since I first knew you and I feel that if you don't love me more, you do not now, in my old age, love me less. And oh darling how dear, how very dear are you to my fond and grateful heart![8]

According to Fagan, who knew her well, Mary's intellect was 'of the masculine order',[9] critical and strong. But all this flew out the window when it came to her *vision* of O'Connell. At various times during 1830, she wrote fondly to him in London, 'At this rate I expect one of these days to be the wife of the Prime Minister of England, Daniel O'Connell. Really, love, it is what you may look forward to without sacrificing one inch of your principles. They will see they cannot do without you';[10] 'I fancy [you] . . . looking as independent as if you were already Prime Minister of England . . . Darling you have brought a blessing upon yourself and your family, and your example has done more for the Catholic Church than ever was done by a layman at any period';[11] and 'My heart overflows with gratitude and pride for being the wife of such a man.'[12]

O'Connell was not the man to be outdone in any language, least of all that of endearment. Typical were the salutations of successive letters in mid-1831, 'My own sweetest love' and 'My own darling Mary'. Equally typical were his preface to the first, 'I have the Corporation case [a major malversion suit] to argue this day at the Rolls and I ought not to consume time from it *even in writing to you*, my own sweetest darling Love',[13] and the expression of his solicitude in the second, 'Darling, my own darling, why will you injure your health by fretting [about a formerly threatened duel]? . . . I should be as happy as *the day is long* if I could overcome your uneasiness. Mary,

I have a plan to go down with you to Windsor before the business of the House actually commences.'[14] All this was private discourse, between the two, meant to be read only by one another. But we can at least claim, in defence of intrusion, that it also had profound 'public' implications. When they were apart (now relatively rarely) the O'Connells interchanged letters almost daily, and in these O'Connell revealed his inner fears and triumphing, sure of a responsive sympathy or delight. Nor was Mary's mere blind support. At a certain level – that provided by O'Connell himself, the newspapers and Catholic Dublin's *on dits* – her grasp of politics was clear and sure, given her steady bias in O'Connell's favour. By her intelligent sympathy, she took some of the incessant strain off O'Connell's shoulders, and in return his self-revelation and dependence on her approval and applause warmed her by the assurance of her own indispensability and filled her with a sense of vicarious achievement. They also made her feel loved. 'All our children', she wrote to him on 5 December 1830, 'quiz me not a little upon the regularity of your letters. I suppose they are surprised you should think so much of a little old woman as to write to her every post. It is a doubt to me however if even [R.L.] Sheil, who has got so much by his lovely wife [Sheil had recently married an heiress], is as much attached to her as my darling old man is to his fond and grateful old woman.'[15]

Only one of O'Connell's children, his eldest daughter, Ellen, was as yet 'settled' in 1830. Five years earlier she had married Christopher Fitz-Simon, to O'Connell's ultimate benefit, as Fitz-Simon was to prove a tactful and painstaking political supporter and intermediary. It is true that the older boys, Maurice and Morgan, born in 1803 and 1804 respectively, were apparently launched upon careers, Maurice at the Irish bar and Morgan as a cavalry officer, in the Austrian Hussars. But Maurice never practised law energetically and soon ceased to practise it at all, while the charming feckless Morgan had neither the abilities nor the persistence which a poor Irishman required to fight his way upward in a foreign aristocratical profession. O'Connell's other sons, John (born in 1810) and Daniel (born in 1817), were still students, the first reading law in London and the other a schoolboy at the Jesuit college, Clongowes Wood. His daughters Betsey and Kate were as yet unmarried; if they were to be placed on a par with Ellen each would have to be provided with a dowry of £5000.

Thus O'Connell carried as heavy a familial burden as ever in 1830, although it was of course accompanied by the usual complex of parental emotional engagement, itself impossible to quantify exactly in terms of pains and pleasures. Certainly, O'Connell's children cost him dearly in time and care as well as money. He was an effusively affectionate father, especially towards his daughters. He might express his feeling with characteristic lack of reticence or commonplace decorum, as when, at a public meeting, he declared, 'I know what it is to respect as well as love those whom, in parental language, I call my angel daughters . . . whatever storms I may be engaged in abroad, when I return home, I have, as it were, attendant angels waiting about me, and cheering me on to renewed exertion.'[16] But he could also treat them with great sensitivity, as when after Betsey's wedding in 1831 he sent this message to her sister (now the only unmarried girl though Betsey's elder), 'Tell my sweetest Kate I hope to live to see her love a husband more than she loves her father though she may rely on it that her father will never love her less than he does at present.'[17] O'Connell also indulged his sons, even if less exuberantly. He defended Daniel's neglect to write home from school with, 'Darling, why do you fret yourself about Danny? If he was in the slightest degree unwell the Jesuits would write to you at once and, as to the sweet fellow himself, a letter necessarily takes away the play hours of a day.'[18] When Mary changed her mind about his sending a thunderbolt to his sons, he agreed with his usual easy grace, 'I recognized with delight your *mother's heart* in your retracting the *scolding* I meant to give my poor boys.'[19]

At the same time – at any rate, at this time – O'Connell's sons caused him more difficulties than his daughters, and Maurice the most difficulty of all. He had charm and cleverness, but was also lazy, expensive and cursed with the widespread expectation that he would measure up to his father in achievement. Sadly, he was still attempting to imitate O'Connell in his public bearing and even vituperation, like the small boy repeating the conjurer's movements – but without the conjuror's effects – after the party. Whether in despair of Maurice's making a living at the bar or in the hope that his eldest son would turn into his political as well as his legal heir, O'Connell decided in 1830 to introduce him to his own new trade, that of parliamentary politican. He put him forward for Drogheda at the general election of that year, and though Maurice failed both at the polls and in subsequent petitions against his successful opponent, O'Connell found him a seat, albeit at the cost of savage local quarrels, at a by-election for co. Clare in March 1831. O'Connell would never have serious difficulty in finding a compliant Irish constituency for Maurice – or indeed any of his sons; the crux was the cost of a parliamentary career. O'Connell and his wife had long been on the hunt for a rich wife for Maurice, and their efforts became strenuous once again about the time of the by-election. The girl in sight was a daughter of George Bourke Kelly, who had acted as chairman of the English Catholics' committee of the O'Connell Testimonial in 1829. The 'principals' negotiated first, O'Connell writing from London to Mary, who was in Dublin, on 5 March 1831, 'Maurice had better remain with you until I see the Kellys [again]'.[20] The second meeting appears to have gone well, and on 26 May 1831, O'Connell complained to Mary (now in London while he was in Dublin), 'You have not said anything of the young lady of Acton [Miss Kelly]. If she does not *forbid*, it is sufficient. Recollect *that*, darling.'[21] Nothing came of the affair. Perhaps Maurice resisted an arranged marriage. Certainly, he was to leap in the opposite direction sixteen months later.

Meanwhile, O'Connell had inadvertently launched himself on a 'solution' to the problem of his sons' futures. At the 1832 general election, Maurice's brothers, Morgan (who had abandoned the Austrian cavalry) and John, together with their brother-in-law, Fitz-Simon (by now virtually another of O'Connell's sons), joined him in the House of Commons; and eventually even Daniel, whom O'Connell set up in business after he left school, also became an MP. To some extent, this indicated their incapacity to make their own way in the world. But it also manifested O'Connell's new determination to establish a core of totally obedient parliamentary supporters, who could also be deployed at will across the Irish constituencies, as so many pieces in his game of parliamentary nominations and substitutions. A family party within a party was cruelly expensive to maintain and more or less reduced the young O'Connells to the level of political automata, as well as perpetual dependents on their father. But it also helped to make O'Connell himself a parliamentary leviathan – even the greatest British magnate of the day 'owned' fewer members – and, Maurice perhaps apart, seems to have deepened rather than alienated his boys' loyalty and love. After all, his children could scarcely help being minnows to his Triton when it came to public things. Even the arrival of Betsey's first child was announced to the world in terms which did at least as much justice to her father as herself: 'Birth at Darrynane Abbey, the lady of N. J. Ffrench, of Fort William, in the county of Roscommon, Esq., and youngest daughter of Daniel O'Connell, M.P., of a son and heir.'[22]

II

In 1829 O'Connell abandoned his regular practice as a barrister. During the 1830s he toyed at least once with the notion of returning wholeheartedly to his old profession, and occasionally accepted briefs which carried high fees or promised political *éclat*. Sometimes he picked up a few additional cases during a visit to an assize town on special retainer. When in very low water financially in 1839–40, he actually sought business. 'I will give opinions in Dublin', he wrote wryly to P. V. Fitzpatrick on 14 December 1839, 'to any persons unwise enough to pay for them',[23] and in the following summer he appeared in some rather inglorious cases on the unfamiliar western circuit, at Galway and Castlebar. This seems to have been his swansong at the bar. His practice between 1829 and 1840 would not have accounted for more than a tenth of his time or income.

None the less, his thirty years as a prodigiously busy, versatile and successful advocate had shaped him permanently. There seems to be no question that he stood in first rank of counsel. Retrospectively, the *Law Magazine* compared him favourably with the two leading English advocates of his own generation.

It is impossible to conceive a more powerful advocate than Mr. O'CONNELL was, before a Judge and Jury. They who have heard him in Parliament only, can form no notion of the man, such as he was, whilst wielding men's minds in his natural sphere of action. Impassioned and vigorous as BROUGHAM, discreet, argumentative, and zealous for his client, and forgetful of himself, as LYNDHURST, he had a playfulness of humour, a readiness of wit to affix an irresistibly ludicrous epithet, or apply some story fraught with ridicule, in an appalling degree, where he pleased – a power, moreover, of the deepest pathos, to which the former two were strangers. No man that ever spoke, did probably possess the power of moving the feelings and passions of a Jury in the same degree as Mr. O'CONNELL.[24]

His Irish contemporaries were unanimous that, while others might excel him in particular specialisms, none matched him as a professional, all round. 'Every requisite for a barrister of all-work', wrote W. H. Curran in his critical *Sketches of the Irish Bar* in 1823, 'is combined in him; some in perfection – all in sufficiency.' He was a master of procedure and the practical application, on an instant, of general legal principles; he was almost without a rival 'in a vehement and pertinacious talent with which he contends to the last for victory, or, where victory is impossible, for an honourable retreat'. Although his chamber business was immense, his forte was jury cases, and in particular as defence counsel in criminal proceedings. Curran observed that he was unerring in choosing the line best adapted to his auditors.

> But, in addition to the art of heating the passions of his hearers to the malleable point, O'Connell manifests powers of observation of another, and, for general purposes, a more valuable kind . . . Throw him upon any particular class of men, and you would imagine that he must have lived among them all his life, so intuitively does he accommodate his style of argument to their particular modes of thinking and reasoning. He knows the exact quantity of strict logic they will bear, or can comprehend. Hence, (where it serves his purpose) instead of attempting to drag them along with him, whether they will or no, by a chain of unbroken demonstration, he has the address to make them imagine that their movements are directed solely by themselves . . . This of course, is not to be taken as O'Connell's invariable manner, for he has no invariable manner, but as a specimen of that dexterous accommodation of particular means to a particular end, from which his general powers as a nisi-prius advocate may be inferred. And so, too, of the tone in which he labours to extort a verdict; for though, when compelled by circumstances, he can be soft and soothing . . . yet on other occasions, where it can be done with safety, he does not hesitate to apprise a jury, whose purity he suspects, of his real opinion of their merits, and indeed, not unfrequently, in the roundest terms, defies them to balance for an instant between their malignant prejudices, and the clear and resistless justice of the case.[25]

This may be taken as an epitome of his public method. In politics no less than law, his art of persuasion had many tones, including, paradoxically, the defiant and the denunciatory; and not just in the trial room but in everything O'Connell strove for the verdict, rather than effect. Forensically, he was indivisible.

It is curious that O'Connell, who was pre-eminently an efficient counsel, also became a mythical figure through his profession. The folk-hero of Irish legend was preternaturally cunning, dextrous in laying traps for his opponents, adroit in uncovering their deceits, endlessly audacious and resourceful – and of course ultimately triumphant. The popular image of O'Connell as a lawyer was essentially the same, and it was, in part, the secret of his power over the rural masses. A great cross-examiner is a sculptor carving in snow; only on the rare occasions is he extensively reported. O'Connell's last great performance as a criminal barrister, in a case which apparently validated and certainly enlarged his heroic reputation, was one such occasion. It is worth considering in detail.

On Saturday 24 October 1829, a first batch of prisoners, Patrick
O'Leary, a well-to-do 70-year-old farmer, and three others, were
convicted at Cork of conspiring to murder several landlords living
near Doneraile. O'Connell, who had already decided to reduce
severely if not abandon entirely his legal practice, and was then
holidaying at Derrynane, had refused the prisoners' brief. But after the
conviction of O'Leary and his co-defendants a messenger was sent
ninety miles on horseback to Derrynane to implore O'Connell to take
up the cause of the remainder. In keeping with the melodrama already
infusing the affair, O'Connell responded to the desperate appeal by
driving himself from Derrynane throughout the night of 25–6
October, breaking his journey only at Macroom for three hours' sleep.
In the mysterious country fashion, the word of his dash for Cork had
got abroad, and there were knots of people to cheer him on at every
crossroads and straggle of cabins along the way. The court, sitting at 9
am on 26 October, refused an application for an adjournment until
O'Connell should arrive, although he was expected within the hour.
As the swearing in of the jury reached its end, however,

> there was a buz in the avenues to the Court, produced by the appearance of
> Mr O'Connell, who ... was received, as usual, with unequivocal
> demonstrations of applause by the populace. The learned gentleman's
> outward appearance testified that he had been travelling all night, but after
> throwing off his top covering, he seemed quite fresh and ready for business,
> and some refreshment being sent to him, he seemed in a few minutes to
> forget everything but the case he had undertaken.[26]

The fables of the subsequent encounter were built around O'Connell's
superior command of law, protracted and vituperative duel with John
Doherty (the solicitor-general, who led the prosecution), and con-
founding of the crown's witnesses by a cross-examination which
seemed to read their secret purposes as if through glass. Stripped of
their embellishments of witty and plangent exchanges, the popular
stories showed a real grasp of the progress of the trial. O'Connell's
repeated objections soon halted the stream of hearsay and leading
questions which had slipped by in the course of Saturday's hearing; his
every objection was upheld. His sustained assault upon Doherty's
affectations and unprofessional conduct of the case told in the end on
the attitudes of even the bench, the fellow-counsel and the jury. During
O'Connell's second day in court, the presiding judge Pennefather and
the other prosecuting barristers – with a decided air of 'the lady doth
protest too much' – took the extraordinary step of vouching publicly
seriatim for Doherty's probity. Later the court refused to entertain a

counter-affidavit from Doherty after O'Connell had charged the prosecution 'with a suppression of evidence, and a withdrawal of witnesses for the prisoners'. 'Perchance', the court ruled, 'the reading of the replying affidavit might militate against the prisoners at the bar'.[27] By that stage the compact front of judges and prosecuting counsel, then usual in cases of agrarian crime, was in complete disarray.

But O'Connell's *chef-d'oeuvre* was the breaking down of the prosecution's four chief witnesses, whiteboys who had turned king's evidence. The newspaper summary of some of the passages of cross-examination of the first witness, Daniel Sheehan, will suffice to illustrate O'Connell's method of entanglement: the lines of questioning can be readily inferred.

[Witness –] I cannot recollect how often we [Patrick Daly and he] met together; I was once in a house drinking porter with him, but I do not recollect how often we were drinking together; . . . I do not recollect that I swore I was not in company with Daly.

Mr O'Connell – You are a great fellow at recollection; you are a perfect *non mi ricordo*.

It was Colonel Hill who sent me to Dublin; I was sworn in a whiteboy only five or six years ago; the third time I was sworn in was about twelve months ago; my second swearing in was in winter, and of a Sunday . . . I cannot say what time I was last sworn in as a whiteboy . . . I do not recollect from one year to ten when I was last sworn in a whiteboy.

Mr O'Connell – Well, what am I to do with this fellow? Witness – On the trial last Friday I thought I was not bound to Mr M'Carthy, since I was not sworn a witness for him; I am not as honest a man to-day as I was on Friday; I know I am obliged to answer you, Sir; . . . I do not recollect how long this Doneraile business is going on; I know what a month is, but I do not know how many there are in a year; I don't recollect when Dr Norcott's carriage was fired at; I know Michaelmas and Christmas; I can't say whether Mr Low was fired at before or after Christmas; Mr Low was fired at before the attack on Dr Norcott's carriage; I do not recollect which was fired at; the Doneraile meeting was the first; I know not how many years ago the Doneraile business happened; at the meeting held there, Leary, Magner, Hickey, Wallis, Shine, and William Nowlan were present; these are the same names I told Sergeant Goold; Michael Nowlan was also there; he was a relation of William Nowlan's.

After Mr O'Connell had, with considerable perseverance, and much time been occupied in endeavouring to obtain from the witness an answer as to whom Michael Nowlan was, he acknowledged that there was no such person.[28]

The evidence of the other whiteboy witnesses was similarly trans-muted by O'Connell in a babel of contradiction and inconsequenti-ality; one of them was driven in his misery to cry out, "tis little I thought I'd meet you here to-day, Counsellor O'Connell!'[29] The discrediting cross-examination proved crucial. The juror who held out against conviction, in the teeth of sustained pressure from his fellows and the bench, told the judges, 'My Lords, . . . I cannot agree with them [his brother jurors], for the character given by the witnesses for the prosecution of themselves was such, that I would not believe a single tittle of their evidence.'[30] With a hung jury, the second set of defendants (less one acquitted already) was discharged – ostensibly to be retried later, but in reality for good.

In the third trial, which followed immediately, O'Connell held the initiative throughout, and so pursued his earlier onslaught on the crown's evidence that even Pennefather, in his summing-up, described its witnesses, variously, as 'wretches', 'miscreants, who have steeped their hands in repeated acts of blood', 'monsters' and 'base'. The jury took only twenty minutes to find the latest contingent of defendants 'not guilty'. Thereupon the prosecution announced that it would not proceed with the charges against those still untried, primarily because of 'the character of the evidence'[31] – that is, the evidence after it had passed through O'Connell's mangle.

The *Freeman's Journal* reported that 'every tongue was loud in praises of Mr O'Connell, to whose exertions the result is universally attributed'.[32] The accolades were well-earned. There can be little doubt that more than a dozen men would have been hanged had he not taken command of the defence. As it was, the lives of even the first four prisoners were saved as, retroactively, his devastating cross-examination caused their sentences of death to be commuted to transportation. O'Connell's role as the almost magical deliverer was confirmed in the popular conception. He stood forth as the peasants' bulwark against the state, even when, as was almost certainly the case at Doneraile, they attempted to defend their means of living by a scheme of selective assassination. It was advocacy in such agrarian *causes célèbres* which cemented his union with the rural masses. Yet, once the verdict was in, he addressed the people in the tones of the sheriff of Nottingham rather than Robin Hood, and aligned himself firmly with the cause of public order. He made his peace with the opposing counsel (Doherty excepted), discountenanced any overt celebration of his triumph and told the peasantry to take warning from the trial of the utter ruin into which Whiteboyism and any similar excursion into conspiracy and violence must lead them. The final courtroom exchanges were mutually congratulatory.

> Mr O'Connell . . . If ever the people had an opportunity of witnessing the pure administration of justice, it has been afforded to them on this occasion; and if ever there was a practical lesson held out to the perpetrators of crime that there is no fidelity to be placed in their companions in guilt – no matter what obligations of secrecy were entered into by the confederacy – the present Commission has fully demonstrated it; while what I cannot but call the majestic impartiality with which justice has been administered by the bench must inspire confidence in all. I beg pardon, my Lords, for having thus intruded, but I could not help saying so much.
>
> Baron Pennefather – Those trials have been brought forward by the Crown, and defended by the counsel for the prisoners, in a manner which, in the name of the Court, and I think I may say in the name of the public, has been most satisfactory . . . It is right too, to say, that while the prisoners have been defended with great power and ability, that defence has been conducted with perfect regard for the due administration of the laws.
>
> Mr O'Connell bowed to the Court.[33]

In several ways, O'Connell the counsel provides us with keys to understanding O'Connell the public man. In both roles he combined aggression and dauntlessness in the popular cause with a most careful adherence to the rules and conventions governing the system in which he was operating. In both, he threw himself into the 'case' of the moment, but, win or lose, proceeded to the next with undiminished appetite for, and commitment to, the succeeding struggle. No one had more settled general principles than he, but neither was anybody more absorbed in the immediate. In both roles, O'Connell was fertile and variable in tactics, loud and eager in the thick of conflict, yet ready and even anxious to settle for lesser gains the moment the larger ones appeared unattainable. In both, he alternated the gravely responsible and demotic notes, as need suggested. He treated, for instance, the judges in the Doneraile trials with all formal respect, making his submissions with professional decorum. But every so often he played to the groundlings in the courtroom, as in mimicking Doherty's mincing dismissal of a witness, 'You may go down, sir', with 'Naw! daun't go daune, sir',[34] or in adding to his supporters' treasury of remembered sallies with

> Court – Mr O'Connell, from whence do you take your definition of perjury?
>
> Mr O'Connell – My Lord, I take it from the Catholic cathechism.[35]

In changing his occupation from law to parliamentary politics in 1830, O'Connell merely exchanged one forum for another. His methodology and mental predisposition remained the same. They had been stamped into him by virtually a lifetime's practice at the bar. Not that there was any reason for him to try to put on a new man at the age of fifty-five. He had already mastered the arts of popular domination, and of working within – often just within – the bounds of official structures. He had forged and tempered an extraordinary range of tools for public use; they would do practically as well in one place as another.

III

In abandoning his regular practice at the bar O'Connell lost the staple of his income. In money terms, he probably sacrificed about £6000–£7000 per annum, and came to depend instead on Irish public subscription – a species of 'compensation' – to provide him with the bulk of his resources. This soon became settled into a more or less annual 'Tribute' to himself; sporadically, a 'Rent' was also collected for various political movements or emergencies. It is impossible to say exactly how much these levies raised; the sums varied significantly from one phase of activity to another. But an annual average of some £12,000 would seem a reasonable estimate for 1831–45. His landed and other income was probably £4000–£5000 per annum.

None the less O'Connell found it almost impossible to make ends meet. He was chronically extravagant and careless with money, and drew no real distinction – if indeed there were any to be drawn – between his 'public' and his 'private' funds. His political expenditure was in itself enormous. As well as supporting his family party of MPs, he contributed heavily to his own associations and campaigns and the dissemination of information and propaganda. Even the maintenance of a third residence in London – a set of rooms in lodgings or a rented house, during the parliamentary session – and his incessant travel between Ireland and Great Britain and within both countries, were considerable burdens. General elections were the worst of all. He had sometimes to meet the costs of several contests, two or three of them for ruinously expensive county seats, and then to defend his gains, once more from his own pocket, against the inevitable petitions.

It is not surprising that with steady drains and sudden large demands on an income partly dependent on the caprice of the Irish public, O'Connell should have fallen from time to time into terrible financial trouble. It was no novelty for him to be close to bankruptcy. In fact, this might be said to have been his usual condition before, first, the legacies falling into his lap on the death of his uncle Maurice (Hunting Cap) O'Connell in 1825, and then the national testimonial raised for him on the attainment of Catholic Emancipation in 1829, lifted him for a short while well above the slough. After 1830 things were still worse in certain ways. A man in his later fifties – even an O'Connell – could not sustain the buoyancy of spirit, and the hope of somehow or other working his way out of calamity, which had been so remarkable a feature of his early manhood and middle age. Besides much more – in the form of still proliferating family charges, the expectations of benefaction deriving from his higher social station, and, above all, the carriage of what was virtually a separate political system on his own shoulders – now hung on his remaining solvent. Yet although O'Connell was still to suffer occasional desperate crises and days (and once or twice a week or so) of dark despondency, he was free of the near-constant financial frets and fears of the years before 1830.

This wonderful relief is chiefly to be explained by O'Connell's acquiring a financial manager in 1830. Patrick Vincent Fitzpatrick, born in 1792, was the son of Hugh Fitzpatrick, a Catholic bookseller and publisher who had been imprisoned for libel in 1813 in the course of an attempt by Peel to destroy O'Connell's agitation. P. V. Fitzpatrick, as a young barrister, became a member of O'Connell's entourage at the Catholic Association in the mid-1820s; and it was actually he who induced O'Connell to stand for co. Clare in the fateful by-election of 1828. He also – happy augury – undertook to raise sufficient money for the contest, and well over the required sum was speedily gathered in. This led on to Fitzpatrick's appointment as an organizer of the O'Connell testimonial in the following year – again with remarkable success, O'Connell sending him on 10 May 1830 his 'most sincere and cordial thanks . . . some occasion may arrive when I may be able to show you how deeply obliged I am, and how sensibly I feel my debt of obligation to you'.[36] Apparently off his own bat, Fitzpatrick next proposed that a 'Tribute' be raised regularly; for on 24 June O'Connell assured him, 'Your plan of a "Collection Sunday" I highly approve of'.[37] Fitzpatrick had thoroughly made his way into O'Connell's confidence and affection. In August 1830 O'Connell wrote to his brother James in Kerry,

> This will be handed to you by my very kind and particular friend Mr P. V. FitzPatrick. He is the eldest son of the late Mr Hugh FitzPatrick. He has been one of the most useful, if not the most perseveringly useful, of the

managers of 'the Fund'. All the articles in the [*Dublin Evening*] *Post* on that subject have been written by him. I cannot describe to you how grateful I am to him. He is now going to the South of Ireland. I recommend him to you in the strongest terms. Invite him to your house whilst he remains in Kerry. Show this letter to John [O'Connell's other brother], and take care to *forward* him throughout the kingdom of Kerry.

I leave this letter open that he may show it in Cork to our friend Charles Sugrue, Tom Fitzgerald, etc.[38]

Fitzpatrick demonstrated his mastery of his craft when raising the successful Tribute of 1831. He proved to be patient, prudent, tactful, systematic and wonderfully informed. Thereafter not only was he charged with the organization of the national collections (on a percentage basis) but he also took over, step by step, the management of O'Connell's own finances. The second task called for all the considerable calm, resourcefulness and powers of persuasion at his command; but he never failed his master. Fitzpatrick was much more than O'Connell's man of business. He rapidly became a sort of general adviser and arranger, and, especially after Mary O'Connell's death in 1836, O'Connell's chief confidant and nearest friend. But his vital role was that of shield between O'Connell and financial trouble. He could not insulate him completely from the consequences of over-spending and the reckless extension of commitments. But he saw to it that O'Connell was hauled out of each successive scrape. He gave him the opportunity to concentrate, almost all the time, upon the primary business of his life. He was Mazarin to O'Connell's Louis XIII, except that his loyalty was not to an abstract kingship but to a hero of his own. He was often called, even in his lifetime, O'Connell's *fidus Achates*; and so he was.

IV

In most, though not all, forms of political and cultural ideology, O'Connell was in the advance guard in 1830. During his remaining seventeen years of life, he moved further up the van in certain places; in others he fell back. Often it was the world about him that changed position rather than himself. Generally his views were constant.

Outside politics and morals, he tended to follow the drift of the day. Let us take creative literature as an illustration. Here his shifting taste was always conventionally good. Like most educated people, he somehow accumulated a wide knowledge of Shakespeare, perhaps in the style of Henry Crawford in *Mansfield Park*, 'Shakespeare one gets acquainted with without knowing how'.[39] As a young man, he was deeply impressed by the quintessential novel of sensibility, Mackenzie's *Man of Feeling*. A decade and a half later, he was taken with Byron and Scott. Byron's biting critiques of contemporary society and politics often matched his own, and Scott both resembled O'Connell remarkably in background and disposition and responded in much the same way, imaginatively, to the past. 'There never was such a novelist', O'Connell observed after re-reading all Scott's works in succession in 1841, 'and there never again will be another such.'[40] O'Connell's retrospective romanticism focused, however, on religion quite as much as – or perhaps more than – pageantry or the hierarchy and mutuality of traditional Gaelic society. He was 'an enthusiastic admirer of the cathedrals of England', especially Canterbury; in fact, he commissioned a painting of Becket's martyrdom to be hung in his Dublin parish church. It was at Canterbury that, according to his own account, he astounded the 'female guide' with the information that every prelate interred in the great 'pile' was a papist.

> 'Bless me!' cried the woman, in astonishment, 'I never knew that before.' – I then described the effect of the high altar lighted up for the celebration of mass in Catholic times; when the great aisle, now boxed up into compartments by the organ loft, stretched its venerable and unbroken length from the altar to the portal, thronged with kneeling worshippers. The picture delighted the woman. 'Oh!' cried she, clapping her hands, 'I should like to see that!' – 'God grant you may yet,' returned I.[41]

Like thousands of other readers, O'Connell became immediately enamoured of Dickens's early books. On 4 September 1837 he demanded that the new issue of *Bentley's Miscellany* be sent to him at Derrynane at once. 'The story of "Oliver Twist" is continued in [it], and I am most impatient to see it.'[42] Again like thousands of readers, he was, however, infuriated by the death of Little Nell, and in a storm of outraged sentimentality threw the volume which had recounted it away. Bulwer Lytton was among his later favourites.

He admired most of the leading Irish writers for the contemporary London market, chiefly Moore whom he virtually idolized for both his 'melodies' and his political novels such as *Captain Rock*, which was 'to the struggle for Catholic Emancipation what *Uncle Tom's Cabin* was to the abolition of slavery'.[43] But he also warmly praised the books of the Banim brothers and Gerald Griffin. Griffin's *Collegians* had a particular appeal, for O'Connell had defended the murderer unsuccessfully in the case on which the novel was based. (It was a rare instance of his rejoicing in an adverse verdict: 'I do not feel any the most slight regret at his conviction', O'Connell told his wife, 'It is very unusual with me to be *so* satisfied, but he is a horrid villain'.[44]) Significantly, the Irish authors whom O'Connell particularly liked – Moore, Griffin and the Banims – had Catholic backgrounds and, however prudently concealed or muted, nationalistic instincts similar to his own. Contrariwise, Maria Edgeworth's *The Absentee* jarred on him, ostensibly because he saw in it a covert attack upon himself, but more probably because he divined that by the 1830s Edgeworth had reverted to the standard Ascendancy condescension towards and suspicion of his class.

V

Thus, with a few Irish aberrations, O'Connell's pleasure reading generally followed the mainstream as it flowed. But the doctrine of one comparatively obscure novel, which had much impressed him when he was young, suffused his public conduct all his life. The novel was William Godwin's *Caleb Williams*, and the doctrine, as developed systematically in Godwin's *Political Justice*, was to provide him, as we have seen, with two of his master principles. The first of these was epitomized by O'Connell himself in the proposition that that government was best 'which laid fewest restraints on private judgment'.[45] The second was an absolute repudiation of violence in seeking political or any other ends. By itself, Godwin had argued, human reason was capable of producing infinite social amelioration; blood-shed halted progress, or rather drove things back. Public opinion was the ultimate source of every power; change that opinion, and accordingly government was changed. In a letter of advice of 16 February 1830 to Thomas Attwood, who had just set up the Birmingham Political Union, O'Connell translated Godwin's visionary philosophy into the language of the practical agitator.

There are two principal means of attaining our constitutional objects which will never be lost sight of. The first is the perpetual determination to avoid anything like physical force or violence and by keeping in all respects within the letter as well as the spirit of the law, to continue peaceable, rational, but energetic measures so as to combine the wise and the good of all classes, stations and persuasions in one determination to abolish abuse and renovate the tone and strength of the representative system. The other is to obtain funds by the extension of a plan of collection which shall *accept* from no man more than he can with the utmost facility spare even in these times of universal distress. The multiplication of small sums, of very small

sums, should be the proper as it would be the efficacious popular treasury
. . . The people should incessantly call for reform until their cry is heard
and *felt* within the walls of Westminster.[46]

Godwin's first principle, the utmost freedom from restraint, virtually subsumed the whole range of O'Connell's political objectives; it
also classified O'Connell's type of early-nineteenth-century radicalism. It was no chance that by 1830 he was commonly termed
'liberator' or 'emancipator'. These terms indicated precisely how
O'Connell saw his general task – as the unshackling of people from all
the fetters imposed by ascendancy, discrimination or prejudice, as well
as by tyranny itself. O'Connell did not follow Godwin to the uttermost
limits of *Political Justice*; he did not seek, for instance, the eradication
of such 'coercive' institutions as monarchy, aristocracy or the law of
contract. But overall he adhered to an extreme programme of
individual rights. This programme was essentially negative in character, a grand procession of 'freedoms from'. But it could also be
regarded positively, as the steadfast pursuit of civil equality.

With much justice, O'Connell claimed the name of universal
egalitarian. He represented his struggles to achieve parity for
Catholics and Irish as mere particular manifestations of a general
aspiration. Typical was his powerful and consistent advocacy of
Jewish 'emancipation'. As he assured the leader of English Jewry, Isaac
Goldsmid, towards the close of 1829, 'you will find in me the constant
and active friend to every measure which tends to give the Jews an
equality of civil rights with all other the king's subjects, a perfect
unconditional equality. I think every day a day of injustice until that
civil equality is attained by the Jews.'[47] He was as good as his word.
Although Jewish relief was a highly unpopular cause in Britain (it was
opposed even by many radicals, including Cobbett), O'Connell was
foremost in support of the removal of Jewish disabilities bill in the
House of Commons in 1830. He made short shrift of the cant which
commonly clothed racial prejudice. He would have none of the
arguments that equality for Jews would de-christianize the state and
establish an 'alien' body in the polity. During the debate of 22
February 1830, he declared that instead

> of separating the Legislature from Christianity, by conceding the claims of
> the Jews, we should prove ourselves still more Christian by doing as we
> would be done by, and carrying into effect the principle of perfect freedom
> of conscience, – a principle that already manifested its beneficial tendency,
> and which would be the more beneficial the more widely it was extended.[48]

Later, on 17 May 1830, he dealt masterfully with the attack on Jews for their outer loyalties. A Jew 'might still remember the traditionary home of his father . . . [but] he was still obedient to our laws. Let them not, therefore talk of the name of Christianity, when it was used to do evil instead of good.'[49]

Racial prejudice or exclusion he attacked with cold reason, but colour prejudice and slavery he attacked with passion: these fired him to savage and contemptuous denunciation. He would never visit the United States: it was a slaveholding country. He would never shake the hand of an American who in any way – even by mere residence in a 'bond' state – condoned the abomination. 'I should be sorry to be contaminated by the touch of a man from those States where slavery is continued', he told an anti-colonization meeting in London in 1833.[50] His earnestness cannot be doubted. During 1843–5 he persisted in his public condemnations of slavery in the United States. Even at the cost of ultimately destroying his entire support system in the United States, he did not yield to the sustained pressure of the American Repealers either to maintain silence on the subject or to declare Irish independence to be the political priority. The Young Ireland faction, and indeed many others within his home movement, generally argued that Ireland's need for overseas sympathy and resources should be paramount. O'Connell would have none of this. A deeply entangled politician, he sometimes hedged initially. But from the start to finish he never really deviated from the line that the American Declaration of Independence was a lie before God, while men, women and children were bought and sold, used and looked upon, as chattels: he would, he said, recognize no man as an Irishman who failed to repudiate this institution. Moreover, O'Connell's 'brotherhood of man' embraced all victims of Western colonialism. In a speech to the Aborigines Protection Society in 1840, for example, he denounced colonialism in Australia and New Zealand as carrying ruin and genocide in its train; 'no other human event led to evils so multitudinous'.[51] 'There', he once declared, 'are your Anglo-Saxon race! Your British blood! your civilizers of the world . . . the vilest and most lawless of races. There is a gang for you! . . . the civilizers, forsooth, of the world!'[52] His hatred of supremacism, colour-discrimination and servitude had been formed and settled long before 1830. From early in the century he had been a leading figure in the main European abolitionist organization, the British and Foreign Anti-Slavery Society, and during the years 1830–3, he was to play a critical part in the successful campaign for West Indian 'emancipation'. Despite the compensation of the former slaveholders (which he deplored) he later 'looked upon [this victory] . . . as one of the glorious acts of nineteenth-civilization, a symbol of the inevitable progress of man'.[53] His last decade in politics was the same; he continued to pour out time, words and political powers in the cause of black and other 'coloured' liberation. Small wonder that he was already in 1830, and would remain until his death, a hero of heroes to the American negroes and many abolitionists.

What of that other great body of deprived, women? As a young man, O'Connell had reasoned himself into an affirmation of full sex equality on general individualist principles. But in the world in which he was to live, female 'emancipation' was scarcely even a debated issue; and, more or less automatically, O'Connell accepted the dominant concept and practice of sharply separated spheres for men and women. When, however, he was suddenly forced to decide on a question of women's public rights, his inherent individualism conquered conventionality. On 17 June 1840, Lucretia Mott, an American delegate to the General Anti-Slavery Conference then taking place in London, asked O'Connell for his opinion on the conference's rejection of women delegates on the grounds 'that the admission of women being contrary to English usage [it] would subject them to ridicule, and that such recognition of their acknowledged principles would prejudice the cause of human freedom'.[54] O'Connell's lengthy reply was testimony to his ultimate candour as well as his underlying liberality.

> I should premise by avowing that my first impression was strong against that admission, and I believe I declared that opinion in private conversation. But when I was called on by you to give my personal decision on the subject, I felt it my duty to investigate the grounds of the opinion I had formed; and upon that investigation I easily discovered that it was founded on no better grounds than an apprehension of the ridicule it might excite if the Convention were to do what is so unusual in England – admit women to an equal share and right of the discussion. I also, without difficulty recognised that this was an unworthy and, indeed, a cowardly motive and I easily overcame its influence.
>
> My mature consideration of the entire subject convinces me of the right of the female delegates to take their seats in the Convention and of the injustice of excluding them . . . Mind has no sex; and in the peaceable struggle to abolish slavery all over the world, it is the basis of the present Convention to seek success by peaceable, moral and intellectual means alone, to the utter exclusion of armed violence. We are engaged in a strife not of strength but of argument. Our warfare is not military; it is Christian. We wield not the weapons of destruction or injury to our

adversaries. We rely entirely on reason and persuasion common to both sexes . . .[55]

O'Connell never spoke, nor was he ever called on to speak, on women's political rights, and certainly, following the orthodoxy of the day, he took their role to be essentially domestic. But he did discern that the voting powers of women shareholders in the East India Company and the Bank of England made nonsense of the notion that women had no place in public affairs; and the rigour of his individualist principle renders it likely that, had he entered politics in 1860 instead of 1830, he would have been among the first to press women's suffrage and their constitutional equality in general.

All in all, his claim to universality as a liberator can be sustained. Gladstone's posthumous tribute was essentially just.

> He was an Irishman, but he was also a cosmopolite. I remember personally how, in the first session of my parliamentary life [1833], he poured out his wit, his pathos, and his earnestness, in the cause of negro emancipation. Having adopted the political creed of Liberalism, he was as thorough an English Liberal, as if he had had no Ireland to think of. He had energies to spare for Law Reform, for Postal Reform (a question of which he probably was one of few to discern at the time the greatness), for secret voting, for Corn Law Repeal, in short for whatever tended, within the political sphere, to advance human happiness and freedom.[56]

VI

In his letter of late 1829 to Goldsmid, O'Connell wrote:

> To my mind it is an eternal and universal truth that we are responsible to God alone for our religious belief and that human laws are impious when they attempt to control the exercise of those acts of individual or general devotion which such belief requires. I think not lightly of the awful responsibility of rejecting true belief but that responsibility is entirely between man and his creator, and any fellow being who usurps dominion over belief is to my mind a blasphemer against the deity as he certainly is a tyrant over his fellow creatures.[57]

This was his proclaimed position on religious toleration in 1830, as it had been in 1813 when he declared that 'perfect liberty of conscience [was] ... eminently, almost exclusively the hope of liberty' in Ireland,[58] and as it was to be in 1841 when he told the Earl of Shrewsbury that the 'respect which each person would claim for his own opinion would require of him to treat with equal justice the opinion of others'.[59] In general O'Connell lived up to his professions.

His normal state of bitter struggle with 'Orangeism' and the church establishment in Ireland was truly, as he claimed, an opposition to a political ascendancy based on confessional allegiance. He even strove for compensation for Protestants displaced in the course of Irish reforms. 'I want to work out political changes', he declared, 'but I am equally desirous to avoid inflicting individual injury. I war against systems, not against men'.[60] At one level, O'Connell was a hot religious partisan. He eagerly counted up Catholic converts and hailed the advance of Puseyism as an inadvertent tribute to Catholic principle; he exulted that his religion was 'daily making progress – it receives an impulse from various and opposite quarters'.[61] But this was a far cry from deviating from public impartiality or abating his innate magnanimity towards persons.

It was characteristic that O'Connell should have warmly supported, in April 1830, the re-instatement of an Anglican army officer who had been dismissed from the service for refusing to fire signals at a Catholic ceremony in Malta, and equally that, in a sect-torn society, O'Connell should have himself employed a Protestant attorney, a Protestant land-steward and at least one Protestant manservant. He was a tireless advocate of the English dissenters' causes, from the abolition of religious tests for office to the abolition of church rates, and despite the chasms in creed he remained on good terms with almost all, and in particular with the Society of Friends. 'Friend O'Connell', the Quaker veteran, Joseph Pease, once told him on parting, 'I have for many years watched thine actions closely; I have kept mine eye upon thee, and I have never seen thee do aught that was not honest and useful.'[62] The solitary blemish on O'Connell's non-conformist record was an outburst of 1 August 1839 against 'the filthy slime of Wesleyan malignity'.[63] The Methodists were perhaps the bitterest contemporary assailants of Catholicism, and the issue at stake was perhaps the most inflammatory of all, proselytization. Besides, O'Connell was despondent at the time. None the less, he lapsed equally in charity and taste.

For a nineteenth-century Catholic, O'Connell was as remarkable for his commitment to the total separation of church and state as for his unqualified defence of the individual's liberty of conscience. On 11 September 1830, he wrote, in a letter intended for the public eye, of the recent revolution in France whereby the Bourbon monarchy had been superseded:

There is one feature in this great and satisfactory change which as a Catholic I hail with the most profound conviction of its utility – it is the complete severance of the church from the state. Infidelity, . . . which has deluged France with the blood of the Catholic clergy, was losing ground by degrees since the concordat obtained by Napoleon but the progress of Christian truth and of genuine piety was much impeded since the return of the Bourbons, by the unhallowed commixture of zeal for religion with servile attachment to the Bourbons. 'La religion et le Roi' were put in juxtaposition . . . Religion was thus placed in a false position. Catholicity in France was situate somewhat as Protestantism has been, and to a certain extent still is, in Ireland. It was considered to be the enemy of the people and of liberty.

I heartily rejoice that the last glorious revolution has altered the position. Religion left to its own intrinsic merits may sustain some slights and will certainly be exposed to many calumnies but those merits and the heavenly beauty of its precepts and practices will be likely to win their way with more facility now that they cannot be ranged with any hostile party . . . France has set the great and glorious example . . .[64]

This remained O'Connell's credo. He was later to dismiss the Orleanists in France as false liberals. But this he regarded as confirmation rather than contradiction of his principles; their active anti-clericalism and repressive legislation represented, in his eyes, an invasion of religious liberty by the state.

It was no wonder that O'Connell had become already the paladin of the nascent Catholic liberal movements on the Continent. In fact, at the very time that he wrote his manifesto of 11 September 1830, the young Comte de Montalembert had arrived as a pilgrim at Derrynane, to make obeisance to the great champion of Catholic liberty. When, however, Montalembert, together with his fellow-liberals Lamennais and Lacordaire, sought papal approbation of their advocacy of freedom of conscience and the separation of church and state, the new pope, Gregory XVI, elected in 1830, rejected them and their journal, *L'Avenir*, out of hand. His encyclical *Mirari vos*, promulgated in 1832, condemned most liberal tenets including unlimited freedom of assembly, of speech and of the press, and 'the erroneous and absurd opinion – or rather, derangement – that freedom of conscience must be asserted and vindicated for everyone'.[65] Moreover, to the embattled defender of the papal states, the separation of civil and spiritual authority seemed the very emblem of irreligion.

Yet, although Rome obliquely reproved O'Connell's political activity from time to time, by forbidding the Irish clergy to engage in any form of agitation against established government, O'Connell himself remained unscathed. No censorious line or word ever issued from the Curia. On the contrary, during 1838 Gregory XVI, as marks of particular regard, granted two special indulgences to the O'Connell family, another indulgence to any person who prayed in O'Connell's private chapel at Derrynane, and the privilege of a portable altar to O'Connell himself – this last being normally reserved for heads of state. For his part O'Connell, to counter doubts cast upon his orthodoxy, had written in the preceding year,

> I revere in all things the authority of the Holy See. I really believe (in so far as I know myself) that there is not a single person who pays more sincerely than I do, and with all my heart, the submission – in the widest sense of the word – to the Holy See which the Catholic Church demands of her children. I have never said and shall never say a single word which I would not subject to her authority with profound obedience. I am attached to the centre of unity with the most ardent desire never to separate myself from it either in thought or word or action, and if I should ever deceive myself in the opinions I express, I hope that they will be interpreted according to my sentiments because my submission to the authority of the Church is complete, whole and universal.[66]

How is O'Connell's high favour, let alone his exemption from censure, to be explained? He had several advantages: he was a layman; he was devout; he made no pretence to knowledge of theology; he had long struggled for, and ultimately won, the most famous Catholic victory of the age; he was sincerely, as well as prudentially, deferential to the Church; most Irish bishops were on most occasions his admirers. Secondly, the principal 'error' of contemporary liberalism, singled out for special condemnation in *Mirari vos*, was religious 'indifferentism'. Here O'Connell was orthodox beyond all question. He fully accepted the precept 'no salvation outside the Church', even if, characteristically, he also held that no one had a 'right to judge his neighbour's conscience'[67] or to suggest that a rejection of Catholicism might not be serious and sincere. Finally, the most important difference between the contestants may well have been which way, on the time scale, they faced. Whereas Gregory XVI and his kind were still fighting the intellectual battles of the *ancien régime*, O'Connell's was the prophetic role: poles apart, a line yet ran straight between the two. Grounded in benign individualism and universal concepts of human rights, O'Connell anticipated the sort of theology which was to be released in the Roman Church by the Second Vatican Council. As Helen Coldrick puts it, he had 'adopted the advanced view that religious freedom possessed a positive moral content . . . Because man was rational and free, he enjoyed the right to decide for himself ultimate matters of belief and commitment.'[68]

It is true that, during his last years, O'Connell seemed increasingly rigid in religious – or, more strictly, ecclesiastical – concerns; there were also suggestions of clericalism in some of his public utterances and stances. But these were largely the product of circumstance. The O'Connellite party among the Irish episcopate (on whom he depended politically from 1840 onward) was also, doctrinally, the narrowest and most truculent. Moreover, Peel's ministry (1841–6) deliberately raised divisive religious issues in the hope of alienating the more 'moderate' or 'broader' section of the Irish Catholic prelacy from O'Connell's movement. In such conditions, politics demanded that O'Connell bend a little to the ultramontanist wind. In any case, his every instinct would have warned him against Greeks – in the shape of English tories – bearing gifts. He was also led to the edge of sectarian asperities in 1845–6 by Young Ireland insinuations that he headed a 'priests' party' and that some at least of his lieutenants were striving, by fair means or foul, for Catholic ascendancy in Ireland. Again, however, O'Connell was essentially responding to a political challenge, with the additional provocation – as he saw it – of being lectured or patronized by Johnny-come-lately recruits to his cause, some young enough to have been his grandsons, others as suspicious of popery as any of his Exeter Hall assailants. All things fairly considered he adhered remarkably to his earliest definitions of individual and institutional rights in matters of religion. He was as truly tolerant, both by nature and deliberate endeavour, as might reasonably be asked of anyone – not only of his own but also of almost any other time.

VII

In general, in the fields of human rights and religious freedom, O'Connell held positions analogous to those attained by most Western liberals by the 1960s. *Pari passu*, he became, if anything, a more rather than a less 'advanced' radical during 1830–47, for in these years reactionary opinion clarified and conservative opposition hardened at certain points. Economic freedom was, however, a much more complicated business. By upbringing and inheritance, O'Connell was a lesser Irish landlord of the indulgent, non-improving, uncommercial kind. He occasionally supported agrarian reforms in the tenant interest, and his native kindliness and *quieta non movere* attitudes certainly earned him universal or near-universal popularity on his estates. But, practically speaking, he had no clear policy towards Irish land beyond the encouragement of residency, and of his own particular type of paternalism and chieftainship, among proprietors at large. It would scarcely be an exaggeration to approximate his landed philosophy to the Dickensian 'spirit of Christmas'. Correspondingly, although he repeatedly visited industrial towns and cities in the English north and midlands, he understood little of the fundamental structure or implications of British industrialism. He was at home in the old world of craftsmen and artisans, but that was all.

On the other hand, O'Connell applied his radical individualism as confidently and rigorously to the commercial and manufacturing as to any other fields. He was a doctrinaire free trader and the keen enemy of all constraints on trade or the supply of labour. Before 1830 this had little significance in his public life; it led to nothing more than occasional *obiter dicta* on distant things. Thereafter, however, in consequence of O'Connell's being both a leading member of the House of Commons, and a close ally of English middle-class and artisan radicals, his economic principles had a considerable bearing on politics on both sides of the Irish Sea. He had warmly approved the repeal of the Combination Acts (which had in effect rendered trade unions illegal and strikes criminal offences), but only because he was committed to the principles of the 'free contract' and personal liberty of choice and action. He did not favour trade unions as fighting forces, for the very same principles led him also to assert every individual's right to enter into his own wage contract. Hence O'Connell's firm backing for the prohibition by the Trade Unions Act of 1825 of 'intimidation', 'protestation', 'obstruction', the 'closed shop' and even peaceful picketing – a concatenation which made it extremely difficult to conduct a lawful strike. 'It was fair for them [workers] to combine . . .', he was to declare in 1838, 'but the moment they attempted to coerce others, the moment that they carried the effect of their combination to any other individuals, that instant crime commenced, and they were not only guilty of a crime in the eye of the law, but also of a moral crime, and they inflicted a robbery upon others.'[69] O'Connell was unconcerned by working-class denunciation, when it came, for 'he felt satisfied in his own conscience that he was acting as their best friend'.[70] By this he meant that restrictive labour practices were inimical to employment, and thereby ultimately to wages too. 'They [workers] were not entitled to wages out of capital; they were only entitled to them out of profits, and if their employers made no profits the wages must decrease. Wages, which were the price of labour, must depend upon the demand.'[71] Such reasoning was later to be execrated as Gradgrindism, and would eventually seem 'gothick' to the enlightened. But, to keep perspective, we should recollect that O'Connell was merely repeating the most advanced economic precepts of the day, and that he was to be in his grave for almost thirty years before (by means of the Conspiracy and Protection of Property Act of 1875) the law ceased to uphold most strictly the attitudes towards unionism which he expressed. Nor can it be doubted that he believed that his was the humane as well as the scientifically proven answer to the labour problem of the 1830s.

There are, however, other fields of ideas in which, after 1830 and still more after 1840, O'Connell began to seem a man of the past rather than the future or the present. Ideologically, he had been bred, as we have seen, a rationalist and a universalist, with an essentially atomistic view of society. Certain trends in Ireland and, to some extent Great Britain, worked against all three during his final years. They had made no great headway before he died, yet quite enough for his unease with, and resistance to, them to become apparent.

First, extra-rational politics broke the surface. If only in a half-hidden way, several of O'Connell's fundamental presuppositions came under challenge. The Germanic type of romanticism and idealism which infused the *Nation* newspaper and the more ardent element in Young Ireland placed the emphasis on the race rather than the person, the group rather than the individual, instinct and emotion, rather than reason, cultural rather than constitutional liberation, and a subjective and creative rather than a formal and negative concept of independence. Secondly, in part because of the passion generated by such a view of nationality, but also because there were few left who, like O'Connell, had had direct experience of the French Revolutionary turmoil and the Irish risings of 1798 and 1803, doctrines of armed resistance – if only in hypothetical form – began to circulate in Ireland once again before O'Connell died. To him, they were anathema. He was not himself above administering the heady stuff of ancient violent glories to his public. He even chose as the motto for his *Memoir on Ireland, Native and Saxon*, Moore's braggart lines,

> On *our* side is Virtue and Erin,
> On *theirs* is the Saxon and Guilt,

which, every Irish reader would have known, followed directly

> But onward! – the green banner rearing,
> Go, flesh ev'ry sword to the hilt.[72]

But this was merely to use the long-dead past as a momentary intoxicant. It could not – horror of horrors! – have any current or future reference.

In the third place, the new concept of 'the nation' was accompanied by a new notion of its supremacy. For O'Connell, the Irish nation meant simply all the inhabitants of Ireland, 'Catholic, Protestant and Dissenter'. In its political manifestation, it existed primarily to ensure fair play for all its members. Each denomination should have equal claims, in law and civil rights, within its bounds. But 'the nation' conceived of as a spiritual entity demanded much more of its component individuals, and this was to become of increasing importance as the public domain expanded in the third and fourth decades of the nineteenth century. Again some of O'Connell's basic presuppositions were under challenge. Let us take education, which was now becoming a governmental or partly governmental concern, as an example. Was it 'the nation's' function to facilitate the individual, be he Catholic, Protestant or Dissenter, in exercising his 'right' to educate his own children, or was 'the nation' to be itself responsible for inculcating 'national' values in the young, relegating their Catholicism, Protestantism or Dissent to the region of private instruction and belief? Did 'the nation' ultimately imply the secular state? These were the sorts of issues suddenly confronting O'Connell before he died. Finally, there was the surreptitious advance of incipient collectivism. Who in 1830 would have dreamt that, by 1847, public health, arterial drainage, industrial safety and factory hours would have been among the leading domestic issues of the day? Certainly not O'Connell, whose idea of the state was largely confined to the staples of late eighteenth-century central government – national defence, national revenue, foreign affairs, constitutional arrangements, and law and order in their largest aspects.

Thus, in his final phase, O'Connell anticipated in many ways our modern world. But there were other things in which he followed faithfully in the main line of contemporary thought, and yet others where he stayed deaf to the first whispers of the future. Meanwhile, he stood, in 1830, on a sort of plateau. Emancipation was behind him, Repeal before. The climb would be more difficult than ever.

CHAPTER 14

The Houseman

1830–1

I

'Othello's occupation's gone!': so men thought of O'Connell on the eve of his entry into the House of Commons in February 1830. For a quarter of a century he had been an agitator outside the walls of the legitimate political system. It was hardly to be expected that, approaching the age of fifty-five, he should take up successfully a new business, which was, so to speak, the very inversion of his old. He had, moreover, forced himself into a closed circle by hateful means. In the eyes of the British political classes, he had recklessly aroused the passions of the mob, and dangerously weakened the barriers to violence, licence and dispossession. As a popular agitator, he seemed to personify the force which threatened their hereditary domination. As Irish, as Catholic and as a mere bullyragging counsel, he was regarded as an intruder upon a company of gentlemen all the more so as he would no longer accept challenges to duels. As a public man, his intemperate vilification and open passion were adjudged 'low', and he was generally regarded as unprincipled. Charles Greville, a faithful reflector of upper-class reactions, summed him up in his journal at the end of 1830:

> Utterly lost to all sense of shame and decency, trampling truth and honour under his feet, cast off by all respectable men, he makes his faults and his vices subservient to the extension of his influence, for he says and does whatever suits his purpose for the moment, secure that no detection or subsequent exposure will have the slightest effect with those over whose minds and passions he rules with such despotic sway. He cares not whom he insults, because, having covered his cowardice with the cloak of religious scruples, he will resent no retaliation that can be offered him.[1]

Correspondingly his 'party', when it came to be formed in the Commons, was despised as cads. Even Le Marchant, an advanced and well-informed young liberal, noted in his diary in 1833:

His [O'Connell's] immediate followers are not [a] very creditable looking set. Fergus O'Connor has the appearance of a country attorney. He was involved some time ago in a charge of robbing the mail, and he did not come off with very clean hands . . . Daunt and O'Dwyer have more of the ruffian about them. Lalor shews that he has never been in gentleman's society before. I believe it was only last year that Sir Henry Parnell . . . presented [him] with a coat, being the first he had ever been the owner of, to appear in. Some of the others are not a whit better.[2]

Much of this was simple vulgar prejudice of the type more economically displayed by Wellington in his celebrated complaint about the 'shocking bad hats' to be found in the first 'Reformed Parliament'. But it also expressed the inveterate resentment of the elite, for O'Connell had ranged against him the peculiar combination of insolence and frightened ruthlessness which marks a privileged order under threat.

None the less Othello did make his way. O'Connell became one of the handful of men who came late to Parliament with a large reputation, and retained it undiminished. When one adds to his name those of Cobden, Joseph Chamberlain and Ernest Bevin, one has practically exhausted the category. With his marvellous plasticity, he caught 'the tone of the House' at once. Even his first appearance on the parliamentary stage, arguing the case for his own admission at the bar of the House on 18 May 1829, had been adjudged 'in manner and tact beyond what could have been conceived, and all that it should be';[3] and the following passage from his maiden speech proper on 4 February 1830 coruscates with the irony, clarity and deceptively simple art which rendered him immediately effective in the Commons:

What did it [the King's speech] contain? The first point was, that foreign nations continued to speak in terms of peace; but did they ever do otherwise when a war was on the point of breaking out, or even when the war itself had actually commenced? The next information was, that the Russian war was at an end. That was an important discovery, indeed; and, of course, none of them knew that before. They were then told that nothing was determined as to Portugal. And why? Ah! they were not told that. Was the character of Don Miguel then doubtful? Did any one doubt that he had usurped the throne of another, and endeavoured to cement his seat by the spilling of innocent blood? If so, why did the government of England shrink from the decision to which it ought to come? They were next told of the partial distress of the country. But was that a fact? He thought that the expressions which had fallen from the three hon. members on the other side who had supported the Address, were – the one, that the distress was general; the second, that the distress was extraordinary; and the third, that the distress was overwhelming. The chancellor of the Exchequer, however, had made one happy discovery; he had found an 'Oasis in the desert' – a country where no distress at all existed: and, who would have thought it? – that country was Ireland.[4]

It had been generally believed that a demagogue who fed on adulation would fail before an inimical, intimate and sophisticated club. Far from it: he could strike the right note at once. After his appearance at the bar of the House in May 1829, Lord Lansdowne told him, through Tom Moore, 'that from report he had conceived that, however suited to a popular assembly or mob, [O'Connell's] eloquence would not answer for the *refinement* of Parliament, but that he was now decidedly convinced of the contrary'.[5] Correspondingly, Greville reported on his maiden speech in a journal entry of 5 February 1830, 'O'Connell [made] his *début*, and a successful one, heard with profound attention, his manner good and his arguments attended and replied to.'[6] Nor was that speech an isolated oratorical piece. Four days later, he assured his friend James Sugrue that he was rapidly learning to handle the House and would soon be 'a constant speaker'.[7] In fact, during his first week in the Commons he spoke briefly or intervened at almost every sitting, and J. C. Hobhouse, an old parliamentary hand, observed that he invariably performed 'sensibly';[8] in context, there was probably no higher praise. From this beginning until three months before his death in 1847, O'Connell was a major (though often execrated) parliamentary figure. Some even considered him, in his prime, the most complete speaker in the Commons. One American observer wrote after visits to England in 1834 and 1837 during which

> I made it a point of professional duty . . . to hear the leading orators of the age; and . . . I would place the illustrious living in the following order of precedence. O'CONNELL, I think, is the finest orator of the age, for his rare concentration of intellectual gifts. He is logical, profound, sarcastic, bitter, humorous, playful, – and has a masterly command of all the earnest and touching passions. I have heard him at least fifty times, and in every variety of question; and every new display gave me a higher opinion of his varied, astonishing, and exquisite powers. In the commons, next to him, I would rank Lord STANLEY; then, Sir ROBERT PEEL . . . they are master of debate.[9]

As telling a tribute to O'Connell's personal dominance as any of the laughter and huzzas and howls which accompanied his speeches in the 1830s were the silence and murmurs of pretended agreement with which his final broken rambling was heard when he last addressed the House, a trembling, piteous shadow of his former self.

In many respects O'Connell was fortunate in the timing of his entry into Parliament. In British terms, 1830 represented one of those formative moments when one type of politics is in final disarray, with its successor still obscurely in the making. The eighteenth-century political system, in which the use of crown patronage and influence provided the basis of government, had lost its mainspring by 1815. The decay was not only virtually complete but also universally apparent after the death of Lord Liverpool in 1827. O'Connell's victory in the Clare by-election of 1828 had, therefore, a significance quite beyond either the immediate Catholic question or Irish disaffection. It seemed to sound the beginning of the end of the effortless ascendancy of the nobility and squirearchy in national politics. It was this aspect of the result which most deeply impressed such men as Wellington and Peel. What was to follow no one knew. But it seemed clear that some degree of power-sharing with other classes was inevitable, that the representative principle would advance, and that party would gradually shift its base from self- or family interest towards sectionalism and ideology, and ultimately supplant patronage as the main supplier of guaranteed House of Commons votes. As a conventional British radical on all these matters, O'Connell had at once a clear programme to push and a considerable body of potential allies.

In terms of Irish politics as well, 1830 marked a formative moment. The constitutional implications of the Act of Union were by now fully apparent. On the one hand, the Protestant interest as a whole had moved over to support the Union; a quasi-colonial government for Ireland, in the form of a lord lieutenancy and its surrounding apparatus, had, contrary to the original expectations, been retained; and successive British cabinets had opted for a species of 'indirect rule' based upon a privileged position for, and the near-monopoly of office and favours by, the loyalist minority. On the other hand, the Catholic Relief Act of 1829 had weakened and, in a limited sense, even broken into this redoubt; O'Connell had established independent sources of power, both by capturing county seats and by gathering and organizing intimidatory masses; and, in the process of attaining these objectives, he had succeeded in associating the Catholic Church with agitation, hostility to British rule and pressure for denominational equality. Thus, he occupied an interesting bridgehead. In which direction he would try to move, and how, and with whom, were still dark questions. But never since 1801 had Irish circumstances been nearly so uncertain or unfixed.

II

O'Connell spent his first two months in parliament learning his new craft. Generally, he made his own openings by getting up petitions in Ireland. This was not difficult; as he himself had said three years earlier, 'really we are so used to petition that we can get them drawn in every village by men from the highest to the poorest classes among us'.[10] During February and March 1830 he arranged through various Irish friends and agents for a large number to be forwarded to him for presentation in the House of Commons. These inspired petitions, which constituted the majority he received, reveal his initial strategy. Most of them concerned the exactions of the established church, municipal corruption or Catholic needs, though a few raised politically neutral grievances about bridges, market places and the like. Significantly, only two of the petitions related to Repeal of the Act of Union.

The matters which first engaged O'Connell closely were, however, different from these. On 4 February 1830 he procured a petition for a new and comprehensive legal code from his old ally, Edward Dwyer, the former secretary of the Catholic Association. Dwyer had gathered 10,000 signatures for him. 'Rational' legal reform had long been to the forefront in O'Connell's programmes. As he said of himself a few days after he had received Dwyer's petition, 'there never lived a more complete, entire, unchangeable enemy to law abuses as they exist – a more determined advocate for the *domestic* instead of the *factitious* – the *summary* in contradistinction to the *technical* form of procedure'.[11] This brought him close to the English radicals, in particular Bentham. O'Connell's other leading concern in his first session in the Commons was an Irish bastardy bill brought in by the government to equalize Ireland and England in this regard. O'Connell opposed the bill fiercely, arguing that to enable unmarried women to secure maintenance for their children from whichever unmarried man they nominated as the father would undermine Irish (as it had already undermined English) sexual morality. He even appealed directly to at least two Irish bishops for their aid in denouncing the proposed measure. All told, his opening parliamentary campaign may have been busy and eccentrically radical, but it was certainly not nationalistic.

On 6 April 1830, while in Dublin for the Easter recess, O'Connell set up the Society of the Friends of Ireland of all Religious Persuasions to promote the causes for which he had gathered petitions earlier in the year, as well as a handful of new issues. Repeal was one of the objectives, but the Society's initial emphasis was on financial rather than political 'Justice for Ireland' – the abolition of the malt, paper and coal duties and resistance to the government's proposed increase in the taxes on newspapers and spirits. Though its programme was generally moderate (with Repeal half-lost in the multitude of other appeals), the Society was suppressed by vice-regal proclamation within three weeks of its inauguration. Wellington's government had determined well beforehand to leave O'Connell no square of agitatory ground to stand on. The experience of the Catholic and New Catholic Associations of 1824–9 had steeled it against all cries of 'arbitrary rule'.

Possibly because of this gross provocation, possibly because he had learned while in Ireland that his mild conduct in the Commons was unpopular – his election agent in Clare thought it 'right . . . to tell you that people here seem to think you have made "a bad fight" in Parliament'[12] – O'Connell took the offensive upon his return to London. This took the form of virtually individual combat with his old court-room antagonist, the Irish solicitor-general, John Doherty. At the beginning of May 1830 O'Connell brought the Doneraile Conspiracy, and another recent case, in which Doherty had been accused of professional misconduct in his zealous pursuit of verdicts for the crown, before the Commons. In the sympathetic arena of the House, Doherty had the better of the first exchanges; O'Connell withdrew one motion and lost a second heavily. Doherty counter-attacked when, a little later, O'Connell appealed publicly for a run on the banks in Munster in the hope of weakening the Wellington administration. Proud of attaining and retaining office, Doherty mocked O'Connell as a strolling player who would wreck the theatre because the company refused to hire him. Proud of his own capacity as a lawyer and contemptuous of Doherty's incompetence, O'Connell, in return, mocked the 'stage trick, scenic skill and forensic management'[13] with which the solicitor-general strove to hide his professional inadequacy. O'Connell declared himself pleased with his own performance. 'I assure you', he told his friend, R. N. Bennett, on 25 June 1830, 'I taunted him very successfully upon his sore point – his ignorance. I also flung off the attack upon me gaily and with sufficient contempt for all parties concerned in it.'[14] But jousting with Doherty was a futile exercise, all too likely to be dismissed as a slanging-match of Dublin coal porters by supercilious English members. However ready a learner and effective a speaker O'Connell had proved himself to be, he had still not settled upon a profitable track to follow in the House of Commons.

A leading reason for his uncharacteristic tentativeness during the first half of 1830 was the supposed imminence of George IV's death, for this would precipitate a general election and a fresh parliament. Even before he entered the Commons, O'Connell had evidently planned, to some extent, for this occurrence. On 4 February 1830 Dwyer forwarded to him in London proposals for particular election agents for himself in co. Clare, his son Maurice in Drogheda, his son-in-law Christopher Fitz-Simon in co. Wicklow, and his admiring young supporter, Michael Quin, in co. Tipperary – evidence, as well, that, even at this early stage, O'Connell had hopes of building up a parliamentary 'connection' of his own after the eighteenth-century fashion. No one could predict how long the king would last. On 21 April O'Connell told Bishop Doyle of Kildare and Leighlin, 'the dropsy in his chest is believed quite incurable. He may live these four or five months – he may die in a week.'[15] Two months later he reported, 'There is nothing new. The Ministry, tottering, despised and despicable. The King lingering beyond expectation.'[16] In fact the king died on 26 June, almost immediately after this was written; but during the long months of waiting and uncertainty O'Connell had more or less mirrored the House of Commons as a whole in being both directionless and loth to make commitments.

Curiously, his dealings with his own constituency, Clare, took on something of the same colour. The achievement of Emancipation had transformed Irish electoral conditions. The disenfranchisement of the 40s. freeholders in the counties had suddenly swept away at least three-quarters of the voters. The Catholic hierarchy had solemnly enjoined their priests, on 3 February 1830, to refrain from any further political activity. Above all, the movement which O'Connell had constructed in the 1820s had achieved its specific goal and was practically demobilized. Rev. John Kenny, parish priest of Kilrush and (despite the episcopal prohibition) still a zealous electoral agent for O'Connell, told him frankly on 20 April 1830, 'Though the landlords could not secure the return of two [members for co. Clare] they could by threats, bribery etc. certainly return one.'[17] Kenny believed that O'Connell could retain the remaining seat, but also that he was unaware of the difficulties in the way of his success. In the first place, James O'Gorman Mahon intended to stand for the county, and although he was unlikely to defeat O'Connell, he could certainly embarrass him. O'Gorman Mahon's local following was considerable and he was prepared to spend a fortune (his new wife's dowry) both legally and illegally on a campaign. But, much worse, O'Connell had promised his friend Major William MacNamara in 1829 that he would back him in the next Clare election. O'Connell claimed that MacNamara had subsequently absolved him from this undertaking. This MacNamara denied, and since he had O'Connell's promise in writing and O'Connell could appeal only to a private conversation, the Major had the upper hand throughout. Tangled and increasingly public and bad-tempered exchanges culminated in a challenge from O'Connell's son, Morgan, which MacNamara, though a noted duellist, refused. By 9 July 1830 O'Connell had decided that the game was up in Clare: 'I am bound . . . too strictly', he privately confessed, 'that is the fact.'[18]

With the general election pressing, he wished desperately 'to be able to take a *decisive* course'.[19] Almost three months earlier he had prepared a fall-back position at Drogheda where Maurice would stand down in his favour should he decide to contest that seat. Since then he had either made or responded to electoral overtures in no less than six counties other than Clare – Wexford, Waterford, Cork, Galway, Louth and Meath – and would have gone for Kerry had not Lord Kenmare's brother been standing there. Finally, for whatever reason, O'Connell chose co. Waterford, although this placed him in direct competition with Thomas Wyse, the architect of the Catholic Association's crucial electoral victory there in 1826, for the popular vote. On 13 August 1830, after two days' polling, O'Connell proposed to retire in favour of Wyse, so disastrous were the consequences of dividing the liberal camp. Wyse took the hint, and instead retired in O'Connell's favour; at last, the 'Liberator's' return to parliament was assured. From beginning to end, it was a lamentable performance by one who had set up to be a professional politician. O'Connell had disturbed arrangements, strained supporters' loyalties, alienated Wyse and offended potential colleagues in at least half a dozen constituencies – and his son lost Drogheda into the bargain. Whatever parliamentary skills he had already demonstrated and however deep his reservoir of public gratitude in Ireland, it was high time for him to work out definite purposes and *modi operandi* outside as well as within the House of Commons.

III

Meanwhile, help came adventitiously. The 'July Revolution' in 1830 in France seemed not only to O'Connell but also to all other Irish liberals both a model and a confirmation that even more oppressive regimes than Wellington's might be suddenly and almost bloodlessly superseded. On 3 October one of his young supporters exulted in the 'aid that you [O'Connell] *must* derive from the exhilarating events that are every day springing up, an almost miraculous illustration of your principles and doctrines'.[20] Two days later, O'Connell congratulated himself on the latest turn of events: the 'Belgic revolution' against the Dutch was proving even 'more important than the French',[21] for – to him, at least – Belgium provided the additional analogy of a Catholic people freeing itself from an enforced union with a more populous, despotic, Protestant power. The British government saw things in much the same light as O'Connell. Although this augmented O'Connell's practical problems (in the increased use of vice-regal power to stifle agitation) it was none the less encouraging to learn that Peel was looking down the same vista as himself and seeing Dublin following the same insurrectionary road as Paris, unless restrained or diverted by one means or another.

Heartened by all this, O'Connell in effect launched a new campaign at a public dinner in Killarney on 7 October 1830. The original object was the celebration of the French and Belgian revolutions, but O'Connell turned it 'in truth, [into] a meeting for the repeal of the Union'.[22] Soon after, he set out his programme and priorities in a letter to Michael Staunton, editor of the *Morning Register*:

The Union should now be agitated in every possible shape . . . [including] the formation of a permanent society. A permanent society is absolutely necessary in order to collect funds *in primo loco*, to collect funds *in secundo loco*, and to collect funds, thirdly and lastly, because we have both mind and body within us and all we want is the means of keeping the machine in regular and supple motion. Corruption was said by Burke to be the oil that makes the wheels of government go. Money is as necessary to keep in due operation the springs of popular excitement . . .

On Friday [8 October] we got up a most numerous meeting in honour of the French and Belgic revolutions in the court house of Tralee and passed many honest resolves. On Saturday another meeting in the same court house, and resolutions in favour of petitions against the Subletting and Vestry bills, for radical reform and the Repeal of the Union. Today [11 October] I attend a dinner . . . at Kanturk; tomorrow I get a public dinner in Cork; on Wednesday [13] October], a meeting for redress of grievances in Youghal; on Thursday, a public dinner in Waterford; on Friday, a meeting in Waterford for redress of grievances . . .

AGITATE! AGITATE! AGITATE![23]

It was a measure of O'Connell's determination to end the hesitancy and uncertainty of the spring and summer of 1830 that he should, in the space of ten days, have addressed nine public meetings or banquets –for he immediately continued his 'progress' from Waterford to New Ross and Enniscorthy. Never before had he canvassed so intensively; never before had he given up so much of his sacrosanct 'vacation month', October, to work of any kind. Everywhere he was met with adulation. 'The manner', a contemporary observed, 'in which he was received during the journey from Darrynane [sic], until his arrival in Cork, was beyond anything he had ever before experienced. On the roads as he passed, crowds of peasantry met him, cheering for REPEAL as his carriage drove by.'[24] Everywhere, Repeal was in the forefront of the political demands; the city and county meeting at Waterford had been summoned for the sole purpose of getting up a petition in its favour. Dublin Castle responded on 18 October with a proclamation against an 'association . . . formed, or . . . about to be formed in the city of Dublin, under the name of the Irish Society for Legal and Legislative Relief, or the anti-union Association'.[25] It may also have inspired the 'Leinster Declaration' of 29 October (so-called because the Duke of Leinster chaired the meeting at which it was drawn up) repudiating the current agitation for Repeal and supporting 'the permanence of the British connection'.[26] O'Connell was producing not only a fresh agitation but also a fresh political polarization in Ireland; many of the 100 peers and MPs who signed the Declaration were whigs or liberals.

As soon as Parliament reassembled, Peel carried the war into O'Connell's camp. On 2 November 1830 he told the Commons that, through his Repeal agitation, O'Connell intended to sever Ireland's links with Britain by force, and that his movement must end in a revolution like that which had just overthrown the Bourbon regime in France. O'Connell of course denied that Repeal implied either violence or repudiation of the crown; and in the end he was unexpectedly supported. His letter to Dwyer next day described his triumph.

The scene last night in the House was a most extraordinary one. There never was yet any man so beset as I was when I went into the House and, during the first speeches, every allusion to me of an unkind nature was cheered. Although Peel attacked me directly, he sat down amid rapturous applause. I got up at once. They at first were disposed to slight me but I rebuked them with indignation and certainly took my wicked will of them fully and to my heart's content. I cannot be a judge of my own speaking but

I know that I threw out in my old [Catholic] Association style. I also know that the result was most cheering for me for the men who had been standing off from me before, and were not only cool but hostile, became of a sudden most cordial in their manner and confidential in their declarations. One perceives a change of this description better than one can describe it, and the change was complete.[27]

The change probably owed as much to the whigs' need of his support to bring down the tory government – he had pointedly described himself as the representative of Ireland rather than Waterford alone – as to his eloquent self-defence. O'Connell was about to be wooed politically, brief though the initial courtship proved to be.

Meanwhile, although he devised a series of 'Repeal breakfasts' in Dublin to circumvent the prohibitory proclamation of 18 October, there was little O'Connell could do immediately towards building up a permanent political organization. But he could pursue the other major objective set out in his letter to Staunton, collecting funds. He did not, however, follow the course which this letter had implied, the initiation of a 'Repeal Rent' after the pattern of the 'Catholic Rents' of 1824–9. Instead, as we have seen, on the advice of his new Admirable Crichton, P. V. Fitzpatrick, he decided to renew and render permanent the personal 'tribute' to himself, the O'Connell Testimonial of 1829. On 31 August 1830 he told Fitzpatrick, 'The elections are over ... The harvest is getting in. The periodical distress is for the present over. This is the time to do something for the Fund. This, of course, is confidential; that is, it must not be known to come from me.' He warmly approved the scheme which Fitzpatrick had sketched out already for a designated Sunday (varying from diocese to diocese) when an annual collection would be taken up at the church doors. This was a variant of the method used in collecting the Catholic Rent, but O'Connell's financial goal remained exactly what it had been in 1824: 'one shilling each from one seventh of the Irish Catholics would be one million of shillings or £50,000; more, in fact, than could be necessary'.[28] Fitzpatrick assured O'Connell that he had 'never for a moment ... lost sight of the fund', and in particular approved of O'Connell's suggestion that it was best to begin at Waterford, if its new bishop, Abraham, who was a whig and an enemy of Repeal, could be manoeuvred into sanctioning a diocesan collection. A 'select deputation' could then be mustered to beard Archbishop Murray of Dublin: 'his cooperation..., if obtained, will almost beyond doubt secure the rest of the bishops'. The final step would be a visit to each important district before the appointed Sunday 'to put the collectors in harness'. Fitzpatrick concluded with a foretaste of his skill as political manager, not least in his tactful management of his 'master':

> The idea of the shilling subscription is good but its promulgation must be immediately antecedent to the day of actual collection. It must apply to the 'great public' and by no means be permitted to interfere with the contribution of larger sums from those able and willing to give such. It was my intention this morning to have suggested to you to write some letters to the journals on attractive topics or declaratory of your intended course of proceedings in the next Parliament. Such things are useful stimulants and I am happy to perceive you have anticipated me by a communication to the Waterford papers . . . You will of course appear in the shape of an eloquent eulogy [by public letter] on the French Revolution . . . It may be well timed to pay a compliment in some of your earliest papers to the bishops and clergy. There will be little difficulty in doing this from the general admission that no praise can in their regard savour of flattery.[29]

Already we can see why Dr Angus Macintyre concluded that 'In O'Connell's political machine, the discreet, efficient and charming Fitzpatrick ... played an unobtrusive but vital part, the full significance of which is missed if he is described simply as O'Connell's faithful supporter or as his financial agent.'[30] Early in October 1830 he proceeded to execute the first part of his plan in Waterford. He worked on Abraham, not directly, but through friendly priests at a diocesan assembly at Cahir. Lest Abraham suspect that he was being manipulated, Fitzpatrick 'quarter[ed] myself at Clonmel where I shall have it in my power to canvass quietly some of the influential clergy as they pass to the meeting'. Characteristically, he did not confine himself to the matter immediately in hand. Having noticed that O'Connell had recently offended J. M. Galwey and his supporters, who were important in Waterford politics, by a chance reference in a public letter, he suggested 'the *possible* good policy of your dropping in upon Mr. Galwey on your route from Cork. He may be and I believe *is* worth "whistling back", particularly as I find "the unfriendly" in this district in somewhat greater force than I was prepared to expect.'[31]

It was clear that, in Fitzpatrick, O'Connell had at last found answers to the problems of financing his agitation and monitoring and maintaining a national political machine. At the same time he had found in the Parliamentary Intelligence Office which he set up in Dublin and its 'curator', Dwyer, a metropolitan centre and management safe from repression even under the current laws and exercise of vice-regal discretions. In short, O'Connell had rapidly acquired or thrown together the nucleus of a major movement before he returned to the House of Commons in the late autumn of 1830.

IV

'I attend the House constantly from its sitting to its rising', O'Connell wrote on 3 December 1830.[32] This claim to assiduity was thoroughly justified; and between being assailed as a demagogue and charlatan for raising the Repeal cry in Ireland, and himself assailing the Irish administration (and especially Doherty) as brutal and unscrupulous, he had been the storm centre of many a debate during the preceding month. In a typical exchange, on 9 November, a junior minister, George Dawson, called him 'a man of vulgar mind and mean ideas';[33] while O'Connell rejoined that he would not be intimidated by 'placeholders, who revel on the hard earnings of the people'.[34] When, however, Wellington resigned on 16 November 1830 and the whigs under Earl Grey took office after decades in the wilderness, it looked for a while as if O'Connell might become a regular government supporter, or at least be politically neutralized. After all, when his entry into the Commons had first seemed imminent, he had observed to the Knight of Kerry, 'I need not tell you that if I get in I will be a Whig but certainly one "des plus prononcés" because my opinions upon reform are of the most strong description'.[35] Moreover, it was still generally assumed in the British governing circle that O'Connell was in politics for money and other personal ends. Accordingly, an attempt was made to buy him off as soon as – or possibly just before – the whigs gained office.

The Marquess of Anglesey, destined to be the new Irish lord lieutenant, interviewed O'Connell at least twice in London about this time. 'Lord Anglesey', O'Connell wrote later, probably with reference to a meeting between them in mid-November, 'sent for me and talked to me for two hours to prevail on me *to join* the Government, . . . he went so far as to discuss my private affairs in order to prevail on me to repair my fortunes.'[36] Rumour had it that O'Connell was offered the Irish mastership of the rolls and other judgeships (including the chief justiceship of Calcutta!), and his own statement seems also to imply an invitation to accept a political office. The mastership of the rolls, with a knighthood and perhaps ultimately a peerage, would certainly have been attractive earlier in his career. For years O'Connell (and still more Mary) had looked forward to his ending in eminence on the bench, with a large, secure income, an elevated social standing and ample leisure. But by now he would have been generally condemned at home as the betrayer of his country had he taken the king's shilling in any form – and by no one more grievously than Mary. 'My dearest love', she wrote to him on 1 December 1830,

> Thank God you have acted like yourself, and your wife and children have more reason to be proud of you now than they ever were. Had you acted differently from what you have done it would have broken my heart. You cannot abandon the people who have always stood by you, and for whom you have sacrificed so much . . . Had you been betrayed into an acceptance of the terms offered by Government you would die of a broken heart before six months expired. You now stand firmly on the affections and on the love of your countrymen, and when that country is aware of the *splendid sacrifice* you have made for them, . . . they will strain every nerve to reward you. I shall hold up my head higher than ever I did. I shan't be afraid to look at the people as I certainly should if you were a titled pensioner of the Government . . . I never saw anything like the pleasure that danced in their [his children's] eyes when assured of your refusal. May God bless you, my own love! Words are inadequate to tell you how I love and respect you for this late act, so like and so worthy of yourself.[37]

The government, however, gave him no credit for principle. Even Anglesey, who probably judged O'Connell more charitably than any other of the whig leaders, concluded that he was 'flying at higher game than a judgeship . . . he is secure of a better income from the deluded people than *any Government* can venture to give to *any Person* whatever'.[38] Anglesey also attributed the reason given by O'Connell for rejecting whig pleas for support – that is, their retention of Doherty as Irish solicitor-general – to pique and fear of '*his Master* (for so Doherty certainly was in the H. of Commons)'.[39] Despite, or perhaps because of, this, no less than three separate attempts were made between mid-November and mid-December 1830 to win O'Connell over to the whigs' side. After the failure of the last, however, Anglesey decided that there was nothing for it but war to the death against O'Connell in Ireland, and accordingly began to strike military postures before himself and others, even prior to his setting sail for Dublin. 'I saw him [O'Connell] yesterday, for an hour and a half', he wrote to the Irish whig Lord Cloncurry on 16 December 1830,

> I made no impression upon him whatever; and I am now thoroughly convinced that he is bent upon desperate agitation . . . For the love of Ireland I deprecate agitation . . . But if the sword is really to be drawn, and with it the scabbard is to be thrown away – if I, who have suffered so much for her [Ireland], am to become a suspected character, and to be treated as

an enemy – if, for the protection of the State, I am driven to the dire necessity of again turning soldier, why then I must endeavour to get back into old habits . . .[40]

Conversely, O'Connell blew hot and cold in his attitude towards the whigs over the same period. At one point he endorsed a plan 'for a procession to meet the Marquess of Anglesey' upon his landing at Dublin.[41] But almost immediately he changed his mind. 'I decidedly think', he re-instructed Dwyer on 1 December, 'the anti-unionists ought not to give him any *glorification*. This is the result of my deliberate judgment.'[42] Six days later, in response to a fresh government overture asking him to state his demands other than Repeal, he re-iterated his refusal to accept any office or favour for himself and set out an alarming catalogue of twelve political 'wants'. Significantly, several of these were specifically 'Catholic' in character, while others aimed at breaking the exclusive Protestant hold upon the Irish corporations and grand juries. O'Connell may well have decided, before he returned to Ireland for the parliamentary break, that the Catholic card was now the one to play. From London, he tried to stir Archbishops Curtis and Murray, as well as MacHale of Killala and perhaps other Irish bishops, into raising publicly the issue of Catholic education.

From the moment that he reached Dublin, Anglesey seemed set upon a policy of destroying O'Connell's Repeal movement in all its manifestations. Between 26 December 1830 and 13 January 1831 he issued no less than four proclamations suppressing meetings in favour of Repeal, the 'Repeal breakfasts', the Parliamentary Intelligence Office and the long-promised 'permanent organization' for the agitation, which O'Connell attempted to institute on 6 January. Anglesey also tried to forestall any repetition of the various legal manoeuvres by which O'Connell had kept the Catholic Association alive by proclaiming – blanket-wise – 'any adjourned, renewed, or otherwise continued meetings of the same, or of any part thereof, under any name, pretext, or device whatsoever'.[43] Finally on 18 January 1831 he had O'Connell and five of his lieutenants arrested on thirty-one charges of 'evading' either the recent proclamations or the Proclamation Act itself.

All this was sailing very close to arbitrary government. Shortly before he left England, Anglesey himself had stated publicly that, although he was a determined opponent of Repeal, he considered agitation on its behalf perfectly allowable. In the same vein, Melbourne, the home secretary, told the lord lieutenant that, while any attempt to revive the methods of the Catholic Association should be stamped on, the historic constitutional rights to discuss and petition must not be infringed. Thomas Wallace, a leading Irish liberal lawyer, who disapproved strongly of both the Repeal movement and O'Connell's current conduct, none the less spoke of Anglesey's charges as 'savour[ing] strongly of *illegality* and *oppression* . . . to an extent which *greatly* endangers public liberty'.[44] Given the whigs' self-image as the party of civil and religious freedom, and the consequent embarrassment if they persisted for long with government by ukase in Ireland, it seems likely that the real purpose of the repression was to force O'Connell to abandon Repeal and compose his differences with the government. Similarly, it is difficult to credit that O'Connell believed his own repeated assertions that Repeal was imminent. It seems much more probable that he was trying, through whipping up a campaign for Repeal, to bring the whigs to more satisfactory terms on Irish issues – and, equally important in his eyes, in the filling of Irish offices. Viewed in this light, the apparently dramatic series of events, set in train by the respective arrivals of O'Connell and Anglesey in Ireland, may perhaps best be interpreted as the continuation – by other means – of the bargaining of November-December in London.

At any rate, in the game which followed his arrest, O'Connell 'proceeded to outwit and outmanoeuvre his opponents'.[45] He worked on several fronts. Former Irish liberal and whig allies were used to canvass in London and Dublin on his behalf. Two of them, Cloncurry and Lord Meath, were pressed to join in a reform campaign, in which the issue of Repeal would be omitted. A run on the banks in Munster was attempted, though only tentatively, lest the provincial economy be really injured. More important, O'Connell used all his legal lore and ingenuity – ultimately successfully – to find a way out of the dilemma, a course by which he himself might escape all penalties without the government having to lose face by dropping the prosecutions. His secret negotiations with the ministry – which neither side would admit to having initiated but which began soon after his arrest –make it certain that he was well aware of, and prepared to allow for, the government's difficulties, and also that his price for dropping the Repeal agitation was an official programme of Irish amelioration. But his most effective move of all was his decision to oppose his close friend, the minister Lord Duncannon, in a forthcoming by-election in co. Kilkenny, should the government persist with its prosecutions. 'Lord Duncannon', he wrote to the go-between, R. N. Bennett, on 7 February 1831, is a man for whom I have the highest respect, esteem and regard but he is now 'one of my prosecutors' and as the Ministry are determined to *crush* me, I must carry the political war into their quarters. He must expect opposition if the prosecutions go on. I have arranged materials for a powerful opposition. I have entered into the details of finding money and attornies and I believe he will find it a hard task to succeed, coming forward in the shape of one of my prosecutors.[46]

O'Connell had left it much too late to defeat Duncannon. But his intervention even at the eleventh hour reduced the majority – on Duncannon's home ground – to a mere sixty-one votes. As Dwyer claimed on 26 February, 'Had a committee been formed a week earlier or had you not been prevented by other arrangements from going to Kilkenny, there can be no doubt but the Colonel [Butler, Duncannon's opponent] would be the sitting member.'[47] The lesson for the whigs was unmistakable: that they might well lose up to twenty Irish seats in a general election, should O'Connell oppose them, and that meanwhile it would be dangerous to appoint any Irish county member to ministerial office since this would bring on a by-election. O'Connell's readymade solution to their problem was now tacitly accepted. He pleaded guilty to certain of the charges in the knowledge that he would not appear for judgment until after the Proclamation Act had expired and the measure under which he had been prosecuted become inoperative. When the case came up again in May, it simply fell to the ground as lacking any current legal basis.

For his part, O'Connell was freed from the obligation of attempting to renew the Repeal agitation by the introduction of a widesweeping parliamentary reform bill on 1 March 1831. This he could hail (in a letter to the 'People of Ireland') as a measure deserving 'the ardent and decided support of every friend of national liberty';[48] its passage was now the foremost political objective. The whigs reciprocated by welcoming O'Connell's return to the Commons. 'You cannot conceive', he told Mary on 5 March, 'what a change there is already towards me in the House.'[49] None the less he feared for his reception when his turn would come to speak upon the bill. 'Only think', he wrote to her again on 8 March, the sixth day of the debate, 'of my being so absurd as to feel nervous in the rascally House. Yet so it is . . . My own darling heart, my fame as a parliamentary orator depends on this day and I am speaking to an exhausted subject.'[50] But he triumphed. Next day Greville noted, 'O'Connell was very good, and vehemently cheered by the Government, Stanley, Duncannon, and all, all differences giving way to their zeal.'[51] Congratulations poured in, but the praise which he seems to have valued most was that of the English attorney- and solicitor-general who pronounced his to have been the most effective and magnanimous speech in the entire debate. At last, he and the whig government were effectively in alliance. In the general election of May 1831, which followed the House of Lords' rejection of the first reform bill, O'Connell worked in complete harmony with and for the ministry, parcelling out Irish candidatures, helping to secure the return of ministers such as Parnell and Duncannon, and even suggesting to Duncannon that he should be supported from whig party funds if he abandoned his safe county seat and used his name to try to wrest some borough from the tories. It is not surprising that he should have been swept up in the enthusiasm for reform (one of his life-long political passions) or happy to find himself flattered and courted by the administration. But neither was it altogether wise to have responded so unreservedly. In particular, in his eager pursuit of reform in Britain, he failed to exploit his current power, which was very great, to secure an equivalent advance in Ireland.

V

O'Connell was necessarily a Janus-faced politician. He was a member of Parliament because he was supported by the masses; his power in the House of Commons derived ultimately from their compacted power. Grey observed in 1831 that O'Connell's mastery of the Irish people had provided him 'With the greatest opportunities & the most powerful means that almost any man ever possessed of raising his own character, & serving the Publick',[52] and such an influence over millions needed to be constantly cultivated. But it would not do for *vox populi* to employ the same accent or forms of speech inside as outside the House of Commons. O'Connell's other political role was that of a gentleman in an assemblage of gentlemen, governed by complex rules of conduct, and (in the strict sense) highly conventional in its mode of debate and acceptable tone of oratory. Like many others, Stanley made much of the contrast between the O'Connell of Westminster and the O'Connell of the Dublin public meeting, who 'habitually bespattered' his opponents 'amongst the mobs'.

> For no two persons could be more different from each other than the hon. member for Waterford speaking in that House, and the same hon. Member elsewhere, or rather somebody who bore his name, for he could scarcely

believe it to be the same person, when 'courting the most sweet voices of the rabble'.[53]

It is worth exemplifying the dualism at length; it goes to the heart of O'Connell's difficulties in blazing the trail of the democratic parliamentary representative. First let us take an extract from his speech in the debate of 12 May 1830 on the Doneraile conspiracy trial. O'Connell's accusations were grave. He charged Doherty with tampering with or manufacturing evidence in order to secure convictions (and with them death sentences) in a murder trial, and the British government with appointing a juvenile incompetent, Lord Francis Leveson Gower, as Irish chief secretary, with the task of defending these malpractices. Yet O'Connell's language never crossed the bounds of controlled derision and disdain and licensed parliamentary invective.

What care I, then, for the unwise arrogance – the unfounded presumption – the overweening vanity of his [Leveson Gower's] censure. May I continue to deserve it! His office is, indeed, one of great promise. It is part of his public career. He is on his road (for such is the miserable destiny of this country) to still higher station. He is an apprentice in politics, and he dares to censure me, a veteran in the warfare of my country. His office is a mere apprenticeship. The present premier [Wellington] was Secretary in Ireland – the present Secretary of State [Peel] was Secretary in Ireland – so was the present Chancellor of the Exchequer [Goulburn]. Their juvenile statesmanship was inflicted upon my unhappy country. I have heard that barbers train their apprentices by making them shave beggars. My wretched country is the scene of the political education of our statesmen, and the noble Lord is the shave-beggar of the day for Ireland. I have done with the noble Lord – I disregard his praise – I court his censure – I cannot express how strongly I repudiate his pretensions to importance – and I defy him to point out any one act of his administration to which my countrymen could look with admiration or gratitude, or with any other feelings than those of total disregard. His name will serve as a date in the margin of the history of Dublin Castle – his memory will sink in contemptuous oblivion.[54]

This was classical public speaking. The short, driving sentences; the triple flourishes, the epigrammaticism and antitheses; the banked fire and finely calculated satire; the precision of terminology – 'proper words in their proper places'[55] – all manifest O'Connell's eighteenth-century training. The *beau ideal* of his boyhood had been Grattan; Douai and St Omer had grounded him in Cicero and Renaissance exercises for forming public men, in 1791–3. But form and dexterity apart, the passage was aglow with a master-image. 'Shave beggar' expressed both perfectly and passionately Ireland's resentment of the contemptuous relegation of its government to the second or third level of significance, and of the contemptuous assumption that it harboured merely a mendicant and subjected race. For nearly two decades, the phrase was to be wielded, often with deadly effect, in Irish assaults upon British policy and administration.

The contrasting declamation was occasioned by a proclamation for the suppression of dangerous societies issued by the then Irish chief secretary, Sir Henry Hardinge, in the absence of the lord lieutenant, on 18 October 1830. At a public dinner in Dublin four days later O'Connell, to the accompaniment of 'cheers and laughter', denounced 'English soldier-scribes, illegal proclamations and tall, raw-boned Scotchmen'.

I arraign that paltry, contemptible little English soldier [Hardinge], that had the audacity to put his pitiful, and contemptible name to an atrocious Polignac Proclamation (loud cheers) – and that too in Ireland, in my own country – in this green land – the land of Brownlow – the country of Grattan – now in his grave – (hear) – the land of Charlemont and of the 70,000 volunteers – the heroes of the immortal period of '82 (cheers). In that country it is that a wretched English scribe – a chance-child of fortune and of war, urged on by his paltry, pitiful lawyerlings – puts his vile name to this paltry proclamation putting down freemen (cheers). I would rather be a dog and bay the moon, than the Irishman who would tamely submit to so infamous a proclamation. I have not opposed it hitherto, because that would implicate the people and give our enemies – the English Major-General and his lawyerling staff – a triumph (hear, hear, hear). But I will oppose it; and that too, not in the way that the paltry castle scribe would wish – by force. No; Ireland is not in a state for repelling force by force. Too short a period has elapsed since the cause of contention between Protestants and Catholics was removed – too little time has been given for healing the wounds of factious contention, to allow Ireland to use physical force in the attainment of her rights or the punishment of wrong . . . as yet the progress of reconciliation is not completed, and until it is, Ireland – being divided – would be too weak for the physical force of her enemies. I do not advocate the display of physical force at any time. God forbid that such a desire should influence my conduct. I only allude to the circumstance to show that even were physical force justifiable, Ireland is not now in a condition to warrant its display (cheers). Well, I obeyed – the people obeyed the proclamation – they did not submit to the base mandate of a paltry Englishman (cheers). No; I never will submit to such audacity; and I here promise that I will never cease to pursue the – miscreants shall I call them? – no, that would be too hard a phrase; – but I will call them the despicable, base, miserable, paltry creatures, with bad heads and worse hearts, who issued that nefarious proclamation (cheers) – in that place, where, and at that period when, reason shall be listened to. I do not mean to say that I shall be attended to in the rotten, borough-mongering Parliament. But I trust the day is not far distant when reason shall be heard, and when fine and imprisonment shall mark the foul conduct of Secretary Major-General Sir Henry Hardinge (loud cheers).[56]

The audience being predominantly middle class, this was a higher order of bombast than O'Connell used at outdoor popular meetings. None the less, it might be dismissed, at first sight, as rhodomontade. It was pitted with apparently meaningless abuse – 'paltry', 'base', 'vile', 'lawyerling' and the like. It shamelessly thumped the sentimental-patriotic drum, with scarcely a pretence of relevance. It was, practically speaking, self-contradictory – the audience was enjoined to obey but not to submit to the proclamation, and O'Connell promised to 'pursue the miscreants' in Parliament, but not until after it had been reformed!

Yet it would be quite mistaken to write off such a speech as mere rambling braggadocio. On the contrary, it was calculated rhetoric. In effect, O'Connell was instructing his followers to conform to the proclamation and abstain from violence. But it would not do for an order of this kind to be issued in plain language. Demagogues need their own sort of tact. O'Connell had therefore to cover the retreat, by vague – in fact, illusory – indications of future legal and parliamentary challenges to the proclamation, and by working up his audience to a sense of their unimpaired power and pride by references to the glories of 1782 and the force at Ireland's command once sectarian divisions were obliterated. It did no harm to hint that this force might be physical, before rapidly repudiating such a thought. Still more to the purpose, the degradation of opponents through personal abuse, in order to diminish their seeming formid-ability, or if possible render them ludicrous instead of fearsome figures, was part of O'Connell's stock-in-trade. This explains his strange antistrophes upon the unfortunate Hardinge, whom he and his audience alike must have known to be the mere instrument of official policy in this case.

It was only to be expected that the Aunt Sallies of these affairs should resent the rain of verbal missiles. In accordance with the accepted code, Hardinge desired 'satisfaction' for the insults heaped upon him. O'Connell had, however, long made it clear that he would fight no further duels. They were, he now argued, against both conscience and reason – an exchange of pistol shots being quite irrelevant to the rights and wrongs of any political dispute. He was, he said, always ready to disavow an established *error of fact*, but nothing more. All this was rehearsed in O'Connell's reply to Hardinge, published in the Dublin newspapers on 24 October 1830. But his principal defence was that he had spoken of Hardinge only as an official, not as an individual. 'He [O'Connell] spoke of Sir Henry Hardinge in his *public* capacity as an instrument of despotism. He did not say one word of him in his private capacity.'[57] It was natural enough that O'Connell should take this line. From his standpoint, the scurrility ladled upon Hardinge was purely in the line of business. It had nothing to do with Hardinge personally. Simply, the exigencies of agitation demanded that any relevant officer of the crown should be so assailed. But it was also natural that Hardinge, learning that he had been paraded in public as a 'paltry, contemptible little English soldier . . . a wretched English scribe, a chance-child of fortune and of war', should feel that he had been intolerably affronted. If not the horsewhip, at least the challenge was the ordained response. O'Connell's refusal to conform to the most elementary rule governing 'satisfaction' exposed him to the scorn of his social equals. Cowardice was the usual explanation of his conduct, counter-scurrility and slander its common consequence. Worse still, his attitude tended to place him in – to use the contemporary phraseology – the blackguardly as against the gentlemanly class. During 1832, for instance, the Irish chief secretary, E. G. Stanley, and the former Irish solicitor-general, Philip Crampton, declared that O'Connell had no claim to being a gentleman because he insulted opponents while refusing the consequent challenges to duels. Nothing could be more hurtful to his *amour propre*, or more harmful to him in the high politics of Westminster, than to be pronounced *déclassé*.

Yet O'Connell's two voices, the parliamentary and the popular, were not really disconnected. Each was a means of attaining and exercising influence. Largely by his forensic skill, he accumulated political capital in Ireland, and largely by his forensic skill, he spent it judiciously in the House of Commons. It was, in the last analysis, a single process. Unfortunately for O'Connell, his particular popular and professional techniques, although well-tried and proven over quarter of a century, necessitated his playing contradictory public roles, with contradictory lines, styles and intonations. But to abandon either would have impoverished, perhaps even rendered nugatory, his performance.

CHAPTER 15

Systole and Diastole

1831–2

I

In the general election of 1831, O'Connell fought something akin to a national campaign. He did not, however, fight on his own behalf but, as has been said, made common cause with the 'Reformers' generally. He busied himself arranging 'liberal' candidatures and electoral committees in at least nine of the Munster and Leinster counties, as well as in several boroughs; and almost uniformly he succeeded. His dealings reveal a remarkably close knowledge of, and capacity to manipulate, the local power-systems. Correspondingly, his zeal in 1831 extended his range of influence. Perhaps the most striking instance of his control of things was his response to Lord Duncannon's plea for an uncontested re-election in co. Kilkenny. At a word from O'Connell, Duncannon's opponent withdrew, although O'Connell modestly disclaimed all the credit. 'Col. Butler', he told Duncannon on 29 April 1831, '*put* the compliment on me of having declined in consequence of my letter to him. But I am too candid to do so by you. All, however, is safe in that quarter.'[1] He acted in such a masterful fashion in this case because Duncannon was his main link with the government in London. It was through Duncannon that he pressed (not always in vain) requests for minor return-favours. Duncannon was also the conduit for his demands that the Irish administration cooperate in securing the return of members favourable to the reform bill. Here he was less successful. Anglesey and Stanley appear to have allowed their dislike and distrust of O'Connell to outweigh the normal duty and interest of a government at election times, which was of course to use its official influence on behalf of 'friends'.

O'Connell's manoeuvres created difficulties for himself. In his current constituency, co. Waterford, he attempted a complex play in order to increase the 'Reform' representation all round. This involved securing the Hon. George Lamb, a junior minister, for his running mate. When Lamb refused to stand, O'Connell too withdrew from Waterford and at the eleventh hour plumped instead for co. Kerry, although this offended some of his warmest Waterford admirers. When it seemed as if he might have a dangerous contest on his hands in Kerry after all, he worked might and main for an invitation (duly received) to stand for co. Tipperary. In the end, however, he and another 'Reformer' won Kerry easily, after he had put the family political machine into rapid operation by writing to his brother John on 2 May 1831,

> You must now instantly begin to work. You must ransack the county. Speak to the bishop. Engage every voter. Write every priest. Send Maurice and Charles Brenan [O'Connell's cousins] in every direction where a voter can be had. Write to James [O'Connell's brother] to come home at once and assist us. Do not deceive yourself as to my majority . . . I suppose the members of the [Tralee] Chamber of Commerce will become my committee. If proper arrangements can [be] made the expense will be as nothing.[2]

Significantly, O'Connell's platform in Kerry was limited to two specific issues, the great reform bill and the abolition of negro slavery. Neither in public nor in private did he so much as mention Repeal – or any other specifically Irish matter – during the entire campaign. If his opponent, the Knight of Kerry, is to be believed, however, O'Connell's supporters did not hesitate to enlist religion on their side. In excusing his own early withdrawal from the contest, the Knight reported,

> The Priesthood were marshalled under a Jesuit Bishop. I was depicted as a traitor at once to King and Country . . . my vote [against] Reform was an attack on the People and their Religion . . . – the effect was a general fury equal to that raised against Vesey [Fitzgerald] in Clare [in the by-election of 1828] and with much more of personal rancour. The effect would have been the detaching of almost every Catholic freeholder from even the best Landlords – and in the conflict I should have polled little more than the Protestants giving Dan a universal triumph . . .[3]

Only slowly did O'Connell's informal alliance with the whigs (who triumphed in the general election, most of all in Ireland) begin to crumble. He forbore to resent Stanley's repulsive formality both during and immediately after the electoral campaign, and returned to Westminster at the beginning of June 1831 in high hope that the government would reward his loyalty by a more conciliatory approach to Irish issues. But after interviews in London with both Anglesey and Stanley, he concluded that although 'they desire to do good to Ireland' their leading principle was 'English domination . . . [and] as the control of Ireland *must* be obtained as the *primary* object, everything Irish is looked at through that medium'.[4] This reading of official policy was vindicated all too soon. When a new version of the Irish parliamentary reform bill was presented, it ran on lines markedly different from those designed for the remainder of the United Kingdom. The government gave Ireland only five additional seats whereas Scotland received eight. This left Scotland with almost twice as high a parliamentary representation per head of population. The new English and Welsh representation was more than twice as high as the Irish – indeed, in terms of county seats (in general the most 'open' and 'popular' part of the system) the disproportion was almost 5:1. Meanwhile, several Irish boroughs with electorates well below the new British minimum were retained intact. Franchise reform showed a similar disparity. The 40s. freeholder was enfranchised in England and Wales but remained unenfranchised in Ireland; and the English registration machinery was now incomparably superior. But even the lack of uniformity was not uniform. The government insisted upon a £10 household suffrage in English and Irish boroughs alike, although it was well recognized that the true Irish equivalent would have been a £5, and not a £10, valuation. This correspondence had, however, precisely the same motivation as the various distinctions. The ministry was determined to avoid, wherever possible, changes which would increase either the democratic or the Catholic element in the Irish electorate. The whigs' desire to do Ireland (or even their own party) 'good' was indeed secondary to their desire to keep Ireland secure under Britain's domination.

O'Connell, unpleasantly surprised when Stanley re-presented the Irish parliamentary reform bill in the Commons on 1 July 1831, described the few changes from the original measure (minor concessions on the county leasehold franchise), as 'Stanley's humbug "improvements" '.[5] But he was inhibited from pressing home his attack by his own tactical error in having welcomed the first Irish bill warmly in the course of his 'generous' reform speech of 8 March. He compounded this mistake by parleying privately with various ministers during the summer and early autumn of 1831. By the end of the parliamentary session, he had gained nothing more than further trivial amendments in the leasehold franchise clauses. All the great matters – the number and size of the Irish constituencies and the principal qualifications for enfranchisement – remained untouched. O'Connell blamed Stanley exclusively for this failure; he believed that the other members of the cabinet whom he had seen were genuinely sympathetic to his representations. Meanwhile Stanley had given further offence by introducing an Irish arms bill, also on 1 July 1831. 'It is an atrocious act . . .', O'Connell wrote next day, 'if passed, [it] would just come to this that whilst the Orange Yeomanry got arms from Government, the people were to be deprived of all means of preventing their throats from being cut with impunity.'[6] At this stage, still counting on his utility to and his cordial relations with the whigs, he was as confident of securing the withdrawal of the arms bill as he was of winning substantial modifications in the Irish reform proposals. He had no doubt that Stanley and 'the hare-brained and vain Anglesey' would have to retreat 'under the pressure of public opinion'.[7] But once again the government yielded little; the arms bill was eventually enacted with only one significant amendment.

Gradually, the enmity between O'Connell and Stanley deepened. On O'Connell's side, the seeds of rancour were probably first sown at the time of his arrest in January 1831 when (as he later put it), under Stanley's directions from Dublin Castle, 'common thief-takers were sent to his house, to drag him from the bosom of his family'.[8] Stanley's hauteur, contempt for 'inferiors', dexterity in debate and unconcealed support for the continuance of Protestant Ascendancy in Ireland, perfected O'Connell's enmity. For his part, Stanley resented O'Connell's incessant attacks upon the partiality, corruption and incompetence of his administration in Ireland; on 10 August 1831 he broke out against O'Connell's 'coming down there [the House of Commons] night after night and without proper notice charging the Irish Government with having acted unfairly in this case, in that case, or in the other case'.[9] Correspondingly, O'Connell scarcely exaggerated when he spoke of 'the anti-Irish party which he [Stanley] commanded in the Cabinet'.[10] Their parliamentary exchanges soon became virtually individual combat.

None the less, O'Connell did not yet break with Grey's government, and the Lords' rejection of the second (or 'great') reform bill on 8 October 1831 brought him back, immediately and fully, to its support. Even before this happened the more liberal faction in the cabinet, led by Lords Brougham and Holland, had been pressing hard to win (or rather buy) O'Connell over to a permanent alliance with the whigs. Grey himself, though he loathed both O'Connell and his politics, admitted that his power was extraordinary, and his backing necessary for the carrying of reform. The details of the government's consequent offers and approaches to O'Connell are once more obscure. But we can guess something of their nature from two letters to Richard Barrett, editor of *The Pilot*, in which O'Connell wrote, on 5 October 1831, '*Strictly, strictly private* and most confidential. I COULD be Attorney-General – in one hour',[11] and on 8 October, 'Expect to see me about Tuesday week [18 October], *not* Master of the Rolls nor Sir Daniel but honest and true and your sincere friend'.[12] We know certainly that, at the request of Sir Henry Parnell, the secretary-at-war, Bishop James Doyle proffered him some post or other about this time, and on 26 October he actually received a patent of precedence admitting him to the inner Irish bar – an honour and advantage which he had coveted for twenty years. A few days earlier Grey had expressed the hope that this favour (already in train) together with the promise of a post for one of his sons-in-law (probably Nicholas Ffrench who had recently married his daughter, Betsey) would prove 'only preliminaries to a more useful connection with him [O'Connell]'.[13]

Although Doyle told Parnell on 17 October 1831 that his interview with O'Connell was 'more successful than I anticipated',[14] there is no evidence to suggest that O'Connell seriously considered accepting either political or judicial office at this time. But he was certainly ready to enter into an informal concordat with the whigs in return for the introduction of a sort of spoils system in the Irish administration. He expected it to be systematically 'liberalized'. As he put the point to Duncannon on 19 October,

> The government [at Dublin Castle] is, in point of fact, as essentially anti-Irish and Orange as it was in the days of Peel or Goulburn . . . allowing, as I readily do, that the intentions of the ministry are good, of what value is that when all their appointments are almost without exception from the ranks of their present and *continued* enemies? . . . I can now pledge myself that if the government will act with vigour on their own principles, Ireland will be a source of strength and comfort to them.[15]

A subsequent speech by a member of the ministry, Lord Ebrington, was taken by O'Connell to have given the necessary assurance that the Irish administration would be thoroughly 'reformed' according to his wishes, and with that he proceeded to put his part of the supposed bargain into effect. He himself described the sequel thus in a letter of 4 December 1831:

> I did think that Lord Ebrington spoke *advisedly* and that, therefore, my principles would be adopted in the management of Ireland and my popularity transferred to the King and the King's government. So far I was

not only ready to assist, but I did assist. For on my arrival there [Dublin], I found a formidable Anti-Union organization complete, called the Trades' Union, headed by a man [Marcus Costello] of popular qualifications and capable, I fear, of misleading. I took them out of his hands. I not only turned them but I can say I turned the attention of the rest of the country from the overpowering question of Repeal to the suitable one of Reform, and I actually kept matters in suspense in this state for a month after my arrival.[16]

This was a reasonably accurate abridgement of the story of O'Connell's activity after his return to Ireland on 18 October 1831. He found that the artisans of the capital had been organized into a powerful combination, the Dublin Trades Political Union, radical in tendency and wholeheartedly committed to Repeal. Immediately, he established a corresponding middle-class association, the National Political Union, with the much more moderate programme of assisting the ministry to carry through reform, and – instead of Repeal – the achievement of all the 'benefits . . . which could possibly be procured by a domestic and local legislature'.[17] Next, he attacked the D.T.P.U. as divisive (in setting the working and middle classes against each other), and proceeded to infiltrate it with his own supporters. Within a month, he had in effect captured it for his own purposes. The artisans' association changed both its constitution and its name (to the National Trades Political Union), threw Repeal overboard and endorsed O'Connell's current collaborationist policy. Thus he was fully justified in telling Duncannon on 4 December that he had brought the divergent agitation into line in support of the whig government. It was true of course that he was also serving his own political ends in subordinating a potentially independent movement and crushing a potential rival for popular leadership in Dublin, Marcus Costello. But this did nothing to diminish the whigs' obligation to him for his strenuous political exertions.

Thus he had good reason to feel aggrieved when the government failed to provide a quid pro quo. As he pointed out to Duncannon on 4 December, there had been no change whatever in either the manning or the conduct of the Irish administration during the previous two months. The Irish legal establishment had, similarly, been left intact. Perhaps naively, O'Connell had expected the process of Irish concilia-tion to begin with the replacement of Stanley as chief secretary. Instead, 'Mr. Stanley, the snappish, impertinent, overbearing High Church Mr. Stanley, Mr. Stanley of Crimes Bill notoriety, who spoke of the "tried loyalty" of the Orange Yeomanry, was sent over again to be chief and only real governor.' O'Connell now menaced the ministry directly.

> Mr. Stanley MUST be put out of the government of Ireland . . . or the ministry *must* expect to lose the support of the Irish members . . . I say six [members] because so many have actually put themselves into my hands. If I, however, said twelve and went on to twenty, perhaps I would be nearer the truth. I know how easy it is for the friends of Earl Grey in England . . . to *bravely* exclaim against dictation. But all that is folly. The people of Ireland must have a party to support their interests; that party cannot certainly be the Tories. Alas! It is not the Whigs. Who are to be the friends of Ireland? We must form – I am forming – an Irish party, a party without religious distinction.[18]

He gave immediate substance to his threat by announcing that he would not return to the Commons when parliament reassembled on 6 December 1831, but instead devote himself to the more important business of building up the National Political Union at home. He also publicly condemned Bishop Doyle's current support of Anglesey's administration, adding, sadly, that his lordship had been taken in by 'Castle smiles'.[19] These were comparatively daring steps, and O'Connell tried to cover himself by also proclaiming his willingness to return within forty-eight hours to Westminster should the reform bill really be endangered, and by assuring Doyle that he had not meant to insult him personally. But Doyle, who evidently retaliated by threatening O'Connell with the loss of the Catholic Church's backing, was never fully reconciled.

Eventually, O'Connell retreated and agreed to attend the Commons again after the Christmas recess of 1831. Duncannon's earlier, anxious flattery – 'I need not assure you how necessary your presence here will be and how great a triumph your absence would give to the opponents of the Reform Bill'[20] – may have had some effect. But, more important, a prolonged absence would have damaged O'Connell's own cause. He had a vital interest in the achievement of parliamentary reform in Britain; he also believed that his best hope of altering the Irish bill lay in operating himself in the House of Commons. He considered that he had gone as far as he safely could in teaching the government that his support was not automatic, but must be paid for, politically. At the same time, his moves towards forming an independent Irish party, however accidental in origin, were by now seriously meant. Indeed, they were a logical development of his entire parliamentary experience of 1831.

II

Both the whigs and O'Connell had been exploring unknown terrain throughout the year. The systematic, continuous interaction of parliamentary and extra-parliamentary power was a new phenomenon. Isolated events or issues, such as the Wilkes episode or the anti-slavery campaign, had produced interesting specific novelties in the past. But a separate, or potentially separate, group in the House of Commons, with an unchallengeable leader, secure constituency bases and mass popular support, was quite unprecedented. How were the traditional parties to deal with such a group? How was *it* to traffic with *their* system? The whigs swung from the extreme of attempting to imprison or at least intimidate O'Connell to that of trying to recruit him to the ministry or remove him to a judgeship. They also set his 'political price' much too low, for they refused even to weaken significantly the 'Orange' hold upon Irish government. Duncannon pleaded, on 26 December 1831, that 'you [O'Connell] make no allowance for the situation in which they [the cabinet] came into power and the difficulty of altering old habits and prejudices'.[21] But the truth was that men like Grey and Stanley had no intention of advancing O'Connell's influence at the expense of that of the Ascendancy. Correspondingly, between May and December 1831, O'Connell moved from campaigning furiously for a whig victory in the general election to withdrawing from the Commons in protest against their inactivity. He, too, overvalued his hand. It was altogether unrealistic to expect that Stanley would be removed from Ireland, or even that Irish bills would be materially amended, at his *ipse dixit*.

None the less, each party was gradually learning the grammar of the new sort of politics. The main lesson drawn by O'Connell was that, having nothing to hope for from the English tories at Westminster, he must endeavour to increase his bargaining power *vis-à-vis* the whigs, and that, paradoxically, the best means of doing so was to create and control an independent Irish party. At the same time, he was prepared to ally, if he could, with the Irish tories against the two main British groupings. The purpose of this improbable combination would be to dictate, or at least profoundly influence, the Irish policy of whichever of the major parties happened to be in power. Throughout 1832 O'Connell was to oscillate between these strategies – or, more precisely perhaps, to pursue the first while trying also to knit into it something of the second.

O'Connell's parliamentary performance in 1831 is also worth

consideration as a whole for it reveals the range not only of his participation but also of his techniques and tactics in the business of the House of Commons. There is point moreover in looking to the beginning of whig rule in considering O'Connell as a parliamentarian. Only when the liberals were in power was he a true believer in – or at any rate a true practitioner of – 'the parliamentary method' in Irish politics. Under conservative rule, he instinctively assumed that progressive legislation would dry up, that the government's Irish policy would be unpalatable, and that the power of the state would be thrown behind the Protestant Ascendancy. For good measure, Peel (almost as deeply antipathetic to O'Connell as O'Connell was to him) was master of the tories almost to the end of O'Connell's period in the House. During phases of tory government, therefore, O'Connell turned towards extra-parliamentary agitation and attempts to organize pressure from without. His attendances at parliament during Peel's second ministry, 1841–6, were meagre and his performances perfunctory. Only when, in late 1845, the prospects of the liberals' return improved was 'the parliamentary method' once more in the ascendant.

On the seventy-seven sitting days on which he attended the Commons in 1831, O'Connell spoke 283 times. Some of these were mere interjections, but more were considerable, often very considerable, speeches. Almost all were powerful or telling. The meaning of the parliamentary method for him was immediately apparent in his approach to the dominant issue of 1831, parliamentary reform. He was of course committed to the full radical programme, down to universal male suffrage, the secret ballot, triennial parliaments and equal electoral districts. Lord John Russell's original bill fell very far short of this. Yet O'Connell accepted it – and on suggestive and prophetic grounds: first, as an instalment, and secondly, on trial for its capacity to provide radical political ends by other than radical political means. As he later observed, 'This measure gave none of these [the radical demands] . . . but it was in other respects so liberal and so extensive, that . . . it would demonstrate one of two things – either that further Reform was not necessary . . . or that it would give all these at a further period, . . . safely, certainly, and rationally.'[22] His entire handling of such an issue as Repeal was already foreshadowed here. Other expressions of O'Connell's radicalism also had revealing accompaniments. He was second only to Joseph Hume in pressing for reductions in public expenditure, and especially for the abolition of useless offices, both to save money and to limit government support resting on patronage. But his drive for municipal reform in Ireland soon passed from pressure to suppress offices in the gift of Irish local bodies to pressure for a share in them. Similarly, he warmly supported freedom of expression, and this became a significant issue in 1831 because of proposed curbs upon the press. But O'Connell formulated his opposition to controls in terms of counter-productivity rather than of principle. The threatened *Republican* and *Poor Man's Guardian* were, he said, 'ridiculous and disgusting trash'. They would be the only gainers from a prosecution. 'It was an excellent puff for ... seditious publications, and the author must be much obliged to him [the Minister] for having pitied the sorrows of a poor old libeller who must otherwise have starved.'[23]

Foreign affairs were pressed into the background during 1831, but the aftermath of the Continental revolutions of 1830 occasionally engaged parliament's attention. Whereas, in as well as out of the House of Commons, O'Connell warmly supported the Belgian and Polish struggles for independence, he now strongly opposed the new Orleanist regime in France. The explanation of the disjunction, and of the sudden turnabout in his attitude to the government of Louis Philippe, was of course the anti-clericalism which the Second Monarchy had soon displayed. Since 1810 at least, O'Connell had distinguished French *liberaux* from true liberals in this regard. To some extent, his attitude towards the Belgians and Poles was determined by a romantic approbation of peoples striking for liberty: he spoke of their revolts as classic cases of 'the cause of poor downtrodden Man'. But they also illustrated 'this lesson, that one nation cannot continue with impunity to wrong and oppress another'.[24] What could be more apropos Ireland? In the cases of both Belgium and Poland, unions with more powerful alien states had been forced upon them; in both, Catholic peoples had been subjected to heretical or schismatic overlords. Finally, slavery apart, his approbation of the United States – 'the meridian splendour of American independence',[25] as he had called it in 1829 – was constant. His old vision of the whole western world engaged in a supra-national conflict between the forces of tyranny and freedom was far from dissipated.

When attention turned towards Ireland directly, the House's time and O'Connell's interventions were devoted mainly to affairs of the moment, such as affrays over tithes or malign crown prosecutions, or to the interests of specific groups which he was asked to support, such as turnpike trustees, tobacco growers or whisky distillers. But when on one occasion he raised the larger political question of Repeal in a debate, he repeated substantially the pattern of argument which he had used for parliamentary reform. First, he asserted his fundamental principle: 'if the Union were not repealed, Ireland would indeed soon cease to be a constituent part of the British Empire. It was necessary to the welfare and happiness of Ireland that she should have a domestic Legislature.'[26] Almost in the same breath, however, he hinted at a 'Justice for Ireland' experiment. Let them see whether a liberal, reforming government could and would provide Ireland with the same benefits which she might hope to gain from parliamentary independence:

> the object of those who advocated the Repeal of the Union was, to obtain a cheap government, and a just administration of the laws . . . The Repeal of the Union was merely a means to attain an end, and those who advocated that measure, expected now to attain their object without going through that ordeal . . . they were now willing to try the effects of a reformed House of Commons.[27]

In turn, this line of argument led into a demand for equal treatment for Ireland under the Act of Union, for standardizing practices in Ireland and Great Britain, for substituting a true marriage of kingdoms for a form of subordination. Such flexibility epitomized O'Connell's dialectical manoeuvres in the house, for his early 'moves', like opening gambits in chess, were often substantially the same.

The other striking characteristic of O'Connell's Irish 'policy' in parliament in 1831 was his relentless hostility to the influence of the Ascendancy. One curious corollary of this was a predilection for direct British rule as against sub-government by the loyalist minority. Even at the cost of open conflict with Hume, and despite his unvarying hostility towards the current incumbent, Anglesey, he argued for the retention of the lord-lieutenancy in Ireland as a brake on Castle influence. A constant theme in O'Connell's speeches during the year was denunciation of the Irish yeomanry as a partisan, 'Orange' force – ill-led, ill-conducted, cruel and vindictive – and the desirability of replacing them by regular British troops. Again, he pressed repeatedly for filling the Irish offices hitherto monopolized by the 'Orange faction' by a counter-balancing number of Catholics and liberal Protestants. Thus, although O'Connell's formal demand was full self-government for Ireland, his 'provisional position' amounted to a threefold demand for, first, the reduction of the power, privileges and monetary rewards of the Ascendancy, secondly, the advancement of Catholics in their place, and thirdly the maintenance of British and central authority in Dublin as the best hope of attaining these objectives.

It was only at the close of 1831, when he had temporarily abandoned the House of Commons, that he began to consider a fundamental change in his parliamentary tactics. Meanwhile, throughout the year he had laid down a new pattern at Westminster, whereby 'the Irish question', backed by popular agitations at home, would engross much of the time, and shape much of the business and many of the outcomes in the House of Commons. He had achieved this almost single-handedly and in particularly unfavourable conditions in that the sessions were dominated by a single, essentially non-Irish issue, the reform bill. Although his specific political successes were few and small in scale, he had succeeded generally as a politician, in a chill climate and an unfamiliar place.

III

O'Connell did his duty by the great reform bill in the spring parliamentary session of 1832 – but little more. He appears to have spent a mere five weeks in London, from late January until 1 or 2 March. Before he left for Westminster he had busied himself with inspiriting and developing his National Political Union in Dublin, and he broke his journey from Holyhead to London to visit Staffordshire and Warwickshire, the heartland of contemporary English radicalism. The Wolverhampton Political Union had sent him a flattering invitation to accept an address after he had been escorted into the town by a promised ten thousand working men:

> the Council of the Wolverhampton Political Union [wishes] to express our sentiments of approbation and esteem for the uniform, zealous and uncompromising exertions you have ever evinced in the cause of Reform and to mark our admiration at the vastness of your genius and the magnificence of your eloquence. Grateful for what you accomplished time past, the *emancipation of the seven millions*, for which and your patriotic efforts to restore us to our political rights, we earnestly desire to express our feelings of unfeigned thankfulness, and humbly solicit an opportunity to present an address as a memorial of our gratitude to the *Great Liberator* of religious disabilities.[28]

Having been duly fêted at Wolverhampton on 19 January 1832, O'Connell proceeded to a still larger reception arranged by the more celebrated Political Union at Birmingham: the Birmingham crowd was reported to have been 15,000–20,000 strong.

O'Connell, who was also being courted at this time by other Political Unions, was ready to champion the English radicals' demand for 'the whole Bill, and nothing but the Bill', in return for equal treatment for Ireland in terms of parliamentary reform. This meant, as he told the crowd at Birmingham, an increase of twenty-five members in the Irish representation, the elimination of the most scandalous Irish pocket and rotten boroughs, and the restoration of the 40s. freehold franchise. Although he was backing the government's own measure for England and Wales, the whigs were none too pleased at O'Connell's alliance, however temporary, with the English 'democracy'. Even the 'advanced' liberal Col. Leslie Grove Jones wrote to him from London on 22 January, 'You have not shown and have, I fear been making a *dinner* speech at Birmingham. I like you best in the House of Commons.'[29] But O'Connell was in no mood to be flattered into complaisance.

It is not clear whether he had already planned a popular campaign in Ireland when he returned to Dublin on 4 March 1832. One reason for his leaving the House of Commons so early in the session, and with crucial debates on the Irish tithes question due shortly to come on, seems to have been legal engagements during the spring assizes on the Munster circuit. He was involved in at least one case in Tralee and probably in other suits in Cork a little later. He was apparently contemplating at this time – perhaps only in an hour or two of gloom – the abandonment of parliamentary politics and a return to the Irish bar. On 11 February 1832 he had written to Fitzpatrick of the time 'When I leave the House and return to my profession'[30] in a context which suggested that this would happen comparatively soon. But whether it developed out of his going on circuit or had been long designed, a popular campaign in Munster dominated O'Connell's 'vacation' from parliament in March and April 1832.

It began with a wildly enthusiastic reception, on much too large and complex a scale to have been merely improvised, when he entered Tralee on 11 March. This was followed by a public dinner in his honour two days later. From Tralee he progressed – no lesser word will do for O'Connell's quasi-royal journeying – through Mitchels-town and Cahir to another grand reception and public dinner at Clonmel. Everywhere the pattern was the same. For miles outside the towns the roads were lined with people, and throngs of horsemen, carriages, bands and banners accompanied O'Connell to and from each main street or square. As he had prophesied to his wife on 13 March, 'You will hear a flaming account of my various receptions.

347

Everything is arranged for a most *amazing* entry into Cork [on 18 March]. If the day be fine we shall have one hundred thousand persons in my train.'[31] In fact, Cork's greeting exceeded even O'Connell's high expectation: on a wretched wet windy Sunday more than 200,000 people assembled for his welcome. O'Connell stayed ten days in Cork, and then embarked upon another round of processions and public dinners at Cahir, Cashel, Roscrea and Athlone between 29 March and 2 April.

The receptions were striking even when O'Connell was only passing through some little place. For example, the Millstreet correspondent of the *Cork Chronicle* reported,

> On Thursday morning [15 March], it having been known in Mill-street that the Liberator was to drive in from Killarney and breakfast at Murphy's hotel, on his way to Clonmel, which place he was to reach that day, the people of this town, with the Rev Mr Fitzpatrick, P.P., about seven o'clock went on about three miles on the Kerry road to meet him. When, after anxious expectation for some time, the Liberator appeared, he was received with deafening shouts. On two occasions the people almost insisted on taking the horses from his vehicle, but on no account would he admit them to do so. Having reached Mill-street, the crowd of people amounted to a large multitude. After breakfast, Mr O'Connell, having procured a chair on which he stood outside the door of the Hotel, addressed the people. Every sentence of his address was received by the people with loud cheers and every demonstration of pleasure and gladness.[32]

The massive Cork demonstration required very considerable organization – even more perhaps than it received, for there was confusion at some of the assembly points. The cortege took nearly four hours to reach the centre of the city from the point on the outskirts at which O'Connell's travelling carriage was met by the procession; it took about one hour and a half to pass any given station along the way. Not only was the entire route lined on either side, but also the river, to the left, was thronged with small craft and every street window and 'even the house-tops themselves' were crammed with people. The 'Morality Societies' and nearly fifty of the trades of the city mounted elaborate displays; they had drawn lots for their places in the parade. The trades' displays provide the clearest indication of the elaborate behind-the-scenes orchestration of the affair, for almost all of them were decked in orange and green, thus symbolizing the motifs which O'Connell now wished to be in evidence, union between Irish Protestants and Catholics and their common interest in the causes of

Reform and Repeal. The majority of the banners specified this in one form or another, generally linking O'Connell with Repeal. Typical were the mottoes on the Glass Makers and Glass Cutters flags: 'William IV and Reform' and 'O'Connell and Repeal'. Equally significant was the legend borne by the little company of the Cotton and Worsted Weavers, 'Twenty-eight Protestants – eighty Catholics', for O'Connell was also bent on presenting his current agitation as supra-denominational. But the artisans were only one element in this great manifestation of O'Connell's drawing-power. The celebrants ranged from beggars and labourers to the richest provision merchants and local manufacturers.

It is worth quoting O'Connell's speech in Cork extensively, for it perfectly exemplifies both his mastery of the demagogue's craft and his mode of signalling to the masses his current political priorities. O'Connell, reported the *Cork Chronicle*, 'came forward on the handsome platform of green and orange . . . and thus addressed the countless thousands that heaved and stirred like the waters of an ocean in an earthquake, beneath him . . .':

I have not . . . the presumptuous vanity to suppose, that I am master of any language that could possibly be adequate to express the sentiments and feelings that are overflowing in my bosom at this moment, at that mighty exhibition of national strength and national determination (cheers). But there is one thought which rises to my mind, above all others, and to which I must give utterance. It is the heartfelt gratification – the delightful feeling – the exquisite consciousness of knowing that the magnificent and undeserved compliment is paid me, not alone by the liberated Catholic, in requital for his freedom, but by my fellow-countrymen of all classes and creeds, and shades of religious opinions (tremendous cheering for some minutes). Yes, the compliment is enhanced by the fact of my Protestant fellow-countrymen joining with their Catholic brethren in paying it (loud and long continued cheering). Catholics (he continued, leaning his folded arms on the railing of the balcony, and addressing with the ease, affection, and familiarity of a father the stirless and silent immensity of human life below him) – Catholics, you and I are even (cheers). I did you a favour, and you do me another – and what a favour! – in requital. But, Protestants! in what terms can I thank you? What words can give expression to my feelings of gratitude for the honour you have done me this day? But I will do you a service too, for I will elevate your beloved country – our beloved country – (cheers) – into a powerful kingdom. I will take her from the position of a paltry province, and I will make her once again a kingdom, and independent (tremendous cheering) . . . I'll ask Lord Grey whether with such a shout ringing in his ears he should have selected such a man as

349

Stanley to rule this country? Stanley of tithe-system notoriety – Stanley, merely because he is an aristocrat in temper and habits, and the son of a peer . . . the shouts of the men of Cork many of whom are Orangemen – see I am a piece of an Orangeman myself, for I wear an orange lily in union with the shamrock (and he exhibited his green travelling cap, on the broad band of which were orange lilies and green shamrocks interwoven – while the repeated shouts of the thousands below him showed their satisfaction at the proceeding) – I say the tradesmen of Cork – the people of the country have spoken the word, and tithes are no more in Ireland (tremendous cheering). My friends, the meaning of the meeting to-day is this, that Ireland is too much oppressed – that she feels herself too much trampled upon to be so any longer (cheers) . . . we will once more have a parliament of our own in College green (tremendous cheering for many minutes). That is no sectarian meaning; that is no sectarian object (cheering); it is one in which every Irishman should feel a vital interest; it is one in which every Irishman does feel an interest (cheers); it is one in which we are all equally concerned, for it is one which comes home to every tie of our hearts and spirits (awful cheering).[33]

O'Connell was not presenting a precise programme but attempting to generate political excitement and expectation; and it was an additional advantage that his annual Tribute was being collected at this time. In so far as his Cork speech – like all the others delivered during his spring campaign of 1832 – had a major chord, it was Repeal. But this was blended with an appeal for continued support for parliamentary reform, a denunciation of alien rule in Ireland (and in particular, Stanley's) and the celebration, albeit premature, of the death of Irish tithes. The supposed victory on the tithes issue was coupled, once again, with a diatribe on Stanley's malignancy. In Cork, O'Connell embellished these basic themes with several references to the decline in the city's trade caused by the Act of Union; he usually found some local manifestation of depression to drive home the lesson that the Union was destroying Irish employment or reducing Irish incomes. But this too fitted into the final general demand for the restoration of Irish parliamentary independence. Thus O'Connell kept Repeal in the foreground but surrounded and interlinked it with other slogans; nothing was really pressed home. As he explained his strategy in a letter of 17 May 1832:

I do not urge on the Repeal when it could interfere with Reform but I utterly decline making any bargain on this head. I will not postpone the Repeal by contract although I tacitly allow it to stand over for a fitter season which is now very near. The English Reform Bill will be law in ten days [in fact, this did not occur until 7 June], and from that moment the

Repeal will be our cry; it will serve every purpose. In the first place it will compel a better Reform Bill for Ireland in order to disarm some of those who would otherwise join in the Repeal. Secondly, it will prepare the English mind for the more direct and constant agitation of the Repeal measure. It is absurd to suppose anything else could serve Ireland.[34]

Most noteworthy of all in his 1832 campaign was O'Connell's deliberate wooing of the Irish Protestants. No longer did he assail the Orange engrossment of public offices, honours and favours in Ireland. He was even silent on the subject of Dublin Castle's own mismanagement, as against Stanley's and the British government's oppression. All this was of course designed to persuade Protestants to make common cause with him in the forthcoming Repeal campaign. O'Connell believed that he was making headway. After his processional entry into Cork on 18 March, he boasted to Fitzpatrick of 'the respectable and *considerate* thousands who shouted for it [Repeal] yesterday – Protestants, Catholics and Presbyterians'.[35] Soon afterwards he stated publicly that, in supporting a motion on the Irish freeman vote earlier in the year, he had not been deterred by the fact that it favoured Protestant as against Catholic artisans. 'I think that if the Orangemen of the North understood my views', he added, 'there would be little difficulty in reconciling all Irishmen to each other and thus becoming so strong in our mutual cooperation as to be soon able to restore to Ireland legislative independence.'[36] In July, O'Connell's protracted and arduous efforts to secure recompense for an old Orange enemy, Sir A. B. King, who had been dismissed abruptly from his official post when the whigs came to power, at last succeeded. O'Connell had been moved to act primarily by his own good nature and pity for an aged man's sudden destitution. But he was also a political calculator. 'I do not think the act will be thrown away when we come to our next effort for conciliation', he told Fitzpatrick on 19 July 1832.[37] He ensured that the Dublin Protestants knew of his magnanimity when he was courting them later in the year. 'Are you aware', he asked William Scott, the former city sheriff,

that it was I who fought out Sir A. B. King's pension for him? I can positively assert that he never would have got it but for me. I tell you these things to show the freemen that, although King was Deputy Grand Master of Orangemen and had, on the king's visit, behaved treacherously to myself yet I got an act of justice done for him when his own party literally threw him overboard.[38]

There is some evidence that O'Connell's large-mindedness was not politically wasted. King himself, who was still a respected figure in

Dublin Orangeism, wrote in gratitude, 'To *you*, Sir, to whom I was early and long politically opposed, to you, who nobly forgetting this difference of opinion, and who, rejecting every feeling of party spirit, thought of my distress and sped to succour and support me, how can I express my gratitude?'[39]

About the time that O'Connell succeeded in King's case, he was in grave danger of featuring in a public scandal, when an Ellen Courtenay, who accused him of having assaulted her and fathered her child, called on the Rev. Charles Boyton, the leading Irish Orange polemicist, and Remigius Sheehan, the editor of the leading Orange newspaper, the *Dublin Evening Mail*, to publicize her charges. Later she demanded that they report her threatened proceedings against O'Connell in the Dublin lord mayor's court. Both steadfastly refused to give Courtenay publicity. O'Connell was profoundly grateful. On 17 July 1832 he asked Fitzpatrick to call on Sheehan and

> express to him for himself and for Dr Boyton my hearty thanks as a private gentleman and quite independent of politics . . . it has enabled me to see the personal good qualities and high-mindedness of men who have been, and are upon principle, my very violent and most decided political enemies. It is pleasant to find that Irishmen are better than our passions and prejudices make us imagine.[40]

Boyton and Sheehan may well have been influenced by O'Connell's advocacy of their friend King's cause. But they may also have been obeying a sort of tacit code of honour which often mitigated the asperities of nineteenth-century Irish communal conflict, at least at the higher social levels. Perhaps in so small and interactive a middle and upper middle class as Dublin's it was only prudent that certain restraints should be observed.

Of course, O'Connell tended to inflate every manifestation of private kindliness or forbearance into a sign of coming union. He responded, for example, to the news of Boyton's and Sheehan's repudiation of Courtenay with, 'I trust . . . that the day is not distant when we will join our "little senates" [their respective political associations], and compose only one body concerting together for the good of Irishmen of every class and persuasion.'[41] It was true that Sheehan 'set great value' on O'Connell's compliments and spoke largely of the important changes which might ultimately be 'produced by the interchange of such kindly sentiments between parties hitherto so actively belligerent'.[42] It was also true that on particular – though rare – occasions or issues, the Irish political classes, Catholic and

Protestant, or portions of each, might temporarily coalesce. But to read into all this the promise of ultimate constitutional agreement was to miscalculate completely the determining forces in Irish society. From boyhood, however, O'Connell had, off and on, pursued this will o' the wisp; he would do so, off and on, until he died. Never did he pursue it more ardently or pertinaciously than in 1832.

IV

On 24 April 1832 O'Connell left Dublin to resume his seat in the House of Commons. As before, he made a leisurely journey to London, addressing meetings of reformers and radicals on the way. His primary purpose was, as before, to assist in carrying the English and Scottish reform bills, and to induce the government to recast the Irish bill on the same lines as the other two. In partial imitation of his Irish spring campaign, he spent almost as much energy in popular agitation in London as in supporting the 'Reform' ministry in parliament. He could count only on the backing of radicals such as Cobbett and of such organizations as the English National Union of the Working Classes when he demanded that Ireland be treated equally in parliamentary reform; the government merely strove to evade the issue of parity for all parts of the United Kingdom. The British bills were eventually carried; but so too was the Irish – with a solitary significant amendment. O'Connell had especially objected to the retention of the traditional Irish registration system which was conducted by assistant barristers, 'a totally irresponsible body – already encumbered with more business than they can well discharge and five-sixths of whom were appointed for their high and inveterate Tory principles'.[43] But Grey and Stanley absolutely rejected the proposal that Irish registration be placed upon the same basis as the English. O'Connell fared no better with his secondary parliamentary objective, the defeat of Stanley's Irish tithe bills. Both the tithes arrears bill, whereby the state took over, in part, responsibility for the collection of tithes overdue, and the tithe composition bill, which transferred the liability for tithes from tenants-at-will and yearly tenants to their landlords, were duly carried. The second especially was anathema to O'Connell, 'the most violent invasion of private property I ever read of'.[44] Not only did it leave tithes intact; it also, in effect, involved landlords (including O'Connell himself) in their collection. Small wonder that he was soon eager to leave London, 'this vile town'[45] – or that he should have abandoned the House of Commons well before the ending of the current session.

Even while O'Connell was in London, he attempted to sustain an Irish agitation. During May 1832 he issued three public letters for reproduction in the Dublin newspapers in order to signal his immediate political concerns. The first asked for a pledge in favour of full parliamentary reform, should the government be forced to call a general election; the second denounced the bias and ill-will of Anglesey's administration in Ireland; and the third repeated his call for an Irish reform bill fully equal to the English in all particulars. Through Fitzpatrick and Edward Dwyer, he kept up a mild flow of meetings and demonstrations in Dublin, and flagged his directions to the movement as a whole. With an eye to the next general election (whether or not it preceded the attainment of reform), he also maintained a correspondence with key men in various Irish constituencies. His fund of knowledge of local political circumstances and combinations throughout Leinster and Munster was expanding all the time. Fitzpatrick's rapidly swelling store of political information was also at his disposal.

It may have been just one such piece of information which led O'Connell to insist upon a Repeal pledge from 'his' candidates in the forthcoming general election. On 19 July 1832 Fitzpatrick reported that a '*good* authority assured me yesterday that no man will be returned by the county [Dublin] that refuses the pledge of *Repeal*. The same is averred of the city of Limerick with the addition that the "Representative Aspirant" must exhibit *your* introductory letter.'[46] After a month's political reading and rumination at Derrynane, O'Connell fell in with Fitzpatrick's proposal that he himself should run for Dublin city. The Repeal pledge was to be a *sine qua non* for the metropolis: 'no candidate should be tolerated but a Repealer'.[47] According to O'Connell's scheme, however, his running mate was to be a tory. Best of all would be the sitting conservative member, Frederick Shaw, if only he could be induced to take the pledge. In a letter of 29 August 1832, O'Connell declared a whig to be 'much worse' for Ireland than a conservative:

A Conservative has but one fault, which is indeed a *thumper*: he wants ascendancy – a thing impossible to be revived. But he is, after that, Irish, often very very Irish, and whilst in opposition he may be made more Irish than the Irish themselves. An *Angleseyite*, on the contrary, is a suffocating scoundrel who would crush every Irish effort lest it should disturb the repose of our English masters.[48]

But his scheme for Dublin city, probably chimerical from the outset, foundered when the National Political Union put forward E. S. Ruthven, a second Repealer, on 30 August. To make matters worse, O'Connell's 'beloved friend', Cornelius MacLoghlin, was later asked to stand for the city, presumably if O'Connell himself withdrew.

O'Connell was furious. 'Why,' he demanded of Fitzpatrick on 29 September,

> in the name of all that is absurd not wait until you know your strength before you talk of candidates, at least before you pledge yourself to them or make them pledge themselves to stand? The game *was* this. A Corporator [an 'Orange' member of Dublin Corporation] and an Agitator should have coalesced on the Repeal principle. The coalition should have preceded any declaration of any candidate. I believe it might have been well if I were the Agitator – well not for me, but for the cause. That plan, however, is knocked on the head by the premature starting of Ruthven . . . thereupon you go dreaming of another popular man to the total exclusion of a Corporator, and to the prevention of our taking the first great step to Repeal.
> I can hardly tell you how you annoy me.[49]

None the less, he still strove, up to November 1832, to find a conservative Repealer for Dublin, although in the end he had to stand with Ruthven against two tory anti-Repealers. O'Connell was practically alone in striving for an alliance with the Orange party upon the common platform of Repeal. Strangely enough perhaps, he could not understand his isolation. 'How shortsighted, how blind', he exclaimed on 7 November, 'must be the men who do not see the advantage of increasing their own forces by taking deserters from the enemy unless those deserters give themselves up tied hand and foot!'[50] This last referred to other causes, such as the abolition of tithes and church rates, additional radical measures of parliamentary reform and the overthrow of the grand jury system, which almost every Repealer (led indeed by O'Connell himself) was to advocate in the course of the campaign.

From an early stage, the Repeal pledge emerged as the startling novelty of the election. During 1828–9, demands on candidates for specific prior commitments arising out of the Catholic issue had been made, irregularly. But never before had subscription to a formula been systematically required in a general election. Now O'Connell determined to use the pledge to establish his (and his followers') complete independence of the whig-liberal party. He wrote, for example, of his close friend and fellow-counsel, Michael O'Loghlen,

I love him as my son and would trust him exactly in the same way . . . I would share my heart's blood with him. But I deal with him as I do with Maurice. If Maurice refused to give the Repeal test I would oppose him, decidedly oppose him, if I could get a *Repealer* in his place. I should bitterly lament to be in any species of hostility with O'Loghlen but 'Angleseyites' are now the bane of Ireland. Repealers are its only chance.[51]

O'Connell was not in fact so absolute in applying the Repeal formulary as this might suggest; and the ultra-democratic trades associations and political unions elaborated it into a catechism too particularized – and offensive to candidates – for his liking. But overall, through his organizations, his obedient newspapers and his personal influence, he pressed the pledge in almost every Irish constituency outside Ulster. Repeal had, therefore, a vital function in the general election of 1832. It was the instrument whereby O'Connell created the first prototype of the modern political party, with a distinct entity, a popular base, an agreed 'platform' and a universally acknowledged leader.

O'Connell's leap in the dark proved remarkably successful. Even when allowance is made for the later disqualifications, thirty-nine clear Repealers were returned. In only three constituencies, the close borough of Dungarvan and the counties of Limerick and Mayo, did a whig or liberal overcome a Repealer. O'Connell's principal difficulty was not defeating opponents but finding enough worthwhile candidates to run in Repeal colours; as he himself had put it earlier, 'Repeal appears to me to want nothing but sincere and uncompromising advocates'.[52] In nine counties, only a single O'Connellite stood (all successfully); a second would probably have been returned in each had there been another Repealer on offer. Similarly, seats almost certainly went begging in cos. Galway, Sligo, Wexford and Wicklow for want of Repeal candidatures. Thus, if fortune had consistently run O'Connell's way, and men with sufficient time, ambition, money and standing could have been found for every likely constituency, he would have captured at least half the total Irish representation in 1832. Even as things went, he had reason to feel complacent. To have built up quite a formidable Irish party, within six months and in the teeth of both government and the official opposition, was certainly a striking index of his power. The questions now were, how to keep this power intact until the next general election, and how to deploy it meanwhile in parliament, in so far as it could be maintained. Immediately, however, O'Connell could rejoice. Even before all the returns were in, he wrote on 20 December 1832, in the midst of successful electioneering in Tralee, to Fitzpatrick:

> Everything has – blessed be God! – hitherto passed in the most satisfactory manner. If Meath and Dublin county do as well [they did], why we shall be all triumph – and the best kind of triumph, that which furnishes hope and indeed appears to reduce hope into the certainty of being able to accomplish something for Ireland. My return for Dublin unsolicited, and even unavowed by me, is perhaps the greatest triumph my countrymen have ever given me.[53]

V

On 20 December O'Connell had written to his wife as well as to Fitzpatrick from Tralee. 'In short, darling, everything appears quite prosperous', he had reported.[54] It was of the general election that he spoke, but the phrase might serve as a motto for his fortunes generally during 1832. It certainly applied in its most commonplace sense, to money. Probably for the first time since boyhood, O'Connell was flush with funds, if not altogether free from debt. Fitzpatrick set out to raise £1000 per month for the O'Connell tribute for 1832, and easily exceeded his goal during the calendar year. O'Connell responded to the rising financial tide with his usual panache. His steward John Primrose may well have been astonished to receive, on 14 April 1832, not a demand for cash, but a declaration of O'Connell's intent to clear the '*principal money* of my Iveragh debts'. He announced that he was now

> in a hurry to get rid of all my debts all over the world. *I have £5000* lent on a mortgage of stock to keep by me. This I do not touch. I have settled that is paid off or deposited £2000 out of Betsey's fortune. Blessed *be the great God* I expect soon to be quite independent and not to have my income cut down by auditors [creditors]. Is there anybody that teazes you particularly for money [?]. If so, state it to me and we will, with the help of God, get rid of that auditor.[55]

His brother James was probably still more startled when O'Connell offered him, out of the blue, a loan of £5000 to purchase land for the benefit of James's younger children. With characteristic grimness – on the edge of irony – James rejected 'a purchase which I have no occasion for . . . if I should be able to save as much money as will provide for *my other children*, without leaving a heavy debt on my small landed property, it will in my humble judgment be the most prudent course . . . Borrowing money to purchase land has generally been found a most ruinous speculation.'[56] Undaunted, O'Connell proceeded, in the late spring and early summer of 1832, to deposit £3500 at the Hibernian Bank; lend (it would seem) £1000 to the parish priest of St James's, Dublin; pay off several Cork and Kerry debts; spend a little on his houses at Carhen (his birthplace) and Derrynane; distribute through Fitzpatrick small sums to various religious charities; and take his chaise and four to Liverpool to travel 'comfortably and sufficiently expeditiously' to London.[57] But perhaps the best index of all of O'Connell's unwonted 'prosperity' was the absence of any reference whatever to money in his extensive correspondence in the months preceding the general election of 1832, in which three of his sons, besides himself, were candidates.

In addition to the Tribute and his rents, O'Connell earned something at the bar in 1832; but it can only have been comparatively little. He joined the Munster spring circuit half-way through its course, but soon departed for his March-April political campaign. His notion of abandoning parliament for law was evidently evanescent. Despite very heavy pressure from Ireland he did not leave London in time to act for the accused in the very important Carrickshock tithe trial held at the Kilkenny assizes on 20 and 21 July. 'Your non-appearance caused great disappointment and dismay', Fitzpatrick told him[58] – although in fact acquittals were secured. But though he practised only occasionally, O'Connell's reputation as a counsel never shrank. Shrewdly Fitzpatrick attributed this to 'the *Caesaren vehis* feeling which induces the Irish people to rely so much not only upon your great powers but also on your *fortune*'.[59] Many much humbler persons agreed with Bonaparte that luck was the final virtue.

O'Connell suffered some illness, or at least depression, during his last three weeks in London in July 1832. He went so far as to seek a resident 'young physician or surgeon of sufficient skill'[60] for Derrynane while the family resided there from August to November – though this may have been principally for his wife's sake, as there are several references to her ill-health throughout the year. Possibly his concern for himself related to a rheumatic disorder – as well as to his everlasting battle against fatness – for his prescriptions seem always to have run along the lines of horseriding for exercise and regular hot baths. At a guess, his real trouble was the temporary over-taxing of his body; he was now fifty-seven years of age. Certainly, he did not suffer either before or after his summer sojourn in London. In the course of his arduous spring campaign in Ireland, he had written to Mary, 'I was not one bit fatigued by my exertions yesterday [29 March 1832], and never had a more refreshing sleep. I could rave of the scenes I have gone through';[61] six days later, he had reported that he 'never was better in health or spirits';[62] and these spirits appear to have stayed buoyant until he returned to Westminster in mid-April. They also revived almost as soon as he reached Kerry for his long vacation. He told Fitzpatrick on 11 August that his health was quite restored. 'I now enjoy my pristine elasticity of animal sensation. There never was so great a change in the tone of animal functions in any man within so short a period. I enjoy my mountain hunting on foot as much as ever I did and expect, with the help of God, to be quite prepared for as vigorous a winter campaign as ever I carried on.'[63] Though the winter campaign was vigorous indeed, O'Connell never complained of illness or even weariness throughout its length. His habitual 'elasticity of animal sensation' seems to have been re-enthroned in the last five months of 1832.

The glow of O'Connell's family feeling can be glimpsed only occasionally in his correspondence for 1832. During the year he was rarely parted from his wife, the principal recipient of his private hopes and fears. But he did report to her – *couleur de rose*, of course – the well-being of all her children who remained in Ireland when she went to London in the spring. On his visit of 1–2 April to his 'own Betsey' and his 'darling Kate', who was staying with her in co. Roscommon, he found 'Betsey thin but looking well . . . Catty [Kate] is perfectly well. So are Morgan [his son] and Ffrench [Betsey's husband].' Morgan was indeed 'as stout as a lion'.[64] O'Connell also called at Clongowes to see after his youngest son Daniel, who was still a pupil there, and then told Mary, 'Banish all kind of uneasiness on his account. It is not possible for him to be better . . . They [the Jesuits] praise him to the skies.'[65] Finally, he journeyed to co. Wicklow to call upon his eldest daughter, Ellen. Meanwhile he heaped praise on Maurice who had stayed in London with Mary and was acting, currently, as O'Connell's 'voice' in the House of Commons. Knowing how Mary would warm to praise of her first-born, he ardently applauded Maurice's speech on the Irish tithe bill on 27 March 1832, and told her, a few days later, that the priests at Clongowes 'are in raptures about Maurice – *so am I, sweetest*'.[66]

But no one, except presumably his bride, could have been enraptured by Maurice's elopement later in the year with Mary Frances Bindon Scott, the daughter of a tory Protestant landowner in co. Clare. It was certainly a romantic escapade. Maurice sailed his yacht into Cahircon, close to the Scotts' home, bore off Mary Frances across the

Shannon estuary, and then descended to Tralee where the pair were married, at a Catholic ceremony, on 29 September, and to Kenmare, where they married two days later according to the rites of the Church of Ireland. Subsequently, O'Connell said that he had agreed to Maurice's making proposals to Bindon Scott, but not of course to his marrying his daughter without Scott's consent or even knowledge. It is hard to believe that O'Connell liked the match, quite apart from the impropriety of its execution. Mary Frances's fortune, £6000–7000, was rather larger than those of his own daughters. But O'Connell and his wife had had much higher hopes for Maurice, and, in any case, Mary Frances was – immediately – a penniless acquisition, for her father at first disowned her. Worst of all perhaps was the fact that the Catholic champion's heir had married out of his own church, with the possibility that the female children of the union, at least, would be lost to the faith. But whatever his immediate reaction to the news of the runaway wedding, O'Connell soon drew Mary Frances into the family cocoon. 'Darling little Mary', he wrote to his wife from Tralee (where he was electioneering on behalf of Maurice) on 26 December 1832, 'has a sore throat and she stayed in bed all day nursing it. I have determined that she and Maurice should travel more slowly [than himself] to Dublin . . . so as to dine with us on . . . New Year's Day . . . Maurice and little Mary write in love to you.'[67] All that remained, it seemed, was to secure the new Mrs O'Connell's fortune and paternal pardon. The little domestic cloud had been driven off – for the time being – by O'Connell's resolute pursuit of family felicity.

VI

As we have seen, a much more threatening cloud had hung over O'Connell's own reputation at the beginning of the year. On 25 November 1831 the radical Henry Hunt had forwarded to him a letter from Ellen Courtenay accusing O'Connell of having raped her some fourteen years earlier and of being the father of her illegitimate son, born in November 1818: Hunt claimed that Courtenay had sent him this in 'applying to me for pecuniary relief'.[68] Courtenay's (or perhaps we should say Hunt's?) move was the first step in an attempted blackmail. Blackmailing public men for sexual misconduct (real or invented) was then a common practice, and even guiltless victims sometimes paid for silence in order to avoid a scandal. O'Connell denied all knowledge of Courtenay – and the evidence would seem to establish his complete innocence. But early in January 1832 his friend

Grove Jones warned him of 'the calumnies that were in circulation against him' in London.[69] O'Connell, widely feared, disliked and already classified as 'ruffian' rather than 'gentleman' (a 'gentleman' would, of course, according to the code, support his bastards), was extraordinarily vulnerable to hostile gossip among the political classes. None the less, he refused to buy off or have any truck with Courtenay.

Her next ploy was to issue from the debtors' prison in which she was detained a pamphlet setting out her charges against O'Connell in full horrid detail. Still, he held to his line of ignoring the accusations while endeavouring to prevent their coming to wider public notice. Thus, he wrote to his young relative, Walter Baldwin, in London on 29 April 1832:

> you must not publish anything about *my fair friend*. What she wants most is to have a controversy raised and I am sure that no friend of mine who appreciates her attack at its just value will indulge her in a controversy. You therefore, let me say it, *must* not indulge you *cacoethes scribendi* on this subject as I am sure that my request which is very unequivocal will decide you not to publish one line upon the subject. Nothing could annoy me on this subject but a publication purporting to come from a friend.[70]

Courtenay's final – and futile – fling in 1832 was, as we have seen, to ask the Irish tory press to print her story, and – this failing – to enjoin the editors to send reporters to the Dublin mayoral court when she would make an application before it. O'Connell's reputation may have suffered, to some small extent, from the whispering which must have accompanied the 'scandal', particularly as it was uncountered by open denial. But the brave course of defying Courtenay, and maintaining silence, was probably the wisest, too. No one took up or even made public reference to Courtenay's cause, despite all her efforts. O'Connell had come through practically unscathed: 1832 was indeed his prosperous year.

CHAPTER 16

The Uses of Repeal

1833–4

I

During 1832 O'Connell's politics had been, in one particular sense, built upon Repeal. But he was using Repeal as a political instrument rather than pursuing it as a goal. He employed it to justify his associations, to launch his agitations, to frighten the whigs into concessionary measures or appointments, to lead into 'Justice for Ireland' demands, to demonstrate good faith to British politicians when he shelved it, or to mark off a distinct political grouping of his own when he slapped it down upon the counter once again. But Repeal also lived on quite another plane; in fact, its natural habitat was the ideal. The young Michael Doheny, destined to become an insurrectionist in 1848 and the author of the famous fiery *Felon's Track*, wrote to 'the Liberator of our country' on 27 November 1832 from Clonmel gaol (where he was incarcerated for his part in resisting tithes):

> These are decisive times. The next few weeks will be teeming with events important to Ireland and much will depend on the energy of the people during that brief period. What a glorious object the people have to struggle for! How magnificent is even the hope of national liberation! As all bitter feelings against petty injustice and local tyranny are merged in the nation's predominant aversion to the Union, so all the mind and the might of the people should be directed to its *Repeal*.[1]

Had O'Connell, after the wear and tear of nearly thirty years of daily politics, lost his hold upon this visionary dimension of Repeal? No, by no means altogether: but his attitude was by now most complex. It deserves a full analysis, at the point at which he emerged, in January 1833, as the leader of a considerable parliamentary party committed to that single, but ramifying, principle.

Let us start by asking, what did O'Connell mean when he called for the repeal of the Act of Union? No one should have known better than he that his frequent demand for the 'simple repeal' of the British statute passed in 1800 contradicted the entire trend of his political activity since that date. Literally interpreted, it was nonsensical. He could not have meant to propose the re-constitution of the eighteenth-century Irish constituencies, controlled, as almost all had been, by crown, patrons, proprietors or bribes. Nor could he have accepted the re-imposition of those Roman Catholic disabilities which had been removed statutorily since 1800. Yet both of these 'safeguards' had been pre-conditions of 'independence' for the great majority of Irish Protestants before 1800. In fact, the Union had come about, so far as they were concerned, because they had come to feel that even these defences were too flimsy for the maintenance of the Protestant Ascendancy, or even Protestant security or possessions. On the one hand, the events of the 1820s in Ireland – in particular, the loss or potential loss of control in many of the parliamentary constituencies and the proven power of Irish popular agitation – had further weakened Protestant 'securities'. On the other, O'Connell could scarcely have contemplated reversing a series of changes which he himself had done most to bring about. Further, as the Repeal movement developed in the early 1830s it was closely linked, by and through O'Connell, to the full radical reform programme – manhood suffrage, vote by ballot, equal electoral districts, triennial parliaments, and the abolition of the property qualifications for MPs. Isaac Butt was surely right to contend later on that 'Repeal was a revolution . . . the proposition was not to return to any state of things that previously existed in Ireland – not to adopt the constitution of any European state, but to enter on an untried and wild system of democracy.'[2]

Thus, O'Connell could certainly not have intended what he often formally proposed, the turning back of the constitutional clock to 1799. Why, then, did he present the issue in such terms? Various types of answer may be proffered. First, Repeal appeared to evidence extraordinary political consistency, given the great length and variety of O'Connell's public appearance. Throughout his long campaign for Catholic civil rights, he had lost no opportunity of emphasizing its secondary nature: religious liberation, he always said, was ultimately meaningful only in the context of Repeal. Even his abatement of Ireland's claims, during the course of his first parliamentary flirtation with the whigs in 1831, was presented as contingent, and was in fact apparent rather than real. When, therefore, towards the close of 1832 he committed himself, at last, to a direct and total assault upon the Union, the mature man of fifty-seven may have looked back in imagination to the young man of twenty-five, and told himself that in his beginning was his end. The very Act which he had opposed in 1800 he still opposed in 1832; all that he had ever sought was the restoration of the status quo. Thus, Repeal gave unity to O'Connell's long career. He could present himself, even to himself, as changeless from first to last, tacking perhaps to contrary winds, but unvarying in his destination, a Fabius among national liberators. This may have been important. Demagogues may live through a temporary failing in applause, but hardly disbelieving in themselves.

Secondly, O'Connell was not only an Irish nationalist but also a leading British radical, in certain senses the leading British radical of his day. In radicalism, he could reconcile his personal ambitions and his early grounding in the ideology of the Enlightenment. Resentment of, and refusal to acquiesce in, the condition of inferiority into which, as an Irish Catholic, he had been born, were the steady urges in his life. His consequent passion for parity could be readily articulated in terms of civil equality. That O'Connell was the complete egalitarian, in the formal and legal senses in which contemporaries understood the word, there could be no reasonable doubt. One could find no measure of civil rights which came within his sphere of action or comment which he did not earnestly support. Thus, he could honestly present his drive for formal political equality for Irishmen and Catholics within the United Kingdom as a particular manifestation of a general and absolute principle. Repeal fitted with equal neatness into his universalist radicalism. The demand for legislative independence could be paraded as the apotheosis of egalitarianism, while serving, at the same time, as a burning glass for all the bitterness which racial and religious discrimination had engendered.

There was, however, another level at which O'Connell's radicalism helps to explain his emphasis on the repeal of a particular statute. As a political technique, as distinct from a body of ideas, British radicalism for the first two-thirds of the nineteenth century centred on the removal of clearly specified abuses or restraints. The classic form of campaign, beginning with the anti-slavery movement, was to institute an agitation for the abolition of a particular evil by parliamentary action. Each campaign was a separate undertaking with a separate target; happiest of all if the target were a specific Act of parliament. To present the constitutional rearrangement of the British Isles in the same sort of terms as the abolition of the slave trade, or church disestablishment, or the repeal of the corn laws, was therefore a natural action for O'Connell. His long and successful campaign for

Catholic Emancipation had taken precisely this form, down to casting the objective in terms of, to use the official phraseology, the removal of the statutory 'Disabilities ... imposed on the Roman Catholic Subjects of His Majesty'.[3] Focusing on a single repealing measure had, moreover, for the purposes of mass agitation, the solid advantages of limpid simplicity and the clear identification of a visible enemy. That this enemy was a comparatively recent Act of parliament, and one besides of so large a sweep that almost every contemporary misfortune could be plausibly ascribed to it, were further significant advantages for a popular movement. Thus, both the nature and the art of contemporary mass politics suggested the wisdom of a campaign for 'simple repeal'.

Thirdly, it should never be forgotten that O'Connell had to work in and through the political system of the United Kingdom. He had to move British opinion, a British ministry and a predominantly British House of Commons – and behind all these, requiring a still greater force to overcome, the British crown and House of Lords. He could use threats, blandishments, demonstrations, dangers and discomfort – but violence was disavowed. In the best of circumstances, it was a daunting journey. But had O'Connell announced in so many words that his objective was to advance to a novel state of things which, whatever its constitutional form, implied mass democracy, tenant right and disestablishment of the Church of Ireland, it would have been pointless for him to have ever put one foot before the other.

Instead, the chosen issue was well designed to counter the British 'great fears' – of revolution, of popery and of separation. The choice of 'simple repeal', with its implicit as well as explicit invocations of '1782', could scarcely have been bettered as a device for allaying the *furor Britannicus*. 'Simple repeal' was meant to convey the ideas of restoration and of Protestant security, if not of actual Protestant domination. The repeated use of 'Grattan's Parliament' and 'College Green' in O'Connell's Repeal oratory suggested mere moderate colonial nationalism and even perhaps the acceptance of renewed Ascendancy leadership, if freed of its former sectarian oppression. The backward references also commonly included the comforting incantation of 'king, lords and commons'; and fervent expressions of adherence to the crown were from first to last a leading feature of each O'Connellite campaign. O'Connell inscribed 'Loyal' on his banners with all the purposive ostentation of an Orange Lodge; he called incessantly for cheers for His Majesty with all the sentimental hyperbole of a two-bottle parson. On the surface, it was difficult to assail any of this as unconstitutional. Thus, Repeal constituted, in O'Connell's view, the safest means of exerting mass, extra-parliamentary pressure and represented the highest opening bid which an Irish agitation of the 1830s could safely make.

Fourthly, as this last point suggests, the truth would seem to be that O'Connell did not intend to put forward a specific proposition or make a specific demand in launching his movement for Repeal. It was, in lawyer's language, an invitation to treat rather than a firm offer. What he probably intended in 1830–2 was to elicit a proposition from the British government. Repeal was only apparently a demand. Its true counterpart was not so much Catholic Emancipation, tithe abolition or Irish church disestablishment as Parnell's 'Home Rule'. Like O'Connell, Parnell avoided, so far as possible, specification of his objective. Like O'Connell's, Parnell's pressure appears to have been designed to force out a counter-offer, which might be accepted, rejected as insufficient, or used as a start for bargaining. The essential similarity of O'Connell's situation and leadership to Parnell's is apparent in this extraordinary passage towards the close of the great Mansion House debate of 1843 upon the desirability of Repeal:

> a Parliament inferior to the English Parliament I would accept as an instalment if I found the people ready to go with me, and if it were offered me by competent authority. It must first be offered me – mark that – I will never seek it. By this declaration I am bound thus far, that if the period should come when I am called upon practically to act upon it, I will do so; but I will not give up my exertions for the independent legislation until from some substantial quarter that offer is made . . .
>
> Upon this subject I must not be mistaken, I never will ask for or look for any other, save an independent legislature, but if others offer me a subordinate parliament, I will close with any such authorized offer and accept that offer.[4]

Despite the initial hedges of 'an instalment' and 'the people ready', O'Connell was showing more of his hand that Parnell would ever do. Still, he worked within the same ambience. Each man sought to force a declaration from a British party, and to make none himself. Some apparently specific goal had to be announced; otherwise a movement could never have been set afoot. Parnell's devices were silence and an ambiguous and amorphous name and programme, 'Home Rule'; O'Connell's, garrulity, inconsistency and an impossible ostensible object, 'Repeal'. But this was a mere difference of mode and style. They were at one in being 'comparative separatists', who recognized that the *degree* of separateness would be determined ultimately in

Great Britain, and who committed themselves to no abstraction or ideal form of state.

O'Connell came nearest, perhaps, to particularizing his conception of the relations between Great Britain and Ireland after the Union was repealed in a speech delivered to the reformers of Bath in May 1832. It was an occasion for minimizing the degree of autonomy which the rupture would entail. O'Connell was anxious to lead British radicals on from making common cause on parliamentary reform to making common cause on the constitutional rearrangement of the government of the British Isles. He was reported as saying:

> The Irish have been accused of wishing to have a separate Legislature, and to be divided entirely from England. Nothing can, however, be more untrue than this. We are too acute not to be aware of the advantages which result particularly to ourselves from our union with this country. We only want a Parliament to do our private business, leaving the national business to a national assembly; for it is well known to all who are acquainted with the subject that the private business of the House of Commons, if properly attended to, is quite enough to occupy its entire consideration. Each of the twenty-four States of North America has its separate Legislature for the dispatch of local business, while the general business is confined to a national assembly, and why should not this example hold good in the case of Ireland?[5]

He was immediately assailed in Ireland for having abandoned the Repeal cause. His use of the phrase 'our union with this country' was seized on as the very ensign of surrender. O'Connell may well have spoken loosely or inadvertently of 'union', but the context makes it clear that in no sense was he arguing for the maintenance of the Act of 1801. In any event, as commonly happened, he claimed to have been misreported and that the word which he had employed was not 'union', but 'connexion'. He went on, in his public letter of explanation to 'the People of Ireland', to make it clear that he saw Repeal as issuing in a federal system for Great Britain and Ireland. He proposed that a domestic legislature, consisting only of a House of Commons, should be created for each country. These legislatures should meet in the last quarter of each year, and deal with such issues as law and order, agriculture and commerce within their respective territories. Then in the following January or February, an imperial parliament should meet in London to determine matters of common concern to Ireland and Great Britain, war and peace and imperial and foreign relations.

Despite the lack of detail and the impracticality of the machinery in

O'Connell's proposal, it is deeply interesting. At first sight, his domestic legislature might appear a meagre objective, especially when he employed the direct analogy of the states of the American union. It seemed to fall far short of parliamentary independence. But the independence of 'Grattan's parliament', the holy grail of the Repeal movement, had been largely illusory. The British cabinet, through its control of the crown, the Irish executive and, normally, the majority of votes in both the Irish houses of parliament, had been the ultimate authority in Ireland throughout 1782–1800. O'Connell's domestic legislature was meant to be *exclusively* effective in the areas which concerned him most, the economy, the civil service, local government, and the legal and police systems. Secondly – and perhaps still more important to O'Connell – his proposal reduced Great Britain to the same constitutional level as his own country. The British domestic legislature would have no greater range of business, no larger powers, than its Irish counterpart. The equal footing of the two was driven home by the further proposal of a joint imperial parliament to deal with external and colonial relations, and everything that bore on these, such as the armed forces and the foreign service. It is true that the imperial parliament would be dominated by its British members – to say nothing of its embracing the current House of Lords. None the less its very character, composition and duties would imply that Ireland was no less a mother-country, no less a nation, than Britain herself. No less than the domestic assemblies, it would serve as a symbol of political equality.

All this probably expressed O'Connell's fundamental purposes throughout his Repeal agitations. His notion of 'internal' affairs may have been ill-defined and certainly failed to come to grips with the inherent problem of how economic policy and the levels of taxation and public expenditure should be determined. But his general division was clear enough. Ireland should govern itself in what concerned itself alone; and so should Britain. In matters which concerned the outside world – physically speaking – he was prepared to allow Britain the substantial power, provided that Ireland was *formally* accepted as an equal partner. Parity was the key to all his thinking on Repeal, no less than to all his thinking on Emancipation. The great driving force of his politics from first to last was his revolt against inferiority of condition. But he was ever a pragmatist; and while the accidents of his Bath speech and its aftermath may have drawn from him a comparatively specific avowal of his ideal settlement, he never again allowed himself the indulgence of detailed speculation, but rather used Repeal *sans phrase* as a popular rallying-cry, a mode of intimidating governments and a hoped-for bargaining counter.

II

The general election of 1832 had scarcely ended before O'Connell attempted to broaden the base of his support in the House of Commons beyond the Repeal MPs. He seized upon Richard Barrett's proposal of 30 December (conceivably inspired by himself) that a 'national council' of all Irish MPs and representative peers be called to consider the state of the country. Immediately, O'Connell summoned a meeting of the 'council' in Dublin, before the beginning of the new parliamentary session. By publishing the responses to his 'invitation' in the newspapers, he exerted the utmost pressure on the freshly elected Repeal members and even on liberals returned for 'open' county constituencies, to present themselves before him. Similarly, when on 10 January 1833, he still considered it possible that his son-in-law's brother Nicholas Fitz-Simon, MP for King's Co., might not appear, he saw to it that Fitz-Simon received this message: 'Let him not listen to base advisers. He is ruined for ever if he shrinks from the people at this juncture.'[6] In fact, all the Repeal MPs either attended the 'council' or provided good reasons for not doing so. Dr Macintyre has described the outcome succinctly:

> of the 30 to 35 MPs who attended the Council's two sessions in a hotel opposite the old Irish Parliament on College Green, only three were not Repealers. The Council heard a report on Irish revenue, taxes and funded debts from Michael Staunton, the editor of the *Morning Register*; it discussed the soap and paper trades, grand jury reform, the abolition of tithes and various measures of franchise reform, but there was no discussion of Repeal itself, and in general the results of the Council disappointed those like Henry Grattan and John O'Connell who hoped that it would lead to unity of purpose and action and that it would act as the working model of an Irish legislature.[7]

There is no evidence that O'Connell ever thought of the council (which never met again) as a dry run for a future Irish House of Commons. It is much more likely that in gathering together whatever parliamentarians he could, he hoped to establish more firmly, and to expand, an independent Irish pressure group at Westminster. Clearly, Repeal had served its purpose for the moment. It was not to be pressed further immediately. Instead, O'Connell brought to the foreground the Irish issues of common concern, doubtless to draw some non-Repeal liberals into the fold. Another of his purposes in promoting the council may well have been the confirmation of his personal authority and leadership.

All the same, O'Connell hedged his bets. On the one hand, he prepared the way for another sustained agitation at home. On 3 January 1833, he replaced the National Political Union by a 'Society of Irish Volunteers for the Repeal of the Union'. The precedent of 1782 was not only deliberately invoked but even declared to be the model for the sort of action called for now that parliamentary reform had been achieved. On the other hand, he put what pressure he could upon the new whig government to appoint a more sympathetic and amenable Irish administration. 'You are the only person connected with power', he told Duncannon on 14 January, while the national council was meeting,

> to whom I could write what I know and what I believe and indeed I should not feel at rest if I did not tell you that the Government cannot appreciate the exact state of this country. Stanley has had considerable success in enforcing the Tithes. He has overawed many, very many parishes, and there was an adequate force for that purpose but the result is just what those who know Ireland foresaw – the spirit which is curbed by day walks abroad by night. Whiteboyism is substituted for open meetings. *There is almost universal organisation going on.* It is not confined to one or two counties. It is, I repeat, *almost universal*. I do not believe there is any man in the rank of a comfortable farmer engaged, not one man probably entitled to vote. But all the poverty of our counties is being organised. There never yet was, as I believe, so general a disposition for that species of insurrectionary outrages . . .
>
> I know you will excuse me for my cause in troubling you at this length. But, indeed you who are acquainted with the history of Irish affairs, must have been prepared for this result. The insanity of delivering this country to so weak a man as Lord Anglesey and so obstinate a maniac as Stanley, is unequalled even in our annals.[8]

O'Connell had thus devised a multiple strategy at high speed, in the three weeks between the conclusion of the general election and his departure for London on 23 or 24 January 1833. He was trying, simultaneously, to produce a disciplined parliamentary party, a national support organization, and a shift in the Irish policy of Grey's re-elected ministry. As all this filtered through to the liberals at Westminster, it seemed that it was 'evidently the game of O'Connell to keep the Repeal question out of Parliament, but to agitate and stir up Ireland from its foundations with the question; to embody the whole population of Ireland as unarmed Volunteers, [and] to make Repeal of the Union the prevailing sentiment of that body'.[9] These were three-quarters truths at least. Throughout the session, O'Connell made only one considerable speech on the Union; and until the 'Society' was suppressed by proclamation on 10 April, he strove, so far as was practicable from a distance, to breathe life into his re-created Volunteers. Moreover, with Fitzpatrick as his channel of communication, he renewed his efforts to entice the Orange party into the Repeal camp. Hoping to build upon a common hostility to the whigs, he went to the limit to render Repeal palatable to a wounded and resentful Ascendancy. On 21 February, through his faithful intermediary, he offered these generous terms to Boyton, the Dublin Protestant champion:

> My plan is to restore the Irish parliament with the full assent of Protestants and Presbyterians as well as Catholics. I desire no social revolution, no social change. The nobility to possess lands, titles and legislative privileges as before the Union. The Clergy, *for their lives*, their full incomes – to decrease as Protestantism may allow that decrease. The Landed Gentry to enjoy their present state, *being residents*.
>
> Every man to be considered a resident who has *an establishment* in Ireland.
>
> In short, salutary restoration without revolution, an Irish parliament, British connection, one King, two legislatures.[10]

A month later, he asked (again through Fitzpatrick) 'Would *they* [the Irish tories] take up *the Repeal* as founded on the basis of a local parliament for *local objects* merely and the present 105 members to come over to the Imperial Parliament for all *general* purposes, as at present? In short, see what we can do to satisfy him [Sheehan, the Dublin Orange leader] and his.'[11]

But all this was a secondary theme. O'Connell was perforce not active but reactive once he got to parliament. He was immediately confronted with a king's speech which, at Stanley's direction, threatened throughgoing repression in Ireland. He was moreover pitched at once into the old hand-to-hand combat with Stanley himself. As Le Marchant described the opening night's debate on 5–6 February 1833,

> O'Connell's speech, artful and persuasive in a very high degree, made a deep impression. It required a very skilful answer, and certainly did not receive it from Stanley. His invective upon O'Connell, though pointed and forcible, did more injury to himself than to his opponent. It was not

accompanied by a proper confutation of O'Connell's changes, so it looked like invective alone, and the evening ended by O'Connell standing in a much higher position than in the last Parliament. The new members thought he had much right on his side.

Luckily for ministers O'Connell was not satisfied with this moderate success. He must needs shew his strength, or perhaps shew the Repealers in Ireland that they had not sent so many representatives to the House in vain. One after another these Hibernian orators rose to repeat in lengthy and declamatory harangues their complaints of the wrongs of their country and their accusations against the ministry. Their coarse manners, fierce deportment and baseless assertions, at length heartily wearied the House . . . It cannot be denied that many of the facts stated in his [O'Connell's] speech were far from being satisfactorily answered. Still his injudicious tactics produced the same effect as if they had been.[12]

The familiar diastole and systole, the alternate dilation and contraction in O'Connell's relations with the whig government, also re-emerged. Initially, he was softened by the Irish Church temporalities bill introduced by Althorp in the Commons on 12 February. The bill proposed to substitute a tax on clerical incomes for church cess (which Irish Catholics as well as Irish Protestants had to pay), the abolition of nearly half the Church of Ireland bishoprics and archbishoprics, and – by the so-called 'appropriation' clause – the sale of episcopal estates to build up a surplus fund which might possibly be drawn on, inter alia, for the support of the Catholic clergy. Though O'Connell regarded this as 'very short of what it ought to be in point of extinction of burden', he was, overall, delighted with the measure. 'It establishes valuable principles', he told Fitzpatrick, ' – first, that Parliament is to *cut down* the magnitude of the *establishment* (admitting, by way of parenthesis, that the establishment is too large) to a reasonable extent. It establishes, also, the parliamentary right to manage *that* species of property.'[13] O'Connell was at one with Pusey in seeing in the appropriation clause the beginning of the end for the traditional Anglican pretensions.

He was equally pleased with the setting up on 14 February 1833 of a select committee, with himself among its members, to inquire into the workings of the municipal corporations: it seemed to him a heaven-sent opportunity 'to prove the entire System of Dublin Corporation abuses'. Next night, however, the whigs showed him their other face when Grey introduced the government's Irish coercion bill in the Lords. Even the tories were amazed at its severity, Ellenborough describing it as 'a compound of the Proclamation Act, the Insurrection

Act, the Gagging Bill, the Suspension of the Habeas Corpus Act, & Martial Law'.[14] Grey justified the harsh measure as called for by O'Connell's mastery of Ireland. The truth was that the cabinet had swallowed lock, stock and barrel the wild account of the Irish situation which Anglesey had sent them on 6 January: 'We have to deal with a widespread conspiracy ... I apprehend the greatest possible danger must result, from allowing the People of Ireland to labour under the delusion that the Repeal of the Union, is an object which it is within *their* power ... to accomplish.'[15]

O'Connell was outraged at Grey's 'project of Ministerial despotism ... the Irish [MPs], of course, will fight it inch by inch'. Lest, however, the ardour of some might cool, he told Fitzpatrick on 17 February, 'There is nothing so necessary as to pour the vial of popular indignation on all the Irish members who are liable to popular influence and yet desert their colours on this vital occasion.'[16] This was seriously meant, and executed. A fortnight later, for example, the Athlone Trades Political Union publicly condemned their liberal member for failing to support O'Connell in a division, and resolved 'to displace him if he does not reverse his conduct'.[17]

According to the general judgment, O'Connell was worsted in the initial – by now almost ritualistic – bout with Stanley when the coercion bill, having sailed effortlessly through the Lords, was introduced in the lower House on 22 February. Even the moderate liberal, E. J. Littleton, who was comparatively well-disposed towards O'Connell, reported that Stanley

> made one of the most masterly and effective appeals to the House ever heard ... O'Connell was quite subdued, and could hardly falter out a shuffling explanation of his conduct at a city meeting a day or two before, where he had spoken of the House of Commons as 'six hundred scoundrels'. The Mob King seemed completely humiliated.[18]

But in the long run O'Connell redeemed his promise to '*emasculate* the act at the very worst'.[19] Although a meeting of nearly sixty Irish MPs which met at Palace Yard rejected his formal proposal that the coercion bill be systematically obstructed in the Commons, in practice he achieved this end. At every stage in the bill's progress, he used delaying tactics, constantly insisting upon divisions, extending both the length and scope of the debates on particular clauses, and using the various forms of the House to hold up business. Once again, O'Connell, at bay, proved a remarkable political innovator. His coercion bill campaign of the spring of 1833 foreshadowed, decidedly if crudely, the celebrated disruptive tactics pursued by Parnell's party in the opening parliamentary session of 1881. Moreover, O'Connell had to work with much less reliable tools and in less favourable circumstances. It was uphill toil for him to mobilize even the Repeal MPs, and several 'popular' Irish liberals actually supported the government's measure in the end. 'I am afflicted beyond measure', he wrote on 11 March 1833, 'at the conduct of many of the Irish members: Lambert of Wexford – atrocious; Keane of Waterford County – trecherous [sic] to the last degree; Evans [MP for co. Dublin] – very, very bad.'[20]

None the less by 21 March he had secured so many important amendments (such as the abandonment of retrospectivity and the exemption of the press from the new courts martial clause) that he could claim, with much justice, that it was 'now more a foolish than an infernal bill. To be sure it tramples on great principles, masking the rascality of those who bring it forward but it contains little that is formidable in its powers.'[21] Moreover, his guerilla warfare held back the passage of the bill until 2 April, and left a considerable number of the English liberal MPs disenchanted with their masters. The government had been shown up as both repressive and vacillating, and gibbetted by O'Connell as a mere bundle of whig men and tory measures.

III

As the session proceeded, O'Connell's emnity towards the whigs deepened. His sourness intensified with each exercise of obstruction; he was making no progress towards his cherished objective of reforming Dublin Corporation; and when the ministry dropped the appropriation clause from the Irish Church bill, he became contemptuous of the remaining concessions and rounded fiercely on the entire measure. 'I have no doubt', he wrote on 27 April at a moment when Grey's government seemed tottering, 'that the scoundrel . . . Whigs are out, and I have done my best to give them the last kick. The base hypocrites, with Liberty in their mouths and tyranny of the worst kind in their hearts!'[22] Yet already the pendulum was swinging again in the opposite direction. Indeed, in one sense, the worse O'Connell's relations with the whigs, the more he expected some junction with them. As he himself put it, 'To be respected by them they must feel one to be a formidable enemy. They have always courted their enemies. I look to success *with* them only from attacking them with virulence until they believe me formidable.'[23] But also his sky was lightened when, on 29 March 1833, Stanley exchanged the Irish chief secretary-ship for the colonial office; for three years Stanley had stood as the greatest single obstacle to O'Connell's political designs, as well as his most effective opponent in the House of Commons. Stanley's immediate successor, J. C. Hobhouse (whom O'Connell soon dismissed as 'only milk and water'),[24] served a mere seven weeks; and Littleton, who replaced him as chief secretary on 17 May, was quite amenable to negotiation with the Repeal contingent. The second factor which opened the way to some degree of rapprochement with the whigs was a protracted governmental crisis. From late April, when it suffered a temporary defeat in the Commons on its proposed malt tax, until mid-July, when it secured the Commons' re-endorsement of its Irish Church bill, the ministry's fate hung in the balance. Its dependence upon O'Connell's support grew evident. As early as 6 June, he saved Grey's government when it was threatened in a vote of confidence on its foreign policy. As he noted next day,

> I joined [with] the Whig ministry last night and contributed perhaps a good deal to the extent and satisfactory nature of their victory. I have helped them at this crisis which, however, is not yet over . . .
> My speech and vote last night gave me a *proper introduction* to Mr Littleton. If anything can be done it is now. I am, I think so at least, formidable as an enemy. I have shown an act of unmerited friendship. We shall see whether anything can be done. Littleton will be in town this day.[25]

The imminent prospect of the tories returning to power had had its usual effect upon O'Connell; but he had two further reasons for moderating or intermitting his opposition to Grey's government. First, on 6 April 1833, before Littleton took over the chief secretaryship, the Irish executive instituted a prosecution of Barrett for having published in the *Pilot* an allegedly seditious letter from O'Connell to 'the People of Ireland'. Dublin Castle's immediate purpose was to force O'Connell to accept responsibility for the publication or, if this failed, to show him up as a poltroon who hid behind editors and printers, and thereby intimidate 'his' press. Probably correctly, O'Connell discerned the more general object to be an attempt 'to suppress the agitation of the Repeal of the Union. It [the charge] states it to be *seditious* to bring the Union into what the law terms *contempt*.'[26]

He had no intention of proffering himself as a victim in Barrett's place. He had warned Barrett beforehand of 'the fact that every letter I ever published *could* be declared a libel . . . you knew the risk and accepted it'. But when it looked as if Barrett (under the influence of another editor, Staunton of the *Morning Register*) might throw him to the Castle wolves, O'Connell truly feared imprisonment. On 7 June, he appealed to Barrett,

> there never yet was a moment of my political life in which it was so essential to the interests of Ireland that I should be *at large*. My power of locomotion in England as well as in Ireland is, I think, essentially necessary, for the sake of Ireland, to be preserved at this critical juncture. To be sure, I may be mistaken; I may be deceiving myself; but I would not have published one line in Ireland if I thought such publication would put me in a situation to be withheld from action for *three years*, a period which the Court of King's Bench would readily inflict on me.[27]

In fact, Barrett was to remain true to O'Connell, who guaranteed him complete indemnification – so far as money could indemnify him – should he be convicted. None the less, until the trial took place O'Connell could not feel altogether safe. Nor could he, as tribal chieftain, relish the possible exposure of his inability to protect a follower who was about to suffer grievously for his fidelity. With all this, good relations with the whigs became suddenly desirable. Should it seem worth their while, the government could drop or (as in the case of O'Connell himself in 1831) deliberately mismanage the prosecution. They had the power to lift, more or less at will, the financial, political and moral burden from his shoulders.

O'Connell's second reason for coming to terms, if possible, with the whigs was that such an accommodation would stave off, for another term, the raising of the Repeal issue in parliament. Anxious to postpone the humiliating defeat which awaited any motion in favour of Repeal in the House of Commons, he had omitted the subject entirely from the agenda of his national council, when it had met in Dublin in January 1833. Down to the passage of the coercion bill on 2 April, he could argue that the struggle against this odious measure must take priority. But thereafter pressure mounted in Ireland for him to test the water at Westminster by bringing Repeal forward to debate. Several young Turks, chief among them the newly elected MP for co. Cork, Feargus O'Connor, openly denounced his procrastination (O'Connor doubtless saw this as the first step in a challenge to O'Connell's leadership); and partly through their agitation, though partly independently, demands for immediate action on Repeal began to be heard in various parts of Ireland during May. All this helps to explain the olive branch implicitly offered to the government by

O'Connell when he saved them from defeat in the House of Commons on 6 July. A whig effort to conciliate Ireland would be his best security against the importunate rashness of his would-be rivals.

O'Connor, however, threatened to press a Repeal motion on his own, and O'Connell was forced to summon two meetings of the Repeal MPs at Westminster in order to hold him back. O'Connell carried the day, but only barely. At the meeting of 10 June 1833 his motion opposing the raising of Repeal during the current parliamentary session was carried by a mere 12 votes to 10, with 10 abstentions; even two of his own relatives, his cousin Herbert Baldwin and his brother-in-law W. F. Finn, voted with his opponents. After O'Connor had challenged this vote, the decision was confirmed a few days later; but again the number voting and the margin of O'Connell's victory (17 to 7) were far from reassuring. Meanwhile, Fitzpatrick had warned O'Connell that the pressure for a Repeal motion was growing so rapidly in Dublin that it would be dangerous to run athwart it. Even had O'Connell received this warning before the first meeting of the MPs, he would have ignored it. 'I am bound in candour', he replied,

> to tell you that the advice of my friends in Dublin would not induce *me* to consent to bring it on this session because I know that any rational discussion upon it is impossible in this advanced and complicated state of the public business. We should have been either deprived of a house by members going away or we should be treated with contempt and ridicule by men who are now thinking of nothing else save *escaping* from London and getting rid of the session. You have no idea of the effect which must be produced in this country as well as in Ireland by the total and ludicrous failure of the attempt to debate it *now*. It would literally be equal only to the plan of 'privateering after the war' . . .
>
> One great reason why I would not bring on the Repeal this session is, that it would give a fictitious patriotism to men who have been voting badly through three fourths of the session; and indeed it is just such men who in general are for forcing it on at present . . . *working up* their popularity by giving a vote for Repeal just at the moment when no rational result could ensue . . .[28]

None the less, O'Connell was still on the defensive. A number of influential ill-wishers – chief among them, the alienated editor of the *Freeman's Journal*, Patrick Lavelle, and the Dublin radicals, Thomas Reynolds, vice-president of the National Trades Political Union, and Patrick O'Higgins, a warm friend of O'Connor, who was later to be called 'The Irish Chartist' – maintained the campaign against him. On 19 June 1833 they carried a motion at a parish meeting of St Audeon's,

Dublin, deprecating the decision to postpone raising the Repeal issue in the House of Commons. O'Connell felt this repudiation deeply. From London he reproached the faithful Fitzpatrick on 22 June; 'how is it possible that you should not in all that parish have been able to procure fifteen more friends of mine to turn the scale?' He grieved to learn that the merchant Thomas O'Connor on whom he could normally rely was

> arrayed in the adverse ranks. I thought he knew me better than to believe that anything but the impossibility of doing good and the certainty of doing harm would have induced me to postpone a discussion. It does, I confess, mortify me especially after your representations on the subject.

O'Connell proceeded to list for Fitzpatrick's (and presumably, through him, for others') benefit the current parliamentary issues in which he was playing a vital part, whether in opposition or support. These included the church temporalities, anti-slavery, Bank of England charter and East India government bills, and O'Connell concluded, in pique, 'I repeat this thing to you because I feel dissatisfied and disgusted with the triumph that has been had over me by Reynolds and O'Higgins and beings of that description'.[29] This coda is revealing. It brings out not only O'Connell's vision of himself as a Gulliver in Lilliput but also the chasm between Westminster and Dublin politics.

None of this was likely to allay the Irish resentment of his backsliding on Repeal. Yet O'Connell could play the kingmaker in the Commons only by reason, ultimately, of his Dublin political base, and it was he himself who, by making Repeal the touchstone in the general election of 1832, had forged the very weapon which his domestic enemies were now brandishing in his face. Moreover, Feargus O'Connor was emboldened (and perhaps also manipulated) by the opposition at home into declaring that – the adverse votes of the 'party' in London notwithstanding – he would introduce a resolution in favour of Repeal before the conclusion of the current parliamentary session. Without even apprising O'Connell beforehand, he put down his motion for 16 July 1833. Lavelle saw to it that this was duly publicized, and lauded, in the *Freeman's Journal*.

O'Connell was now in a still more awkward fix. His wife, who was with him in London, declared herself 'strongly against [his] taking any part'. He himself thought that he should 'merely stand by' and do no more than reply to some speaker towards the close of the debate. 'It is cruel to have my plan deranged by this interloper [O'Connor]', he fretted, 'His debate can do nothing but mischief.'[30] Whether or not O'Connor had been bluffing or whether he was sobered by O'Connell's threat virtually to disavow him, O'Connor in the end withdrew his motion, though only on the very day set down for it to be debated. But meanwhile O'Connell had been trapped. Earlier he had promised his own parliamentary 'party' that he would himself propose a motion in favour of Repeal when parliament re-assembled in 1834. In giving the undertaking (to which he was driven by fear of defeat in one or other of the meetings held earlier in June), he had argued that the delay was necessary in order to prepare the ground by petitions and to ensure full and fair reportage in the press. Even if this was not altogether disingenuous, O'Connell's dominant objective was postponement *per se* – much in the spirit of St Augustine's prayer, 'Lord, give me chastity, but do not give it yet.'

He may well have hoped, originally, to evade his commitment for the next parliamentary session: he had, after all, proved himself to be the Houdini of Irish Political Promises over many years. But the maintenance of the campaign for the immediate discussion of Repeal by O'Connor, Reynolds and Lavelle rendered escape virtually impossible. O'Connell bowed – temporarily, at least – to the inevitable, and began to prepare 'the People of Ireland' for an offensive by a series of public letters. 'There is', noted the young Dublin physician, William Stokes, in his journal on 27 June 1833, 'a bawling fellow under the window just now crying, "Counsellor O'Connell's most important letter to the People of Ireland to *terrify* them to have the Parliament in Ireland, for the small charge of one halfpenny." This *is* a most comical country!'[31] In a mood of gloomy resignation, O'Connell told Fitzpatrick on 5 July, 'I will now begin in earnest to prepare myself for the contest. All my fame, alas, as an orator and statesman depends on *this* exertion.' So low had his spirit sunk that he went on to instruct Fitzpatrick, who was about to set forth from Dublin on a tour of Ireland to raise money for the O'Connell Tribute, 'Wait a few days before you begin *your circuit*. Let the *discussion* question be at rest first.'[32]

Perhaps O'Connell did not despair altogether of putting off Repeal beyond even 1834. He certainly cultivated Littleton (who fully realized that he was the target of 'O'Connell's coaxing' and himself hoped to tempt O'Connell out of politics by offering him the Irish Mastership of the Rolls) during the remainder of 1833. As early as 24 July, Littleton recorded that

O'Connell today thanked me privately in the House of Commons for having muzzled in some degree the Irish newspapers, as far as personal abuse of him went; and told me that I was the only Irish Secretary who had ever evinced a disposition to afford publicity and enquiry into Irish abuses – which I really believe to be true.[33]

In wooing Littleton, O'Connell may well have hoped to gain enough concessions from the whigs to warrant his launching a 'Justice for Ireland' experiment. Not the least merit of such a move, in his eyes, would be that Repeal could be held in abeyance until it was apparent that the 'experiment' had failed. It was probably with some such objective in view that, on 20 October 1833, O'Connell sounded his Cork 'manager', William Fagan, about arranging a meeting which he might address. He was uncharacteristically tentative. 'Let the matter drop', he told Fagan, 'if there be any indisposition to put it on its *right legs* again.' Obviously in the hope of winning back O'Connor, he asked that the county members be invited: 'O'Connor may be a little self-willed occasionally, but he is calculated to be a useful man.'[34] This proved a gross mistake. When at the public dinner held in his honour in the Cork Chamber of Commerce on 4 November, O'Connell invited the government to undermine Repeal by introducing generous remedial measures, O'Connor challenged him repeatedly with contemptuous interjections. When it came to his turn to speak, O'Connor called on all Irishmen to fight for 'repeal, the whole repeal and nothing but repeal',[35] and with fatal aptness described O'Connell's attitude to Repeal as akin to Frankenstein's towards his monster. This finally turned the key upon O'Connell. To be shown up before the 250 leading nationalists of the leading nationalist city in the country was unendurable. Now there really was nothing for it but to face the music in the House of Commons.

IV

'The year 1834', wrote O'Neill Daunt much later, 'was rendered remarkable by the introduction of the Repeal question into the House of Commons. O'Connell told me he was forced to take this step, bitterly against his will. "I felt", said he, "like a man who was going to jump into a cold bath, but I was obliged to take the plunge." '[36] Despite his announcement in June 1833 that he would 'bring them [notices of his motion] on the next thing after the King's Speech is dismissed',[37] O'Connell selected a comparatively late date in the session, 22 April 1834, for the commencement of the debate. He seems to have put off his preparations as long as possible; but by early April he could delay no longer. He soon felt himself to have been all too well justified in his earlier foreboding. 'I never felt *so nervous* about anything', he told Staunton on 9 April,

as I do about my Repeal effort. It will be my worst. I sink beneath the load. My materials are confused and totally without arrangement. I wish you *could* come here and bring MacCabe [the chief reporter on the *Morning Register*]. I would readily be at the entire expense; but you should come without delay. In fact it is at the last moment I venture to write to you on this subject. I say venture, because I am convinced there will be nothing in my speech deserving recollection or any extraordinary exertion, by my friends. It is quite true that I have often desponded before a public exertion and afterwards succeeded, but this cannot now be the case. I feel for the first time *overpowered*. Well, can you come to me? Can you bring MacCabe? If I had in the Galleries here such a reporter as he is of my speeches, sinking the weak points and mending the best, I would stand high among orators. But it is in vain to dwell on minor points.[38]

He showered Fitzpatrick with requests for reference books and other materials for his address, and oscillated wildly between hope and dejection. In successive sentences, he planned to turn his speech into a pamphlet, if MacCabe would help him; observed, 'But, after all, I can make but little, miserably little, of my subject. Would to God it were in abler hands!'; and resolved to reorganize the Repeal agitation radically the 'moment we are defeated'![39]

O'Connell's speech introducing his motion for a select committee to inquire into the effects of the Act of Union reads flatly. The 'case' he stated was exclusively legal and utilitarian. For five hours he trawled through Irish history since 1246 for evidence that Ireland had been constitutionally wronged and economically sacrificed by her more powerful neighbour. The fact that he was interrupted only once – and that after his first few sentences – probably tells its own story. 'O'Connell', one sympathetic listener noted, 'was encouraged by the cheers of the Irish voices alone, and, as far as any symptoms of the perception of his argument by any of the English members present was concerned, his orations might as well have been bestowed upon the inmates of a deaf and dumb asylum.'[40] O'Connell was mildly boastful once it was over. 'I never felt more buoyant in spirits . . .', he told Fitzpatrick, 'When an accurate report of my speech appears, as it will without delay, from the notes of Mr McCabe, with the documentary illustrations, I *do* think it will make an impression in Ireland.'[41] But this may have been nothing more than the ordinary light-headed reaction to the end of a long-dreaded ordeal. While he was delivering his speech, he could not but have felt that he was undergoing a prescribed, mechanical, and ultimately unmeaning exercise.

After O'Connell's speech had been countered by a still lengthier address from Spring-Rice (now chancellor of the exchequer), the hostile majority became increasingly impatient as the 'debate' meandered over three more nights. A personal attack on O'Connell by Henry Lambert, a Catholic liberal MP for co. Wexford whom O'Connell had denounced for his tergiversation on the Irish coercion bill, provided their solitary interval of glee. Lambert declared that the Tribute which

> once was a voluntary effusion, now became an exaction of contrivance and a management of tact and business; and when he reflected, that places of public worship were desecrated, and made scenes of dissension and turbulence, for the sake of collecting this rent from the impoverished peasantry, he felt it his duty to . . . express his feelings to the House . . . his family were obliged to abstain from a place of worship, merely to avoid Mr O'Connell's jackalls [sic], who, during the whole Sunday were enforcing the tribute.[42]

Lambert was to pay dearly for his half-hour of British glory; O'Connell saw to it that he never sat again for Wexford or any other seat. His own Repealers remained steadfast; all but one supported him in the lobbies – even if rumour had it that some bewailed their commitment privately. But he secured no other vote except that of an eccentric English opponent of Repeal who none the less approved of an inquiry into the workings of the Act of Union. On 29 April 1834 the motion was defeated by an immense majority, 523 to 38.

Now O'Connell truly was released. Superficially, he had been humiliated, his weakness nakedly exposed. How could he hope to gain thirty British votes in the House of Commons, let alone the three hundred he would need to carry Repeal through even the first stage of its journey towards enactment. He had stirred English nationalism, and it had rent him, politically, limb from limb. Yet it was not with false jauntiness but with a genuine ease and renewal of confidence that he wrote to Fitzpatrick ten days after his defeat, 'Now I laugh at the chuckling triumph of our silly and mercenary Irish Unionists. Poor creatures! they are like the Indian savages who occasionally in dark nights fear that the sun is extinguished for ever and will never rise again. Naboclish!!*[43] O'Connell's happy recoil is far from incompre-

*A corruption of the Gaelic 'Ná bac leis', meaning 'Never mind'.

hensible. It was only on the surface that O'Connell's own politics in 1833–4 (or 1830–2, for that matter) appeared to be 'manic-depressive' in type, with rapid swings from enthusiasm to revulsion. Such an impression obscures their steady trend. Beneath the incessant public gyrations we can discern a persistent endeavour to reach an understanding with the whigs. It was, in O'Connell's eyes, the strategy that promised most advantage at least cost. He had no desire to campaign squarely for Repeal or to launch another mass agitation if he could make significant political progress otherwise. Each was useful, even necessary, as a threat. But both seemed, at this juncture, distasteful, unpromising, and dangerous as actualities. Thus, the defeated motion – and not least the scale of the defeat – was far from an unmitigated loss. It freed O'Connell to deploy a hopeful strategy which the campaign to bring Repeal before the House of Commons had long immobilized.

The essence of the strategy was to exploit the disagreements in the whig cabinet and party on the issue of Irish tithes. It was clear by 1834 that the Grey-Stanley faction would swallow a degree of internal reform of the Church of Ireland, but insist on its retaining its revenues intact lest this bulwark of British control in Ireland be undermined. Conversely, Russell, Althorp and their followers regarded the 'surplus' of these revenues as a sort of stake-money which might be drawn on to buy some relief from the Irish pressures in the House of Commons; to them, moreover, the Irish established church constituted the least defensible of all the anomalies in the machinery of British rule. Only three days after the defeat of the Repeal motion, O'Connell's friend, David Roche, MP for Limerick city, proposed a resolution for reducing the tithes *in toto* by 20 per cent, and their burden upon the occupiers by 60 per cent. O'Connell himself renewed this proposal on 6 May, with the additional object of procuring 'a share of the fund for Hospitals, Infirmaries, Dispensaries and [Catholic] Glebes'.[44] Although the government refused to endorse the scheme, O'Connell's principal purpose in promoting it was secured when Lord John Russell (without informing any of the colleagues) announced – in effect – that he accepted the principle of appropriating Irish ecclesiastical surpluses for secular ends. In little more than a week the wheel had come full circle. It was now O'Connell's turn to capitalize, if he could, upon the embarrassment of his antagonists.

He proceeded to play out the rubber with great skill. Through Sir Francis Burdett he let the government know that 'he would answer for quieting' Ireland should his tithe plan be adopted;[45] meanwhile all agitation would be suspended and Repeal lie dormant. But how was such a programme of inaction to be sold to the faithful at home, who smarted under the brutal rebuff of 29 April? As Reynolds had already set in train the calling of major protest meetings in Dublin and perhaps elsewhere, O'Connell ordered Fitzpatrick on 7 May 1834 to call upon the firebrand immediately and

> beg of him not to agitate for a Repeal meeting for the present. This is a critical moment and I am endeavouring to make the most of it for Ireland. Either the Ministry will concede to me the Tithe question or they will not. If . . . no concession is made, then I will be able to recommence the Repeal agitation with tenfold force after having given this fair and fortunate trial to the British Parliament.
>
> You must not suppose that there is the least relaxation in my opinions on the subject of the Repeal. My conviction on that subject is really unalterable, but I will get *what I can* and use the Repeal *in terrorem* merely until it is wise and necessary to recommence the agitation. It is quite discreet not to give the Ministry any excuse for further coercive measures or for continuing any part of the Coercion Bill.[46]

Next day he followed this up with a still more desperate appeal to beard

> my friend Reynolds as speedily as possible, and give him in strict confidence my most anxious advice not to call any meeting *directly* or *indirectly* on the subject of the Repeal for some weeks. He is not a man to yield to mere authority although I do believe he has some confidence in me, but he will yield to a just and sound reason. Now that reason is, that the parliament are ready to enact any law, however atrocious, to meet Repeal agitation. My game therefore is, and it ought to be that of every sound Repealer, to suspend any demonstration on our part until the session shall be so far advanced as not to leave time for any other Coercion Bill . . . If, while I take this line on the one hand and Ireland is silent on the other, any further coercive attempt is made, see on what strong grounds I shall be able to oppose it, and what a Repeal reawaking speech I shall be able to make in that opposition! Put this view before Reynolds and other honest Repealers and I think they will be likely to concur with me in a short postponement of any meeting. I am working the Tithe question *well* . . . Implore, then, of Reynolds and of the other honest Repealers to allow my experiment its full development. He may depend on it that the cause of Repeal will not, and *shall not*, suffer by a short postponement of *direct* agitation.[47]

But O'Connell's initial letter had sufficed to stop the Dublin radicals in their tracks. As Fitzpatrick later recalled, its arrival 'prevented the publication of a formidable requisition for a meeting to renew the Repeal agitation. The requisition was actually in type, but the subscribers deferred at once to O'Connell's recommendation.'[48]

The policy of 'lying-doggo' paid its first dividend on 27 May 1834. In the absence of Irish pressures which might have re-cemented their unity, the whig ministry split on the appropriation issue; Stanley, Sir James Graham and two other ministers resigned from the cabinet. O'Connell was disappointed in the replacements – 'There never was a mountain in labour [which] produced a more ridiculous mouse' – although he was pleased that Stanley, 'the worst of the bad in everything which relates to Ireland', was gone, and that in the general reshuffle his Irish liberal friend, Richard More O'Ferrall, became a lord of the treasury: 'it is a brain blow to [the] Orange party . . . in Ireland'.[49] But he confidently expected that the reconstituted ministry would at least allow the Irish Coercion Act, due shortly for renewal, to lapse. Accordingly, his fury was unbounded when he learned, from Althorp's statement in the Commons on 16 June, that 'this mean, dastard, rascally administration have determined to renew the Coercion Bill! The scoundrels!!!' At once, he told Fitzpatrick to announce to Ireland that his Repeal speech was being prepared for publication, as the first shot in a new campaign.

> I will set about preparing it without delay. I have begun and will proceed with 'the Repeal'. My experiment has been perfectly successful. I have shown that the most energetic anxiety to conciliate the British Government and British Parliament is totally useless. We humbly ask for bread; they give us a stone. Well, can there be one wretch so base found as to consent to wait longer before he becomes a Repealer?[50]

The threat had immediate effect. As Macintyre observes, 'the section of the Cabinet anxious to conciliate O'Connell were prepared to go to any lengths' to prevent his being driven into hostility again.[51] After hurried internal negotiations with other ministers, Littleton, with Althorp's approval, met O'Connell privately and left him with the distinct impression that the key clause to which O'Connell objected, the ban on public meetings, would be dropped. In fact, the prime minister, Grey, in terror that this would open the door to a fresh Repeal agitation, insisted upon its retention. Of course, this second 'betrayal' relit O'Connell's rage, and he proceeded to reveal to the House of Commons his version of Littleton's approach to him on 20 June, and the subsequent parleying *sub rosa*. Though Littleton disputed this account, O'Connell's exposé precipitated yet another cabinet crisis, which this time ended in Grey's resignation. Melbourne succeeded him as prime minister.

Generally speaking, O'Connell was justified when he laid claim, about 11 July 1834, to the role of arbiter in the current parliamentary circumstances.

> It was I, in fact, that turned out the Administration. I get this credit from everybody; and if the next be not better we will turn that out also. From the moment Littleton told me that Lord Wellesley [the Irish viceroy] and he himself were adverse to the Coercion Bill, the game was in my hands if I did not throw it away . . . My victory is therefore admitted by everybody to be complete, and its ultimate results will, I think, be eminently useful to Ireland. We are on the way from a half Whig, half Tory Government to one half Radical, half Whig, without the slightest admixture of Toryism. The moment such a Ministry is formed there will be a famous *turning off* in Ireland. The Attorney-General will certainly be dismissed, and the entire Orange clique will go with him.[52]

Less than three weeks later O'Connell proved his power when on 30 July he proposed and carried two vital amendments to the government's Irish tithes bill. Under the revised bill, all tithe arrears were to be forgone, and the tithe burden on occupiers was to be reduced by 40 per cent, half of the shortfall to be met by the state and half to be absorbed by the Church of Ireland itself. This concluded neatly the counter-attack launched by O'Connell on 6 May. He had gained (so far as victory in the Commons could do so) the substance of his original proposal which had meanwhile served to re-shape the cabinet to his liking.

It was a masterly recovery from the débâcle of the Repeal motion. Yet we should not forget that for more than a year and a half, ever since the general election of 1832 was first bruited, Repeal had been O'Connell's broadsword in working towards a transformation of the whig government and preparing the way for some lasting compact with them. It was of course ironic that the issue of Repeal was of most use to O'Connell when he undertook finally not to use it! But this was in the nature of the game to which he was committed, and did not necessarily imply a cynical indifference to constitutional ends. There remained a level at which O'Connell saw himself as still pursuing Ireland's legislative independence. No rock-climber (he might have said) would attempt to ascend directly to the summit, or even to ascend continuously; Odysseus did not despair of ultimately gaining the Ithacan shore because he was continually diverted.

CHAPTER 17

St Martin's Summer

1834–6

I

And we'll plant a laurel tree,
And we'll call it 'Victory',
Said the Shan Van Vocht,

so O'Connell exulted in a letter of 31 July 1834 to Fitzpatrick.[1] He
was cheering his own achievement in securing the amendments to the
Irish tithe bill in the House of Commons, the repudiation of all claims
to arrears and the reduction of future tithe payments by 40 per cent.
These were, he continued, ' "pour commencer," as they say at Paris
. . . I see no reason why more of the same dose may not be useful for the
next *draft*.'[2] This struck the note of political joyousness which
O'Connell was to sustain, with scarcely a break, throughout the long
campaign to consolidate his initial victory. Immediately he met
disappointments. His amendments, together with the Irish tithe bill as
a whole, were thrown out by 'the scoundrel Lords' on 11 August;[3] and
his first trial of his influence with the new ministry – a ferocious
attempt to get the serving 'Orange' attorney-general, Blackburne,
removed from office – failed completely. But he was quite undaunted,
and looked to the next parliamentary session for another assault not
only on tithes but also on the Irish municipal corporations. What
sustained him was the shift in the power centre of the whig-liberal
party. Melbourne himself was scarcely less reactionary, or disdainful
of O'Connell and his tail, than Grey; and he also spoke for such
ministers as Lords Lansdowne and Palmerston, to say nothing of the
king. But leading liberals in and out of the new cabinet, in particular,
Duncannon, now home secretary, Edward Ellice, the party manager,
Littleton and the 'advanced' Henry Warburton, were reconciled to the
necessity, and perhaps even desirability, of Irish reform and of frank
and open dealing with O'Connell. Between August 1834 and April

1835, O'Connell's primary objective was to secure the dominance of this element within a whig ministry which depended on Irish votes for its survival.

O'Connell returned to Derrynane by way of Waterford ('the state of cholera in that town [Dublin] . . .', he wrote, 'makes me unwilling to go there'[4]) on 18 August 1834, and remained in Kerry for almost three months. Although he threw himself into hare-hunting and the entertainment of his numerous visitors with his accustomed gusto, much of this time was spent in managing politics, from a distance. His first care was to play down Repeal and direct popular pressure into more profitable channels. As Fitzpatrick advised him on 20 August, when a revival of the Dublin Trades Political Union threatened, 'your most judicious course would be to address the *quondam* Trades at once exhorting them not to give a chance to their enemies . . . by renewing a description of agitation inapplicable to the crisis and the objects of the country'.[5] This particular danger was averted. 'The Repealers will, I hope,' O'Connell laid down, 'see the propriety of allowing the Tithe question to take precedence.'[6] In a series of public letters, he declared that he had at last abandoned his attempt to conciliate the Orange faction as hopeless: 'I am now – and for ever – convinced that Orangeism must be put down.'[7] Practically, his new policy implied a concentrated attack on the privileges of the established church and the municipal corporations, which in turn implied cooperation with the ministry. The government had foreshadowed reforms on both these fronts in the king's speech closing parliament. On 27 August O'Connell told Fitzpatrick that

> the impulse should be given by the establishment of County Liberal clubs and Liberal clubs in every town. Parochial meetings to get up petitions for the abolition of tithes should also be held as speedily and as numerously as possible. It is of vital importance that a great stir should be made as soon as possible to show the determination of the people universally to get rid of the blood-stained impost of tithes. I am greatly inclined to confine the agitation as much as can be to the tithe question. If we could but get an universal expression of detestation of tithes, it would secure our victory in the next session.
>
> The Corporate Reform will be the first measure of that session. The present Ministry *must* carry that measure; and what a blow it will be to the late ascendant party![8]

No formidable anti-tithe campaign was developed during the autumn of 1834; still less was the scheme for a universal Irish network of Liberal Clubs realized. None the less O'Connell's general strategy succeeded. Repeal was quietly and rancourlessly withdrawn from the public's attention – apart from an occasional healthy reminder to the whigs that it might readily be wheeled on-stage again. Meanwhile, the declaration of war upon the Irish tories enabled O'Connell both to press harder for changes in the personnel of the Irish administration and to forge further links with the forward section of the liberal party. It also enabled him to demonstrate to the government that he could 'deliver' his Irish support, as well as restrain the violence and disorder of the masses. As he made the point delicately to Duncannon on 2 October 1834, 'I had no notion that I could so long keep down active agitation by the popular party. But I perceive that there is more of tact in the public than I could have believed. They see, as I do, that our business is to allow the Orange faction to display its hostility.'[9]

While keeping the chosen Irish issues at a comfortable simmer until parliament reassembled in November, O'Connell focused his energy on securing more congenial Irish appointments. Law offices took pride of place: he believed that these largely determined the character of executive action. Accordingly, he renewed his importunities to seize the chance of a vacant judgeship to remove Blackburne from the attorney-generalship, stipulating that it was of equal importance that he be not replaced by the solicitor-general, another anti-O'Connellite, Crampton. On 2 September he even sent Duncannon a list of 'the liberal barristers fit for that office [the Irish attorney-generalship]' – Holmes, Michael O'Loghlen, Perrin, Richards, Keatinge and 'Mr Pigot, a young man but of great, very great legal knowledge . . . Would be, I trust will be one day, an ornament to the Bench'. O'Loghlen and Pigot were Catholics, and O'Connell added the significant rider, 'if emancipation is not to continue to be a dead letter, you will not pass over Sergeant O'Loghlen'.[10] He followed up his pressure on Duncannon, which also took the form of four public letters published between 5 September and 11 October 1834, by similar appeal-menaces directed to Ellice and another sympathetic and influential liberal, James Abercromby.

As things fell out, it was Crampton who was raised to the judiciary; Blackburne remained attorney-general and O'Loghlen filled Crampton's place. O'Connell was furious. Yet, had it not been for accidents of personality, Blackburne would have ended on the bench, with Perrin, the third of O'Connell's nominees, attorney-general. This is what the government had attempted to achieve. Such men as Duncannon, Ellice and Abercromby were already anxious that O'Connell should be satisfied, so far as practicable. In fact, in several ways the episode foreshadows his later dealings with the whigs in power. Often he did not gain immediately the appointment for which he pressed. If he had 'friends' in the upper ranges of Melbourne's administration, so also had he enemies or ill-wishers – Melbourne himself and his coterie, and chief of all William IV. Equally, however, 'O'Connell's men' rarely failed to get their preferment in the end. Four of the Irish attornies-general appointed during Melbourne's second government (1835–41) were drawn from O'Connell's original list of six. Of course, it does not follow that the credit for this belongs – sole and entire – to O'Connell. Some were obvious choices for the liberals. None the less the desire, or supposed necessity, to appease him was a major consideration in every such decision.

Although it was still early days, with the high whig repugnance to O'Connell as yet scarcely tempered by experience, his applications during the autumn of 1834 extended well beyond the range of legal offices and were answered with extraordinary compliancy by his governmental allies. Despite O'Connell's bitter words in private and calculated public *exposés*, Duncannon kept on terms, insisting that he sincerely welcomed and would do his best to adopt O'Connell's 'suggestions' for preferment, even though 'I must now repeat to you that I should be acting unfairly by them – those with whom I am particularly connected – if I made promises or gave assurances that it did not depend on me to perform'.[11] Ellice pleaded the difficulties of making sudden and sweeping changes, and of dealing with the vested interests of incumbents. 'In saying this however', he went on,

> I do not mean to express an opinion in favour of the employment of adverse or unwilling instruments in the direction and execution of liberal measures. On this point I have long entertained sentiments not dissimilar from those you express and Ireland is not the only country, or the administration of her affairs the only department in which the Whig Government have suffered serious inconvenience and injury from a policy for which too much respect for the feelings and interests of individuals and an accession to power after fifty years' exclusion are the best excuse.

As an earnest of goodwill, Ellice acceded to O'Connell's request to take up the case of the widow of his cousin, Darby Mahony, formerly an officer in the 16th Foot: she sought an army pension. 'Although in principle ... an economist', Ellice assured O'Connell, 'I am no advocate for saving public money at the expense of meritorious officers.'[12] While we may discount a little for judicious flattery, there is no reason to believe that the leaders of the liberal *avant garde* were

substantially disingenuous in dealing with O'Connell. Their fundamental interest marched side by side with his – for the stretch of road
now coming into sight, at least. They were deeply anxious to check a
tory revival – above all a tory return to power – and to increase their
own influence and share of offices within the whig-liberal complex;
they were also sincere advocates of a radical reform of the finances of
the Church of Ireland. Obviously, O'Connell held the key to even the
partial realization of their hopes.

O'Connell's immediate gains in September and October 1834 may
have been small, but the very fact that he had begun to make inroads
on the exclusive system of local Irish power was enough for present
jubilation. When Melbourne assumed office in July 1834, no Catholic
had yet been appointed a judge or a law officer or a stipendiary
magistrate. None had ever been an O'Connellite supporter, scarcely
any, even an active liberal. It was this which made the first shoot or
two, with the promise of a much greater crop to come, seem so
significant in the later months of 1834. On 22 October, *The Times*,
which still backed the right-wing whigs, expressed its and their
outrage at 'the monster's' pretension. His public letters, it declared,

> all said in plain, though not the most civil or modest, language – I,
> O'Connell, am 'the people of Ireland;' and if you don't put the
> Government of the country into the hands of the *'people of Ireland*,' you
> shall be d—— everlastingly ... To that Moloch [the Repeal cause] he
> would sacrifice not merely all the freedom and discretionary power of the
> King's advisers in their present and future nominations to office, but, to
> multiply the victims of his ferocious idol, he would, without a shadow of
> equity, decency, or apology, dismiss from his situation every man who has
> not been baptized in the waters of bitterness and hatred against the existing
> Constitution, and against the connexion of Ireland with Great Britain ...

This was the cry of a raging wounded animal, of a caste whose
monopoly was being breached. Conversely, O'Connell himself was
blithe as air. 'My own opinion of politics', he told Fitzpatrick on 11
November, 'is to the last degree favourable to Ireland. I do think we
are approaching a great national triumph.'[13]

II

Meanwhile O'Connell believed that he was about to breach another
monopoly of the ruling caste, and to approach another national
triumph, during the second half of 1834. He founded a bank. At first
sight this may seem bizarre. O'Connell had lived most of his adult life

on the edge of financial ruin, and for years his time had been engrossed by the most strenuous politics of every kind. But, although a marplot in handling his own affairs, he was otherwise a first-rate man of business, with serious, if sometimes eccentric, views on current fiscal and economic issues. Correspondingly, his incursion into Irish banking was, primarily, politics by other means. He may have hoped to increase his capital and London dignity thereby. But his principal purpose was to reduce the domination of the Ascendancy in Ireland, and strengthen instead the nationalist-liberal-Repeal interest.

On 13 June 1834 O'Connell told another would-be entrepreneur that 'the "Irish National Bank" . . . is about to be formed under my auspices . . . The more banks in Ireland the better, provided they be founded on a sound banking principle, and not merely got up by schemers or over-speculative persons.'[14] Three weeks later he and his committee, which included his son Maurice and several others of his personal following in the House of Commons, issued the prospectus of what he now termed the 'National Bank of Ireland'. This stressed its anticipated commercial superiority to the Bank of Ireland and Provincial Bank, which then largely monopolized Irish banking but lacked, the prospectus continued, 'the ability, from the nature of the principles on which they are founded, to confer any decided advantages, on Ireland'.[15] The Bank of Ireland was still primarily a central and metropolitan bank, with a statutorily established monopoly of branch banking within a radius of some sixty miles of Dublin. The Provincial, despite its name, had set up a mere 21 branches in its nine years of operation. The prospectus allowed that the Provincial could boast some remarkable achievements, but discerned two fundamental weaknesses in its development, over-centralization and the failure to 'unite itself with a body in Ireland, with whom to share its profits, as well as to fortify itself on a principle'.[16] 'O'Connell's Bank' would remedy the first by devolution – subsidiary local banks owned half locally and half by a London parent company – and the second by extending Irish banking facilities much more widely geographically and much deeper socially. Under the first head at least, the National lived up to its word. After a year's operation – its doors first opened for business at Carrick-on-Suir on 28 January 1835 – it was running twenty-seven branches, and several of these in places without any existing bank. In O'Connell's own county, Kerry, for example, it was already serving not only Tralee but also Cahirciveen, Listowel, Killarney and Killorglin. From the start the National set out to attract small capital as well as large, by paying interest on current accounts, by preferential interest on deposit accounts below £30, by offering extra-banking financial services for a small commission and – significantly – by waiving all charges for religious and charitable institutions. By the beginning of 1836, it had already more share-holders than the Provincial (773 to 644).

The prospectus failed, however, to mention O'Connell's leading reason for launching a new financial institution. The 'new bank . . .', he wrote confidentially to Fitzpatrick on 8 July 1834, 'has been for a great while a subject of anxious speculation with me. I have sensibly felt the want of a counter-check to the rascality of the Bank of Ireland and of the Provincial Bank. You know that they play into the hands of the Anti-Irish party. I want a *mutual friend* at the other side.'[17] With some justice, O'Connell regarded the Bank of Ireland as a bulwark of the Anglo-Irish (and in particular the Dublin mercantile) establish-ment; and although the Provincial was less tory in complexion as well as governance (Spring-Rice was one of its leading spirits), it was certainly no friend to nationalists. In O'Connell's estimation, the major Irish banks had long denied his camp both capital and credit. He therefore had no scruples about making them (together with local Munster savings banks), the targets of 'runs for gold' in 1830, 1831 and 1833, in order to bring pressure on governments in various crises. None of the runs proved especially damaging financially. But O'Connell had undoubtedly added a small weapon to his political armoury. It was costly and laborious to carry and distribute sufficient quantities of gold to meet these sudden demands. At the least, he could preen himself on causing trouble and creating expense for his Irish enemies.

As usual, sectarianism intertwined with politics. O'Connell, like many others of his class and kind, believed that the Bank of Ireland and Provincial were deeply inimical to Catholic as well as nationalist interests, although – business being business – they of course included some Catholics among their customers. In response to the conviction that they were discriminated against, a group of Catholic merchants in Dublin had established their own bank, the Hibernian, in 1825, in which O'Connell himself took a small amount of stock. But the Hibernian was discriminated against in turn. Unlike the politically influential Provincial, it was confined to Dublin and denied the right to issue notes which, in contemporary circumstances, doomed it to operate on a very small scale. Thus, while secure enough in its Dublin Catholic mercantile base, the Hibernian was no answer to what O'Connell thought of as the pressing need, a bank for Catholics and

Repealers upon a national scale. 'We want a bank of our own', he declared in Dublin on 5 December, in which customers would be neither rejected nor disadvantaged because of their 'politics and religion'.[18]

In the title of his bank, 'National' was really meant in two senses. It set out to provide both a comprehensive network for the whole island and a financial organization for Repealers. As well as eight of the originating committee being Repeal MPs, four of the first directors were O'Connell himself (as Governor), his son, Maurice, and his son-in-law, Fitz-Simon, and Cornelius O'Brien who sat for co. Clare. Indeed, the whole venture depended on O'Connell's Irish fame. Two of the resolutions passed unanimously at a meeting of the Bank's organizing committee held on 15 October 1834 read, 'That it would be of very great importance to the welfare of the Bank that the Bust of Mr O'Connell should appear upon all the notes of each Branch' and 'That Mr Reynolds shall be desired to consult with Mr O'Connell as to holding meetings and establishing Committees in three or four additional influential [Irish] Towns, without delay.'[19]

At the same time, the founding committee included some City MPs and the first board some London moneymen, among them, T. Lamie Murray, an able disciple of the great banking reformer, Thomas Joplin. Thus, despite its Irish nationalism, the National had access from the start to London capital and expertise, and these must have contributed something to its early success. Moreover, the prospectus notwithstanding, it rapidly moved back to an 'over-centralization' as marked as the Provincial's. Indeed, it was always more centralized than its launching rhetoric would suggest, for the London parent company retained 'supreme control' of lending as well as a veto over all proposed new subsidiaries and local directorates. As O'Connell had written at the outset, when – but only when – 'a sum large enough to establish a branch bank in any locality is subscribed, the London managers will double the amount'.[20] In any event, as early as 1837 the subsidiary company system had proved so cumbersome that all these companies except two (Clonmel and Carrick-on-Suir) were amalgamated with the London parent; and within two decades even the two survivors were swallowed up.

Thus the whole enterprise was paradoxical in a way that reflected a dualism in O'Connell's own situation and disposition. On the one hand, the National was the most cosmopolitan and sophisticated of Irish banks. It alone was asked to join – at that at a comparatively early stage – the profoundly influential London Clearing House; it alone had a London headquarters and close and continuous connections with the City. On the other hand, initially at least, it reached lower and spread wider in Irish society than either of its major rivals. It drew even the middle class of farmer and shopkeeper into its clientele; it tapped even the very small depositors; above all, it was the natural resource of the ordinary Catholic customer, and especially of the Catholic Church in its rapidly developing need of financial services. It does not seem extravagant to see all this as mirroring O'Connell's double-sidedness, as, on the one hand, an extra-Irish giant, the very symbol of European liberal Catholicism and secular British radicalism, and, on the other, the great Irish ethnogogue – to use Gladstone's telling word. At the second level, the National Bank promised jobs – to say nothing of jobbing – for O'Connell's particular circle and class. He told Fitzpatrick shortly before the bank's foundation, 'it is [a matter] of course that if we succeed it will be my anxious study that you, your brother [Hugh] and brother-in-law [J. C. Ayre], should participate in that success'.[21] In practice, O'Connell must have often come, in later years, to curse the power and patronage which was assumed to reside in him as Governor. He was to be subject to endless embarrassing appeals, from influential priests and other key Irish supporters, to intervene in Bank appointments or promotions, or take sides in local wrangles. None the less, the National was, in its own particular and circumscribed fashion, an exercise in self-government – at any rate, in O'Connell's estimation.

Viewed in certain lights, therefore, O'Connell's establishment of the National Bank might appear to have been a form of alternative or parallel institution, to provide a vital service for an alienated and frustrated element in society. Although his own financial, as well as other sorts of, ecumenism was genuine, the National was widely regarded, in its early years, as essentially confessional in character, essentially the bank of Irish Catholics and the Catholic Church. O'Connell's earlier venture into the most dynamic field of Dublin manufacture, porter-brewing, already dominated by the Protestant firm of Guinness, might be similarly represented. Unlike the formation of the Bank, the purchase of Madder's – re-named O'Connell's – Brewery in 1831 proved a failure. He himself lauded its product as 'the very best Irish porter I ever tasted . . . It is really superlative';[22] but too few of the public shared his taste. For all that, O'Connell's essay into a 'Protestant' business, and in particular his entrusting the management of the brewery to his son Daniel, Fitzpatrick and other Catholics, might perhaps also be regarded as an attempt to set up a rival structure in Ireland to match the island's underlying duality.

None the less, these appearances are probably deceptive. O'Connell would never countenance an open division in Irish society or national exclusiveness in any of his undertakings. Herein lay an as-yet hidden difference between him and the coming generation of Irish nationalists. One of the first manifestations of this divergence was Fagan's critique of O'Connell's rejection in 1838 of a proposal by a body of Cork merchants to institute a run on gold in protest against the House of Lords' rejection of an Irish municipal reform bill.

O'CONNELL's reason for . . . connecting himself with the Banking system of the country was because of the monopoly – the religious monopoly – carried out in the management of the Bank of Ireland, and because of the political influence exercised by that establishment. These were undoubtedly good reasons for getting up such a Company as the National Bank of Ireland, provided always that it was an Irish Bank . . . But be that as it may . . . we assert, as a truism, that a political agitator leading on millions, in a peaceful course, to obtain from a reluctant legislature their rights, should be unwholly unshackled and freed from a monetary system, the great principle of which is to leave things as they are, not to risk ruffling the surface of society, and to bear existing ills sooner than encounter unknown evils. In the ordinary affairs of life, these maxims may do well; but when a nation is struggling for justice, its leader should have no connexion with such a system. We therefore, always, since 1836, felt that there was an inconsistency in O'CONNELL's position as Governor of a Bank.[23]

But whether or not he was influenced by private or occupational interest in the particular case which Fagan criticized, O'Connell's was generally the larger and the wider view. He found no difficulty in inhabiting both an English and an Irish world. He saw no incompatibility between the flattering appearance of City man with access to the *arcana* of international money, and the uncomfortable realities of an agitator whose finances depended upon the pennies and threepences of the poor. London and Dublin were simply different fields of combat; the struggle itself was everywhere the same. Of nothing was this more true than politics proper, and never did these seem to open into more interesting possibilities than in the phase in which he set the National Bank afoot.

III

British politics were transformed by the death of Earl Spencer on 10 November 1834, which removed his heir Lord Althorp to the House of Lords, leaving behind the problem of who should succeed him as leader of the Commons. The obvious choice, Lord John Russell, was too close in views to the Duncannon group for Melbourne's comfort. William IV abruptly solved the whigs' conundrum for them by using the prime minister's difficulties as a pretext for replacing them in office by the tories. O'Connell's immediate reaction was one of contemptuous irritation. 'I have just heard of the change of Ministry . . .', he wrote, 'It is well that we are rid of the humbuggers.'[24] But this was merely the reflex response of disappointment. As soon as it was clear that the tories, although a minority in the Commons, would form a cabinet – it was not yet certain that Peel, then on vacation in Italy, would take over the premiership – O'Connell swung back immediately to his set position. '*We* are out. The Whigs are out', he wrote to his wife on 18 November 1834 from Cork, where he had just been fêted at a banquet in his honour,

> Peel is on the Continent and cannot be heard of for some weeks. In the meantime it is likely that the Radicals of Great Britain will rally and recommence political unions and all manner of agitation. We, Repealers, must take a dignified station. I believe I will be able to give the proper tone, at least I think so. I am on the whole exceedingly pleased. I do believe that you never were so near being the wife of a Minister of State as you are. But God's will be done. Whether it be so or not, if Wellington does not succeed in forming a Ministry or if he be turned out, our time will come in either case.
>
> The dinner here went off splendidly, nothing could be better, your husband the cock of the walk as usual.[25]

Although speaking specifically as a 'Repealer', he had leapt forward in imagination to taking up station himself in the next liberal administration or even cabinet!

Three days later, he summoned a meeting in Dublin of all 'sincere friends of Reform . . . to consider the best means of combining all the friends of Political amelioration, in opposition to the supporters of oligarchy and monopoly in Church and State'.[26] A number of Irish and two English MPs who happened to be in Dublin (one of them William Cobbett with whom O'Connell was currently on the warmest terms of friendship) attended: 'a great meeting', O'Connell rejoiced to Mary, 'where I . . . got them unanimously to agree to postpone the agitation of the Repeal until we drive Wellington from the ministry. I was greatly cheered.'[27] A Dublin tory journalist confirmed O'Connell's account in reporting to Wellington 'the presence of a good many of the Whig lawyerlings. Conway, the editor of the [*Dublin Evening*] *Post*, the government organ, appeared and made his peace with O'Connell – so that your Grace may be prepared for an *unprincipled* agitation'.[28] O'Connell had tested the water and felt its temperature to be right; and he proceeded on 24 November to launch his Anti-Tory Association, open to all Irish whigs, liberals, radicals and Repealers. O'Connell threw himself into the work. 'The new Association is going on swimmingly', he told Mary next day, 'We have already 110 [fully-subscribed] members, more in fact than we had after a year of the Catholic Association. We are preparing everywhere for battle.'[29] According to Fagan, O'Connell remained the Association's 'moving spirit'. It met three times a week, and 'At every meeting he delivered a long and effective speech. It has often been a subject of amazement, how even his fertile mind could thus day after day pour forth on the same topic a stream of uninterrupted eloquence and each day in a different form ... as a working speaker, untiring and practical, no man ever approached near him.'[30]

Many of the Irish liberals both resented and feared O'Connell's assumption of control over, and driving management of, the general election campaign. Even his 'protégés', Perrin and O'Loghlen, attempted – unsuccessfully – to set up an independent organization in Dublin. Perrin, in particular, believed that O'Connell was endeavouring to establish the 'principle that no liberal person shall come into parliament [for an Irish constituency] who shall not be bound hand and foot by him'.[31] But O'Connell had undercut the ground of Irish liberal 'independence'. 'This is a peculiar election', he told Mary on 3 December 1834, 'at which we [the Repealers] are ready to allow every or almost every anti-Tory in possession to continue so.'[32] In fact, with the sole exception of Lambert (whom O'Connell had earlier sworn would never again represent co. Wexford), all sitting Irish whig and liberal MPs were guaranteed O'Connellite support. This was much too tempting a prospect for any of them to run athwart him in the end, however great their initial anger at the demagogue's exorbitance. Even Perrin tried eventually to bargain with him on Lambert's case. The Repealers also swallowed what was for some a very bitter draught. Thus, Fr John Sheehan wrote from Waterford about the incumbents for the city:

To secure unanimity here I have made up my mind to support Barron and Wyse at the election . . . But I assure you that in doing so, I make a very great sacrifice of feeling. For Wyse's sense I have the poorest possible opinion. No man but a fool could in times like the present have a contempt for the people such as he has manifested. In Barron's honesty I have very little confidence . . . However as the cause of reform requires that we should take them I am satisfied to do so.[33]

A Killarney Repealer wrote in the same vein that although the 'conduct in private life [of Mullins, sitting member for co. Kerry] exceeds in turpitude his political recreancy . . . I have no doubt but the liberal men of Kerry would agree with you that for the purpose of defeating the enemy it is advisable to support' him.[34] Conversely, O'Connell exercised prudent restraint where necessary. His son John stood for Youghal not as a Repealer or even specifically as his father's supporter but as 'a reformer': this enabled the whig Duke of Devonshire's agent to let him run unopposed.

Once the Irish polling dates had been set for 9–27 January 1835, O'Connell threw himself tempestuously into electioneering. He remained in Dublin until late December, arranging candidate adoptions, funds and tactics in constituencies throughout the south and east. He seemed to touch everything, to be in touch with everyone; he practically forced himself into acceptance as a sort of national commander of the 'anti-tories'. Generally, he continued in tearing high spirits, sending cheerful news or predictions almost every day to Mary. 'Have you a mind to be Lady O'Connell, my own heart's darling love?', he asked her, on one occasion, 'Tomorrow you shall know more. Now I can only say I expect that this change [Melbourne's dismissal] will have the most fortunate results.'[35] His sole worry was his 'family party': three of his sons, his son-in-law Fitz-Simon and his nephew Morgan John O'Connell were also candidates. He fretted that Maurice's lackadaisical behaviour might lose him Tralee – 'I hope Maurice has not left Tralee too soon. It would be better for him to be there more frequently',[36] he told Mary on 5 December – and towards the end he began to fret lest he himself should fail in Dublin city: he feared that many of his freeholders would be disqualified because of their rates arrears or perjure themselves by falsely claiming to have paid them up to date. In the event, his entire family 'tail' was returned successfully, although his apprehension for himself was eventually justified when on 16 May 1836 Ruthven (his running-mate) and he were unseated for Dublin on petition.

Although the 'anti-tories' lost nine Irish seats in all, they remained in a large majority in Ireland, 65 to 40. With justice O'Connell claimed that he controlled at least 60 of the Irish 'liberal' members; 34 of these might even have been classified as Repealers, though of varying degrees of fervour. Given this result, was he to attempt again to constitute an independent Irish party? From the day that the whigs lost office, he had endeavoured to make common cause with them and the English radicals. This was not necessarily a permanent commitment. Obviously, his course after the general election depended on its final outcome, even if his own preference would be to continue the alliance which he himself had done so much to initiate and sustain. As things turned out, his parliamentary contingent held, theoretically speaking, the balance of power in the House of Commons. While precision in allocating members to parties was impossible in 1835, it looked, after the general election, as if the tories might muster up to 300 votes, the whig-liberals up to 200, and the assorted radicals 90 or so between them. It seemed, on paper, the ideal 'Parnellite' situation in which an Irish 'brigade' of members could make and unmake British governments.

But this appearance was misleading. O'Connell in the 1830s could not conceivably have played the part of a Parnell in the 1880s. First, political allegiance was much looser in the earlier phase. In 1834–5, it seemed quite on the cards that, given over-pressure by O'Connell, a considerably body of the whigs might coalesce with the Peelite tories to form a secure centre party. Secondly, O'Connell's control over his 'tail' fell far short of Parnell's iron command of a ferociously disciplined party; in particular, a fair number of the O'Connellites were prepared, not to say eager, to be lured, by place or office, to the official benches. Thirdly, O'Connell (unlike Parnell) was still deeply enmeshed in the Catholic question; the fight to *realize* Emancipation, even for the superior classes, was still in its beginning stage. Some share in state power seemed vital if any of the discriminatory system were to be dismantled and replaced; and in 1835 – as against, say, 1845 – there was no hope that the tories would enter any bargain with the Catholic clergy which might diminish the strength of their Irish 'garrison'. Finally, it must be stressed again that O'Connell was the pathfinder in popular-parliamentary politics. Parnell had all the maps deriving from O'Connell's explorations at his disposal, but almost every journey undertaken in the 1830s was a journey into the political unknown. Fifty years later the ground then being traversed was thoroughly familiar to conservatives, liberals and nationalists alike. They, too, were in their own way pioneers but not in the sense of

O'Connell's absolute originality. Nor should we forget, when all is said and done, that Parnellite 'independence' ended in a still closer and more 'fatal' liberal alliance than O'Connell's. An alliance was, after all, the logical conclusion to the accumulation of parliamentary treasure: sooner or later it must be spent in a commitment, or it would rust.

At any rate, O'Connell never wavered in course after the general election of 1835 was concluded. It was the high whigs who tacked backwards and forwards. The key question was whether or not they would pay the price of partial dependence on O'Connell in order to regain office; and the central figure in this decision was Lord John Russell. Ultimately, Russell was prepared to pay the price; his own reward would be leadership of the House of Commons and a decisive role in cabinet. But it was necessary for him to work through at least one layer – and possibly two layers – of intermediaries in reaching an understanding with O'Connell. He had to conceal any such dealing from Melbourne, initially, and, in the long run, from the world at large. It was also in O'Connell's interest that there should be no overt agreement – provided that the tacit bargain was firm and unambiguous.

The issue on which to challenge Peel's government was chosen carefully. Whigs, radicals and Irish of every hue would, it was hoped, rally behind the nomination of James Abercromby for the speakership. It was Warburton who, in respectful and even deferential letters to O'Connell, recruited him to the cause. On 20 January 1835 he wrote to O'Connell 'to enquire . . . (and I shall report your answer to the Whigs) whom you feel disposed to support as Speaker. All on this side of the water agree in thinking Abercromby the fit man . . . But in case he would not consent, whom would your friends agree to support? Spring Rice, Cutlar Ferguson, Bernal, Sir James Graham? or whom?'[37] But Abercromby proved complaisant – as of course did O'Connell in proferring his support; and, with Russell's implicit connivance, Warburton took the decisive step of sending O'Connell a bundle of printed invitations from Russell to attend the pre-sessional meeting of liberal MPs on 18 February at Lichfield House, Westminster. Duncannon probably acted as a secondary channel of whig communication with O'Connell at some stage in the business of his enlistment.

O'Connell responded eagerly to the invitation, writing directly to Russell on 13 February 1835 that he could count on the 62 or 'at the very lowest' 60 Irish MPs at O'Connell's disposal. Using the pretext of averting civil war in Ireland now that Peel had set loose 'the sanguinary Orange gang', O'Connell went on to

> promise that the Irish members of the popular party will avoid all topics on which they may differ with you [Russell] and your friends, *until the Tories are routed*, and that you will find us perfectly ready to cooperate in any plan which your friends may deem most advisable to effect that purpose. In short, we *will be* steady allies without any mutiny in your camp.[38]

Russell replied cautiously and coolly. His letter would have been still more frigid had not Duncannon (who said from the start that the election results 'had imparted an almost sovereign sway to O'Connell'[39]) told Russell boldly that the whigs might as well throw up the game if they began by 'trembling at shadows' and 'quaking' at the prospect of Irish and radical support.[40] O'Connell, however, continued serenely upon the path of cordial collaboration, attending faithfully all the liberal party meetings held in 'the dusty unfurnished drawing-rooms of that dingy-fronted mansion [Lichfield House]' during the spring,[41] and ardently supporting Russell in each of the seven defeats which he inflicted on Peel in the House of Commons between 17 February and 7 May 1835. O'Connell cheered every liberal triumph like a schoolboy. 'Victory! I write on my knee in a crowded room. Victory, victory!', he crowed to Fitzpatrick after Abercromby's election to the Speakership.[42] A later success was greeted with, 'The scoundrels [Peel's ministry] are, I believe, in point of fact, *out certainly* . . . Blessed be the great God for this prospect! . . . It is joyful to think that the iron rule of Orangeism is so nearly at an end . . . I would give a pound for an attested copy of Shaw's [Shaw was tory MP for Dublin University] visage as he went just now into the House. I cannot describe my delight.'[43] By the end of March O'Connell had openly accepted the whigs' leadership; and on the night of 18 April, in a historic scene, O'Connell and his followers joined the mass crossing from the opposition to the ministerial benches, as the government changed hands. But he had already stipulated his 'terms of support'. On 26 February he had declared in the Commons,

> If I am asked if I give up the repeal of the Legislative Union, my answer is, that I suspend it. But for what? To give time for carrying into full operation the three measures I have described [Irish tithe, parliamentary and municipal reform]; to give them a fair trial, to see if they will amend the condition of Ireland, and if they fail, then again to resort to repeal; but if they succeed, then to give it up for ever.[44]

All this represented the essence of the notorious 'Lichfield House compact' between O'Connell and the whigs, whose very existence both parties to the supposed bargain consistently denied. Still, as even Russell himself allowed in later years, 'an alliance on honourable terms of mutual co-operation undoubtedly existed'.[45] The understanding with O'Connell was no less a contract for being unwritten and in part implicit. Tacitly, O'Connell promised the whigs support in the House of Commons except when their government was not at risk *and* so long as they gave him a considerable degree of influence over Irish measures and appointments. Tacitly, they promised him, not necessarily his full demands, but at least ten shillings in the pound. As he himself saw it, O'Connell had at last advanced significantly in his post-Emancipation or second grand campaign. The prospect of sharing power, and enjoying an equal standing in their native land was finally unfolding before Irish Catholics – of the middle class, at least. It seemed a decisive stage in the process of turning the emancipists into the truly emancipated.

IV

O'Connell, as we have seen, had repeatedly written to his wife in the preceding months as if he expected to benefit himself, and handsomely, from the coming change in government. When in mid-April 1835 Melbourne made his first attempt to form a ministry, O'Connell wrote confidently to Fitzpatrick, 'You may be convinced that I will not accept offers of any kind without distinct pledges. Nor is there any office I should accept save [Irish] Attorney-General or Secretary for Ireland.'[46] We may well take this with a grain of salt. O'Connell must surely have known that no British government, however well-disposed or necessitous, would contemplate placing him in either of the two controlling positions in their Irish administration. In fact, he virtually indicated as much when he added, to Fitzpatrick, 'there may be objections in the prejudices of the King against me which may render it unwise to have me named to any situation. The result, however, will be that the less of personal advantage I acquire the more of national benefit shall I stipulate for.'[47] Moreover, on the very same day he pressed Ellice to have O'Loghlen rather than Perrin succeed to the attorney-generalship. O'Connell's benignity was undisturbed when it finally became clear that neither William IV nor Melbourne (to say nothing of other influential whigs) would agree to his being offered any post whatever. Russell, as in honour bound, informed O'Connell that he would not participate in the new government should O'Connell feel seriously aggrieved at his exclusion. But not only was O'Connell unoffended, he may even have been relieved to have escaped an awkward choice: it is noteworthy that for all his apparent preliminary hesitations he was invariably to end by rejecting invitations to take office. There can be little doubt that he was consulted about – or at least informed beforehand of – the whigs' proposed appointments to the major Irish posts. It was he who on 13 April 1835 passed on to the Repeal newspapers in Dublin the correct predictions that Lord Mulgrave would be the new lord lieutenant, Lord Morpeth the new chief secretary, and Blackburne removed from the attorney-generalship. It would be absurd to conclude from this that O'Connell virtually nominated the new Irish administration. Despite his urging, Perrin was preferred to O'Loghlen for the senior legal office, although it is true that both had been among O'Connell's original nominations. On the other hand, he left the whigs in no doubt that 'the Corporation and Orange factions' must go – 'Delenda est Carthago is my device as opposed to that horde'[48] – and we can be sure that the incoming ministry at least heeded this, and was extremely careful to appoint nobody in Ireland of whom O'Connell disapproved.

That the composition of the new Irish administration was the most urgent of all questions in his eyes was clear from his first speech on returning to Dublin after Melbourne's second administration had been formed. Then, he set out for his audience the price of his support: 'That the power and malevolence of the vile Orange faction must instantly cease . . . That the country will cease to be governed by its unrelenting enemies . . . [and] that the administration in Ireland will be purified.'[49] He said nothing about legislative programmes. O'Connell had no qualms in laying his implicit concordat with the whigs, and the consequent shelving of Repeal, before his Irish public. Fitzpatrick had supposed that he would be chary of openly admitting the *entente*. For once the diligent student misread his master. On his way back from London, on 22 April 1835, O'Connell briskly replied:

You seem to wish that I should shrink from public meetings or exhibitions. I totally disagree with you. I have no apprehension of unruly Repealers. I should desire to give them a public opportunity of discussing their views in contrast with mine. I am as much a Repealer as ever I was but I see the absolute necessity of confuting those who say we prevented the Union from having a fair trial in the hands of a friendly Ministry, and also of giving a decisive check to Orangeism . . . I have two objects – to overthrow the Orange system and to convince the most sceptical that nothing but a domestic parliament will do Ireland justice. With these views of the present aspect of affairs, the sooner I come before the Irish public the better. I know the magic of being right. I never saw that which was founded on common-sense defeated at a public meeting. Commonsense sanctions and directs my present course – the experiment I am making to confound the Orange party and to give a fair trial to the measures of those who declare themselves our friends. I will therefore attend every public meeting and every public dinner I possibly can.[50]

Of course, O'Connell was justified by the event. He could always, as Lecky observed, 'play on an Irish popular audience like a great musician on his instrument, eliciting what tone and what response he pleased'.[51] Instinctively he understood the interior rhythms of Irish agitation; now he could exploit what Moore once described as the characteristic national mood, 'a burst of turbulence dying away into softness'.[52] Moreover, like the prudent advocate, O'Connell had multiplied his defences. He could place his emphasis on either Irish government or Irish legislation, as he willed; he always could fall back upon Repeal; he could demand good works from the Union while yet denying faith in its durability.

O'Connell needed all the ebullience he was displaying. As it became clear that he was the pivot on which the change of government in Britain and the control of Irish patronage would turn, he became the direct target of malign toryism. He felt this first in purse. Although almost half the Irish seats were uncontested in the general election, opponents were found for all six of those in which the members of O'Connell's 'family party' stood. His three sons and his nephew and himself were later subject to more or less expensive petitions against their returns. 'The Orange party hate me with a most malignant hatred', O'Connell wrote to J. D. Mullen on 11 March 1835, 'They have involved me in the expenses of four [*recte* five] petitions';[53] and six days later he continued in the same despondent vein:

> Even my health and strength are leaving me. The whole burden of the city of Dublin petition in all its arrangements, the whole expense of that and four other petitions are thrown upon me after having sustained the expenses of five contested elections. The Orangemen are determined to crush me and only think the subscription in Dublin to sustain the election is not sufficient to pay the local expenses there – that is – the expenses of clerks, attornies, porters, printing and stationery ... For the first time in my life I am disposed to feel heartbroken but God's holy will be done.[54]

By 25 March, however, he was his old dauntless self, telling Fitzpatrick that he had overcome his 'mental agony respecting the elections and these petitions . . . intended certainly, to ruin me . . . my mind has, thank God recovered its tone and energy'.[55] None the less, more than a year of electoral troubles and expenditure still lay ahead, and the final cost to O'Connell of the 1835 general election and its aftermath may well have reached as high as £15,000. Small wonder that in a later moment of dejection, he confessed to his 'comforter', Fitzpatrick, 'Really, I sometimes almost despair. I must, I think, mortgage perhaps all my family property [to meet petition expenses] but do not breathe a word of this to anyone.'[56]

Secondly, in 1835 as never before, O'Connell aroused a species of national rage in Britain, deriving from intense distaste for his vulgarity and still more intense fear of his supposed, as against his declared, intentions. In celebrated doggerel, *The Times*, which had swung over to the conservatives largely because of the whigs' junction with O'Connell, expressed on 26 November 1835 the personal detestation and congeries of prejudice which had kept up tory (and Greyite whig) hatred of him throughout the year:

> Scum condensed of Irish bog!
> Ruffian – coward – demagogue!
> Boundless liar – base detractor!
> Nurse of murders – treason's factor!
> Of Pope and priest the crouching slave,
> While thy lips of freedom rave;
> Of England's fame the vip'rous hater,
> Yet wanting courage for a traitor.
> Ireland's peasants feed thy purse,
> Still thou art her bane and curse . . .
> Safe from challenge – safe from law –
> What can curb thy callous jaw?
> Who would sue a convict liar?
> On a poltroon who would fire?

As the last jibe in particular showed, the spearhead of the attack was social: a man who insulted others without affording 'satisfaction' was beyond the pale. This was the point made by Lord Alvanley in challenging – or more precisely not challenging – O'Connell on 21 April 1835, 'I can hardly hope that you will make an exception in my favour, by doing what any other gentleman would do.'[57] O'Connell who had, after some provocation, given offence by rounding on Alvanley as a 'bloated buffoon' in the House of Commons,[58] responded with the expected denunciation of duelling. 'I treat it', he told Alvanley through George Damer, Alvanley's 'second', on 1 May, 'with the most sovereign contempt, as a practice inconsistent with common sense, but, above all, as a violation, plain and palpable, of the divine law.'[59] Thereupon Alvanley set in train a motion to have O'Connell expelled from the whig club, Brooks's, for, in effect, conduct unbecoming an individual with pretensions to gentility: it is impossible to say whether or not Alvanley had intended such a move from the beginning. Surprisingly, several even of the whig oligarchs rallied to O'Connell's defence and the managers of Brooks's, led by Ellice and Duncannon, saw to it that the motion for O'Connell's expulsion was declared inappropriate for the club to consider. The new political bonds between O'Connell and his English allies had taken the strain with ease.

In turn, the Brooks's rejection did lead to a duel – but between Alvanley and Morgan, O'Connell's second son, who sought satisfaction for Alvanley's attempted social degradation of his father. Hard on the heels of this affair (which ended in the harmless exchange of shots) came a challenge to Morgan from Disraeli. Disraeli, now a young tory on the make, had abused O'Connell at the general election as an 'incendiary and traitor' of 'bloody hand'. Of course, his victim replied with interest, out-O'Connelling even himself with, 'England is degraded in tolerating, or having upon the face of her society a miscreant of his abominable, foul, and atrocious nature.'[60] Disraeli purported to believe that Morgan had set himself up as his father's duelling *alter ego*, and, when Morgan sensibly refused to take up the endless work of shooting in defence of O'Connell's vituperation, promised a later vengeance in the House of Commons. With characteristic floridity, he told O'Connell, 'We shall meet at Phillipi.'[61] Six months later Sir Francis Burdett (a recent convert, like Disraeli, from radicalism to conservatism) again proposed that O'Connell be driven out from Brooks's, now because of the low tone and scurrility of his public speeches. Once more, Ellice and Duncannon held the fort. This time, however, it was at the cost of some 100 resignations from the club, though many of these had, like Burdett, already passed over from the liberals. Unquestionably, O'Connell was damaged by the sustained barrage. But though Melbourne himself fully shared the general aristocratic disdain of O'Connell's 'ruffianism' – 'Why, you know', he remarked, having encountered O'Connell at dinner, 'after one has had O'Connell, one may have anybody!'[62] – the whigs *en bloc* refused to throw him over. The bonds of political interest still held. In fact, the practice of mutuality had rendered them more secure.

V

It would be a mistake to attribute the solidarity between O'Connell and the government, which developed steadily during 1835, solely to the self-interest of the parties. We should also recognize, as Dr Ó Tuathaigh has done, that there was 'warmth and . . . genuine loyalty and respect . . . [on] both sides of this alliance'.[63] The foundation for mutual sympathy was the character of the new Irish executive. From O'Connell's standpoint, it could scarcely have been bettered. He would have preferred O'Loghlen to have been attorney – rather than solicitor-general, but both Perrin and O'Loghlen strove for impartiality (tempered, if anything, by a leaning towards the 'Catholic' side) in the administration of the law. Lords Mulgrave and Morpeth, lord lieutenant and chief secretary respectively, were able and sincere liberals, Mulgrave excelling in affability and the common touch, Morpeth in depth of knowledge and practical efficiency. Equally important was the replacement in July 1835 of the tory under-secretary, Gosset, by Thomas Drummond, generally adjudged the greatest Irish public servant of the nineteenth century. Drummond was high-principled, fearless, torrential in his energy and acutely intelligent; above all, he both knew Ireland well (having spent 1825–30 in its countryside working for the Ordnance Survey) and loved it as his adopted country. Finally, the entire executive was extraordinarily harmonious, aiming at agreed objectives by agreed means. Small wonder that the regime has been described as 'a St Martin's summer in the long winter of the Union'.[64]

This is not to say that O'Connell was wholly satisfied by the new government of Ireland. It was impossible that he should have been. It would have taken much more time and ruthlessness than Melbourne's administration was granted or possessed for the entire structure of Irish rule to have fallen into liberal and nationalist hands. At the beginning of 1835, Irish government was, practically speaking, an exclusive tory preserve. Six years later, at a rough estimate, about one third of the Irish judges, magistrates, sheriffs, assistant barristers and other important officers of national management belonged to the 'anti-tory' camp. At a still rougher estimate, some 30–40 per cent of the new appointments were of Catholics.

O'Connell may have complained repeatedly at the slow pace of the substitution, Dublin Castle's over-caution and the ministry's timidity in the face of a House of Lords ever-ready to charge it with favouring papists and subversives. But this should not disguise his steady joy at what seemed to him a marvellous transformation, not least in the incorporation of Catholics in the national system of power. He spoke of the Relief Act of 1829 as 'one portion of Catholic emancipation . . . that Act was but a part of the justice we looked for'.[65] The benign rule of Mulgrave, Morpeth and Drummond was the next instalment. It mattered little that the majority of the replacements of office-holders were moderate or liberal Protestants. As yet, comparatively few Catholics possessed the necessary property or formal qualifications for the posts or functions; indeed, a modest degree of positive discrimination was exercised on their behalf. What counted was the parity implicit in recruiting them at all. Hence the notes of pride and confidence struck by O'Connell in writing to Fitzpatrick on 4 September 1835 of O'Loghlen's promotion to attorney-general:

> I know of my own personal knowledge that the Government . . . are resolved to discountenance the Orange faction everywhere and in every respect. We have for the first time in near two centuries a Catholic Attorney-General . . . His ears will be open to the complaints of the Catholic Clergy as well as of the Catholic laity upon every act of oppression and tyranny practised against the poorest of the people. Every care will be taken to give the Commission of the Peace to every liberal man qualified for it. The Attorney-General will not allow jurors to be packed against the people. And if the Orangemen or police commit any more murders, they will be prosecuted seriously . . .[66]

Hence, too, the note struck by the O'Connellite *Pilot* when it reported in 1840 the swearing in of David Pigot, the *fourth* Catholic Irish attorney-general to be appointed by the Melbourne government. The newspaper noted that both the officers concerned, the acting chancellor and the clerk of the hanaper, were also Catholics, 'a situation unthinkable a decade before'.[67] It might have added that two of the three were close friends of O'Connell, and the third his son-in-law.

The advancement of what was coming to be called (to avoid former, now-embarrassing names) the 'popular party' was one side of the equation. The other was curbing the power of the Ascendancy. The whig government, heavy with proprietorial interests, would never countenance – nor would O'Connell have welcomed – a direct attack on Irish landlordism. The Grand Jury Act of 1836, which introduced some central surveillance and eradicated the very worst of the old corruption but left the gentry still in command of major county expenditure, represented their utmost boundary of reform in this regard. But 'Orangeism', by which O'Connell meant not merely the

Order itself but also Protestant supremacism in general, was quite another matter. Here he confidently called on Mulgrave to help in cutting back the most galling manifestations of Ascendancy; and luck played into his hands when in July 1835 a select committee of the House of Commons reported on the operation of Orange lodges in the army, thereby causing a public revulsion against their clandestine and occasionally sinister activity.

O'Connell lost no time in pressing the government to counteract Orange dominance in Ireland. Skilfully, he presented this as the precipitant of mass disorders. 'The restoration', he reported confidentially to Ellice on 11 May 1835, 'to power of the Orange faction under the late Peel administration was followed by such a virulent display and practical *exertion* of the worst and most sanguinary passions of the Orange faction that the country from one end to the other felt as if handed over to the most vexatious and insulting oppression.' The natural and inevitable consequence was the rapid revival of the conspiratorial, terrorist Catholic counterforce, the Ribbon Societies.

> Since the new ministry was formed there is a sensible decline in this faction. The Catholic clergy are beginning to be listened to by many of the Ribbonmen and if the Orange party continues to be discountenanced by the Government, we shall be able *once again* to put down the spread and strength of Ribbonism without any legislative interference or much public display if any.[68]

Throughout the remainder of 1835 O'Connell maintained his pressure on the government: the Orange peril was the constant theme of his correspondence. In his last surviving letters of the year to Mulgrave (4 and 8 December) he concentrated upon the forthcoming nomination of the county sheriffs, who among other things, controlled the jury panels.

> We have party judges, we have still party sheriffs and of necessary consequence we must have partisan jurors. It really is the only thing to be wondered at, that the people are *so* patient, for really I have beheld scenes in our courts that would drive the most apathetic mad . . . you have before you the great game – the all-important selection . . . What must the condition of the people be if the judges, instead of being checked by juries, find that they have sheriffs to aid them by giving juries who, instead of resisting, will favour party spirit, give party verdicts and enable the judges to distribute vengeance not to administer justice. The state of Ireland requires a firm hand of power to stem the torrent of oppression legal as well as practical.[69]

O'Connell added a particular plea that Samuel Hickson, a local enemy of the O'Connells and 'of the Catholic clergy', should not be appointed sheriff of co. Kerry.[70] Mulgrave proved responsive. Not only was Hickson passed over but also the Irish government eventually took the audacious and much-denounced step of departing altogether from the customary judges' lists of prospective sheriffs whenever these lists would 'force' an outrageous Orange or gross supremacist appointment upon the lord lieutenant. This was in line with the settled policy of the new Irish government. By the threat, and effective deployment of adequate force, it had ensured that The Twelfth (12 July) in 1835 would not be marked by the usual violence or provocations; and two months later the privy council actually disallowed the election of a mayor of Cork because he was an avowed member of the Orange order. There can be no doubt that O'Connell saw the clipping of the 'faction's' wings as critically important to Irish reform. As he wrote to Fitzpatrick on 4 September 1835, 'when the Orange faction ceases to have political existence there is *nothing* Ireland cannot command',[71] and, a week later, 'if the Orange faction were put down, the combination [of the ministry and himself] in Ireland would be too strong to permit any misgovernment. Indeed, indeed, I do anticipate better days.'[72] Whether disingenuously or not, he even justified the shelving of Repeal in terms of the struggle against Protestant supremacism: 'the cry for the Repeal would only give increased strength to the vile Orange faction, who are violent anti-Repealers, that they may have the appearance of being devoted to British connection. We must not strengthen their bonds.'[73]

All this was hard political business for O'Connell, but no business could have been more delightful. It was with real gusto that he threw himself into the importuning of Dublin Castle for favours or appointments for his friends and connexions. Equally satisfying was the baulking of his enemies, with its superadded pleasurable sensation that the world of Irish patronage had turned upside down. While there is no evidence that he was greedy on his own account, O'Connell's natural expansiveness was deeply gratified by feeling that the good things of office were, to some extent at least, at his disposal. In promising his daughter, Betsey Ffrench, for instance, to put her husband forward for a commissionship of the projected Shannon improvement authority, he wrote joyously on 23 June 1835, 'We are a great support to the Ministry so that I am as able I think, as I know I am willing, to be of use to him [Ffrench] . . . Never did father love a daughter better than I do, my own Betty.'[74] Well in the spirit of the

1830s, O'Connell was more concerned with the securing of a place than with which place was secured. A characteristic letter – to J. D. Mullen, currently his main support in the fight to retain his seat for Dublin against petition – ran:

> I need not tell you that I made every exertion to succeed in procuring the nomination for you of the tide surveyorship. I got my final answer only yesterday. It is unfavourable. 'The appointment belongs to the Board of Customs. It goes by seniority amongst the officers of that Department. A new man cannot be brought in.'
> I do believe, if the thing were possible, you would at this hour be the man. But there is as good fish in the sea as ever was caught. We will have a remodelling of the paving board and of the police magistracy within six months, and assuredly you shall be *one* if I live . . . *Rely on me.*[75]

It must not be supposed, however, that O'Connell attempted to aggrandize on behalf of his own family to any considerable extent or that he spent his influence chiefly in the pursuit of personal favours. The bulk of his applications were more generally political in objective, such as the securing of favourable (and the frustration of inimical) assistant barristers – who oversaw the registration of parliamentary voters in the counties – or the counterbalancing of 'Orange' by 'popular' magistrates. Whichever form of request he made, O'Connell was met with courtesy and, quite commonly, compliance. This was as true of Russell in London as of Mulgrave in Dublin Castle. Small wonder that O'Connell maintained his air of jubilee and elation throughout the year. Even if only at second hand he was tasting a little of the sweets of power. When 1835 had all but run its course, he summed it all up for Fitzpatrick,

> Tomorrow [1 January 1836] I begin agitation afresh. The last, after all, was a glorious year! One other such and the faction is down for ever. I am, blessed by God, in the best health and the highest spirits.
> Goodnight, God bless you![76]

VI

O'Connell's satisfaction owed nothing to Irish remedial legislation, for none was passed during 1835. On assuming leadership of the House of Commons in April, Russell had confirmed, in general terms, the new government's willingness to accept O'Connell's conditions for support and to propose Irish electoral, municipal and tithe reform bills. Electoral reform proved difficult, but on 26 June 1835 Lord

Morpeth introduced in the House of Commons an Irish tithes bill, which fixed a rent charge of 68.5 per cent in lieu of tithes and appropriated £58,000 'surplus' revenue of the Church of Ireland for other purposes. As this approximated closely to O'Connell's own proposal of the preceding year, he welcomed it warmly and supported it pertinaciously; in fact, it was the votes of his 'tail' which provided the necessary majorities to carry it through the lower House.

The tithe issue had never been especially close to O'Connell's heart. We might describe it as a passion of his supporters rather than himself. It was far otherwise with the next whig measure, the Irish municipal corporations bill introduced by Perrin on 31 July, for this held the keys to various treasuries of local power. Accordingly, O'Connell greeted the proposal with 'infinite pleasure and delight'. It would, he declared in the House of Commons, 'For the first time . . . identify the people of Ireland with the British Constitution'.[77] This was a flamboyant acknowledgement that his original demand that Irish municipalities be placed under popular – that is, middle-class and artisan – control had been met. The whig government would have conceded less had it not been for their English municipal corporation reform bill, currently embattled in the House of Lords. As Spring-Rice, the chancellor of the exchequer, wrote privately, 'we were bound by English Bill analogies . . . If we depopularized the Irish Bill by a measure of less extensive reform than was conceded to [England] and Scotland we gave an immediate countenance to the cry of Repeal'[78] – a confession which vindicated most remarkably O'Connell's strategy. Perrin's bill rendered Irish municipal government fully elective, with householder qualification (£10 in places above 20,000 in population and £5 in those below) for the franchise, and a large measure of corporation control of the formerly autonomous commissions for such urban matters as lighting, paving and sanitation. It was less democratic than its English counterpart. £10 and £5 minima were, effectively, much more restrictive qualifications in Ireland than in England; the largely Protestant freeman vote was retained intact; and the Irish lord lieutenant was given powers over the appointment of borough magistrates and – later – sheriffs which had no equivalent across the Irish Sea. But to O'Connell all these mattered little in the light of the massive shift in urban management which the bill promised even as it stood.

This was, however, the limit of success in 1835. The House of Lords rejected the appropriation clauses of the tithe bill by a majority of more than 3 to 1; and since this was the issue which had originally fused whigs, radicals and O'Connellites, the government dropped the entire measure for the present. The Irish municipal corporations bill passed the House of Commons on 17 August 1835 without a division but only because, as one tory observed, the House of Lords could be depended on to defeat it. They were not required to do so. The government was in difficulty enough with English municipal reform – which it was forced eventually to lop and crop in order to ensure its passage – and accepted the plea that it was too late in the session for the upper House to proceed beyond the first reading of the Irish bill. Thus O'Connell left Westminster empty-handed. But by no means did he consider his comparatively long sojourn in London – he spent more time on parliamentary business in 1835 than in any other year – a failure. The House of Commons had endorsed two of his three major legislative demands, in forms which he could accept wholeheartedly, and the remaining obstacle to their enactment now stood clear and naked before the world. It was evident from the character of its opposition to the English municipal corporations bill that the House of Lords was bent upon systematic obstruction of the whig measures of domestic reform. It was clearly their hope to force a general election in which the impetus of the tories' revival (already manifest in the January polls) would carry the party forward into power. The logic of the situation, as O'Connell saw it, was to campaign against the upper House itself, and so far as practicable to mobilize British radical and liberal opinion in a cause similar to that carried to so triumphant a conclusion in the Reform Act of 1832.

O'Connell used an invitation to address the Manchester liberals to launch what he called a 'Mission to the people of England and Scotland'. Although brief, extending only from 11 to 21 September, it included mass meetings and public dinners in four of the great northern cities, Newcastle-upon-Tyne, Edinburgh and Glasgow, as well as Manchester. O'Connell shot at a single target, the

> impediments now thrown in the way of all amelioration of our institutions by a factious majority of the House of Lords . . . Liberty is an empty name and constitutional rights are vile delusions if any two hundred men, no matter by what titles or denominations styled, can prevent every improvement in the social system and continue every abuse.[79]

Instead, he proposed an upper house of 150 popularly elected peers. O'Connell chose this theme in order to maximize the appeal to British reformers while striking at the main citadel of resistance to his 'Justice for Ireland' programme. He himself was delighted at his reception. As he wrote excitedly to Fitzpatrick after the conclusion of the Manchester dinner, there never was anything more enthusiastic than my reception here. The procession of the trades, notwithstanding the wetness of the day, exceeded thirty thousand. I made ten or twelve thousand hear me in a spurt of about an hour . . . I never was so well received in Ireland [as at the dinner]. It is a strong measure to say so and yet it is true . . . You may imagine that I must have been encouraged by applause of an enthusiastic nature to go on or I would have sooner terminated. Indeed, it is impossible to give you in the compass of a letter any idea of the sensation I made . . . The prospects for Ireland brighten. I am beginning to think that I shall be a Cabinet Minister next session, with the rule of matters in Ireland officially committed to me.[80]

Throughout the 'Mission', O'Connell employed the techniques of demagogic denigration and self-projection so well tested before Irish mass-audiences. The House of Lords was dismissed as 'the soaped pigs of Society', Wellington as 'a stunted corporal' and Lord Lyndhurst as 'a contumelious cur'; and he arrayed himself (according to the *Caledonian Mercury* of Edinburgh) in 'a green surtout vest, and pantaloons, with a green travelling cap, encircled by a gold band . . . The people crowded round his carriage in their eagerness to get a near view of him, and he replied to their salutations with the greatest affability and good humour.'[81] Despite much mobbing of this kind, O'Connell was painfully adrift when he declared that it 'is only now that the people of England are beginning to understand me'.[82] The hostile British press pounced with glee upon his gutter language; the *Annual Register* for 1835 pronounced it a mere intoxicant for 'the ignorant rabble . . . instead of being fitted to convince and convert the rational and sober-minded, it only excited disgust and some degree of alarm'.[83] This was a partisan view; many 'respectable' British radicals closed their ears to the Billingsgate and simply enjoyed the novel spectacle of the haughty being pulled along the mire. It was true, however, that O'Connell made only a superficial and temporary impression on English and Scottish opinion: he was sowing on very stony ground, and though the seed sprouted fast, it died as quickly. But this was to be hidden from O'Connell until well into 1836. Meanwhile he carried his euphoria with him into his winter, or more exactly his autumn, quarters at Derrynane.

O'Connell spent an extraordinarily lengthy 'vacation' at Derrynane, from late October 1835 to mid-January 1836, and, on the evidence of his surviving correspondence, devoted much less of it than usual to politics. One letter, for example, explored the early history of Calvinism; another rehearsed, in delightful counterpoint, two of his cherished enthusiasms, Irish spirituality in the sixth and seventh centuries AD and the modern progress of personal rights.

> I rely on the fragment of Gildus and on Bede for my notions of Ireland in the Dark Ages. That there was *all* the learning of the times, a high spirit of religious devotion, much ascetism, is perfectly true but what must be the state of civil policy when the lands were held not by individuals but by the clan, when the succession to the chief power and property was governed by no rule of descent but belonged to the nearest relation who was also the *bravest* man. That ingredient in the right had all its natural effects.[84]

Apart from laying in materials for the demolition of Peel when parliament re-assembled, and striving to keep Mulgrave up to the mark, O'Connell's only significant political venture, while at Derrynane, was an attempt to launch an 'Irish Reform Society' which would draw in the few Irish liberal peers and landed magnates. 'I regret to see', he told Lord Cloncurry on 14 December 1835, 'that all my efforts appear insufficient to excite to the formation of a "government party" of rank and fortune in Ireland [although] the odious Orange party rally at once round a Tory party.'[85] This is a significant indication of the way in which O'Connell's mind was moving during his Kerry break. He was to 'plunge' more heavily than ever before upon the whig alliance.

That he was ready to raise and re-raise his stake with seeming recklessness became apparent during the series of public meetings (at Tralee, Tuam, Stradbally in Queen's county, Dublin and Liverpool) which marked his slow progress to Westminster in the second half of January 1836. At each Irish meeting, he took the supreme gamble of asking his audiences to release him from his commitment to Repeal should Britain provide Ireland with true justice. As he himself fairly described the outcome at the Liverpool meeting of 27 January,

> I have very lately been entertained in Kerry I said to my countrymen there, 'if we get justice will you give up repeal?' What was their reply? 'Get us justice and give up repeal' (hear). At the great Connaught meeting in Tuam . . . I have said to 50,000 of my countrymen, 'If I get justice will you give up repeal?' – and one and all replied 'get us justice, and give up repeal' (hear, hear). I have put this question in various other places and have received the very same reply. On Monday last [25 January] I put it to my constituents in Dublin. If any men could have an inducement to seek a resident parliament, it was the tradesmen of Dublin. They would all be fully and well employed, and would have opportunities of making their fortunes (hear). Well, I put the same question to them. I asked the Trades' Political Union, if they got justice would they give up repeal? I put this to them clearly and distinctly,

and what was their reply? 'Give us justice' (hear, hear, hear) . . . Now, here I am, authorized by my country to give up repeal at once and for ever, if England will barely do us justice; and what kind of people are those who would deny this to us (hear)?[86]

As Lecky observes, 'With any other public man, such a course would be dangerous in the extreme',[87] all the more so as O'Connell had, even in Ireland, pressed his language of prospective loyalism to the limit, with, for instance, 'The people of Ireland are ready to become a portion of the Empire . . . they are ready to become a kind of West Britons, if made so in benefits and justice; but if not we are Irishmen again'[88] or 'Ireland is now ready to amalgamate with the entire empire. We are prepared for full and perpetual conciliation.'[89] He seemed even to reduce his former Repeal demand to the level of a trick when he told his Liverpool audience that it was his 'flapper [cudgel]' to counter the 'flapper' of tory oppression in Ireland.

> I too have found it necessary to use a flapper; and the flapper I took up was of no ordinary size . . . I took up a cudgel, and that cudgel was the repeal (hear, hear). [I] was like the gun beggar in Gil Blas, who begged with a gun, and was the most successful beggar on the road (laughter). He looked at the gun occasionally, and pointed to it before travellers, but he always asked charity in the name of Heaven (laughter and cheers). That was the very nature of the political charity of those who had misgoverned Ireland (cheers).[90]

O'Connell banked successfully on being the nonpareil among politicians, the father of his country, the accepted expressor of the national will. In part, his strength lay in his capacity to convince himself, as the preliminary to convincing 'the Irish people', that he was their constant reflex. 'I am nothing', he had proclaimed the year before, 'but the straw rolling on the surface of the stream. I show by the manner in which I am carried along, the strength, the rapidity, and the course of the current.'[91] The most interesting question is not why his faithful listeners accepted all he told them without demur but why he now announced so plainly his apparent eagerness to be assimilated to, or absorbed in, a British imperial structure. The very words 'West Britons' – even if, patently, they did not carry for O'Connell their later vilely-perjorative connotations – suggested gross servility. Was Moore's terrible insinuation of 1834 –

> Say, is it that slavery sunk so deep in thy heart,
> That still the dark brand is there, tho' chainless thou art. . . ?[92]

all too well justified by the event?

There can be no question that by the canons of later nineteenth-century (and still more twentieth-century) Irish nationalist orthodoxy O'Connell stands condemned from his own mouth. But a higher court – on the daring assumption that such could exist! – might well reverse this judgment on appeal. The first explanation of O'Connell's extraordinary rhetoric of January 1836 is the tactical. He had already attempted to sap the enemy's main institutional defence-work, the House of Lords. Now, with the positive encouragement of the cabinet as channelled through Warburton, he was assailing the Lords' main support in English public opinion by stressing that he asked no more than the rest of the *soi-disant* United Kingdom had already won, and that as grievances disappeared so too would *inimical* differentiation. It was a carefully designed offensive directed at specific objects. Secondly, we should note that O'Connell was not really deviating from his settled 'justice' policy. He was merely drawing out more boldly, for persuasive ends, its ulterior implications. When he declared – as often in this set of speeches – that Ireland was now prepared to amalgamate completely with the empire, he invariably added some such proviso as 'But for this purpose equality – perfect equality of rights, laws and liberties – is essentially necessary'.[93] He did not add, as he had been wont to do and was to do again, that he did not expect his condition to be met. These were not the circumstances for expressing dubiety out loud. But doubtless he made due mental reservations. Thirdly, when he said, 'but if not we are Irishmen again',[94] he spoke only of political formalities. In O'Connell's pre-modern view of nationality, constitutional arrangements had little bearing on cultural identity. He lacked the new sense of organic historical development; shaped intellectually by older values and presuppositions, he would have found such concepts as 'anglicization' or 'mental colonialism', in the last analysis, incomprehensible. It would never have occurred to him that his offer – if seriously meant – to merge 'his' Ireland in the empire generally implied even a diminution of its *haecciatas* or inherent singularity. Finally, we may well question whether the offer *was* seriously meant. 'Justice for Ireland' was O'Connell's own coinage. He, and only he, could say when it had been attained. Perhaps instinctively rather than by deliberate design, he had given himself all the elasticity he might need. Even the best-disposed British government conceivable in the 1830s must fall far short of providing perfect equality for its Irish constituent; and well-disposed British governments were bound to be succeeded, sooner or later, by their opposites. The return of the tories to office would certainly be taken by O'Connell to presage the return of 'Injustice for Ireland'. Thus, not only need there not be but also there could not be any final commitment on his part. In short, we should see the apparent extravagance of January 1836 as another stage in O'Connell's eternal tacking. This audacious tack was probably as far rightward as he could safely go; the swollen sail must almost have touched the Irish water. It was certain, however, that, early or late, the time would come when he would put about and attempt to catch a wind blowing from the contrary direction.

Yet the very fact that O'Connell was stretching so intently to conciliate the British political classes is an index of his hopefulness of success. On the eve of parliament reassembling, on 4 February 1836, he looked forward confidently to the generation of sufficient public pressure to cow the Lords into substantial surrender on the forthcoming Irish tithe and municipal corporation bills. It was still a season of joy. Well might he have repeated – blithely indifferent of course to the irony of plundering a revolutionary anthem –

> And we'll plant a laurel tree,
> And we'll call it 'Victory',
> Said the Shan Van Vocht.[95]

CHAPTER 18

Liaisons

1836–8

I

If 1835 had seemed the best of years to O'Connell, 1836 might well have seemed the worst. Parliament had barely reassembled when on 11 February a backbencher, John Hardy, moved for an inquiry into the alleged sale by O'Connell of one of the co. Carlow seats at a contested by-election in June 1835. O'Connell offered no opposition but declared the inquiry to be necessary to clear his name. The charge was very grave and the implication that he had profited financially still more damaging.

The affair was complicated. In his eagerness to win co. Carlow for the anti-tories at the general election of January 1835, O'Connell had, at considerable cost to himself, put forward his own son Maurice and another 'Repealer', Michael Cahill. They were defeated by 33 and 34 votes respectively, but the successful conservatives were unseated on petition; meanwhile Maurice had been victorious at Tralee. When the new writs for co. Carlow were issued, O'Connell, desperate to increase his numbers when the whig government's regular majority was precarious, threw himself into the search for fresh candidates. In the end, he induced a London 'City man', the sheriff of Westminster, Alexander Raphael, as well as a local liberal, N. A. Vigors, to stand. 'Mr Raphael's principles are all that we can desire . . .', he told Vigors, 'His opinions on the Corporation Reform and Tithe system are those which you and I cherish.'[1] Perhaps Raphael's business habits were less to O'Connell's liking. O'Connell had to provide him, on 1 June 1835, with a written statement of the terms they had agreed on.

> You [Raphael] having acceded to the terms proposed to you for the election of the County of Carlow, viz. you are to pay before nomination £1000 – say one thousand pounds – and a like sum after being returned, the first to be paid absolutely and entirely for being nominated, the second to be paid only in the event of your having been returned, I hereby undertake

to guarantee and save you harmless from any and every other expense whatsoever, whether of agents, carriages, counsel, petition against the return, or of any other description. I make this guarantee in the fullest sense of the honourable engagement that you shall not possibly be required to pay one shilling more in any event or upon any contingency whatsoever.[2]

Although Raphael and Vigors were duly elected on 19 June 1835 by considerable majorities, a petition against their election was launched immediately; and while this was being heard, O'Connell pressed Raphael, in very peremptory terms, for the payment of the second £1000. Presumably Raphael's argument was that he had not yet been 'returned' – although he had in fact taken his seat – but on 28 July he reluctantly lodged the additional money, with a proposal that the difference of interpretation of the agreement should be arbitrated by some 'mutual friend'.[3] A week later (according to his own account) Raphael discovered that he was bearing the cost of defending the Carlow seats alone, and called upon O'Connell 'as an act of justice to me, to fulfill your engagement'.[4] Meanwhile, O'Connell had dangled the consolation prize of a baronetcy before him: 'Tell me, in the strictest confidence', he wrote, 'whether you have any wish to be a baronet. Of course I do not ask you without a sufficient reason'.[5]

Raphael and Vigors were unseated on 19 August 1835, and no baronetcy coming Raphael's way, he made public his belief that he had been swindled. Eventually, as we have seen, the entire business, complete with correspondence between the combatants, landed up before the Commons inquiry. O'Connell won through. On 11 March 1836, the inquiry exonerated him from all charges of corrupt practice, although it declared that his conduct in relation to the by-election had been intemperate.

> Your Committee cannot help observing, that the whole tone and tenor of this Letter [O'Connell to Raphael, 1 June 1835] were calculated to excite much suspicion and grave animadversion; but they must add, that, upon a very careful investigation . . . no charge of a pecuniary character can be attached to Mr O'Connell.[6]

Little he cared for such reproof. He had been cleared of the potentially disastrous accusations, explicit and implicit, of dishonest behaviour. He had been able to establish that he had paid over the £2000 (in fact, by his own error, £2015) to Vigors. This was the vital thing, for O'Connell had in his usual careless way mixed the 'political' with his private money. The innuendo that he had gained personally from the transaction had represented his gravest danger. After some digging for the necessary vouchers and receipts, he could also fairly claim that the money had gone to meet electoral expenses. 'Why', he declared,

> no usurer ever made so good a bargain as this man [Raphael] did. No man ever was subject to a worse bargain than that which, in his absence, I made for Mr Vigors, but which he at once adopted and ratified . . . Surely it is only necessary to say, that no man ever yet had a five days poll for a county who would not rejoice at having but £1000 to pay as his moeity of the expenses – sheriff, sub-sheriff, booths, poll-clerks, deputies, agents, inspectors, books, paper, printing, advertising, carriage of voters to the assize towns, and a tremendous train of et ceteras. If there should be no petition, I agreed, on the part of Mr Vigors, that the greater part of the second £1000, more than one-half of it – whatever might be the amount of the election expenses – should be applied to the formation of a fund to indemnify the voters, and their friends and relations, from that persecution which the Carlow landlords then threatened and have since exercised. This plan Raphael . . . approved . . . [7]

Members of the Commons in 1836 would have had little difficulty in crediting that £2000 or even £4000 might soon be swallowed up in any county contest; and voter indemnification funds had been common in Ireland since 1826. O'Connell may have been aided too by a feeling among MPs that Raphael's insistence upon highly restrictive conditions for his advance bordered on sharp practice; many of them would have been all too familiar with electoral accounts soaring beyond the original 'tenders' for expenses. Certainly, O'Connell was aided by the government, in whose interests, ultimately speaking, he had acted. When on 21 April 1836, Hardy attempted to have the report of the committee of inquiry set aside, Russell and other ministers came to O'Connell's rescue and, in a vote on substantially party lines, crushed the renewed assault.

Despite his 'acquittal', the episode damaged O'Connell – and by extension the ministry which supported him. Some mud always sticks, and plenty had been thrown. Moreover, O'Connell's correspondence with Raphael, now widely known, showed him in some unpleasing lights, alternately wheedling and threatening, trying to buy Raphael off and sliding over the apparent promise to see Raphael clear of petition expenses over and above those covered by his £2000. O'Connell tried to rebut the last charge by claiming that Raphael had

> admitted, that although, VIGORS was bound to pay all the expenses as long as he saw any prospect of a successful issue, he was not bound to continue the contest after expending the [second] £1000 and, that, when he had no adequate motive to expend more money, he was under no

obligation to go further. If RAPHAEL afterwards employed an agent, and counsel of his own, he did so upon the most explicit understanding, that he had no claim upon any person for his voluntarily choosing to do so.[8]

O'Connell also protested strongly 'against the treacherous practice of publishing letters, written in that careless and confidential way, which results from the belief that what one writes can never meet the public eye'.[9] But even these defences (let alone Raphael's counter-claims) were grist to the tories' mill; and their newspapers ground them gleefully to the last.

Meanwhile, more grist had arrived. Soon after O'Connell's return to London, Ellen Courtenay and a youth claiming to be O'Connell's son began to follow him each Sunday as he walked from his residence in Langham Place to mass at the Spanish chapel; on the way they importuned him for support. At last, on Sunday 13 March 1836, John O'Connell, who accompanied his father, strove to drive the boy away, in the end hitting him several times with his umbrella. Three days later, he found himself before the Bow Street magistrates, charged with assault. John was fined 20s., but the self-styled 'Henry O'Connell' gained no other satisfaction. The magistrates refused to listen to his claim and, in effect, instructed him to stop dogging O'Connell in the streets. O'Connell himself did not appear in Bow Street but John was supported by his brothers Maurice and Morgan and his brother-in-law Fitz-Simon in a brave show of family solidarity.

Apart from a brief but total denial of Ellen Courtenay's and 'Henry's' allegations, made through Fitz-Simon in court, O'Connell adopted the same tactic as in 1832; he maintained public silence. He should have been secure. As one of the magistrates told 'Henry', there were 'legal and proper modes of redress' open to him if he had any claim upon O'Connell,[10] and neither 'Henry' nor Ellen Courtenay appears ever to have pursued these. But with the hostile press, led by *The Times*, in full cry after O'Connell, and even English liberal newspapers bound to notice so rich a potential scandal, the affair was widely publicized. In an oblique attempt to counter the damaging gossip Mary O'Connell, despite her failing health, accompanied her husband on a brief midlands and northern tour (3–12 April 1836) to rouse the English radical reformers. It can scarcely have been a coincidence that 'the ladies of Nottingham' (where he spoke on 4 April) added to their gift to her of a locally-made lace veil 'a testimony of their estimation of her husband's services . . . and of admiration of the domestic support and zealous encouragement which she has always given him in his political career, especially in periods of the greatest trial, difficulty, and discouragement'.[11]

Inadvertently, O'Connell revived the 'scandal' when in a letter read to a meeting in Dublin on 25 August 1836 he threatened to 'bring, in all its proper bearings, before the public the hideous details' of Lord Lyndhurst's life:[12] Lyndhurst was his current *bête noire* for both his recent denigration of the Irish majority as 'alien in language, loyalties and religion'[13] and his close association with *The Times*. O'Connell appears to have had only Lyndhurst's political misdeeds in view, although he did refer, in an unspecific fashion, to a former 'partnership'. But *The Times* made itself an opening by warning the 'unredeemed and unredeemable scoundrel' of what he might expect should he attempt an *exposé* of Lyndhurst's intimate affairs. 'As surely', it 'thundered' on 29 August,

> as he dares to invade the privacy of the life of Lord Lyndhurst, or of any other man, woman, or child, that may happen by themselves or their relations to be opposed to him in politics, so surely will we carry the war into his own domiciles, at Darrynane and Dublin, and show up the whole brood of O'Connells, young and old.

The Times may have had O'Connell's son Maurice in its sights: Maurice fathered, writes Professor M. R. O'Connell, 'several illegitimate children'.[14] In turn, O'Connell 'hurl[ed] defiance' at those 'vile instruments', the editors, and their still 'more vile employers [the Walters]', on his family's as well as his own behalf. They were, he exclaimed, 'blessed be God! [as] unstained as they are cherished'.[15] To answer at all was probably unwise as every word from him fed rather than doused the controversy. Even the support of such liberal newspapers as the *Morning Chronicle* and *Examiner* merely gave new life to the war of words; and the tone of their tory counterparts may be gauged from this conclusion to a *Standard* editorial, 'no other combination of letters that can be put upon paper so comprehensively describes all that is vile, cruel, sordid, and false as the name "Daniel O'Connell" '.[16] Small wonder that O'Connell spoke of 'a political and personal meanness hitherto unknown'.[17] But of course he had only his own success, atop his own scurrility, to blame.

As the Raphael and Courtenay affairs developed during February and March 1836, O'Connell was also embattled on another front, as the committee hearing of the petitions against his and Ruthven's return for Dublin in 1835 at last got under way. Here he faced a host of difficulties. Initially, he was hopeful. After the committee ruled on 9

March 1836 that voters should not be disqualified for non-payment of paying taxes unless they were more than six months in arrears, he wrote, 'I believe this makes us safe'.[18] By 22 March, however, the inquiry had taken so unfavourable a turn that he confessed to Fitzpatrick that the 'expense and vexation are so great that I really am not competent to do any other business until this matter is closed. My own expectations are very gloomy.'[19] He had already solved his leading problem, where to find another constituency should he be unseated. Richard Sullivan, the Repeal MP for Kilkenny city, had given him a letter of resignation from the House for use at his discretion. Sullivan had also arranged for O'Connell to succeed him in the Kilkenny representation at a moment's notice. Well might O'Connell assure his loyal supporter, 'I never can and never will forget your kindness. You have paid me one of the greatest compliments that one man could to another.'[20] But what if the committee determined upon a new election in Dublin? In that case, O'Connell faced a further range of problems. First, Ruthven was at death's door (he died on 31 March) and it was proving most difficult to find another potential candidate; secondly, the tories would ensure that the second contest was at least as expensive as the first; and thirdly, if O'Connell stood again for Dublin, he could scarcely take up Sullivan's offer in the meantime, and would perforce be absent from the House during the most critical phases of the session. If, on the other hand, the committee seated O'Connell's conservative opponents, he wished to counter-petition against them on the ground of bribery. But the timing and form of such petitions were nice questions of tactics, as well as of comparative expense.

With all these hypothetical outcomes and expedients before him, O'Connell was pegged down by glum electoral calculations and precautions throughout the spring of 1836. The one unpalatable certainty was the ruinous expense. The original Dublin contest had cost O'Connell some £650 'exclusive of the sum subscribed in that town',[21] and he had to bear the entire cost of the committee hearing (over £7000) alone. He told Fitzpatrick on 13 May that he would find him

> at the loss of full £8000 at the lowest calculation. It has cost the opposite party four or perhaps five times that sum but what comfort is *that* to me? ... Why am I thus attacked? It is a compliment the Orange faction pay to my utility.
>
> This may be glorious but it is very vexatious. You, therefore, will see at once that the expenses of my large family here — . But I am sick, heartily

sick of thinking on this subject. There is nothing fictitious in the fury with which I am pursued and persecuted. The worst is that I have lost more than a year from active agitation. I felt, pending this petition, like a winged wild fowl.[22]

It may well have been a relief to O'Connell when, on 16 May 1836, the committee finally declared the conservative candidates to be elected, in place of Ruthven and himself, for Dublin city, and when, soon after, his own petitions against the substitution were rejected. O'Connell lost only one day's membership of the House, for, by Sullivan's skilful arrangement, he was returned for Kilkenny on 17 May. At least, he was clear of one morass, even if, as he said himself, 'with heavily encumbered fortune'.[23]

In fact, his long and costly struggle to retain his Dublin seat had won him some sympathy among English liberals and 'respectable' radicals; and after the adverse decision was made known, an 'English testimonial' was set up to compensate him for his losses. About £3000 was subscribed at the meeting to launch the appeal; the 'whole amount he received after deducting expenses, was £8489'.[24] So far so good: O'Connell more or less recouped his heavy Dublin costs, and, in the process, called forth public evidence of substantial English support.

But even this was not without alloy in his unhappy year. He had meanwhile fallen into another trouble. On 10 May 1836 he and his 'tail' voted for the second reading of a government factory regulation bill, although he had earlier assured Lord Ashley that he would back his alternative 'ten-hours' measure. The government bill, having been carried by a majority of only two, was then dropped; but O'Connell was widely denounced for both his tergiversation and his cruel indifference to the sufferings of the factory children, who would continue to work more than ten hours on certain days. It was soon rumoured that he had been bribed. The July number of *Blackwood's Magazine* reviled him for selling out 'the infant supplicants for mercy ... The sordid Judas of these days betrayed them for gold';[25] this typified the charges made freely in the tory and working-class press. They would seem unwarranted. The 'English testimonial' (which somehow served as the basis of the indictment) was not set afoot until well after the vote on the factory bill, and there is no evidence to suggest that it was inspired by any consideration other than the Dublin debt, which had been incurred as much on the government's behalf as on his own. Nor should O'Connell's claim that he had been persuaded to change his mind by the statistics and 'authorities' quoted in the debate be scouted out of hand. The matter was not (despite its popular presentation) a simple issue of right and wrong but rather 'nothing less than a deplorable contest in inhumanity'.[26] *The Times* was not far from the truth when it observed that the mill owners had 'found in Mr P. Thomson [the president of the board of trade, who introduced the bill] a ready tool of their cupidity, and the right hon. gentleman, on looking at his primer, found that "the less labour is interfered with the better" '.[27] But Ashley's bill was equally defective. It implied the raising of the weekly total of the children's hours from forty-eight to fifty-eight; by abandoning any attempt to provide checks on age, it opened the door wide to the employment of children under nine; and it totally ignored education, safety and welfare. A much more likely charge against O'Connell is that he switched his votes in order to stave off the government's defeat; this would have been in keeping with his general line of conduct in 1836–41. None the less, it was the charge of pecuniary corruption which dominated in the furore of mid-1836.

Fuel was added to this particular fire by a concurrent rumour that O'Connell had accepted a douceur of £5000, through the agency of Pierce Mahony, to carry a Dublin-Drogheda railway bill through the House of Commons. Certainly, O'Connell had chaired the meeting which recommended that such a bill be prepared, and he regarded the projected railway (later built) as 'a speculation of the utmost value if in nothing else in expending £400,000 in labour'.[28] But such railway schemes and acts were a commonplace of the time, and there was nothing in itself sinister in either O'Connell's conduct or his views. Mahony publicly repudiated the charge as a downright lie and challenged the anonymous 'slanderer' to declare himself, so that he might hale him before the courts for defamation. As to O'Connell, Mahony declared,

> he owed it to that most eminent man to state, that he did not believe there was one existing more above the suspicion of entering into so base an arrangement; and after a confidential intercourse of nearly 25 years, he did not hesitate to avow that, upon Mr O'CONNELL'S honour, he placed the most entire reliance . . .[29]

The shortlived 'scandal' was of small importance in itself, but undoubtedly significant as an index of the extent to which O'Connell's reputation for personal probity had by now been stained – at least, in the eyes of his innumerable British ill-wishers.

As if his cup of controversy were not already full, he was also assailed during the summer of 1836 for the Roman Church's supposed endorsement of intolerance and persecution, as revealed by one of its text-books of moral theology: the point was of course to establish the perils of handing over even municipal government – let alone an independent parliament – to a driven rabble of Irish papists. O'Connell was challenged to participate in a grand debate at Exeter Hall on 12 July (symbolic day!), the arrangements for which were to be drawn up by a body of MPs nominated in equal numbers by O'Connell and the British Protestant Association. Sensibly, O'Connell refused to be embroiled. In a public letter to the reverend secretary of the Association he mocked the proposed 'mummery' and good-humouredly bade the meeting to 'resolve away' to its heart's content.[30] This did not of course silence the rabid Protestants, who formed yet another corps in the army of O'Connell's denigrators.

As if he stood in a pillory, variegated tory missiles had flown at him from all directions throughout the parliamentary session of 1836. At the very least, they ate up his time and broke his concentration on his essential business. Kevin O'Higgins' depiction of his own plight in 1922 seems remarkably apropros O'Connell's in 1836 – 'standing amidst the ruins of one administration, with the foundations of another not yet built, with wild men screaming through the keyhole'.[31]

II

A still more grievous blow was to fall on O'Connell later in the same year: his wife died. It is impossible to fix in time the onset of Mary's final illness. As early as 13 September 1835 O'Connell wrote to her from England, 'how I do long to hear . . . of your health being reestablished'.[32] But between this date and the end of January 1836 she appears to have journeyed from Derrynane to Dublin, back to Derrynane and thence eventually to London, which suggests, though not certainly, a considerable measure of recovery. As we have seen, she also accompanied O'Connell on his brief tour of English industrial cities in early April, but she was by then clearly an ill woman. Within four or five weeks she was in Tunbridge Wells, taking the waters, under the direction of O'Connell's friend, the Harley Street physician, John Elmore. On 30 May O'Connell expressed his relief at her report that this treatment was 'agreeing with' her, though he suspected that she might, out of a mistaken kindness, have misled him as to her improvement. In the usual sad and probably unmeant fashion, he begged to be told 'nothing but the truth'.[33]

In August 1836 the O'Connells returned to Derrynane. Possibly

Mary had stayed in Tunbridge until their departure from England. At any rate, her case was clearly hopeless by the time that she reached Kerry once again. In a 'Strictly confidential' letter of 4 September to Barrett, O'Connell struggled to come to terms with his impending loss:

> God help me! my ever beloved is in a state of much suffering and daily losing ground. I do most potently fear she cannot recover. She may linger weeks. One week may ... Oh God help me ... !
>
> The purest spirit that ever dwelt in a human breast. She did not believe in the existence of evil. I am incompetent or too womanish and too weak to do my public duty and this is what she would condemn. But I think I can rally.
>
> She would advise me to devote my energies, even in misery, to Ireland. I need not smile for that would resemble a crime; but what am I writing! Only, after all, my great consolation will be a dogged and determined activity in the cause of Ireland.[34]

In mid-September she was moved to John Primrose's house near Cahirciveen in the desperate hope that it might prove a healthier place. But she was soon returned to Derrynane to die. Throughout her decline, O'Connell made no mention of his affliction in his letters, except for those to close Irish political friends. Even to them he wrote with uncharacteristic restraint – to Pierce Mahony, 'This is a subject not to be obtruded on others. Its pressure is alas mine own';[35] to Richard Sullivan, 'my domestic prospects are not brightening';[36] and to Fitzpatrick, 'Hope, which comes to all, comes not to me.'[37]

O'Connell was suffering doubly for he feared that Maurice might also be on the way to death – apparently from tuberculosis. 'Maurice is in a very precarious state', he told Barrett, 'I will act upon your hint and send him to a warmer climate for the winter.'[38] Of Mary he despaired, but almost worse was the agony of doubt about his son's survival. On 9 September 1836, telling Fitzpatrick of his great alarm, he added, 'These afflictions impair my public ability, as well as tear to pieces my private affections.'[39] Maurice came through a very severe 'attack on the lungs' in mid-October, but O'Connell had been so frightened that he decided to leave Mary temporarily in order to

> take up [to Dublin] an exact statement of his case and ... have a consultation of medical men – Crampton, Colles, and White – on my arrival ... I must decide about Maurice. At his time of life it is the saddest of the sad but I *must* think of something else. If he is to go southward for the winter, there is no time to be lost.[40]

On 26 October, he wrote to Fitzpatrick: 'Expect me in Dublin on the 2nd of November . . . Mrs O'Connell is in that state that she will not perceive that I am away. She may linger on week after week with nothing but despair of amelioration. Alas, alas! I cannot describe to you my own *mental* state.'[41] He never reached Dublin, however; he had got no further on his way than Killarney when on 31 October word reached him that his wife had died. She was 58 years old.

Mary O'Connell was buried in the same tomb as Hunting Cap on the Abbey Island at Derrynane. There are obvious ironies in the old antagonists being gravemates and in Mary's coming finally to rest in a place from which she had striven so often to escape. But there are fitnesses as well. A single slab covers the two persons who did most to shape O'Connell's life; and they lie at the far extremity of that strip of land which O'Connell thought of as woven into his very being – within the broken monastery walls among the dunes and grasses of the wave-torn spit which runs from the house and pleasure ground of Derrynane into the sea.

O'Connell's private grief is necessarily beyond estimation. Part of his very being had been cut away, in a sort of surgery without anaesthetic. Even his 'public' loss was irreparable. For more than thirty years, Mary had received and responded independently to his inner political thoughts. In his first surviving letter after her death, he described her as 'the most right-thinking woman *I ever knew*', adding 'It is however passed, and I only remain to recollect.'[42] Three years before, on the crucial question of canvassing Repeal immediately in the House of Commons, he observed, 'My wife – who in almost all my political resolves has been, I believe, uniformly right – is strongly against my taking any part.'[43] It would be absurd to suppose that he followed her political dictation, or always sought or heeded her political advice. But, unquestionably, he believed her judgment to be sensitive and sound; it would always be frankly yet delicately delivered, and ever-coloured by a fierce regard for his reputation, especially his integrity and consistency. There could be no substitute for such a confidante. Even shrewd, loyal intimates such as Fitzpatrick and Barrett were far from privy to all O'Connell's mind; nor would they dare to open their own minds completely to one who so towered above them in name and station. Moreover, they could not provide the reflective sympathy which O'Connell, like most men, needed – or at least yearned for – to sustain his confidence in himself. On Christmas Day 1834, for instance, he had described in considerable detail to 'the most tender of wives, my own darling Mary!' his marvellous forensic triumph in *Hodgens* v. *Mahon*, which had just been decided. 'I was most vehemently cheered', he concluded, 'and even the judge did not intervene to prevent it, that is, the continued cheers. Darling, I indulge my vanity that you may share in it.'[44] Never again would there be anyone to whom he could write such words or say such things or look to for glowing comfort. The well that he had drawn on for a third of a century or more was now sealed and soundless.

III

O'Connell had entered 1836 confident (he asserted) of sweeping advances towards his declared legislative objectives, parliamentary, municipal and tithe reform. The first was much the least important because the cabinet would not entertain the proposals from which he might have gained significantly – an enlargement of the Irish electorate, an increase in the number of Irish seats, or an equalization of the Irish constituencies – but instead focused on the single issue of voter registration. Although O'Connell himself had taken a hand in the drawing up of the government's 1835 registration bill, which had been rejected by the Lords, it was far from certain that his party stood to profit from its passage; and when its successor, introduced on 10 March 1836, was later dropped, the O'Connellites were relieved rather than resentful.

The key measure of the year was of course the Irish municipal corporations bill. It was to counter this that the tories, with *The Times* and Lyndhurst in the van, unleashed their intensive and protracted campaign against O'Connell, both personally and as the main subversive. The animus of O'Connell's assailants sprang from their penny-dreadful fears that the Ascendancy's loss of control of the Irish municipalities would prove the first step towards surrendering the entire 'sister' island to the forces of priestcraft and revolution. O'Connell seemed to them to give some substance to this horrid vision, when, early in the debate on the 1836 bill, he announced that each reformed Irish corporation would constitute 'a Normal school for teaching the science of peaceful political agitation'.[45] In fact, the new bill was practically identical with that abandoned in 1835, when parliamentary time ran out. The only substantial change came in the committee stage when, to O'Connell's fury, the government conceded that the vital office of sheriff should no longer be partly elective but instead filled at the lord lieutenant's nomination. For internal conservative party ends, Peel eventually took up the counter-policy of the 'abolition of all [Irish] corporations without exception', with the corollary of 'direct rule' of the Irish municipalities by Dublin Castle.[46] This alternative fared badly in the House of Commons where the government secured resounding majorities of more than 60 in each of the critical divisions. Greville (prematurely) read these triumphs as a sign that the storm against O'Connell had blown itself out: 'the Tories . . . have overdone their attacks on him, and as it has been their sole *cheval de bataille*, they have ridden it till it has not a leg to stand upon'.[47]

The House of Lords, however, fastened on the simple 'solution' of abolishing the corporations and 'amended' the government's bill accordingly. Strangely, O'Connell's initial reaction was to acquiesce in this attempted *coup*. After all, spoiling the Egyptians was an inviting prospect. As he explained himself to Barrett on 16 May 1836,

> For my own part, I will candidly confess that my first impression was that the extinction of the present Corporations would be a substantial benefit. That they interfere with the administration of justice, and render it partial and corrupt, is now admitted by everybody. There cannot be found any man in either House to offer the least defence, or even palliation, of the conduct of our infamous Corporation[s]. Only think what an avowal by those who were hitherto the protectors of those very Corporations, that they were too bad to be allowed to exist longer, and yet Ireland has endured these now avowed evils! . . .
>
> I thought no sacrifice too great to get rid of such a system; but that is not now my opinion . . . We should be, I think, disgraced if we were to accept it, and we may trust that the people of England will assist us effectually to have 'justice done to Ireland.'[48]

O'Connell's conclusion gives us the key to his about-face. Lyndhurst had challenged his entire strategy for 1836 when he told his fellow peers on 9 May that to apply 'the same principle . . . to different places must produce dissimilar results, and could not lead to equal justice'.[49] Not merely did Lyndhurst imply that the Irish majority was unfit for even municipal 'liberty' but also he struck at the heart of O'Connell's 'Justice for Ireland' reasoning. Mulgrave appreciated what O'Connell had now at stake. 'I believe', he wrote to Russell from Dublin on 15 April,

> that there is no other question on which there is more general anxiety [in Ireland], not perhaps that they anticipate any very great actual advantages from it [municipal reform] except in the large towns but because they consider it as embodying the principle of *equal justice to Ireland* . . . the [Irish] Liberal Party will unite in counting the Municipal Bill as the last of

433

equal Rights on points not connected with the Church, and it would be very difficult to ensure continued confidence in the Government with our submitting to be beat upon such a point without an appeal to the people.[50]

Russell tried to save something from the wreck by proposing, as a *pis aller*, that only the eleven largest Irish municipalities should retain their corporations, the remaining towns to be directly administered by the crown. Most reluctantly, O'Connell fell into line, but, as he later told Pigot, was happily rescued from the consequences of this embarrassing surrender by the Lords' intransigence. 'The Corporate Reform Bill was *amended* by Lord John against my consent. I protested in private against the compromise but was driven in public to support *the party*; and it is now well I did so, as we have had the credit of moderation without being tied to any restrictive enactments.'[51] The Lords' second rejection was enough to stiffen the government's resolve. Russell went so far to appease O'Connell as to advise the creation of new peers to offset the tory majority in the upper House. Although there was no possibility that Melbourne would endorse such a step on any Irish issue, Russell's gesture of solidarity had its effect in re-binding O'Connell to the whigs. As he himself affirmed on 30 June, during the debate on the Lords' obstruction,

> I know the present Government are disposed to do all they possibly can in order to obtain justice for the people of Ireland. Let my support of them be misrepresented as it may, I shall support them because I know there is no alternative between a system of uncompromising despotism in Ireland, and the maintenance in power of the present Ministry.[52]

None the less, the cabinet support promised to O'Connell was a barren sort of satisfaction. The fact remained that Irish municipal reform, the leading prize of the parliamentary session, was lost for 1836. O'Connell would have to try again in 1837 to mount sufficient Irish and English popular pressure to force the Lords' hand. It was all ominously reminiscent of the fruitless successes of Catholic Emancipation in the House of Commons before 1829, and the grinding toil to be re-commenced with every failure. This might be balanced by consciousness of the eventual triumph; but no man in his sixties can afford to invest much in 'the long run'. Moreover, the fate of the new tithe bill seemed to form a gloomy precedent. The 1836 tithe measure was practically a copy of that defeated in the upper House in 1835, and it followed, with depressing fidelity, the sad course of its predecessor. Having passed its third reading in the Commons on 4 July 1836, it quickly foundered in the Lords, where the essential appropriation clauses were rejected. Was it not all too likely that the municipal corporations bill would fall similarly in 1837 at precisely the same obstacle as had brought it down in 1836?

O'Connell responded to his political repulses in his customary way. He proclaimed a new agitation and, with lightning speed, designed an organization to control it. Significantly, it was to MacHale, the leader among the sympathetic clergy, that he first announced his project. 'I intend . . .', he wrote to him on 2 July 1836,

> to propose the revival of the Catholic Association in a new name and somewhat broader basis. It will bear the name of 'The General Association of Ireland', to be dissolved so soon as full corporate reform and a satisfactory adjustment of the tithe are obtained by law.
>
> I intend to have the 'Irish rent' to replace the Catholic rent and to find a friend to indemnify *tithe victims* but this part of the arrangement will require discretion, tact, and some cautious management. You will see my plans fully developed in the *Pilot* of Wednesday [6 July].[53]

The great curiosity of this mass movement was its specific commitment to support the current government and preserve public order; and in fact it did serve the general liberal as well as Irish interests. But primarily it was meant, as its author clearly implied, to replicate the Catholic Association in machinery and fervour. As an agitator, O'Connell was nothing if not practical. 'The Government will *not* discountenance us', he assured Fitzpatrick, also on 2 July,

> Our organisation will be complete. Treasurers, Finance Committee, Committee for each Province, a person responsible for each county, Registry Committees *out* of Dublin . . .
>
> Every man who subscribes one shilling will have his name enrolled. Every man who subscribes a pound to be a member, being proposed and seconded. In short, all and more than the Catholic Association has done. This is the precious moment to set to England one example more. I am determined that nothing shall prevent me from working out my plan. One way or the other, we must succeed in obtaining justice for Ireland.
>
> I write to Barrett a letter, a short one for publication [in the *Pilot*]. This is private, that is, not for the newspapers. Can you get me ten names of men who will work? If I had but *ten* real *working* men it would be quite enough. Surely ten such men can be found. The day of meeting must be *Thursday*, to give the weekly papers time to send the debates to the country.[54]

In several respects, the General Association was one of the more successful of O'Connell's popular excursions, especially after Mary's death and Maurice's recovery released him for serious management and campaigning. He was fortunate in having a readymade enemy to rouse the necessary element of passion in his following. Irish tories had formed a Church Property Protection Association which, in the spring of 1836, resurrected an antique form of writ by which they successfully pursued tithe defaulters, even to the point of arrest and imprisonment – in the process compelling the reluctant Irish executive to employ the police and army to execute court orders. Nothing was better fitted to enflame tenant resistance and clerical indignation, and thereby fuel O'Connell's movement. The General Association could busy itself with counter-actions on behalf of the defaulters. These had, from O'Connell's standpoint, the sterling merits of both stirring up enthusiasm and belligerency and justifying the call for generous subscriptions. As always, 'Rent' was O'Connell's chief measure of an agitation's health, and by this criterion the Association flourished. As one of his faithful disciples put it in May 1837,

> see the silent and increasing influence the General Association is acquiring through the agency of Justice Rent. Observe the alarm of the lordly aristocrats of England. How well and surely does their experience enable them to calculate the result. Why is this? Not in consequence of the power money of itself bestows; but because it is a sure and steady index of the People's feelings – because it is the thermometer by which the warmth of those feelings can be best ascertained, and in proportion as the contributions increase or diminish in such proportion are the National sentiments indicated.[55]

None the less, O'Connell trod on delicate ground in basing much of his appeal upon the tithe issue. As early as 1 July 1836, Sharman Crawford, an independent and crochety Ulster liberal, challenged him in the Commons to revert to his original demand for the total abolition of Irish tithes. O'Connell dismissed Crawford as the sort of visionary who would invariably sacrifice an achievable good for an impossible ideal. Although a mere half-dozen O'Connellite MPs backed Crawford, it was irritating that a persistent dissentient voice should be raised in parliament on a matter deeply engaging the sympathies of the Catholic clergy and substantial tenant farmers. Worse still, Crawford also raised it again at meetings of the Association late in 1836, adding to his demand for complete eradication strong denunciations of O'Connell for sacrificing Irish to governmental interests. This did little to disturb O'Connell's mastery of his movement, but it certainly placed him on the defensive, in particular with the bolder spirits among the priests and bourgeoisie. A rift with MacHale began to open.

The *contretemps* was all the more unfortunate because it was clear to O'Connell by the end of 1836 that he would have to make more instead of less concessions on Irish tithes. A possible compromise was beginning to be mooted at Westminster whereby the House of Lords would allow the substance of the Irish corporations bill to pass in return for the abandonment of the appropriation clauses in the tithe bill. O'Connell succumbed privately to the temptation and confessed himself ready to yield up appropriation should need be. 'I wish with all my heart', he told the cabinet on 29 December 1836 through his usual intermediary, Warburton,

> the Ministry were decently freed from that *Dilemma*. If there were a proper deduction from the burden of the tithes, there would for the present be no surplus; and it is really too bad to risk *on such* a point a ministry who are for the first time in history conquering the 'Anti-Saxon' spirit of Ireland and adding eight million to the King's subjects.

As a *quid pro quo*, O'Connell sought the restoration of the clause in the corporations bill which left the shrievalty a primarily elective office. 'This plan', he justly pointed out, 'was abandoned as a concession to the Tories who made use of it as an argument against any new corporations in Ireland.'[56] But even if he were to gain his point, it would be but a miserable offset to his numerous large, yet fruitless, retreats on Irish bills throughout the year.

Thus O'Connell ended 1836 not only with no legislative trophy to display for all the labours and obloquy he had endured but also with the centrepiece of tithe reform virtually given up, Irish parliamentary reform virtually forgotten, and the battle for the municipal corporations unresolved. Even had he not lost Mary, it might still be counted as the worst of years.

IV

Was the crescendo of all O'Connell's strivings since July 1834 to be nothing more than an Irish municipal corporations bill in 1837? Apparently – but this should not be written off as necessarily negligible, by O'Connell's measurement, at least. First, he was faced by a large tory majority in the House of Lords bent on systematic obstruction. The degree of intransigence varied. Wellington was comparatively pliant, Lyndhurst, an ultra of ultras. But all were ready to use their blocking power to kill liberal Irish legislation, steeled in their resolve by widespread public support and the belief that the conservatives might well win the next general election. O'Connell's logical course, to campaign seriously for the abolition of emasculation of the House of Lords, was not really a practicable proposition in the 1830s. His best counter was to increase popular pressure; and, accordingly, during January and February 1837 he whipped up meetings and petititons of the General Association not only in favour of the Irish bills but also in support of such general radical reforms as the secret ballot; he also strenuously wooed the British non-conformists by throwing himself into their current campaign for the abolition of church rates. But his Irish agitation was respectable (in all senses) rather than a menacing concentration of the masses. Fagan, one of its principal managers, wrote afterwards, that although it

> had all the appearance of a political crisis it passed off like a dark but fleeting cloud. It was but a transitory exhibition of feeling . . . In fact, none, but those who complied with them can know how deep was the disappointment of the people, at the adjournment of the great question, for the success of which they felt an intense anxiety, and for which alone they have an inclination – the question of Repeal. O'Connell while in England, aided, by letters addressed to the people of Ireland, and to the National [i.e. General] Association, the agitation for Justice – and, like every act of his, it had its effect amongst the middle classes, but the people had but one all-absorbing interest – the attainment of Repeal, and, until he opened that bright prospect to their view, it was difficult to urge them into exertion.[57]

O'Connell's English meetings also failed to win a fiery response. His radical support in Britain had been both narrowed and weakened by the events of 1836.

Secondly, although the municipal corporations governed only one-tenth of the Irish population, their capture was a dear objective to O'Connell. Albeit with some over-simplification, we might specify this as the third of his major emancipationist goals – the first being the removal of Roman Catholic disabilities and the second a share in the exercise of Irish central power, a voice in the shaping of Irish policy and a hand in the filling of Irish offices. The corporations may have been generally impoverished and often futile. But any important constituent in the system of Irish Ascendancy was *per se* a prime target for O'Connell. He coveted moreover their hoards of petty patronage, rights of local legislation, magisterial courts and influence over parliamentary elections. Finally, they represented, on however small a scale, a form of the self-government for which O'Connell craved. Shaw once said of nationalist movements in general, that they were 'only the agonising symptom of a suppressed natural function';[58] the dictum applied fully to O'Connell's eagerness to control even a City

Hall. All this helps to explain the seeming extravagance of the price he was prepared to pay for municipal reform. Both practically and symbolically it appeared to him the next stage in a long and difficult advance.

Meanwhile, it looked as if the major parties were moving towards the sort of compromise on Irish legislation to which O'Connell had consented at the close of 1836. He prepared the way for it in Ireland by a carefully worded letter of 18 February 1837 to Fitzpatrick. In this, he considered Peel's likely terms, 'to allow the Irish Municipal Reform Bill to pass *both Houses*' in return for an appropriation-less tithe bill, with the commutation fixed at 70 per cent. 'Should they [the government] accede,' he continued,

> the Irish members will probably feel it their duty to protest against any compromise on the subject of the tithes and accept the deduction merely as an instalment . . . Certainly something would be gained by carrying into effect the bargain between Peel and the Ministry but none of the Irish popular members could commit themselves to the plan.[59]

Clearly O'Connell was ready, for the sake of his Irish public, to withhold support from the government on the major Irish issues, *provided* that it was safe to do so. If Russell and Peel came to an understanding, a favourable majority was assured in the House of Commons, and O'Connell could abstain, or even oppose, secure in the knowledge that the clause or measure in question would be carried none the less. He would not of course take any action which might actually endanger the corporations bill, all the more so as the ministry had yielded to his wishes on the election of sheriffs issue.

As the parliamentary session progressed, the conditions of a tacit settlement between the liberal and conservative leaderships gradually clarified. Peel insisted on the establishment of an Irish poor law – which the whigs already favoured – partly in the hope that a new rating system might do something to preserve tory interests in the municipalities. O'Connell reluctantly consented. For almost a decade he had fought against any such measure, even at the cost of endangering Bishop Doyle's support in earlier days. His reasons were a characteristic compound of traditionalism and 'modernity'. On the one hand, he argued that a poor law would obliterate Christian charity and compassion, and weaken the human interdependency which he idealized as the mark of his own sort of landed proprietorship. On the other, political economy told him that it was folly at the least to disturb the market forces; in particular, communal support of the able-bodied would be disastrous for themselves as well as the precarious Irish economy. Nor should we forget that O'Connell was himself a landlord, open to the usual landlord nightmare of Irish property sinking under the immeasurable weight of Irish pauperdom. Despite all this, O'Connell yielded to political necessity in 1837, and when on 13 February, Russell introduced an Irish poor relief bill modelled on the English workhouse form of 1834, he greeted it with assumed benignity, announcing that he 'cheerfully acced[ed] to the proposed plan'.[60] One other element in the legislative amalgam is worth noting. The government added a clause to the tithe bill imposing a tax of 10 per cent on the incomes of Church of Ireland ministers for general (and not merely Anglican) educational purposes. It was hoped that this would, *inter alia*, help O'Connell to justify his change of front at home.

O'Connell's position was now set. He would support the ministerial package of the three major Irish bills, with the proviso that he might formally oppose specific clauses where the government ran no risk of defeat. The grand scheme, however, foundered, more or less accidentally. Twice the House of Lords postponed consideration of the Irish municipal corporations bill (which had passed through the lower house unscathed) until it could legislate on tithes and poor relief. But on 20 June 1837, before either of these measures could be settled, William IV died. This meant a new general election and the ruin of the entire legislative programme of the session. O'Connell was – by his own view of things – badly out of luck. Despite Wellington's initial reluctance to follow Peel's line in accepting the trinity of measures, and Lyndhurst's inveterate opposition to them all, the three bills would probably have passed the House of Lords had the parliamentary process not been interrupted; and two of them, the corporations and tithe bills, were much more advantageous to O'Connell than the measures subsequently enacted. Besides, he had surrendered his position on the poor law without any counterbalancing gain, and uselessly given up considerable ground on tithes. Meanwhile, this last had precipitated a serious revolt in Ireland.

On 26 May 1837 MacHale sent O'Connell a petition from the clergy of the Tuam archdiocese protesting hotly against the concessions made in even the 1837 tithe bill. Pointedly, MacHale used O'Connell's own formula 'Justice for Ireland' as his frame of reference. 'The Tithe Bill', he concluded, 'they [the people] took on as the test of the justice which has been so long promised but of which the performance is, they complain, so long delayed. Wishing you many happy years to aid in the consummation of that justice which the country expects.'[61] Alarmed, O'Connell reported to Fitzpatrick, 'Dr MacHale's resolutions have made a considerable sensation . . . Unless he shall relax, the Connaught members will vote against us.'[62] He pleaded for reconsideration, or at least delay in presenting the petition. Attempting at once to frighten, flatter and feed the sectarian animus of the archbishop, he wrote on 31 May,

> I am, I own, timid and could have wished that this blow had not been given to the falling fabric of ministerial power. I do believe it will be decisive of their fate. But do not understand these as tones of reproach. I may be sorrowful but, in plain truth, I can have no elements in my mind which could create anger when, as in this instance, the wise and the good adopt a course too bold for my humbler temper. What I grieve at is simply that it should have been necessary for your Grace to have adopted that course at the moment of all others most critical to the continuance of the only bearable government Ireland ever experienced since the fatal day when the followers of the murderers of Becket polluted our shores.[63]

O'Connell went on, in labyrinthine self-justification, to argue that the 1837 tithe bill had surrendered comparatively little. But MacHale would have none of this. For him, it was enough that the 'enemy' was rejoicing. 'What confirms the distrust of the people . . .', he told O'Connell on 4 June, 'is that the bill is palatable to many of the parsons of the country and to the Tory landlords.'[64] MacHale had come to distrust both O'Connell's leadership and his judgment. The breach now opening up between the two was to last until 1840. In effect, O'Connell had lost his political control of the western province.

Immediately, however, he was absorbed in the forthcoming general election, to be fought out during August 1837. On 28 June, he instructed the General Association of Ireland to reconstitute itself 'The Friends of the Queen' for the purpose of conducting the electoral campaign. This purported to be, literally speaking, an ultra-loyal body: 'we must all', he wrote in his public letter to the Association, 'with one accord, rally round the throne of the Queen, and in support of her Majesty's government'.[65] In fact, O'Connell meant simply to revive the election strategy of 1835, whereby all Irish 'anti-tories' – whigs, liberals, radicals and Repealers – made common cause, refraining entirely from opposition to one another. The bonds would be all the stronger now that O'Connell could claim the Queen as a liberal sympathizer and point to the liberals' 'proven' Irish record while in office. With extraordinary fidelity, the pattern of the last general election was repeated. O'Connell was again the great

energizer, accommodator, manipulator and dictator – as circumstances suggested – of the Irish campaign. Again he suffered all the
anxieties of conniving the safe, and where possible cheap, return of his
family connection. He even played once more the difficult game of
arranging a fall-back position for himself in Kilkenny city, should he
fail in Dublin; he was determined to win back the capital if he could,
writing 'confidentially' to Fitzpatrick on 1 July, 'You know that I can
be *compelled* to stand for Dublin.'[66] Similarly, Maurice proved as
negligent as ever in his 'contest' of Tralee. Having learnt that his son
intended soon to leave the county town for Derrynane, O'Connell
wrote on 11 July to one of the local managers of the campaign, 'See
him [Maurice] and tell him from me that I shall be utterly offended if
he leaves Tralee without my express permission. Read this passage for
him, and if you coincide with me in opinion, pray urge him to remain
until after the assizes at least, nay, until I tell him he may go to
Derrynane.'[67] In fact, O'Connell won Dublin city, and despite
Maurice's temporary loss of Tralee (he was later seated on petition)
could claim an Irish triumph overall. Whereas the liberals lost
considerable ground in Britain, the Irish 'anti-tories' of 1837 carried
71 of the country's 105 seats as against 67 in 1835.

The Melbourne ministry now depended absolutely on O'Connell's
Irish votes for its existence. Without them it would have been in a
minority of at least 25 in the House of Commons on several of the
main contested issues. Theoretically, then, O'Connell held the balance
of power in the lower house and with it the capacity to make or destroy
British governments *ad nauseam*. But, as has been said, such a
mechanical model of the Commons bears little relation to the realities
of the mid-1830s. Party discipline was still weak. Even O'Connell
suffered from regular defections from his 'tail', as for example his
injunction of 21 April 1837 to Barrett of the *Pilot* makes very clear:

> *write a paragraph* – observe, a paragraph IN LEADS, upon the Irish
> Members. Mention Mullins of Kerry, who has been *missing* ever since the
> recess. Mention the folly of pairing as to election petitions. Mention Smith
> O'Brien's refusal to vote on the late division respecting the Irish Legion . . .
> Take care that this should not appear to originate with me. Comment upon
> the absence of every other member who was absent but of course, treat the
> real friends lightly.[68]

About fifty of the British members still followed the old practice of
normally supporting the government of the day, whatever its political
complexion. Moreover, the idea of constituting a permanently

independent Irish party, let alone an independent Irish opposition, was altogether foreign to O'Connell's concept of the contemporary political alignments in both Britain and Ireland. The liberal as against the reactionary cause was the essential divider everywhere. It would be equally anachronistic to visualize the conservative party of 1837 considering for a moment a junction with O'Connell for the sake of office. Part of their *raison d'être* was his defeat and if possible destruction, just as the very principle of their post-1886 successors was perpetual and absolute resistance to Home Rule.

In such conditions, the general election of 1837 should be regarded as greatly weakening instead of strengthening O'Connell's political position, all the more so because the liberal losses in Great Britain had been largely among radical MPs. This meant a serious diminution of his natural sympathizers in the House of Commons, and a consequent rightward swing in ministerial policy and conduct. O'Connell felt the change immediately, when the government put pressure on him to wind up the General Association. He yielded without a struggle, comforting himself with the reflection that he could recreate a national organization whenever suited. 'The Ministry', he wrote to Fitzpatrick from Derrynane on 4 September 1837, 'wish to dissolve the Association and I see no reason why we should not gratify them. It is easy to start another whenever necessary.'[69] When he announced his decision publicly in the following month, he presented it as a spontaneous avowal of faith in the Irish executive: 'I think we are arrived at a period when we should give this proof of our satisfaction at the improved state of the administration of the government in Ireland, and of our confidence in the good intentions of our gracious Sovereign, and in those of her Majesty's ministers.'[70] Although O'Connell retained his Dublin 'Registration Office', now under T. M. Ray, for the scrutiny of electoral qualifications, the dismantling of the Association symbolized a further contraction of his political independence.

A second blow fell when parliament re-assembled in November 1837, and Russell, capitalizing on the diminution of the radical numbers in the Commons, rejected out of hand their demands for the secret ballot, triennial parliaments and the extension of the franchise as 'nothing else, but a repeal of the Reform Act [of 1832]'.[71] This was deeply embarrassing for O'Connell. Only a short time before he had urged the English radicals to agitate strongly 'in favour of short parliaments, extended suffrage and the ballot ... The less the Ministers do, the more remains to be done by the reformers. Let each of us then bestir himself to do his share of the work. Ireland at least will support us.'[72] There could be no clearer identification of himself with the cause of further parliamentary reform or of Irish with British radicals. But once Russell had spoken, *salus imperii, suprema lex*: upholding the Melbourne ministry overrode all else. O'Connell's difficulty came to a head at a major rally in Birmingham on 14 December 1837 at which he was guest of honour. While he fully endorsed, of course, the entire reform programme, he pleaded with the meeting to continue to support the government, for Ireland's sake. The chairman, Joshua Scholefield, MP for Birmingham, rebuked him gently, 'You must however be guarded when you meet us again and say *rather less* in praise of the present Administration . . . The men of Birmingham claim you as one of their own kindred and are jealous that any preference should be given *by you* to Ireland over England!'[73] When, however, O'Connell, on reaching Dublin, declared that only a handful of the Birmingham audience of 7000 demurred at his appeal to keep the whigs in power, a young radical, P. H. Muntz, who had spoken at the meeting, left him in no doubt about the depth and bitterness of English radical opposition to his waiving parliamentary reform in the interest of maintaining a friendly government in Dublin. In the name of members of the Birmingham Political Union, Muntz wrote, on 1 January 1838, that

they knew well that Lord Mulgrave was almost the sole boon the Whig government had given to Ireland; they knew that you had no guarantee for a continuance of that boon an hour longer than the Whig administration lasted; they knew that that administration as now composed could not exist many years if even many months . . . Their [the whigs'] object has been to lull the people of Ireland, under your auspices and with promises of future benefits, into security; to quiet them by poor laws and a constabulary force. . . . Ireland in chains, a coalition between Whig and Tory would take place and both would then laugh at you when you found yourself in the position you were in 20 years ago, and the power which might have saved your native country glided from your hands. . . . You pleaded for a government which had declared its deadly hostility to those reforms which the people demand, and then you quitted the meeting without giving any reason for what you asserted. Sir, the people of Birmingham . . . care little whether you call yourself Whig or Radical, they want deeds, not professions . . .[74]

V

O'Connell had meanwhile precipitated a conflict with other radicals – this time Irish and working-class. His return to Dublin from Derrynane at the beginning of November 1837 more or less coincided with the worst of a long series of trade union outrages. On 5 November 'an employer named Armstrong, in company with his wife, four children and another family, was attacked by thirty armed carpenters, while the police looked on'.[75] Next day at the Trades Political Union O'Connell denounced not only the brutal attack but also the associations themselves. They were both a-political (evidently an offence in O'Connell's eyes!) and committed to 'objects connected with the regulation of trade and wages, which they assume the control and management of'.[76] This was the opening shot of a brief but fierce engagement.

O'Connell's liaison with the Dublin artisans (some of whom were Protestants) had its basis in their common interest in Repeal. That the Act of Union had destroyed the city's prosperity was an article of faith among the tradesmen, and O'Connell was always ready to second this belief. Astonishingly, his comparatively good relations with the unions had survived his capture, in November 1831, of their new, independent organization, the Dublin Trades Political Union, and his turning it into an instrument of his own. It was otherwise with O'Connell's postponement of the Repeal issue in 1833, and again after the defeat of the Repeal motion in the House of Commons in 1834. This did arouse working-class hostility. But, as Dr D'Arcy observes, 'Working-class discontent with the shelving of repeal agitation could indeed only be expressed by implication since the artisans now lacked an organ of expression following the domination of the Trades' Political Union by non-artisan elements after 1831.'[77] Besides, O'Connell had endeared himself at the Dublin unions when at the end of 1833 he had refused to align himself with the city's employers in anathemizing a recent wave of labour violence. He told the employers, at their public meeting, that they 'should not have cast the imputation of crime upon the people and then shrunk from coming forward to substantiate their charges'.[78]

A sort of mutual forbearance kept O'Connell and the artisans more or less in harmony until his outburst of 6 November 1837. He ignored – publicly, at least – the trade union outrages which grew apace during 1836–7. They ignored – publicly, at least – the calls from British unions to repudiate him for his 'betrayal' of the factory children in

1836. But the Armstrong bloodshed proved to be one of those 'last straw' cases which bring a train of scandals to a head; and in the general Dublin furore it was only to be expected that O'Connell, then back in residence in the city, should give a lead. This was especially the case because most of the current industrial 'crimes' were conspiracies issuing in the savage use of armed force, precisely what O'Connell had persistently condemned in the agrarian secret societies. Moreover, his contretemps over factory legislation in the preceding year had led him to consider and declare himself on trade associations in general. His speech of 6 November made it clear that while he conscientiously supported the freedom to form such combinations, he considered that the refusal to admit apprentices, the closed shop and the minimum wage all offended the fundamental principles of political economy. Since the Dublin unions were striving to enforce all three, direct conflict was now inevitable.

At first the unions, after the usual fashion of reluctant rebels, blamed the king's evil advisers rather than the king himself. O'Connell was declared to have been deceived by the employers' misrepresentation of the case. The secretary of the stonecutters union, for example, announced that it would grieve him deeply 'should [it] be for a moment supposed that the trades of Dublin had any quarrel with Mr O'Connell. It was with those by whose false and calumnious communications Mr O'Connell had been misled that they contended.'[79] Such pious pretences were sustainable for a time because O'Connell was out of Dublin, in attendance at the House of Commons, for most of November and the first half of December 1837. But when, on his return, the unions memorialized for a chance to be heard by him in their own 'defence' at the Trades Political Union, 'the same place where the charges were made',[80] he left them in no doubt of his utter opposition to their three offensive practices. This led in turn to a mass meeting of the artisans on 26 December at which not only O'Connell's opinions but also his conduct and character were assailed. The chairman called on the meeting to 'make daggers of their tongues and use them against that man who attempted to lower them in the scale of civilized society';[81] one stab was sneers at O'Connell's shuffling on Repeal.

It had always been a merit and mainstay of O'Connell's popular leadership that he answered challenges to his authority immediately and decisively. On 8 January 1838, virtually single-handed, he confronted the artisans in a pre-arranged public disputation in the Corn Exchange rooms. During his three and a half hour opening harangue, he re-traversed his original objections to the unions' restrictive and dictatorial practices, with lengthy excursions on the law of molestation and intimidation and the economics of pricing labour. But he also threw aside, on this occasion, all Queensberry rules of debate and verbally gouged and rabbit-punched his opponents (and especially the artisan's leader, Patrick O'Brien) like a street fighter. He insinuated repeatedly that they were the dupes of his tory enemies and that some at least of the unions were deeply implicated in the trade burning, beatings and murders of the past two years. He played not only the sectarian, but even the spiritual card. Those who refused apprenticeships, he said, denied their own and other children the right to work.

> I, therefore, turn upon you, and tell you, the tradesmen of Dublin, that you are doing that which is unjust and illegal – that which is contrary to religion. There are many of you who frequent your religious duties, and of you I ask do you think that when this speech is read by the Catholic clergy, and the question brought in its true and real light before them, that they can, in the just fulfilment of their duty, give the sacraments to any Catholic who belongs to this system (hear, hear, and confusion).[82]

To the taunts that he had betrayed Repeal, O'Connell responded with a blend of braggadocio and personal denigration:

> But should I fail in attaining that justice [for Ireland], Irishmen, do you imagine, I despair (no)?
>
> > 'Hereditary bondsmen, know ye not,
> > Who would be free, themselves must strike the blow!'
>
> If I fail, I will come back to repeal, if the tradesmen of Dublin do not allow any portion of the faction or any blockhead which may be placed at the head of you to divide you and me (hear, and cheers). As to that Paddy O'Brien, I pity him. I remember once saying of a great squire in the country, that he had a great deal of hair outside his face and nothing at all inside of it (laughter). He was a great man – poor Paddy O'Brien was a great man the day he was at the head of the trades; but I do implore the tradesmen of Dublin to fling away from them any man who attempts to sever the friend of Ireland from the objects of his patriotism (hear, and cheers).[83]

He ended with a well-calculated personal appeal, which also conjured away the 'factory children' charges:

> The calumny of the Manchester children is among the most grievous of those charges, and when I hear it repeated without any ground, and the charge made by the tradesmen of Dublin, I cannot help exclaiming – who,

after me, would serve his country (tremendous cheers, followed by uproar)? Am I not to be treated with even ordinary respect? Am I not old or venerable enough? Am I to be told that that is Irish respect; or have I no tradesmen of Dublin to stand round me (cries of plenty, and cheers – a voice in the crowd exclaimed that it was Orangemen, and none but Orangemen, who produced the confusion). I require that that man hold his tongue; now I put it to every honest Irishman whether he could stand by that man, Mr O'Brien, (cries of no, no,) by him who has calumniated me – the only person who has never deserted the cause of Ireland (loud cheers) – who am doing a painful duty – a duty more to you than to myself. . . . I call on all trades to witness that this man has made use of the subject of the Manchester children as a calumny against me (cheers).[84]

It was a cruel and unscrupulous use of oratorical power. As one of the unionists exclaimed, 'As well might the lion be let loose on the lamb as Mr O'Connell attack such a one as Mr O'Brien, so unable to defend himself against a powerful antagonist like him'.[85] On the other hand, O'Connell was fighting for his political life. The Dublin artisans were an important constituent of his power base. He was also fighting against much initial hostility and continual challenges and interruptions; it seems clear that he was at times in danger of physical assault. Archbishop Whately later speculated – perhaps in hope! – that it might all end in O'Connell's assassination. 'What a curious Acteon-like fate would it be if O'Connell were to be murdered by a mob! . . . In his speeches on Poor-laws, and much more against the combinators, he has shown his usual skill, but a courage which he certainly never displayed before.'[86] Moreover, O'Connell's claims and counter-charges were far from baseless. Before the Corn Exchange meeting, he had gathered evidence from artisans of the violent courses being urged on the Dublin trades committee, of prohibitions on apprenticeships and of successful competition from outside. 'I have also to state', one tradesman testified, 'that in the stone cutting a man can procure a chimney piece 30 per cent cheaper in Glasgow, Belfast or Armagh than in Dublin, taking all charges into calculation. All other manufactures in proportion.'[87] As early as 24 December 1837, O'Connell had concluded that he could show the Commons select committee into combinations, which he intended to propose, 'that in Dublin these combinations have had the most important and unhappy effects on wages and employment'.[88]

The really extraordinary feature of the meeting of 8 January 1838 was O'Connell's crushing and unalloyed success against the odds. Even before it closed, he had cut off the trade union leadership from the mass of their followers, and indeed O'Brien from the remainder of the leaders. When he again met the unions, at a public meeting which they organized some three weeks later, his triumph was complete. There was no counter to his demonstration of the illegality of the critical union practices. It was, however, far from a mere matter of silencing a sullen opposition; O'Connell appears also to have converted the Dublin labour movement *en bloc* to his own creed of using 'public opinion and the press' instead of 'the bludgeon or the "knobstick" ' to achieve its ends.[89] While a simple *post hoc propter hoc* explanation of this extraordinary charge may be unwarranted, the fact remains that, from the day of the Corn Exchange confrontation until after O'Connell's death, Dublin labour disputes were virtually free of violence and even of much that we should now regard as legitimate coercion. Undoubtedly, O'Connell's return to the serious agitation of Repeal in the 1840s enlarged the ground for common action with the trades. But the rapprochement was quite as much methodological as political. He had, it seems, convinced the unions of the superior utility of peaceful agitation and systematic propaganda. When, for example, the journeyman bakers were fighting for better working conditions in 1842, they declared that they might 'have effected the object they had now in view by means of combination, but they had learned a lesson from O'Connell, and thought with that great man that there was no social or political advantage that could not be most easily and most advantageously acquired by means of moral force, and the irresistible impulse of public opinion'.[90]

O'Connell's handling of the Dublin crisis of November 1837–January 1838 was a remarkable exhibition of political virtuosity. It is true that he possessed an immense store of accumulated prestige so that there was a bordering of *lèse majesté* in any challenge to his Olympian command. Even before the meeting at the Corn Exchange, six of the Dublin unions had dissociated themselves from all personal criticism of O'Connell, and a seventh proclaimed its fealty to him when the proceedings opened. None the less, he showed consummate resource and skill in winning back, slowly but surely, a body of angry men who had already thrown over his authority and 'freed' themselves from their habitual respect. To induce others to adopt opinions directly opposite to those with which they started is surely the final achievement in the art of public persuasion. However unscrupulous the means – and O'Connell drew on his full demagogic repertoire of ridicule, mob-humour, vituperation, pathos, particularity, sensitivity and cunning misdirection in his crucial speech – it was the performance of a master.

Yet, however much we distinguish the different elements, or admire the skill, we cannot wholly explain, or exactly appreciate, such works of politics as O'Connell's coups of 1831 and 1838 *vis-à-vis* the aberrant Dublin tradesmen. As well as all else, some strange, irrecoverable chemistry of the relations between man and man must have worked its spell. Nothing less could account for his success. But it is one thing to assert as much, another to know what actually happened. The cramped and smeared columns of the contemporary press may pile up detail after detail of the events; but they still leave us ignorant – we can only infer even the necessary existence – of the final factor. What is to be said when the limit of re-creating the dead reality has been reached?

> I am satisfied with that,
> Satisfied if a troubled mirror show it . . .
> An image of its state. . . ?[91]

CHAPTER 19

Declinations

1838–41

I

When parliament re-assembled after the general election of 1837, O'Connell's first and most anxious concern remained the survival of the liberals in power; but he was bound also to hold them so far as possible to their Irish legislative programme. Peel, now strengthened in the House of Commons, would no longer consider the threefold compromise, and although on 5 December 1837 Russell re-introduced the Irish municipal corporations bill, practically unchanged, there was little hope that it would pass the Lords. On 10 February 1838, O'Connell told Fitzpatrick that, despite the ministry's powerlessness to press the bill in the upper house, 'I do believe that there will be a yielding on the part of Wellington's party sufficient to carry it through. My own opinion is that it will be law this session.'[1] But this was rank wishful thinking; O'Connell had no ground whatever for his 'opinion'.

He was now free to oppose the Irish poor law bill, also re-introduced in December 1837. It would no longer serve as a *quid pro quo* for favourable municipal and tithe reform. With the whigs and tories vying in the bill's support, there was no danger to the ministry in O'Connell's opposition, and he could securely recant his earlier acquiescence, even to the point of confessing publicly that it sprang from his own want of 'moral courage'.[2] On 18 December 1837 he denounced the poor law bill as proposing 'a species of social revolution in Ireland [which] will necessarily create a new and heavy charge on property'.[3] His principal fear was for the 'responsible' landlords who would carry much of the burden properly belonging to their evicting and absentee brethren. But he also pleaded on behalf of the future paupers who, denied outdoor relief, faced nothing but 'imprisonment in a workhouse'.[4] As a gesture towards conventional Irish values and apprehensions, O'Connell actually moved the rejection of the bill on 9 February 1838. He must have anticipated a miserable defeat, even if not by the actual ignominious margin of 277 votes to 25. 'Never was cant more conspicuous', he mourned to Fitzpatrick next day, 'than in the cry of some of our Poor Law mongers. Others imagine that, because they point out distress and destitution, they make a case for a Poor Law. Yes, they forget that Poor Law affords less relief than it inflicts injury, but the delusion will end in greater misery and more dissatisfaction. I have done my duty.' Characteristically, however, he ended this letter with the postscript, 'The Ministers are quite safe. All right with the queen.'[5] There could be no doubting his priority.

Tithe was the third major Irish issue left hanging when William IV's death had precipitated a parliamentary dissolution. By then, it had driven a wedge between O'Connell and MacHale, as well as certain of the other Catholic clergy; and in an attempt to recover this lost ground, he proposed on 9 November 1837 an entirely new approach whereby the state (through the Consolidated Fund) would take over responsibility for a commuted tithe in return for the cost of the new Irish Constabulary being borne by a local tax. Thus, while achieving a not dissimilar result, O'Connell ingeniously avoided the contentious and hitherto fatal issue of direct appropriation of the Church of Ireland 'surplus' for general purposes. Even MacHale was coaxed at first into part-approval. He told O'Connell on 27 February 1838 that 'to have the payment of the Protestant clergy charged on the Consolidated Fund . . . [would be] an excellent instalment since we could securely calculate on the cooperation of England and Scotland in finally doing justice as far as regarded the Protestant Establishment.'[6] The scheme had also some attraction for a government caught between the devil of commitment to the principle of appropriation and the deep sea of a House of Lords committed in the opposite direction. Russell's proposals for a new tithe bill, revealed at last in March 1838, generally resembled O'Connell's outline. The main addition was a rent-charge, fixed at 70 per cent of the tithe composition of 1832, which was to finance the Irish Constabulary and some other 'secular' expenditures. O'Connell was so gratified by a plan close to his suggested *via media* that he promised publicly to meet his own tithe debts, to pay '*all* my parsons' the accumulated arrears of several years.[7] His euphoria was short-lived. Conservative pressure in both houses soon transformed the bill. The quasi-appropriation and state funding clauses were dropped and the rent-charge raised from 70 to 75 per cent of tithe composition. The consequent tithe act of 1838 was a meagre return for almost a decade of agitation. Yet O'Connell, who had declared only a year before that they 'might sell the very bed from under him but he would never consent to pay a single fathing for tithes',[8] backed the final measure, even at the cost of dividing his supporters in the House of Commons. This endorsement is difficult to explain other than as a recognition of the *force majeure* represented by the tory majority in the upper house. O'Connell had lost not only a grievance which had helped his movements throughout the 1830s but also an important target for popular indignation. With tithes now absorbed in rents, the Church of Ireland was removed from the direct line of O'Connell's fire. By the same token, his capacity to mobilize the Catholic clergy as his auxiliaries was diminished. MacHale had written to O'Connell condemning even Russell's initial proposal as falling

> far short of what the Ministry was pledged to and the people of Ireland expected. It has no appropriation clause. It does not reduce one of the supernumary parsons even where a single Protestant is not found. Nor does it, out of the proposed reduction of thirty per cent., . . . give any advantage to the occupying tenantry.[9]

The cabinet's subsequent pusillanimity, and what the archbishop regarded as the ultimate triumph of the parsons, did nothing to endear O'Connell to him.

II

On 15 February 1838 O'Connell had written excitedly to Fitzpatrick that the queen desired him to attend the next *levée*, in order, he believed, to discuss the conciliation of Ireland. The wish must have been father to the thought. There is no evidence that the queen so much as mentioned Ireland to him when, six days later, he and his sons were presented to her at St James's Palace. None the less, it is interesting to observe that the 'great objects' which he had intended to lay before her were still 'the final settlement of the Tithe question, [and] the completion of the corporate reform and of the electoral franchise in cities and counties'.[10] The tithe question was, as we have seen, finally, though humiliatingly, settled later in the session. But municipal reform suffered, first, from backsliding by the ministry in their anxiety to come to terms with Peel, and subsequently from so many and such drastic amendments in the House of Lords as to be no longer worth pursuing. As to the Irish parliamentary franchise,

O'Connell would very shortly find himself on the defensive, as the conservatives launched a powerful campaign to have its conditions altered in their favour.

Thus by mid-1838 even O'Connell would have had to own that the liberal alliance had failed to produce worthwhile legislative fruit. 'Justice for Ireland' seemed as far off as ever, and hope so repeatedly deferred had sickened the heart of Irish agitation. To many, O'Connell seemed to have reduced himself and his parliamentary faction to a mere governmental instrument. He had dismantled even the innocuous General Association to placate Dublin Castle. The Paris newspapers *Courier Français* saw this last as a marvellous instance of a demagogue's dominion.

> The work of difficulty was, not to set in movement these mighty masses, and make every impulse obedient to his will, but when in the conscious possession of power, and within view of the great object of their contest, thus to induce the voluntary surrender of their matured organization, and implicitly confide in the Government, of which they had so long experienced the oppression, is a source of astonishment and admiration, and evidence of the highest moral influence which man can exercise over his fellow man.[11]

But the complete indifference which greeted the Association's dissolution was also a sure indicator of the current apathy.

For O'Connell, however, the very occupation of the government benches by so 'well-disposed' a ministry as Melbourne's more than compensated for its legislatory weakness and double-dealing. After all, each month brought its trickling increment of change in the composition of the Irish administrative system. It was O'Connell's habit to speculate gleefully on the effects of each gain in time, as the successive parliamentary crises were surmounted. For instance, on 4 May 1838, he wrote confidentially to Fitzpatrick,

> I am delighted to tell you the Ministry is *safe*. I was yesterday in great alarm . . . You may therefore reckon with certainty that the present ministry will have all the coronation [June, 1838] patronage, and without any difficulty another year of office. This, after all, is cheering for Ireland, as it leaves with us Lord Mulgrave and gives us another winter *to kill* our worthless judges. They will stick fast as long as they can, the vagabonds!![12]

It was his unshakable conviction that the Irish tory judges hung on in office, in the hope of surviving long enough to have their successors appointed by a conservative administration! There was moreover a steady stream of offices appearing on the 'market', in which to place his political creditors and friends. Within one fortnight, between 18 September and 1 October 1837, he applied to either Drummond or Morpeth for a stipendiary magistracy for J. D. Mullen, a filizarship (a legal appointment on the chancery side) for Patrick Costello and the clerkship of the rules for his attorney, William Woodlock. Even when, as sometimes happened, O'Connell failed in applications such as these, the successful candidates were usually men of his own party or inclination, so that his strategic end of 'popularizing' the Irish public service was still being met. This was especially important with the many posts to be filled in the new constabulary. One parish priest pressed O'Connell to secure regular recruitment on the basis of religion: 'Could not a rule be made . . . that at least one half of those that are added to the Police should be Catholics[?]'.[13] Even well short of this, a considerable number of Catholics (including Archbishop Slattery's brother) did become officers of the new force.

The greatest single gain, in O'Connell's eyes, from the continuance of the liberals in office was the widespread changes wrought by the Morpeth administration in the Irish magistracy in the spring of 1838. O'Connell was very early in cheering on what he regarded as potentially a 'brain-blow' to Orangeism in Ireland. 'Will you be so good', he wrote to Drummond from Derrynane on 25 September 1837,

> as to let me know all that is *tellable* about the forthcoming revision or restriction of the commission of the peace. There are some very improper persons in the Commission in this county [Kerry] but as they are Protestants – that most uncandid thing in the world – the affectation of over candour will I fear prevent Lord Kenmare [the deputy-lieutenant] from striking them out or concurring in that measure. Besides we are literally *inundated* in this quarter with parsons as *justices*. I wish much to know what precautions you think will be taken to purify these nuisances.[14]

It was just as important that Dublin Castle should remain viligant against 'Orange' excesses among the surviving JPs, and Drummond's later strong and well-publicized interventions against a handful of grossly 'unreconstructed' magistrates brought equal joy to O'Connell's heart. The abasement of his hereditary Irish enemies struck a chord at least as deep as that set singing by the advancement of his Irish friends. A few years before, a fellow-barrister had caught well – in fun yet seriously – the expression, even in his very gait, of O'Connell's ferocious hatred of the inferiority imposed upon him by Irish circumstances:

As he marches along through the [Dublin] streets to court, he . . . flings out one factious foot before the other, as if he had already burst his bonds, and was kicking the Protestant ascendancy before him; while ever and anon, a democratic, broad-shouldered roll of the upper man is manifestly an indignant effort to shuffle off 'the oppression of seven hundred years'.[15]

When it came to social and religious 'liberation', the heart had the same reasons as the reason, and was much the more powerful engine. Of course, O'Connell was too reflective and acute a politician to miss the fact that the centralizing and expansionist tendency of the Morpeth administration could be used later by a conservative government for the advantage of *its* Irish partisans. But he also knew that the 'popular' layer being gradually inserted into the Irish forces of law, order and local authority could never be totally eradicated, and that the precedents of comparative impartiality in the running of the country could never totally dismissed. Besides, he was already old: sufficient unto the day . . .

Yet even the warming sense of governmental favour and of influence over the distribution of patronage no longer afforded O'Connell its original satisfaction. For one thing, he was worn down by the multiplicity of applications. Even, or perhaps particularly, those issuing from the ranks of his Irish opponents meant inroads on his time and energy. These ranged from the unknown daughter of the 'late Dep. Judge Advocate of Ireland' begging his support in a pension claim to a co. Limerick parson soliciting his 'good word' in applying for the deanery of Dromore. He often grieved that he was exhausting his credit with government by the great number of his requests, although his inbred courtesy and politician's wariness forbade him to reject any suitor for grants or offices out of hand. He also protested, with some justice, that his very power in Ireland held the administration back from over-indulging him with favours lest it be paraded as his mere marionette in the inimical British press. 'It is also strictly true', he told one of his Kerry relatives in 1837, 'that instead of a readiness to comply with my request there is a jealousy in certain quarters of being supposed to be dictated to by me which dispossesses me of my share of patronage.'[16] Worse still, failure to secure an objective led to resentment in supporters. When O'Connell failed to stave off the appointment of an enemy of the formidable Fr Sheehan of Waterford as JP, Sheehan wrote to him in anger: 'Dr Jones has been sworn in a magistrate. There never was a more unworthy appointment. It is calculated to bring Lord Mulgrave's administration into contempt.'[17] One of O'Connell's bursts of counter-irritation, in a letter to Richard

Barrett, serves to show how grievous a burden all this place- and prize-dealing might become:

> Really private, I did what I could for Mr [James] Birch [an Irish journalist]. There is this cruel treatment which I receive from everybody – that when I do not succeed for any applicant, which is the case in 99 instances out of every 100, I am blamed for want of zeal or sincerity. 'ONE WORD' – how I hate that 'one word!' – from him would have done it!! In future I ought to say no, bluntly, to every application. I feel that I ultimately get the same displeasure and have all my trouble for nothing. I must say Mr Birch has treated me badly in complaining to you. I explained to him, as far as I could, without mentioning names, what I had attempted on his behalf and the nature of the obstacles in the way of having his wishes complied with, whereupon he *disavowed* the present Administration and left me without as much as one expression of thanks for the effort I made. I wish I were in opposition again but I must say you and Birch treat me most unjustly.[18]

By a final irony O'Connell was practically debarred from using his influence on his own behalf. He was tempted most sorely of all in June 1838, with his fortunes, pecuniary and political, at almost their lowest ebb, by the offer of a baronship of the exchequer or alternatively the Mastership of the Rolls. But, as he told Fitzpatrick on 15 June, 'my friends may (but most confidentially) know that I do not intend to accept any office whilst Ireland is so totally unredressed. I nail my colours to my country's mast.'[19] Although we may detect in this a hint of leaving the door not completely closed, three days later he confirmed his rejection of the offer. 'The die is cast. *I have refused office* . . . You know that, if I took anything, it would be the Rolls. But I could not bring myself to accept it. My heart is heavy but *I have made this sacrifice.*'[20]

In doing so he referred back to Mary. 'If SHE was alive I should have my reward and my consolation, but *her* memory casts a protection about me which will prevent me from abandoning my struggles for Ireland save with my life.'[21] The recollection of his dead wife deepened the wound but also helped him to cauterize it by a revived feeling that he was true to his chosen track. Ireland was to consume him always.

III

When parliament rose on 9 August 1838, O'Connell found himself in a most complex political position. He was immensely relieved that the whig ministry still held office. 'Blessed be Heaven', he told Fitzpatrick on 11 August, 'that the Session is over and that we have a respite from the enemy and good government for another year!'[22] On the other hand, the cabinet had by then given way on two critical Irish issues. It had surrendered the appropriation clause of the tithe bill (the original cause of Melbourne's accession to power) and agreed to the substitution of a £8 for a £5 valuation as the basis for the municipal franchise in its forthcoming Irish municipal corporations bill. O'Connell had had to stomach the first as the price of the continuation of whig government; and while denouncing the second as 'only going over to the enemy . . . It will almost annihilate the franchise in Dublin and at £8 render it quite exclusive',[23] and predicting (correctly) that this first 'compromise' would lead in time to a second, raising the qualification to £10, he had no intention of breaking with the ministry on that account. But worse than his own dissatisfactions were the dangers, first, that the government would throw in its hand as hopeless, and, second, that it would be repudiated by many Irish nationalists and, in particular, by many of the Catholic bishops and priests. Russell's refusal to consider any further measure of parliamentary reform had driven the British radicals into semi-revolt; a sufficient number of them might well move on to a full insurrection, which would cost the government its bare working majority in the House of Commons. Correspondingly, the whig failure (increasingly read as a failure of will or of desire) to carry its Irish legislative programme had alienated considerable bodies of O'Connell's supporters. His control of the popular movement seemed under threat.

To this intricate problem, O'Connell responded intricately. On 18 August 1838, immediately after his return to Dublin, he launched the Precursor Society of Ireland at a meeting of his constituents. Its declared objective was the mobilization of 'the national will . . . [in] a last attempt to procure from the British legislature full justice to Ireland' before instituting a Repeal association.[24] O'Connell set the time limit as the end of the parliamentary session of 1839, and once more listed as the principal items of 'full justice' the total abolition of tithes and complete parity with Great Britain in parliamentary and municipal reform. O'Connell sought to speak with many voices. To MacHale, he argued that with 'steady and universal exertion [the Precursor Society] would free us from the incubus of the State-paid Church and obtain for us all we desire besides'. Lest MacHale should suppose that he had abandoned Repeal, he added, implausibly, that this achievement would render 'ninety-nine out of every hundred of the Irish of every persuasion friendly to a domestic Parliament'.[25] He tried to persuade a liberal editor that the '*agitation*' raised by the

Society would help 'to show the Tories that they cannot possibly hold office'.[26] He told Pigot (for transmission to the Irish administration) that

> we have no hope from the Ministry in England. I solemnly assure you that, in dealing with them on the Irish bills, I found the same repulsive coldness last session that I experienced in Lord Grey's time. In the Irish phrase, they 'neither love us nor like us.'
>
> We must act for ourselves, we must raise the cry again all over Ireland. It is the only mode to obtain anything for the country. I believe it to be the only mode of fencing the Ministry in office but at all events we must rely on ourselves. We have nothing else to rely on.
>
> As to the 'Precursor', instead of its being a Repeal society it is directly the reverse. It is a society to prevent the necessity of seeking Repeal. I have called on enemies to Repeal to join us in order to consolidate the Union.[27]

Finally, he handed down to Fitzpatrick, for the benefit of a recalcitrant supporter, the oracular pronouncement that the Society 'may precede justice to Ireland from the United parliament and the consequent dispensing with Repeal agitation. It may precede Repeal agitation – and will, shall, and must precede Repeal agitation if justice be refused'.[28]

Despite this fan-spread of appeals, the Precursor Society was coolly received. MacHale stayed aloof, and some priests continued to assail O'Connell for his tergiversion on the tithe issue. O'Connell was careful to cultivate friendly bishops, and obtain their approval, or at least consent, before holding a Precursor rally in their dioceses. 'I am bound', he assured Archbishop Slattery on 7 October 1838, 'to struggle for the religion and liberties of Ireland but I am deeply convinced that these struggles to be useful must merit the sanction or at least avoid drawing down any censure from the high dignitaries of the Catholic Church in Ireland.'[29] As to agitation, O'Connell set up the usual sort of headquarters at the Corn Exchange and, from Derrynane, on 15 September promised ' "a progress" on my way to Dublin in November'.[30] This aroused small enthusiasm. Nearly six weeks later, O'Connell confessed to Fitzpatrick that he had 'as yet received only four invitations' to hold meetings.[31] In the end, he managed to agitate decorously (his own phrase) at public dinners in co's Kerry, Cork (where there were three venues, Kanturk, Youghal and Cork itself), Tipperary, Waterford, Limerick and Galway, in an adequate but unexciting circuit. One reason for O'Connell's rather *piano* performance was Dublin Castle's strong disapprobation of the Precursor Society, which was conveyed to him in letters from Pigot.

O'Connell was apparently undisturbed when Pigot told him that the Society was in breach of the Convention Act of 1793, thereby rendering its leaders liable to imprisonment. Even if Pigot were right in law, it was most improbable that the Irish executive would prosecute those who were still its best Irish friends. But when Pigot followed this up by the threat that supplies, in the form of further patronage, would be cut off ('the Government, I am convinced, would find themselves unable to advance to public office any individual . . . pledged' to adopt Repeal if the Precursor programme were not achieved 'within *one year*')[32] the blow appears to have struck home. Although O'Connell did not respond to this immediately, within a month of his return to Dublin from Derrynane he dissolved the Society and reconstituted it in what he hoped would be an inoffensive form. 'Every reference to the Union has been omitted', he told the new viceroy, Lord Ebrington, 'and its purposes are now quite consistent with the *objects* avowed by the Irish government.'[33]

This signalled, not the end of the Precursor, but a fresh understanding with the whigs. In general, O'Connell used both brake and accelerator in directing the Society. When a tory government threatened, he held back in the interests of maintaining the liberals in power; but when the liberals seemed secure in power, he attempted to increase the pressure on them. But he also braked when it seemed that his influence over Irish appointments was falling off. In deleting Repeal from the Precursor programme at the end of 1838, he was moved in part by fears that Melbourne's cabinet was losing its appetite for office and that Irish intimidation might, in consequence, prove counter-productive, but mostly by his intense desire to have a say in filling the vital legal position of lord chancellor, which he then believed would soon be vacant. He pressed Ebrington on 3 January 1839 to support 'the popular cause with the Irish Bar, with whom *we* are but too weak already . . . I owe it to you in candour to state that the Irish Government have no small occasion to take a leaf out of the Tory book wherein it is written, "Oppose your enemies, back your friends".' As a sweetener, he added, 'if the Radicals [Chartists] in England give you any trouble you can withdraw from Ireland by a few arrangements *all* the regiments now here'.[34] Conversely, when the supposed crisis was over, and the whigs had settled back, in apparent security, in power, O'Connell changed tack. 'With respect to Ireland', he wrote to Fitzpatrick from London on 6 February 1839,

there is a thorough indifference in both parties. In the Whigs, coldness and apathy; in the Tories, suspended hostility. They equally desire to keep Ireland out of sight and to let her people continue in, I may call it, hopeless servitude. I am thoroughly convinced that my plan of going back [to Dublin] once a fortnight [to address Precursor Society meetings] is of the utmost importance.[35]

In fact, O'Connell did return for meetings of the Society in Dublin several times during the parliamentary session; he also maintained his siege on MacHale, imploring him to countenance the spread of the Precursor into Connacht. Thus, he constantly changed emphasis according to immediate circumstances. During one 'braking' phase, he told MacHale, 'There was never anything more hopeless than to attempt to bully them [the liberal ministry]. *I know it from experience*.'[36] But an earlier letter had run, 'I have been written to menacingly ... but their menaces, I need not tell your Grace, I despise.'[37] It was quite true that O'Connell had been and would be 'menaced'. But the Precursor Society was itself a 'menace'. In short, in the half-cock agitation of 1838–9, each side attempted to exert pressure on the other while yet avoiding conflict.

IV

O'Connell's serene assumption that the ministry was safe at least for the current session died suddenly on 7 May 1839 when, on the issue of the Jamaican constitution, the government's majority fell to five; Melbourne resigned next day. Some radicals, alienated by the whigs' resistance to further parliamentary reform, had opposed the ministry, and much to O'Connell's chagrin, two of his Irish 'supporters' failed to appear in the division lobbies. He was still more infuriated by the defection of William Smith O'Brien, liberal MP for co. Limerick, who voted with the tories. 'He is an exceedingly weak man', O'Connell exclaimed soon after, 'proud and self-conceited ... You cannot be sure of him for half an hour.'[38] But abusing the renegades brought small comfort in the crisis. 'I do not know when I felt so uneasy and unhappy', he told his ministerial friend, More O'Ferrall, on 7 May, and implored him to do all in his power to persuade the cabinet to hold on to office and 'preserve Ireland from the [Orange] faction as long as they possibly can'.[39] Next day, in a public letter to 'the People of Ireland', he proposed, not an intensification of activity by the Precursor Society, but the formation of a new Irish reform association to bring together all anti-tories. O'Connell probably believed that a general election was imminent. At any rate, the resignation of

Melbourne's government brought home to him how greatly his current political position depended on its continuance.

Then, fortune came to the rescue. In the so-called Bedchamber crisis, Queen Victoria refused to accept Peel's nominations for her ladies of the household; Peel thereupon refused to assume office; and, the old cabinet having conciliated the recalcitrant English radical reformers, Melbourne returned to power. Meanwhile, Russell had tried to make the whigs' assurance of O'Connell doubly sure by writing to him on 9 May,

> It is a pleasure which I cannot refuse myself to acknowlege the constant and disinterested support which you have given to the Ministry in which I held a department chiefly connected with the affairs of Ireland.
>
> I am glad to see that [in the public letter of 8 May] you exhort your countrymen to abstain from acts of violence and I feel little or no doubt that, although you differ from me with respect to several measures relating to Ireland, you will persevere in refraining to press for Repeal while there is any prospect of equal justice to be obtained by other means.[40]

But O'Connell's support was never in doubt. 'Hurrah for the darling little Queen! Peel is out; Melbourne is in again', he wrote excitedly to Fitzpatrick on 10 May 1839,[41] and, next day, 'The queen has behaved nobly. To her we are indebted for our safety.'[42] He proceeded to arrange a form of political *Te Deum*, held in Dublin on 23 May – 'an Irish demonstration',[43] to use his own terms – at which a solemn address of gratitude to Victoria was drawn up.

For a considerable time, O'Connell was happy enough to report to Fitzpatrick merely that Melbourne's government was surviving. But of course he expected some reward (over and above a finger in the disposition of Irish patronage) for his fidelity. The Dublin demonstration of 23 May had called once more on the government to equalize Irish and British municipal and franchise reform; and, at a lower level, O'Connell also pressed for an Irish railways bill and amending legislation sought by two influential Irish lobbies, the vintners and the grocers. By the end of June 1839 it was clear that he had failed at every point. The ministry had blocked his parliamentary efforts to achieve his lesser ends; and although the Irish municipal corporations bill was still before the Commons its voting qualification had been set at £8, and even this would probably be rejected by the Lords. 'Nothing will be done for Ireland', he now cried, 'and, in fact, Ireland has nothing for it but the REPEAL.'[44] It was, however, a vapid, unmeant threat. O'Connell was not yet nearly desperate enough to break with or even endanger the ministry. This became painfully apparent when the

House of Lords so altered the municipal corporations bill as to win back ground for the almost entirely Protestant freeman voters and raise the property qualification for the rest from £8 to £10. O'Connell was outraged, at first. The mangled measure, he exclaimed when he learned of the lords' amendments on 5 August, was 'impossible to take ... I cannot sacrifice my conscientious convictions'.[45] But almost immediately he began to yield ground, and within three days surrendered unconditionally. When, in a letter dated 6 August, Ebrington pressed O'Connell to accept the changes, arguing that even the lopped bill was better than none at all, and that there was no 'reasonable prospect of obtaining better terms by further delay',[46] O'Connell fell into line with distressing alacrity and parade. 'I do therefore yield', he replied,

> any doubts I may have had to your superior judgment, and although I am bound – but this is consistent with your advice – to protest very strongly against considering this a full or adequate measure of corporate reform yet you have convinced me that I ought not to risk any opposition to the bill and of course I will not do so, being indeed well pleased to have this opportunity though small in itself, to testify how entirely your Excellency's Government of Ireland commands and obtains my entire and respectful confidence.[47]

Thus the £10 franchise and the other tory limitations on the reform of the Irish muncipalities, against which O'Connell had struggled for so long, became law at last virtually without resistance from him.

Perhaps in self-disgust at what he must have believed to be a necessary abasement, perhaps because he feared that the latest humiliation would finally destroy his support in Ireland, O'Connell sank into a rare despair. 'I am, I confess, very unhappy', he wrote to Fitzpatrick 'in the most strict secrecy' on 7 August 1839, 'I do not believe I will long survive the blow I apprehend from the desertion of me by the country at large. It weighs upon my heart.'[48] Expecting that the Tribute for 1839 would fail, he continued next day,

> God help me! What shall I do? I think of giving up my income, save an annuity of a small sum to myself and my two sons, and going, if I am received, to Clongowes, and to spend the rest of my life there. I want a period of retreat to think of nothing but eternity. I sigh when I look at the present agitated aspect of affairs, foreign and domestic, and vainly think that if Ireland thought fit to support me I might still be useful; but it is plain I have worn out my claim on the people. You are aware that Connaught [i.e. MacHale] is, of course, estranged from me . . . Still I do not regret that I gave up my profession and refused office.[49]

As usual Fitzpatrick steadied and cheered him, and by 21 August his natural resilience had done the rest. While claiming – improbably – that if left to his own wishes he would 'retire altogether from political life' because of the 'disgusts' he had received, he launched into schemes for fresh agitation in both England and Ireland, ending with the aim of 'animating' the Irish 'quietly and cautiously' for the Repeal.[50] He was an indomitable and incorrigible politician.

He was, however, far from ready to go wholeheartedly for Repeal as yet. On 2 September 1839, almost immediately after he returned to Dublin, he dissolved the Precursor Society, replacing it by a Reform Registry Association in which Irish whigs and liberals could participate. The grand emphasis was now on rousing 'all Ireland for the Queen and Constitution',[51] the particular, on the registration of voters against the next general election. O'Connell could never formally forgo Repeal. But he reduced its current function to that of a far-off prospect. Ebrington reported on 8 September, after a confidential meeting with O'Connell,

> though he said he could not dissolve the Precursor without holding out Repeal in the distance as his remedy for the political grievances of his countrymen, he assured me that he would agitate as little as he could, & would not be a party in forming any Society except that which he had announced for revising the Registration.[52]

The Irish government meanwhile attempted to cut off any retreat on O'Connell's part by announcing that Repealers would not be considered in future for official appointments.

In setting up the Reform Registry Association, O'Connell soon found the Irish whigs to be, as usual, slothful and devious allies. Despite his assurance that only a little money was needed 'to secure Ireland to the Melbourne Cabinet', they failed to fulfil their original engagement to pay £1000 into the new organization. 'If I had kept on foot any *agitating* body', he wrote angrily from Derrynane to More O'Ferrall on 29 November 1839, 'we should have friends in abundance, but because I have dissolved my poor Precursors I am left on the strand with the tide out.'[53] Off and on, O'Connell considered schemes for refloating himself as a popular leader during the last months of 1839. In particular, he toyed with raising the tithe issue in another form, that is, to applying the tithe rent-charge either to offset the new poor rate or for general public purposes. This was not promising material for a national campaign, but at least it was aimed at what O'Connell saw as the essential problem at this stage, how to re-engage the Catholic Church in Irish politics. One difficulty was the continued estrangement of MacHale, and O'Connell sought – though vainly – to ensnare him by a blatant appeal to his fierce religious partisanship. 'The time is come', he wrote to MacHale on 23 December 1839,

> when all Catholic Ireland should rally – should form a strong and universal combination.
>
> The Tories are united. You perceive that they are daily becoming less careful to conceal their intentions. They avow their bitter hostility to the religion and to the people of Ireland.
>
> The furious and most sincere of the British Tories avow their intention to re-enact the Penal Code, whilst the more wily declare their designs not to go farther than to render the emancipation act a mere dead letter . . .
>
> We want protection for the Catholic against all parties, Ministerial as well as Tories. My object would be once again to organise all Catholic Ireland in an effort of resistance to all our enemies.[54]

A second stumbling-block for O'Connell was the bitter and persistent conflict between MacHale and his ecclesiastical province and Archbishop Murray and the majority of the other Irish bishops over acceptance of the national education system. Whatever one prelatal party might support was likely to be opposed by its rival. Perhaps O'Connell's most hopeful sign was the rapid spread of Fr Theobald Mathew's new temperance movement in the last months of 1839. Mathew himself had no wish to be linked with O'Connell or nationalist politics in any form; this might hinder, perhaps even destroy, his work. But his recruits were largely those whom O'Connell had recruited earlier in his political mobilizations: Mathew's emphasis in order, discipline, respect for institutions and, of course, sobriety was identical with O'Connell's ground-plan for all his agitations; and, in the early days at least, even the forms of the temperance rallies – their banners, procession songs and slogans – were those developed in the O'Connellite agitations. Significantly, O'Connell declared at a public banquet in Bandon on 5 December 1839 that he was watching the influence of the temperance societies before unfurling the banner of Repeal. If they succeeded, there was *ipso facto* material for him to work with. So indeed it was eventually to prove.

Meanwhile, O'Connell placed at least as much emphasis on English as on Irish agitation. He considered that the English middle-class radicals, especially the advanced parliamentary reformers and the anti-corn law men, offered the best prospect of vivifying and securing the liberal ministry. Before he left for Ireland at the end of the parliamentary session of 1839 he chaired, on 18 August, a London meeting from which a Precursor of Reform Society, committed to household, artisan and even some lodger franchise, emerged; and he had of course long been a principal advocate of the leading reform issue of the year, the secret ballot. Correspondingly, O'Connell cooperated warmly with Richard Cobden (who disliked and distrusted but also needed and flattered him) in promoting the Anti-Corn Law League. He assured Cobden that Ireland, presumably under *his* direction, was safe for the cause, and on 13 December 1839 accepted Cobden's invitation to 'star' at the great League dinner to be held at Manchester in the following month. O'Connell proposed that a 'meeting of Operative Reformers to organise for a struggle to obtain an *effectual* extension of the suffrage and to put down the physical force Tories' be also held at Manchester on the following night.[55] Cobden having given him a *carte blanche*, he intended, he said, to include a defence of the Irish government's promotion of Catholics to office in his banquet speech.

'The meetings [on 13 and 14 January 1840] in Manchester', O'Connell told Fitzpatrick as soon as he reached London, 'were most glorious. It was utterly impossible to be received better than I was.'[56] He had assailed not only the corn laws but also the Chartists, and warned the workers of Manchester against being tempted into violence. This set the tone for the first quarter of 1840. Up to the end of March, O'Connell was the complete ministerialist, largely taken up with British issues and the local manoeuvrings at Westminster, and exulting in every repulse of a tory assault on Melbourne's government. His first accounts to Fitzpatrick from London were uniformly complacent and almost proprietorial in terms of the exercise of power: 'I have pleasure to tell you that the political prospects are daily becoming more bright';[57] 'Be joyful and rejoice and thank God for the Tories are completely discomfited. They are in absolute despair of gaining office';[58] and 'we are now soberly engaged in enjoying our triumph, and the certainty of the Ministers remaining in office'.[59] Correspondingly, Dublin Castle conveniently ignored its own resolution against placing or promoting Repealers in office – at least, when it came to the O'Connells. At the beginning of 1840, O'Connell's second son, Morgan, was appointed assistant registrar of deeds, and O'Connell's appeal for a stipendiary magistracy for his son-in-law, Charles O'Connell (who had, he said, 'like so many other Irish gentlemen "outbuilt" himself'[60]) was met most sympathetically by Ebrington. 'I have delayed', the lord lieutenant wrote to O'Connell on 22 February, answering your letter of the 18th because I could not bring myself to give the denial which I fear I must at least for the present, to the touching appeal returned herewith though it almost brought tears into my eyes when I read it. You do me justice in believing that that appeal does not lose its force in my estimation from its coming from a member of your family, backed by a recommendation from yourself. I have never hesitated to express to you my strong disapprobation of those parts of your conduct in which I thought you liable to blame, and I have with equal readiness and greater satisfaction done you full justice for those where I considered you entitled to praise and particularly for your late most essential service to the cause of social peace and tranquillity by the exertion of your influence in keeping away Chartism from these shores. If, therefore, I consulted only my own wishes and feelings, they would very much incline me to comply with your wishes but I am greatly pressed at present for the next two or three appointments of stipendiary magistrates whenever the vacancies may occur, besides which I must candidly confess my apprehension that it would not be advantageous either to the Government or yourself that so near a relation and a namesake of yours should be put into the place of a stipendiary magistrate so soon after the late appointment of your son, Mr Morgan.[61]

None the less, Charles eventually got his stipendiary magistracy.

V

The days of security ended abruptly on 26 March 1840 when Lord Stanley carried the second reading of his registration of voters (Ireland) bill in the House of Commons by 250 to 234. This essentially tory measure aimed, by its clauses enjoining annual registration and the withdrawal of registration certificates, at restricting the Irish franchise, greatly to O'Connell's detriment. O'Connell was cast into despondency. He genuinely feared that the measure would be carried (it did in fact reach the committee stage despite the government's opposition) and the ministry was, concurrently, also in danger of defeat on a motion condemning its conduct of the 'opium war' with China. In these straits, he sounded MacHale once more on 'making a *great* popular movement or a movement which I hope to be *great* . . . a "Justice or Repeal" association'.[62] Pride of place was to be given to attacking the privileges of the Church of Ireland; the remainder of the programme consisted of the usual demands for parity in Irish and British parliamentary and municipal reform.

O'Connell attempted to undercut the principal cause of MacHale's coldness.

You were in your former letters pleased to labour with me to use my influence with the present Ministry to adopt a more liberal course of legislation in Ireland or, I should say, *for* Ireland; and you conveyed the idea to my mind that I ought to obtain from the government that adoption by menacing to desert them at their need and to allow the Tories to put them out. It was in vain that I assured your Grace that the leading men of the present Ministry and, especially, Lord John Russell desire and anxiously desire an honourable opportunity of giving up power.

They do not cling to it, *believe me*. I do beg of you to believe me, for I know the fact, they do not cling to office with that tenacity that would make such a menace of the slightest avail. Now do, my dear and most revered Lord, believe me that this is the simple fact. Nay, they menace me to resign unless I satisfy them in my conduct.[63]

If O'Connell was disingenuous in promising a new campaign against the established church in Ireland, he was truthful in saying that it was the ministers who were threatening him with resignation rather than his threatening them with the withdrawal of his support. By now this must have been apparent even to MacHale, for he immediately blessed O'Connell's undertaking. 'Whilst the franchise remained', he replied on 11 April, 'there was yet hope for a peaceful assertion of our rights – take that away and the people are left without any arms in their hands . . . Come, then, among us as early as you can find it convenient and you will have a *céad míle fáilte*.'[64] In turn, O'Connell acted quickly. Four days later, he launched the 'National Association for full and prompt Justice or Repeal' in Dublin;[65] as with the Precursor Society, he promised to adopt Repeal if 'justice' were not attained during the parliamentary session. Although O'Connell's address from the Association to 'the People of Ireland' on 21 April 1840 emphasized Repeal and called for the collection of a Repeal Rent, he maintained his old pursuit of the liberal alliance in parliament. Characteristic was his use of the plural in reporting to Fitzpatrick on 30 May: 'We lose a Welsh county and, they say, the County of Monaghan. Ireland is in foolish apathy. May God help us!'[66] Correspondingly, he expressed deep relief when at last, on 30 June, it looked as if Melbourne's ministry would endure into 1841. Once more the queen had come to the rescue. After a government setback during the committee stage on Stanley's bill, O'Connell , as he wrote,

did much apprehend that the ministers would . . . throw up the game in despair . . . I confess my heart sank within me at the dismal prospect that resignation would open for Ireland, especially as there are so many base and sluggish amongst our own people and, in particular, amongst the wealthy classes, to countenance any government that condescended to play the hypocrite ever so little. The restoration to power of the Orange faction would be accompanied with such horrible vexation as to render it impossible to calculate how long we should be able to preserve the peace. But I need not for the present dwell on these things because one of the men in power told me they were determined that nothing should induce them to resign until after the birth of the Queen's child . . . Thus we are sure of remaining in our present position until next February. In the meantime many a card may turn up a trump.[67]

It was all a curious beginning to a movement which was to culminate in 1843 in much the greatest and most menacing demonstration of Irish popular strength during O'Connell's lifetime!

On 13 July 1840, on a brief visit to Dublin, O'Connell transformed his Justice or Repeal Association into the 'Loyal National Repeal Association', dedicated simply to the achievement of Repeal. This may seem a strange response to the prolongation of the life of Melbourne's government. But O'Connell was convinced that Stanley's bill had been only scotched, not killed; the struggle would be renewed next session. All the arguments in favour of an Irish agitation stood, and experience had shown that the complex and contingent objective, or pseudo-objective, of 'Justice or Repeal' roused no one outside the circle of his own particular acolytes. Repeal per se, he now declared, was 'the only topic that can animate the entire mass of the population'.[68] The further involvement of MacHale, who would respond eagerly to the more extreme demand and was the bellwether of the more 'advanced' prelates, may well have been a secondary reason for the change. O'Connell was obsessed by the supposed need to start serious campaigning in Connacht; and, practically, this depended on MacHale's yea or nay.

The archbishop proved gracious, and O'Connell immediately enlisted his aid in getting up a requisition to hold a Connacht provincial Repeal meeting at Tuam on 13 August 1840, and in ensuring some respectable attendance. 'Excuse me being thus tediously particular', O'Connell ended, 'but I am most thoroughly convinced that the Repeal alone can keep secure the religion and the liberties of the Irish people.'[69] The Tuam meeting was moderately satisfactory, the attendance being reported at 10,000; and O'Connell, having spent the month of September at Derrynane, undertook a series of rallies throughout Munster, as well as a Leinster provincial meeting at Kilkenny, during October 1840. It was not an impressive tour. Of course, O'Connell drew respectful crowds and could call out some influential supporters in every town and city in the south and west. But it seems clear that the initial response to 'pure' Repeal was unenthusiastic, perhaps even apathetic. Joseph Hayes, a shrewd Cork merchant and O'Connellite, in the ungrateful role of candid friend, provided O'Connell with a devastating analysis of his current problems. It is worth quoting at considerable length.

There is no imaginable *phasis* which hatred or hostility to English domination, legislative or social, can assume, which shall not have my best wishes ... To agitate such a subject as Repeal, however, requires more than such individual feeling. It requires capability in the individuals undertaking it, willingness in the public mind to receive the impulsion, and that the question shall have some practicable shape as well as practicable result in view. On the former occasion that the Repeal was agitated here, the public crowded the ranks, regarding the agitation as auxiliary to the carrying of the elections then in progress. Many who allowed themselves to be ranked as Repealers laughed at the agitation and at themselves, so soon as the fever subsided and may I be allowed to say to you that the swappings and changes in the nature and character of the associations, which followed, have not tended to alter their feelings in relation to it. At present, then, I may say that there is great indisposition on the part of the people, who may be called of the middle classes, to join in agitation for the Repeal. This is chiefly grounded on the conviction that its attainment is impracticable and hereon, I must be candid to say, for myself, that I firmly believe England would war to the knife before she would legislatively concede the question. That to win it and wear it we must fight for it, and before we pursue such a course we must be prepared to say we have a rational chance of success. Have we that chance? If we have, we are justified in the hazard or is such a speculation nonsense?

'To die for treason is a common evil
To hang for nonsense is the very Devil.'

Thus is it reasoned among the people with whom I talk politics and I would feel altogether at a loss where to point for the material of an effective agitation. We have no lawyer now among us who will speak one word on the subject. There are offices for public prosecution, clerkships of the Peace and of the Crown to be occasionally given away, and a Repealer solicitor, nay a solicitor attending political meetings distinct from elections, will be as far from filling one of them as Yorick's head was from fitting a mitre. And writing of mitres, how are the clergy affected? Almost to a man withdrawn from Repeal, at least the secular order of that body. The Trades are no longer in any force here ... Some few of them of the best capacity for business have obtained situations ... and of course they are *hors de combat*. In fact a process of corruption has been going on through the instrumentality of place giving and, wherever a member of a family has been started a candidate for public employ, the whole division of kindred deem it necessary to eschew Repeal, lest of its embarrassing the speculation.[70]

The substantial truth of Hayes' critique was borne out by the difficulty O'Connell experienced in finding local leaders prepared to sign the requisition for the Leinster provincial meeting and by the ill-tempered wrangling in both Limerick and Waterford as to who should arrange his visits. Meanwhile, Ebrington had further depressed the prospects of professional and middle-class (and even ambitious tradesman) participation in the new Repeal movement. In a speech of 30 September 1840, he identified Repeal with separation and the destruction of the empire, and laid down that 'whatever favour or patronage the government were wont to bestow on its supporters, for those who take part in this agitation, whatever other claims they may have to consideration no application will on any account be attended to'.[71]

In one important regard, O'Connell himself began to hedge even before he undertook his autumn tour in Munster. He overrode every objection to drawing on the Repeal Rent to pay for work on the Dublin register of parliamentary voters, although all past experience had shown that this served the general liberal rather than any specific Repeal interest. He became still more ambivalent in the last two months of 1840. By-elections in cos Carlow and Mayo brought him back to his basic principle of striving to defeat the tories on every front. He was piqued when his offer to help in the Carlow campaign was rejected by the local liberals. 'Alas!', he grieved to Fitzpatrick, 'that they [would] not join in the Repeal cry'.[72] On 21 November 1840, he attempted to insert his son John into the canvassing, instructing him

> to volunteer your services at the Carlow election and at the preceding agitation. Write down to Arthur French or to Mr Fitzgerald who acts as secretary – [T. M.] Ray will give you his address – and offer any aid in your power to the success of Mr Ponsonby's [the liberal candidate's] election. Say that you will go about agitating or working in any other way in which you could be useful.
>
> Let these offers come as emanating from yourself and not at all as suggested by me.[73]

But John was not asked to join in the campaign. O'Connell was better placed in co. Mayo (MacHale was a power in that constituency) and tried to take a hand in the election. In an address to the electors of

Mayo, published on 7 December, he assailed the tories and warmly endorsed the choice of the Mayo Liberal Club, Mark Blake; his address ignored the issue of Repeal. He also offered 'my presence in Mayo . . . or my son John would go *agitating* there, if you [MacHale] thought that advisable'.[74] No invitation came for either, even though O'Connell proposed 'to assist *privately* the Mayo men'[75] (apparently from the Repeal Association's funds), and also made it known to Dublin Castle, through Fitzpatrick and some hidden intermediary, that he was ready to serve as a secret channel for any money the government might wish to spend on Blake's behalf. Again, he was rebuffed – although politely. Nothing could have been more galling to O'Connell than to have been treated as irrelevant in an Irish by-election – and one in which the liberals triumphed, into the bargain! What else could he expect, however, when he strove to hunt with the hounds of government while still running with the hare of his Association?

Thus O'Connell ended 1840 in a strange balance between political independence and collaboration. He drew, as he put it, a 'melancholy consolation' from the defeat of the liberal candidate in co. Carlow on 5 December: 'It proves that the Whigs cannot prosper without the Repealers.'[76] But he had no stomach for antagonism in this case. He refused to denounce publicly an Ulster Constitutional Association set up by liberals in Belfast to counter the Repeal movement; and when, at the beginning of December 1840, his liberal friend, Pierce Mahony, proposed a general meeting of Irish reformers, O'Connell seized the apparent opening for joint action with alacrity. 'I highly approve', he wrote to John from Derrynane on 4 December, 'of Pierce Mahony's Requisition [for the meeting]. It does not imply any dereliction of Repeal, and that I will *practically* prove . . . put my name and Maurice's to that Requisition. Tell Mahony . . . that I approve of and sign his Requisition.'[77]

At the same time, O'Connell maintained the regular organization of the Repeal Association, with its weekly meetings at the Corn Exchange and steady if small returns of Rent. During the last four months of 1840 he largely delegated the chairmanship of the Dublin meetings to John, whom he was 'educating' politically by a series of minute instructions such as 'I send an address on the subject of the registries. . . . Go and read it before the meeting so that you may read it *at* the meeting *legibly* . . . Move 1st. The admission of Dr Cantwell, the Bishop of Meath . . . 2nd. Move the admission of Dr Blake, the Bishop of Dromore . . . Read his letter, move its insertion on the minutes, and that I be requested to send him a suitable reply';[78] or 'Determine on *making* topics to speak upon. You will delight me by *doing* business.'[79] Ray (whom at this stage O'Connell described to John as 'just the best man in his station I have ever met with, beyond any comparison the best'[80]) managed – and helped to manufacture – the Association's ordinary proceedings. Barrett's *Pilot* served more or less as its official organ. Thus, for all his anxiety that Melbourne's government should remain in office and for all his readiness to work wholeheartedly with the liberals in Ireland to this end, O'Connell had no intention of dismantling once again the basic structure for an agitation. Stanley's registration bill would certainly be revived in the coming parliamentary session; meanwhile the whigs' ennui and purposelessness in office were growing month by month. In the midst of these dangers, the Repeal Association was (O'Connell hoped) a form of reinsurance, a mode of laying off his main political bet. Possibly it might not be needed – for the present – for anything more than marking time and disturbing Dublin Castle. But at least it constituted a reserve. The fact that Repeal had not caught on at first would not have daunted O'Connell overmuch. Thirty years of mass politics had taught him that a great deal of dreary labour had to precede the blaze of a crusade – and indeed that it was often more profitable to preach and prepare for one than to set out, in true earnest, for a Holy Land.

VI

O'Connell's *prime* objective was still to keep the whig government in power. This was tacitly recognized by Russell when he 'whipped' O'Connell (though courteously and tactfully) to appear in the Commons when parliament re-assembled on 26 January 1841. It was also noisily assumed by various English radicals who strove for O'Connell's attendance, as a leading lion at public demonstrations in favour of parliamentary reform, when he made his way southwards from Liverpool to London. He remained convinced that the greatest political evil of all would be the tories' return to government; and his current agitation of Repeal, no less than Reform, appears to have been directed specifically to preventing this. As he told Fitzpatrick, on his arrival in London,

It is believed they [the whig government] will hold out another session, and if the Repeal agitation becomes imposing in Ireland, and a new Reform

473

agitation takes place, as I believe it will in England, the Tories may be kept out for ever. But their exclusion can be effected by nothing else unless the Repeal agitation becomes formidable.

How I wish that our friends in Ireland would all see this matter in its true light by first considering what will become of Ireland if the Repeal be not agitated. It is certain, in that case, that the Tories will come into power. It may be said that the Repeal will not prevent them but is it not clear that there is nothing else that will? Are they not on the very verge of being in office?[81]

O'Connell had several reasons for wishing the whigs to cling to power. First, 'with France arming, America threatening, the East unsettled, war in India, war in China, distress and Chartism in England',[82] conditions – all of a sudden – seemed unusually favourable for the application of Irish pressure. Secondly, he was ill-prepared to face a general election. The unreadiness ranged from the neglect of the voting registers and the decay of local organization to a marked paucity of likely candidates; but he was most worried by the lack of clerical enthusiasm for or commitment to his cause. 'If *all* our clergy aided the Repealers', he complained, 'we might make a noble demonstration, but, alas, the Whigs while in office will allure many.'[83] It was ominous that even so warm a friend as Archbishop Slattery of Cashel should have remonstrated with O'Connell, on 16 January 1841, for declaring publicly that he and his clergy had promised to become Repealers should Stanley's Irish registration bill be carried. (O'Connell was driven, lamely, to plead that he had been misreported and that 'Such a line of conduct would be ... consistent with the patriotism and good sense evinced by your Grace upon all occasions'[84]). Given the tepid temperature of Irish politics, episcopal support was indispensable if the priests were to be enlisted in great numbers in the forthcoming campaign; and O'Connell tried his best to attract at least some of the bishops by presenting Repeal as the principal safeguard of the Catholic gains of the past decade. On 10 April he told the sympathetic O'Higgins of Ardagh, doubtless in the hope that it would be spread among the hierarchy,

I hold the prelacy of Ireland collectively and individually in too much respect to dare to do anything but bitterly regret that they are not all Repealers. I regret it the more because of my thorough conviction that we Catholics cannot hold what we have got without the Repeal and *a fortiore* that we cannot get anything that Ireland wants without an Irish parliament. The Orangist party will – it is manifest – be soon again in power, and the Irish people will have to feel all the active and unceasing virulence of that truculent party. I could weep tears of blood at seeing that the opportunity of now making a great and powerful rally for Catholic Ireland is lost owing to the unworthy selfishness of some of our influential laymen and also owing to the mistakes of some of our otherwise most deservedly respected clergy. God help us. It is indeed heartrending to see that the opposition to the Repeal is not left to the congenial spirit of Orangism but has alas mixed up with it some of our most excellent prelates. It is the first time that the people and any part of the Irish hierarchy were divided.[85]

Four weeks later, O'Connell sounded Fitzpatrick on the chances of discreet lobbying, 'Could you privately convey to Catholic dignitaries the propriety of assisting to agitate?'[86]

The third reason why O'Connell strove to maintain the whigs in government for as long as possible was, of course, the access to influence which had accompanied their rule. He regarded the corporation elections, due to be held in the autumn of 1841 under the new Irish Municipal Reform Act, as of special significance: if the tories were in command at Dublin Castle, the whole might of the administration would be thrown against Repeal, liberal and Catholic candidates. There was, moreover, the usual slow but cumulative effect of having a voice in appointments and awards to be considered. In replying to a letter of 27 April from O'Connell, at a time when it still seemed possible that the whigs might hold out until 1842, Fitzpatrick reiterated these arguments:

> The intrusion of the faction previous to the new municipal organisation could not fail to have a calamitous effect upon the construction of the different bodies. This gives an additional and important reason for *keeping them* [the tories] *out* if it can continue to be done. Another year's blockade too can scarcely fail to reduce some part at least of the stubborn Bench.[87]

A final depressing prospect was that O'Connell might have to meet the costs of several contests in the course of a general election. 'For my part', he observed dejectedly to Fitzpatrick on 19 February 1841, 'I will have to sustain four elections [his own candidature and those of his sons Maurice, John and Daniel]. Where shall I get money? The tribute has not been successful this year.'[88] He even caught a black glimpse of himself as a finished man, with the work, which only he could do, undone.

> It comes across my mind that my career will terminate just at the moment that Ireland ceases to have friends. I am, you perceive, disposed to be gloomy . . . I do believe that Ireland is capable of being made once more

and thoroughly a nation and that her hour is arriving but my vanity or self-reliance makes me think that I am wanting for the completion of a bloodless and not illegal change. Pardon me, my good friend.[89]

The government held on throughout the spring of 1841, despite a net loss of four seats in a round of English by-elections and the defeat of a major official measure, Morpeth's Irish registration bill, which O'Connell had warmly supported. By the end of April, however, it was apparent that its budget would be rejected. A general election would then become inevitable. This, wrote O'Connell sadly on 4 May, would certainly be 'destructive to me. I know not what I shall do . . . It will be a triumph of the enemies of Ireland if I am driven from the field.'[90] Still, he struggled to postpone the evil day, and to persuade the ministry to fight on to the last. 'I object', he told Morpeth on 7 May,

> to the present Ministry's resigning the management of her Majesty's counsels so long as they can *possibly* hold their station at the head of public affairs. They are placed as a kind of moral promontory between the people of Ireland and that furious and fanatical party, who have so often driven a kindly and naturally faithful people to the very verge of actual rebellion and into the gulf of agrarian crimes and of local but sanguinary outrages.[91]

But even more important to O'Connell than spinning out the time in office was the government's using, eventually, its power to dissolve and fight a general election, rather than resign. Otherwise, the tories would be entrenched in Ireland at polling time and 'the Orangists no longer restrained by superior power will come armed to each hustings, the command of the police and of the army will be in their hands'.[92] A tory-dominated Dublin Castle would mean both bloodshed and the loss of perhaps as many as ten seats. In his anxiety to avoid such an outcome, O'Connell virtually promised to offer no opposition to official candidates and to require no pledge whatever from his own.

> I do not want to promote my own peculiar opinions. I am quite certain that no supporter of her Majesty's Government would at any Irish election be embarrassed by being asked for any pledge beyond the unequivocal support of this Ministry or of opinions as, for example, respecting the Ballot which some more or less of that Ministry have avowed.[93]

For once the whigs did not disappoint O'Connell. They held on to office until Peel's motion of no-confidence in their administration, carried by a single vote on 6 June 1841, forced them to surrender; and even then Melbourne did not resign but used his single remaining power to dissolve parliament instead. Even more, the issuing of writs for the Irish elections was, at O'Connell's insistence, held back to the very last.

None the less, O'Connell had been in no doubt since the beginning of May that he would soon have to face the polls. His own seat was his first concern. He was unlucky in being a sitting member for Dublin city, for the tory strength in freemen votes in the capital meant that the issue would always be doubtful and the contest costly. He had a double hand to play. It was, he believed, important that he avoid having another Repealer as his running mate, for this would lessen his own chance of success. But better still if he could escape to another constituency without loss of face. He gained the first objective in the end: the other sitting member, Robert Hutton, a liberal who would not support Repeal, was re-endorsed *faute de mieux*. But the second failed: O'Connell's best hope here was that the young whig Lord Kildare (the heir of the Duke of Leinster) would also accept nomination, but Kildare refused to run, leaving O'Connell no choice but to go forward. Next came his family. O'Connell managed to save some money by substituting his son John for himself (whom the electoral committee wanted) as candidate for Kilkenny city. Athlone, for which John had sat in the preceding parliament, needed cash spent on it; Kilkenny was practically free. Nor would Maurice's return prove expensive. 'Tralee', O'Connell predicted correctly on 9 June, 'will cost from £100 to £150, not more.'[94] His nephew, Morgan John, could look after himself in co. Kerry. O'Connell also expected – wrongly as things turned out – that Carlow, where his son Daniel was put up with a whig, Ashton Yates, to wrest the country from the tories, would cost *him* nothing.

He had been talked into contesting Carlow against his better judgment. Fitzpatrick had told him on 17 May that 'it is understood that Carlow will be positively recovered from [Col. Henry] Bruen',[95] and his son-in-law Fitz-Simon made an equally confident prediction eight days later, adding 'it being understood Yates should bear the expense'.[96] On 28 May O'Connell gloomily acquiesced. 'If they can get no other candidate to stand along with Ashton Yates', he wrote to his son John,

> I suppose I must give them your brother Daniel though it will be very hard on me to have to bear the expense of so many elections. I will of course go down to Carlow at once when wanted and go from parish to parish *agitating*. I will write off for Dan at once and meanwhile hold myself in readiness to go down at call and work for him. But those who are urging me

to this trouble, risk and expense must recollect that protection for the tenantry by some species of an indemnity fund will be absolutely necessary as there will assuredly be plenty of evictions after the struggle. My accounts from Carlow say that under the circumstances I mention we should succeed, *viz.* ultimate protection for the tenantry, immediate and extensive agitation, and a son of mine.[97]

Once he had yielded to the pressure, however, O'Connell threw himself into the Carlow contest, declaring that 'My great object is to make Carlow the Clare of Repeal'[98] and setting about snaring the local bishop (Haly, an anti-Repealer), at least to the extent of exhibiting benevolent neutrality.

O'Connell's first general problem, how to run both a Repeal and a pro-government campaign, was comparatively easily solved. The advanced nationalists like Thomas Davis were told privately that 'the want of funds is a decisive reason for not urging the Repeal . . . This is really the secret of our weakness.'[99] Where need be, as in co. Tipperary, O'Connell intervened openly to restrain the rash and zealous from opposing liberals whom he wished to see returned. Meanwhile, he brought the nationalist press into line, ensuring that it was (as Fitzpatrick put it)

> . . . to their [the whigs'] faults a little blind
> And to their virtues *very* kind . . .[100]

The 'People of Ireland' were instructed in an open letter of 19 May to return Repealers in preference to radicals, radicals in preference to whigs, but any of them in preference to a tory: the essential order was to 'Oppose the Tories everywhere, and in everything'.[101] This blessed formula enabled O'Connell to have the best of both worlds, for Repealers, radicals and whigs did not stand against each other but only against conservatives.

Finding tolerably good anti-tory candidates – in some cases finding an anti-tory candidate at all – was a much greater problem. In Ireland as well as Britain, liberal politics had gone slack after ten years of almost unbroken whig rule. O'Connell still had useful lieutenants in some constituencies; generally the local political bosses were leading priests. Fitzpatrick and to a lesser extent Ray could provide other political intelligence, particularly for Dublin. Fitz-Simon and Richard More O'Ferrall, both in office, were further sources of political information, as well as go-betweens with constituency organizations or potential candidates in particular cases. O'Connell also regarded Fitz-Simon 'as a safe and discreet channel of communication with the government',[102] and used him in his efforts to secure government money for the Carlow contest, and to obtain final favours for friends or clients while the whigs were still in office. His son John, whom he had despatched to Ireland in mid-May, served, more than any other, as his confidential agent. 'I think', O'Connell wrote to him on 21 May, 'I *must* go to Dublin next week [he did not do so until 11 June] but in the meantime act for me as if I was *not* to go over – cautiously but *firmly*.'[103] All this provided national political machinery of a sort. But it was a ramshackle and defective form of management, supported by woefully inadequate resources. As O'Connell told Fitzpatrick at the outset of the campaign, 'these are disastrous times to me in my pecuniary prospects ... how ought my heart to sink at these contingencies, coupled with what I fear will be a failing fund! My heard is indeed sore but, I would hope, submissive.'[104]

Given these adverse circumstances, O'Connell fared remarkably well. The tories gained only six Irish seats in the end (leaving them with 38 out of the 105), and twenty of the successful anti-tories were Repealers. But Dublin city and co. Carlow were among the tory victories. O'Connell appears to have expected defeat in Dublin. From the outset, he considered alternative constituencies and was in fact elected for two, co. Cork and co. Meath (he chose to sit for Cork); and he took no part himself in the Dublin election. Instead he spent almost the entire election time, from mid-June to mid-July 1841, canvassing, cajoling and speechifying on behalf of Daniel in co. Carlow. It seems to have been a remarkably pietistic bout of electioneering. One of the Sisters of Mercy at St Leo's, Carlow, wrote later,

> He remained a month in town, and every evening from a raised platform in front of his hotel, he addressed his crowded audience, and having done speaking he would retire as if to take a short rest, but really to beg God's blessing on his labours; Father [James] Maher [O'Connell's Carlow 'manager'] told us, that those moments were always employed by the grand old patriot, in saying his beads. On Sundays he went to Confession in our Sacristy or rather in the screened off portion of our chapel, when his fervent act of contrition could be distinctly heard by all outside, then heard Mass and received Communion most devoutly. He also breakfasted here on these occasions together with His Lordship and some of the priests.[105]

At first, O'Connell was quite hopeful. Soon after he arrived in the constituency, he reported, 'We have glorious prospects here if we could but work them out. The people are rousing, and the Catholic clergy are, for the first time for years, taking their station.'[106] But his final assessment, during polling, was more realistic. 'We are fighting a good fight', he reported to Fitzpatrick on 13 July 1841, 'I hope we shall succeed though, you know, I am apt to despond.'[107] When the count ended next day, Daniel and Yates were trailing their opponents by eight and seven votes respectively in a total poll of 1401. O'Connell bore the blow with all his usual resilience and good-humour. 'Grieving is a folly', he exclaimed on 19 July, 'Hurrah for the next movement.'[108] None the less, it was most curious that the 'national' leader should have spent the entire campaign in a single doubtful constituency. It cost him dearly, in the literal sense at least. Although the government appears to have contributed, under cover, a considerable sum towards the expenses, he probably paid £500 or more out of his own pocket – as well as about £1000 from the Repeal Association's funds, in protecting tenants who had supported Daniel and Yates from landlord reprisals. It was nonsense for O'Connell to speak of co. Carlow as 'the Clare of Repeal'. Repeal was not an issue in the campaign, and O'Connell was neither flanked by perfervid orators nor swept forward by hordes of directed enthusiasts. The decision to spend the critical electoral month in a modest provincial town and the second smallest county in the land is very difficult to explain. When we have said that it gave O'Connell a sort of political vacation, and removed him from the clangours and disappointments of the metropolitan struggle, we seem to have exhausted the benefits which his curious excursion may have conferred upon him.

Ultimately, however, neither his comparatively respectable showing in Ireland as a whole nor the narrowness of his defeat in Carlow mattered much. The tories were resoundingly successful in Great Britain and emerged from the general election with an overall majority of more than eighty. In defeat, the whig leader, Russell, determined to repudiate O'Connell; he and his party were by now thoroughly sickened of the alliance. It would be, it seemed, a long, hard winter at Westminster for the Irish cause.

CHAPTER 20

Divagations

1841–2

I

With the tories in secure control of the lower as well as the upper house of parliament after the general election in 1841, O'Connell saw no alternative to making Ireland the field of operations once again. On the morrow of the polls, he informed Fitzpatrick that there was now nothing for it but unwavering systematic opposition under the banner of Repeal.

> Repeal is the sole basis which the people will accept . . . We attempted half measures – registry franchise associations – and failed although we had the patronage of Government. A cobweb association of that kind may be attempted with a colour of success while the Whigs are in but it would be at best an abortion and should be flung away as a delusion, worthless and disagreeable, so soon as the Tory power begins. No, the Repeal and the Repeal alone is and must be the grand basis of all future operations, hit or miss, win or lose. The people will take nothing short of that and I bitterly regret to tell you that the popular excitement is of so exasperated a character that they will rush into insurrection unless my influence checks and controls them, and that cannot exist or operate unless I take the highest tone and make the most constant exertions in favour of Repeal . . . I say there can be no other basis of association save the Repeal, the glorious Repeal.[1]

Fifteen months, however, were to pass before O'Connell acted, with either determination or consistency, on his own resolution. The Irish Municipal Reform Act was shortly to be put into effect; its implications and immediate consequences were to engross him down to the end of October 1842.

The Act had deprived Irish civic authorities of several functions which even their reformed English counterparts retained. But it had at least opened up patches of local government and prestige to an elective process. Even with the new Irish municipal electorate reduced, proportionately, to little more than one-third of its English counterpart, O'Connell calculated that all the corporations outside Ulster could be captured by his supporters. The most crucial was of course Dublin, which he would contest himself. Winning and running the capital were to consume his energies for a considerable time. It was a welcome diversion in what otherwise promised to be his leanest season in nineteen years.

Meanwhile, comparatively speaking, Peel's government enjoyed a respite from Irish pressures. According to the usual pattern of British administrations in these conditions, it exercised a sort of negative opportunism – that is, it seized the opportunity to do nothing beyond satisfying, so far as practicable, the claims of the rival factions within its own ranks. The first two years of Peel's ministry were characterized by a sort of dualism, or even schizophrenia, in the response of Dublin Castle to O'Connell. In part (mainly, the executive part), the Irish administration reverted to the traditional tory 'Protestant' policy; in part (mainly, the legislative or parliamentary part), it toyed with continuing the whig policy of moving gradually towards parity between conflicting Irish interests and religions. The dichotomy was epitomized by the appointment in 1841 of Earl De Grey, a right-wing tory with Irish Protestant connections, as lord lieutenant, and of Lord Eliot, a liberal conservative, as chief secretary. O'Connell might well have thought himself back in the 1820s when the tory ministries of Liverpool, Canning and Goderich regularly 'balanced' their Irish administrations by alternate 'pro-' and 'anti-Catholic' viceroys and chief secretaries.

Certainly, during 1841–3 the new Dublin regime closely resembled those of the earlier epoch. De Grey, backed by O'Connell's old political enemies Sugden and Blackburne (now, respectively, Irish lord chancellor and attorney-general), attempted to turn the clock back in his appointments. Within the Church of Ireland, he advanced only those who were known to be opponents of the national education system, and, within the police force, only Protestants. He restored Orange magistrates who had been dismissed by his whig predecessor, and eagerly encouraged prosecutions of the press for 'libels' on his administration. This was precisely the form of British indirect rule which O'Connell had always resented most deeply, and ceaselessly assailed. Conversely, Eliot favoured the whig type of minimal, 'judicious' concession to Irish pressure. He defended the 'democratic' franchise of 1832, the Irish poor law of 1838 and the national board of education: he beat off an Irish tory campaign for state support for the

Church of Ireland schools. He also pressed for occasional Catholic legal appointments and a modest programme of legislative reform. The cabinet rejected his proposals for an increase in the Maynooth grant and an extension of the Irish franchise, and the Irish tory opposition secured the defeat of bills which he introduced in 1842 to reform Irish medical charities and the grand jury system.

Eliot succeeded occasionally in minor matters, but it was De Grey who generally carried the day in 1841–3. This is ultimately explicable only in terms of the cabinet's absorption, during these years, in extra-Irish matters – economic distress and social disaffection in Great Britain, troubles in India and dangerously deteriorating relations with the United States and France. For there was no shortage of Irish experience in the upper ranks. Almost half of Peel's cabinet consisted of ex-viceroys and ex-chief secretaries of Ireland; and Peel himself and the colonial secretary, Stanley, had developed during their secretary-ships particularly clear and elaborate views of the proper government of Ireland. Peel's in particular should have opened the way to ambitious 'remedial' measures. He was to write, on 19 October 1843:

> mere force, however necessary the application of it, will do nothing as a permanent remedy for the social evils of Ireland. We must look beyond the present, must bear in mind that the day may come – and come suddenly and unexpectedly – when this country may be involved in serious disputes or actual wars with other Powers, and when it may be of the first importance that the foundations of a better state of things in Ireland should have been laid.[2]

Perhaps Peel and his cabinet, their foreign and domestic preoccupations notwithstanding, would have followed and developed Eliot's line during 1841–3 had O'Connell not been correspondingly diverted from applying any serious pressure on them either in Ireland or elsewhere. But on the parliamentary front – with a secure majority in both Houses, O'Connell generally absent and most of his followers idle, feeble or inept – the tories had practically nothing to fear. So far as Irish agitation went, the government for long dismissed O'Connell's current Repeal movement as a gigantic sham – 'a failing concern' was Peel's contemptuous judgment;[3] and there was no increase in Irish violence or disorder during 1841 or 1842. Thus Peel did not feel himself impelled to work out any coherent Irish policy beyond alternate checks to the exuberance of Eliot and De Grey – for he and Graham made sure to rein-in not only the conciliators but also the ultra-tory party whenever it threatened to bolt too far back along the road of learning nothing and forgetting nothing. This *far niente* policy proved a costly error. O'Connell had been written off much too soon. In the event, he succeeded in turning his enforced holiday from agitation into the basis for a much more formidable agitation in the future. He returned from it like a giant refreshed.

II

O'Connell's lord mayoralty of Dublin (1 November 1841–31 October 1842) has been, in all senses, badly noticed. Contemporary British mockery of his peacocking in the robes of office and glee in the title 'Lordship' (Thackeray squeezed these 'jokes' dry in his *Irish Sketch Book*) has been occasionally recalled. But generally historians have dismissed his year in the Dublin Mansion House as an aimless interlude, interesting only in so far as it emblemized a further significant decline in the domestic sway of the Irish – and in particular the metropolitan mercantile – Ascendancy.

This is a serious misjudgment. O'Connell did glory, child-like, in the lord mayoral parade and fritteries; he did exult, on the morrow of his victory, that his enemies

> have no longer the power to hurt us. To be sure, there never was such a corrupt, bigotted, jobbing, robbing corporation (laughter), but now they are gone, and there's an end to them . . . and we will put for an inscription over them – 'Here lies the Rotten Corporation of Dublin; it did no good when living, and it is a burden to the earth when dead' (shouts of laughter).[4]

But O'Connell's vision of his office soared high above its trappings or the novelty of the Repealers' triumph. He saw it as offering a first trial in self-government. Dublin Corporation was not exactly College Green *in parvo*. But, in O'Connell's eyes, its management presented him with the chance to show the world at large that the 'mere Irish' could order their affairs with impeccable propriety, probity and dispatch. He justified his own aspiration

> to the dignity of Lord Mayor . . . [by] his habit of business and his familiarity with the rules of debate [which] conferred upon him advantages which might not, perhaps, be easily found in another person, and which he conceived might be of great service in ensuring the maintenance of strict order, regularity and decorum in the proceeding of a new corporation.[5]

A la Johnson and Thrale's brewery, O'Connell saw in the lord mayoralty the potentiality of political riches beyond the dreams of avarice, rather than a parcel of boilers and vats!

It was, of course, extraordinarily convenient for O'Connell to find another arena for activity just as his prospects in parliament were dimmed. It was also convenient that the Irish corporation elections were scheduled for 25 October 1841, only eight weeks after the whigs were at last forced from office; this minimized the tories' capacity to manipulate the local electoral system to their advantage. O'Connell had to sacrifice his beloved Kerry vacation to the cause. 'It is a cruel disappointment to all here', wrote his son John from Derrynane, 'There was quite a *scene* upon the mountain yesterday when Denis McCrohan told the huntsmen that you could not come. Two or three of them, led by Cormac, fairly sat down and cried.'[6] But the Dublin municipal election required the rapid construction of a new political machine. The first essential was revision of the electoral roll, and this was frantically pursued almost up to the election day itself. Beyond the grind of roll-scrutiny, O'Connell based his campaign upon parish clubs which were to select the candidates for the fifteen city wards. Their lists constituted what he termed 'the whole ticket', which he repeatedly instructed the burgesses (or local electorate) to support *en bloc*. A week before the polling date, he was confident of carrying thirteen of the fifteen wards, provided that the burgesses troubled themselves to vote, and obeyed the order to 'stand true to the whole ticket . . . If any man breaks through the ticket, we are lost; if any man does not vote for the whole ticket, he is not for Ireland.'[7] To drive these points home, O'Connell secured (and publicized) a resolution from the Repeal Association, 'That any burgess enrolled on the Liberal interest who does not vote for the whole ticket at the ensuing municipal election is an enemy to the principle of civil and religious liberty, injures the cause of the depressed Irish manufacturers, and is a foe to the Repeal of the Union.'[8] All fell out more or less as O'Connell planned. If he did not make quite a clean sweep in the thirteen 'popular' wards, he carried 'the whole ticket' in eleven, and more than three-quarters of all seats in the new corporation (47 out of 60). He also headed the poll himself in two wards – thereby securing an ordinary vote as well as that which he would possess as chairman. His political genius had not failed; he had conjured up, almost on the instant, a set of tactics and cadre of lieutenants to deal with the novel circumstance.

Doubtless John O'Connell mirrored his father's view of his elevation when he boasted that the capture of Dublin corporation was

second only 'to that glorious and *certain* event', the restoration of the
Irish parliament. 'You have', John continued,

> a legally recognized *lordship* from *the people*, utterly unconnected with
> court favour or aristocratic usage ... We rejoice, my dear Father, that
> Dublin has paid you such a tribute of respect as to take you for its first
> freely chosen chief magistrate, but still more that you should thus have
> opened to you one additional and most available means of advancing that
> great measure which will be the compensation for all your labours and
> sufferings, as it is and has been the great object of your life, the raising
> Ireland to her proper condition as a nation.[9]

But though O'Connell had succeeded by a ruthless, though brilliantly
executed, exercise in street politics, grounded in his Repeal organization and appeal, he at once declared that he would eschew both party
and partisanship during his lord mayoralty. Of course, such
olympianism would help him to display his remarkable executive
powers; it was the nearest he would ever get to membership of a
government. But, much more important, supra-factional rule would
tend to verify his life-long assertion that Irishmen of all creeds and
antecedents could work together in their own country for the common
good. In postponing Repeal as an immediate issue, he hoped, he said,
to persuade Irish tories that they had nothing to fear from their
compatriots.

Even had he wished to do so – which was, of course, far from being
the case – O'Connell could not have buried the triumphal fact that he
was the first Catholic lord mayor of Dublin since 1688, or have fled
mob adulation on every public occasion. But he certainly cultivated
the image of selfless political impartiality. Inevitably his term of office
began with a taste or two of the spoils system. The replacements for
certain of the corporation officers had evidently been decided well
before the municipal election. John O'Connell told his father on 4
November that he had informed an applicant for patronage 'that
whatever might be at the disposal of the Corporation had been long
ago bespoken'.[10] But thereafter O'Connell seems to have striven
earnestly both to reduce the number of corporation officials, and to
prevent jobbery, even in the Repeal interest. On 8 December 1841 he
hotly resisted a motion of Councillor Callaghan and Alderman
Purcell, both Repealers, that all officers should be elected by ballot as
the 'best means' of ensuring the council's independence (Callaghan
wished his own son to be appointed junior counsel to the corporation,
and despaired of his succeeding in open voting). O'Connell threatened
immediate resignation.

He had, he perceived, sat too long in that chair (loud cries of no, no, no, and great confusion) ... and he had, therefore, prepared a notice which he would give into the hands of the Town Clerks, for the election of a new Lord Mayor (loud cries of no, no, and great sensation). It was of too much importance that even the quantity of influence which he possessed in Ireland – should be preserved by him chaste and undefiled (cheers) ... in point of law he was bound to say that publicity was the principle of the new corporations, and any thing which went to prevent that would not only make him leave the chair, but the assembly also.[11]

The 'rebels' instantly surrendered, and a counter-motion begging O'Connell to withdraw his impending resignation was carried with acclamation.

> O! it is excellent
> To have a giant's strength; but it is tyrannous
> To use it like a giant.[12]

Unquestionably, O'Connell had acted, in effect, the bully. But the original motion was a direct challenge to his political as well as his civic authority.

The only open deviation from his vaunted neutrality as chairman came in response to tory provocation. On 23 December 1841 the 'Orange' councillors proposed that the corporation congratulate De Grey on his appointment as lord lieutenant. 'The notion of the reformed corporation of Dublin consenting to such a proposition', O'Connell broke out, 'could not be entertained by any man.' De Grey governed for a party that

> seemed to despise the opinion of the people, and who assisted in restraining their [the corporation's] own powers by giving them a corporation bill far inferior to what had been granted to any of the towns in England (hear) ...
> [De Grey] has no public character but that which he ought to be ashamed to hear – that of making professions of impartiality and liberality, while he is doing the work of the partizan.

Of course, the vote, which went on party lines, favoured O'Connell. He himself, however, by no means considered his stance political. His concluding outburst revealed his inward thought – or perhaps unconscious assumption – that *he* was the embodiment of *national* will, and the opposition a mere nexus of *frondeurs*. 'The [O'Connellite] party referred to', he declared, 'consisted of the people, who were not a party, but who were opposed by a section of the country, that might properly be termed a party.'[13]

In this vein, O'Connell, while pouring fishwives' abuse upon Peel and De Grey at weekly meetings of the Repeal Association, treated their supporters with a sort of elephantine forbearance when acting or speaking as lord mayor. He ordered the statue of William III in College Green to be painted 'bronze' so that the Dublin Orangemen (having a colour near enough to their hearts presumably) need no longer try to deck it with garlands on their celebratory days, and thereby provoke sectarian disturbances. He cast off his official regalia at the doors of the Catholic Pro-Cathedral on New Year's Day, 1842, with the aside (for the benefit of the surrounding mob) that although the lord mayor was a Catholic, his robes were Protestant. He abandoned the traditional lord mayor's proclamation calling for the solemn observance of Good Friday. 'It was a rule with Roman Catholics, and they all knew he was one', he told the corporation on 23 March 1842, 'to leave these things with their clergy . . . He was disposed to pay the same respect to the clergymen of every other religious domination.' When this decision was generally applauded, O'Connell allowed himself a single flick of asperity. 'Such a feeling was certainly to be commended . . . the more particularly when it was recollected, that in the room in which they them met the most rigorous exclusion on account of religion was perseveringly adhered to.'[14] His momentary lapse from magnanimity was trifling, however, compared with the undying bitterness of some of his Orange opponents. Councillor Mackay, for example, decried the O'Connellites in the corporation as 'men who had neither principle, honour or character – the dupes and slaves of the greatest tyrant who ever lived . . . and amongst them, he was sorry to say, there were a great many Protestants, who attached a degree of respectability to the contemptible set'.[15] But O'Connell was finally rewarded for his laborious supra-sectarianism. On the day that he retired from office, he was eulogized in the corporation (to general cheers) as a tyrant who enslaved by the heart and not the hand. A motion 'expressing our . . . approbation of the impartial manner with which Alderman Daniel O'Connell discharged the duties of Lord Mayor' was also carried, unanimously.[16]

Some of O'Connell's gestures – the bronzing of William III's statue or the abandonment of his robes and chain at the church door – were comical enough. He also paraded, and was paraded, as Mob King. Immediately after his election, he appeared at the open window of the council chamber and asked the delighted crowd whether they knew him still in his new finery, and whether his cocked hat became him. For weeks after, as he rode about in the civic coach, flanked by footmen in a livery of green and yellow, his tattermadalion followers called 'Hats off!' to all spectators, tearing away the headgear of the reluctant. But it must be allowed that, as popular politician, O'Connell was more or less a licensed public performer. His role as lord mayor resembled his professional 'part' of barrister. Both occupations were akin to acting in being replete with rituals and costume, and in the prescribed emotional reactions, cultivation of rapport with audiences, and dispensation (for the time being) from many of the conventions governing ordinary life. All this was second nature to O'Connell – as well as first artifice.

Once in the council room, O'Connell was a very different being. His executive efficiency was at least as striking as his 'impartiality'. Early in his term, he set up finance, law, property and water committees, each under his own chairmanship – forgoing at the same time that portion of the lord mayor's allowance which was a charge on the impoverished pipe-water estate. Characteristically, he drew up, unaided, a complete pipe-water bill in twenty-four hours in order to give it the necessary notice to be considered in the next session of parliament. Equally characteristic was his flamboyant offer of his professional services free of cost to the corporation during a wrangle over the expense of employing legal officers. O'Connell was punctilious in his weekly attendance at the lord mayor's court and (if the absence of any charges to the contrary is conclusive) in adhering to his original undertaking to deal with litigants only in open court, and to see none in the Mansion House. A petition presented in the Commons on 6 May 1842 complained of his inactivity in admitting freemen to the franchise; but, in reply, he claimed to have missed only one admission day, and that through illness. It is true – as tory councillors kept pointing out – that he was absent from Dublin for considerable periods. He spent some eighteen weeks in attendance at the House of Commons; he also holidayed in Derrynane in September, although for less than half his usual time. Even O'Connell (when it suited him) allowed that his opponents had ground for dissatisfaction in this regard. In declining an invitation to stand a second time for the lord mayoralty, he told the corporation on 16 August 1842 that he 'was obliged to be absent more frequently that he would wish, which was an exceedingly wrong principle'.[17] Less grandly, he vowed a month later that he 'would not consent for any offer to forfeit my prospect of being here [Derrynane] all October in the ensuing year'.[18]

None the less, Dublin must have gained much more from his intelligent and decisive management for seven months of the year than it lost from having to suffer a *locum tenens* for the remaining five. It was not flummery when O'Connell was lauded for his 'distinguished ability [and] unwearied assiduity' in the corporation immediately after his retirement.[19] He had applied himself with his customary zeal. 'I never was worried out of my existence', he wrote on 4 December 1841, 'until after I became a great *City* Lord.'[20] So it remained to the concluding weeks of his term of office. Between 2 and 16 October 1842 (the fortnight allotted by law) he completed the revision of the burgess roll, labouring nine hours a day up to the 16th, when he worked almost until midnight. He also pushed through a reform of the weighmaster system at Smithfield market during the week that he retired. It is true that much of the substance of municipal government, as we see it, was ignored during O'Connell's no less than earlier regimes. He had nothing to say on sanitation, arterial drainage, housing, roads, gas lighting and similar matters, critical to the comfort and even tolerability of urban life, although these were the subjects of rapid change in both theory and practice in contemporary Europe. The omission was important. People dwell, wash, walk, play, live noisomely or not, live in light or dark, die young or old, as well as brandish tokens and struggle for vicarious power. But the fault lay at least as much with the politically-inspired limitations of the Irish Municipal Reform Act as with O'Connell himself, and in fact he can scarcely be blamed for not seeing the city which had been his chief home for nearly half a century – wrapping him round like an old familiar garment – with fresh eyes. By all the customary criteria of Dublin civic government, he was a remarkably efficient, even an imaginative, lord mayor.

The effectiveness of O'Connell's administration was the more remarkable because the new corporation was encumbered by the accumulated debts (over £300,000) and ill-kept financial records of the old. His first action as lord mayor was to institute an investigation into the accounts of the late treasurer, Sir John Kingston James. Eight and a half months later, James had still failed to produce detailed accounts. On 16 August 1842, O'Connell reported to the corporation that 'not a single date when any payment was made could be found. The entire affair looked as much like a fraud as anything he had ever seen.'[21] By the end of September 1842, James still having failed to divulge even the dates on which debentures and the interest on them had been issued, O'Connell moved from the chair that he receive no compensation or back salary. Meanwhile, the corporation had been in desperate financial plights. On 2 April 1842 seven of its wealthiest O'Connellite members had had to subscribe £500 each in order to procure the release of its estate from chancery.

Significantly, O'Connell himself was not among the subscribers. The reason was simple: his own finances were by then in little better state than the corporation's. The lord mayor's allowances under the new Act did not meet the outgoings which O'Connell (ever lavish) deemed indispensable, and his suspension of party politics, even if only when acting in his official role, dried up the contributions to his Tribute and the Rent. On 25 July 1842, he wrote to Fitzpatrick 'overwhelmed with affliction. It almost drives me mad . . . [Edmond] Smithwick's bill for £420, due on Wednesday week, *comes upon me*. I write again to him today in great anxiety.'[22] He did indeed write anxiously to Smithwick, one of his most loyal and necessary supporters:

> Unhappily I have this month made payments to the extent of some thousands of pounds, and next month is also heavy though comparatively light. I did not however foresee or make provision for your bill, foolishly thinking it impossible that I should not get it renewed. It makes me quite unhappy lest it should go back on you for want of my being ready to take it up . . . I really cannot describe my anxiety. What am I to do? If the bill goes back on you under present circumstances I never can forgive myself.[23]

Once more, however, the indefatigable Fitzpatrick came to the rescue; he arranged for all O'Connell's bills to be accepted. 'May God bless you!', replied O'Connell in relief on 29 July, 'I was actually in despair'.[24]

III

O'Connell could have ill-afforded a second term as lord mayor. But it was not this that moved him to reject it; never in his life had he regulated his actions by what he could or could not afford. It was the cost to his public life which really mattered. He had already creamed the office of such *éclat*, and opportunity to display administrative talent, as it had to offer. Meanwhile, his failure to make headway with any of his main objectives during the second parliamentary session of 1842 appears to have clinched his determination to revert from the municipal arena to the national. On 6 August 1842 he announced to Ray from London that he proposed 'to proceed at once to the perfect organisation of the·Repeal agitation', and instructed him to prepare immediately accurate returns of the Association's activities throughout Leinster since the preceding 25 March. 'The apathy', he went on,

> by which the spirit of patriotism is paralysed must soon give way to the conviction that Ireland has nothing to depend on but her own exertions . . .
>
> But shall we despair? I will try the thrilling trumpet that has often before caused despair to hope and torpor to be roused into energy. I do not despair, nor does the chill of an ungenial Legislature diminish the glow of hope which I derive from the subdued but reviving flame of genuine Irish patriotism. The People of Ireland are true to the heart's core. The Clergy of the People are as sincere in their love of fatherland as they are eminent in Christian zeal and fervent piety. I do not despair . . .
>
> Have, I repeat it, prepared a list of all the parishes in Leinster, with the names of the clergy of each parish and of every layman therein, who shall have taken at any bygone time an active part in the Repeal agitation. It is by detailed and persevering exertions that public opinion will recover its tone and energy in Ireland.[25]

We should note the prominent role which O'Connell evidently envisaged for the Church. For some time, he had been steadily cultivating the hierarchy, acting more or less as their agent in various pieces of legislation which touched ecclesiastical interests; and on 9 May 1842 he had written to Paul Cullen, rector of the Irish College at Rome, on the multifarious benefits which would flow to Irish Catholicism from the repeal of the Act of Union. 'British!!!', he exclaimed in the course of his apologia, 'I am not British. You are not British. When the British north and south fell away and dissipated amongst the profligate and the renegades of Protestantism and of every species of infidelity, the inheritance of the Lord amidst the land, the Irish Nation and the Irish Church were the victims of and not the participators in these crimes.'[26] When on 9 September he ordered his personal secretary O'Neill Daunt to commence 'arrangments [sic] for opening the campaign of agitation', he also warned him to advance only with clerical concurrence. 'Be sure to have the approval of the Catholic clergy in every place you move to.'[27]

Well before his term of lord mayor ended, O'Connell set afoot what he called 'provincial agitation for the appointment of Repeal wardens in every parish'.[28] In mid-September 1842, the principal organizers of this preliminary work were dispatched to Munster, Connacht and Leinster. He himself was released from 'office' on 1 November, but the accumulation of business in arrears and the need to restore himself once more at Derrynane precluded him from wholehearted campaigning for a time. When the New Year began, however, he was ready for a full agitation. On 7 January 1843, he told Fitzpatrick, 'I intend to spend less time in London this Session than ever I did.'[29] In fact, he spent none. No skirmishing at Westminster could compare in significance with the onslaught which he rapidly succeeded in mounting at home. The lord mayoralty had served its purpose. O'Connell had played the part of sober and judicious statesman, in the utmost glare which the Lilliputian theatre of a city council could provide. Now it was time to take to the open air and use an entire country for his stage, and, by turns, Coriolanus, Brutus and Mark Antony for roles.

IV

A most striking feature of O'Connell's winning and wearing of the Dublin lord mayoralty was, as we have seen, his recovery of energy and spirit. The press of new work was nothing as against its accompanying colour and excitement. Rather, it was a break from care, from the anxious years of hand-to-mouth political existence, when the survival of the whigs in office – all-in-all to him – seemed practically forever at the hazard. Thus in late 1842 he came back to serious politics quite restored, with all 'the gloss of freshness'[30] once again.

His renewed exuberance and revitalization while in office were a remarkable testimony to O'Connell's power to subordinate the private to the public man, for, interiorly regarded, the early 1840s were not easy years. Central to everything which touched him individually was his religion, and O'Neill Daunt's record of his conversations with O'Connell during 1840–2 throws some light on this. O'Connell's belief tended to be grave and rigid. In a contention with Daunt (a convert to Catholicism) on 'whether errors in faith, or errors in morals, were the more dangerous to the soul and the more offensive to God', O'Connell argued strongly for the first:

Nothing short of a thorough and perfect sincerity – and, moreover, a cautious sincerity, – could acquit the holder of erroneous faith from the guilt of heresy. Of course, every person thus thoroughly and cautiously sincere, was free from heretical guilt; but those who belonged not to the Catholic church laboured under the grievous disadvantage of being deprived of true sacraments; or, in other words, they were deprived of those ordinary channels of grace and modes of reconciliation with God, of which *all* stand in need, inasmuch as *all* have at one time or another sinned mortally. Even though a Catholic should have sinned more grievously than a person without the pale of the church, yet the position of the former was in *one* respect better – namely, that he stood a better chance of obtaining the grace of true repentance.[31]

Even when he spoke of the astonishing rise in the number of 'male communicants' over the past quarter-century or so, O'Connell took it at its lowest computation – as an indication of greater earnestness in religion, and not necessarily of spiritual progress: 'Every Sunday you will see many more than you then saw at Easter or Christmas; and this is, at all events, an evidence that the persons who communicate, *intend*, at least, that they will not live in sin.'[32] It seems significant that one of O'Connell's two favourite Latin hymns, which he was accustomed to recite aloud when travelling, was that generally heard by Catholics on Good Friday only, when the Way of the Cross was being commemorated.

> Stabat Mater Dolorosa,
> Juxta crucem lachrymosa
> Dum pendebat filius. *[33]

Although he continued to deplore the temporal power, possessions and pretensions of the pope, and to assert that 'In fact, the democratic spirit is more favourable to the cause of morality and religion, than the monarchical', he took an absolutist view of papal authority in the field of faith and doctrine.[34] He wrote on 9 September 1841, for instance, that

> the spiritual authority in all its effulgence [is] the Apostolic See, the centre of unity, the safeguard of the Church. That authority is assailed in our day by the spirit of absolutism in many Catholic and other sovereigns, who not content with Caesar's portion claim what belongs to God. It is also assailed by the restless genius of false liberalism which whilst it affects to seek liberty principally desires to uproot religion.[35]

He cherished Dryden's lines exalting the inerrancy of the papacy,

> But Gracious God! how well thou dost provide
> For erring judgments an unerring guide . . .
> O, teach me to believe thee thus concealed
> Nor further search than what thyself revealed

---

*The sorrowing mother stands
In tears next to the cross
While her son hangs from it.

But her alone for my director take
Whom thou has promised never to forsake.[36]

It is silly as well as arrogant to believe that one can make windows into people's souls. But, for what they are worth, the outward signs suggest that O'Connell was an ultra-conscientious, fearful, straitened type of Catholic, almost morbidly observant. There appears to have been little or nothing in him of the spiritual joyousness and easy resilience which one might have predicted from his public bearing. He may even have been a victim – to a small degree – of a form of religious neurosis. Certainly, he had a thorough knowledge of the textbook responses to scrupulosity. During all this period, and indeed after he had died, his youngest daughter, Betsey Ffrench, was (intermittently, at least) in deep religious distress, though the specific subject of her 'scruples' is unknown. When O'Connell first learnt of her condition, in June 1839, he prescribed the set ecclesiastical remedy of utter submission to direction:

> It is quite true that you are in a state with which it is the inscrutable will of God to try the souls of His elect – a state of great danger if the spirit of pride, of self-esteem, or of self-will is mixed with it, so as to make the sufferer fall into the snare of *despair*. Despair is your danger, your only danger. Oh, generous God, protect my child from despair! If you by humility, submission, humble submission, to the church in the person of your spiritual director – if you give up every thought and throw yourself into the arms of God by OBEDIENCE and submission, you will soon be at peace and be so for life, and in an eternity of bliss . . . If your scruple be such as you cannot communicate to your father, go at once and consult Dr MacHale about it. Determine, before you go in the presence of God, to submit to whatever the Archbishop shall say to you.[37]

When Betsey's reply revealed her to be still caught in her maze of fears, O'Connell repeated the orthodox instruction:

> There is one remedy, and *only one*. That is, absolute, unqualified submission to your director – unreasoning submission. Do not argue with anybody. Let nobody reason with you, but *submit*. Do exactly what your director requires. In your case your director may – and, I think, should, compel you to go to communion without going to confession at all. Many persons in your condition have been perfectly cured by perfect submission.[38]

Had O'Connell himself been among the 'cured'? Certainly, he occasionally manifested something like obsession in seeking to make reparation for some past real or imagined wrong. He, whose Lenten mortification was often awesome, grieved over some self-exemptions from fasting in earlier days. He even worried – in his rare flushes of affluence – about distant, doubtful debts. He once wrote to his former steward, for instance,

> I cannot express to you how uneasy I feel about the money I received out of Segerson's lands after his death. I must satisfy my mind to the last shilling. I have an impression I received £72. I will pay it all over again if I [one word illegible] and if I should not recollect it, *it must be paid* . . . Where are the Brennans I put out of Bahaghs? It was for putting them out I made some compensation. There was a balance due to them of a bond debt by Segerson . . . Really this subject is troubling my mind and conscience.[39]

Ten days later, he followed up this *cri de coeur* with, 'I also earnestly request you will *at once* find out all particulars of the Brennans of Bahaghs . . . I cannot, my dear John, bear delay in this matter.'[40] All this may signify no more than bouts of extraordinary conscientiousness. But there seems little doubt that O'Connell's religion was very serious, in both the general and the contemporary evangelical senses. An acute awareness of (to use his own words) 'the evil of sin in its offending God and subjecting us to deserve punishment hereafter'[41] did not conduce to private comfort – not that O'Connell would have spoken of his spiritual pains, whatever they might have been, as anything other than part of the Christian dispensation, of the purifying design of (his own words again) 'a loving God who, in the excess of his love, died on a cross' for him.[42] 'Alas, alas,' he once asked O'Neill Daunt, '. . . of what use will future fame be to me when I am dead and judged?'[43] This rings authentic.

Despite the docility of his family, O'Connell's path as a father was steep and broken. Although the eldest was 39 years old in 1841 and the youngest 22, none of his children had really thrown off their early dependence on him, nor had he lost his old fearful solicitude or sense of responsibility for their affairs. One or other or even several of them, and their families, stayed with him, often for weeks at a time, at Derrynane or Merrion Square or in London. For all his control of the domestic timetables, this must have eaten into his working-time and concentration, as well as money. As with all his family cares, the loss of Mary told on him here. She (according to her daughter Ellen) had known that it

> was necessary for the success of affairs both of law and politics . . . that he should never be troubled with household affairs; and she therefore, while regulating his family with the great exactness, took care never to harass

him with her domestic troubles ... On the contrary ... [even] when engaging a governess, she was wont to stipulate that no chidings of the children should ever take place in their father's presence, but should be reserved for the schoolroom.[44]

Mary was no longer there to screen him as best she could from all that was disagreeable in a household.

To be pressed in by the business of his family was far from simply troublesome to O'Connell. He slipped naturally into, and revelled in, the part of patriarch; he enjoyed crowded tables and a domestic audience. He also doted on his grandchildren, calling them by the usual sort of childish names (Fanny Fan-Fan or Duck-a-day), and full of the usual foolish wonder at their infant talk; he remained almost cloyingly affectionate towards his own daughters and younger sons. But, as we have seen, a heavy tax was paid on such emotional commitment. The death of his favourite grandson struck O'Connell to the heart, and there is no doubting the reality of his anguish when he first learned of Betsey's sad condition: 'Represent to yourself your darling boy in mental agony and then you will read my feelings of utter misery at your state of mind. This, I own, is the severest blow that ever I experienced, to have you, my angel daughter, consuming your heart and intellect on vain, idle, and unprofitable scruples';[45] or again, 'I write to you by your pet name, to recall to your own tenderness your fond father's affection. I see your case clearly, and it breaks my heart to think of it.'[46]

Another blow was the break-up of Maurice's long-troubled marriage early in 1841. Evidently, Mary Frances deserted her husband, for Maurice wrote to O'Connell on 20 March, 'It has struck me that *her* family may set up insanity as a defence and I think that this ought to be considered.'[47] At first it looked as if some 'quiet arrangement' might be reached, but on 18 May 1841, through her brother, Mary Frances told her solicitor that 'she would listen to no terms under £300 a year [roughly, the income which her dowry would have earned], that she would not appear in Dublin and that she had been served with her citation'.[48] O'Connell was privy to the negotiations, and although his comments have not survived there can be no doubt that the marital scandal would have hit him hard. Such affairs generated a family-wide, ill-differentiated air of disgrace in early Victorian Ireland; and besides O'Connell had now to provide further support, domestic and financial, to Maurice and the four children who had been left upon his hands. There are also some indications that O'Connell fretted lest his little grand-daughters be deprived of

Catholic education. At the time, it was common in 'mixed marriages' for daughters to be reared in their mother's religion, and sons in their father's. Probably O'Connell feared that what was cruelly but all too accurately described as a '*habeas animam*' struggle might follow Mary Frances's departure. In fact, she appears never to have demanded more than the £300 per annum for her own maintenance. But O'Connell must have been sick with apprehension, and the shame of the whole business, for a while.

Whatever the final settlement with Mary Frances, ultimately he would have borne the additional expenses, for, Atlas-like, he still carried the majority of his family on his shoulders. Although Maurice had a small independent income, O'Connell appears to have given him, as heir, an allowance of £700 a year. It also seems that O'Connell had to underwrite (at an annual cost of £85 for a life assurance premium) that portion of Mary Frances's dowry which even yet remained effectively in the hands of the Scott family. His second son, Morgan, who had been appointed Irish assistant registrar of deeds in 1840 and married in the same year, was no longer a financial burden; in fact the roles may have been temporarily reversed in 1841 to judge from Fitzpatrick's request of 27 January to O'Connell (the first of three such notes) for 'a cheque for £750 to pay Morgan's acceptance for your accommodation due early next week'.[49] Similarly, O'Connell's eldest daughter, Ellen, was more or less independent, although in 1841 her husband was complaining to O'Connell of 'the present too small salaries' of Irish public servants: 'I boldly assert the salary of "Clerk of the Hanaper" [his own office] is already too low at £600 a year'.[50] O'Connell helped his other daughters, Kate and Betsey, with occasional small gifts of money; neither was well-off. But his other sons were major charges. Despite the injection of considerable outside capital and more skilled management, 'O'Connell's Brewery' had proved an unsuccessful venture, and was sold – to re-emerge, appropriately enough, as the Phoenix – in 1840. Thus Daniel was back again, more or less, on O'Connell's hands. John, for whose marriage settlement O'Connell had had to borrow £5000 in 1838, was also in some measure a dependant. '*Instead of money for agitating expeditions*,' he wrote to O'Connell from Dublin on 9 December 1840,

I am obliged, my dear father, to ask you to let me place to your account one or two of my heaviest *household* bills (not wine) since you left town. I have no choice as the money I calculated upon has *suddenly* failed me. House property is so precarious that after getting £200 a year these 2 years as my third of Eliza's [his wife's] joint property, I now learn I am not to get more than what I have received this year, viz., £130 – deficit £70 *on one third alone*, making on the whole £210. This, with the £70 Eliza's illness cost me, renders me a beggar for the rest of this year but *it shall be the last time*. I have had to raise money to meet Eliza's illness which will give some idea of my condition.[51]

The basis of O'Connell's financial troubles in the 1840s was probably expenditure, past and current, on his family. Such crises as the failure to meet Smithwick's bill in July 1842 had their roots in his chronic indebtedness, which in turn derived, to a considerable degree, from earlier spending on his children. At the very least, O'Connell had laid out £20,000 in financing their marriages, and their yearly drain upon him must have meant further borrowing. Early in 1842, the Board of the National Bank was so concerned about his rising overdraft, which by then totalled almost £30,500, that it set up a special committee to tackle the problem of its Governor's affairs. The minutes of their committee reveal something of the awkwardness of the extraordinary situation:

When [on 27 February 1842] the chairman presented to his Lordship [O'Connell] their Report, and in proposing to read the same he said it was unnecessary as he would read it over, himself, his Lordship then entered into some verbal explanations, when the Committee intimated that they would prefer having a reply in writing and which his Lordship promised to furnish, on the following Tuesday, the 1st of March.

In consequence of no reply being received from his Lordship on the 19th of March the Chairman with the concurrence of the other Members of the Committee, addressed the following Letter to his Lordship, the The Rt Honble Daniel O'Connell MP

My Lord,   19 March 1842
    Not having had the pleasure of meeting your Lordship at the Court [Board meeting] this day, and, in consequence of the inquiries which have been made respecting the result of the Report now in your Lordship's possession, I have as Chairman of the Special Committee, and in accordance with the wishes of my Colleagues to solicit the favor of your furnishing us with the written communications as agreed upon when we first had the honor of an interview with your Lordship.[52]

When on 27 March 1842 O'Connell at last tendered his written submission, it was clear that the bulk of his security consisted of assurance policies on various lives, his own included. It was also evident that several of the policies had been entered into in order to secure capital sums, or underwrite commitments, for Maurice, John and perhaps other of his children. The premiums on the policies alone amounted to over £1250, and the overdraft interest to some £600, per annum. To these outgoings was soon to be added the obligation to reduce steadily his ill-secured overdraft at the bank. With it all, his younger sons at least remained in a precarious condition. Could O'Connell always keep out of mind the grim warning of his brother James, a few years earlier, 'a long experience of the cold heartedness of the world makes me fear these young men [in particular, "poor little Dan"] may, in the event of your being suddenly taken out of their life, be left without the means of existence'?[53]

In this way, O'Connell's public rebound of 1841–2, his outward gaiety, the renewal of his zest and sparkle, are to be set against his enveloping private cares. How did he keep such heart-sicknesses at bay, quite out of sight? Explain it as we will – by ferocity of ambition, by indomitability of nature, by matchless powers of recovery or the politician's innate sense of stage – it still seems a marvel of control. Whatever hidden weights he carried, he was, at the end of 1842, ready to spring, as lightly as ever, into the contest of his life.

CHAPTER 21

The Big Bang

1843

I

As we have seen, the new Repeal Association advanced little during its first two years in being. Yet, curiously enough, this slow progress was partly responsible for the development of something like a general programme for the movement. In his efforts to widen his appeal, O'Connell took aboard various popular demands, especially those attractive to the small tenant farmers. The abolition of tithes was one obvious example. Another was the replacement of the new Irish poor law by a quasi-charitable system financed by a tax on incomes of over £500 per annum, or better still by a state-aided scheme to succour the sick poor: the farmers were groaning loudly under the novel burden of the poor rate. But the most promising adoption was for fixity of tenure. This was rather a misnomer, as the Association's proposal amounted to little more than compensation for tenant improvements and a minimum of twenty-one years for leases. None the less, it was a radical demand in the climate of the early 1840s.

Similarly, O'Connell set up committees of the Association to sustain interest in, and manufacture business for, the weekly meetings. The committees (whose membership was identical and determined solely by O'Connell, the invariable chairman) investigated and reported on such subjects as the passage of the Act of Union, Ireland's financial relations with Great Britain, the progress of Repeal, and the restoration of the Irish House of Commons. The main consequence of these reports was to enlarge O'Connell's own oratorical armoury and to keep up the spirits of the faithful. Even the report on the progress of Repeal was much more an essay in propaganda than an attempt to remedy serious organizational failings. But the committees also led, almost accidentally, to the acquisition of policies at several points. By its very failure to take off politically, 'simple repeal' ended up with various shreds and patches of an extra-constitutional platform.

The critical change came in late 1842 when O'Connell's term as lord mayor ended and the inefficiency of the existing organization could at last come under serious attention. As a first step, the Dublin wardens were re-ordered. Next, inspectors of wardens, charged with the establishment and maintenance of a thorough-going system of propaganda, fund-collection and communciation with the centre, were appointed for the towns and groups of parishes, with chief inspectors for still larger regions. This was of course a harking back to models provided by the Catholic Association in 1827–8. O'Connell also began to emphasize much more strongly the importance of the wardens' work, and the need to recruit them widely. Leading members of the Association, notably W. J. O'Neill Daunt, Tom Steele and later Maurice O'Connell, were despatched on tours of the provinces to organize meetings, select officers and generally establish a network for agitation. Rapidly, the parishes were supplied with one, two, three or even four wardens. In turn, the wardens usually appointed collectors to gather in the Repeal Rent; and they themselves were subject to the control and direction, immediately of the inspectors, and ultimately of the Association headquarters at the Corn Exchange. As usual with O'Connell's movements, Munster led the way. But the enlistment extended rapidly, though in varying degrees of effectiveness, in every county south of, say, a line drawn from Sligo to Dundalk.

Thus well before the great Mansion House debate of 28 February 1843, when O'Connell virtually proclaimed a crusade for 'simple repeal', the foundations of the mass movement of that year were being laid. The new stress on organization was not without some ideological implications. Total community mobilization was being attempted. This meant extensions of the notions of internal policing and internal legal adjudication, which had been only intermittently applied or vaguely adumbrated during the Association's early years. Repeal police and a Repeal arbitration system for land disputes pointed in the direction of alternative government from below and the supersession, in part at least, of the official agencies of law and order. Again, the exigencies of agitation were adding new political dimensions to Repeal. When after large and enthusiastic popular meetings had been held in widely-dispersed places during November and December 1842, O'Connell was emboldened to declare that '1843 is and shall be the great Repeal year',[1] further developments were foreshadowed. The movement which he proclaimed was necessarily dynamic; it had to produce the impression of continuous growth, in both scale and intensity, if the strain on the British government were to be maximized. This implied in turn a climax to the season of agitation. An ultimate, apparently practicable, culmination to the campaign season had to be devised. At the dinner following one of the earliest monster meetings, held in Sligo on 4 May, O'Connell announced that once the first goal had been attained and three million members enrolled in the Association within three months – that is by early August 1843 – each 'district' in Ireland would express 'confidence' in particular persons who would meet 'spontaneously' in Dublin as the Council of Three Hundred. He added that the council would at once draw up 'Bill no. 1' to repeal the Act of Union, and 'Bill no. 2', to re-institute the Irish House of Commons.[2] It seemed to be implied that further parts of the Association programme would be taken up similarly, seriatim. Clearly, O'Connell was promising the unilateral establishment of a virtual parliament. But, equally, the 'expression of confidence' rather than polled votes, and the 'spontaneous' assemblage of individuals rather than the summoning of elected representatives, were meant to keep the Association within the boundaries of the law. There could be no doubt however that, under the pressure to formulate a climax, Repeal had taken a further massive step in the direction of something very different from its original character, that is, towards becoming a prototype Sinn Fein.

Secondly, the nature of the enterprise of 1843, with the need to marshal and inspirit many tens of thousands of people every week and to evoke and release sentiments of historic resentment and mass-attitudinizing, inevitably led the orators to the brink of the martial. As an English visitor described the meeting at Mullaghmast, co. Kildare, on 1 October 1843, 'The men yelled and danced with rage; the women screamed and clapped their hands. The vast multitude – I believe there were really 100,000 present – moved and moaned like a wild beast in agony.'[3] O'Connell guarded his language very carefully: bombast was one thing, words capable of being construed as seditious quite another. But in practice it was not possible to resist all military or minatory flights in the charged emotional exchange between demagogue and people. At the dinner following the Kilkenny monster meeting of 8 June, for example, O'Connell broke out,

> We stand at the head of a body of men that, if organized by military discipline, would be quite abundant for the conquest of Europe. Wellington had never such an army as we saw today. There was not at

Waterloo on both sides so many stout, active, energetic men as we saw here to-day . . . They would be as ready to obey their Repeal Wardens as if they were called sergeants and captains.[4]

Three days later, having been inflamed by a vast public meeting (reported as 400,000 strong!) at Mallow, O'Connell was led on by the thunders of applause and the presence of a ladies' gallery at the evening banquet to the fiery topic of Cromwell's massacre of women of Wexford.

300 of the grace, and beauty, and virtue of Wexford were slaughtered by the English ruffians. Sacred Heaven! (tremendous sensation, and cries of 'oh, oh'.) I am not at all imaginative when I talk of the possibility of such occurrences anew (hear, hear); but yet, I assert there is no danger of [sic] the women, for the men of Ireland would die to the last in their defence. (Here the entire company rose and cheered for several minutes.) We were a paltry remnant then; we are nine millions now.[5]

A short time earlier, he had cried out, in the celebrated 'Mallow Defiance', 'I say they may trample me; but it will be my dead body they will trample on, not the living man.'[6]

In short, the very scale and pace of the agitation of 1843 helped to reshape 'Repeal'; and the equivalent was of course true of the groups whom O'Connell had to recruit as sub-managers and local organizers. We have seen already how the programme was developed to appeal to the tenant farmers; attempts were also made to involve both shopkeepers and tradesmen by the establishment of Repeal boards of trade in Dublin and provincial cities such as Limerick. But much more important – indispensable, in fact – was active participation of the bulk of the Catholic clergy. The support, or at the very least neutralization, of the bishops was a pre-requisite, as they effectively controlled the lower clergy. This had been substantially secured by the beginning of 1843. As soon as O'Connell began serious campaigning, in 1840, Archbishop MacHale of Tuam and Bishops Browne of Galway, Blake of Dromore, Cantwell of Meath, O'Higgins of Ardagh, and Foran of Waterford and Lismore declared publicly for Repeal, and were ready to engage actively in the struggle as O'Connell's allies. Over the next two and a half years, eleven other members of the hierarchy committed themselves to Repeal. Slattery of Cashel was coaxed out of his non-combatancy, and Bishops MacLaughlin and Maginn of Derry, McNally of Clogher, Kennedy of Killaloe, Keatinge of Ferns, Feeny of Killala, Burke of Elphin, Coen of Clonfert, French of Kilmacduagh, and O'Donnell, Browne's successor in Galway, all became members of the Association, and most of them zealous partisans into the bargain. These adhesions accounted for a clear majority of the Irish episcopate, and in their dioceses the priests were active repealers almost to a man. Even in dioceses where their lordships were 'neutral' or covertly hostile, a large number of the clergy worked for the Repeal Association. This was important, for in the countryside at least it was the ordinary parish priests, and to a lesser extent their curates, who carried the movement on their shoulders.

When the Association was reconstructed in the winter of 1842–3, it was almost invariably the parish priest (as often as not O'Connell knew him personally) whom the organizers from Dublin first approached. He would arrange the initial meeting, nominate likely persons for wardenships, supervise the local Repeal rooms once they were established and largely plan the monster meeting if one were to be held later in the vicinity. A typical case was that of the Rev Mr McEvoy, parish priest of Kells. The Repeal organizer stayed with him on his first visit, and through him arranged the initial meeting. It was McEvoy who selected the Repeal wardens, and acted as general organizer of the later mass meeting of over 100,000 people which O'Connell addressed. He also served as host to O'Connell on the occasion, and from first to last was the channel of communication between Kells and the Association's headquarters. Many of the priests became Repeal wardens, though they by no means constituted a majority of the corps. Almost always, outside the cities and the larger towns, they filled the critical office of inspector. Even where they were not officially inspectors, most of the dealings with the wardens took place through them, and it was they who generally distributed the Association's circulars. The chief speakers at the monster meetings stayed at the local parochial houses; and clergy constituted a high percentage of the platform party at both the meetings and the evening banquets where one of the inevitable toasts was that drunk to 'The clergy of Ireland'.

This is not to say that the Repeal movement of 1843 was overtly or even substantially sectarian. Its difference in this regard from the Emancipation agitation of the 1820s was continually stressed in speeches and publications. Every Protestant recruit (especially if he were a clergyman) was fêted as a lost sheep found. None the less the Catholic priests and bishops were accorded the full deference which their indispensability to the organization and agitation deserved. After investigating one dispute at Waterford, O'Connell censured all 'language of a disrespectful nature' to the Catholic clergy, and threatened with expulsion any member of the Association who used such terms.[7] As it happened, no religious issue arose during 1843, and O'Connell was required to go no further in respecting clerical susceptibilities or in serving clerical interests than public flattery of the grossest kind.

Like the Catholic Association, the Repeal Association was overwhelmingly Catholic in membership, with a small number of eccentric or ultra-liberal Protestant adherents. But it had one unique component. The 1820s had produced no equivalent to the young intelligensia epitomized by their newspaper, the *Nation*, first published in October 1842. Its founders, Thomas Davis and John Blake Dillon, respectively Protestant and Catholic graduates of Trinity College Dublin, and Charles Gavan Duffy, an Ulster Catholic journalist, were archetypal of a new generation of Irish nationalists. Davis was indeed something more – their prophet, expositor and conscience, all in one. Significant differences of emphasis, and even of basic principle, between O'Connell and this Young Ireland group were eventually to emerge. Their anti-sectarianism passed far beyond his demand for parity among religions; it practically relegated religious belief to the sphere of the private and the personal, and proffered 'national consciousness' as a universal, overriding public creed. Moreover, the nationalism of the Young Irelanders derived – partly via Davis – from German Romanticism and the Prussian example, whereas O'Connell's was essentially a product of the eighteenth-century Enlightenment. This meant as has been said above that the Davisites stressed cultural rather than constitutional distinctiveness; group or collective rather than individual rights sympathies and antipathies rather than forms and institutions as the substance of political independence – and, of course, in the long run, on race and language, as in the Fatherland. At each of these points, O'Connell differed from the Young Irelanders fundamentally.

None of these differences, however, reached the surface before or even during 1843, and in the meantime the *Nation* and Young Ireland party strengthened O'Connell's hand and underpinned the Association in several ways. First, they generated enthusiasm and fervour of a different order from O'Connell's now-conventional, popular rapport. Secondly, they spoke for the young, and especially for the urban and educated or semi-educated young, from within a movement led by a man nearing seventy years of age whose primary appeal was to established respectability and the rural masses. Thirdly, they wrote

MAJOR REPEAL MEETINGS HELD IN IRELAND
DURING 1843

O'Connell himself attended (or in the case of Clontarf would have attended) the meetings held in those places printed in italic type. The map has been compiled from the newspaper reports of meetings in the *Freeman's Journal* and *Nation*.

507

and propagandized in the current idiom; they furnished the popular patriotic, often chauvinistic, literature on which not only the Repeal agitation of the 1840s but also all later nineteenth-century Irish nationalism could feed. They provided a much larger bank of sentiment, stances and rhetoric than O'Connell ever had before at his disposal – as well as a new bank of spirited speakers and activists. In their own way they were as indispensable to the great demonstrations of 1843 as the supporting Catholic bishops and their clergy.

II

The first public meetings of 1843 in Clare, Cork and Queen's County maintained the momentum of late 1842; but it was to his motion of 28 February 1843 before Dublin Corporation in favour of Repeal that O'Connell looked for the true launching of the new year's campaign. The subsequent three days' debate was closely followed and widely publicized, not only in Ireland but also in the British press. O'Connell triumphed. The motion was carried by 41 votes to 15; but much more important was the success of his own speech of more than four hours' duration. He did what he had invariably excelled in through his long professional career; he stated a case which he had had sufficient time and inclination to prepare thoroughly and to plan with forensic care. On this occasion he chose to pitch his oration in a conciliatory rather than a defiant tone, stressing his own respect for law, property and the social order, and the moderation of his objectives. He even made clear that, short of full Repeal, he was open to any reasonable offer. In repudiating violence, he was passionate and unbounded:

> Soon must I leave this fleeting scene. What is the world, and what are the world's glories, to me, that in order to grasp them for an instant I should imperil my immortal soul? Not for all the universe contains would I, in the struggle for what I conceive my country's cause, consent to the effusion of a single drop of human blood, except my own. Any other man's blood I dare not spill.[8]

O'Connell repeated his familiar formulae for agitation. Meetings were to be held for the sole purpose of petitioning parliament to repeal a statute: this was no more than the hallowed right of every British subject. These meetings must be orderly, no matter how large or how provoked. They must be peaceful, not only issuing in no disturbance but also offering no menace beyond that which the continued frustration of millions necessarily implied. They must ask for nothing more than equality, seeking no supremacy or favour, but only parity for all sects and parties.

It is not clear when or with what degree of premeditation the subsequent 'monster' Repeal meetings of 1843 were planned. The term 'monster' was an invention of *The Times* – although gladly adopted by the Association – and some of the earliest meetings after the great debate appear to have come about more by accident than purpose. One or two were, seemingly, casual appendages to public banquets held in O'Connell's honour. Moreover, his own initial scheme was that the other nationalist corporations should imitate Dublin in passing, amid popular acclaim, resolutions in favour of immediate Repeal. On the other hand, it was clear soon after the first post-debate mass meeting (held at Trim, co. Meath, on 16 March) that a larger project was quickly taking shape. On 24 March, O'Connell wrote to his friend and supporter, Charles Bianconi:

> And now, my good friend, is it not a crying shame that your noble county [Tipperary] should remain in such apathy and torpor when all the rest of Ireland is rousing itself into a combined effort for the Repeal? I want a Repeal meeting either at Clonmel or Cashel or Thurles. I want to see from 60,000 to 100,000 Tipperary boys meeting peacefully and returning home quietly, to adopt the petition [in favour of Repeal] and to organise the Repeal rent. Now you know you *must* get into motion, there's no use at all in hanging back any longer when you set about it. I know you will do the thing right well.[9]

Four days later the *Freeman's Journal* announced a series of meetings, at Sligo on 4 May, Cork on 7 May, Mullingar on 14 May, south Tipperary (Cashel was later nominated) on 23 May, and north Tipperary (Nenagh was lated nominated) on 25 May. This programme – with the subsequent addition of a meeting at Charleville, co. Cork, on 18 May and a meeting at Cork on 21 May after the one scheduled for 7 May had been transferred to the Curragh – was in fact faithfully fulfilled. The crowds at these assemblages were estimated at 300,000 or more in most cases. Thus, even if the 1843 campaign began as a renewal of the extra-metropolitan agitation of late 1842, it was turned almost at once into a deliberate and massive demonstration of numerical strength and organizational capacity.

Some forty of the outdoor rallies of 1843 might fairly be classified as 'monster meetings'. Between late March and late September, an average of nearly two a week were held, most of them on Sundays or church holidays, but also many in mid-week. Only two or three took place at 'historic sites'; the great majority were in strategically located country towns. We can safely infer that, from a comparatively early date at least, the places were chosen with a view to 'covering' almost the entire countryside, Ulster excepted. Contemporaries generally agreed that the meetings drew people from up to sixty miles away. But even if we halve this figure and use a radius of only thirty miles, we find that the meetings blanketed the provinces of Leinster, Munster and Connacht, apart from a few coastal extremities and the tips of elongated peninsulas. In addition, parts of cos Monaghan, Down, Armagh, Fermanagh, Tyrone and Donegal fell within the circles.

O'Connell was of course the very heart of the mighty movement. Not only did he dictate all the larger organizational work and manage the regular Dublin sessions and committees, but also he formed the centrepiece of no less than thirty-one of the monster meetings – a considerably higher degree of personal participation than in the equivalent Emancipation agitation of 1826–8. The 1843 campaign was O'Connell's Indian summer, his final blaze. Although he was sixty-eight years old before it was complete, he was tireless and exuberant to the end. The monster meetings he attended entailed over 5000 miles of travel in carriages or open cars, hours as the cynosure of every eye among multitudes of people, and open-air and banquet speeches, two or three times each week. It was a giant's theate, and virtually a year's long play. As the meetings settled into a pattern, their staging became ever more elaborate. For a day – or even two days – before a meeting, crowds began to converge from all directions, on foot, in carts or by horse, often in compact bodies carrying banners or green boughs, sometimes led by bands. Near the site, Repeal wardens, their hats inscribed 'O'Connell's Police', began to marshal them into sections. In the centre stood a huge wooden platform; on the outskirts, on every side, 'cavalry' and carriages eventually formed the perimeter. A German traveller, Jacob Venedey, thus reported O'Connell's arrival at the Athlone meeting of 15 June 1843:

> Now there arose a cry such as never before had greeted my ears; now all hats were raised in the air, and there burst forth the unanimous shouts: 'Hurrah! hurrah! hurrah! Long live O'Connell! Long live the Liberator!' A hundred thousand voices sent forth these salutations to the man whose magic power had circled them around him. He sat on the box-seat of a carriage drawn by four horses, and answered the salutation with head, hand, and cap. It was with the greatest difficulty that a passage could be forced from the carriage to the platform. How he made his way I do not even to this day comprehend, for there was not room for a person to fall, much less to walk. 'Make way for the Liberator!' was the charm word

which accomplished the wonder that otherwise had been an impossibility.[10]

Bulwer Lytton, present at another of the mass meetings, described in memorable verse O'Connell's undiminished power of voice and command of the reactions of a mass audience:

> Walled by wide air and roofed by boundless heaven;
> Beneath his feet the human ocean lay,
> And wave on wave flowed into space away.
> Methought no clarion could have sent its sound
> E'en to the centre of the hosts around.
> And, as I thought, rose a sonorous swell,
> As from some church tower swings the silvery bell;
> Aloft and clear from airy tide to tide,
> It glided easy as a bird may glide.
> To the last verge of that vast audience sent,
> It played with each wild passion as it went:
> Now stirred the uproar, now the murmurs stilled,
> And sobs or laughter answered as it willed.
> Then did I know what spell of infinite choice
> To rouse or lull has the sweet human voice.
> Then did I learn to seize the sudden clue
> To the grand troublous life – antique to view,
> Under the rock-stand of Demosthenes,
> Unstable Athens heave her noisy seas.[11]

In certain respects, the monster meeting was a people's festival, though one marked by sobriety and regimentation rather than licence. Perhaps the most striking, in terms of size and discipline at least, was the great demonstration on the Hill of Tara, co. Meath, on 'Lady Day', 15 August 1843. The lowest published computation of the numbers present was 800,000. Such a figure may seem to us necessarily – and perhaps also wildly – inflated, and it was of course in O'Connell's interest that his support be represented as immense. But even the Association's leading enemy *The Times* reported the crowds at Tara at approximately one million; and given the proximity of Dublin, the 'basin' – at least fifty miles in circumference – from which the attendance was drawn, and the regular organization of contingents, it certainly seems possible that over half a million persons were assembled. The fields for miles around the open sweep of country about the Hill were filled with vehicles; the mounted escort, told off in lines of four by the Repeal 'police', was generally estimated at 10,000 horsemen; it took O'Connell's open carriage two hours to complete the final stages of his journey through the throngs. Masses were said all morning at six altars scattered about the site; two bishops and thirty-five priests were among the hundreds of 'leaders' finally assembled on the 'Liberator's platform'; a vast dining pavilion was also erected on the Hill. Patently, all this constituted a spectacle, mass celebration and physical and emotional experience which would have impressed scores of thousands of people lastingly. What impressed – and alarmed – the opponents of the movement was the absence of disorder and the virtually mechanical obedience of so immense and diverse a body.

The audiences were far from passive receptacles of oratory. They shouted, groaned, laughed, scorned or exulted, according to their cues. The interaction was of course more concentrated and immediate at the public banquets which followed the monster meetings. At Mallow on 11 June, for instance, the dinner speeches were preceded by a singer rendering one of Moore's 'melodies'. When he reached the end of the verse,

> Oh, where's the slave so lowly,
> Condemned to chains unholy,
> Who, could he burst
> His bonds accursed,
> Would pine beneath them slowly?

O'Connell leaped to his feet and, raising his arms wide, exclaimed, 'I am not that slave!', and in a scene of passion all the room copied his very action, shouting over and over again, 'We are not those slaves! We are not those slaves!'[12] O'Connell the revivalist, the precipitator of something not unlike the conversion experience, was never more evident than in 1843.

The affairs were staged with care. At Tara, O'Connell's carriage was preceded by a car on which a harper sat enthroned playing Moore's 'Harp that once through Tara's Halls' – with its resonance of ancient coronations of the Irish high-kings upon the Hill. At the meeting at Mullaghmast (the scene, in popular belief at least, of the most notorious act of sixteenth-century English treachery), O'Connell wearing his alderman's red robes was 'crowned' by the sculptor, John Hogan. The 'crown', a green velvet cap edged with gold, was supposed to conform to the original Gaelic symbol of kingship. The sculptor, who had just completed his celebrated marble statue of O'Connell for Dublin's City Hall, was 'supported' by a painter and a graphic designer who had also worked on supplying 'art' for the agitation.

Hogan was a fine if conventional artist, but most of the visual expression, artefacts and decoration of O'Connell's movement would have been condemned three generations or so later as nationalist kitsch. The dominant motifs of everything from membership cards to Conciliation Hall (the Association's grand new assembly place in Dublin completed in October 1843) were wolfhounds, round towers and shamrocks, rendered with congruent sentimentality and convolution. Yet this was, after all, merely a variation of the Early Victorian mode, a fragment of a Europe-wide phenomenon. It also conformed to the general contemporary impulse to simplify and didacticize. Here it matched the design and conduct of the monster meetings. Their rhetoric, signals and responses were as bright, crude and singular as the paints in a child's first box. But if the art and interplay of the Repeal movement were naive, they were also direct, natural and, fundamentally, sincere. The unselfconscious gusto, crowd-warmth and delightful exitements and excesses of the monster meetings and the 'monster' banquets were of a piece with their accompanying pageantry and pictures. Richard Pares once wrote that men are 'in politics not only for party and for profit, but most of all for the due exercise of the talents God gave them, and for fun'.[13] With this in mind, let us remember that even the participating-listeners had some claim to being 'men in politics' in 1843.

If O'Connell was the distant, worshipful father-figure of millions, he was also the close, astute instructor for thousands, perhaps even tens of thousands of party helpers. The number undergoing education in political management, at various levels and with various specializations, was clearly very large. The Association's headquarters staff grew fivefold during 1843, to fifty clerks; but the proportional increase in active workers all through the country would have been greater still. Each of the later monster meetings required long and elaborate preparations, from the lowliest needs of crowd control to the planning of themes and the orchestration of popular indoctrination. Especially west of the Shannon, comparatively new ground for O'Connell, many fresh recruits to agitation had to be raised. The great upsurge in the Repeal Rent and in the public's resort to the Repeal arbitration system also drew in numerous political assistants. Everyone involved either had been, or was being, grounded in O'Connell's practised political methodology, for his writ ran and his hand stretched down to the humblest office-holder or occasional draftee. Many of his pupils were future emigrants. Seeds of the politics of the entire English-speaking world in the third quarter of the nineteenth century were being broadcast throughout Ireland in the course of the great campaign.

III

Dublin Castle showed no alarm at the continued growth of the Repeal movement during January and February 1843 or at the course or outcome of the Dublin Corporation debate. Even the development of the monster meeting in late March and the specific announcement on 6 April 1843 of a 'great tour' of Ireland to demonstrate the extent and peaceful character of the demand for Repeal were ignored. But with swelling audiences and ardour at the succession of meetings held in April, the Irish administration suddenly took fright. On 4 May the lord lieutenant, backed by the Irish law officers, asked Peel for emergency legislation to render the meetings illegal: he excused his earlier silence upon the dangers of O'Connell's latest move by claiming that until a few weeks before the agitation had been 'utterly undeserving of notice'.[14] Even at this point, De Grey was more concerned at O'Connell's growing middle-class and clerical support than at his extraordinary power to rouse the masses.

Peel would not be panicked by De Grey. O'Connell had chosen the right to petition parliament as his ground, and this was dangerous for any British minister to assail. He had also defended another flank by ensuring that his movement was strictly orderly: even Graham, the home secretary, had to admit as much in the House of Commons on 26 May. Moreover, any legislation directed against the Repeal Association would raise the question, 'Why is not the Anti-Corn Law League similarly suppressed?', for the League was essentially the same in organization, conduct and method as O'Connell's movement. Peel would certainly avoid, if he could, any direct junction of interest, let alone of action, between the two agitations. Instead, he attempted to compromise by a solemn statement on behalf of the government in the House of Commons on 9 May 1843 that the Union would be maintained at all costs and hazards: even civil war was preferable to the dismemberment of the empire. O'Connell saw at once that Peel had failed to find any illegality in the current Repeal campaign, and he proceeded, as Professor Nowlan puts it, to 'answer defiance with defiance'.[15] Before an Association meeting in Dublin on 18 May, he proclaimed, 'I will observe the spirit of the law – the letter of the law. I will, to be sure, shear it to its closest limits, but I will obey; and I set their blustering at defiance'.[16] Publicly at least, O'Connell made little of Peel's extraordinary undertaking, in the name of the queen as well as of the British people, to hold to the Act of Union to the death. Peel, he declared, was the very man ultimately to concede Repeal. Patently he meant his listeners to infer that because Peel had already 'betrayed' the tory cause by supporting Catholic Emancipation in 1829 and by acquiescing in parliamentary reform in 1833, he was likely to yield a third time if sufficient pressure were applied. O'Connell proceeded to increase the pressure through his monster meetings, to such effect that – to take one obvious yardstick – the Repeal Rent which had risen to a weekly average of £360 in March, and again to £600 per week in April, leaped to £2000 per week in May.

O'Connell was aided by a false step taken by Peel to appease Dublin Castle. In mid-May the government consented to the Irish executive's long-pressed proposal to remove leading Repealers from the magistracy. On 23 May Sugden, the Irish chancellor, withdrew the commission of the peace from thirty-four members of the Association, including Lord Ffrench, O'Connell himself and his son John, although no warning had been issued, or justification of the 'punishment' attempted. One predictable effect was to add impetus to the agitation. In mild and painless fashion the movement had acquired nearly three dozen martyrs headed by O'Connell himself. A less predictable but more important consequence of Peel's *faux pas* – or, perhaps we should say, sacrificed pawn – was the resignation, in protest, from the magistracy, of a number of Irish whigs, led by Lord Cloncurry, Henry Grattan and Smith O'Brien. It was not a costly gesture on their part, and it helped to bridge the gap which had been rapidly opening up between orthodox Irish liberals and Repealers.

None the less O'Connell was concerned that the government should have conceded at all to Dublin Castle's cry for repression. He had further cause for uneasiness at the beginning of June 1843. When Edward Lucas, the Irish under-secretary, threatened to resign because of Peel's and Graham's pusillanimity in dealing with O'Connell, he was persuaded to remain in office by the government at the cost of a further concession. Such yieldings seemed to give substance to the recurrent rumours that legislation to suppress the monster meetings was about to be introduced. All this helps to explain O'Connell's 'martial' speeches at Kilkenny and Mallow on 8 and 11 June: they were oblique warnings of the sea of troubles on which the government would launch itself should it attempt to abrogate the right to petition for Repeal. Even at Mallow, when O'Connell was, to some extent, carried away by the excitement of the moment, his careful briefing of reporters before his evening speech makes it clear that he intended to raise the stakes in the game of menaces in which he was engaged with Peel and Graham. He soon came to fear, however, that he might have stepped beyond the limit of safety from prosecution or proclamation in speaking of laying down his life: his 'Defiance' at Mallow was to be the high-water mark of his disaffection. Eleven days later, at the monster meeting of Skibbereen, he signalled a change of course. 'I am not determined to die for Ireland', he now announced, 'I would rather live for her (cheering), for one living Repealer is worth a churchyard full of dead ones.'[17] This prudent retreat was matched – or perhaps we should say answered – by Graham's public withdrawal of his earlier refusal to consider any 'measures of further conciliation' in Ireland,[18] and by the government's assurance, at last, that the right to petition would not be suspended. The initiative was still O'Connell's.

Throughout June and July 1843 the monster meetings continued to grow in size. Attendances of half-a-million persons were regularly reported, and however we scale this down, indubitably the numbers were immense. Moreover, O'Connell was now opening up new territory systematically. By 31 July, meetings had been held in the majority of the counties of the three southern provinces, and considerable portions of the other counties were sufficiently close to the meeting places to supply further legions of attenders. The momentum of his movement was also gathering in more and more of the Catholic clergy. As early as 15 May, at the dinner after the Mullingar monster meeting, Bishop O'Higgins of Ardagh proclaimed

> that virtually you all have reason to believe that the bishops of Ireland were Repealers; but I have now again formally to announce to you that they have all declared themselves as such, and that from shore to shore we are now all Repealers (great cheering) . . . If they attempt, my friends, to rob us of the daylight, which is, I believe, common to us all, and prevent us from assembling in the open fields, we will retire to our chapels, and we will suspend all other instruction, in order to devote all our time to teaching the people to be Repealers in spite of them (cheers).[19]

This, as we have seen, exaggerated the degree of episcopal support for Repeal. Six of the bishops of the ecclesiastical provinces of Cashel, Tuam and Dublin still held back from joining the Association. But these constituted a small minority, and even they refrained from any overt opposition to O'Connell. Generally speaking, he could rely upon the Irish Catholic Church, and it was the clergy's deep commitment to his agitation which most alarmed the British government in the midsummer. 'It is a religious struggle', wrote Graham on 16 July, 'directed by the R. Catholic Hierarchy and Priesthood, on which we are about to enter; and I very much doubt whether any political considerations enter much into the causes or objects of this strife, which will lead to blood-shed and convulse the Empire.'[20]

No less significant than the mass enrolments and clerical enlistments was the impact of the campaign upon the Catholic, and even (albeit to a much lesser extent) the Protestant, upper and upper-middle class. In particular, the success of the monster meetings was forcing Irish whigs and liberals into a fresh series of positions. A minority actually declared themselves for Repeal. Doubtless, most of such converts were rich Christians, men who, in Palmerston's phrase, 'have of Course been compelled by Fear of Constituents to become Repealers pro Forma'.[21] But even these were scalps to be displayed on O'Connell's belt. Short of joining the Association, others, especially MPs from Irish 'popular' constituencies, were forced along the path of concession, or attempted concession, in the hope of countering O'Connell's influence. On 18 July a group of Irish whig members proposed that meetings be mounted in England to advertise the urgency of redressing Irish grievances. Although this was rejected by the English whigs, a larger body of Irish MPs later signed a collective protest against the government's failure to introduce reforms in Ireland. The list of areas marked out for reform is interesting: the church establishment, landlord-tenant relations, the parliamentary franchise, local government and the practical exclusion of Catholics from public office. O'Connell's list would have been identical: the MPs were asking, in effect, for what he had long termed 'Justice for Ireland'.

This raises the question of O'Connell's true purposes and anticipations in launching his campaign of 1843. He certainly could not have expected to achieve 'Repeal' in any substantial form within the year. No one knew better than a veteran of the long struggles to win Catholic Emancipation and parliamentary reform how slowly the entrenched interests yielded ground, even where (unlike the present case) powerful British parties supported the advance. On the other hand, he was already an old man; he could not afford to spend even half a decade in pursuit of an objective. Moreover, Britain's economic crisis of 1842, the resultant unrest and the rapid expansion of the Anti-Corn Law agitation all rendered the time propitious for the application of massive Irish pressure. Given these various considerations, O'Connell may possibly have hoped (and no more optimistic politician ever breathed) that the British government would offer some modified and circumscribed form of local assembly for Ireland before 1843 was out. In fact, as we have seen, he virtually angled for such an offer in his 'inaugural' speech to Dublin Corporation in February.

But even O'Connell must have acknowledged to himself that the odds against any quick accommodation were very long. Repeal had no extra-Irish support in the House of Commons. It was almost universally opposed in Britain at large. To most Irish, and to virtually all Ulster, Protestants, it was anathema: Wellington, in fact, was shortly to propose the arming of northern Unionists in order that they might crush Repeal by force. In such circumstances, it was far more likely that an attempt be made to undercut O'Connell's agitation by concessions on other fronts than that the Act of Union itself should be disturbed. O'Connell, for forty years a politician, must have understood this thoroughly. It is well to recall that his Association began its life in 1840 as a body dedicated to 'Full Justice or Repeal'. Such a formula permitted O'Connell to pursue simultaneously the goals of liberal reform and constitutional disruption. It could safely be assumed that no Irish reform programme adopted by a British party would exceed mere *partial* 'Justice': Repeal need never be abandoned except for some grand, final, negotiated settlement of the Anglo-Irish relationship. At the same time, Repeal could be held *in terrorem* over the heads of British politicians, and the more it was overwhelmingly and menacingly endorsed by the mass of the Irish population, the more the politicians would be driven to argue that the true source of Irish disaffection was not nationalism or separatism but economic, social or ecclesiastical ills, and to attempt accordingly to kill Repeal with kindness. Placed in this context, O'Connell's 1843 campaign seems rather to conform to than deviate from his customary tactics. If so, it was already bearing fruit when Irish whigs began to call for changes in land and church relations, the local representative system and the distribution of political spoils, and when even Peel's government began to consider what concessions might be made in these very fields. It is true that O'Connell had named 1843 'Repeal Year' and promised a climax to the monster meetings which would, in effect, challenge Dublin Castle's right to rule in Ireland. But he had never found it difficult to cover over a retreat while keeping his force intact, and he had no reason to suppose that, if need be, he could not safely re-order his priorities and re-arrange his timetables as the current season drew to its close.

IV

In fact, by September 1843 there were signs that O'Connell was extricating himself from his earlier commitments. On the 9th he manufactured an occasion for despatching a letter to Campbell, one of the whig law lords, in which he sought to bestir the opposition to take up an extensive programme of Irish reform as a 'counter' to Repeal.

Allow me to say . . . that the Whig leaders do not behave well towards their supporters. Our Irish movement has at least this merit that it has roused the English nation from slumber. There can be no more dreams about Ireland. Our grievances are beginning to be admitted by all parties and by the press of all political opinions to be afflicting and not easily endured. I ask – of course without expecting an answer – why the Whig leaders are not up to the level of the times they live in? Why do they not propose a definite plan for redressing these grievances? Peel, while in opposition, used to enliven the recess by his state epistles, declaratory of his opinions and determination. Why does not Lord John [Russell] treat us to a magniloquent epistle declaratory of his determination to abate the Church nuisance in Ireland, to augment our popular franchise, to vivify our new Corporations, to mitigate the statute law as between landlord and tenant, to strike off a few more rotten boroughs in England, and to give the representatives to our great counties? In short, why does he not prove himself a high-minded, high-gifted statesman, capable of leading his friends into all the advantages to be derived from conciliating the Irish nation and strengthening the British empire?[22]

Simultaneously, O'Connell sought to inveigle Archbishop Murray (who had so far evaded joining the Association) into blessing his exertions for Repeal. He sought sanction for a novena of supplication, although – with matadorial skill – Murray successfully side-stepped the charge. 'I hasten to assure you', he told O'Connell, 'that the novena of prayers which you contemplate does not by any means require my sanction. The throne of Grace is all times open to those who seek to approach it through the merits of Christ for such purposes as you propose, namely, the promotion of the *honour and glory of God and the good of religion.*'[23]

Moreover, O'Connell had as yet prepared no plans for the summoning of the Council of Three Hundred, although a month before, at the Baltinglass monster meeting, he had promised that it would meet before Christmas. Possibly he knew or guessed that, currently, Graham was considering the use of armed force, if necessary, to prevent the Council from assembling. At any rate, on 17

September O'Connell told the 'Connemara' monster meeting, held at Clifden, co. Galway, that he might have to delay the sitting of the Council, and was quite prepared to brave the sneers with which his enemies would greet this news. A fortnight later at Mullaghmast he appeared to shift his emphasis decisively from Repeal to practical reforms, although, as usual, he swathed his message in gauzy generalities.

> I will see every man of you having a vote, and every man protected by the ballot from the agent or landlord. I will see labour protected and every title to possession recognised, when you are industrious and honest (loud cheers). I will see prosperity again throughout your land – the busy hum of the shuttle and the tinkling of the smithy shall be heard again. We shall see the nailer employed until even the middle of the night, and the carpenter covering himself with his chips (laughter). I will see prosperity in all its gradations spreading through a happy, contented, religious land. I will hear the hymn of a happy people go forth at sunrise to God in praise of his mercies – and I will see the evening sun set down amongst the uplifted hands of a religious and free population . . . Stand by me – join with me – I will say be obeyed by me, and Ireland shall be free.[24]

It was by now evident that the climax of the 1843 campaign would not be the constitution of an independent extra-legal legislature but merely the final monster meeting per se! This ultimate assemblage, scheduled to gather at Clontarf on the outskirts of Dublin on 8 October, was planned on a heroic scale. Not only the metropolis but also the surrounding counties and even the Irish communities on Merseyside and Clydeside were to be drawn upon to compose an immense audience and array. The size and fervour, and the stupendous pageantry, of the open-air demonstration at the close of a strenuous season would at least testify to O'Connell's continued power.

Meanwhile, throughout September 1843, the government's resolve was hardening. Fears that it would all end in violence grew rather than diminished. Additional troops were sent from Britain to strengthen the Irish garrisons; ammunition and provisions were accumulated in the Irish depots; and the number of warships at Irish stations and about the Irish coast was considerably increased. Graham took the decision to suppress the Council of Three Hundred by force should O'Connell summon it into existence, and became more and more impatient with what he regarded as the timorousness of the Irish law officers (and especially of the attorney-general, T. B. C. Smith) in not instituting proceedings against the Repeal press. Even Peel, who was less alarmist than Graham, and much less so than Wellington – he knew O'Connell better than either of them, after all – believed that there might well be outbreaks in Ireland before the year was out. But policy as well as fear seemed to demand a denouement with O'Connell. By the autumn of 1843, as Nowlan writes, 'the ministry was in agreement on the necessity of adopting new and more effective measures to tranquillize Ireland and to weaken the Irish opposition to the Government by winning some Catholic support. The repeal agitation and O'Connell's power stood in the way.'[25]

Unfortunately for himself, O'Connell's defence seemed to have slipped for a fatal moment when, on 24 August, he had injudiciously criticized the Queen's speech in opening parliament. At last the Irish law officers opined that his words laid him open to a charge of sedition. It is uncertain, however, whether this would in itself have led to any action in the end. The scale was tipped by the rash rhetoric of the Association's notice of the Clontarf monster meeting, which spoke of the assembly of 'Repeal cavalry' and lapsed unguardedly into other 'military' language. Forty years of legal fencing with the Irish Administration had rendered O'Connell acutely sensitive to danger, and as soon as he discovered the wording of the notice, on 2 October 1843, he repudiated it, publicly. But the damage had been done; the Irish executive had been steeled by the Association's indiscretion into a decision to proclaim the Clontarf meeting.

Dublin Castle's lingering faintheartedness led it to put off issuing the proclamation until 3.30 p.m. on 7 October, the day before the monster meeting was to take place. Peel later condemned this gross and dangerous tardiness, 'It is very fortunate that there was no collision at Clontarf. The shortness of the notice would have imposed a heavy Responsibility.'[26] In fact, the government was saved by the very efficiency, elaborate machinery and iron discipline of O'Connell's Association. The executive committee was in session on the afternoon of 7 October when a messenger arrived hotfoot from the Castle with a copy of the proclamation. Instantly, O'Connell decided on submission to the lord lieutenant's prohibition; not a person in the room demurred. There and then, he sat down to dictate to Ray an address to 'the Irish people', enjoining them to abide by the proclamation unswervingly. Within minutes, this was dispatched to the printers. Meanwhile the workmen were ordered to dismantle the great platform which had been erected already at Clontarf. Well-known members of the Association set out on each of the main roads leading to the capital to turn back the bands of people already converging on Dublin. By the morning of 8 October no one was moving towards the city any longer; and not only throughout Dublin but also in the towns and villages all about, O'Connell's announcement of the abandonment of the meeting, and appeal for calm and acquiescence, was posted up in the various public places. The 'Head Pacificator' himself, Thomas Steele, was pacing the ground at Clontarf, driving away the few who had assembled there, and leaving the field to detachments of the 60th Rifles and the 5th Dragoons, who possessed it in – literally – empty triumph. There was little heart in O'Connell's counter-move at the immense meeting of the Association held next day. Though he condemned the proclamation as 'the grossest violation of the law', he also condemned resistance to it until its illegality had been established.[27] Emboldened by the unexpected totality of its success, the Irish executive, two days later, arrested O'Connell, his son John, and seven other prominent Repealers (including two priests) upon the curious charge of conspiring to 'unlawful and seditious opposition and resistance to . . . [the] government and constitution'.[28]

Conventionally, O'Connell's spiritless submission to the proclamation of 7 October 1843 has been judged a crushing defeat. Even so indulgently sympathetic a biographer as Michael MacDonagh concluded sadly, 'O'Connell's game of bluff and make-believe had failed. He had mistaken the stuff of which Peel was made.'[29] This is much too crude an evaluation. First, the very suppression of O'Connell's last meeting, and his subsequent arrest, were in themselves an oblique testimony to his success. It was his earlier pressure which had forced Peel and his cabinet, at last, onto the path of concession in Ireland; and, once committed to that path, they saw the breaking of O'Connell's power as the necessary preliminary to a course of Irish reform. The fact that it was a tory and not a whig administration which intended to yield ground should not blind us (as it often blinded O'Connell) to the essential fact that it was a *British* government which would yield, in the face of an Irish agitation. O'Connell himself had repeatedly, if partly rhetorically, begged to be put out of business – the business of Repeal – by being outbid by 'Justice for Ireland'. Up to a point, this was precisely Peel's intention – to undercut O'Connell's movement by concessions. Secondly, the direct assault upon O'Connell and the Repeal Association was, in one sense, a confession of defeat by Peel and Graham. Throughout 1843, they had tried to hold the line that the agitation was no more than froth. Now they were committed to an about-face whereby they would have to argue that it threatened the constitutional stability of the United Kingdom. This meant moreover that O'Connell had gained the moral advantage. In effect, Peel's government had been driven to abandon 'the rule of law', for few who considered the matter dispassionately could truly believe that the Repeal Association was, in any sense, a proto-military organization, or that, in pressing for the repeal of a comparatively recent statute, O'Connell was preaching national subversion. Despite the show of legal issues, the fact remained that the government had been driven to resort to brute force, to act as if Ireland were a crown colony instead of an integral part of a united polity.

O'Connell's third gain was being rescued from impending political bathos. What remained after Clontarf but to retire, so to speak, to winter quarters? A popular agitation was, however, a far cry from an eighteenth-century army. It could not be easily re-assembled, let alone re-kindled, especially when the promise of victory within a single season had been the mainspring of the last campaign. Dublin Castle's intrusion rejuvenated the agitation. It provided the missing climax to the year's excitement, kept O'Connell in central focus and rendered him a likely martyr. In fact, the Association made striking immediate gains – in terms of public attention, Rent returns and even influential adherents. As a gesture of sympathy with O'Connell, several leading Irish liberals, such as William Smith O'Brien and Caleb Powell, soon threw their lot in with Repeal.

But it would be absurd to present the suppression of the Clontarf meeting and his own prosecution as, essentially, a victory for O'Connell. For one thing, they clearly exposed his limits as an agitator to the enemy's gaze. It was now certain that he would not resist direct repression, except in the arena of the law courts. Worse still, he had demonstrated only too well that his control of his followers was absolute, and that they would follow him blindly into non-resistance. In lightening ship, O'Connell had thrown a great deal of his minatory power overboard.

A second ill-consequence was the opening up of deep ideological divisions within the Association, though these took some time to reveal themselves fully. Initially, the young men of the *Nation* group acquiesced unreservedly in O'Connell's decision to call off the Clontarf demonstration. They rallied to him at once in his own troubles; in fact, Gavan Duffy himself was a 'traverser', to use the term generally employed for those charged and arrested on 11 October. But when O'Connell instinctively attempted to weave his way out of his new difficulties by presenting Repeal as a much more modest proposal than it had hitherto appeared, the *Nation* recoiled. On 13 November

1843, he announced that he was ready to settle for an 'Irish parliament [which] should have control within Ireland ... for all other administrative functions the British parliament would have the control'.[30] This was – doubtless deliberately – vague. It might have meant, more or less, the form of government foreshadowed in Gladstone's first home rule bill. But it might also have meant something still more circumscribed, a sort of magnified county council. Uneasily and implausibly, the *Nation* interpreted the new formula as 'all the power she [Ireland] possessed in 1783'.[31] Within a month, on 27 November, O'Connell withdrew his feeler altogether. By then it had greatly disquieted the advanced Repealers without attracting any of the Irish federalists whom he had hoped to tempt onto this new ground. Thus, open disagreement in the movement was avoided, for the time being. But the profound difference between O'Connell's mode of thought and style of politics and those of the *Nation* group had been already glimpsed. It was bound sooner or later to re-appear. O'Connell's authority had also been diminished. Just as he was no longer quite the frightening figure that he had seemed to the British public in the high summer of 1843, he was no longer quite the old titan of the agitation in the eyes of the increasingly confident and critical young men who had enrolled recently under his banner.

More important than all else perhaps was the stage in O'Connell's life at which he had received the decisive check. He was now in his sixty-ninth year. To have mounted and sustained a mass movement such as that of 1843 had been a marvel. Gladstone was little older when he conducted the celebrated Midlothian campaigns of 1879–80, which were far shorter in duration and made far fewer calls upon tongue, mind or body. Was it to be expected that O'Connell could ever again marshal the powers and endurance required for a national mobilization of such intensity, or over such a protracted stretch of time? His relief at the suspension of exertions, and welcome for at least an interval of passivity, were evident in his letter of 9 December 1843 to Fitzpatrick. He had at last escaped to Derrynane. 'We had a delightful journey down', he wrote,

> I have already been out hunting two days and am glad to tell you that, although the distemper killed some noble dogs of mine, yet I have a very fair pack remaining. I already feel the immense benefit of my native air and my delightful exercise. I am regaining strength and vigour to endure whatever my sentence may be ...
>
> All is peace and quiet in this county; although the people are as ardent

Repealers as any in the entire Kingdom it is understood to the most remote of the glens that there must be peace in order to succeed.[32]

The pieces tossed about by the upheaval of October 1843 may have fallen on either side of the advantage line for O'Connell. But had the player himself any longer the physical strength or hunger for mastery which the game demanded?

CHAPTER 22

The Fall Out

1844–5

I

O'Connell filled the Irish stage in 1844, but the play was now tragicomedy rather than heroic drama. Initially, he had feared that he might be indicted for high treason, and, oppressed by his memories of 1798, believed that he might very well be hanged. The actual charge, seditious conspiracy, came almost as a relief. Striking the anti-climactic note that was to be heard so often during the year, he told his son John, 'I do not think two years' imprisonment would kill me. I should keep constantly walking about, and take a bath every day.'[1]

The trial opened, so to speak, by being postponed. It did not formally commence until 14 January 1844, more than three months after O'Connell's arrest. It could not be denied that the special list from which the jurors would be chosen was badly out of date; and since Protestants outnumbered Catholics by about fifteen to one on the current list, and since it was assumed on all sides that the jurors would give their verdicts on strictly sectarian grounds, the first defence plea was, of course, for a revision. This could not be reasonably resisted. The new list increased the Catholic proportion, perhaps to as much as one in four. But while it was being drawn up, two pages of the names added to the list by the Recorder were mysteriously lost or abstracted; and the majority of those omitted were Catholics. Thus, even before the court sat, there were widespread allegations of foul play and claims that the wells had been poisoned in advance. The crown challenged all the eleven Catholic jurors who were eventually drawn by lot so that the jury consisted of twelve Protestants in the end.

In today's terms, it is difficult to see that O'Connell was being charged with more than conducting a massive political campaign: the 'crime' consisted of its success in mobilization and its objectives. As Thackeray, playing the plain blunt Englishman, later summarized the indictment and result, 'If you did not organise a conspiracy, and meditate a separation of this fair empire – if you did not create rage and hatred in the bosoms of your countrymen against us English – if *you* did not do, in a word, all that the Jury found you guilty of doing – I am a Dutchman.'[2] In British eyes, the real offence was, apparently, the very demand for Repeal (on the assumption that it would lead finally to imperial dissolution), and the very agitation which *faut de mieux* O'Connell was forced to mount in order to gain Britain's attention.

O'Connell defended himself (literally, for he acted as his own counsel) against different charges – those actually set out in the indictment. He strove to establish the altogether peaceable and constitutional character of his movement. Even the police evidence confirmed that no one had suffered the slightest physical injury; that no female had been 'exposed to the slightest indelicacy'; that not 'one shilling's worth of property' had been 'destroyed at any one of those meetings'.[3] O'Connell had, he claimed, merely repeated his proceedings in the Catholic Emancipation campaign – indeed, adhered to the principles that had governed his politics for more than forty years.

From the day when first I entered the arena of politics until the present hour, I have never neglected an opportunity of impressing upon the minds of my fellow-countrymen the fact, that I was an apostle of that political sect who held that liberty was only to be attained under such agencies as were strictly consistent with the law and the constitution – that freedom was to be attained, not by the effusion of human blood, but by the constitutional combination of good and wise men; by perseverance in the courses of tranquillity and good order, and by an utter abhorrence of violence and bloodshed. It is my proudest boast, that throughout a long and eventful life, I have faithfully devoted myself to the promulgation of that principle, and, without vanity, I can assert, that I am the first public man who ever proclaimed it. Other politicians have said – 'Win your liberties by peaceable means if you can,' but there was *arrière pensée* in this admonition, and they always had in contemplation an appeal to physical force, in case other means should prove abortive. I am not one of these. I have preached under every contingency, and I have again and again declared my intention to abandon the cause of repeal if a single drop of human blood were shed by those who advocated the measure.[4]

In delivering his judgement later on, Mr Justice Burton made the extraordinary admission that O'Connell 'had that design [achieving the repeal of the Union without bloodshed] rooted in his mind, and that it was by the great influence which he possessed as a leader ... that he kept the country, or part of the country where he resided, from the dreadful operation of civil war and the shedding of human blood'.[5] It seemed that the court itself believed, as O'Connell put it, that his only conspiracy was one to prevent a revolution!

None the less, on 10 February 1844, after a hearing of more than three weeks, O'Connell and his fellow-defendants were found guilty on several counts. The trial had an air of macabre carnival from the beginning. On the opening day, the 'traversers' were solemnly escorted to the Four Courts by the lord mayor and corporation of Dublin, in full regalia. O'Connell himself immediately donned, and continued to wear, his wig and gown. With each defendant separately represented, the prosecuting barristers correspondingly numerous, three judges on the bench and the court overflowing with the fashionable curious, it was the spectacle and sensation of the season. Even after the verdict was delivered, the affair continued in the same extraordinary strain. Sentence having been postponed, O'Connell crossed immediately to England where he was to receive continual sympathetic ovations. When he entered the House of Commons on 15 February – having passed through throngs of enthusiastic supporters in the Palace Yard – it was as if on cue: D. R. Ross, the liberal member for Belfast, was speaking in his defence. After the cheers from the opposition benches died away, Ross continued, 'Let the House judge by the reception which the head conspirator has just met, whether there be much cause for triumph. You may put that man in gaol – but what will you gain?'[6]

Next day O'Connell reported delightedly to Fitzpatrick that he had been 'admirably received in the House and outside the House, and my name was cheered to the echo at the [weekly anti-]Corn Law League meeting',[7] and, on 20 February, that he 'certainly did not expect anything half so generous or so kind'[8] as his popular reception in London. On 12 March about a thousand people, including several peers, a contingent of British MPs and his erstwhile antagonist, the doyen of 'old' English Catholicism, the Earl of Shrewsbury, attended a public banquet in O'Connell's honour at the Covent Garden Theatre: his treatment was denounced and his health drunk with equal fervour. One of the banquet organizers, W. Simpson, wrote to him later, 'when once aroused by a sense of injustice their [Englishmen's] determination and enthusiasm is unbounded, and I will venture to say that hearty cheer which reverberated through Convent [sic] Garden Theatre on Tuesday last has never had a parallel in any other country'.[9] No less was O'Connell fêted in Birmingham, Wolverhampton and Liverpool when, on invitation, he visited those towns. He was, however, chary of encouraging similar demonstrations in Ireland lest they be treated as an 'aggravation' of his offence when it came to sentencing. Instead, he tried to set in train in Dublin the 'appointment [of a] day of "humiliation and prayer". If universally adopted it would have a magnificent effect upon the enemy, besides being in its own nature most desirable.'[10]

II

When on 30 May 1844 O'Connell at last received his sentence – one year's imprisonment, considerably less than he had feared – he and his co-prisoners processed, in carriages, accompanied by thousands of well-wishers, to their place of incarceration, Richmond Penitentiary, almost in festival fashion. He was received with deference by the governor of Richmond, whose handsome residence was made over for his use and that of his son John. Again he was 'welcomed' as he crossed the threshold, this time by his daughters, Ellen and Betsey, and John's wife, who were alternately to act as his companions-cum-hostesses in the new ménage. It was martyrdom-de-luxe, not merely for O'Connell but also for the other prisoners who shared his comforts, in an appropriately lesser measure. Each had a suite of rooms, a servant or servants, and a resident wife if he were married. It was ultra-gregarious rather than solitary confinement. A few days after O'Connell's imprisonment began, the *Freeman's Journal* reported

> that the crowd of gentlemen pressing for admittance at the prison gate was greater than any we have ever seen blocking the doors of any place of public interest on occasions of the highest-wrought expectation. We saw gentlemen of the highest respectability content to take their places on the exterior of the crowd, and wait while numerous batches were admitted, until gradually they themselves approached the gate, and obtained the coveted entrance.[11]

Shortly afterwards, perhaps at O'Connell's instigation, specific visiting days and hours had to be set down. But Charles Gavan Duffy, who was a fellow inmate, later recalled that 'immediate political associates' still dined daily with the traversers. 'O'Connell', continued Duffy,

> was a genial and attentive host, full of anecdote and *badinage* while the ladies remained, and ready, when they withdrew, for serious political conference or the pleasant carte and tierce of friendly controversy. An artist's studio and a daguerrotypists camera were set up within the precincts to multiply likeness of the prisoners . . .[12]

O'Connell at Richmond was a sort of Lear inside-out. He was very careful to remain in health: like the ocean-liner passenger (and his imprisonment bore more than one resemblance to a protracted voyage in the first-class), he measured his daily perambulation around the interior perimeter so that it amounted to a three-mile walk. So far from being in ceaseless conflict with rejected or immoral daughters, he was cosseted by his. He was said to have sat often with his hands clasped in theirs. In fact, he seems to have developed a penchant for young female company and adulation. Clearly, he was on close terms with Margaret O'Mara, the half-sister of his eldest daughter's husband, even before he entered Richmond. On 23 May 1844 he had her escort him to a local convent, having written beforehand, 'My dear Margaret ... I will go down without my breakfast so that unless you give me a cup of tea before ten I must starve till I return at one to the Association. If *your ladies* choose to come up with me I will have places kept for them.'[13] Less than a week later, he visited Margaret again, telling her later, 'I do not know when I spent so delightful a day.'[14]

The probable reason for his delight was that Rose McDowell was among Margaret's '*ladies*' at that time. Rose, on a lengthy visit to her close friend Margaret, was the daughter of the liberal Presbyterian, Robert McDowell, of Belfast, who had chaired the Repeal banquet held in the city in O'Connell's honour in January 1841. She was twenty-two or twenty-three years of age in 1844; later she was spoken of – with what justification it is impossible to say – in such conventionally-laudatory terms as 'charming', 'lively' and 'culti-vated'.[15] Certainly, she moved in the 'upper' Repeal circles while in Dublin. Possibly she was one of O'Connell's young devotees. At any rate, he fell victim to her attractions. Most accounts of the sequel derive from the reminiscences of Duffy, who was close at hand in Richmond:

> During the whole period of the imprisonment O'Connell was an unsuc-cessful wooer. He was labouring under the most distracting influence that can possess a man of his years – a passionate love for a gifted young girl, who might have been his grand-daughter. His family were naturally alarmed by this incident, and the more so doubtless that the lady whom he proposed to place at the head of their house differed from them in race and religion, and their feverish anxiety could not fail to react upon him. Their fears were allayed in the end by the lady's persistent refusal to become his wife, but this result was not calculated to restore the composure of O'Connell. In truth, it left him discontented and perturbed in a high degree.[16]

Duffy went on to assert that O'Connell was simultaneously suffering from the onset of 'softening of the brain'; and the conjunction has been widely read as implying that O'Connell's 'infatuation' sprang from 'senility'. It would have ill-become Duffy if this were what he meant to say or insinuate: he himself was sixty-five years old (only three years younger than O'Connell in Richmond) when he married and set about breeding a family for the third time. In fact, O'Connell's pursuit of Rose McDowell needs no pathological explanation. The last spurt of passion, the desperate urge to rise up against encroaching age, the cumulative loneliness of outliving others, are common enough, if wretched, experiences of the old; nor was O'Connell the first or last old man to succumb to a woman but a third his age. If, in fact, he did propose marriage, it was probably soon after he entered Richmond, for on 21 June 1844 he wrote to Margaret O'Mara,

> If Wednesday [26 June] about two o'clock suited yours and your dear mother's convenience I should take care to have you at once admitted. I need not tell you that I should be most gratified if Rose would condescend to accompany you *here*. She is indeed all you describe her and more both in head and heart. In fact she is *one* of the most superior women I ever met with intellect, sound judgment and facinating [*sic*] sweetness. Unless she comes with you I suppose I shall never see her again.[17]

This was, apparently, the pathetic end of the affair.

O'Connell put a brave face on the humiliation of being gaoled. The weekly bulletins on the traversers' condition at Richmond which he sent to be read to the Repeal Association meetings were generally ebullient, even jaunty, in tone. The most celebrated ran, 'The prisoners are all looking right well, and getting fat'![18] On 1 August 1844 he told his daughter Betsey that 'all enjoy excellent health and spirits. We are quite gay and cheerful as larks.'[19] He also professed to be gratified by his enforced suffering in the cause of Ireland. 'My imprisonment is not irksome to me', he told a visiting party of American sympathizers,

> for I feel and know that it will, under Providence, be the means of making our country a nation once again. I am glad I am in prison. There wanted but this to complete my political career. I have laboured for Ireland, refused office, honour, and emolument for Ireland. There was just one thing wanted – that I should be in jail for Ireland. That has now been added to the rest, thanks to our enemies, and I cordially rejoice at it.[20]

Underneath, however, he was embittered, and especially hostile towards the Irish liberals. When, soon after his imprisonment, Thomas Wyse moved in the Commons for a select committee to inquire into the composition of the special jury list at the state trial, O'Connell was contemptuously dismissive. 'I do not care a twopenny ticket for Wyse's motion. . . . All [it] will accomplish will be a knitting together once more the *disjecta membra* of the present party in power.'[21] He proceeded to round also upon his old ally Sheil, whom he now classified as another of the pusillanimous Irish whigs:

> Oh; plague take the shabby set! the Duke of Leinster – his name operates like a vomit – is getting up with Peter Purcell dinners for pig feeders and calf fatteners! Lord Miltown sent me a salmon – good for Friday – and Lord Cloncurry sent me his card. I am amused at condescending to have even the appearance of being angry with such beings. The Irish Orangemen are more friendly to Ireland than the Irish Whigs. But I have cheerfully done with them.[22]

Even when the Repeal Association took up Wyse's point, and insisted on making it the ground for an appeal to the House of Lords against the convictions, O'Connell remained sourly gloomy. He had, as he informed Betsey, 'no rational expectation of the writ of error being decided in our favour';[23] he told Fitzpatrick that there was 'not the smallest shadow' of a chance of his being set free.[24]

The more sensitive of O'Connell's supporters caught the sombre note to be heard beneath the surface jingle. Richard Dowden of Cork (to take one instance) was overcome by a profound sense of *lèse majesté* when he visited O'Connell at Richmond. He allowed that O'Connell's degradation served Ireland's cause. But even this scarcely outweighed his melancholy and anger. 'I own when I visited you *within the walls of a prison*', he wrote on 11 August, 'my sense of what you were working out forsook me, and I only saw in grief and indignation our country's true servant and eminent leader a prisoner because of his power and his virtue. I am not nor cannot get free of those feelings.'[25] Even O'Connell's political enemies, if they were sufficiently perceptive, felt the enormity of the 'king's' imprisonment. Macaulay, addressing the government benches, exclaimed,

> My belief is that, as regards the end that hon. Gentleman has lately been pursuing, it is not only mischievous but wholly unattainable. I regard with deep disapprobation some of the means pursued to obtain that end; and in saying this, I wish to speak with the respect that is due to eminence and misfortune; but with the respect that is due to truth. I must say too, that the position which Mr O'Connell holds in the eyes of his fellow-countrymen, is a position such as no popular leader in the whole history of mankind ever occupied.[26]

Some such feeling may have affected the outcome of the appeal in the House of Lords. Four of the judges appear to have voted on party lines, with the two decided whigs favouring the appeal. But the fifth, Lord Chief Justice Denman, although originally a whig, was widely regarded as non-partisan, and his support of the appellants may have been influenced by the consideration that justice should manifestly be seen to have been done in so portentous a prosecution. The deficiencies in the special jury list was the ground of his decision. At any rate, on 4 September 1844, the judgment on O'Connell and his co-prisoners was reversed by a majority of three to two.

Something of the original air of solemn farce-cum-fiesta was immediately restored to the affair. Desperate journeys (ending in a race of horsemen from the Westland Row railway terminus to the Richmond prison) were undertaken so that O'Connell might receive the good tidings as soon as possible, although, in fact, he did not believe them until confirmed by one of the traversers' solicitors. Upon his official release next day (6 September 1844), he remained in the penitentiary until evening, holding a sort of levee in the governor's garden, as thousands of admirers filed past him, shaking hands. After spending the night at home, he returned to Richmond with the other 'martyrs' for a formal, celebratory liberation. During the morning of 7 September, in a sort of royal gesture for the occasion, he procured the release of forty-two other prisoners.

> In his moment of triumph he remembered that within the same walls which had confined him and his fellow-martyrs there were other captives – captives more for human frailty than for depravity, who, guilty of assaults and other light offences, had been sentenced to pay fines, and being unable to discharge them were now languishing in gaol. Mr O'Connell . . . paid the fines of forty-two who had been sentenced in various amounts ranging from smaller sums up to sums of 5l and 6l. Thus, some of the poor prisoners of Richmond shared the happiness of the day, and the Liberator had the satisfaction of hearing that there was gladness in their hearts before he left the prison to enter on his own triumph.[27]

At 2 p.m. the prison gates were again thrown open and O'Connell re-emerged to mount his triumphal car. He climbed to the topmost level of this precarious equipage; on the middle platform sat an aged harper playing national airs; and beneath him, on the carriage floor, were ranged O'Connell's grandchildren, clad in green velvet tunics and white-feathered caps. The car, huge, ramshackle and splendidly decorated (it was draped in purple and gold and drawn by six dapple-grey horses), epitomized the celebration. The procession took more than two hours to pass each stage, and was headed by a chain of open carriages bearing the lesser traversers, their attornies, and, in an enormous volume, the indictment. The lord mayor and aldermen wore their scarlet robes; the Head Pacificator brandished a green bough aloft; the trades flourished successively their gorgeous banners; even 'the shipping on the river displayed their gayest bunting, floating in many colours from the mast heads'.[28] O'Connell's old showmanship had not gone to rust. When he reached College Green, he halted the cortège, tore off his Mullaghmast cap and pointed in silence to the former Irish houses of parliament, while he pivoted above the surrounding sea of faces. Nor had he cast aside any of his old shibboleths or catchcries. 'There must be no illumination this night,' he told the crowds beneath his balcony when he at last attained his house in Merrion Square,

> – tell that to everybody you meet, and say it is my advice – aye, and say it is my command (hear, and cheers) . . . Conciliation is what we want – Protestants, Catholics, Dissenters, Irishmen of all classes, let us combine them all . . . Yes; I am glad that I was permitted to suffer for Ireland (cheers). I rejoice that I was permitted to dwell in a prison for your sake. The Liberator wanted to be liberated himself for three long months (loud cheers and laughter) . . . My course is a course of morality and peace. We have won much by it and by it we will achieve yet more (cheers). Ours is no sectarian cause.[29]

Two days later, O'Connell addressed the weekly meeting of the Repeal Association. Of course, this opened the door to another burst of popular rejoicing, and Conciliation Hall duly 'quaked and trembled with the applause'.[30] But the consuming interest was to discover O'Connell's future strategy. Even the most faithful of the faithful must have been disappointed in the result. He expended the majority of his rambling speech in a review of the twists and turns of the trial and appeal, ending with a startling recantation of his year-long denunciation of the whigs.

> And now I am going to make atonement to a public body – a class of men whom I often assailed . . . Yes, we owe a debt of gratitude to the Whigs, and as I was never tardy in censuring them . . . I am now equally eager to award them that meed of eulogy which it is their unquestionable right to receive . . . I rejoice with an exceeding great joy at the escape we have had from the fangs of injustice – an escape for which we are, under Providence, indebted to the dignified impartiality by which the bench has been ornamented through the judicial appointments of the Whigs.[31]

His new programme (in so far as any emerged clearly from the address) followed much the same lines. He proposed the impeachment of the judges of the Queen's Bench, the Irish attorney-general and the British ministry! Around this fantastic scheme he laid a smokescreen of apparent violence and energy by scurrilous personal attacks upon the 'foul-mouthed letter-opener, Sir James Graham' and the 'monster liar of Parliament', Peel.[32] Not a word was uttered on the subject of a fresh agitation, other than a bombastic reference to a coming campaign *in England* to drum up support for the impeachment. Repeal itself was practically ignored. No one could doubt that O'Connell had yielded ground. By the time that he concluded, it was clear, even to his servile audience, that he had no intention of trying to revive or repeat the stirring demonstrations of 1843. Davis had been all too right when he observed, during the course of the Richmond incarceration, 'O'Connell will run no more risks . . . from the day of his release, the cause will be going back and going down'.[33]

III

Before the end of September 1844 O'Connell left Dublin for Derrynane. He travelled directly, being too worn out to halt for demonstrations on the way, although he promised to make good his omissions when he would return some two months later. Derrynane worked its usual magic on him. 'I found my pack in the high pride of beauty,' he told Fitzpatrick on 3 October, 'It would delight any strong being capable of delight to see them and hear them *trail*. I had a splendid hunt yesterday',[34] and, a few days later, 'I have had great hunting. My pack is splendid.'[35]

He had now the leisure and spirits to consider the political future carefully. The hare-brained impeachment scheme had served its immediate purpose – to help him through the difficult first meeting of the Association after his captivity – and could now be cast silently away. Since the autumn of 1842 he had virtually abandoned the House of Commons; since his emergence from Richmond – if not indeed since the Clontarf débâcle – he had virtually abandoned popular agitation; and the whigs totally ignored the oblique invitation to a new concordat which his address to the Repeal Association on 9 September had probably contained. So, with the avenues of parliamentary pressure, mass demonstrations, and inter-party confederacy closed, it was natural for O'Connell to explore the possibility of widening his national front at home.

With the sharp polarization of Repeal and unionism in Ireland in 1843, a body of 'moderates' seeking a way between the two 'extremes' gradually came together around the apparent compromise of federation. The federalists were never a coherent or organized body, nor was there ever an agreed definition (or even perhaps any clear concept) of political federation in the British Isles: in fact such notions as emerged suggested mild devolution for Ireland rather than a federation of states or peoples. The federalists were of mixed political origin: some of them Catholics, most Protestants, some of them whig-liberals, most liberal-radicals or liberals plain. It would be misleading to speak of federalist 'leaders', but some were at least prominent in the cause, in particular, Sharman Crawford and the Hon. Henry Caulfield in the north, and the businessmen, William Murphy and Robert Hutton, in Dublin. In fact, the movement had two 'capitals', Dublin and Belfast. Federalism had a special appeal for those Belfastmen who, although habituated to regarding themselves as radicals in politics, found separation from Great Britain repellent or frightening. Some years earlier, the *Northern Whig* had explained or rationalized the attitude of this group in economic terms: 'We are not devoid of national feeling as Irishmen, but as an industrious and enterprising people we are a thousand times more closely bound up with Liverpool and Glasgow, with Lanarkshire and Lancashire, than with all Munster put together.'[36]

Clearly, then, there were difficulties in O'Connell's coming to terms with a heterogeneous body that lacked both a formal organization and a mouthpiece among the newspapers. But he determined, apparently quite suddenly after his removal to Derrynane, to fish openly for an understanding with them. He had, he believed, stirred the Dublin federalists into activity before he left for Kerry. 'The first step', he wrote on 1 October to Smith O'Brien, who had formally headed the Repeal movement during his imprisonment and whom O'Connell now professed to treat as a species of co-leader,

> will be for the Federalists to display themselves. The second to appoint a committee of arrangement at which you and my son John should attend to secure us all from any compromise tending to render precarious the right of Ireland to 'legislative self-protection'. I do believe the men who are *about* to be prominent are sincere and inclined to go the full necessary length with us. Of course our duty is to avoid every delusion. And as to any compromise, *that* is not to be thought of.[37]

Despite this last assurance, O'Connell's essential purpose seems to have been to put additional pressure on the government to concede something tending towards 'home rule'. As he confided to Fitzpatrick, 'The truth is that a strong Federal display made by and with men hitherto non-Repealers would induce the Ministry to strike and to canvass the terms on which the Irish legislature should be re-established.'[38] But as the days slipped by without any public 'display' by the Dublin federalists, he began to fret. As early as 3 October he confessed to 'becoming very impatient to hear *authentically from "the Federalists"*'.[39]

A week later, O'Connell's patience snapped. The protracted fatal illness about this time of his eldest grandson, to whom he was deeply attached, may have increased the strain upon him; and on 12 October he mourned, in a letter to Fitzpatrick, 'the loss of my sweet boy, one of the noblest creatures that ever lived'.[40] On the same day he abruptly issued a manifesto from Derrynane announcing his own preference for a form of federalism over simple Repeal, and calling for a 'Declaration' from the federalists.

> I do at present feel a preference for the Federative plan, as tending more to the utility of Ireland and to the maintenance of the connection with England than the mode of simple Repeal. But I must either deliberately propose or deliberately adopt from some other person a plan of a Federative Union, before I bind myself to the opinion which I now entertain.[41]

This move did not perhaps represent so extensive a retreat as it has ever since been regarded. He himself does not appear to have seen the two objectives as clearly antithetical – to Smith O'Brien he had written of 'federative Repeal',[42] and to Pierce Mahony of 'the repeal Cause – federalist or otherwise'[43] – and it was altogether reasonable, even if politically unwise, for him to reject absolute distinctions. The federal system which O'Connell now sketched in outline consisted of a single imperial parliament with two subordinate legislatures for Great Britain and Ireland. This was essentially the same definition of the 'Repeal demand' that O'Connell had given at Bath in 1832 when under pressure to be specific. It reflected his own constitutional dualism, which embraced the notions of both national independence and participation in a worldwide empire. In certain respects, in particular, in placing Great Britain and Ireland on a level domestically, it was a more advanced demand than that of Home Rule in a later generation. Moreover, Davis himself was negotiating with the northern federalists at much the same time as O'Connell appealed to them from Derrynane, and, in part, for the same reason – that an infusion of new men and tactics might revive the national movement. None the less, O'Connell's ploy was presented to posterity as a surrender, and for this he had, if not himself directly, at least his fundamental strategy to blame. As he expressed this to Fitzpatrick on 8 October 1844, 'When you enter into details you give *handles* to your enemies to trace out difficulties and start objections.'[44] One of the major political uses of the Repeal slogan had been its deceptive simplicity and negativity. But the obverse of this agitatory merit was that any variation of the plain and specific demand seemed, to the general mind, a retreat.

Perhaps, in the absence of any formal federalist party, O'Connell's pronouncement had to be *urbi et orbi*. But it was carelessly made, with little preparatory private correspondence with either his lieutenants or the federalist leaders or influential critics in the Repeal movement. It was immediately repudiated by the *Nation* group on the grounds that the Repeal Association could not work against its own *raison d'être*, and that federation would perpetuate Ireland's cultural subordination to Great Britain. Even the faithful O'Neill Daunt was deeply embarrassed by O'Connell's apparent about-face. On 29 October 1844, he wrote to his 'dear Liberator':

> Do not think me factious, for I premise by saying I will either *act* or *not act* as you think best. I am not so unwise as not to know that *you* see farther than *I* do.
>
> I was desirous (subject to your approval) to speak in the Conciliation Hall to the effect that my own impressions gave a distinct preference to 'simple Repeal' as compared with Federalism, that having already given the reasons for such preference, which remained unaltered, I would not now repeat them but that, notwithstanding my unequivocal convictions on this head, I was not the less sensible of the wisdom of expanding the basis on which a struggle for local legislation could be made and that *this* was the policy of your recent letter on the subject. I meant to work out this last idea somewhat in detail. The utility of such a speech would in my mind consist in showing how an out-and-out 'simple Repealer' could yet consistently concur in the *policy* of your letter. It is on this head principally there are misconceptions aflow.
>
> Federalism is not new in the Association. But a *preference* for it on the part of our leader is new. For when I made the speech last winter sustaining the superiority of simple Repeal to Federalism, you then distinctly told me you thought I argued conclusively.
>
> I think you may trust my discretion in not doing mischief. At all events I shall be guided by your judgment.[45]

Even this political obeisance failed to save Daunt from bitter reproof, as his description of his next meeting with O'Connell makes clear.

> I rose to greet him on his entrance. His irritation at the public dissent from the policy of his recent experiment was visible in his manner.
>
> 'I am quite well,' said he, as he shook hands with me; 'that is to say, quite as well as a man can be who is opposed by one-half of his friends and deserted by the other half.'
>
> 'You cannot class me', said I, 'amongst either the opponents or the deserters.'
>
> 'Certainly not amongst my opponents,' said he, 'but as to the deserters – um! – I am not quite so sure.'[46]

The Ulster federalists simply failed to respond at all, despite a meeting held in Belfast on 26 October 1844, presumably to consider O'Connell's overture. From Dublin there came only (and even at that from an unspecified group) a timid devolutionary scheme that went no further than proposing that local taxation, the poor law, and industrial development should belong to an indigenous Irish assembly. There was nothing in this on which to build a new departure, and O'Connell hastily retreated. A second declaration from Derrynane, written on 8 November 1844, a month after the first, chided the federalists for their silence and the *Nation* group for its precipitate utterance, and wound up the whole business with a characteristic piece of compass-boxing – a gloss to the effect that O'Connell had never meant to accept for Ireland 'less' than she had enjoyed before 1801; as things had fallen out, it would be 'much better to limit our exertions to simple Repeal'.[47]

This exhausted O'Connell's resources. For the present, there was nothing left but thundering in Conciliation Hall, struggles to keep the Repeal organization in good repair, and his blessedly unfailing Micawberism. In June 1845 he was reduced to asking Smith O'Brien to decide for him whether his long absence from parliament should continue. 'Decide for me as well as for yourself . . . It will be no small sacrifice to give up my visit to my loved mountains but if you *continue* to think that sacrifice necessary I will readily make it.'[48] The sacrifice was made; but, as we shall see, quite in vain. What was there now to do at Westminster but to watch the skies for signs of another liberal dawning?

IV

Towards the end of 1843 the radical leader Charles Buller had canvassed O'Connell's ideas on Irish reform. In his response of 9 January 1844, O'Connell artfully eluded both the issue of the indispensability of Repeal and any clear commitment on his own part to the programme which he now proffered the British liberals.

> I am not telling you what would satisfy me personally but I will tell you what I know would deprive me of many of my present adherents. As for myself, you admit that the slightest shrinking from the Repeal is at the present moment impracticable. Even my usual doctrine of instalments would under existing circumstances have the appearance of cowardice or at least of paltry timidity. But as I have no notion of keeping up a party at the expense of sacrificing any measures useful to Ireland, I will candidly tell you what I think would mitigate the present ardent desire for Repeal.[49]

Pride of place went to the disestablishment of the Church of Ireland – significantly, on the ground of psychological rather than material satisfaction for Irish Catholics. 'If you reflect for one moment on the galling nature of the infliction of making one Hierarchy inferior and degraded, and making the other Hierarchy proud, inflated and exalted, you will not be surprised at this being the monster grievance which festers in the mind of the Catholic clergy'.[50] Secondly, O'Connell proposed two modest measures of land reform, the repeal of the several post-Union statutes which had, in various ways, strengthened the landlord's hand in destraining and evicting for non-payment of rent, and some form (unspecified) of fixity of tenure; he also suggested a heavy tax upon absentee landholders. His third antidote was movement towards political equality between Great Britain and Ireland. Practically, this meant a large extension of the Irish county franchise to end the scandalous disparity between the two countries in this regard; placing the Irish municipal corporations upon the same basis as English in terms of power and scope; and abolishing the Irish freeman suffrage – 'an ancient Protestant nuisance'[51] – to prevent the system being grossly distorted in favour of the Orange faction. As a parthian shot, O'Connell told Buller that he did not believe for a moment that the British people would make the necessary concessions to Ireland until, as in the case of America, too late. In particular, the whigs

> won't do it. The principal part of them will necessarily be under the control of Lord John Russell and he will never permit anything like justice to be

done to the Catholic people of this country. I know him well. He has a thorough, contemptuous, Whig hatred of the Irish. He has a strong and I believe a conscientious abhorrence of Popery everywhere but I believe particularly of Irish Popery.[52]

Greville, to whom Buller showed O'Connell's letter, responded in the privacy of his journal, 'There was nothing . . . to lay hold of; he passed over the real evils which weigh down the people, and their causes – poverty, hunger, nakedness, no employment, no capital flowing there to set them to work.'[53] But Greville was wrong in one particular. There was something to lay hold of in O'Connell's letter. In fact, Peel's design for the conciliation of Ireland followed the same track, in part. Peel and his main advisers on the Irish question, Graham, Stanley and Eliot, may not have appreciated the opportunities of splitting Irish nationalism which O'Connell's arrest and subsequent imprisonment afforded them. Here they sowed the seeds of division inadvertently. But they certainly aimed – as Peel had put it earlier – at detaching 'a considerable portion of the respectable and influential classes of the Roman Catholic population' from the Repeal movement.[54] Three of the five major proposals to emerge from the cabinet papers and deliberations of the winter of 1843–4 were directly religious. Whereas, however, O'Connell wished to draw down the Church of Ireland to a lower civil and social level, Peel planned to narrow the gap between the churches by a handful of judicious concessions to the Catholics.

The first Peelite measure, the charitable donations and bequests bill, damaged O'Connell badly. The bill, representing an attempt to remove one of the leading Catholic grievances – the difficulties in the way of the Church receiving gifts or legacies – set up a new donations and bequests board of thirteen, including five Catholics, three of whom were to be Catholic prelates. Property might be vested in the board in trust for the maintenance of Catholic clergy or churches. It was immediately denounced by O'Connell and MacHale as discriminatory against the religious orders, insulting in annulling bequests made less than three months before the testator's death, and dangerous in facilitating outside intervention in the domestic concerns of the Catholic episcopate. Despite the fact that only seven Irish MPs opposed the measure, O'Connell assailed it on 24 August 1844, from Richmond prison, in the most violent terms, as 'very dangerous', 'very pernicious' and 'untechnical'.[55] He did so as a professional lawyer, delivering an 'opinion'; and although O'Connell himself suspended his condemnation while he was parleying with the federalists, it was on the strength of his authority that MacHale and twelve other Irish bishops issued a 'Protest of the Hierarchy and Clergy of Ireland' on 9 October, and that Paul Cullen and other Irish ecclesiastics at Rome condemned it unreservedly. In fact, O'Connell had spoken rashly. He had made the elementary error of basing part of his argument on words in the bill which were deleted before enactment; and he had pronounced, 'layman though I be, nothing can, to my humble judgment, be more manifest than the uncanonical nature of this Commission jurisdiction',[56] although he was largely ignorant of canon law.

The true reason for his opposition was, doubtless, apprehension lest the issue would divide the Church and render a portion of it sympathetic to the tory ministry. It was the government's intention (as MacHale put it) to associate Catholics 'with the old and inveterate enemies of our faith, detached from their brethren, and acting against the interests of their religion; dependent on the crown, fearful of its displeasure, and fawning on its caresses'.[57] Unless three 'fawning' prelates could be found to join the board, however, the Act would be a dead letter, and the government correspondingly humiliated and rejected. Thus the matter became another trial of strength between Peel and O'Connell, with the Repealers, the Repeal press, and the Repeal bishops exerting the utmost pressure against any prelates who might be invited to take seats on the board. They failed. After some wavering and at least one defection, the archbishops of Armagh and Dublin, and Bishop Denvir of Down and Connor, were gazetted as members. Unquestionably O'Connell had suffered a moral and (with a breach now open between some leading churchmen and the Repeal Association) also a political defeat. Dublin Castle exulted: 'The "Roman Catholic party" as such has ceased to exist. O'Connell can no longer rely on the support of the church', wrote Eliot.[58] 'We have erected a barrier – a line of Churchmen – ', Heytesbury, the new lord lieutenant, added, 'behind which the well-thinking part of the Roman Catholic laity will conscientiously rally, and aid us in carrying out . . . measures of conciliation.'[59] While this exaggerated both the government's success and its significance, there could be no doubt that O'Connellism had been severely wounded.

Peel's and Graham's second proposal, to treble the annual grant to Maynooth (from £8,928 to £26,360) and to make it a permanent charge on the revenue, while providing a capital grant of £30,000 for the college buildings, struck at O'Connell in another way. Here the government batted on a plumb wicket. The bishops had privately requested assistance in 1841 and 1842, and could not but welcome the new offer, all the more so as Peel would have to brave a Protestant furore in Britain and confess to past illiberality in making it. Tacit acceptance was O'Connell's only course: though asked to do so, he did not speak when the Maynooth bill was at last debated in the Commons on 11 April 1845. It was all the more galling for him to know that the boon could be conferred only by a tory government; even had the whigs wished to grant it when in office, they would probably have been defeated in the House of Lords.

Most awkward of all for O'Connell was the government's declared intention to take up the Irish university question. This would certainly divide the Catholic hierarchy and educated laity. MacHale and his faction among the bishops would probably settle for nothing short of denominational tertiary (no less than primary) education. This faction more or less co-incided with the O'Connellite 'party' in the episcopate; and, reciprocally, O'Connell's stance on the university issue was substantially the same as theirs. He laid the ground of opposition carefully. As early as 2 December 1844 O'Connell stated at a meeting of the Repeal Association that 'in whatever college was made, every religion should be free', and that 'education in literature and religion should not be separated, but each persuasion should have the means of partaking of both';[60] and in the next month he sought, and secured, the endorsement of these principles by sympathetic bishops. Cantwell of Meath assured O'Connell of his 'unbounded confidence in your enlightened and *truly Catholic* views'; he added, 'I tremble at the very idea of the projected colleges and the *mixed system* of education which it is, I believe, intended to establish among the *middle* and *higher classes*.'[61]

But long before Graham introduced his academical institutions (Ireland) bill at the beginning of May 1845, it was apparent that a considerable proportion of 'the *middle* and *higher* classes' disagreed. Almost half the Irish bishops, almost all the Irish liberal and 'moderate' Repeal MPs and the bulk of the Young Ireland element in the Repeal movement were ready to accept it, at least as a *pis aller*, and to work within the new system. O'Connell saw the danger that his 'party of the sincere and practical [practising] Catholics' would be assailed 'as being supporters of narrow and bigoted doctrines'.[62] But though he carried the main body of Repealers with him, there was little he could do to counter such a representation of his support, all the more so as the exigencies of the campaign and the ardour of his clerical allies compelled him to play the card of denigrating Graham's proposed non-denominational colleges as 'godless' and 'infidel'.[63] Indeed, concessions made by Graham while the bill was in progress through the Commons drove O'Connell deeper into 'narrowness' and 'bigotry'. To Graham's amendment permitting separate denominational halls of residence, for instance, he could only respond, 'See what an advantage this gives to the Protestants who are rich over the Catholics who are poor!'[64] All this was but token resistance, its only value public show; and O'Connell left London before the bill passed through even the lower house. *'There is not the least use* in our staying here', he wrote dejectedly to Fitzpatrick on 27 June 1845, 'and we would incur some of the responsibility for the details, if we were to remain uselessly to battle upon the subject. The Ministry have a most overwhelming majority, especially in favour of any measure opposed by the old Irish.'[65] O'Connell's final words are most revealing. In common Irish usage, the 'Old Irish' signified the indigenous Gaelic and Catholic element in the population as against *all* the rest.

The remaining items of Peel's conciliatory initiative of 1844–5 did little damage to O'Connell. The further measures encroached directly on either Orange power or the interests of landed property and met a proportionately powerful conservative resistance. First, Peel and Graham considered steps towards rendering the Union more an association of equals and less an expression of British superiority and decided on a £5 freehold franchise for Ireland, which would do something to reduce the gross disparity between the voting qualification in the two countries. But they did not persist with the registration bill embodying this proposal beyond the second reading; it would almost certainly have cost the tories Irish county seats. Furthermore, they made no attempt to equalize English and Irish municipal corporations, perhaps the most scandalous and certainly the most recent instance of the double standard operated by British governments. It was, as O'Connell wrote on 25 April 1845, 'a bitter insult and a palpable injustice and a direct contradiction of anything deserving of being called a *Union* that the people of Ireland should not have the same corporate powers in point of law with the people of England and Scotland'.[66] Correspondingly, O'Connell's plea for substantial agrarian reform – 'it is the Repeal Association and the hopes it excites which prevent a rebellion . . . the mischief is most pressing, and a powerful remedy is alone applicable to the case', he informed the ministry through a private intermediary on 26 April 1845[67] – met with a timid response. At the beginning of June, Stanley introduced a meagre compensation for improvements bill in the

House of Lords, but encountered such fierce opposition that he abandoned it (together with all hopes of other ameliatorative agrarian measures) almost immediately.

Thus, Peel's counter-offensive, though conceived along O'Connellite 'Justice for Ireland' lines, in fact succeeded only in the religious field. But this single success was enough to render insecure, for the remainder of his life, O'Connell's major power base, the united 'national front'.

V

It was not only through its legislative campaign that the government pushed religion ever further towards the forefront of Irish politics from mid-1844 on. It also adopted the whig device of opening public offices to Catholics, thereby draining off a little more of O'Connell's middle-class support. Much worse, it attempted to use Rome to deprive him of all episcopal backing.

O'Connell's imprisonment had rallied, temporarily, even the most conservative prelates to his side. In fact, a national novena (nine days devotion) in petition for a favourable outcome of the House of Lords appeal, had been approved by the entire Irish episcopate; and Archbishop Murray himself had presided at the solemn *Te Deum* held in the pro-cathedral in Dublin on 8 September 1844 'in thanksgiving to Almighty God for the deliverance of the beloved Liberator to his country, and his fellow-martyrs from unjust captivity'.[68] Conversely, as we have seen, O'Connell desisted, for the time being, from his denunciation of the donations bill. Within a few weeks, however, the British government's pressure on Rome produced a fresh source of discord. Working directly through their agents in Italy and indirectly through Metternich, Peel and Graham induced the pope to reprove publicly all members of the Irish clergy who involved themselves in political agitation. Although the papal rescript of October 1844 was milder than Peel had hoped, it was none the less severe. A prohibitory injunction of 1839, it complained, had been ignored, to the discredit of the Holy See; and ecclesiastics were sternly reminded of their sacred duty to separate themselves from all secular concerns, and to dissipate popular excitements.

The O'Connellite bishops remained unmoved. Some took the line of Cantwell of Meath that it was 'conduct and language . . . unbecoming our sacred characters' and not participation in Repeal meetings or banquets which had been condemned.[69] Others, like O'Higgins of

Ardagh (who dismissed the rescript as 'very harmless') argued that 'being purely hypothetical, it leaves matters precisely as they stood before'.[70] MacHale and Browne of Galway went directly from the synodal meeting of 20 November 1844 which 'welcomed' the papal injunction to attend a Repeal dinner held in O'Connell's honour! None the less, O'Connell's cause was injured in two important ways. First, the new injunction emboldened the considerable minority of bishops who wished to distance themselves from O'Connell's politics to declare publicly their neutrality or even opposition. Secondly, it tended to deepen the division of the Irish hierarchy into two camps, and thereby paved the way for the emergence of a 'conciliatory' episcopal party, prepared to meet the government halfway. We have already seen some of the effects of this development, in producing significant episcopal support for such measures as the donations and colleges bills and rendering O'Connell himself half a prisoner of the MacHaleite faction, during the first half of 1845.

It was ironic that in his seventieth year O'Connell should have fallen foul of an important section of his native Church. His Continental reputation as Catholic champion was never higher. Only a year before, Montalembert, about to launch a fresh campaign against anti-religious education in France, had made a pilgrimage to receive his 'blessing' and encouragement in London. Correspondingly, O'Connell's personal piety (in the mechanical sense, at least) was even intensifying. He acquiesced in the attribution of his deliverance from Richmond to the intercession of the Blessed Virgin; and he maintained his own novena of petition to the end despite his release before the nine days were up. Early in 1845, he received a 'very great privilege' from Rome. This was, in the words of his intermediary, Rev F. J. Nicholson, 'a plenary indulgence *on every day* you may wish to obtain one, on compliance with the specified conditions. This indulgence, as you will perceive, is applicable by way of suffrage to the suffering souls in purgatory.'[71] Moreover, O'Connell continued to regard the papacy as the 'centre of unity', the safeguard of true religion.

> That authority is assailed in our day by the spirit of absolutism in many Catholic and other sovereigns, who not content with Caesar's portion claim what belongs to God. It is also assailed by the restless genius of false liberalism which whilst it affects to seek liberty principally desires to uproot religion.[72]

These two sentences reveal much of O'Connell's self-view as a Roman Catholic. He saw himself as balancing – but serenely –the claims of liberty and faith. For him, liberty was essentially the absence of privilege, compulsion or restraint. In terms of religion this implied that church and state were clear different spheres; that denominations should be both autonomous and publicly on a level; and that individual persons might choose, as they wished, amongst beliefs and spiritual practices.

For decades O'Connell had maintained this position without serious difficulties at home. But a concatenation of inimical forces formed quite suddenly in the early 1840s. First, the Young Ireland concept of nationality gave a new primacy to citizenship. Implicitly, it subordinated religion to the needs of national identity and unity, wherever (as in education) the two tended to conflict. Secondly, Irish Catholicism had rapidly become more confident, triumphalist and aggressive. By now, the MacHale school at least was prone to identify Catholic and Irish values, and sought to mould the new society –which they believed would soon succeed the old in Ireland – upon specifically Catholic lines. Thirdly, British Protestantism was likewise growing in confidence, triumphalism and aggression, while the main body of Irish Protestants (who participated fully in the general increase in zeal) were also deeply frightened by the prospect of even partial concession to Repeal. Finally, Thomas Davis, who was especially influential in shaping 'advanced' opinion within the Repeal movement and among the young intelligensia as a whole, was neurotically suspicious of popery and quick to detect schemes of priestly tyranny. This produced a series of flashpoints. Thus, O'Connell's world-picture, in particular his special ideas of 'the free church' and 'the free state', came to seem less and less apropos as the collective and the passionate began to replace the individual and the 'rational' as the master-notes of Irish political discourse.

VI

O'Connell was first awakened to some of the unpalatable consequences of his success in attracting Irish Protestants to Repeal when Smith O'Brien proposed to him that a reception in Cork which he had planned for Sunday, 7 April 1844, be brought forward to the preceding day lest offence be given to Church of Ireland and nonconformist members. O'Connell good-humouredly complied, 'I am quite sure you are right. The strictness of the Protestant practice . . . is the safer course.'[73] None the less, as Denis Gwynn observed, 'it must have seemed strange, after so many years of popular agitation which

O'Connell had habitually conducted after Mass on Sundays'.[74] As time went on, the temperamental discordance springing from the differences in religious background passed far beyond such specific issues as sabbatarianism. On 26 July 1845, Davis told his fellow-Protestant, O'Brien, 'between unaccounted funds, bigotry, billingsgate . . . [and] crude and contradictory dogmas . . . any cause and any system could be ruined'.[75] There may have been nothing specifically religious in finding scurrility in public speeches, or the mingling of public and private monies, or demagogic manoeuvring, disdainful. But Davis's charges certainly expressed the Irish Protestant's characteristic sense of superiority (reflected in the self-images of rectitude, candour, manliness and plain dealing) to the 'peasant' values by which he found himself surrounded. The crucial charge, however, was the directly sectarian, 'bigotry'.

Soon after O'Connell's release from Richmond, Davis's gathering fears of priestly domination of the national movement had broken out in a letter to John O'Connell, in which he denounced the censorship exercised in Catholic Italy, the attribution of the House of Lords decision to 'a miracle', the hooting and abuse in Cork of a convert to the Church of Ireland, and an article in the *Dublin Review* in which another Cork convert to the Church of Ireland, D. O. Madden, was dismissed as an untrustworthy witness on the character of the religion which he had abandoned. Evidently, Davis expected that his catalogue of grievances would be forwarded to O'Connell, whom he appears to have regarded as, in some sense, ultimately responsible for the excesses of his co-religionists. At any rate, O'Connell took up the challenge, replying to Davis at length on 30 October 1844. He granted that Davis and the *Nation* should enjoy the 'fullest liberty' to abuse Italian censorship and 'the State Trial miracle' (though Catholics had an equal liberty to credit it); and he repeated an earlier condemnation by himself of 'the Cork attack upon a Protestant proselyte'. On Madden, a bitter anti-O'Connellite, however, he would not yield ground. 'Would you not have a right', he asked Davis, 'if a person who from being a Protestant became a Catholic and abused the Protestant clergy, to state that his evidence against them ought to be considered as suspicious or even unworthy of belief?' O'Connell then staked his claim to be the true liberal in matters of religion, implicitly transferring the charge of 'bigotry'.

I really think you might have spared the insinuation that you and other Protestants were 'pioneering the way to power' for men who would establish any sort of Catholic ascendancy. I know this, and I declare it most solemnly, that in the forty years I have been labouring for the public I never heard one bigoted expression, not only in our public meetings but in our committees and private discussions, from a Catholic but I have often felt amongst *some* of the liberal Protestants I have met with that there was not the same *soundness* of generous liberality amongst them as amongst the Catholics.

I hate bigotry of every kind, Catholic, Protestant or Dissenter, but I do not think there is any room for my interfering by any public declaration at present. I cannot join in the exaltation of Presbyterian purity or brightness of faith. At the same time I assert for everybody a perfect right to praise both the one and the other, liable to be assailed in argument by those who choose to enter into the controversy at the other side . . . As to my using my influence to prevent this newspaper war [between the *Dublin Review* and the *Nation*] I have no such influence that I could bring to bear. You really can much better influence the continuance or termination of this bye-battle than I can.[76]

All this reveals a new polarization; fresh but deep cross-purposes are appearing. Davis no less than O'Connell prided himself upon his liberalism. His leading objective was to maintain the rights and standing of the minority in the new Ireland; and his natural response to the growing identification of 'Irish' and 'Catholic' was to attempt to impose a supra-sectarian view of social institutions and objectives. The logical conclusion was the secular state; Davis was foreshadowing the substance of what is generally regarded as 'liberalism' in contemporary Ireland. But O'Connell could also flaunt some modern 'liberal' credentials. He was the complete political democrat (where Smith O'Brien, for one, opposed the raising of such issues as household suffrage or the secret ballot), and, as we have seen, so thorough an opponent of slavery as to sacrifice in the end his American support–network to the cause (whereas Davis, for example, placed the forwarding of Repeal ahead of asserting the 'principle' of negro emancipation). Moreover, as his letter to Davis made clear, O'Connell saw himself and Irish Catholics in general as magnanimous, as well as correct, in claiming no advantage on account of their overwhelming preponderance in numbers. He could not (to be sure) be ever on his guard against a slip of tongue or pen which revealed his interior consciousness of the disparity. But he was satisfied that he allowed all practicable liberty of belief to every fellow-countryman and -woman. It was for him a very plain and simple matter of indefeasible individual right: such was the 'liberalism' which had been stamped indelibly on him in his early manhood.

The crux came when the nation and the state (in their modern senses) emerged upon the scene, for these implied, or might well be taken to imply, the 'privatization' of such matters as religious practice. To O'Connell, such a conclusion was illiberal: his liberalism regarded the indoctrination of the young as the concern of the responsible individual – and, by extension, of the individual's church – rather than a means of achieving social ends. Hence, with both claiming 'liberal' sanction, Davis could end by arguing for 'mixed' education, in the national interest, and O'Connell by standing on the individual's religious liberty, which perforce included the choice of his child's instruction. Looked at in one light, it was the 1840s challenging the 1790s; looked at in another, it was the opening skirmish in a campaign which grips Ireland still.

The issue was not, however, coolly classified in this fashion in the critical nine months from September 1844 to May 1845. Instead, Davis was driven to magnify a number of trivial incidents in his attempt to raise the alarm at the apparent Catholicizing of Repeal, while a clericalist faction, charging or insinuating that Davis and the *Nation* were anti-religious in tendency, began to form within the Association. From February 1845, when the government's colleges bill was announced, the sectarian antagonism between these extremities of the Repeal movement grew ever more embittered. O'Connell postponed formal discussion of the bill for as long as possible. Smith O'Brien tried to avoid expressing publicly his approval of the principle of 'mixed' education; he fully recognized, he told Davis, 'the importance of my maintaining sincere, unreserved and friendly co-operation with O'Connell'.[77] But the conflict was irrepressible; there was no hope that university education could be left an 'open' question in the Association.

When the bill was at last considered at a general meeting of the Association on 26 May 1845, it was Davis who precipitated a 'scene'. O'Connell may have irritated him initially by vigorously applauding M. G. Conway (a glib but disreputable young journalist who had jumped on the 'Catholic' bandwagon) when he lauded denominational university education to the skies. Davis followed immediately and immediately offended.

I have not . . . more than a few words to say in reply to the useful, judicious, and spirited speech of my old college friend, my Catholic friend, my very Catholic friend, Mr Conway.
Mr O'CONNELL: It is no crime to be a Catholic, I hope.
Mr DAVIS: No, surely no, for –

Mr O'CONNELL: The sneer with which you used the word would lead to the inference.[78]

But Davis went on to further provocation, claiming, in a passage of perverse and contorted reasoning, that he and the Irish bishops were at one in their objections to the colleges bill. In fury, O'Connell rose to expostulate that whereas the 'mixed' system had been 'met with the unequivocal and unanimous condemnation' of the Irish bishops,

> [t]he principle of the Bill has been lauded by Mr Davis, and was advocated in a newspaper professing to be the organ of the Roman Catholic people of this country [the *Nation*], but which I emphatically pronounce to be no such thing. The section of politicians styling themselves the Young Ireland Party, anxious to rule the destinies of this country, start up and support this measure. There is no such party as that styled 'Young Ireland'. There may be a few individuals who take that denomination on themselves. I am for Old Ireland. 'Tis time that this delusion should be put an end to. Young Ireland may play what pranks they please. I do not envy them the name they rejoice in. I shall stand by Old Ireland; and I have some slight notion that Old Ireland will stand by me.[79]

It seems significant that, in such a context as a Repeal meeting, O'Connell should have identified himself with, and spoken for 'the Roman Catholic people of this country'. Was he too – for all his picture of himself – being sucked into public sectarianism at last? But perhaps the most significant feature of the outburst was his designation (even if only to belittle it as a handful) of a 'Young Ireland party'. So far this had scarcely existed, either in substance or in name, outside on the pages of the hated Madden's book. It was Madden who had coined the phrase, but to little effect as yet. When Smith O'Brien protested in a whisper, O'Connell withdrew the term at once, as 'disclaimed by those to whom it was applied'.[80] But the damage had been done; fatal words had been uttered; its very naming went far towards rendering a schism actual.

As to the rest, the *mores* of the day took over; sentimentality provided a 'resolution'. Davis rose to his feet again, disavowed factionalism, declared that he and his friends were 'bound . . . by a strong affection toward Daniel O'Connell' – and thereupon (in the words of Duffy) 'broke into irrepressible tears'.[81] O'Connell was not to be outdone; he also rose once more, reciprocated the warm expression of personal regard, and throwing his arms about him cried, 'Davis I love you'. One at least of Davis's friends was disgusted by his no less than O'Connell's theatricality. 'Mr O'Connell's attack on Young Ireland', wrote Thomas MacNevin next day, was what I expect from his years and irritability – the candle stinks as it waxes low on the socket. His retraction was shabby: and his hugging of Davis more like the clumsy pantomime of an ox than any display of manly sincerity.

As for Davis, I know not what to say. 'Exit Hibernia in tears'. Ah – what stuff for a politician. What was there in the vulgar assault made on himself and his friends to authorise these pearly drops or this quivering emotion?[82]

But Davis himself was quite satisfied with his 'success'. O'Connell too believed that he had succeeded, that the old lion had both tamed and reconciled his cubs. All this was quite illusory. Not only had the protagonists failed to conjure the divisions away: they eventually ran all the deeper for having been displayed. Once the genii of religious fear and vainglory had been released, within an ailing movement, there was no returning them to their bottles. Peel had, at long last, won his duel with O'Connell. At one blow, he had split both Catholic politics and Repeal.

CHAPTER 23

The Widening Gyre

1845–6

I

The effects of the momentarily-open rupture at Conciliation Hall on 26 May 1845 were not immediately apparent. O'Connell 'had', Gwynn writes, 'lived through so many much more tempestuous and emotional scenes, that he could scarcely have any deep feeling of resentment'.[1] At any rate, he showed no sign of either renewed anger or alarm during the coming months. Conversely, Davis had both publicly repledged his fealty to O'Connell and felt an afterglow of self-satisfaction at the manner in which he had comported himself in the exchange. Moreover, only four days after the 'scene' in Conciliation Hall, a national levée to commemorate the anniversary of O'Connell's imprisonment was held in the Rotunda in Dublin. This, preceded by processions through the streets and attended by delegations from all over Ireland, was an occasion for sentimental demonstrations of renewed loyalty to the Liberator and Repeal. These were repeated at the corresponding celebration in Cork on 8 June 1845, when O'Connell, entering the city on a vast triumphal car, was received with fervid enthusiasm by dignitaries, trades and populace alike: 'The exhibition here was truly magnificent', he wrote, 'It actually exceeded that in Dublin.'[2] It was not difficult, amid such euphoria, to relegate the collision of 26 May to the category of minor and temporary misunderstanding.

The sudden death of Davis on 16 September 1845 at the age of thirty seemed at first to vindicate completely such a view. O'Connell wrote at once from Derrynane in a letter to be read to the Association:

My mind is bewildered and my heart afflicted. The loss of my beloved friend, my noble-minded friend, is a source of the deepest sorrow to my mind. What a blow – what a cruel blow to the cause of Irish nationality! He was a creature of transcendent quality of mind and heart; his learning was universal, his knowledge was as minute as it was general. And then he was

553

a being of such incessant energy and continuous exertion. I, of course, in the few years – if years they be – still left to me, cannot expect to look upon his like again, or to see the place he has left vacant adequately filled up; and I solemnly declare that I never knew any man who could be so useful to Ireland in the present stage of her struggles. His loss is indeed irreparable. What an example he was to the Protestant youths of Ireland! What a noble emulation of his virtues ought to be excited in the Catholic young men of Ireland! And his heart too! It was as gentle, as kind, as loving as a woman's. Yes, it was as tenderly kind as his judgment was comprehensive and his genius magnificent. We shall long deplore his loss. As I stand alone in the solitude of my mountains, many a tear shall I shed in the memory of the noble youth. Oh! How vain are words or tears when such a national calamity afflicts the country. Put me down among the foremost contributors to whatever monument or tribute to his memory shall be voted by the National Association. Never did they perform a more imperative or, alas, so sad a duty!

I can write no more – my tears blind me. . . .[3]

All this was rather in the nature of a lapidary inscription, in which, notoriously, a man is not on oath; and O'Connell was just the person to respond unrestrainedly, even hyperbolically, to the pathos of Davis' death. None the less, with its clear implication that the Repeal cause had been struck a devastating blow, the letter amounted to a public declaration that the disagreements between Davis and O'Connell had been, at most, trivial differences in emphasis.

This was far from true. Religious shibboleths continued to work their poison in the movement after 26 May. O'Connell himself, who habitually attached scurrilous epithets to the objects of his aversion, almost invariably referred to the new Colleges Act as 'infidel' or 'godless'.[4] Naturally such adjectives entered the general currency of Repealers and tended to be transferred – whether carelessly or maliciously – to at least some of those who supported the measure after it had been enacted. O'Connell's son, John, adopted the role of *intransigeant* upon the issue; and as he was at once much of an age (and consequently in something of rivalry) with many of the Young Irelanders; the conductor of proceedings in Conciliation Hall in his father's now-frequent absences; and commonly assumed to be O'Connell's political 'heir', sectarian bitterness was kept fresh and lively throughout the summer of 1845. At the same time, Davis contributed his share before he died. During July and August he drew to Smith O'Brien's attention various signs (as he saw them) that the Repeal movement was degenerating into a mere priests' party. Distinct and hostile factions were becoming ever more evident within the

Association. Even the circumspect secretary, Ray, told Maurice O'Connell on 31 July, apropos the non-denominational colleges and parliamentary reform, 'There is assuredly a difference of opinion on these matters between Mr O'B[rien] and a majority of the people of Ireland.'[5]

Meanwhile, O'Connell had been humiliated during his brief attendance at the House of Commons towards the end of June 1845. 'The Ministry', he wrote to Fitzpatrick from London on the 27th, 'have a most overwhelming majority, especially in favour of any measure opposed by the *old Irish*. In fact, though you may think it vanity, I cannot but assert that the Ministry *seem pleased* to have me so completely in their power, as I necessarily am in the present House of Commons.'[6] He returned to Ireland apparently determined that the parliamentary Repeal party should recover the respect and influence which it had enjoyed in the mid-1830s. His correspondence evidences an unwonted concern with parliamentary representation; and in a letter sent from Derrynane on 8 August 1845 to be read aloud at the next Association meeting in Dublin he set out a plan of revival and renewal. O'Connell's declared objective was the return of sixty to seventy Repeal MPs at the next general election. If this were realistically intended, it meant that he hoped to carry at least twenty of the thirty-two Irish counties, an extremely difficult though not absolutely impossible undertaking. To this end, he proposed a scheme of 'registry wardens', one to be appointed in each parish, with the specific duty of promoting the registration of sympathetic voters. Ray reported to him shortly afterwards that both the mustering of Dublin voters and the preparation of the nation-wide scheme were well in train. 'We have just received', he told O'Connell on 25 August, 'a return from the [Dublin city] Registry, today 19 Repealers to O. . . . We are working the wards well. . . . We are doing all we can to work out the Registry Plan. We have sent the enclosed circular to the Clergy to get "Registry Wardens" named, and the Instruction Papers etc. are printed in quantity.'[7]

But little was achieved. Outside the cities and the 'jurisdiction' of the occasional enthusiast, the 'Plan' was practically ignored. Even O'Connell's intense interest in his own brainchild appears to have been shortlived. When he left Derrynane late in September, it was principally to undertake a short series of general Repeal rallies in the south and west. These were small, decorous affairs, a far cry from the monster meetings of two years before. O'Connell's intention was in part to re-rouse the faithful and in part to preach patience where agrarian disturbances were once more upon the increase. 'Kerry wants a stimulant. Tipperary, if anything, wants restraint', he told O'Brien on 17 September 1845.[8] Between 26 September and 15 October 1845 O'Connell addressed Repeal assemblies and banquets at Killarney, Thurles, Castlebar and Sligo. Everywhere he was greeted with the old deference, and to that extent his little autumn circuit was useful confirmation of his commanding position within the movement. But he was, at best, marking time. Essentially, his home resources for an offensive were exhausted, and he could do little more than await the arrival of some *deus ex machina* – the whigs' return to power perhaps or a general election which would end luckily in the Repealers holding the balance in the House of Commons.

Although O'Connell himself remained publicly sacrosanct, his loss of persistent drive and direction took its toll, and during the third quarter of 1845, the Repeal Association began to suffer badly from the malaise of weakening central power. In Cork, it was said, the local organization was so spiritless that the return of two Repeal members for the city could no longer be assured. In London, a serious quarrel broke out in July between the priest-inspector and some wardens, and several branches were disbanded, at least temporarily. Soon afterwards, the Repealer John Reynolds caused an uproar in Dublin, and provoked O'Connell's direct intervention, by his attacks upon the Repeal-dominated Corporation. O'Connell's favour was fought over in other places. His friend, William O'Donnell, warned him on 9 September that if he accepted the hospitality of the 'advanced' Repealer, Michael Doheny, he would offend other parties in co. Tipperary: 'You can't go to Doheny's. It would not answer . . . his house I would not consent to have you at.'[9] In Limerick, O'Connell became, in effect, the bone of contention between the Repeal mayor, Dr W. H. Geary, and the main body of local Repealers, as both Geary and his opponents strove, in late July, to secure him as guest of honour for a banquet. O'Connell agreed at last on 29 August 1845 to attend a dinner in the city but would fix no date. As he explained to O'Brien some three weeks later, 'You must have perceived in my answer to their [the Limerick Trades'] invitation that I have given myself time to play the long game and I therefore can postpone the dinner till there is a prospect of unanimity amongst all Repealers in Limerick.'[10]

The most serious conflict of all occurred in Waterford, and O'Connell inadvertently added fuel to the blaze when he declared at the Association meeting of 27 October 1845 that he would move a vote of thanks to the local 'radical' Repealer, James Delahunty, for his registration work were it not that to do so might seem as if he were taking sides in the city quarrel. This drew down on him an angry rebuke from his old friend, his Waterford manager and 'fixer' for quarter of a century, Rev. John Sheehan. 'There is no part of your doctrine as an agitator which I admire more', wrote Sheehan on 30 October,

> than your saying that you would not bring about the greatest possible good at the expense of one drop of human blood. This is the true principle of the moral force revolutionist, and the announcement of it has secured for you the active cooperation of thousands amongst those who, looking only to their eternal interests, would not on any other terms consent to be implicated in the turmoil of political agitation.
>
> I am sure that however just may [be] my own abhorrence for the spilling of blood, it is not stronger than your detestation of any course which would bring the bishops and the Catholic clergy into contempt amongst the people . . . Read, I pray you, my letter and I ask if I have not established incontestably a case against Mr Delahunty, my own parishioner whom, under an erroneous impression no doubt, you are now sustaining against the Bishop [Foran] and the two parish priests of Waterford. What can you think of a party who cast the vilest and most contumelious imputations upon such a man as Dr Foran? He was lately closing a series of most instructive lectures and he found it necessary to advert in very strong terms to . . . the uncharitable and vituperative speeches made at the nocturnal meetings of the Waterford Repeal Association . . . He was replied to by one of the party whom you are now sustaining: 'What a pity it is that Dr Foran does [not] take the pledge from Father Mathew' . . .
>
> If Mr Delahunty says that without following up the course he is pursuing, you cannot have two Repeal members, for this city, he is making an unfair representation.[11]

Although O'Connell did call on 'the popular party' to apologize for its disrespect to the clergy, he also declared that each side was 'in the wrong to a certain extent', and offered his own services as mediator.[12] It was a far cry from his former easy mastery of the agitation.

These various divisions by no means reflected a simple Old Ireland–Young Ireland dichotomy. In fact, Geary, who was later to lead a Young Ireland faction in Limerick, was at this stage in trouble for his 'whiggish' conduct. Occasionally, there were indications that a clash owed something to antagonism between 'advanced' and 'moderate' elements within the Association. Most clearly did this seem to be the case in Waterford where the traditional clerical leadership was being challenged; moreover, Sheehan's heavy stress on moral force suggests that this too was a ground of battle. On the whole, however, the dissensions did not spring from generational or ideological dispute, but from failure of morale and the consequent diminution in O'Connell's control and direction of the movement.

> Turning and turning in the widening gyre
> The falcon cannot hear the falconer;
> Things fall apart; the centre cannot hold . . .[13]

Moreover, the falconer's voice was no longer clear or decisive. The separate 'knots and bodies' (as Ray called them) within the local Associations were no longer commanded to coalesce; some groups of wardens were beginning to challenge, and even flout, instructions from the centre. 'I greatly dread the relaxation of our Rules', Ray wrote to O'Connell on 8 September 1845 concerning a demand that monies be retained by a branch instead of forwarded as normally to headquarters, 'There is hardly a place where troublesome spirits are not anxious to break through and the great danger is that, if it transpired that any privilege was allowed to Limerick, we would risk speedy disorganisation elsewhere . . . The Rent today is low.'[14] O'Connell's chosen barometer of his agitation's state of health told the essential story: the weekly national Rent now sometimes fell below even £200.

II

In the final months of 1845, O'Connell's attention was drawn away from the Repeal movement proper to two new, but interrelated, factors. The first was the partial failure of the potato crop in Ireland. Its significance was not immediately recognized. In fact, as late as 11 September Fitzpatrick reported to O'Connell that the 'comparatively prosperous state of the country ought to make it [the collection of the Tribute] very successful'.[15] But by the following month the blight was manifest in no less than eleven of the counties. O'Connell himself, moving widely around Munster and Connacht about this time, was among the first to appreciate the extent of the disaster. It was probably at his instigation that Dublin Corporation, on 21 October 1845, set up a special committee to inquire into the causes of the potato failure; at any rate, he dominated its proceedings from the start. His initial objective may have been narrowly political, to seize the opportunity created by the distress to drive home the 'lesson' of Irish misgovernment under British rule. But he was soon horrified by the evidence of suffering which came streaming in: 'my attendance on the Mansion

House committee', he wrote to Smith O'Brien before the year was out, 'has made me acquainted with the frightful certainty of an approaching famine; and you know pestilence always follows famine, the prospect is really frightful'.[16] Immediately, he proposed restricting the output of the breweries and distilleries in order to conserve barley, and the placing of limitations upon the export of other foodstuffs; his next step was to call on the government to provide 'ample means of employment and [put] within the reach of the labouring classes a sufficient quantity of food, to be paid for out of the money they receive as wages'.[17] O'Connell's desperate concern, sense of frustration at his own impotence and fear that an incalculable number would 'perish in Ireland within the next twelve months'[18] are not to be doubted. But, automatically, he translated everything that he experienced into political terms, as well; and the potato blight was of critical importance not only in itself but also in contemporary British politics, because it would compel Peel's ministry to come to a determination on the repeal of the corn laws, an issue which deeply divided the conservatives. This was the second new factor of late 1845.

For some time, Peel and his particular supporters within the cabinet had been moving towards the immediate relaxation of the restrictive legislation; and the incipient Irish famine served powerfully to strengthen the case against 'dear food'. Peel was thus driven to search about for some compromise with the protectionist majority of his own party which would allow the import of cheap grain to Ireland. O'Connell was quick to see a possible advantage in all this. Co-operation with Peel was, as ever, out of the question; but the whigs were likely to move farther and faster towards corn law repeal, which he himself, as a free trade radical, in any event supported. He was doubtless sincere when he declared at the Repeal Association meeting of 3 November 1845, 'If I had only the alternative of keeping the people alive or giving up the repeal, I would give up the repeal.'[19] But it was his rider, that the whigs had not asked him to make any such choice, which told the audience which way the wind was blowing – that a new whig alliance might become practicable politics at last. Conversely, the Young Irelanders (the name was by now in general currency) took alarm; from late November onwards the *Nation* regularly demanded complete independence of the whigs no less than of the tory government.

Having failed to find a new corn laws formula which would leave his cabinet united, Peel resigned office on 6 December 1845, and Lord John Russell was called on to form a new liberal administration.

Through his friend, D. R. Pigot, O'Connell privately informed Russell that he could rely on the support of the Repeal MPs in return for reasonable concessions. O'Connell laid most emphasis upon the need for a reform of the Irish franchise (on which the building up of a strong Repeal party in the House of Commons to some extent depended) and an amendment of the Irish Municipal Corporations Act. On 15 December, he made the substance of his position public when he told a Repeal Association meeting that he was confident that he could make some progress with Lord John Russell.

This precipitated a head-on clash with Smith O'Brien. The corn laws themselves produced a secondary collision. As on most other general issues, O'Brien stood to the right of O'Connell, favouring a gradualist modification of the laws rather than complete repeal. Claiming (quite wrongly) that nine-tenths of the Irish electorate opposed the removal of protection, he demanded that, at the very least, the corn laws remain an 'open question' in the Repeal Association. But the main field of battle was an impending 'whig alliance'. 'I cannot describe to you', O'Brien wrote to O'Connell on 18 December 1845,

> the solicitude which I feel with respect to the policy of the Repeal Party in connection with the recent change of Government. I entertain the most sincere conviction that upon the conduct which we shall adopt during the next three months depend not only our chance of witnessing the accomplishment of the Repeal of the Union but also the character of the Irish nation. If all our exertions, our pledges may I say, our *sacrifices* are to end in placing the Irish nation under the feet of the English Whigs, I cannot justify to myself the part which I have acted nor do I think that the Repeal agitation will have conferred upon Ireland anything but injury and disgrace.

Not merely did O'Brien insist that the Repeal MPs should remain aloof from both British parties, but he also proposed that they should form what was later to be termed an 'independent opposition': the 'alternative which ought be presented to the minister is in my opinion not "If you give us these measures we will support you" but "If you do not give us these measures we will oppose you".' Finally, he excused his 'frankness' by claiming that it was the most effectual mode of countering the current tory newspapers' reports that he and o'Connell were now rivals for the leadership, and that the Repeal Association was being steadily 'O'Brienized'.[20]

Typically, O'Connell dealt with the personal issue first. 'I have passed

50 years of my life in agitation', he replied to Smith O'Brien on 20 December, 'and I never was jealous of any man . . . the more any of my fellow-labourers earned the popular applause and the good opinion of wise men, the more I rejoiced and this feeling it is that makes me exult in your present popularity.'[21] If this seems a very generous, it was also a misleading response. On the one hand, the notion of a duarchy, which O'Connell himself occasionally suggested in writing to O'Brien, could not have been seriously meant. O'Brien was not to be spoken of in the same breath as O'Connell as a popular leader; and his political standing at large still depended on O'Connell's patronage, which in turn sprang from the symbolic value of the adherence of O'Brien, a comparatively able and thoroughly respectable member of the Protestant landowning caste, to the Repeal cause. On the other hand, the Young Irelanders were unquestionably seeking to ensnare O'Brien for their leader, and through him ultimately to dominate the Association. It was also true that O'Brien's stances coincided increasingly with those adopted by the *Nation*. His lack of personal ambition and honourable sense of what was due to the movement as a whole (and perhaps also to O'Connell for past and current favour) continued to hold him back. None the less, circumstances were forcing him gradually towards the role of O'Connell's rival.

As we have seen, the corn laws issue itself divided the two sharply. In his reply of 20 December, O'Connell argued the inevitability of their repeal and the absurdity of calling on the British government to furnish the employment and food needed to stave off mass starvation while yet 'vot[ing] against provisions being as cheap as they might otherwise be'. He added that 'the great majority of the Repealers' agreed with him: this was a safe assertion, they always did! 'However', he told O'Brien, 'as you require that the Corn Law question should be an open question in the Association, I of course at once comply. You are most completely entitled to have your opinion respected to the extent of having no question considered as *closed* which you are convinced ought to be open.'[22]

O'Connell was determined to be conciliatory. He went on to profess his concurrence with O'Brien's policy of complete parliamentary independence, with the sole qualification (if such it was) that 'our neutrality ought not to be a *sulky* neutrality'.[23] But O'Connell's easy acceptance of the formula that every 'good' British measure should be supported and every 'bad' one opposed, irrespective of its whig or tory provenance, meant little, practically. For, to him, government signified much more than pieces of proposed legislation; and a ministry whose decisions he could hope to influence, which was not altogether inconsonant with his general radicalism, and which would allow his party some share in Irish patronage and some voice in the filling of Irish offices, was *ipso facto* to be preferred. As we have seen, he was well into political trading with a prospective whig government at the very time that he proclaimed to Smith O'Brien his continued adherence to 'neutrality'.

It will be obvious that two different political languages were being spoken in the exchange of 18–20 December. O'Brien's was the language of 'principle', or at least of unconscious predeliction or prejudice which presented itself to the locutor as 'principle'. But O'Connell's was the language of advantage. It was characteristic of him that, although an inveterate opponent of the corn laws on free trade 'principle', the argument which first sprang to his mind in December 1845 should have been the crass inexpediency of continued resistance to their repeal. In the same fashion, he had never seen an inconsistency – but rather the contrary – in alternately agitating and shelving the Repeal issue, as occasion served. What matter whether the stick or carrot was employed, provided the donkey moved. Nor had he ever seen a contradiction between taking up a formally 'independent' position in the House of Commons and accommodating a whig government – at a price. For him, whatever he gained as the price of such support, whether in terms of posts, statutes, amendments or advancements, was *not* gained at the expense of ultimate Repeal, but instead brought it a little closer. This complex attitude was epitomized by his comment of 22 December 1845, when he learned that Russell had failed to form a government after all and that Peel would be restored to the prime ministership *malgré lui*, 'If we could have managed to play our cards well in Lord John's Government, we should have *squeezed out* a great deal of good for Ireland without for one moment merging or even postponing Repeal but on the contrary advancing that measure.'[24]

Peel's return to office brought the interchange to a halt, immediately. But meanwhile the seeds of still greater troubles had been sown. John Mitchel, Davis's replacement as leader-writer of the *Nation*, was an Ulster unitarian, suspicious of clericalism generally as well as popish priestcraft, and more violent in both views and language than his predecessor. On 22 November 1845, in response to a London newspaper comment that the railways would greatly speed troop movements about Ireland, he wrote in an editorial,

The military uses (or abuses) of railways are tolerably well understood; but it might be useful to promulgate through the country, to be read by all Repeal Wardens in their parishes, a few short and easy rules, as to the mode of dealing with railways in case of any enemy daring to make a hostile use of them ... To lift a mile of rail, to fill a perch or two of any cutting or tunnel, to break down a piece of embankment, seem obvious and easy enough ... Hofer, with his Tyroliens [*sic*], could hardly desire a deadlier ambush than the brinks of a deep cutting upon a railway.[25]

O'Connell was aghast. Not merely had the *Nation* envisaged future armed resistance, but it had also doled out recipes for conducting a guerilla war. This struck at the heart of (in all senses) the very first principle of his politics, the repudiation of physical force in every form. By referring specifically to the Repeal wardens, it had opened up, as well, the prospect of another indictment for sedition. O'Connell had spent a political lifetime striving to secure himself and his movement against just such a prosecution, and his Richmond experiences had deepened, if possible, his horror of incarceration. He immediately protested to the *Nation* and secured the publication of a formal acknowledgement in the following issue that the newspaper 'had neither connexion with, nor control over, Repeal Wardens'.[26] As a further safeguard, O'Connell, at the next meeting of the Repeal Association which he attended, vehemently repudiated the editorial: the safety of the Association, he insisted, must on no account be imperilled by offering the slightest countenance to such statements. But, once more, this was, despite the immediate appearances, unfinished business. Unknowingly – though doubtless he would have been delighted had he known – Mitchel had placed a time-bomb, still more destructive than the issue of truckling to the whigs, in the midst of O'Connell's following.

III

Somehow or other, absurdity kept breaking in upon O'Connell. In the midst of encroaching famine and deepening division he spent much of the last quarter of 1845 in ludicrous denunciation of, and counter-denunciation by, a correspondent of *The Times*. In the autumn of 1845 the newspaper commissioned a barrister, T. C. Foster (thereafter elevated to 'the Commissioner'), to write a series of letters on the condition of the Irish people similar to those which he had recently provided for Wales and the Scottish Highlands. As a matter of course,

O'Connell distrusted *The Times*; he may also have been happy to have a new hare to pursue. Accordingly, he pelted Foster with abuse ('the gutter Commissioner', 'liar', 'scoundrel', 'traducer of my brave people') at the weekly meetings of the Association. It was often a grotesque performance. The 'gutter commissioner', he told the meeting of 27 October,

> introduced himself to my revered and accomplished friend Dean O'Shaughnessy, of Ennis . . . he [Foster] said he saw enough of Ireland to convince him that the Irish were not entitled to a Repeal of the Union . . . Sir, said the Dean, I am not in the habit of being discourteous to any person, but if I were not in my own house I would tell the servant to show you out (cheers). Off went the gutter commissioner . . .[27]

When Foster reported that the Dean had written to confirm that this story was entirely baseless, O'Connell told the next meeting, 'He [Foster] denied altogether that he had been threatened to be kicked out of the house of Dean O'Shaughnessy . . . All, he had to say was that . . . he ought to have been. (Loud laughter and cheers)'.[28] Foster, however, by no means saw himself as a protagonist in a Punch and Judy show. Outraged, he set off to inspect O'Connell's own property in co. Kerry, and in due course provided *The Times* with 'a minute and merciless description of the squalour in which the Liberator's tenants lived', including the graphic detail that there was 'not a pane of glass in the parish [of Derrynanebeg], nor a window of any kind in half the cottages'.[29] Foster's report was probably accurate. W. H. Russell, whom *The Times* sent to confirm Foster's findings, wrote later, 'I believe the tenants of Derrynanebeg were squatters, the evicted refuse of adjoining estates, who flocked to the boggy valley, where they were allowed to run up their hovels of soddened earth and mud.'[30] This would have been quite characteristic of O'Connell's conduct as a proprietor. It was precisely because he allowed his tenants – and squatters – 'to live their lives in their own traditional, slatternly way'[31] that he was popular on his estate. None the less he was stung by Foster's charges into devoting much of December 1845 and the beginning of January 1846 to attempted refutations and the (remarkably successful) drumming up of testimony, from Irish tories as well as whigs, to his merits as an open-handed and indulgent landlord. Among other things, the episode can be seen as an exercise in O'Connell's customary demagogic skills; they had not slackened yet. Burlesque and buffoonery had always been important items in his repertoire for managing the masses; and the politics of the diversion had repeatedly proved useful when – as in his current dealings with the whigs – O'Connell might appear to have been trapped between contradictory commitments. Moreover, he had discerned that this was an occasion – they were rare – for the successful playing of the supra–sectarian card, whereby the latent Anglo-Irish resentment of British assumptions of moral, organizational and social superiority could be temporarily enlisted on his side.

It certainly was the case that the Ascendancy generally was disaffected at the end of 1845 and in the opening months of 1846. 'Just as the possibility of the Whigs returning to power had increased the tension within the Repeal Association,' writes Nowlan, 'so also the break-up of Peel's party weakened the bonds which had secured the body of Irish landlord opinion to English Conservatism.'[32] Smith O'Brien attempted to exploit this disarray by negotiating an agreement with the English tory protectionist, Lord George Bentinck, to accept the temporary import of duty-free grain to Ireland. O'Connell would have none of this. Correctly, he saw O'Brien's move as an attempt to provide the Repeal movement with an alternative to a 'whig alliance'; and, again correctly, he deemed it to be politically inept. There could be no durable combination between Irish nationalists and British diehards and disgruntled landlords. Instead, O'Connell set out from the start of 1846 seriously to court, and be courted by, the liberals. The proper theatre for such operations being Westminster, he returned to the House of Commons on 25 January. Apart from two very short spells of attendance, he had ignored parliament for over three years, since August 1842. He was now to devote himself to it for almost six months on end.

Happily, an ample justification for his about-face lay to hand. Partly because the agrarian crime rate had risen with the onset of distress in 1845 but also because of exaggerated fears that O'Connell's modest, county meetings of October were but the prelude to another massive agitation, Peel was preparing a draconian Irish coercion bill for the coming parliamentary session. O'Connell seized this opportunity. At a meeting of Irish Repeal and liberal MPs in Dublin, which he summoned on the eve of his departure for Westminster, he promised unremitting opposition in parliament to the threatened coercion. Such a programme was by no means the ideal basis for co-operation with Lord John Russell. Like most high whigs, Russell inclined instinctively towards any measure which promised to impose 'firm' government on Ireland. But their common interest in eventually displacing the

conservative ministry was sufficiently powerful for Russell to help
O'Connell at least to the extent of delaying the progress of Peel's bill –
thereby undercutting Peel's argument that its swift passage was, in
every sense, a matter of life and death.

It was of course always best to deal with the whigs from a position of
strength, and O'Connell used the occasion of a by-election for co.
Mayo to demonstrate his continued power in the constituencies. On 2
March 1846, after 'a fierce struggle', his Repeal nominee, J. M.
MacDonnell, defeated the strong liberal candidate G. H. Moore
(father of the novelist, George Moore), who was both popular locally
and a Catholic. O'Connell had called personally for support, contributed to the electoral expenses and, working through MacNicholas,
the bishop of Achonry, as well as MacHale of Tuam, enlisted the
clergy as his political agents. On 26 February 1846, Moore's mother
appealed to O'Connell

> in behalf of your fellow creatures in this country many of whom, unless you
> exert yourself, will probably become victims to the fury to which I lament
> to say the priests of our religion are exciting them . . . I do not attempt to
> interfere with your plans as to the representation of this county. All I
> implore of you is to use your influence with Doctors McHale and
> McNicholas to restrain those priests in their respective dioceses who seem
> so heedless of the consequence of their harangues . . .
>
> [Rev] Mr Coghlan, who has patronised Mr McDonnell in his speech at
> Swinford, says 'It is not in *tens* nor in *hundreds* but in *thousands* that you
> should go to the hustings and prevent anyone from voting for Moore.'
>
> Now, sir, it is not in *my* name that I address you but in the name of
> humanity that I implore you to put a stop to projects which, if carried [into]
> effect, must cause bloodshed . . .[33]

Clearly, the Repeal party had to strain every nerve in order to defeat
Moore; the margin was only seventy votes. 'It was a bold undertaking', O'Connell wrote later to MacHale, 'and would have been
fatal if unsuccessful. Your Grace's energy and all-commanding
influence, aided by the patriotic clergy, have achieved the most
valuable triumph for Ireland since the Clare election.'[34] Though this
last was a palpable exaggeration, it is an index of how seriously
O'Connell was now setting about the building up of leverage in
parliament. He himself participated regularly in the business of the
House of Commons throughout the spring of 1846, in pressing for
Irish famine relief, in the corn laws debates and, above all, in
combating Peel's coercion bill. He compelled a reluctant Maurice to
join him at Westminster, writing to him in Derrynane on 26 March,

'You must be here for the second reading of the Coercion Bill immediately after the Easter recess. It is impossible to dispense with your presence';[35] and he busied himself with arranging for the return of his youngest son Daniel at a forthcoming borough by-election. For the first time since leaving Richmond prison, his course seemed really set.

IV

Suddenly O'Brien ran athwart O'Connell's new strategy by another exercise in the politics of principle. On 3 April 1846 he refused to serve on a parliamentary committee, dealing with English railway business, to which he had been appointed. This move originated in a scheme which Davis had mooted, while the 'traversers' were imprisoned in 1844, that the Irish MPs should deliberately absent themselves from parliament in protest. Nothing came of it until, a year later, O'Brien and John O'Connell adopted modified forms of abstention from the Commons; but they did so too late in the summer session of 1845 for any counter-action to be practicable. O'Connell had warmly supported this demonstration; it broke the current political doldrums, if only feebly, and he persuaded himself, if no other constitutional lawyer, that the House of Commons had lost its controlling power over Irish MPs by the Act of Union. From the beginning of 1846, however, O'Connell had changed his tack completely. Parliamentary participation was now the order of the day. Accordingly, John O'Connell accepted committee membership, and O'Brien's adherence to the old resolution was, to say the least, embarrassing.

When O'Brien's contumacy was considered by the Commons on 28 April 1846, O'Connell pleaded that 'it was not the intention of his hon. Friend [Smith O'Brien] to be guilty of any contempt . . . He had merely acted from a mistaken feeling of his duty.'[36] John O'Connell, while praising O'Brien's highmindedness, argued that 'his services to Ireland would have been better rendered in still further opposing the Coercion Bill':[37] he himself had accepted committee membership lest he be rendered 'unable to oppose the Coercion Bill, which he regarded as a higher duty to Ireland'. O'Brien did not anticipate imprisonment for contempt. 'I cannot believe', he wrote to O'Connell in the course of a comparatively cordial discussion of tactics just before the debate, 'that the House will enter into a contention which must be attended with great inconvenience in regard to public business as well as to its results upon public feeling in Ireland. I therefore expect that a motion will be made without parade to substitute another member in my place on the Committee.'[38] Instead, however, he found himself confined in the Tower of London. The train of happenings which would rend the Repeal movement in two had started.

There were of course two views of O'Brien's stand. Like many of his fellow-countrymen, he saw himself as the champion of integrity and consistency, ready 'to encounter every personal hazard in giving effect to the resolve of the Irish nation'.[39] But devoted O'Connellites such as Steele spoke of him as the dupe 'of a perfidious clique, that sought . . . to make him their plastic instrument . . . through his own wayward personal impulses'.[40] As O'Brien could justly claim to have acted in accordance with a Repeal Association resolution of 1845, the real issue was the nature and breadth of O'Connell's authority. This became evident immediately. On 30 April 1846 Ray reported from Dublin to O'Connell:

There was a very warm discussion in committee today on Mr Smith O'Brien's affair . . . [with] a very full attendance of the *young men* evidently brought together from the circumstances.

Mr Doheny . . . after a flourishing preliminary harangue proposed that a vote should be passed at the [general Association] meeting on Monday [4 April] of sympathy with Mr O'Brien, of approbation of his conduct and of the determination of the Irish people to sustain him and also of their fullest confidence in him etc.

Mr [J. C.] Fitzpatrick, Barrister, opposed Doheny's views . . . He said that Ireland acknowledged you only as Leader, that Mr O'B[rien] had not acted in unison with you but, on the contrary, took an opposite course, that he did not then see how approving of the course in one case could be other than disapproving in the other . . .

I take it almost for granted that we will have a letter from you on Monday to guide us. As things are, it is absolutely necessary we should have your directions public or private as we all fear there will be division at the meeting on Monday.[41]

The meeting was certainly divided, but O'Brien's supporters were heavily outvoted when they proposed that the Association should endorse his defiance of the House of Commons. Evidently, O'Connell had instructed his lieutenants to oppose any move which might identify the Association with illegality, and thereby endanger its existence. Unquestionably, O'Connell feared charges of sedition. But equally, as his publicly expressed hope that O'Brien would soon return to combat the coercion bill made clear, he realized that his command of the Repeal movement was under challenge. As Martin Crean, the assistant secretary of the Association, observed to him after a meeting of the Young Ireland-dominated '82 Club held in Dublin on 9 May, 'I am diffident in giving *you* my opinion but it is my duty to say that the *open* and avowed drift of the majority at the meeting was to set up the "Golden [Calf]" in your stead.'

Although Crean ended his report by assuring O'Connell that 'the *people* will never submit' to the new idolatry,[42] popular support for O'Brien was already manifesting itself in certain places, and particularly in O'Brien's own constituency, Limerick. Repeal meetings in the city and Rathkeale on 9 and 10 May 1846 denounced the pusillanimity of the official policy, and the Rathkeale branch resolved to exclude the O'Connellite *Pilot* from its Reading Room because of its 'unmanly attempt . . . to asperse and misrepresent the conduct of William S. O'Brien'.[43] The Limerick trades went so far as to raise the banner of possible insurrection when they declared that O'Brien would remain true to his pledges 'even if it were necessary to lead his fellow-countrymen to the field in defence of the trampled liberties and prostrated constitution of Ireland'.[44] In all, a considerable proportion of the Limerick activists were moving towards secession from the Association – interestingly, with some priestly support, for O'Brien's imprisonment was precisely the sort of personal suffering to evoke clerical sympathy. To a lesser degree, the same tendencies began to show themselves in other large provincial centres, Cork, Kilkenny and Clonmel.

O'Connell had to deal with all this at a distance, at least three days away in communication-time, and through agents fearful of acting on their own initiative. He was careful, in his public letters, to write no word of disparagement of O'Brien; privately, too, he instructed his Dublin supporters 'not [to] take any part against' him.[45] At the same time, he made it quite clear, though only by implication, that O'Brien's was the mistaken strategy, or at least inferior to that of maintaining the struggle against the coercion bill in the House of Commons. In masterly fashion, he undermined the Young Irelanders' emotional appeals by organizing, through the parochial clergy, a series of petitions against O'Brien's imprisonment. O'Brien's supporters were infuriated, for the 'principle' of his stand was totally ignored; and there were arguments and scuffles at various chapel doors. But O'Connell had chosen his ground well: the petitions (he presented over 200 in all to the Commons) channelled much of the compassionate feeling which the affair had aroused into his own rather than the Young Ireland ranks.

O'Connell certainly suffered from the fact that his was patently the 'unmanly' position; he was abasing himself before instead of defying the British parliament. None the less, it was he who held the master-cards. First, none of his opponents dared as yet an outright challenge to his leadership, and secondly none of them wished to abandon or be driven from the Repeal Association which (the wide circulation of the *Nation* notwithstanding) remained their principal platform and source of influence. It was noteworthy that at both the committee and the general meetings of the Association during May 1846 the Young Irelanders invariably retreated when either O'Connell's authority or the illegality of what they proposed was made the specific issue. Even the most candid and reckless of them, T. F. Meagher, did not fight on after Doheny's motion was replaced by an anodyne resolution of sympathy on 4 May. 'Young Meagher', Ray reported to O'Connell after the next general meeting on 11 May,

> opened a speech, brilliant as usual, by reference to the resolution passed last day which he said he thought fell short of what the Association felt but still perhaps it was the more safe and legal. T. Steele took his opportunity to refer to Meagher's expression and took advantage of its proceeding *from Meagher*. He said that the course taken by the Association had your full approval of its indispensable caution.[46]

Correspondingly, O'Brien himself, despite his anger at his 'abandon-ment' by O'Connell, decided to use him to raise in the Commons on 22 May 1846 a technical argument (that the committee of selection had been improperly constituted) against his imprisonment. 'I have no hesitation therefore', he wrote to O'Connell early that day, 'in saying that I prefer to owe my discharge to you than to him [unknown] . . . It is . . . of the utmost importance not to me alone but to "Ireland and Repeal" that every possible effort should be made to obtain a successful debate and division tonight.'[47] O'Connell's motion failed, but this mattered little practically, as the Commons discharged O'Brien – *ex gratia* – before the week was out.

It might have seemed as if reconciliation rather than rupture between the two was on the way. But the tide of general politics ran in an adverse direction. By the beginning of June 1846 it was becoming clear that the days of Peel's ministry were numbered, and the whig-liberals likely to succeed him soon in office. In terms of his own objectives, O'Connell's strategy had been vindicated. The corn laws would shortly be repealed, thereby destroying (in the eyes of all members of the Commons except his own faction within the conservative party) the *raison d'être* of Peel's premiership. Meanwhile, the Irish coercion bill had been fatally delayed. It was now likely that the whigs, tempted by the prospect of a return to power, and the tory protectionists, eager for vengeance on their 'betrayer', Peel, would combine with O'Connell and the Repeal and radical MPs to defeat it at the third reading. All this foreshadowed an imminent change of government and a new ministry dependent on O'Connell's support. A fresh 'whig alliance' – though O'Connell dared not formally shelve Repeal or admit that he intended the record of 1835–41 to be replayed – was stealing over the horizon.

The Young Irelanders attempted a pre-emptive strike against the threatened entente. On 13 June 1846 the *Nation* published no less than three articles denouncing the rumoured alliance of O'Connell and the whigs, and two days later the brilliant Meagher led a similar attack at the weekly general meeting of the Association. As Crean reported to O'Connell,

> The Young Irelanders mustered strong (as their small number will allow) at the meeting to-day. Young Meagher made a long speech in the course of which he said that suspicions were abroad that Repeal would be sacrificed for Whig patronage and in allusion to Davis he said '*we* looked upon him as our leader and our prophet'. In reply Tom Steele took exception to that phrase in particular and called on Meagher to explain if he meant by 'we' the people of Ireland, [and] that if he did [whether] the people repudiated any leader but 'O'Connell.'[48]

It was said later that 'when the fascination of Meagher's speech was off the meeting were entirely against' the Young Irelanders.[49] At any rate, all of them, including Meagher, retreated when confronted with the question, were they disputing O'Connell's leadership? Next day Ray told O'Connell that, in private conversation, Mitchel had tried to 'explain away' Meagher's 'malevolent' speech. 'He appeared to me', Ray continued, 'very anxious to disengage himself and his party from the imputation of any disrespect towards you. We [Ray and Steele] asked him upon what were the speeches and *Nation* articles founded? Confessedly on rumours in the Tory journals adopted by them; and who had power to make any compromise? as they said – but his pretexts were too shallow.'[50]

Meanwhile O'Connell had decided to put an end to this game of tip-and-run. Although the letter is not extant, it was probably on or about 11 June 1846 that he informed his Dublin lieutenants of his intention. 'In obedience to your desire', Crean responded on 15 June, 'I communicated the purport of your letter to *your friends*. They are delighted at your determination to put down this most mischievous knot',[51] and Steele wrote on the 16th that it had 'given your own Old-Ireland people joy beyond measure that on your return [to Dublin] you intend putting these scamps in their proper position'.[52] It seems likely that the impending change in government was largely responsible for O'Connell's decision to act: bargaining with the whigs would be very difficult if there were still an unchallenged and, in effect, 'licensed' opposition to any such move within the Association. But other factors may have weighed with him, as well. He was genuinely afraid that the current Young Ireland rhetoric might lead to the suppression of the Association. Even references to the 'illegality' of the House of Commons' proceedings against Smith O'Brien seemed dangerous, and were in fact deleted by Ray when presenting correspondence to a general meeting. But it was deviations from the Association's principle of strictly peaceful agitation which alarmed O'Connell most – in addition to providing him with his chosen ground for action. Mitchel's original anticipation, in November 1845, of the possible use of force had been since capped by similar oratorical excursions in the course of protests against O'Brien's confinement in the Tower. Doheny's declaration at a meeting of the Liverpool Repealers on 17 May that there were times when 'the strength of man, contending for principle, must be decided by the issue of his own blood' was probably the most disturbing, as it was delivered by a member of the executive committee to a regular branch meeting of the Association.[53] It was easy to envisage Dublin Castle using such a flourish as the ground for proclaiming the organization. Again O'Connell may well have been influenced by hostile reactions to the coat-trailing of the Young Ireland group. Early in June 1846 Dr Magennis, parish priest of Clones, co. Monaghan, wrote to the secretary of the Association:

> I am desirous to tell you with a view of having it communicated to the Liberator and his worthy sons that should this infidel and unprincipled *Young Ireland party* continue to retain their wonted airs of impudent domination, I and every priest and every layman in this vast diocese [Clogher] with the bishop at their head will relinquish all connection with the Association and hold correspondence only with the three I have mentioned.[54]

While Crean's covering observation to O'Connell that Magennis expressed 'the almost unanimous opinions of the clergy of Ireland' was an exaggeration,[55] there could be no doubt that the Church as a whole was rapidly aligning itself against Young Ireland. This was in part a clerical reflection of O'Connell's own changing attitude; but as it developed it presented him with an additional temptation to strike down Young Ireland while the conditions remained favourable.

O'Connell's first move was the dispatch of an open letter from London to the Association on 18 June condemning 'the efforts [of] . . . some of our juvenile members to create dissension', and denying absolutely that the Repeal cause would be 'abandoned, postponed or compromised', even if the whigs came to power: he trusted that this forthright declaration would take away 'some clap-traps from juvenile orators'.[56] It does seem to have left them cowed – outside the columns of the *Nation*, at any rate. Ray reported that they made no difficulties at the general meetings of the Association on 22 and 29 June 1846. 'I think you will have no further trouble with the Young Irelanders', he told O'Connell on 29 June, 'They see clearly that you are determined to follow up the blow.'[57] And O'Connell did follow up the blow, by returning to Dublin in time for the Association's committee meeting of 11 July – Russell having meanwhile succeeded Peel as prime minister. O'Connell bluntly proposed both the formal confirmation of several earlier resolutions rejecting the use of physical force, and the adoption of a fresh statement which concluded, 'We emphatically announce our conviction that all political amelioration, and the first and highest of all – the Repeal of the Union – ought to be sought for, and can be sought for successfully, only by peaceable, legal, and constitutional means, to the utter exclusion of any other.'[58] To allow his opponents no loophole, O'Connell declared 'the principles of the Association to be the utter & total disclaimer of the contemplation of physical force'.[59] Although Mitchel and Meagher demurred, the remainder of the committee voted obediently for O'Connell's motion. The way was now clear for him to present the same declaration to the general meeting of the Association held two days later. Again he triumphed; only three voices were raised in even qualified opposition, and Meagher was the sole dissenter when O'Connell's motion was put to the meeting, and carried with acclamation. Again O'Connell had left no room for equivocation. He told the meeting that he had so phrased his resolution as 'to draw a marked line between Young Ireland and Old Ireland', and that it specifically required members of the Association to eschew the abstract principle as well as the actual practice of violence.[60]

Having apparently secured his rear, O'Connell returned to London and the business of attempting to influence the shape and direction of Russell's new government. On the surface, he had carried the day with ease by the brutal use of his own 'moral force' – his accumulated authority and habit of command. It was certainly a dextrous and audacious political display by a man almost seventy-one years old. He had dared his 'juvenile' critics to defy him as arbiter of the Repeal Association, and only Meagher had had the final hardihood to do so. He had implicitly challenged Smith O'Brien to choose his side in the affair, and O'Brien, still anxious to avoid an open breach with O'Connell, had absented himself from the critical meetings. O'Connell had chosen his issue with great skill, presenting his opponents as the wanton and dangerous innovators who would sacrifice a formidable movement for a 'principle' which they themselves declared had no bearing on the present or even (so far as they then could see) the future. On the field of battle he had simply rolled them up.

V

The *casus belli* chosen by O'Connell was, however, a mere fragment of the Young Ireland case against him. They had, as R. B. McDowell puts it, 'the advantage of being political puritans'.[61] They loathed what they saw as O'Connell's lack of sensibility, vulgar oratory, coarse populism, financial chicanery, truckling to British enemies and clerical friends, love of sycophants, use of creatures to control the Association, jobbery, duplicity and outworn values. None of these had been conjured away by his triumphs of 11–13 July. It is true that, however willing to wound, the Young Irelanders were yet afraid to strike. In a sense, O'Connell had by now realized his boyhood ambition to be the Father of his Country. At least, he was its father-figure; and for the present no one – not even Meagher – was prepared to disobey a solemn and specific parental order, to be cast adrift in a world without known bearings. But the rebellion was almost ripe; and O'Connell's renewed absence from Dublin from mid-July onwards would prove emboldening.

It should be remembered that, from O'Connell's standpoint, his visit to Dublin to suppress Young Ireland was a mere, if necessary, interruption of his principal task – to secure a more favourable Irish administration and legislative programme from the whigs. On 30 June he had informed O'Brien that he regularly told Russell's emissaries 'that they [the new government] must not only leave the Repeal question open, reinstate all the magistrates [dismissed as members of the Association in 1843] but govern Ireland by Irishmen'.[62] This last

was O'Connell's most important immediate concern. He appears to
have had a private hand in the appointment of Baron Brady as lord
chancellor, of J. J. Murphy as master of chancery, of his friend D. R.
Pigot as chief baron of the exchequer, of another friend O'Conor Don
as lord of the treasury and perhaps also of Sheil as lord of the mint.
Covertly he strove to secure the return of the Irish liberals who had
been raised to office by Russell, and hence required re-election. His
leading success, in the teeth of Young Ireland protests, was the
securing of a clear run for Sheil. 'I have stifled all opposition to Sheil at
Dungarvan', he told Pigot, 'The election will not cost him a shilling,
and that is what he likes.' He had to play other constituencies warily. 'I
have been working in an under channel' in Clonmel, he reported
(again to Pigot), for the return of J. H. Monahan, the prospective Irish
solicitor-general. He was not prepared, however, to allow Redington,
the newly appointed Irish under-secretary, to fill the vacant borough
of Dundalk. Not only had Redington been too outspoken an anti-
Repealer, but also O'Connell's youngest son, Daniel, was already
interested in this constituency. 'I have difficulties enough to
encounter', he confessed, 'to keep the Repeal party within bounds
without having those difficulties augmented, even in my domestic
circle.'[63] But the most important objective of all was to prevent the
nomination of a Young Irelander for any of the seats. Even before his
excursion to Dublin, he had written to his local mainstay, Edmond
Smithwick,

> Kilkenny [county] must return a Repealer, and I cannot possibly permit it
> to return either a Tory or Whig or an animal more mischievous than either
> of the others, called a Young Irelander . . . Nothing could afflict me more
> than any leaning to Meagher after his recent misconduct. I really think him
> more dangerous than that undermining fellow – Doheny.[64]

O'Connell's attempt to practise a spoils system through sympathetic
intermediaries by no means stopped short at high judicial and political
office. On 8 July 1846, he had enlisted Pigot's aid to arrange the lower
as well as the upper end of the scale satisfactorily. 'There are details',
he wrote,

> which will contribute much to the popularity of the new Government. I
> mean the appointment, under the Castle, of tradesmen, &c. Hitherto they
> have been almost uniformly violent Orangemen who have got those
> appointments. These things may be thought trivial: they are not so. They
> go much farther, sink more deeply than you imagine. Then it may be said to
> be liberality to leave these persons in their present situations. It is a kind of

liberality that has never been exercised towards the Catholic tradesmen; and whenever an opportunity arose, there never was a more bitter *selector* of Orangeists than that miserable Lord Heytesbury.

I do implore of you, have this matter recommended in the proper quarter, whatever it be, and do have it attended to promptly and distinctly.[65]

Concurrently, O'Connell publicized the Irish measures which he wished the whig administration to adopt. These were familiar: parliamentary reform (of constituencies, franchise and registration), local government reform (of the municipal corporations and grand juries) land reform (in favour of improving tenants and tenants-at-will and punitive of absentee landlords) and an amendment of the Colleges Act. There was nothing immoderate or surprising in this latest Justice for Ireland catalogue, except perhaps the omission of any further design against the Church of Ireland and the inclusion of the university issue, which parliament had settled so recently and with such difficulty. These appear however to have been the nub of the matter for O'Connell at the moment. 'I do not hesitate', he told Russell (through his intermediary, Pigot) on 12 July 1846, 'to place the question of the Protestant church in abeyance but then something must be done respecting education and touching the "*Infidel*" Colleges before Parliament rises.'[66] Who could wonder at the Young Irelanders' outrage when they saw or guessed the true effects, the actual consequences, of O'Connell's continued 'adherence' to the 'principles' of Repeal and independence of the British ministry?

From the standpoint of the *Nation* group, the key to the situation was Smith O'Brien. The *Nation* attempted to save itself by a sort of deathbed moderation. Duffy wrote in its columns on 18 July 1846,

in the fiery enthusiasm of '43 good men may have thought – did think – that a time was at hand when this country would negotiate best . . . with arms in hand . . . [But] it would be the blindest folly to dream that any means but opinion are within our grasp [now]. We rely on no other. We believe in no other as applicable in the smallest degree to our time and condition.[67]

But O'Connell had already determined to disengage the Association completely from the newspaper, and *within* the Association the Young Irelanders felt impotent without an established national leader to command them. O'Brien was pressed hard on either side. O'Connell made his expectations clear when he wrote to O'Brien, also on 18 July, that it is impossible for me to act with any of the avowed Young Irelanders unless they retract their physical force opinions altogether and submit to the resolutions of the Association. Whilst those resolutions stand approved by all the Committee except two and by the entire meeting of the Association (with only one exception) I am for strictly adhering to them. If they be wrong in anything let them be altered or amended in the usual way; but, until changed by the same authority that passed them, I for one do not think I go too far in requiring the Young Irelanders candidly to adopt them or to cease to cooperate with us.[68]

Meanwhile, Duffy told O'Brien that he had failed his supporters by absenting himself from the fateful general meeting of the Association of 13 July. 'One and all, they [the men to be attacked] believe that, having got into this battle in your defence, you left them, when a crisis came, to take care of themselves.'[69] Slowly, it would seem, O'Brien came to a determination to resist O'Connell's fiat. On 28–9 July, at the first general meeting of the Association which he attended after O'Connell's *coup*, the issue of physical as against moral force was raised again. The ensuing conflict carries the air of a set-piece, as if each party had attempted to pre-arrange its actions and reactions. Meagher, in the course of a scintillating address glorifying armed resistance, was silenced by John O'Connell, from the chair, as in breach of the test of membership of the Association laid down by O'Connell on 15 July. O'Brien protested hotly in the name of liberty of speech. Next Meagher attempted to resume his oration only to be ruled out of order once again. O'Brien then led the chief Young Irelanders and 'a section of the meeting who followed and applauded them' from the hall.[70] The secession had come at last.

The scanty evidence which survives suggests that O'Connell was unperturbed by this denouement. He may well have been relieved, or even satisfied that he achieved his end. Certainly, he would now be free of open rows and dissension within his movement, and free both to secure the political succession for his son John and to bargain with the whigs to best advantage. He had the warmest backing of the Catholic Church in general, and of his own episcopal faction in particular. Cantwell rejoiced in the breach, pronouncing the 'physical force' adherents to 'be regardless of their duty as Christians'; O'Higgins declared proudly that 'we have no physical force men in this diocese [Ardagh]. Neither have we, thank God, any schoolboy philosophers, false and sanguinary Repealers or Voltarian newspapers.'[71] Dr Cane of Kilkenny, long a sympathizer with Young Ireland, warned Duffy:

The priests generally will rejoice to hear you are laid prostrate, and all who abide by their views and follow in their track will echo their sentiments. This is an immense power you have to encounter; and any public meeting anywhere in Ireland, would by its majority rule against you, and with the Association.[72]

Finally, the seceders made no move to set up a counter-organization and O'Brien showed no desire to challenge O'Connell for the national leadership, or even to put himself at the head of the schismatics. Thus O'Connell probably counted himself a net gainer. He had re-attained an obedient – if smaller and shrinking – mass following, and re-awakened clerical – if no other – enthusiasm. The loss of talent, fire and idealism would not have weighed greatly with him. After all, that old and trusty indicator, the Repeal Rent, told him that he was right: the average return almost trebled in the weeks immediately following 29 July 1846.

Beneath the bewildering complexity of stands and shifts in the fourteen months between the original public quarrel between Davis and O'Connell and the final public quarrel between the champions of Young and Old Ireland, one simple pattern is discernible. O'Connell was moving back steadily to the parliamentary method, and, with it, to concern with increasing the numbers and effectiveness of the Repeal party in the House of Commons and, ultimately, helping the whigs back to power. This surely meant that conflict with not only the *Nation* group and its sympathizers but also Smith O'Brien himself was inescapable. The wonder, if any, is that the rupture came so late.

CHAPTER 24

The Dying Fall

1846–7

I

When he returned to Ireland from Westminster early in August 1846 O'Connell may have supposed that another cycle of modest, informal power-sharing was beginning. From Dublin, where he spent the next five weeks, he cannonaded Russell, directly or indirectly, with requests, demands and pleas. He asked, for example, for a peerage for Lord de Freyne's younger brother (so that a 'Catholic' title would not die out), for the reinstatement of the Repeal magistrates dismissed in 1843 and the advancement of various minor officials including six chancery court clerks. He even sought the promotion of his own son Morgan in the registry of deeds. He had persuaded the registrar, Moore, to retire early in order to make way for Morgan, and looked to Pigot to arrange the substitution. 'If you think it has the least appearances of a job', O'Connell added, 'I do not press it in the slightest degree. It seems to me to be nothing more than to allow an officer of forty-eight years' service to retire without personal loss.'[1] Pigot concurred, and Morgan duly became registrar.

This pattern was repeated in much larger matters. On 10 August 1846 O'Connell wrote to Pigot, 'for heaven's sake get rid of the arms Bill or mitigate it exceedingly – no branding'.[2] Three days later he issued another frenzied appeal, 'It gives an irritating topic to your enemies in this city and in the country generally. If possible, get rid of it. *At all events*, get rid of as much as you can of it, especially the branding [clause].'[3] The government proved compliant. The entire bill, proposing to renew an Act against which O'Connell had been inveighing for two years, was dropped almost immediately. On 12 August he begged Russell himself to act at once to counter the effects of blight, now manifest again in co. Cork. O'Connell argued that

the forms of the law and of constitutional guarantees must yield to the pressure of a death-dealing famine. And I also submit whether her Majesty's Government may not feel, at such an awful crisis, it right to consider whether Parliament might not, either by a vote or by a short bill, confer upon the Government extraordinary powers of directing, *without any delay*, the execution of works of public utility and of supplying the immediate means of paying the wages of the labourers employed at such works.[4]

Again the governmental response was favourable. On 17 August 1846, without a division in the House, Russell carried a resolution that £450,000 be made available for public works in Ireland. Meanwhile throughout August 1846 O'Connell had been manoeuvring to secure a candidate for the Clonmel by-election who was both formally a Repealer and a friend to accommodation with the whigs, and found him at last in the liberal Hon. Cecil Lawless, who joined the Association at the eleventh hour. In due course Lawless was returned, unopposed, though the deal itself bordered on the scandalous.

Thus, O'Connell's brokerage brought in a small but steady political revenue at first. Although Russell might declare that he favoured non-Repealers for preferment, Dublin Castle, under the lord lieutenancy of O'Connell's old friend, Duncannon (now the Earl of Bessborough), was anxious to placate him whenever possible, in the belief that his influence alone stood between it and serious disorder. But O'Connell was grossly mistaken if he concluded from this that he had succeeded, in effect, in putting back the clock ten years, and essentially restored the conditions and relationships of 1836. First, he was now encountering, for the first time in his political career, a systematic and continuous nationalist critique of his policies and conduct and a coherent and growing opposition to his type and use of leadership. This is not to say that Irish middle-class 'juvenility' was ranged against him *en bloc*. Almost as many of the young Catholic and liberal Protestant bourgeoisie had supported as resisted him in the Association. *Pace* the cynical observation that the 1848 Revolutions were really about jobs in the civil service, the young men of the mid-1840s, whether O'Brienite or O'Connellite, generally ended up as successful public servants, politicians, judges, journalists, lawyers, doctors or engineers. None the less, it was the Young Irelanders who dominated in their generation, especially in tongue, pen, vision and fervour. Forty years before, O'Connell had been foremost of the foremost in just such a thrusting forward of the ardent young. His role reversal was politically expensive as well as most painful to consider.

Secondly, O'Connell's physical strength was failing. It is difficult to say precisely how and when his decline in health became precipitous. Evidently, he went downhill badly in the course of his usual autumn retreat (September–October) at Derrynane. Soon after he reached Kerry he wrote of the pain he suffered as signifying 'the breaking up of [my] constitution'.[5] O'Neill Daunt was shocked by the bodily deterioration in O'Connell when he met him again in Dublin at the beginning of November 1846:

> I was greatly struck with the physical decay of O'Connell. I had not seen him in public for many months, and the change was painfully manifest. His intellect was as strong as ever, but his voice was extremely weak. How different were his faint and feeble accents from the stirring trumpet tones in which I had heard him, on the banks of the Boyne in 1840, rallying the Repealers of Drogheda around him! I doubt if he could now be heard six yards off.[6]

Even the faithful Steele admitted, about the same time, 'It is sad to contemplate the vast difference between the O'Connell of 1843 and the O'Connell of 1846.'[7] O'Connell assured Fitzpatrick that he could still make himself audible if he chose, that 'he purposely economizes his vocal powers'.[8] But in fact he would never again be heard by the Irish masses: the agitator-general was dead already.

Finally, the times were out of joint, politically. As Nowlan notes, 'Had there been no failure of the potato crop for a second time in the autumn of 1846, the course of political development in Ireland might well have confirmed the victory O'Connell appeared to have won in 1846. But that second and, as it proved, total failure of the crop had a most disturbing effect on political calculations.'[9] Russell and his cabinet failed to grasp the magnitude of the calamity – in fact, Russell told O'Connell on 14 August 1846 that he inferred from the paucity of Irish harvest labourers in Britain 'that they found employment in their own country'![10] In any event, the whigs were in general inhibited by their economic and social preconceptions from embarking on state expenditure and intervention to anything like the degree called for by the Irish crisis. As this crisis deepened, O'Connell seemed, more and more, to have backed the wrong horse, so far as both Irish necessity and Irish opinion were concerned. With all this, there would certainly be no return to the prosperous liberal partnership of the preceding decade.

II

On his arrival in Dublin, O'Connell had immediately grasped the significance of the already widespread second blight. Only nine days later he told Russell that the people of Cork 'are not merely menaced but actually engulfed' by starvation, and that 'there is the greatest danger of outbreaks . . . of the population driven to despair from the want of food'.[11] Instinctively, he slipped into the part of responsible landlord, which was to be his predominant approach to the Irish situation during his remaining months of life. On 27 August he pressed Maurice, at Derrynane, to make provision 'to meet the coming emergencies' on the estate, in particular, to store 'Indian corn' and 'American saved beef', which was 'cheap and good and would make excellent rations occasionally for the labourers'.[12] O'Connell's first-hand experience of the distress, when he reached Derrynane for his long vacation, increased his apprehension. After three weeks there, he told Fitzpatrick, 'It would be the absurdest of all absurd things to think of a Tribute in such times as these. They are indeed more awful than you have any notion of. All our thoughts are engrossed with the two topics – endeavouring to keep the people from outbreaks and endeavouring to get food for them. I tell you danger is in our path.'[13] Meanwhile O'Connell used his political weight on behalf of the suffering peasantry of Iveragh. Finding that the necessary public works sanctioned at the baronial presentments for the locality under the new Labour Rate Act had not begun because of administrative delays, and that by bureaucratic ineptitude the government meal depot for the area had been fixed at the impossibly distant Dingle, he put successful pressure on the new chief secretary, Henry Labouchere, to get wages and food moving at last towards the necessitous. So much was O'Connell caught up in the role of humane proprietor that he not only continued to demand a tax upon absentee landlords but also, on 25 September 1846, mooted the idea of joint action by the resident Irish gentry. The famine had become 'so all-absorbing a subject as to banish all politics unconnected with the distress'.[14] A fortnight later, he issued a public call for the formation of 'a central body of Irish landholders meeting in Dublin, and conferring with all parts of Ireland, as well as with the government'.[15] His prime objective was the extension of the provisions of the Labour Rate Act to reproductive works (that is, works benefitting individuals) instead of unreproductive only. Perhaps because of O'Connell's pressure, Bessborough, quite suddenly, allowed the extension. Thereupon O'Connell withdrew from his own initiative – prematurely as things turned out, for the new scheme was practically unworkable. At this stage, he was determined, almost to the point of obsession, to work hand-in-hand with both government and fellow-landlords rather than by mass-action, let alone agitation. In agreeing, on 13 October 1846, to a meeting at Fermoy with some of the co. Cork gentry, clergy and relief committee representatives, he wrote, 'It is scarcely necessary for me to add that my arrival in Fermoy should not be accompanied by any popular demonstration. Our meeting will be constituted by gentlemen of every sect and persuasion and of course should not be tinged by anything of a party or even a political nature.'[16] After he and the remainder of the Fermoy deputation, bearing their list of complaints and applications, had seen Bessborough and his officials on 30 October, O'Connell even expressed sympathy with the administrators of relief who had so many difficulties to contend with!

As befitted one 'standing above' party, O'Connell's range of favour-seekers extended far beyond his customary clientele during the autumn of 1846. He continued to advance his own family in a minor way, asking that Maurice be restored to the deputy-lieutenancy of co. Kerry and that his 'clansman and very dear friend',[17] Jeremiah O'Connell, receive the commission of the peace. Other applications for unknown young men were imperative because of their source. When his well-tried episcopal supporter, Browne, called on 'the father of our country' to seek an assistant barristership for 'the son-in-law of one of my oldest and dearest friends',[18] O'Connell could not but respond. Old Irelanders such as William O'Connell or Thomas Arkins pressed him to find government employment for their sons; he helped to secure a lunacy commission inspectorate for his family friend and personal physician, Dr John Nugent; and rank-and-file Repealers enlisted his aid to secure humble jobs at the disposal of the Post Office or Dublin Castle. But he was equally energetic on behalf of the sons of liberal or whig friends, or even tories. A Church of Ireland minister, a neighbour in Kerry, called confidently for his help in securing the transfer of a living, 'It strikes me now that you are on the spot [in Dublin], that an application from you to the Government would have a good effect.'[19] O'Connell also went to great pains to get an extended leave of absence for R. G. MacDonnell, the Chief Justice of Gambia, solely because of his friendship for his father, 'an old circuit companion of mine ... though ... a Protestant Parson and ... a wicked anti-Repealer'. In pressing this case on the colonial under-secretary, O'Connell concluded, 'You cannot imagine how much you would gratify and delight me if you could assist this young gentleman in his purposes. It will be conferring a great personal obligation upon me.'[20]

Thus O'Connell made little attempt to operate an informal spoils system – except to exclude from office, so far as he was able, Young Irelanders and malignant Orangemen. He openly welcomed the appointments of sympathetic non-Repealers (particularly Catholics) and lauded the government which advanced them. In O'Connell's eyes, at this point in the political cycle, each such appointment was regarded as an advance, however small, towards national self-government rather than the shameful acceptance of a whig douceur. 'It was said', he declared at the general Association meeting of 3 August,

> that there were a great many young men of talent – Repealers in principle – but who were afraid to join the Association lest they should thereby deprive themselves of the chance of obtaining the honors and dignities of their professions. (Hear, hear.) ... Ought we not all be delighted that an opportunity should be given to such men to come amongst us? Ought we not to be grateful to the government that gives it, as we ought to vituperate the government that refuses it?[21]

Contrariwise, the seceders were denounced. 'Talk to me of the paltry Young Ireland party – faugh! There is only one man among them whose loss I regret – that is Smith O'Brien.'[22] Throughout August 1846 O'Connell attempted – publicly – to woo O'Brien back. But the condition which he laid down for the prodigal's return, unreserved concurrence 'in the principles of moral force and moral force alone',[23] seemed simultaneously to present a bar to its ever taking place. Moreover, O'Connell introduced another apple of discord when on 31 August he secured a resolution from the Association withdrawing Repeal Reading Room subscriptions to the *Nation*. Quoting recent editorials envisaging the use of physical force and constitutional separation from Great Britain, he added that

> whoever seeks to repeal a law by force – whoever incites to the use of physical force for such a purpose, is in point of law guilty of high treason. It would be most culpable in me, as counsel for the Association and people of Ireland, to enter into any compromise with the men who hold and preach up those physical force doctrines.
> They were guilty of no overt act, to be sure, and I am glad of it – they only endeavoured to incite others.[24]

That was the end of the malcontents so far as O'Connell was concerned: he now felt quite free to play the statesman.

For a considerable time, the Young Irelanders accepted the situation at O'Connell's valuation. They remained politically inert for more than two months after their withdrawal from Conciliation Hall. In fact, the first move on their behalf came not from any member of the inner group, but from Cane of Kilkenny who on 26 September wrote to Ray proposing that O'Connell make an attempt to win back the secessionists: the breach with Young Ireland, he believed, would ultimately destroy the Repeal movement. Cane was curtly dismissed by the Association's management; and no one in the *Nation* group followed up his initiative or took any step either to counter, or come to terms with, O'Connell until late October 1846. They seemed content to adopt the proposal, which O'Brien had made earlier to Duffy that 'a portion of the *Nation* [be] dedicated to ... propaganda ... with the bold heading "Young Ireland" over its leading column'.[25]

Once again however the terrific consequences of the Irish potato blight turned the course of events. From late September onwards, rapidly rising food prices and unemployment rates in the cities drove numbers of artisans and urban labourers into revolt against an Association now calling (against John O'Connell's and probably O'Connell's own better judgment) for 'PATIENCE, PEACE, AVOIDANCE OF CRIME, CONFIDENCE IN ALMIGHTY GOD, AND RESIGNATION TO HIS HOLY WILL'.[26] The most dangerous manifestation of insubordination was probably a Dublin 'remonstrance' presented to (but ignominiously rejected by) the Association on 26 October 1846, protesting against not only the suppression of free speech on the peace issue, but also O'Connell's collaboration with the whigs. Although the Old Irelander Arkins might dismiss the movers of the remonstrance as 'the low chartists and discontented of Dublin',[27] and Ray describe them as 'an assemblage of obscure creatures not half a dozen of whom do we know',[28] at least one-third of the Repeal wardens of the city were among the signatories. Meanwhile similar outbursts took place in Cork and Limerick during October, often with angry interchanges between the protestors and loyal O'Connellites. These may well have been an additional reason for O'Connell's insistence that his return progress from Derrynane to Dublin in late October be treated as a 'private' journey.

How was O'Connell to react to the implicit pressure, which all this contained, to seek a reconciliation with the Young Irelanders? The received account (mainly *per* Duffy) is of a faltering old man, in Dublin once again in November 1846, so impressed by the growing strength of the opposition as to sanction an approach to O'Brien and his friends – only to have his scheme dashed cruelly by his son John. Duffy 'quoted' an anonymous 'eye-witness' of the crucial scene as to O'Connell's final utterance, 'You see, Sir Colman [O'Loghlen], I am powerless; there is my best beloved son; you hear what he has said; nothing can now be done.'[29] It is true that O'Connell's immediate entourage was fiercely opposed to a *détente*, although John O'Connell did not speak quite so intransigently as Ray or Crean. But others of O'Connell's close friends, such as the much-respected O'Loghlen, were generally bent on reconciliation. Even O'Neill Daunt asked Smith O'Brien privately on 14 October 1846, 'is there no mode in which you can arrange your difference with Mr O'C[onnell], so as to work once more in the Conciliation Hall? . . . If you can manage to fulfil (as I trust and think you can) the earnest popular wish [that you do so], pray command me in any way in which I could aid in achieving a reunion.'[30] Moreover, O'Connell was well aware of the local pressures being placed on his supporters. In late November, for example, the parish priest of Kilkee, co. Clare, in recommending a young man spoke of him as still adhering to 'the old and experienced *pilot*' though 'strongly prompted by different influences to join the Young Ireland party'.[31] Thus, O'Connell was being pulled not in one but in two directions by his trusted followers. There seems no reason to believe that he was materially influenced by either section. In fact, there is no worthwhile evidence at all that he was as yet either incapable of or unwilling to form his own judgment, or that, until late November 1846, he ever wavered in his determination to ignore the secessionists and protesters.

On 20 November, however, one of O'Connell's most steadfast Repeal bishops, Blake of Dromore, intervened with an appeal for unity which could not be ignored. Blake's first letter (to O'Connell initially but meant to be read aloud later to the Association) has not survived; but its substance may be inferred from O'Connell's reply: 'Such a letter, coming from you and making light of the difference between us and the seceders, would be considered by the public and made use of by the seceders as an approval of their physical-force principles; as an approval, in short, of the illegality and treasonable nature of their principles.' O'Connell assured Blake that there was

no practicable sacrifice that I would not make for the purpose of reconciliation . . . But there are things which I cannot do, and which you are certainly the last man living to advise me to do, namely, to sacrifice principle and to risk and put in jeopardy the liberties and even the lives of all the members of the Association.

The point hinges upon this. We, the sincere Repealers, have placed the basis of our exertions on this: the carrying the Repeal by peaceable, legal and constitutional means and by *none other*. The seceders, on the contrary, insist that, in case we do not succeed by peaceable and legal means, we should reserve to ourselves the use in any favourable opportunity of the sword.

Now, my venerated Lord, I solemnly, as a lawyer of many years' standing, assure your Lordship, with the most perfect truth, that the plan of the seceders would, if we were to accede to or even tolerate it in the Association, involve every member of the Association, including your Lordship, in the guilt of high treason.[32]

O'Connell's consistency is worth noting here. For fully a year, ever since Mitchel's original 'indiscretion' of November 1845, he had held unwaveringly to the line that any endorsement, however remote or contingent, of physical force would destroy the Repeal organization. Moreover, he had always argued, the slightest countenancing of violence in Ireland would set in motion a process which could only end in blood.

Blake responded to O'Connell's desperate plea to withdraw his letter ('If I were in your presence, I would go on my knees to ask this favour'[33]) by substituting a milder version. Even this, however, called on O'Connell

to heal those dissensions which distract, and afflict, and strike with dismay *the public mind*: and I hope that all *sincere* Repealers – and they are still very many, even *among the seceders* – will, ... meet your efforts for *reconciliation*, as acts of condescension on your part, and when re-entered into Conciliation Hall, will not only adhere inviolably to your peaceable course ... but will also strenuously ... second your glorious efforts.[34]

Such strong pressure called for some response from O'Connell, all the more so as, by now, the pitiful inadequacy of the government's efforts to halt the spread of disease and starvation over the west and south was manifest. O'Connell would soon have to distance himself – to a degree, at least – from Russell's execrated administration; in addition to its mishandling of the famine crisis, it had rejected out of hand any amendment of the Colleges Act, to which the clerical Repealers still attached first importance. In fact, some of the more forward of the Young Irelanders (who as a group remained even yet wedded to political 'education' rather than political action) had begun to fear that O'Connell would 'scoop' them by abandoning the whigs and launching a national campaign against the ineffectuality and parsimony of the official measures.

A public meeting called by the Dublin 'remonstrants' on 2 December 1846 proved the final turn of the screw for O'Connell. After passing several now-familiar anti-O'Connellite motions, the meeting, which attracted some Young Ireland attendance, resolved to re-assemble in January with the purpose of forming an independent repeal movement. O'Connell responded immediately to this threat. At the next general meeting of the Association (7 December) he deplored the gross failure of the government to cope with the Irish crisis, and proposed the constitution of a national front to press immediate reforms upon parliament and the cabinet. In particular, he called for a junction of the Irish gentry and middle classes and he proposed that a representative committee should consider and try to resolve the whole disputed issue of the peace resolutions. O'Connell had seized the initiative. It was he who emerged as generous and magnanimous in the public estimation.

Divided between those who believed that O'Connell's overture was genuine and those who suspected him of seeking to entrap them, and between those who wished to bargain frankly and those who insisted that every grievance of theirs be met, the Young Irelanders fared ill when their delegates met O'Connell on 15 December 1846. The negotiations quickly failed, but O'Connell retained whatever credit for large-mindedness survived. Although he laid down that the peace resolutions must be accepted (or at least legally adjudicated) before any other item was discussed, he 'conceded' that the peace issue might be limited to Anglo-Irish relations. Contrariwise, the Young Irelanders simply presented a long list of demands, among them, a prohibition on the acceptance of government places; complete freedom of discussion within the Association; the exclusion of paid officers from, and the reconstitution of, its committee; the regular publication of its accounts; the restoration of the *Nation* to Repeal Reading Rooms; and neutrality on 'sectarian' issues. The Young Irelanders were, not altogether unfairly, seen as asking for the impossible – unconditional surrender; and initially at least, they bore the brunt of the blame for the continuance of disunion in the repeal ranks.

It must not be forgotten, however, that reunion with the seceders was, even if sincerely sought, a secondary matter for O'Connell. His primary objectives, as he had developed them at the Association meeting of 7 December 1846, were to arouse the world at large to a knowledge of the frightful character of the Irish calamity and to produce a combination of the Irish gentry to confront Russell's government. This is made clear by O'Connell's draft letter of 10 December to the editor F. W. Conway, seeking to enlist the aid of the *Dublin Evening Post* 'to arouse the fears and excite the attention of the resident landed proprietors of Ireland. They are by no means sufficiently alive to the horrible state of the country.' O'Connell felt warranted in calling on them 'to meet, to consult, to deliberate' at once. As he predicted, with dreadful accuracy, Ireland was only at the threshold of her horrors.

> A NATION, it is starving. If there be any exceptions, they are so few and so far between that they are not worth mentioning or being noticed. I repeat, the nation is starving, and to the all-prevalent famine is now superadded dysentery and typhus in their worst shapes. Nothing can be more appalling than the spread of these diseases. The typhus is setting in in its worst shape.[35]

Oppressed by this black awareness of the impending catastrophe, O'Connell paid scant attention to Repeal or conventional politics of any kind after 15 December. Instead, he was (he believed) his country's last best hope as a rallying-point for the critically important landed classes, as well as for the nation as a whole.

O'Connell had been forced back briefly into domestic politics as the inadequacy of the government's response to the famine, and the threat of an independent repeal movement, became unmistakable. Even then, he had deplored rather than denounced the meagreness of Russell's measures, and striven to present the nationalist division as a legal rather than a political issue. 'I stand altogether upon the law', he told the Young Irelander, T. D. Reilly, just before the negotiations of 15 December, 'My sole difficulty rests upon the legal objection to the admission of the seceders.' In the same letter, while offering to seek and abide by other eminent counsels' opinion, he set out his argument succinctly:

> I take these propositions to be clear in law: – First: That any assembly admitting any species of physical force as part of its means of obtaining a repeal of an Act of Parliament is an unlawful assembly, liable to be dispersed by any magistrate, and its members punished by indictment.
>
> Secondly: That any such assembly is not only unlawful, but that any acts done by it in furtherance of its objects constitute a treasonable fact, rendering the members liable to conviction and execution for treason . . .
>
> It follows, if I be right, that the seceders cannot safely be admitted into

the Repeal Association unless upon the fullest and most explicit disclaimer of resorting to any physical force means to achieve the Repeal of the Union.

In order to be enabled to receive the seceders into the Association again it should be ascertained whether, beyond a doubt, I am right in point of law or not.[36]

After the negotiations failed, O'Connell attempted to keep the matter on the same neutral ground. On 17 December he reiterated to Smith O'Brien his 'professional' opinion that the 'physical force question' involved the personal safety of the Association's members.

I should vote for the readmission . . . of very many of the seceders if they would disavow the physical force principle; or if, without that disavowal, the Association would still be a legal assembly . . . it was to ascertain this point, and this alone, that I proposed the legal conference as a preliminary step to a complete conciliation.[37]

The seceders, divided before the meeting with O'Connell, were at one afterwards in proclaiming him to have been disingenuous. Mitchel declared, 'I never for one moment believed the proposal to be *bona fide*'[38] and Duffy described it as 'a move which had for its object solely to put us in the wrong'.[39] Certainly, O'Connell's 'move' had served his immediate interest. It was he who could present himself to the people as the spurned bearer of the olive branch. But this is not necessarily to say that his conduct was deceitful. That any step, even a rhetorical leaning, towards physical force would endanger the Repeal movement had been (as we have seen) his *idée fixe* from the beginning. Age and frailty could only have tightened his grip upon his supposed security. Moreover, he had put his bargaining position to the hazard. None of the four counsel – O'Hagan, O'Hea, O'Loghlen and Dillon – to whom he proposed to refer the legal issue was a 'servile' O'Connellite, or even (apart from O'Loghlen) an especial friend. It was not inconceivable that the seceding faction might have accepted his nominations for the adjudicating panel or even that, in due course, the joint opinion of the panel might have run counter to his 'professional' interpretation. At any rate, whether and in whatever proportion O'Connell intermixed guile and candour, he certainly strove to minimize his own *political* involvement, and resumed, as rapidly as he could, his role as high priest of a stricken people.

Apart from a few sad, unmeaning genuflections to Repeal – such as, 'How different would the scene be if we had our own Parliament, taking care of our people, of our own resources!'[40] – his sole significant foray into politics proper from then on was undertaken, characteristically, in the cause of Catholic equality. On 22 January 1847 he complained to the new Irish lord chancellor, Brady, that the Dublin magistracy was almost entirely Protestant in composition, adding 'I respectfully submit to your Lordship the propriety of a prompt measure to remedy this grievance.'[41] Brady, whose elevation owed something to O'Connell's good offices, dutifully complied. Almost all the Dublin magistrates appointed during 1847 were Catholics, probably drawn from the list which O'Connell had attached to his submission. There was a certain fitness in his final specifically political excursion being 'Emancipatory'.

III

Technically, O'Connell was himself an absentee landlord throughout 1846 except for a few weeks in the early autumn. His proprietorship was exercised through the resident Maurice. Maurice was also his agent, John Primrose Jr having been replaced some time before, still owing O'Connell a considerable sum on the estate accounts. Possibly Primrose was removed, not for inefficiency, but in order to prepare Maurice for the management of his succession. If so, O'Connell left little to his son's discretion, even though he sensed by the beginning of October 1846 that his end was near.

It was ironic that O'Connell, who had suffered his uncle Hunting Cap's domination for almost half a century, should have meted out much the same treatment to his eldest son, albeit with counter-balancing affection. Maurice, forty-three years old in 1846, was still painfully subservient to as well as dependent on his father. By another irony, O'Connell, who had lived for at least two decades in a Brazilian jungle of unmet obligations and overdue promissory notes, now harangued his son ceaselessly on the evils of accepting bills. Unfortunately for Maurice, O'Connell had a case. 'Don't conceal from me the fact', he wrote to Maurice on 19 August 1846, 'if you have been accepting accommodation bills for any person, and in any event I do most strongly insist that you will not accept an accommodation bill for any person, without my express permission.'[42] Over the next three months, both from Dublin and at Derrynane, O'Connell badgered the wretched Maurice for a full account of his indebtedness. 'I cannot think you would equivocate with me',[43] he told him on 5 November —doubtless meaning the opposite. Maurice's reply tells its own sad story of his father's domination:

I am sufficiently blameable for my conduct with regard to those bills, without any addition particularly of the charge of seeking to deceive you. The bill of Ally [Alice] Primrose's you allude to was mentioned in my letters . . . I mentioned it to you *here*. I stated it to you in the very commencement of this unhappy business. Most assuredly I had and have no design of deceiving you, and in this instance the evidence is multiplied that such could not be my intention.

With regard to my letter from *Hillgrove* [John Primrose's house] I neither drew nor accepted any bill, nor took a pen in my hand [there] at all unless to write unlucky [*sic*] letter to you . . .[44]

Evidently Maurice's bills (according to one list which may have been incomplete) amounted to almost £2000, and O'Connell forbade him ever to accept another 'without letting me know it while I live'.[45] As a melancholy coda bearing witness to the unhappy relationship between the two, we may add Maurice's reply when, after O'Connell's death, one of his executors refused to sanction a heavy expenditure he had proposed: 'I have been too long trained to suppress and sacrifice my own feelings, in order to give way to my dear father's wishes and orders, to suffer much from my struggle against them at present.'[46]

As one might guess from this, O'Connell was no 'absentee' in spirit, but a most exacting principal when managing his property from a distance. Even before the end of August 1846, he upbraided Maurice harshly for not keeping him *au fait* with the state of the potato crop at home and the steps which he was taking 'to meet the coming emergencies';[47] at the same time he ordered reserves of provisions to be fetched from Cork by the family sloop. During his month's stay at Derrynane, O'Connell busied himself with local relief work and the sanctioning of a pier or breakwater to be built close by his house. The distress which he witnessed on every side drove all else – at least temporarily – from his mind. Even after his return to Dublin on 28 October, it continued to obsess him. Government acquiescence in his initiatives did not necessarily mean government action. Maurice had, for example, to complain to him on 18 November,

The outcry for work at Cahir[civeen] continues still loud and vehement and the orders of the Board of Works are, I understand, causing fresh impediments, the last 'ukase' being that no one who has the grass of a cow is to get labour. This would confine the market indeed in this district. All are nearly equally without provisions, and though the cowless creature may be something lower in the scale, yet the wants of the others are equally pressing. The result of all these changeable orders, all nearly equally ridiculous, is delay and while the Board are balancing straws, the people starve.[48]

O'Connell settled this – so far as it could be settled at the mere centre of bureaucracy – by calling on the Board in Dublin and obtaining an immediate assurance that the 'ukase' was quite unauthorized.[49] This was typical of the fashion in which he used his own standing to inaugurate, expedite or sustain official relief measures in his own barony. Regarding him now as the great bulwark against peasant violence, the Irish administration certainly jumped when O'Connell cracked the whip. He secured British naval transport to carry his own food purchases to Cahirciveen in December; and it was only with lengthy and laborious apology that the Board rejected his extra-ordinary request to purchase the entire government supply of meal and biscuit at its depot in the town. Meanwhile, to the end of 1846 and into 1847 he maintained his barrage of minute instructions to Maurice for both immediate action and preparation for the still more fearful future. Characteristically, these included such peremptory admonitions as: 'Take care to have the accounts most accurately kept. Go through the form of giving a ticket to every man employed, and give it previous [to] or on the day of his beginning to work. Be vigilant in matter of form as well as in substance.'[50]

O'Connell was torn between his own increasing impoverishment and the calls of the needy on and about his property. Following the initial rise in the Repeal Rent after the secession of 2 July, it fell away almost to nothing, and O'Connell was compelled to make capital payments from his own resources in order to keep the organization in being. On 16 October Ray thanked him for a draft for £453; he added that the 'balance [in the "account" between O'Connell and the Association] must by this time be very much in your favour and I am uneasy lest you may be inconvenienced by advances. Still, without drawing upon you we cannot go on.'[51] O'Connell had moreover to offer abatement of rents even though it was from rents that Maurice's debts were meant, in the first instance, to be paid. The Derrynane food stores also tied up capital, and these would be sold below cost price at whatever the labourers could afford at the time of sale. Though O'Connell attempted to strike the right balance in his injunctions, he almost always came down finally on the side of mercy. 'I wish you to be as abundant to the people as you possibly can, recollecting however that we have dreadful times before us',[52] he ended his letter to Maurice of 5 December. A few days later, he wrote in one of his last surviving instructions to his son, 'Of course, you should get as much money as you possibly can for corn and bread. If it were nothing else but to help you to pay off the rascally bills. But I know you will not be harsh to the people.'[53]

From mid-August 1846, when the widespread failure of the potato crop became certain, O'Connell's 'politics' tended to be his experiences of and at Derrynane writ large. The prospect of famine (and behind it the spectre of food riots, social disorder and bloodshed) dwarfed all else; and the government, with its power to say yea or nay to the creation of employment, and its command of money and administrative machinery, became the treasury of last resort rather than a body to be coaxed or bullied politically in the normal way. Correspondingly, O'Connell's domestic politics wore the air of *de haut en bas* in place of his customary popular mobilization. He spoke for and attempted to weld together the 'responsible' classes (and especially those with specific responsibilities for their properties such as himself) to engage the common enemy, mass starvation. It is true that he used his own peculiar influence (at this stage) with the Irish administration largely in the interests of his native barony – and possibly at the expense of other districts. But this emblemized his personalization – in every sense – of the great crisis, and represented, in his eyes, the behaviour proper to every dutiful and feeling master of the fates of others. Truckling to the whigs seemed now an empty charge: to whom should not one truckle if it meant the saving of human lives?

IV

After the abortive negotiations of 15 December 1846 – and despite the setting up at last of a rival Young Ireland political organization, the Irish Confederation, on 13 January 1847 – the popular suffering became once more, and remained, O'Connell's engrossing public interest. He stayed in Dublin until the end of January, still attempting to muster the property of Ireland, and (through Bessborough) the Irish executive, in the cause of much larger and more urgent relief. It was London, however, that commanded the resources; and O'Connell, despite his confession to Fitzpatrick on 11 January 1847 that 'he felt himself gradually failing in bodily strength',[54] decided on an appeal in person to the House of Commons. His hope (if he really had hoped) was immediately extinguished. He wrote to Ray from London on 6 February that

> there is, alas! but little prospect of substantial relief on that enormously large scale which is absolutely necessary to prevent hundreds of thousands of the Irish people from perishing of *famine and pestilence* ...
> I trust in God that my health will enable me to take that active part which

594

I desire on behalf of the famishing people. I intend, please God, on Monday [8 February], in sadness and sorrow, to develope my views of what is necessary to save Ireland. The obstacles in the House of Commons are manifold, and there seems to be an ignorance of the real state of horror in which Ireland is plunged. How I wish that it were possible to make Parliament comprehend the enormous and hideous extent of the calamity which cries for a remedy.[55]

Three days later he confirmed to Fitzpatrick that there was 'every reason to despond', adding, however, 'If it be in my power I shall say a few words this evening.'[56] It was barely in his power. He could scarcely stand in the House for trembling, or be heard even in the total silence of a pitying respect. At last he cast himself – as his British mockers had long cast him – as the Big Beggarman. In effect, he held out his hands for alms. He attempted no argument, attributed no blame, threw his country upon the mercy of its foes. The Irish people, the report of his speech ran,

> were starving in shoals, in hundreds – aye, in thousands and millions. Parliament was bound, then, to act not only liberally but generously – to find out the means of putting a stop to this terrible disaster . . . He had not said one word to produce irritation – he had not uttered one word of reproach . . . She [Ireland] was in their hands – in their power. If they did not save her, she could not save herself. He solemnly called on them to recollect that he predicted with the sincerest conviction, that one-fourth of her population would perish unless Parliament came to their relief.[57]

O'Connell's terrible prophecy was fulfilled. If famine-induced emigration is added to famine-induced mortality in making the computation, over two million Irish persons 'perished' in the years 1845–52.

O'Connell made one last call on Lord John Russell – again a mendicant, but this time on behalf of his faithful, but now bereft, Fitzpatrick. He won the promise of a sinecure, the assistant registrarship of deeds in Dublin, a promise that was honoured later when the government could arrange for the current incumbent to retire on full salary. This was part of the process of winding up his life, which O'Connell had begun already when he told Fitzpatrick of his anxiety 'to settle some matters that might cause difficulty in the event of his death'.[58] He was powerless to make better provision for his children. Pierce Mahony, who was trustee for certain of his property, attempted to improve the family's prospects by some form of settlement backed by the further insurance of O'Connell's life. O'Connell was cut to the quick by this *bêtise*. His life, he replied, was 'certainly not insurable'; Mahony should never have presented him with 'such a document . . . I have neither health nor money to embark in the transaction'.[59] Early in February 1847, he added a codicil to his will reducing his bequest to the Repeal Association from £1000 to £630; the bequest carried the pathetic rider, 'I implore that it may be received . . . as in full satisfaction of any demand that body may or could have on me. In short that if more be in anywise due of me that it may be fully and freely remitted to me so as to leave no kind of debt to the association weighing on my soul.'[60] Two and a half weeks later, O'Connell sent Fitzpatrick his final instructions about the disposition of his assets, including the sale of 'another' £1000 of stock. 'My illness', he went on, 'is very expensive, and the times are indeed bad.' The scatter of orders to his trusted agent included, apparently, the destruction of his mementos of Rose McDowell. O'Connell told Fitzpatrick that he would find in the 'standing desk in my bedchamber . . . a correspondence with a lady which you may read yourself because it contains nothing disreputable. Of course, when you have read it, destroy it.'[61] Nothing, it seems, survived of Mary except the caches of loving letters.

O'Connell began his next letter to Fitzpatrick, 'They deceive themselves, and consequently deceive you, who tell you I am recovering';[62] earlier he had written, 'Poor Nugent is so anxious to have me well that he mistakes his wishes for his opinions.' At first O'Connell had hoped to regain his homeland before he died and in particular to be 'within the reach of [the Rev] Dr Miley', his friend and confessor. 'But', he added despairingly, 'that is idle as I am not strong enough to return to Ireland in such weather as this.'[63] Within a few days, however, the convergence of his physicians' wish that he should seek a warmer climate, a pious scheme that he make a pilgrimage to the Holy City, and Fitzpatrick's tactful application to Archbishop Murray that Miley be released to act as chaplain on the way, issued in a plan to take O'Connell, by easy stages, to Rome. O'Connell was overjoyed at Miley's 'kind, kind' acquiescence. On 16 February, he asked Fitzpatrick to make 'with him whatever arrangements are the most suitable and the most respectful for his coming over here. I would not hurry him but the sooner he finds it his convenience to come, infinitely the better . . . Of course you will insist upon his accepting the full amount of his expenses on the journey.'[64] When he reached London, however, Miley discovered that it was spiritual comfort that O'Connell sought rather than a chaplain for a pilgrimage which he was now most reluctant to undertake. Miley joined forces with the physicians in cajoling him to go. Meanwhile he reported, 'Prayer is his [O'Connell's] only occupation. It is at once most edifying and affecting to witness his demeanour in this respect, not alone by day, but by night also. He is perfectly prepared for death, and had rather not be diverted from the thought of it.'[65] Not until 6 March did O'Connell leave London, and even then it was merely to repair to Hastings to build up his strength for the journey being urged upon him. There the sun broke through and his spirits lightened; he recalled that several of the O'Connells had passed ninety years of age; and calls of courtesy from leading English Catholics were at least diverting, if all too patently valedictory. But there were also signs of occasional agitation. On 12 March, for example, he added two codicils to his will on a single day. Later, Fitzpatrick and Christopher Fitz-Simon arrived at Hastings to bid farewell and accompany O'Connell on the first stage of what would be a *via dolorosa* – to Folkestone where he was to embark on the cross-channel steamer on 22 March. 'O'Connell', Fitzpatrick reported to his sister, 'is very reluctant now to travel, except by railway, [but] this comparatively short drive will be so rapidly accomplished that I trust he will be sufficiently reconciled to it.'[66] Before O'Connell took ship, he 'gave me [Fitzpatrick] his blessing, designating me "the best of *all* his friends" '.[67] It was a long- and hard-earned reward. As a political enemy had once observed, Fitzpatrick 'was the tortoise that sustained the elephant that sustained the world of Irish agitation'.[68]

When O'Connell had last crossed the English Channel in 1823, it had been alone – but to join his wife and children to holiday in Paris. Now he was supported by Miley, his son Daniel and his manservant Duggan – but had only a destination, and no meaningful aim, in view. It was as if O'Connell were attempting to run from death – or, rather, as if his guardsmen were hurrying him ahead of a pursuing doom. The 'frequent, though not continuous, fits of depression',[69] which Fitzpatrick had noted even while O'Connell was in Hastings, deepened after he reached France. An abbé who waited on him in Boulogne was struck by his unremitting gloom. The travel itself, however – by steamer on a flat-calm sea and on short runs by rail – was comparatively easy until Paris was reached on 26 March 1847. There at last homage could be paid, in person, to the avatar of Liberal Catholicism on the Continent. Archbishop Affre of Paris (destined to die on the barricades in the Revolution of 1848) called on him at his hotel in the rue de Rivoli. So too did a deputation from the celebrated Society for the Defence of Religious Freedom. Montalembert, who led it, read the tribute.

> We are come to salute in you the Liberator of Ireland – of that nation which has always excited in France fraternal feelings. But you are not only *the Man of one Nation*, you are the Man of all *Christendom*. Your glory is not only Irish; it is Catholic. Wherever Catholics begin anew to practise civic virtues, and devote themselves to the conquest of their legislative rights under God, it is your work. Wherever religion tends to emancipate itself from the thraldom in which several generations of sophists and lawyers have placed it, to you, after God, it is indebted.

In his weakness, O'Connell answered that he was almost silenced 'by sickness and emotion', and could only say that the demonstration of respect was 'one of the most significant events of my life'.[70] It was also the last public happening. How ironic that the European accolades, dammed up for quarter of a century, should have fallen in the end on indifferent ears and a mind absorbed by imminent demise.

From Paris on, travel had to be by road. The dragging of the dying man, over a five-week period, to Marseilles became increasingly macabre. At the Lapalise stage, near Vichy, Fr Miley reported on 8 April to Fitzpatrick that

> his strength, his appetite, and his spirits are daily sinking. For me to attempt any description of the harrowing anxieties I endure under these most depressing circumstances would be utterly vain. Some nights I do not undress at all. Just now, being much depressed, having headache and indigestion, I went out, while Daniel and Duggan were both with him. I was not away twenty minutes, and, when returning, I was met by two messengers, and coming into the room found him in the greatest alarm at my absence. In fact, I cannot be out of his sight a moment.[71]

At Lyons, where the journey was broken for eleven days, O'Connell recovered sufficiently to walk abroad on a few occasions. But, lost in despondency, he seemed scarcely to notice the reverential crowds who followed him; he made no answer to their expressions of sympathy or admiration. It was Miley who bore the brunt of the misery about this time. 'Never have I had such a struggle', he wrote from Lyons on 16 April,

> as from 2 to 4 o'clock last night to keep him in bed or prevent the alarm being given to the whole hotel. At the moment it would have been most unfortunate that any but his own should have seen him . . .
>
> The doctors give hope, but so terrible are his mental agitations, so pertinaciously does he cling to the most gloomy ideas and prospects, that it is next to a miracle that either mind or body can hold out against it. I fear I am myself beginning to sink. Even by day I cannot leave him to walk in the open air for fifteen minutes; as for the night, all its griefs and terrors are on

me, for he will not be satisfied unless I am by his bed; and by day and by night nothing will he ever hear or speak or think of for a moment but his own maladies and misfortunes.[72]

Marseilles was reached on 2 May 1847, and Genoa, by sea, three days later. There after a brief flare of better health and spirits, O'Connell collapsed, physically and mentally. A fearful consciousness of the past and terror of the coming judgment destroyed his nights; by day he was ceaselessly agitated. His entourage, and Miley in particular, pressed him vainly to move on to Rome. Miley complained angrily to Fitzpatrick that the solemn 'compact' which O'Connell had made with him at Hastings, in Fitzpatrick's presence – namely, to throw 'his own mighty will' into the effort of attaining the final goal – was being broken. 'And yet', wrote Miley, 'so entirely unworthy of him does it appear to me, that I cannot and will not abandon the hope . . . of yet persuading him.'[73] This was not perhaps as wantonly blind or cruel as it might seem for the Genoese doctors had (like their French counterparts) spoken initially of improvement. But by 8 May O'Connell's state was desperate. He ceased to eat. Intermittently he became delirious. He shouted defiance of a phantasmagoric Peel and exulted that Repeal was safely in his box. Duggan's diary entry for 11 May reads: 'Asked me had Mr Wyse brought forward his motion and who seconded it. That Wyse was mad, and to call him should there be a division. No food: worse to-day.'[74] He begged Duggan repeatedly to make sure that he was dead before he allowed him to be buried. In between O'Connell clung to Miley for reassurance. Then, forty-eight hours before he died, calm fell on him, and thenceforward he spoke (wrote Miley) only of 'his eternal interests and the bright hopes of eternity'. At 2 am on 15 May 1847 he received the last sacrament in a scene worthy of the brush of Goya though it received nothing better than an ill-drawn oleograph.

The Cardinal Archbishop [of Genoa] having been confined to his bed ever since our arrival here (he is eighty-eight years old), the vicar-general, attended by his curates and the clerics of his church, and followed by several of the faithful, though it was the dead of night, carried the adorable viaticum with the solemnities customary in Catholic countries, and reposed it in the tabernacle, which we had prepared in the chamber of the illustrious sufferer. The Liberator joined fervently and as audibly as his exhausted powers would permit in the prayers which we had been reciting for an hour before . . . he was perfectly in possession of his mind while receiving the last rites . . . his hands were clasped in prayer, except when he stretched them out to receive the sacred unction.[75]

At 9.35 pm that evening O'Connell died. By 9.35 pm many hundreds of other Irish people had died on 15 May 1847. Most had perished of the direct or indirect effects of the great famine, which in another sense had also borne O'Connell down. It made no difference in the grave.

> Scepter and crown
> Must tumble down,
> And in the dust be equal made
> With the poor crooked scythe and spade.[76]

But perhaps the poor starved ones had been the luckier. O'Connell had had to die publicly over many weeks. His priest, and his son and servant, formed a grotesque species of immediate audience. Their surrounding presence led him on to express, instead of consuming inwardly, his terrors and to indulge in an abasing scrupulosity and despair, which his companions must strive to counter. But even this course may have had its natural, to say nothing of any other, use. On 14 May, Miley wrote that O'Connell 'has been long prepared for death; he has *familiarized* himself with the contemplation of his last end'.[77] This may have been the necessary cost-price for his final hours of quiet and submission.

Towards the end, he asked that his heart be sent to Rome. So it was, encased in a silver urn. Symbolically, this seems quite wrong. It should surely have been laid in the Irish ground from which it had drawn, and to which it gave back so much.

References

MISE-EN-SCÈNE

1 4 Oct. 1838, W. J. Fitzpatrick
   (ed.), *Correspondence of Daniel
   O'Connell the Liberator* (London,
   1888), vol. ii, pp. 151–2.
2 ibid., p. 152.
3 M. F. Cusack, *The Liberator
   (Daniel O'Connell) his Life and
   Times, Political, Social and
   Religious* (London, 1872), p. 31.
4 *Freeman's Journal*, 4 July 1828.

CHAPTER 1
Growing Up
1775–93

1 M. MacDonagh, *The Life of
   Daniel O'Connell* (London, 1903),
   pp. 8–9.
2 Mrs M. J. O'Connell, *The Last
   Colonel of the Irish Brigade.
   Count O'Connell and Old Irish
   Life at Home and Abroad 1745–
   1833* (Cork, 1977), vol. i, p. 305.
3 ibid., p. 122.
4 'The Gaelic Background', in M.
   Tierney (ed.), *Daniel O'Connell.
   Nine Centenary Essays* (Dublin,
   1949), pp. 7–8.
5 A. Houston, *Daniel O'Connell:
   His Early Life, and Journal, 1795
   to 1802* (London, 1906), pp. 129–
   30.
6 W. J. O'N. Daunt, *Personal
   Recollections of the late Daniel
   O'Connell* (London, 1848), vol. i,
   pp. 14–15.
7 This was written in 1849 by S. H.
   O'Grady, *Catalogue of Irish MSS
   in the British Museum*, vol. i, p.
   162, and quoted in G. Murphy,
   'The Gaelic Background', in
   Tierney, *Daniel O'Connell*, op.
   cit., p. 5.
8 O'Connell to W. S. Landor, 4 Oct.
   1838, in Fitzpatrick,
   Correspondence of O'Connell, op.
   cit., vol. ii, p. 151.
9 W. Phelan, *The History of the
   Church of Rome in Ireland*
   (London, 1827), quoted in D.
   MacCartney, 'The Writing of
   History in Ireland, 1800–30', *Irish
   Historical Studies*, vol. x, 1957, p.
   361.
10 6 Aug. 1829, M. O'Connell (ed.),
    *The Correspondence of Daniel
    O'Connell* (Shannon and Dublin,
    1972–80), vol. iv, pp. 87–8.
11 D. Gwynn, *Daniel O'Connell*
    (revised centenary edn, Oxford,
    1947), pp. 21–2.
12 6 Oct. 1794, O'Connell, *The Last
    Colonel*, op. cit., vol. ii, pp. 152–3.
13 Daunt, *Personal Recollections*, op.
    cit., vol. i, p. 116.
14 ibid., vol. ii, pp. 77–8.
15 ibid., vol. i, p. 116.
16 *Cork Magazine*, Sept. 1848, p.
    643, quoted in T. Wall, 'Louvain,
    St. Omer and Douai', in Tierney,
    Daniel O'Connell, op. cit., p. 41.
17 16 June 1789, O'Connell, *The
    Last Colonel*, op. cit., vol. ii, p. 80.
18 14 Jan. 1790, ibid., p. 84.
19 2 Sept. 1790, ibid., p. 90.
20 Daunt, *Personal Recollections*, op.
    cit., vol. ii, p. 26.
21 *Irish Monthly*, vol. x, 1882, p.
    336.
22 3 Feb. 1792, O'Connell,
    Correspondence, vol. i, p. 1.
23 O'Connell to Hunting Cap, 16
    April 1792, ibid., p. 2.
24 Wall, 'Louvain, St. Omer and
    Douai', in Tierney, *Daniel
    O'Connell*, op. cit., pp. 34–5.

25 16 April 1792, Fitzpatrick, *Correspondence of O'Connell*, op. cit., vol. i, p. 3.

26 30 June 1792, O'Connell, *Correspondence*, vol. i, p. 3.

27 14 Sept. 1792, ibid., p. 5.

28 O'Connell to Hunting Cap, 14 Sept. 1792, Fitzpatrick, *Correspondence of O'Connell*, op. cit., vol. i, p. 5.

29 14 Sept. 1792, O'Connell, *Correspondence*, vol. i, p. 4.

30 Wall, 'Louvain, St. Omer and Douai', in Tierney, *Daniel O'Connell*, op. cit., p. 45.

31 MacDonagh, *Life of O'Connell*, op. cit., p. 17.

32 Gwynn, *Daniel O'Connell*, op. cit., p. 39.

33 K. F. Roche, 'Revolution and Counter-Revolution', in Tierney, *Daniel O'Connell*, op. cit., p. 69.

34 10 Dec. 1795, O'Connell, *Correspondence*, vol. i, pp. 20–1.

CHAPTER 2
London
1793–5

1 O'Connell, *Correspondence*, vol. i, p. 6.

2 O'Connell to Hunting Cap, 1 July 1793, ibid., p. 7.

3 O'Connell to Hunting Cap, 21 March 1793, ibid., p. 5.

4 1 July 1793, ibid., p. 6.

5 24 Nov. 1793, ibid., p. 9.

6 ibid.

7 26 Dec. 1793, ibid., pp. 10–12.

8 O'Connell to Hunting Cap, 11 March 1794, ibid., pp. 13–16.

9 O'Connell to Hunting Cap, ibid., pp. 13–14.

10 22 Aug. 1794, ibid., pp. 18–19.

11 O'Connell, *The Last Colonel*, op. cit., vol. ii, p. 151.

12 12 March 1794, ibid., p. 148.

13 14 March 1795, ibid., p. 162.

14 26 Jan. 1794, ibid., p. 145.

15 Houston, *Early Life and Journal*, op. cit., p. 93.

16 ibid., p. 95.

17 O'Connell to Hunting Cap, 26 Oct. 1795, O'Connell, *Correspondence*, vol. i, p. 19.

18 10 Dec. 1795, ibid., p. 20.

19 Houston, *Early Life and Journal*, op. cit., 30 Dec. 1795, p. 95.

20 ibid., 31 Dec. 1795, pp. 97–8.

21 ibid., 18 Jan. 1796, p. 115.

22 ibid., 29 Dec. 1795, p. 91.

23 ibid., 10 Dec. 1795, p. 93.

24 Count O'Connell to Hunting Cap, 26 Feb. 1795, O'Connell, *The Last Colonel*, op. cit., vol. ii, p. 157.

25 Houston, *Early Life and Journal*, op. cit., 11 Dec. 1795, p. 70.

26 ibid., 3 Jan. 1796, p. 101.

27 ibid., 13 Dec. 1795, p. 77.

28 ibid., 30 Dec. 1795, pp. 92–3.

29 ibid., late 1795, p. 64.

30 ibid., 19 Jan. 1796, p. 115.

31 ibid., 12 Dec. 1795, p. 76.

32 ibid., p. 75.

33 Daunt, *Personal Recollections*, op. cit., vol. i, p. 35.

34 Houston, *Early Life and Journal*, op. cit., 5 Dec. 1796, p. 129.

35 ibid., 19 Jan. 1796, pp. 115–16.

36 ibid., 18 Jan. 1796, pp. 113–14.

37 W. Godwin, *Enquiry concerning Political Justice and its Influence on Morals and Happiness* (Toronto, 1946), vol. i, p. 274.

38 ibid., vol. i, pp. 251, 259.

39 Houston, *Early Life and Journal*, op. cit., 30 Jan. 1796, pp. 119–20.

40 ibid., 3 Jan. 1796, p. 102.

41 O'Connell to Hunting Cap, 22 April 1794, O'Connell, *Correspondence*, vol. i, p. 17.

42 Houston, *Early Life and Journal*, op. cit., 13 Jan. 1796, p. 110.

43 ibid., 19 Jan. 1796, p. 116.

44 ibid., 20 Jan. 1796, p. 118.

45 ibid., 19 Jan. 1796, p. 116.

46 ibid., 20 Jan. 1796, p. 118.

47 ibid., p. 125 footnote f.

48 O'Connell, *Correspondence*, vol. i, pp. 23–4.
49 Houston, *Early Life and Journal*, op. cit., 31 Dec. 1796, p. 156.
50 ibid., p. 157.
51 ibid., pp. 156–7.
52 17 Jan. 1796, O'Connell, *Correspondence*, vol. i, pp. 22–3.
53 Houston, *Early Life and Journal*, op. cit., 16 Dec. 1795, p. 85.

CHAPTER 3
Dublin
1795–1800

1 O'Connell to Hunting Cap, 17 May 1796, O'Connell, *Correspondence*, vol. i, p. 25.
2 n.d., O'Connell, *The Last Colonel*, op. cit., vol. ii, p. 272.
3 Houston, *Early Life and Journal*, op. cit., p. 166.
4 3 Jan. 1797, O'Connell, *Correspondence*, vol. i, p. 27.
5 Houston, *Early Life and Journal*, op. cit., 18 Jan. 1797, p. 176.
6 ibid., p. 177.
7 ibid., 19 Jan. 1797, p. 178.
8 ibid., 23 Jan. 1797, p. 185.
9 ibid., 24 Jan. 1797, p. 186.
10 O'Connell, *Correspondence*, vol. i, p. 29.
11 Houston, *Early Life and Journal*, op. cit., p. 204.
12 ibid., 29 Dec. 1796, p. 155.
13 ibid., 4 March 1797, p. 206.
14 ibid., 20 Feb. 1797, p. 202.
15 ibid., 22 Jan. 1797, p. 184.
16 ibid., 25 March 1797, p. 213.
17 ibid., 31 March 1797, p. 215.
18 Daunt, *Personal Recollections*, op. cit., vol. ii, pp. 98–9.
19 Houston, *Early Life and Journal*, op. cit., 25 Jan. 1797, p. 190.
20. ibid., 7 Jan. 1797, p. 174.
21 ibid., 25 Jan. 1797, p. 190.
22 ibid., 28 Jan. 1797, p. 193.
23 ibid., 20 Feb. 1797, p. 202.
24 ibid., 28 Jan. 1797, p. 193.

25 ibid., 24 March 1797, p. 211.
26 ibid., 28 Jan. 1797, p. 193.
27 ibid., 13 Jan. 1798, p. 216.
28 ibid., 7 Dec. 1796, p. 129.
29 ibid., 10 Dec. 1796, p. 137.
30 ibid., p. 138.
31 ibid., 5 Jan. 1797, p. 168.
32 ibid., 20 Feb. 1797, p. 202.
33 ibid., 13 Dec. 1796, p. 142.
34 ibid., 10 Feb. 1797, pp. 196–7.
35 ibid., 31 Dec. 1796, p. 159.
36 ibid., 24 Dec. 1796, p. 148.
37 ibid., 7 Jan. 1797, p. 174.
38 ibid., 13 Jan. 1798, p. 229.
39 ibid., 29 Dec. 1796, p. 156.
40 Hunting Cap to O'Connell, 15 Feb. 1798, O'Connell, *Correspondence*, vol. i, p. 31.
41 Houston, *Early Life and Journal*, op. cit., p. 229.
42 O'Connell, *Correspondence*, vol. i, pp. 32–3.
43 W. J. Fitzpatrick, *Secret Service Under Pitt* (London, 1892), p. 357.
44 W. J. Fitzpatrick, *'The Sham Squire' and the Informers of 1798; with Jottings about Ireland a Century Ago*, new edn (Dublin, 1895), pp. 307–8.
45 Hunting Cap to O'Connell, 15 Feb. 1798, O'Connell, *Correspondence*, vol. i, pp. 31–2.
46 Daunt, *Personal Recollections*, op. cit., vol. i, p. 117.
47 Entry in his fee book, *Irish Monthly*, vol. x, 1882 p. 587.
48 Daunt, *Personal Recollections*, op. cit., vol. i, p. 49.
49 Houston, *Early Life and Journal*, op. cit., p. 235.
50 ibid., 4 Jan. 1799, p. 241.
51 'I survived', in J. M. Thompson, *Leaders of the French Revolution* (Oxford, 1948), p. 10.
52 Daunt, *Personal Recollections*, op. cit., vol. i, p. 119.
53 R. L. Sheil, *Sketches, Legal and Political*, (ed.) M. W. Savage (London, 1855), vol. i, p. 205.

54 ibid., pp. 215–16.
55 ibid., p. 208.
56 O'Connell to Mary, 19 Aug. 1806, O'Connell, *Correspondence*, vol. i, p. 155.
57 Daunt, *Personal Recollections*, op. cit., vol. i, pp. 118–19.
58 ibid., p. 202.

CHAPTER 4
Love and Money
1800–15

1 Daunt, *Personal Recollections*, op. cit., vol. i, p. 133.
2 O'Connell, *Correspondence*, vol. i, p. 34.
3 O'Connell to Mary, 13 June 1801, ibid., p. 58.
4 28 April 1801, ibid., p. 49.
5 1 Dec. 1801, ibid., p. 65.
6 9 Feb. 1802, ibid., pp. 69–70.
7 25 May 1801, ibid., p. 54.
8 O'Connell to Mary, 3 April 1822, ibid., vol. ii, p. 364.
9 O'Connell to Mary, 9 Feb. 1802, ibid., vol. i, p. 70.
10 28 Nov. 1800, ibid., p. 34.
11 O'Connell to Mary, n.d., ibid., p. 77.
12 30 Dec. 1802, ibid., p. 85.
13 n.d. [probably Jan. 1803], ibid., pp. 87–8.
14 O'Connell to Mary, 5 Feb. 1803, ibid., p. 91.
15 O'Connell to Mary, n.d. [probably 7 April 1803], ibid., p. 96.
16 O'Connell to Mary, 3 Dec. 1803, ibid., p. 108.
17 18 Nov. 1802, ibid., p. 81. In fact Ellen and Splinter married in 1803.
18 25 Nov. 1802, ibid., p. 82.
19 29 Jan. 1803, ibid., p. 87.
20 1 Feb. 1803, ibid., pp. 88–9.
21 3 Feb. 1803, ibid., p. 90.
22 16 Aug. 1805, ibid., p. 143.
23 9 Nov. 1804, ibid., p. 119.
24 16 Nov. 1804, ibid., p. 121.

25 16 April 1805, ibid., p. 137.
26 10 Nov. 1803, ibid., pp. 100–1.
27 25 July 1805, ibid., p. 141.
28 12 Aug. 1805, ibid., pp. 142–3.
29 31 March 1806, ibid., p. 149.
30 11 Oct. 1810, ibid., p. 238.
31 30 March 1808, ibid., p. 171.
32 30 March 1811, ibid., p. 252.
33 1 April 1811, ibid., p. 253.
34 9 April 1803, ibid., p. 97.
35 29 Sept. and 1 Oct. 1812, ibid., p. 309.
36 15 March 1809, ibid., p. 193.
37 29 March 1809, ibid., p. 198.
38 14 Jan. 1809, ibid., p. 188.
39 16 March 1810, ibid., pp. 217–18.
40 O'Connell to Mary, 24 March 1809, ibid., p. 195.
41 C. Dickens, *David Copperfield* (London, 1907), p. 167.
42 M. R. O'Connell, 'Daniel O'Connell: income, expenditure and despair', *Irish Historical Studies*, vol. xvii, Sept. 1970, p. 204.
43 O'Connell to Denis McCarthy, 20 Jan. 1806, O'Connell, *Correspondence*, vol. i, p. 147.
44 15 April 1806, ibid., p. 153.
45 O'Connell to Mary, 27 Aug. [1806?], ibid., pp. 155–6.
46 n.d. [probably 6 Aug. 1806], ibid., p. 154.
47 9 March 1807 and 12 March 1807, ibid., pp. 159–61.
48 26 March 1807, ibid., p. 161.
49 2 April 1806, ibid., p. 150.
50 2 April 1808, ibid., p. 172.
51 31 March 1808, ibid., p. 172.
52 n.d. [probably 18 or 25 Sept. 1809], ibid., p. 205.
53 16 May 1811, ibid., p. 257.
54 13 March 1815, ibid., vol. ii, p. 14.
55 14 March 1815, ibid., p. 16.
56 21 March 1816, ibid., p. 88.

CHAPTER 5
Public Lives
1800–13

1 J. O'Connell (ed.), *The Select Speeches of Daniel O'Connell, M.P.* (Dublin, 1867), vol. i, pp. 8–9.
2 Hunting Cap strongly opposed and condemned O'Connell's line of argument: 'For me I have always disapproved of what I conceived to be an unwise and intemperate conduct in that body for some years back, whether they assumed the character of the Catholic Convention or of the aggregate or select meeting of the Catholics of Dublin . . . They seem to me totally to have lost sight of what in my humble opinion should be the main object for their consideration and that was, whether it was to the benignant interposition of the executive Government or to the generous and spontaneous liberality of their countrymen who composed the two houses of parliament that they were really beholden for the favours they had received and to which it was, upon sober and rational reflection, they were to look up for a farther extension of them . . . is it not peculierly [*sic*] unfortunate that the Catholics of the metropolis would not attend to that consideration, and not deprive themselves and their brethren of the only support and shelter they had – the countenance and kindness of the executive Government . . . [?]' Hunting Cap to O'Connell, 30 Jan. 1800, NLI, MSS 15473.
3 O'Connell to Captain Seaver, O'Connell, *Correspondence*, vol. vii, p. 202.
4 Daunt, *Personal Recollections*, op. cit., vol. i, p. 203.
5 O'Connell to Mary O'Connell, *Correspondence*, vol. i, p. 99.
6 18 Nov. 1803, ibid., p. 102.
7 O'Connell, *Select Speeches*, vol. i, p. 15.
8 O'Connell, *Correspondence*, vol. i, p. 127.
9 19 Dec. 1804, ibid., p. 131.
10 23 Dec. 1804, ibid., p. 132.
11 19 March 1805, ibid., p. 133.
12 Gwynn, *Daniel O'Connell*, op. cit., p. 81.
13 O'Connell, *Select Speeches*, vol. i, p. 14.
14 R. Dunlop, *Daniel O'Connell and the Revival of National Life in Ireland* (London, 1900), p. 29.
15 *Hansard*, 25 May 1808, vol. xi, col. 619.
16 Collection of Milner's letters published by Sir John Coxe Hippisley in 1813, p. 5, quoted in B. Ward, *The Eve of Catholic Emancipation* (London, 1911), vol. i, p. 74.
17 O'Connell, *Select Speeches*, vol. ii, p. 20.
18 O'Connell, *Correspondence*, vol. i, pp. 193–4.
19 O'Connell, *Select Speeches*, vol. i, pp. 20–4.
20 Daunt, *Personal Recollections*, op. cit., vol. i, p. 101.
21 O'Connell, *Select Speeches*, vol. i, p. 24.
22 Gwynn, *Daniel O'Connell*, op. cit., p. 85.
23 Hunting Cap to James O'Connell, quoted in James O'Connell to O'Connell, 17 Jan. 1811, O'Connell, *Correspondence*, vol. i, p. 245.
24 M. F. Cusack (ed.), *The Speeches and Public Letters of the Liberator* (Dublin, 1875), vol. ii, p. 259.
25 Dunlop, *Daniel O'Connell*, op. cit., pp. 37–8.
26 This phrase was used by Sergeant Howley. See Gwynn, *Daniel O'Connell*, op. cit., p. 88.

27 *A Full Report of the Speech of Counsellor O'Connell at the Catholic Meeting at Limerick, July 24, 1812* (Dublin, 1812), pp. 3, 13.
28 *Hansard*, vol. xxiii, col. 56.
29 O'Connell, *Correspondence*, vol. i, p. 292 n. 3.
30 Dunlop, *Daniel O'Connell*, op. cit., p. 43.
31 ibid., p. 47.
32 ibid., p. 53.
33 A Munster Farmer, *Reminiscences of Daniel O'Connell during the Agitations of the Veto, Emancipation and Repeal* (London, 1847), p. 25.
34 ibid., p. 43.
35 Dunlop, *Daniel O'Connell*, op. cit., pp. 55–7.

CHAPTER 6
Championing
1813–15

1 Munster Farmer, *Reminiscences of O'Connell*, op. cit., p. 18.
2 *Freeman's Journal*, 8 Feb. 1813.
3 O'Connell, *Select Speeches*, vol. i, pp. 244–5.
4 ibid., p. 248.
5 ibid., p. 261.
6 ibid., p. 258.
7 ibid.
8 ibid., p. 267.
9 ibid., p. 303.
10 ibid., p. 269.
11 ibid., p. 255.
12 ibid., pp. 270–1.
13 ibid., p. 297.
14 ibid., p. 301.
15 ibid., p. 304.
16 Munster Farmer, *Reminiscences of O'Connell*, op. cit., p. 31.
17 C. S. Parker, *Sir Robert Peel from his private papers* (London, 1891), vol. i, p. 117.
18 *Freeman's Journal*, 3 Dec. 1813.
19 O'Connell, *Select Speeches*, vol. i, pp. 341–2.

20 *Dublin Evening Post*, 4 Dec. 1813.
21 O'Connell, *Correspondence*, vol. i, p. 347.
22 O'Connell, *Select Speeches*, vol. i, pp. 366–7.
23 Monsignor Quarantotti to Dr Poynter, C. Butler, *Historical Memoirs of the English, Irish and Scottish Catholics, since The Reformation* (3rd edn, London, 1822), vol. iv, Appendix, Note II, p. 522.
24 *Freeman's Journal*, 9 May 1814.
25 MacDonagh, *Life of O'Connell*, op. cit., p. 92.
26 Parker, *Sir Robert Peel*, op. cit., vol. i, pp. 116–17.
27 14 Dec. 1813, O'Connell, *Correspondence*, vol. i, p. 347.
28 MacDonagh, *Life of O'Connell*, op. cit., p. 65.
29 ibid., p. 66.
30 *Freeman's Journal*, 28 Feb. 1814.
31 O'Connell, *Correspondence*, vol. i, p. 360.
32 MacDonagh, *Life of O'Connell*, op. cit., p. 88.
33 O'Connell, *Correspondence*, vol. i, pp. 370–1.
34 18 Sept. 1814, ibid., p. 380.
35 23 Sept. 1814, ibid., pp. 381–2.
36 O'Connell, *Select Speeches*, vol. i, pp. 447–8.
37 15 May 1815, O'Connell, *Correspondence*, vol. ii, p. 35.
38 [1 June 1815], ibid., p. 41.
39 17 March 1815, ibid., p. 19.
40 25 March 1815, ibid., p. 24.
41 2 April 1815, ibid., p. 26.
42 13 June 1815, ibid., p. 49.
43 12 July 1815, ibid., p. 53.
44 O'Connell, *Select Speeches*, vol. ii, p. 17.
45 ibid., pp. 18–19.
46 ibid., p. 32.
47 Nicholas P. O'Gorman to O'Connell, 19 Aug. 1813, O'Connell, *Correspondence*, vol. i, p. 337; *Dublin Chronicle*, 18 Aug.

1813, quoted in O'Connell, *Correspondence*, vol. i, p. 338 n. 5.

48 Nicholas P. O'Gorman to O'Connell, 19 Aug. 1813, O'Connell, *Correspondence*, vol. i, p. 337.

49 Parker, *Sir Robert Peel*, op. cit., vol. i, p. 186.

50 4 Feb. 1815, O'Connell, *Correspondence*, vol. ii, p. 7.

51 MacDonagh, *Life of O'Connell*, op. cit., p. 69.

52 O'Connell to Richard Newton Bennett, 31 Jan. 1815, O'Connell, *Correspondence*, vol. ii, p. 6.

53 MacDonagh, *Life of O'Connell*, op. cit., p. 75.

54 [probably 3 Feb. 1815], O'Connell, *Correspondence*, vol. ii, p. 7.

55 4 Feb. 1815, ibid., p. 8.

56 MacDonagh, *Life of O'Connell*, op. cit., p. 81.

57 Rickard O'Connell to O'Connell, 4 Feb. 1815, O'Connell, *Correspondence*, vol. ii, pp. 7–8.

58 6 Feb. 1815, ibid., p. 9.

59 [probably 3 Feb. 1815], ibid., p. 7.

60 3 March 1815, ibid., p. 10.

61 Parker, *Sir Robert Peel*, op. cit., vol. i, p. 188.

62 Lord Whitworth to William Gregory, 1 Sept. 1815, ibid., p. 189.

63 William Gregory to Lord Whitworth, 3 Sept. 1815, ibid.

64 [1 Sept. 1815], O'Connell, *Correspondence*, vol. ii, p. 62.

65 Robert Peel to O'Connell, 4 Sept. 1815, ibid., p. 63.

66 O'Connell to Richard Newton Bennett, [4 Sept. 1815], ibid., p. 63.

67 5 Sept. [1815], ibid., p. 65.

68 5 Sept. 1815, Parker, *Sir Robert Peel*, op. cit., vol. i, p. 193.

69 O'Connell to Denys Scully, 13 Sept. 1815, O'Connell, *Correspondence*, vol. ii, p. 66.

70 George Lidwill to O'Connell, [25 Sept. 1815], ibid., p. 70.

71 O'Connell to Denys Scully, 16 Sept. 1815, ibid., p. 67.

72 20 Sept. 1815, ibid., p. 68.

73 O'Connell to Denys Scully, 16 Sept. 1815, ibid., p. 67.

74 Extracts kept by Sir Robert Peel, Parker, *Sir Robert Peel*, op. cit., vol. i, pp. 193–4.

75 Henry Drummond to Sir Robert Peel, 8 Sept. 1815, ibid., p. 197.

76 William Cockburn to Sir Robert Peel, 13 Sept. 1815, ibid., p. 197.

77 O'Connell to Denys Scully, 20 Sept. 1815, O'Connell, *Correspondence*, vol. ii, p. 69.

78 30 Sept. 1815, ibid., p. 70.

CHAPTER 7
Entr'acte
1816

1 7 Jan. 1816, O'Connell, *Correspondence*, vol. ii, p. 78.

2 2 April 1816, ibid., p. 93.

3 *Freeman's Journal*, 11 April 1816.

4 *Dublin University Magazine*, July 1839, p. 113.

5 O'Connell to Mary, 26 March 1816, O'Connell, *Correspondence*, vol. ii, p. 89.

6 O'Connell to Mary, 17 April 1816, ibid., p. 102.

7 O'Connell to Mary, 9 April 1816, ibid., p. 98.

8 11 March 1816, ibid., p. 85.

9 20 March 1816, ibid., p. 88.

10 11 March 1816, ibid., p. 84.

11 13 March 1816, ibid., p. 86.

12 26 March 1816, ibid., p. 89.

13 29 March 1816, ibid., p. 91.

14 1 April 1816, ibid., p. 92.

15 O'Connell to Mary, [24 Aug. 1816], ibid., p. 114.

16 13 March 1816, ibid., p. 86.

17 O'Connell to Mary, 4 Aug. 1816, ibid., p. 104.

18 O'Connell to Mary, 8 Aug. 1816, ibid., p. 107.

19 4 Jan. 1816, ibid., p. 77.
20 17 Feb. 1816, ibid., p. 83.
21 22 Jan. 1816, ibid., p. 80.
22 4 Jan. 1816, ibid., p. 77.
23 O'Connell to Mary, 16 Jan. 1816, ibid., p. 80.
24 22 Jan. 1816, ibid., pp. 80–1.
25 4 Feb. 1816, ibid., p. 81.
26 26 March 1816, ibid., p. 90.
27 17 Feb. 1816, ibid., pp. 83–4.
28 29 Sept. 1816, ibid., p. 121.
29 21 Aug. 1816, ibid., p. 113.
30 8 April 1816, ibid., p. 97.
31 13 April [1816], ibid., p. 100.
32 11 March 1816, ibid., p. 84.
33 18 March 1816, ibid., p. 87.
34 13 April [1816], ibid., pp. 100–1.
35 10 April [1816], ibid., pp. 98–9.
36 4 April 1816, ibid., p. 95.
37 Mary to O'Connell, 8 April 1816, ibid., p. 97.
38 1 March 1817, ibid., p. 135.
39 9 Aug. 1816, ibid., p. 98.
40 11 Aug. 1816, ibid., p. 110.
41 22 Aug. 1816, ibid., pp. 113–14.
42 1 March 1817, ibid., p. 135.
43 22 Jan. 1816, ibid., p. 81.
44 10 Jan. 1816, ibid., p. 78.
45 22 Aug. 1816, ibid., p. 114.
46 13 Jan. 1816, ibid., p. 79.
47 1 April 1816, ibid., p. 93.
48 13 Jan. 1816, ibid., p. 79.
49 18 March 1816, ibid., p. 88.
50 26 March 1816, ibid., p. 90.
51 13 Jan. 1816, ibid., pp. 79–80.
52 3 April 1816, ibid., pp. 94–5.
53 5 Aug. 1816, ibid., p. 105.
54 6 Aug. 1816, ibid., p. 106.
55 17 Oct. 1816, ibid., p. 123.
56 24 Nov. 1816, ibid., p. 123.
57 1 Sept. 1816, ibid., p. 117.
58 3 Sept. 1816, ibid., pp. 117–18.
59 17 Oct. 1816, ibid., p. 123.
60 16 Oct. 1816, ibid., p. 122.
61 26 Sept. 1816, ibid., p. 120.

CHAPTER 8
Ploughing Sands
1817–22

1 O'Connell, Select Speeches, vol. ii, p. 38.
2 Dublin Evening Post, 5 July 1817.
3 ibid., 22 July 1817.
4 O'Connell, Correspondence, vol. ii, pp. 159–60.
5 O'Connell to Charles Phillips, 26 Sept. 1817, ibid., p. 165.
6 O'Connell to Owen O'Conor, 21 Dec. 1817, ibid., p. 184.
7 24 Aug. 1818, ibid., pp. 178–9.
8 O'Connell to Mary, 10 June 1817, ibid., p. 147.
9 10 June 1817, ibid., p. 147.
10 O'Connell to Charles Phillips, 26 Sept. 1817, ibid. p. 165.
11 2 Nov. 1818, ibid., p. 183.
12 21 Dec. 1818, ibid., p. 184.
13 11 Feb. 1819, ibid., p. 197.
14 30 Jan. 1819, ibid., p. 195.
15 15 June 1819, ibid., p. 202.
16 21 Oct. 1819, ibid., pp. 225–6.
17 O'Connell to ——, 21 Oct. 1819, ibid., p. 226.
18 O'Connell, Select Speeches, vol. ii, p. 68.
19 Dublin Evening Post, 30 Oct. 1819.
20 O'Connell, Select Speeches, vol. ii, p. 72.
21 1 Jan. 1821, Letter to the Catholics of Ireland, ibid., p. 95.
22 O'Connell to Mary, 19 March 1820, O'Connell, Correspondence, vol. ii, p. 246.
23 ibid., p. 208 n.1. (Supplied by Eric T. D. Lambert.)
24 3 Aug. 1819, ibid., p. 207.
25 27 Aug. 1819, ibid., p. 217.
26 O'Connell to John Finlay, 6 March 1820, ibid., pp. 236–7.
27 17 April 1820, ibid., p. 257.
28 15 June 1820, ibid., p. 264.
29 Morgan to O'Connell, 25 Aug. 1820, ibid., p. 274.
30 13 Oct. 1820, ibid., p. 286.
31 O'Connell to Hunting Cap, 5 Jan. 1822, ibid., p. 346.
32 O'Connell to Thomas Spring Rice, 16 Nov. 1820, ibid., p. 288.
33 O'Connell to Lord Cloncurry, 16 Nov. 1820, ibid. p. 288.

34 O'Connell to Thomas Spring Rice,
   16 Nov. 1820, ibid., p. 288.
35 17 Nov. 1820, ibid., pp. 290–2.
36 24 Nov. 1820, ibid., p. 292.
37 [probably 26 Nov. 1820], ibid., p.
   295.
38 15 Dec. 1820, ibid., p. 298.
39 [11] Nov. 1820, ibid., p. 304.
40 8 May 1821, ibid., p. 322.
41 O'Connell, Select Speeches, vol. ii,
   p. 96.
42 ibid., p. 110.
43 ibid., p. 125.
44 O'Connell, Correspondence, vol.
   ii, p. 314.
45 14 April 1821, ibid., p. 315.
46 23 April 1821, ibid., p. 319.
47 18 June 1821, ibid., p. 326.
48 Dunlop, Daniel O'Connell, op.
   cit., pp. 118–19.
49 MacDonagh, Life of O'Connell,
   op. cit., p. 110.
50 Freeman's Journal, 4 Sept. 1821.
51 ibid., 10 Sept. 1821.
52 O'Connell to Mary, 12 Oct. 1821,
   O'Connell, Correspondence, vol.
   ii, pp. 335–6.
53 MacDonagh, Life of O'Connell,
   op. cit., p. 111.
54 'The Irish Avatar', The Works of
   Lord Byron, (ed.) E. H. Coleridge
   (London, 1922), vol. iv, pp. 559–
   60.
55 O'Connell, Select Speeches, vol. ii,
   p. 139.
56 O'Connell, Correspondence, vol.
   ii, p. 366.
57 William Plunket to O'Connell, 10
   April 1822, ibid., p. 376.
58 see O'Connell to Marquess of
   Wellesley, 11 July 1822, in
   O'Connell, Select Speeches, vol. ii,
   p. 171.
59 O'Connell, Correspondence, vol.
   ii, pp. 404–5.
60 O'Connell, Select Speeches, vol. ii,
   pp. 171–4.
61 20, 21 Dec. 1822, O'Connell,
   Correspondence, vol. ii, pp. 412–13.
62 T. Wyse, Historical Sketch of the
   late Catholic Association of
   Ireland (London, 1829), vol. i, pp.
   194–5.

CHAPTER 9
Reaping Whirlwinds
1817–27

1 O'Connell, Correspondence, vol.
   ii, p. 141.
2 ibid., p. 142.
3 15 April 1817, ibid., p. 144.
4 See James to O'Connell, 18 May
   1817, ibid., p. 144.
5 10 June 1817, ibid., p. 146.
6 12 June 1817, ibid., p. 149.
7 ibid., p. 150.
8 11 Aug. 1817, ibid., p. 163.
9 O'Connell to Charles Phillips, 26
   Sept. 1817, ibid., p. 165.
10 ibid., p. 169.
11 31 May 1817, ibid., p. 145.
12 12 June 1817, ibid., p. 150.
13 24 June 1817, ibid., p. 152.
14 23 June 1817, ibid., p. 151.
15 23 July 1817, ibid., p. 158.
16 10 June 1817, ibid., p. 146.
17 14 July 1817, ibid., p. 155.
18 22 July 1817, ibid., p. 157.
19 O'Connell to Connell O'Connell,
   18 May 1818, ibid., pp. 176–7.
20 A. Trollope, Framley Parsonage
   (London, 1961), p. 203.
21 O'Connell, Correspondence, vol.
   ii, p. 205.
22 3 Aug. 1817, ibid., p. 162.
23 30 July 1819, ibid., p. 206.
24 O'Connell to Mary, 4 Dec. 1827,
   ibid., vol. iii, p. 360.
25 14 May 1822, ibid., vol. ii, p. 388.
26 O'Connell to Kate, 24 May 1822,
   ibid., vol. ii, p. 392.
27 30 July 1819, ibid., p. 205.
28 28 March 1822, ibid., p. 362.
29 22 Dec. 1820, ibid., p. 299.
30 19 April 1821, ibid., p. 318.
31 15 Jan. 1822, ibid., p. 350.
32 17 Feb. 1822, ibid., p. 357.

33 18 Jan. 1822, ibid., p. 355.
34 James to O'Connell, 17 Feb. 1822, ibid., p. 357.
35 28 March 1822, ibid., p. 363.
36 22 March 1822, ibid., p. 362.
37 1 April 1822, ibid., pp. 363–4.
38 5 April 1822, ibid., pp. 369–70.
39 8 April 1822, ibid., pp. 372–3.
40 4 May 1822, ibid., pp. 382, 389.
41 26 May 1822, ibid., p. 394.
42 O'Connell to Mary, 23 May 1823, ibid., p. 475.
43 26 March 1823, ibid., pp. 456–7.
44 12 March 1823, ibid., p. 447.
45 27 Dec. 1822, ibid., pp. 417–18.
46 O'Connell to James Sugrue, 7 Oct. 1822, ibid., p. 411.
47 O'Connell to Mary, 6 March 1823, ibid., p. 444.
48 ibid.
49 22 and 23 May 1823, ibid., p. 475.
50 20 April 1823, ibid., p. 463.
51 14 June 1823, ibid., p. 486.
52 O'Connell to Mary, 14, 16 and 17 June 1823, ibid., pp. 486–7.
53 O'Connell to Mary, 13 June 1823, ibid., p. 483.
54 O'Connell to Mary, 14, 15 and 17 June 1823, ibid., p. 486.
55 13 July 1823, ibid., p. 501.
56 4 Sept. 1823, ibid., p. 505.
57 8 Sept. 1823, ibid., p. 506.
58 11 Sept. 1823, ibid., pp. 507–8.
59 16 Sept. 1823, ibid., p. 508.
60 17 Sept. 1823, ibid., pp. 509–10.
61 O'Connell to Mary, 27 Jan. 1824, ibid., vol. iii, p. 10.
62 4 Feb. 1824, ibid., pp. 17–18.
63 6 Feb. 1824, ibid., p. 23.
64 12 Feb. 1824, ibid., p. 29.
65 16 Feb. 1824, ibid., p. 33.
66 24 Jan. 1823, ibid., vol. ii, p. 429.
67 O'Connell to Mary, 14 May 1822, ibid., p. 388.
68 O'Connell to Mary, 26 Sept. 1824, ibid., vol. iii, pp. 79–80.
69 O'Connell to John Primrose, Jr, 14 June 1825, ibid., p. 184.

70 1 Nov. 1825, ibid., pp. 196–7.
71 4 Dec. 1825, ibid., p. 211.
72 Mary to O'Connell, 18 Feb. 1825, ibid., p. 114.
73 2 Dec. 1825, ibid., p. 209.
74 *Ireland and its Rulers since 1829* (London, 1844–5), p. 19.
75 *The Irish Bar, comprising anecdotes, bon-mots and biographical sketches of the bench and bar of Ireland* (London, 1879), p. 235.
76 8 May 1822, O'Connell, *Correspondence*, vol. ii, p. 385.
77 18 March 1826, ibid., vol. iii, p. 240.
78 30 Oct. 1827, ibid., p. 353.
79 19 May 1827, ibid., p. 315.
80 4 Dec. 1827, ibid., p. 360.
81 8 Dec. 1827, ibid., p. 362.
82 4 May 1825, ibid., p. 160.
83 7 May 1825, ibid., p. 166.

CHAPTER 10
Four Years of Irish History
1822–6

1 Gwynn, *Daniel O'Connell*, op. cit., pp. 143–4.
2 Rules and regulations of the Catholic Association of Ireland, Wyse, *Catholic Association of Ireland*, op. cit., vol. ii, appendix xiv, p. xxxvii.
3 *Freeman's Journal*, 25 Oct. 1824.
4 ibid., 17 May 1824.
5 J. A. Reynolds, *The Catholic Emancipation Crisis in Ireland 1823–1829* (New Haven, 1954), p. 66.
6 *Freeman's Journal*, 2 March 1824.
7 *Dublin Evening Post*, 27 Jan. 1824.
8 G. de Beaumont, *Ireland: social, political and religious*, (ed.) W. C. Taylor (London, 1839), vol. ii, p. 79.
9 *Freeman's Journal*, 17 June 1823.
10 O'Connell to Mary, 9 March

1824, O'Connell,
Correspondence, vol. iii, p. 50.

11 *Freeman's Journal*, 4 Dec. 1824.

12 ibid., 3 Dec. 1824.

13 ibid., 2 Aug. 1824.

14 B.L. Peel papers 40322, f. 119, quoted in Reynolds, *Catholic Emancipation Crisis*, op. cit., p. 51.

15 Robert Peel to J. L. Foster, 2 Nov. 1824, R.I.A., Peel Letters to J. L. Foster, quoted in Reynolds, *Catholic Emancipation Crisis*, op. cit., p. 58.

16 *Saunder's Newsletter*, 17 Dec. 1824.

17 3 Feb. 1825, *Hansard*, n.s. vol. xii, col. 65.

18 10 Feb. 1825, ibid., cols. 171–2.

19 ibid., col. 260.

20 28 Feb. [1825], O'Connell, *Correspondence*, vol. iii, p. 125.

21 Sheil, *Sketches, Legal and Political*, vol. ii, p. 47.

22 O'Connell to Mary, 28 Feb. [1825], O'Connell, *Correspondence*, vol. iii, p. 125.

23 O'Connell to Mary, [7 March 1825], ibid., pp. 131–2.

24 8 March 1825, ibid., p. 132.

25 17 March 1825, ibid., pp. 141–2.

26 Lord Colchester, *Diary*, 17 March 1825, quoted in Dunlop, *Daniel O'Connell*, op. cit., p. 157.

27 4 March 1825, O'Connell, *Correspondence*, vol. iii, p. 128

28 O'Connell to Edward Dwyer, 15 March 1825, ibid., p. 140.

29 Dunlop, *Daniel O'Connell*, op. cit., p. 158.

30 *Sketches, Legal and Political*, op. cit., vol. ii, pp. 29–30.

31 [7 March 1825], O'Connell, *Correspondence*, vol. iii, p. 131.

32 *Dublin Evening Post*, 18 Aug. 1825.

33 Dunlop, *Daniel O'Connell*, op. cit., p. 169.

34 W. J. Fitzpatrick, *The Life, Times and Correspondence of the Right Rev. Dr. Doyle* (Dublin, 1880), vol. i, p. 451.

35 *Freeman's Journal*, 14 July 1825.

36 O'Connell, *Correspondence*, vol. iii, p. 131.

37 Wyse, *Catholic Association of Ireland*, op. cit., vol. i, pp. 286–9.

38 19 June 1826, O'Connell, *Correspondence*, vol. iii, pp. 248–9.

39 O'Connell to Mary, 21 June 1826, ibid., p. 250.

40 *Freeman's Journal*, 6 July 1826.

41 ibid.

42 John Palliser to —, 24 June 1826, I.S.P.O., Official Papers, second series, 58822/915, quoted in Reynolds, *Catholic Emancipation Crisis*, op. cit., p. 96.

43 *Freeman's Journal*, 8 July 1826.

44 ibid.

45 O'Connell, *Correspondence*, vol. iii, p. 265.

46 O'Connell to Edward Dwyer, 31 Aug. 1826, ibid., p. 268.

47 *Freeman's Journal*, 9 Aug. 1826. Coppinger's letter to O'Dwyer was read at the Catholic Association meeting of 7 August 1826.

48 ibid., 8 Sept. 1826.

49 ibid., 11 Sept. 1826.

50 Parker, *Sir Robert Peel*, op. cit., vol. ii, p. 64

51 *Dublin Evening Post*, 11 July 1826.

52 O'Connell, *Correspondence*, vol. iii, pp. 282–3.

CHAPTER 11
The First Hurrah
1827–8

1 O'Connell, *Correspondence*, vol. iii, p. 288.

2 15 Jan. 1827, ibid., p. 287.

3 22 Feb. 1827, ibid., p. 291.

4 23 Feb. 1827, ibid., pp. 292–3.

5 ibid., p. 293.

6 21 March 1827, ibid., p. 300.

7 ibid., p. 301.

8 *Dublin Evening Post*, 19 April 1827.

9 Eneas MacDonnell to O'Connell, 23 April 1827, O'Connell, *Correspondence*, vol. iii, p. 307.

10 Knight of Kerry to O'Connell, 23 April 1827, ibid., p. 309.

11 28 May 1827, ibid., p. 316.

12 9 June 1827, ibid., p. 322.

13 O'Connell to Richard Newton Bennett, 11 June 1827, ibid., p. 325.

14 29 Nov. 1827, ibid., p. 358.

15 9 Aug. 1827, ibid., p. 340.

16 26 Sept. 1827, ibid., pp. 344–5.

17 24 Oct. 1827, ibid., p. 350.

18 O'Connell to Thomas Spring Rice, 29 Nov. 1827, ibid., p. 358.

19 O'Connell to Thomas Spring Rice, 11 Dec. 1827, ibid., p. 364.

20 1 Dec. 1827, ibid., p. 360.

21 Henry Brougham to O'Connell, [28 April 1827], ibid., p. 310.

22 2 Jan. 1827, ibid., p. 285.

23 O'Connell to Edward Dwyer, 5 April 1827, ibid., p. 303.

24 Robert Peel to Lord Anglesey, 7 April 1828, quoted in Earl Stanhope and Edward Cardwell (eds.), *Memoirs by Sir Robert Peel* (London, 1957–8), vol. i, pp. 36–7.

25 Richard Sheil to O'Connell, 30 Sept. [1827], O'Connell, *Correspondence*, vol. iii, p. 347.

26 22 March 1827, ibid., p. 302.

27 *Dublin Evening Post* 22 Dec. 1827.

28 8 June 1827, O'Connell, *Correspondence*, vol. iii, pp. 319–20.

29 9 June 1827, ibid., p. 322.

30 30 Sept. 1827, ibid., p. 346.

31 Wyse, *Catholic Association of Ireland*, op. cit., vol. i, p. 300.

32 O'Connell to Edward Dwyer, 21 March 1827, O'Connell, *Correspondence*, vol. iii, p. 301.

33 *Dublin Evening Post*, 26 July 1827.

34 ibid.

35 O'Connell to Edward Dwyer, 3 Aug. 1827, O'Connell, *Correspondence*, vol. iii, pp. 336–7.

36 Reynolds, *Catholic Emancipation Crisis*, op. cit., p. 102.

37 Wyse, *Catholic Association of Ireland*, op. cit., vol. i, pp. 310–11.

38 ibid., pp. 317–18.

39 ibid., pp. 320–1.

40 O'Connell, *Correspondence*, vol. iii, p. 345.

41 *Freeman's Journal*, 23 Aug. 1827.

42 O'Connell, *Correspondence*, vol. iii, pp. 372–3.

43 27 Feb. 1828, ibid., p. 377.

44 27 May 1828, ibid., pp. 381–2.

45 Thomas Steele, quoted in Wyse, *Catholic Association of Ireland*, op. cit., vol. i, p. 379n.

46 *Freeman's Journal*, 26 June 1828.

47 Bishop Doyle to O'Connell, 27 June 1828, Fitzpatrick, *Right Rev. Dr Doyle*, op. cit., vol. ii, pp. 75–6, and *Freeman's Journal*, 28 June 1828.

48 Lord Anglesey to Robert Peel, 23 June 1828, Stanhope and Cardwell (eds), *Memoirs of Sir Robert Peel*, op. cit., vol. i, p. 131.

49 Sheil, *Sketches, Legal and Political*, op. cit., vol. ii, pp. 117–18.

50 W. M. Thackeray, *The Irish Sketch Book* (London, 1843), p. 177.

51 MacDonagh, *Life of O'Connell*, op. cit., pp. 157, 161–2.

52 O'Flanagan, *The Irish Bar*, op. cit., p. 249.

53 Sheil, *Sketches Legal and Political*, op. cit., vol. ii, p. 136.

54 MacDonagh, *Life of O'Connell*, op. cit., pp. 161, 162.

55 ibid., p. 164.

56 *Dublin Evening Post*, 12 July 1828.

57 Fitzgerald to Peel, 5 July 1828, Stanhope and Cardwell (eds.), *Memoirs of Sir Robert Peel*, op. cit., vol. i, p. 114.

58 Robert Peel to Sir Walter Scott, 3 April 1829, Parker, *Sir Robert Peel*, op. cit., vol. ii, pp. 99–100.

59 MacDonagh, *Life of O'Connell*, op. cit., p. 165. See also *Dublin Evening Post*, 12 July 1828.

60 *Dublin Evening Post*, 12 July 1828.

61 O'Connell to Cornelius MacLoghlin, 5 July 1828, O'Connell, *Correspondence*, vol. iii, p. 386.

62 Edward Dwyer to O'Connell, 5 July 1828, ibid., p. 387.

63 ibid.

CHAPTER 12
The Famous Victory
1828–9

1 *Dublin Evening Post*, 26 Aug. 1828.

2 Wyse, *Catholic Association of Ireland*, op. cit., vol. i, p. 45.

3 ibid., p. 408.

4 Lord Anglesey to Robert Peel, 8 Sept. 1828, quoted in speech on 4 May 1829 in debate in House of Lords on his recall from Ireland, *Hansard*, n. s., vol. xxi, col. 999.

5 Duke of Wellington to Lord Bathurst, 24 Nov. 1828, A. Wellington (ed.), *Despatches, Correspondence and Memoranda* (London, 1867–80), vol. v, p. 280.

6 17 Sept. 1828, O'Connell, *Correspondence*, vol. iii, pp. 407–8.

7 Wyse, *Catholic Association of Ireland*, op. cit., vol. ii, p. clxx.

8 O'Connell to Rev. Michael Slattery, 2 Sept. 1828, O'Connell, *Correspondence*, vol. iii, pp. 402–3.

9 11 July 1828, ibid., p. 301.

10 *Morning Register*, 17 July 1828.

11 27 Sept. 1828, O'Connell, *Correspondence*, vol. iii, pp. 414–15.

12 O'Connell to Edward Dwyer, ibid., vol. iv, p. 27.

13 22 Sept. 1828, ibid., vol. iii, pp. 411–12.

14 4 Sept. 1828, ibid., p. 404.

15 24 Sept. 1828, ibid., p. 412.

16 *Freeman's Journal*, 15 Nov. 1828.

17 O'Connell to Lord Cloncurry, O'Connell, *Correspondence*, vol. iii, p. 404.

18 Wyse, *Catholic Association of Ireland*, op. cit., vol. ii, p. 48.

19 *Dublin Evening Post*, 5 Feb. 1829.

20 O'Connell, *Correspondence*, vol. iv, p. 6.

21 17 March 1829, ibid. p. 31.

22 *Freeman's Journal*, 11 Feb. 1829.

23 O'Connell, *Correspondence*, vol. iv, p. 16.

24 3 March 1829, ibid., pp. 17–18.

25 O'Connell to Mary, 6 March 1829, ibid., p. 20.

26 O'Connell to the People of Ireland, *Freeman's Journal*, 12 March 1829.

27 O'Connell to Edward Dwyer, 6 March and 11 March 1829, O'Connell, *Correspondence*, vol. iv, pp. 24, 27.

28 12 March 1829, ibid., p. 28.

29 8 Feb. 1829, O'Connell, *Correspondence*, vol. iv, p. 8.

30 4 March 1829, ibid., p. 18.

31 O'Connell to Mary, 6 March 1829, ibid., p. 20.

32 O'Connell to Edward Dwyer, 6 March 1829, ibid., p. 22.

33 O'Connell to Rev. W. A. O'Meara OSF, 18 March 1829, ibid., p. 32.

34 28 March 1829, ibid., pp. 35–6.

35 11 April 1829, ibid., pp. 43–5.

36 14 April 1829, ibid., p. 45.

37 11 April 1829, ibid., p. 43.

38 11 Sept. 1829, ibid., p. 96.

39 14 May 1829, ibid., p. 59.

40 O'Connell to Knight of Kerry, 12 May 1829, ibid., p. 55.
41 O'Connell to Charles Sugrue, 20 May 1829, ibid., p. 63.
42 Hunting Cap to O'Connell, 16 May 1811, ibid., vol. i, p. 257.
43 15 April 1829, ibid., vol. iv, p. 46.
44 1 May 1829, ibid., p. 52.
45 30 July 1819, ibid., vol. ii, p. 205.
46 *Dail Reports*, vol. ii, p. 11.
47 10 Feb. 1829, O'Connell, *Correspondence*, vol. iv, p. 11.
48 25 April 1829, ibid., p. 50.
49 ibid.
50 13 April 1829, ibid., p. 44.
51 7 July 1829, ibid., p. 81.
52 6 March 1829, ibid., p. 21.
53 8 April 1829, ibid., p. 41.
54 15 April 1829, ibid., p. 46.
55 5 March 1829, ibid., p. 19.
56 13 April 1829, ibid., p. 45.
57 8 Feb. 1829, ibid., p. 9
58 10 Feb. 1829, ibid., p. 11.
59 28 Aug. 1829, ibid., p. 94.
60 11 March 1829, ibid., pp. 26–7.
61 11 April 1829, ibid., p. 43.
62 O'Connell to Mary, 21 May 1829, ibid., p. 66.
63 21 May 1829, ibid., p. 66.
64 O'Connell to Pierce Mahony, 4 June 1829, ibid., p. 74.
65 O'Connell to David Mahony, 14 June 1829, ibid., p. 77.
66 O'Connell to Pierce Mahony, 4 June 1829, ibid., p. 73.
67 30 July 1829, J. Bentham, *Works*, (ed.) J. Bowring (Edinburgh, 1843–59), vol. xi, p. 20.
68 6 Aug. 1829, O'Connell, *Correspondence*, vol. iv, pp. 87–8.
69 O'Connell to John Howard Payne, ibid., pp. 70–1.

CHAPTER 13
A Sort of Plateau
1830

1 1 March 1831, O'Connell, *Correspondence*, vol. iv, p. 131.
2 O'Connell to Mary O'Connell, 2 June 1831, ibid., p. 328.
3 W. T. Fagan, *The Life and Times of Daniel O'Connell* (Cork, 1847–8), vol. ii, pp. 179–80.
4 O'Connell to Mary O'Connell, 28 Nov. 1800, O'Connell, *Correspondence*, vol. i, p. 34.
5 [13 March 1832], ibid., vol. iv, p.404.
6 Mary O'Connell to O'Connell [17 March 1830], ibid., p. 141.
7 [1] and 2 March [1830], ibid., pp. 130–1, 133.
8 24 July [1830], ibid., p. 191.
9 'Her affections were remarkable for feminine strength and fervour. Her intellect was of a masculine order, and good sense was its chief attribute.' Fagan, *Life and Times of O'Connell*, op. cit., vol. ii, p. 582.
10 2 March [1830], O'Connell, *Correspondence*, vol. iv, pp. 132–3.
11 [17 March 1830], ibid., p. 140.
12 [1 Dec. 1830], ibid., p. 240.
13 26 May 1831, ibid., p. 326.
14 2 June 1831, ibid., pp. 327–8.
15 5 Dec. 1830, ibid., pp. 242–3.
16 Daunt, *Personal Recollections*, vol. i, p. 250.
17 O'Connell to Mary O'Connell, 2 March 1831, O'Connell, *Correspondence*, vol. iv, p. 283.
18 O'Connell to Mary O'Connell, 28 Feb. 1831, ibid., pp. 281–2.
19 10 March 1831, ibid., p. 290.
20 [5 March 1831], ibid., p. 286.
21 26 May 1831, ibid., p. 326.
22 O'Connell to Richard Barrett, 29 Oct. 1832, ibid., p. 461.
23 14 Dec. 1839, ibid., p. 291.
24 Fagan, *Life and Times of O'Connell*, op. cit., vol. ii, pp. 626–7.

25 W. H. Curran, *Sketches of the Irish Bar; with Essays, Literary and Political* (London, 1855), vol. i, pp. 172–4.
26 *Freeman's Journal*, 29 Oct. 1829.
27 ibid., 2 Nov. 1829.
28 ibid., 29 Oct. 1829.
29 MacDonagh, *Life of O'Connell*, op. cit., p. 204.
30 *Freeman's Journal*, 29 Oct. 1829.
31 ibid., 3 Nov. 1829.
32 ibid., 2 Nov. 1829.
33 ibid., 3 Nov. 1829.
34 MacDonagh, *Life of O'Connell*, op. cit., p. 204.
35 *Freeman's Journal*, 29 Oct. 1829.
36 10 May 1830, O'Connell, *Correspondence*, vol. iv, p. 163.
37 24 June 1830, ibid., p. 175.
38 Aug. 1830, ibid., pp. 194–5.
39 Jane Austen, *Mansfield Park* (London, 1948), ch. 34, pp. 277–8.
40 Daunt, *Personal Recollections*, op. cit., vol. ii, p. 44.
41 ibid., vol. i, pp. 127–8.
42 O'Connell to P. V. Fitzpatrick, 4 Sept. 1837, O'Connell, *Correspondence*, vol. vi, p. 84.
43 Seamus MacCall, *Thomas Moore* (London, 1935), p. 101.
44 15 March 1820, O'Connell, *Correspondence*, vol. ii, p. 243.
45 Houston, *Early Life and Journal*, op. cit., pp. 119–20.
46 16 Feb. 1830, O'Connell, *Correspondence*, vol. iv, p. 129.
47 11 Sept. 1829, ibid., p. 95.
48 *Hansard*, n.s. vol. xxii, col. 799.
49 ibid., n.s. vol. xxiv, col. 794.
50 13 July 1833, *Daniel O'Connell Upon American Slavery* (New York, 1860), p. 47.
51 *Liberator*, 7 Aug. 1840, quoted in Gilbert Osofsky, 'Abolitionists, Irish Immigrants, and the Dilemmas of Romantic Nationalism', *American Historical Review*, vol. 80, no. 4, Oct. 1975, p. 893.
52 *Liberator*, 6 Dec. 1839, quoted in Osofsky, 'Abolitionists, Irish Immigrants, and the Dilemmas of Romantic Nationalism', op. cit., p. 892.
53 Osofsky, 'Abolitionists, Irish Immigrants, and the Dilemmas of Romantic Nationalism', op. cit., p. 891.
54 17 June 1840, O'Connell, *Correspondence*, vol. vi, p. 337.
55 20 June 1840, ibid., pp. 338–40.
56 W. E. Gladstone, 'Daniel O'Connell', *Nineteenth Century*, vol. 25, no. 143, Jan. 1889, pp. 156–7.
57 11 Sept. 1829, O'Connell, *Correspondence*, vol. iv, p. 95.
58 O'Connell, *Select Speeches*, op. cit., vol. i, p. 376.
59 Cusack (ed.), *Speeches and Public Letters of the Liberator*, op. cit., vol. ii, p. 285.
60 Daunt, *Personal Recollections*, op. cit., vol. i, p. 76.
61 ibid., p. 156.
62 ibid., p. 78.
63 O'Connell to the Ministers and Office-Bearers of the Wesleyan Methodist Societies of Manchester, 1 Aug. 1839, *Freeman's Journal*, 5 Aug. 1839.
64 O'Connell to Christopher Fitz-Simon, 11 Sept. 1830, O'Connell, *Correspondence*, vol. iv, pp. 203–5.
65 Pope Gregory XVI, 'Mirari vos', 15 Aug. 1832, in Colman J. Barry (ed.), *Readings in Church History* (Westminster, 1965), vol. iii, p. 41.
66 O'Connell to a friend in Rome, 1837, O'Connell, *Correspondence*, vol. vi, p. 1.
67 Daunt, *Personal Recollections*, op. cit., vol. i, p. 75.
68 Helen Coldrick, 'Daniel O'Connell and Religious Freedom', PhD thesis, Fordham University, 1974, p. 106.
69 13 Feb. 1838, *Hansard*, 3rd series, vol. xl, cols 1085–6.
70 ibid., col. 1097.

71 ibid., col. 1086.

72 T. Moore, 'The Song of O'Ruark', *The Poetical Works of Thomas Moore*, (ed.) Willia:.. Rossetti (London, [1882]), p. 367.

CHAPTER 14
The Houseman
1830–1

1 C. Greville, *The Greville Memoirs; a journal of the reigns of King George IV and King William IV*, (ed.) H. Reeve (London, 1875), vol. ii, p. 100.

2 March 1833, A. Aspinall (ed.), *Three Early Nineteenth Century Diaries* (London, 1952), p. 314.

3 O'Connell to James Sugrue, 21 May 1829, O'Connell, *Correspondence*, vol. iv, p. 67.

4 4 Feb. 1830, *Hansard*, n.s. vol. xxii, col. 94.

5 O'Connell to Charles Sugrue, 20 May 1829, O'Connell, *Correspondence*, vol. iv, p. 63.

6 Greville, *Greville Memoirs; journal of reigns of King George IV and King William IV*, op. cit., vol. i, p. 275.

7 9 Feb. 1830, O'Connell, *Correspondence*, vol. iv, p. 124.

8 11 Feb. 1830, Lord Broughton (J. C. Hobhouse), *Recollections of a Long Life, with additional extracts from his private diaries*, (ed.) Lady Dorchester (London, 1909–11), vol. iv, p. 8.

9 Fagan, *Life and Times of O'Connell*, op. cit., vol. ii, p. 315.

10 *Dublin Evening Post*, 18 Jan. 1827, quoted in F. O'Ferrall, 'O'Connellite Politics and Political Education', PhD thesis, Trinity College, Dublin, 1978, p. 310.

11 O'Connell to C. Sinclair Cullen, 16 Feb. 1830, O'Connell, *Correspondence*, vol. iv, p. 130.

12 Richard Scott to O'Connell, 24 April 1830, ibid., p. 156.

13 *Dublin Evening Post*, 29 June 1830.

14 25 June 1830, O'Connell, *Correspondence*, vol. iv, p. 177.

15 21 April 1830, ibid., p. 155.

16 24 June 1830, ibid., p. 175.

17 20 April 1830, ibid., p. 154.

18 O'Connell to Richard Barrett, 8 July 1830, ibid., p. 187.

19 ibid.

20 P. V. Fitzpatrick to O'Connell, 3 Oct. 1830, ibid., p. 212.

21 O'Connell to R. N. Bennett, 5 Oct. 1830, ibid., p. 213.

22 *Freeman's Journal*, 12 Oct. 1830.

23 11 Oct. 1830, O'Connell, *Correspondence*, vol. iv, pp. 213–14.

24 Fagan, *Life and Times of O'Connell*, op. cit., vol. ii, p. 54.

25 *Freeman's Journal*, 20 Oct. 1830.

26 *Dublin Evening Post*, 30 Oct. 1830.

27 3 Nov. 1830, O'Connell, *Correspondence*, vol. iv, pp. 221–2.

28 31 Aug. 1830, ibid., p. 200.

29 3 Sept. 1830, ibid., pp. 201–3.

30 A. Macintyre, *The Liberator: Daniel O'Connell and the Irish Party, 1830–47* (London, 1965), p. 79.

31 P. V. Fitzpatrick to O'Connell, 3 Oct. 1830, O'Connell, *Correspondence*, vol. iv, pp. 211–12.

32 O'Connell to Bishop MacHale, 3 Dec. 1830, ibid., p. 241.

33 *Hansard*, 3rd series, vol. i, col. 329.

34 ibid., col. 327.

35 6 Feb. 1829, O'Connell, *Correspondence*, vol. iv, p. 7.

36 O'Connell to R. N. Bennett, 31 Dec. 1830, ibid., p. 247.

37 1 Dec. 1830, ibid., p. 240.

38 Lord Anglesey to Lord Melbourne, 21 Dec. 1830, Plas Newydd Papers, quoted in Marquess of Anglesey, *One Leg. The Life and Times of Henry William Paget, First*

Marquess of Anglesey (London, 1961), p. 378.

39 Lord Anglesey to Lord Holland, 11 Dec. 1830, Ilchester MS, quoted in Anglesey, *One Leg*, op. cit., p. 245.

40 Lord Cloncurry, *Personal Recollections of the Life and Times, with Extracts from the Correspondence of Valentine Lord Cloncurry* (Dublin, 1849), pp. 411–12.

41 O'Connell to Edward Dwyer, 29 Nov. 1830, O'Connell, *Correspondence*, vol. iv, p. 237.

42 1 Dec. 1830, ibid., p. 239.

43 *Freeman's Journal*, 11 Jan. 1831.

44 Thomas Wallace to O'Connell, 19 Jan. 1831, O'Connell, *Correspondence*, vol. iv, p. 257.

45 Macintyre, *The Liberator*, op. cit., p. 23.

46 7 Feb. 1831, O'Connell, *Correspondence*, vol. iv, p. 269.

47 Edward Dwyer to O'Connell, 26 Feb. 1831, ibid., p. 279.

48 5 March 1831, *Freeman's Journal*, 8 March 1831.

49 5 March 1831, O'Connell, *Correspondence*, vol. iv, p. 286.

50 8 March 1831, ibid., p. 287.

51 10 March 1831, Greville, *Greville Memoirs; journal of reigns of King George IV and King William IV*, op. cit., vol. ii, p. 125.

52 Lord Grey to Sir Francis Burdett, 3 April 1831, M. W. Patterson, *Sir Francis Burdett and his times 1770–1844* (London, 1931), vol. ii, p. 586.

53 21 Feb. 1831, *Hansard*, 3rd series, vol. ii, col. 816.

54 12 May 1830, ibid., n.s., vol. xxiv, col. 651.

55 Jonathan Swift, 'A Letter to a Young Gentleman, lately entered into Holy Orders', 9 Jan. 1720, in *Satires and Personal Writings*, (ed.) W. A. Eddy (London, 1932), p. 273.

56 *Freeman's Journal*, 23 Oct. 1830.

57 ibid., 24 Oct. 1830.

CHAPTER 15
Systole and Diastole
1831–2

1 29 April 1831, O'Connell, *Correspondence*, vol. iv, p. 309.

2 2 May 1831, ibid., p. 313.

3 Maurice Fitzgerald to John Croker, 23 Feb. 1831, Croker Papers, Duke University Library.

4 O'Connell to Bishop Doyle, 16 June 1831, O'Connell, *Correspondence*, vol. iv, p. 335.

5 O'Connell to Richard Barrett, 2 July 1831, ibid., p. 337.

6 ibid., p. 338.

7 ibid.

8 18 June 1832, *Hansard*, 3rd series, vol. xiii, col. 805.

9 ibid., vol. v, col. 1122.

10 Fagan, *Life and Times of O'Connell*, op. cit., vol. ii, p. 67.

11 5 Oct. 1831, O'Connell, *Correspondence*, vol. iv, p. 355.

12 8 Oct. 1831, ibid., p. 357.

13 Lord Grey to Sir Francis Burdett, 22 Oct. 1831, Patterson, *Sir Francis Burdett*, op. cit., vol. ii, p. 596.

14 Fitzpatrick, *Right Rev. Dr Doyle*, op. cit., vol. ii, p. 334.

15 19 Oct. 1831, O'Connell, *Correspondence*, vol. iv, pp. 359–60.

16 O'Connell to Lord Duncannon, 4 Dec. 1831, ibid., p. 370.

17 *Pilot*, 25 Nov. 1831.

18 O'Connell to Lord Duncannon, 4 Dec. 1831, O'Connell, *Correspondence*, vol. iv, p. 371.

19 *Pilot*, 7 Dec. 1831, quoted in ibid., p. 388 n. 1.

20 Lord Duncannon to O'Connell, 28 Nov. 1831, O'Connell, *Correspondence*, vol. iv, p. 366.

21 26 Dec. 1831, ibid., p. 389.

22 8 March 1831, *Hansard*, 3rd series, vol. iii, col. 181.

23 28 June 1831, ibid., vol. iv, col. 423.

24 22 June 1831, ibid., col. 247.

25 O'Connell to Charles Rivers Carroll, 21 Feb. 1829, *Morning Register*, 26 Feb. 1829.

26 4 March 1831, *Hansard*, 3rd series, vol. iii, col. 21.

27 4 July 1831, ibid., vol. iv, cols 652–3.

28 3 Jan. 1832, O'Connell, *Correspondence*, vol. iv, pp. 396–7.

29 22 Jan. 1832, ibid., p. 400.

30 11 Feb. 1832, ibid., p. 401.

31 13 March 1832, ibid., p. 404.

32 *Freeman's Journal*, 26 March 1832.

33 ibid., 22 March 1832.

34 O'Connell to James Dwyer, 17 May 1832, O'Connell, *Correspondence*, vol. iv, p. 417.

35 19 March 1832, ibid., p. 405.

36 O'Connell to the *Newry Examiner*, 10 July 1832, quoted in ibid., p. 427.

37 19 July 1832, O'Connell, *Correspondence*, vol. iv, p. 427.

38 25 Oct. 1832, ibid., p. 460.

39 4 Aug. 1832, ibid., p. 434.

40 17 July 1832, ibid., pp. 425–6.

41 O'Connell to P. V. Fitzpatrick, 17 July 1832, ibid., p. 426.

42 P. V. Fitzpatrick to O'Connell, 21 July 1832, ibid., p. 432.

43 O'Connell to Mr Galloway, 28 June 1832, ibid., p. 424.

44 O'Connell to the editor, *Pilot*, 18 July 1832.

45 O'Connell to John Primrose, 17 July 1832, O'Connell, *Correspondence*, vol. iv, p. 426.

46 19 July 1832, ibid., p. 431.

47 O'Connell to P. V. Fitzpatrick, 29 Aug. 1832, ibid., pp. 441–2.

48 ibid., p. 442.

49 29 Sept. 1832, ibid., pp. 454–5.

50 O'Connell to P. V. Fitzpatrick, 7 Nov. 1832, ibid., p. 464.

51 O'Connell to P. V. Fitzpatrick, 22 Sept. 1832, ibid., p. 451.

52 ibid.

53 20 Dec. 1832, ibid., pp. 477–8.

54 ibid., p. 476.

55 14 April 1832, ibid., p. 413.

56 18 April 1832, ibid., p. 414.

57 O'Connell to O'Conor Don, [22 April 1832], ibid., p. 415.

58 21 July 1832, ibid., p. 432.

59 19 July 1832, ibid., p. 431.

60 O'Connell to John Primrose jr, 17 July 1832, ibid., p. 427.

61 30 March 1832, ibid., p. 407.

62 O'Connell to Mary, [4 April 1832], ibid., p. 409.

63 11 Aug. 1832, ibid., p. 436.

64 31 March 1832, ibid., p. 408.

65 [3 April 1832], ibid., p. 409.

66 ibid.

67 26 Dec. 1832, ibid., pp. 480–1.

68 25 Nov. 1831, ibid., p. 363.

69 Note in Grove Jones' letter book, quoted in ibid., p. 400, n. 1.

70 29 April 1832, O'Connell, *Correspondence*, vol. iv, p. 415.

CHAPTER 16
The Uses of Repeal

1833–4

1 27 Nov. 1832, O'Connell, *Correspondence*, vol. iv, p. 471.

2 *Nation*, 4 March 1843.

3 10 Geo. IV c. 7.

4 J. Levy (ed.), *A Full and Revised Report of the Three Days' Discussion in the Corporation of Dublin on the Repeal of the Union* (Dublin, 1843), pp. 191–2.

5 *Freeman's Journal*, 10 May 1832.

6 O'Connell to P. V. Fitzpatrick, 10 Jan. 1833, O'Connell, *Correspondence*, vol. v, p. 2.

7 Macintyre, *The Liberator*, op. cit., p. 57.

8 14 Jan. 1833, O'Connell, *Correspondence*, vol. v, p. 3.

9 Diary of E. J. Littleton, 3 Feb. 1833,

Aspinall (ed.), *Three Early Nineteenth Century Diaries*, op. cit., p. 293.

10 O'Connell to P. V. Fitzpatrick, 21 Feb. 1833, O'Connell, *Correspondence*, vol. v, p. 11.

11 O'Connell to P. V. Fitzpatrick [c. 22 March 1833], ibid., p. 21.

12 Diary of Denis Le Marchant, Feb. 1833, Aspinall (ed.), *Three Early Nineteenth Century Diaries*, op. cit., p. 295.

13 [15 Feb. 1833], O'Connell, *Correspondence*, vol. v, p. 8.

14 Diary of Lord Ellenborough, 15 Feb. 1833, Aspinall (ed.), *Three Early Nineteenth Century Diaries*, op. cit., p. 302.

15 Anglesey memorandum on Illegal Confederacies, 6 Jan. 1833, H. O. Papers 100/241, ff. 79–81.

16 17 Feb. 1833, O'Connell, *Correspondence*, vol. v, p. 9.

17 Athlone Trades Political Union to O'Connell, 4 March 1833, ibid., p. 13.

18 Diary of E. J. Littleton, 26 Feb. 1833, Aspinall (ed.), *Three Early Nineteenth Century Diaries*, op. cit., p. 308.

19 O'Connell to P. V. Fitzpatrick, 6 March 1833, O'Connell, *Correspondence*, vol. v, p. 14.

20 O'Connell to P. V. Fitzpatrick, 11 March 1833, ibid., p. 16.

21 O'Connell to P. V. Fitzpatrick, 21 March 1833, ibid., p. 20.

22 O'Connell to P. V. Fitzpatrick, 27 April 1833, ibid., p. 26.

23 O'Connell to Richard Barrett, 7 June 1833, ibid., p. 40.

24 O'Connell to P. V. Fitzpatrick, 18 April 1833, ibid., p. 25.

25 O'Connell to Richard Barrett, 7 June 1833, ibid., p. 33.

26 O'Connell to P. V. Fitzpatrick, 1 June 1833, ibid., p. 35.

27 O'Connell to Richard Barrett, 7 June 1833, ibid., p. 40.

28 O'Connell to P. V. Fitzpatrick, 13 June 1833, ibid., pp. 42–3.

29 O'Connell to P. V. Fitzpatrick, 22 June 1833, ibid., pp. 48–9.

30 O'Connell to P. V. Fitzpatrick, 26 June 1833, ibid., p. 50.

31 W. Stokes, *William Stokes: his life and work* (London, 1898), p. 104.

32 5 July 1833, O'Connell, *Correspondence*, vol. v, p. 51.

33 Diary of E. J. Littleton, Aspinall (ed.), *Three Early Nineteenth Century Diaries*, op. cit., pp. 351–2.

34 20 Oct. 1833, O'Connell, *Correspondence*, vol. v, p. 82.

35 *Freeman's Journal*, 7 Nov. 1833.

36 Daunt, *Personal Recollections*, op. cit., vol. i, p. 18.

37 O'Connell to P. V. Fitzpatrick, 13 June 1833, O'Connell, *Correspondence*, vol. v, p. 43.

38 O'Connell to Michael Staunton, 9 April 1834, ibid., p. 120.

39 O'Connell to P. V. Fitzpatrick, [c. 10 April 1834], ibid., p. 122.

40 Robert Huish, *The Memoirs private and political of Daniel O'Connell Esq., M.P., his Times and Contemporaries* (London, 1836), p. 709.

41 24 April 1834, O'Connell, *Correspondence*, vol. v, p. 126.

42 25 April 1834, *Hansard*, 3rd series, vol. xxiii, col. 40.

43 8 May 1834, O'Connell, *Correspondence*, vol v, p. 132.

44 O'Connell to P. V. Fitzpatrick, 7 May 1834, ibid., p. 129.

45 Patterson, *Sir Francis Burdett*, op. cit., vol. ii, p. 621.

46 7 May 1834, O'Connell, *Correspondence*, vol. v, pp. 129–30.

47 O'Connell to P. V. Fitzpatrick, 8 May 1834, ibid., p. 131.

48 Fitzpatrick, *Correspondence*, op. cit., vol. i, p. 433.

49 O'Connell to P. V. Fitzpatrick, 30 May 1834, O'Connell,

Correspondence, vol. v, p. 138.

50 17 June 1834, ibid., p. 145.

51 Macintyre, *The Liberator*, op. cit., p. 133.

52 O'Connell to Richard Barrett [c. 11 July 1834], O'Connell, *Correspondence*, vol. v, p. 151.

CHAPTER 17
St Martin's Summer
1834–6

1 31 July 1834, O'Connell, *Correspondence*, vol. v, pp. 158–9 n. 1.

2 ibid., p. 158.

3 O'Connell to P. V. Fitzpatrick, 6 Aug. 1834, ibid., p. 162.

4 O'Connell to P. V. Fitzpatrick, 9 Aug. 1834, ibid., p. 164.

5 20 Aug. 1834, ibid., p. 167.

6 O'Connell to P. V. Fitzpatrick, 25 Aug. 1834, ibid., p. 168.

7 O'Connell to the People of Ireland, 25 Aug. 1834, *Freeman's Journal*, 28 Aug. 1834.

8 27 Aug. 1834, O'Connell, *Correspondence*, vol. v, p. 169.

9 2 Oct. 1834, ibid., p. 189.

10 2 Sept. 1834, ibid., pp. 171–2.

11 Lord Duncannon to O'Connell, 8 Sept. 1834, ibid., p. 180.

12 Edward Ellice to O'Connell, 16 Sept. 1834, ibid., p. 183.

13 11 Nov. 1834, ibid., p. 199.

14 O'Connell to Thomas Mooney, 13 June 1834, ibid., p. 143.

15 *Freeman's Journal*, 2 July 1834.

16 ibid.

17 8 July 1834, O'Connell, *Correspondence*, vol. v, pp. 149–50.

18 Sir Matthew Slattery, *The National Bank 1835–1970* (London, n.d.), p. 5.

19 Minutes of the National Bank of Ireland, in possession of the Royal Bank of Scotland, Committee meeting of 15 Oct. 1834.

20 8 July 1834, O'Connell, *Correspondence*, vol. v, p. 150.

21 ibid.

22 O'Connell to P. V. Fitzpatrick, 25 Aug. 1834, ibid., pp. 167–8.

23 Fagan, *Life and Times of O'Connell*, op. cit., vol. ii, pp. 503–4.

24 O'Connell to P. V. Fitzpatrick, 17 Nov. 1834, O'Connell, *Correspondence*, vol. v, p. 201.

25 18 Nov. 1834, ibid., p. 202.

26 *Freeman's Journal*, 21 Nov. 1834.

27 21 Nov. 1834, O'Connell, *Correspondence*, vol. v, p. 204.

28 James Birch to the Duke of Wellington, 22 [Nov. 1834], Apsley House MS, in A. Aspinall, *Politics and the Press c. 1780–1850* (London, 1949), p. 483.

29 25 Nov. 1834, O'Connell, *Correspondence*, vol. v, p. 207.

30 Fagan, *Life and Times of O'Connell*, op. cit., vol. ii, p. 326.

31 R. D. Craig to E. J. Littleton, Dec. 1834, Teddesley MS, quoted in R. B. McDowell, *Public Opinion and Government Policy in Ireland 1801–1846* (London, 1952), p. 162.

32 3 Dec. 1834, O'Connell, *Correspondence*, vol. v, p. 216.

33 8 Dec. 1834, ibid., p. 222.

34 C. Fitzmaurice to O'Connell, 19 Dec. 1834, ibid., p. 237.

35 28 Nov. 1834, ibid., p. 212.

36 5 Dec. 1834, ibid., p. 217.

37 20 Jan. 1835, ibid., p. 263.

38 13 Feb. 1835, ibid., p. 270.

39 Lord Duncannon to Lord Melbourne, 18 Dec. 1834, Melbourne Papers, 230, quoted in Macintyre, *The Liberator*, op. cit., p. 140.

40 Lord Duncannon to Lord Russell, [17 Feb. 1835], quoted in Spencer Walpole, *The Life of Lord John*

Russell (London, 1889), vol. i, p. 222.

41 John O'Connell, *Recollections and Experiences during a parliamentary career from 1833 to 1848* (London, 1849), vol. i, p. 135.

42 19 Feb. 1835, O'Connell, *Correspondence*, vol. v, p. 271.

43 O'Connell to P. V. Fitzpatrick, 27 March 1835, ibid., p. 287.

44 *Mirror of Parliament*, 1835, vol. i, p. 121.

45 John Earl Russell, *Recollections and Suggestions 1813–1873* (London, 1875), p. 135.

46 10 April 1835, O'Connell, *Correspondence*, vol. v, p. 288.

47 ibid.

48 O'Connell to P. V. Fitzpatrick, 14 April 1835, ibid., p. 289.

49 Fagan, *Life and Times of O'Connell*, op. cit., vol. ii, pp. 371–2.

50 22 April 1835, O'Connell, *Correspondence*, vol. v, pp. 296–7.

51 W. E. H. Lecky, *Leaders of Public Opinion in Ireland* (new edn, London, 1903), vol. ii, p. 157.

52 'Prefatory Letter on Music', *Irish Melodies, The Poetical Works of Thomas Moore*, (ed.) W. M. Rossetti (London, 1911), p. 329.

53 11 March 1835, O'Connell, *Correspondence*, vol. v, p. 281.

54 O'Connell to —, 16 March 1835, ibid., p. 283.

55 25 March 1835, ibid., p. 285.

56 4 Sept. 1835, ibid., p. 330.

57 21 April 1835, ibid., p. 295.

58 20 April 1835, *Hansard*, 3rd series, vol. xxvii, col. 1009.

59 1 May 1835, O'Connell, *Correspondence*, vol. v, p. 300.

60 J. R. O'Flanagan, *Life and Times of Daniel O'Connell with Sketches of his Contemporaries* (Dublin, 1875), vol. ii, p. 589.

61 *The Times*, 6 May 1835.

62 Lady Salisbury, 1 Nov. 1835, Salisbury MS, quoted in Macintyre, *The Liberator*, op. cit., p. 157.

63 M. A. G. O Tuathaigh, *Thomas Drummond and the Government of Ireland 1835–41* (Dublin, 1977), p. 4.

64 Terence de Vere White, 'English Opinion', in Tierney, *Daniel O'Connell*, op. cit., p. 215.

65 30 June 1836, *Hansard*, 3rd series, vol. xxxiv, col. 1097.

66 4 Sept. 1835, O'Connell, *Correspondence*, vol. v, p. 329.

67 Ó Tuathaigh, *Thomas Drummond*, op. cit., p. 18; *Pilot*, 4 Nov. 1840.

68 11 May 1835, O'Connell, *Correspondence*, vol. v, pp. 303–4.

69 4 Dec. 1835, ibid., p. 345.

70 8 Dec. 1835, ibid., p. 347.

71 4 Sept. 1835, ibid., p. 330.

72 11 Sept. 1835, ibid., p. 332.

73 O'Connell to P. V. Fitzpatrick, 4 Sept. 1835, ibid., p. 329.

74 23 June 1835, ibid., p. 314.

75 25 July 1835, ibid., p. 321.

76 31 Dec. 1835, ibid., p. 349.

77 31 July 1835, *Hansard*, 3rd series, vol. xxix, cols 1316–17.

78 Thomas Spring Rice to Sir John Newport, 19 Aug. 1835, Monteagle Papers 551, p. 96.

79 O'Connell to James Aytoun, 18 Aug. 1835, O'Connell, *Correspondence*, vol. v, p. 327.

80 11 Sept. 1835, ibid., p. 331.

81 MacDonagh, *Life of O'Connell*, op. cit., pp. 253–4.

82 O'Connell to P. V. Fitzpatrick, 4 Sept. 1835, O'Connell, *Correspondence*, vol. v, p. 330.

83 *The Annual Register, a record of world events*, 1835, p. 367.

84 O'Connell to John Hill Burton, 3 Dec. 1835, O'Connell, *Correspondence*, vol. v, p. 343.

85 14 Dec. 1835, ibid., p. 348.

86 *Freeman's Journal*, 1 Feb. 1836.

87 Lecky, *Leaders of Public Opinion*, op. cit., vol. ii, p. 157.

88 Fagan, *Life and Times of O'Connell*, op. cit., vol. ii, p. 496.
89 O'Connell to Arthur French, 28 June 1837, Fitzpatrick, *Correspondence*, vol. ii, p. 105.
90 *Freeman's Journal*, 1 Feb. 1836.
91 Fagan, *Life and Times of O'Connell*, op. cit., vol. ii, p. 333.
92 'The dream of those days', *The Poetical Works of Thomas Moore* (London, 1853), vol. iv, p. 103.
93 O'Connell to Arthur French, 28 June 1837, Fitzpatrick, *Correspondence*, vol. ii, p. 105.
94 Fagan, *Life and Times of O'Connell*, op. cit., vol. ii, p. 496.
95 O'Connell to P. V. Fitzpatrick, 31 July 1834, O'Connell, *Correspondence*, vol. v, pp. 158–9 n. 1.

CHAPTER 18

Liaisons
1836–8

1 7 June 1835, O'Connell, *Correspondence*, vol. v, p. 309.
2 O'Connell to Alexander Raphael, 1 June 1835, ibid., p. 308.
3 Alexander Raphael to O'Connell, 28 July 1833, ibid., p. 323.
4 5 Aug. [1835], ibid., p. 325.
5 O'Connell to Alexander Raphael, 3 Aug. 1835, ibid., p. 324.
6 Report of the Select Committee on Carlow Election Petition, 11 March 1836, *Commons Papers*, 1836, vol. xl, p. iii.
7 Fagan, *Life and Times of O'Connell*, op. cit., vol. ii, p. 593.
8 ibid.
9 ibid.
10 *Annual Register, a record of world events*, 1836, p. 30.
11 Fagan, *Life and Times of O'Connell*, op. cit., vol. ii, p. 527.
12 O'Connell to Arthur French, 18 Aug. 1836, *The Times*, 29 Aug. 1836.
13 9 May 1836, *Hansard*, 3rd series, vol. xxxiii, cols 734–5.
14 M. R. O'Connell, *Irish Times*, 6 Aug. 1975, and 'Daniel O'Connell and his family', in D. McCartney (ed.), *The World of Daniel O'Connell* (Dublin, 1980), p. 23.
15 *The Times*, 22 Sept. 1836.
16 Quoted in ibid., 23 Sept. 1836.
17 ibid., 22 Sept. 1836.
18 O'Connell to Joseph D. Mullen, 9 March 1836, O'Connell, *Correspondence*, vol. v, p. 356.
19 22 March 1836, ibid., p. 361.
20 O'Connell to Richard Sullivan, 10 March 1836, ibid., p. 357.
21 O'Connell to P. V. Fitzpatrick, 13 May 1836, ibid., p. 371.
22 ibid., p. 372.
23 ibid.
24 Fagan, *Life and Times of O'Connell*, op. cit., vol. ii, p. 537.
25 *Blackwood's Magazine*, July 1836, p. 116.
26 O. MacDonagh, *Early Victorian Government* (New York, 1977), p. 58.
27 *The Times*, 11 May 1836.
28 O'Connell to P. V. Fitzpatrick, 13 May 1836, O'Connell, *Correspondence*, vol. v, p. 371.
29 Fagan, *Life and Times of O'Connell*, op. cit., vol. ii, p. 577.
30 ibid., p. 585.
31 E. Holt, *Protest in Arms: the Irish Troubles, 1916–1923* (London, [1960]), p. 300.
32 13 Sept. 1835, O'Connell, *Correspondence*, vol. v, p. 333.
33 O'Connell to Mary O'Connell, 30 May 1836, ibid., p. 376.
34 4 Sept. 1836, ibid., p. 393.
35 6 Sept. 1836, ibid., p. 395.
36 6 Sept. 1836, ibid., p. 396.
37 9 Sept. 1836, ibid.
38 4 Sept. 1836, ibid., p. 393.
39 9 Sept. 1836, ibid., p. 397.

40 O'Connell to P. V. Fitzpatrick, 26 Oct. 1836, ibid., pp. 400–1.
41 ibid., p. 400.
42 O'Connell to William Howitt, 7 Nov. 1836, ibid., p. 402.
43 O'Connell to P. V. Fitzpatrick, 26 June 1833, ibid., p. 50.
44 25 Dec. 1834, ibid., p. 242.
45 4 Feb. 1836, *Hansard*, 3rd series, vol. xxxi, col. 98.
46 Sir Robert Peel to Duke of Wellington, 10 Feb. 1836, Parker, *Sir Robert Peel*, op. cit., vol. ii, p. 322.
47 Greville, *The Greville Memoirs; a journal of the reigns of King George IV and King William IV*, op. cit., vol. iii, 10 March 1836, p. 347.
48 16 May 1836, Fitzpatrick, *Correspondence*, vol. ii, p. 58.
49 *Hansard*, 3rd series, vol. xxxiii, col. 734.
50 Russell Papers, PRO 30/22/2B.
51 2 July 1836, O'Connell, *Correspondence*, vol. v, pp. 384–5.
52 *Hansard*, vol. xxxiv, cols 1097–8.
53 2 July 1836, O'Connell, *Correspondence*, vol. v, p. 383.
54 O'Connell to P. V. Fitzpatrick, 2 July 1836, ibid., p. 386.
55 Fagan, *Life and Times of O'Connell*, op. cit., vol. ii, p. 669.
56 29 Dec. 1886, O'Connell, *Correspondence*, vol. v, pp. 412–13.
57 Fagan, *Life and Times of O'Connell*, op. cit., vol. ii, pp. 529–30.
58 Preface to 'John Bull's Other Island', *Prefaces by Bernard Shaw* (London, 1938), p. 457.
59 O'Connell to P. V. Fitzpatrick, 18 Feb. 1837, O'Connell, *Correspondence*, vol. vi, p. 16.
60 *Hansard*, 3rd series, vol. xxxvi, col. 486.
61 26 May 1837, O'Connell, *Correspondence*, vol. vi, p. 38.
62 3 June 1837, ibid., p. 42.
63 O'Connell to Archbishop MacHale, 31 May 1837, ibid., p. 39.
64 ibid., 4 June 1837, p. 46.
65 *Freeman's Journal*, 1 July 1837.
66 1 July 1837, O'Connell, *Correspondence*, vol. vi, p. 54.
67 O'Connell to a kinsman in Tralee, 11 July 1837, ibid., p. 61.
68 21 April 1837, ibid., pp. 31–2.
69 4 Sept. 1837, ibid., p. 84.
70 O'Connell to Arthur French, General Association, 19 Oct. 1837, *Freeman's Journal*, 25 Oct. 1837.
71 20 Nov. 1837, *Hansard*, 3rd series, vol. xxxix, col. 69.
72 O'Connell to J. Arthur Roebuck, 23 Sept. 1837, O'Connell, *Correspondence*, vol. vi, p. 86.
73 Joshua Scholefield to O'Connell, 16 Dec. 1837, ibid., p. 106.
74 1 Jan. 1838, ibid., pp. 120–1.
75 SPOI, CSO, RP, Outrage reports, 9/257 (1837), head office of police, 6 Nov. 1837, quoted in F. A. D'Arcy, 'The artisans of Dublin and Daniel O'Connell, 1830–47: an unquiet liaison', *Irish Historical Studies*, vol. xvii, Sept. 1970, p. 231.
76 *Freeman's Journal*, 7 Nov. 1837.
77 D'Arcy, 'The artisans of Dublin and Daniel O'Connell', op. cit., p. 228.
78 *Freeman's Journal*, 11 Dec. 1833.
79 ibid., 22 Nov. 1837.
80 William O'Hanlon to the National Trades Political Union, 16 Dec. 1837, NLI MS1364 (18).
81 *Freeman's Journal*, 27 Dec. 1837.
82 ibid., 9 Jan. 1838.
83 ibid.
84 ibid.
85 ibid.
86 Richard Whately to N. Senior Esq., 25 Jan. 1838, E. J. Whately, *Life and Correspondence of R. Whately* (London, 1866), vol. i, p. 414.
87 James Cosgrave to O'Connell, [c. 21 Dec. 1837], O'Connell, *Correspondence*, vol. vi, p. 115.

88 O'Connell to George Julian Harney, 24 Dec. 1837, ibid., p. 118.
89 *Freeman's Journal*, 27 Nov. 1841.
90 ibid., 21 Oct. 1842.
91 W. B. Yeats, 'Nineteen Hundred and Nineteen', *The Collected Poems of W. B. Yeats* (London, 1963), p. 235.

CHAPTER 19
Declinations
1838–41

1 10 Feb. 1838, O'Connell, *Correspondence*, vol. vi, p. 133.
2 9 Feb. 1838, *Hansard*, 3rd series, vol. xl, col. 948.
3 *Freeman's Journal*, 19 Dec. 1837.
4 O'Connell to Archbishop MacHale, [c. 18 Feb. 1838], O'Connell, *Correspondence*, vol. vi, p. 136.
5 10 Feb. 1838, ibid., p. 133.
6 27 Feb. 1838, ibid., p. 139.
7 O'Connell to John Primrose jr, 4 May 1838, ibid., p. 159.
8 Fagan, *Life and Times of O'Connell*, op. cit., vol. ii, p. 536.
9 26 April 1838, O'Connell, *Correspondence*, vol. vi, p. 156.
10 O'Connell to P. V. Fitzpatrick, 15 Feb. 1838, ibid., p. 134.
11 Fagan, *Life and Times of O'Connell*, op. cit., vol. ii, p. 636.
12 4 May 1838, O'Connell, *Correspondence*, vol. vi, pp. 157–8.
13 James Sheil to O'Connell, 28 March 1837, ibid., p. 27.
14 25 Sept. 1837, ibid., p. 90.
15 Curran, *Sketches of the Irish Bar*, op. cit., vol. i, p. 165.
16 O'Connell to a kinsman in Kerry, 27 March 1837, O'Connell, *Correspondence*, vol. vi, p. 26.
17 19 Feb. 1837, ibid., p. 18.
18 O'Connell to Richard Barrett, 25 Feb. 1837, ibid., p. 20.
19 15 June 1838, ibid., p. 170.
20 18 June 1838, ibid., pp. 170–1.

21 O'Connell to P. V. Fitzpatrick, 15 June 1838, ibid., p. 170.
22 11 Aug. 1838, ibid., p. 174.
23 O'Connell to Viscount Morpeth, 10 June 1838, ibid., pp. 166–7.
24 *Freeman's Journal*, 20 Aug. 1838.
25 6 Sept. 1838, O'Connell, *Correspondence*, vol. vi, p. 175.
26 O'Connell to F. W. Conway, 15 Sept. 1838, ibid., p. 178.
27 30 Sept. 1838, ibid., pp. 185–6.
28 28 Oct. 1838, ibid., p. 196.
29 7 Oct. 1838, ibid., p. 189.
30 O'Connell to F. W. Conway, 15 Sept. 1838, ibid., p. 178.
31 23 Oct. 1838, ibid., p. 195.
32 D. Pigot to O'Connell [c. 27 Sept. 1838], ibid., p. 181.
33 3 Jan. 1839, ibid., p. 202.
34 ibid.
35 6 Feb. 1839, ibid., p. 213.
36 3 Jan. 1839, ibid., p. 204.
37 O'Connell to Archbishop MacHale, 4 Oct. 1838, ibid., p. 187.
38 O'Connell to Rev. Dr Thomas O'Brien Costello, 16 May 1839, ibid., p. 247.
39 7 May 1839, ibid., p. 238.
40 9 May 1839, ibid., p. 241.
41 10 May 1839, ibid., p. 242.
42 11 May 1839, ibid., p. 243.
43 O'Connell to Joseph Parkes, 14 May 1839, ibid., p. 246.
44 O'Connell to P. V. Fitzpatrick, 28 June 1839, ibid., p. 252.
45 O'Connell to P. V. Fitzpatrick, 5 Aug. 1839, ibid., p. 263.
46 6 Aug. 1839, ibid., p. 264.
47 O'Connell to Lord Ebrington, 8 Aug. 1839, ibid., p. 269.
48 7 Aug. 1839, ibid., pp. 266–7.
49 8 Aug. 1839, ibid., pp. 267–8.
50 O'Connell to P. V. Fitzpatrick, 21 Aug. 1839, ibid., p. 277.
51 *Freeman's Journal*, 15 Nov. 1839.
52 Lord Ebrington to Lord J. Russell, 8 Sept. 1839, PRO 30/22/3D.
53 29 Nov. 1839, O'Connell, *Correspondence*, vol. vi, p. 287.

54 23 Dec. 1839, ibid., p. 292.
55 13 Dec. 1839, ibid., p. 291.
56 17 Jan. 1840, ibid., p. 296.
57 29 Jan. 1840, ibid., p. 298.
58 3 Feb. 1840, ibid., p. 300.
59 4 Feb. 1840, ibid., p. 302.
60 O'Connell to R. L. Sheil, 29 Oct. 1839, ibid., p. 285.
61 22 Feb. 1840, ibid., p. 313.
62 8 April 1840, ibid., p. 320.
63 ibid., p. 321.
64 11 April 1840, ibid., p. 324.
65 *Freeman's Journal*, 15 April 1840.
66 30 May 1840, O'Connell, *Correspondence*, vol. vi, p. 333.
67 O'Connell to P. V. Fitzpatrick, 30 June 1840, ibid., p. 344.
68 McDowell, *Public Opinion and Government Policy in Ireland*, op. cit., p. 175.
69 30 July 1840, O'Connell, *Correspondence*, vol. vi, pp. 349–50.
70 14 Aug. 1840, ibid., pp. 352–3.
71 *Freeman's Journal*, 1 Oct. 1830.
72 6 Nov. 1840, O'Connell, *Correspondence*, vol. vi, p. 377.
73 21 Nov. 1840, ibid., pp. 379–80.
74 O'Connell to Archbishop MacHale, 30 Nov. 1840, ibid., p. 385.
75 O'Connell to P. V. Fitzpatrick, 8 Dec. 1840, ibid., p. 388.
76 ibid., p. 389.
77 4 Dec. 1840, ibid., p. 387.
78 6 Sept. 1840, ibid., pp. 358–9.
79 11 Sept. 1840, ibid., p. 361.
80 9 Sept. 1840, ibid., p. 360.
81 26 Jan. 1841, ibid., vol. vii, p. 12.
82 O'Connell to P. V. Fitzpatrick, 10 Feb. 1841, ibid., p. 20.
83 O'Connell to P. V. Fitzpatrick, 19 Feb. 1841, ibid., p. 23.
84 O'Connell to Archbishop Slattery, 17 Jan. 1841, ibid., p. 8.
85 ibid., p. 36.
86 8 May 1841, ibid., p. 50.
87 29 April 1841, ibid., p. 44–5.
88 19 Feb. 1841, ibid., p. 23.
89 ibid.

90 O'Connell to P. V. Fitzpatrick, 4 May 1841, ibid., p. 46.
91 7 May 1841, ibid., p. 48.
92 ibid., p. 49.
93 ibid.
94 O'Connell to P. V. Fitzpatrick, 9 June 1841, ibid., p. 86.
95 17 May 1841, ibid., p. 62.
96 Fitzsimon to O'Connell, 25 May 1841, ibid., p. 72.
97 26 [and 28] May 1841, ibid., p. 75.
98 O'Connell to John O'Connell, 29 May 1841, ibid., p. 78.
99 ibid.
100 P. V. Fitzpatrick to O'Connell, 10 May 1841, ibid., p. 53.
101 *Freeman's Journal*, 22 May 1841.
102 O'Connell to Richard More O'Ferrall, 15 June 1841, O'Connell, *Correspondence*, vol. vii, p. 91.
103 21 May 1841, ibid., p. 67.
104 9 June 1841, ibid., pp. 85–6.
105 Annals, St Leo's, Carlow.
106 O'Connell to ——, 18 June 1841, O'Connell, *Correspondence*, vol. vii, pp. 94–5.
107 13 July 1841, ibid., p. 105.
108 O'Connell to Edmond Smithwick, 19 July 1841, ibid., p. 107.

CHAPTER 20
Divagations

1841–2

1 17 July 1841, O'Connell, *Correspondence*, vol. vii, p. 106.
2 Sir Robert Peel to Sir James Graham, 19 Oct. 1843, Parker, *Sir Robert Peel*, op. cit., vol. iii, p. 65.
3 Sir Robert Peel to Sir James Graham, 2 Jan. 1842, *The papers of Sir James Graham* (Brighton, Sussex, Harvester Press Microform Publications), General Series 1820–1860, Bundle 46.
4 *Freeman's Journal*, 27 Oct. 1841.
5 ibid., 2 Nov. 1841.

6 John O'Connell to O'Connell, 22 Oct. 1841, O'Connell, *Correspondence*, vol. vii, p. 122.

7 *Freeman's Journal*, 19 Oct. 1841.

8 ibid.

9 John O'Connell to O'Connell, 4 Nov. 1841, O'Connell, *Correspondence*, vol. vii, p. 125.

10 ibid.

11 *Freeman's Journal*, 9 Dec. 1841.

12 W. Shakespeare, *Measure for Measure*, Act II, scene ii, l. 107.

13 *Freeman's Journal*, 23 Dec. 1841.

14 ibid., 24 March 1842.

15 ibid., 24 Aug. 1842.

16 ibid., 2 Nov. 1842.

17 ibid., 17 Aug. 1842.

18 O'Connell to P. V. Fitzpatrick, 20 Sept. 1842, O'Connell, *Correspondence*, vol. vii, p. 175.

19 *Freeman's Journal*, 2 Nov. 1842.

20 O'Connell to Betsey Ffrench, 4 Dec. 1841, O'Connell, *Correspondence*, vol. vii, p. 127.

21 *Freeman's Journal*, 17 Aug. 1842.

22 25 July 1842, O'Connell, *Correspondence*, vol. vii, p. 169.

23 ibid.

24 29 July 1842, ibid., p. 171.

25 6 Aug. 1842, ibid., pp. 172–3.

26 9 May 1842, ibid., p. 157.

27 9 Sept. 1842, ibid., p. 173.

28 O'Connell to Thomas Lyons, 17 Sept. 1842, ibid., p. 174.

29 7 Jan. 1843, ibid., p. 183.

30 W. E. Gladstone quoted in John Morley, *The Life of William Ewart Gladstone* (London, 1911), vol. i, p. 332.

31 Daunt, *Personal Recollections*, op. cit., vol. i, p. 228.

32 ibid., p. 304.

33 ibid., p. 87.

34 ibid., p. 303.

35 O'Connell to Rev. W. A. O'Meara OFM, 9 Sept. 1841, O'Connell, *Correspondence*, vol. vii, pp. 114–15.

36 From John Dryden, *The Hind and the Panther*, part 1, ll. 64–71, in O'Connell to O'Meara, 9 Sept. 1841, O'Connell, *Correspondence*, vol. vii, p. 115.

37 O'Connell to Betsey Ffrench, 28 June 1839, O'Connell, *Correspondence*, vol. vi, pp. 253–4.

38 O'Connell to Betsey Ffrench, 8 July 1839, ibid., pp. 258–9.

39 O'Connell to John Primrose Sr, 7 Aug. 1832, ibid., vol. iv, pp. 434–5.

40 17 Aug. 1832, ibid., p. 439.

41 O'Connell to Betsey Ffrench, 8 July 1839, ibid., vol. vi, p. 259.

42 ibid.

43 Daunt, *Personal Recollections*, op. cit., vol. i, p. 238.

44 Memoir by Mrs C. Fitz-Simon, quoted in MacDonagh, *Life of O'Connell*, op. cit., pp. 120–1.

45 O'Connell to Betsey Ffrench, 28 June 1839, O'Connell, *Correspondence*, vol. vi, p. 253.

46 O'Connell to Betsey Ffrench, 8 July 1839, ibid., p. 258.

47 [20 March 1841], ibid., vol. vii, p. 31.

48 Christopher Fitz-Simon to O'Connell, 24 May 1841, ibid., p. 72.

49 27 Jan. 1841, ibid., p. 13.

50 Christopher Fitz-Simon to O'Connell, 28 April 1841, ibid., p. 43.

51 9 Dec. 1840, ibid., vol. vi, pp. 390–1.

52 Committee Book of the Board of the National Bank of Ireland, in the possession of the Royal Bank of Scotland.

53 18 Dec. 1837, O'Connell, *Correspondence*, vol. vi, p. 108.

CHAPTER 21
The Big Bang
1843

1 O'Connell to the People of Ireland, 1 Jan. 1843, *Nation*, 7 Jan. 1843.

2 *Freeman's Journal*, 6 May 1843.

3 J. B. Atkins, *The Life of Sir William Howard Russell* (London, 1911), vol. i, p. 30.

4 *Freeman's Journal*, 10 June 1843.

5 *Nation*, 17 June 1843.

6 ibid.

7 'Report on Waterford', n.d., Loyal National Repeal Association correspondence, MS 3143, NLI.

8 MacDonagh, *Life of O'Connell*, op. cit., pp. 301–2.

9 24 March 1843, O'Connell, *Correspondence*, vol. vii, p. 193.

10 MacDonagh, *Life of O'Connell*, op. cit., p. 319.

11 ibid., pp. 309–10.

12 *Freeman's Journal*, 14 June 1843; MacDonagh, *Life of O'Connell*, op. cit., p. 315.

13 R. Pares, *George III and the Politicians* (Oxford, 1953), p. 30.

14 Lord De Grey to Sir Robert Peel, 6 May 1843, Parker, *Sir Robert Peel*, op. cit., vol. iii, p. 47.

15 *The Politics of Repeal* (London, 1965), p. 46.

16 *Nation*, 20 May 1843.

17 ibid., 1 July 1843.

18 16 June, 7 July 1843, *Hansard*, 3rd series, vol. lxx, cols. 53, 810–11.

19 *Nation*, 20 May 1843.

20 Sir James Graham to Lord Stanley, 16 July 1843, Graham Papers, op. cit., General Series 1820–1860, Bundle 63.

21 Lord Palmerston to Lord Russell, 22 Dec. 1843, Russell Papers, PRO 30/22/4C.

22 9 Sept. 1843, O'Connell, *Correspondence*, vol. vii, p. 224.

23 14 Sept. 1843, ibid., pp. 224–5.

24 *Nation*, 7 Oct. 1843.

25 *Politics of Repeal*, op. cit., pp. 55–6.

26 Sir Robert Peel to Sir James Graham, 16 Oct. 1843, Graham Papers, op. cit., General Series 1820–1860, Bundle 66B.

27 *Nation*, 14 Oct. 1843.

28 Warrant of arrest, *Nation*, 21 Oct. 1843.

29 *Life of O'Connell*, op. cit., p. 329.

30 *Nation*, 18 Nov. 1843.

31 ibid., 9 Dec. 1843.

32 9 Dec. 1843, O'Connell, *Correspondence*, vol. vii, p. 227.

CHAPTER 22
The Fall-Out

1844–5

1 MacDonagh, *Life of O'Connell*, op. cit., p. 333.

2 *Punch*, vol. vi, Jan.–June 1844, p. 248.

3 H. Shaw, *Authenticated Report of the Irish State Trials 1844* (Dublin, [1844]), p. 475.

4 ibid., p. 479.

5 *Freeman's Journal*, 31 May 1844.

6 *Hansard*, 3rd series, vol. lxxii, col. 930.

7 16 Feb. 1844, O'Connell, *Correspondence*, vol. vii, p. 241.

8 O'Connell to P. V. Fitzpatrick, 25 March 1844, ibid., p. 242.

9 19 March 1844, ibid., p. 246.

10 O'Connell to P. V. Fitzpatrick, 25 March 1844, ibid., p. 249.

11 *Freeman's Journal*, 3 June 1844.

12 C. G. Duffy, *Young Ireland. A Fragment of Irish History 1840–45* (London, 1896), vol. ii, p. 60.

13 22 April 1844, O'Connell, *Correspondence*, vol. vii, p. 254.

14 1 May 1844, ibid., p. 255.

15 MacDonagh, *Life of O'Connell*, op. cit., p. 354.

16 Duffy, *Young Ireland*, op. cit., vol. ii, p. 81.

17 21 June 1844, O'Connell, *Correspondence*, vol. vii, p. 258.

18 Daniel O'Connell jr to the Repeal Association, *Freeman's Journal*, 2 July 1844.

19 1 Aug. 1844, O'Connell, *Correspondence*, vol. vii, p. 261.

20 MacDonagh, *Life of O'Connell*, op. cit., p. 344.

21 O'Connell to R. L. Sheil, 19 June 1844, O'Connell, *Correspondence*, vol. vii, p. 256.

22 ibid.

23 1 Aug. 1844, ibid., p. 261.

24 MacDonagh, *Life of O'Connell*, op. cit., p. 347.

25 11 Aug. 1844, O'Connell, *Correspondence*, vol. vii, pp. 262–3.

26 19 Feb. 1844, *Hansard*, 3rd series vol. lxxii, cols. 1185–6.

27 *Freeman's Journal*, 9 Sept. 1844.

28 ibid.

29 ibid.

30 *Nation*, 14 Sept. 1844.

31 ibid.

32 ibid.

33 John Mitchel, *The Last Conquest of Ireland (perhaps)* (Glasgow, [1876]) p. 56.

34 3 Oct. 1844, O'Connell, *Correspondence*, vol. vii, p. 273.

35 O'Connell to P. V. Fitzpatrick, 8 Oct. 1844, ibid., p. 275.

36 *Northern Whig*, 17 Oct. 1839.

37 1 Oct. 1844, O'Connell, *Correspondence*, vol. vii, p. 272.

38 12 Oct. 1844, ibid., p. 276.

39 3 Oct. 1844, O'Connell to P. V. Fitzpatrick, ibid., p. 273.

40 12 Oct. 1844, ibid., p. 276.

41 *Freeman's Journal*, 15 Oct. 1844.

42 1 Oct. 1844, O'Connell, *Correspondence*, vol. vii, p. 272.

43 12 Oct. 1844, ibid., p. 278.

44 8 Oct. 1844, ibid., p. 275.

45 29 Oct. 1844, ibid., p. 285.

46 Daunt, *Personal Recollections*, op. cit., vol. ii, pp. 220–1.

47 O'Connell to T. M. Ray, read at Repeal Association meeting of 11 Nov. 1844, *Freeman's Journal*, 12 Nov. 1844.

48 9 June 1845, O'Connell, *Correspondence*, vol. vii, p. 319.

49 9 Jan. 1844, ibid., p. 235.

50 ibid., pp. 235–6.

51 ibid., p. 237.

52 ibid.

53 Charles Greville, *The Greville Memoirs (second part); a journal of the reign of Queen Victoria 1837 to 1852*, (ed.) H. Reeve (London, 1885), vol. ii, p. 221.

54 Cabinet memorandum by Sir Robert Peel, 17 Feb. 1844, Parker, *Sir Robert Peel*, op. cit., vol. iii, p. 106.

55 *Nation*, 31 Aug. 1844.

56 *Freeman's Journal*, 11 Jan. 1845.

57 To the Clergy and Faithful of the Archdiocese of Tuam, First Sunday in Advent, *The Letters of the Most Rev. John MacHale* (London, 1847), p. 583.

58 Lord Eliot to Lord Heytesbury, n.d., Parker, *Sir Robert Peel*, op. cit., vol. iii, p. 132.

59 Lord Heytesbury to Sir Robert Peel, 20 Dec. 1844, ibid., p. 144.

60 *Freeman's Journal*, 3 Dec. 1844.

61 2 Feb. 1845, O'Connell, *Correspondence*, vol. vii, pp. 303–4.

62 O'Connell to Archbishop MacHale, 19 Feb. 1845, ibid., p. 306.

63 *Nation*, 17 May, 31 May 1845.

64 O'Connell to P. V. Fitzpatrick, 27 June 1845, O'Connell, *Correspondence*, vol. vii, p. 322.

65 ibid.

66 O'Connell to Pierce Mahoney, 25 April 1845, ibid., p. 314.

67 O'Connell to Pierce Mahony, 26 April 1845, ibid., p. 316.

68 MacDonagh, *Life of O'Connell*, op. cit., p. 351.

69 *Pilot*, 15 Jan. 1845.

70 ibid., 24 Jan. 1845.

71 Rev. F. J. Nicholson to O'Connell, 24 May 1845, O'Connell, *Correspondence*, vol. vii, p. 317.

72 O'Connell to Rev. W. A. O'Meara, O.F.M., 9 Sept. 1841, ibid., pp. 114–15.

73 O'Connell to William Smith O'Brien, 2 April 1844, ibid., p. 252.
74 *Young Ireland and 1848* (Oxford, 1949), p. 23.
75 Smith O'Brien Papers, NLI MS 435, item 1371.
76 O'Connell to Thomas Davis, 30 Oct. 1844, O'Connell, *Correspondence*, vol vii, pp. 286–7.
77 1 Dec. 1844, C. G. Duffy, *Thomas Davis. The Memoirs of an Irish Patriot 1840–1846* (London, 1890), p. 308.
78 Duffy, *Young Ireland*, op. cit., vol. ii, p. 175.
79 ibid., p. 177.
80 ibid.
81 ibid.
82 Thomas MacNevin to Smith O'Brien, 27 May 1845, Smith O'Brien Papers, NLI MS 441, item 2288.

CHAPTER 23
The Widening Gyre
1845–6

1 *Young Ireland and 1848*, op. cit., p. 45.
2 O'Connell to William Smith O'Brien, 9 June 1845, O'Connell, *Correspondence*, vol. vii, p. 319.
3 O'Connell to T. M. Ray, 17 Sept. 1845, ibid., p. 342.
4 *Nation*, 17 May, 31 May 1845.
5 O'Connell Papers, NLI MS 13646(24).
6 27 June 1845, O'Connell, *Correspondence*, vol. vii, p. 322.
7 25 Aug. 1845, ibid., pp. 332–3.
8 17 Sept. 1845, ibid., p. 341.
9 9 Sept. 1845, ibid., p. 338.
10 17 Sept. 1845, ibid., 341.
11 30 Oct. 1845, ibid., pp. 345–6.
12 *Nation*, 8 Nov. 1845.
13 W. B. Yeats, 'The Second Coming', *The Poems*, (ed.) Richard Finneran (London, 1984), p. 187.
14 T. M. Ray to O'Connell, 8 Sept. 1845, O'Connell, *Correspondence*, vol. vii, pp. 336–7.
15 11 Sept. 1845, ibid., p. 340.
16 20 [and 22] Dec. 1845, ibid., p. 352.
17 ibid.
18 ibid.
19 Nowlan, *Politics of Repeal*, op. cit., p. 97.
20 18 Dec. 1845, O'Connell, *Correspondence*, vol. vii, pp. 349–50.
21 20 Dec. 1845, ibid., p. 351.
22 ibid., pp. 352–3.
23 ibid., p. 353.
24 O'Connell to William Smith O'Brien, 22 Dec. 1845, ibid., p. 353.
25 *Nation*, 22 Nov. 1845.
26 ibid., 29 Nov. 1845.
27 ibid., 1 Nov. 1845.
28 ibid., 8 Nov. 1845.
29 *History of the Times: The Tradition Established 1841–1884* (London, 1939), vol. ii, p. 9.
30 Atkins, *Life of Sir William Howard Russell*, op. cit., vol. i, pp. 33–4.
31 MacDonagh, *Life of O'Connell*, op. cit., p. 380.
32 *Politics of Repeal*, op. cit., p. 99.
33 26 Feb. 1846, O'Connell, *Correspondence*, vol. viii, p. 7.
34 15 April 1846, ibid., pp. 12–13.
35 26 March 1846, ibid., p. 10.
36 *Hansard*, 3rd series, vol. lxxxv, col. 1161.
37 28 April 1846, ibid., col. 1170.
38 28 April 1846, O'Connell, *Correspondence*, vol. viii, p. 15.
39 William Smith O'Brien to secretary of Liberal Club in co. Limerick, 6 May 1846, Smith O'Brien Papers, NLI MS 436, item 1570.
40 Thomas Steele to O'Connell, 9 May 1846, O'Connell, *Correspondence*, vol. viii, p. 23.
41 30 April 1846, ibid., pp. 16–17.
42 9 May 1846, ibid., p. 22.
43 *Nation*, 16 May 1846.

44 *Limerick Reporter*, 8 May 1846.
45 Edward Brodrick to O'Connell, 15 May 1846, O'Connell, *Correspondence*, vol. viii, p. 30.
46 11 May 1846, ibid., p. 24.
47 22 May 1846, ibid., p. 38.
48 15 June 1846, ibid., p. 46.
49 T. M. Ray to O'Connell, 16 June 1846, ibid., p. 48.
50 ibid., p. 47.
51 15 June 1846, ibid., p. 48.
52 16 June 1846, ibid.
53 *Nation*, 23 May 1846.
54 Quoted in Martin Crean to O'Connell, 15 June 1846, O'Connell, *Correspondence*, vol. viii, p. 46.
55 ibid.
56 *Nation*, 27 June 1846.
57 29 June 1846, O'Connell, *Correspondence*, vol. viii, p. 60.
58 *Nation*, 18 July 1846.
59 Minute (in T. M. Ray's handwriting) of the committee meeting is in the Smith O'Brien Papers, NLI MS 437, item 1660.
60 *Nation*, 18 July 1846.
61 McDowell, *Public Opinion and Government Policy in Ireland*, op. cit., p. 254.
62 30 June 1846, O'Connell, *Correspondence*, vol. viii, p. 61.
63 8 July 1846, ibid., p. 63.
64 23 June 1846, ibid., p. 56.
65 8 July 1846, ibid., p. 63.
66 12 July 1846, ibid., p. 67.
67 *Nation*, 18 July 1846.
68 18 July 1846, O'Connell, *Correspondence*, vol. viii, p. 70.
69 Cahirmoyle Correspondence, quoted in C. G. Duffy, *Four Years of Irish History 1845–1849* (London, 1883), p. 200.
70 Duffy, *Four Years of Irish History*, op. cit., p. 239.
71 ibid., p. 245.
72 ibid., p. 241.

CHAPTER 24
The Dying Fall
1846–7

1 O'Connell to David R. Pigot, 4 Aug. 1846, O'Connell, *Correspondence*, vol. viii, p. 79.
2 10 Aug. 1846, ibid., p. 81.
3 13 Aug. 1846, ibid., p. 83.
4 12 Aug. 1846, ibid., pp. 82–3.
5 Dr John Nugent to O'Connell, 13 Oct. [1846], ibid., p. 126.
6 *Personal Recollections*, op. cit., vol. ii, pp. 255–6.
7 ibid., p. 253.
8 ibid., p. 256.
9 *Politics of Repeal*, op. cit., pp. 110–11.
10 14 Aug. 1846, O'Connell, *Correspondence*, vol. viii, p. 84.
11 12 Aug. 1846, ibid., p. 82.
12 27 Aug. 1846, ibid., p. 87.
13 5 Oct. 1846, ibid., p. 110.
14 Public letter to T. M. Ray, 2 Oct. 1846, *Freeman's Journal*, 6 Oct. 1846.
15 ibid.
16 O'Connell to Stephen Barry, 13 Oct. 1846, O'Connell, *Correspondence*, vol. viii, p. 125.
17 O'Connell to Maziere Brady, 24 Sept. 1846, ibid., p. 98.
18 Bishop George J. P. Browne to O'Connell, 27 Nov. 1846, ibid., p. 146.
19 Rev. Barry Denny to O'Connell, 28 Sept. 1846, ibid., p. 103.
20 O'Connell to Benjamin Hawes, 19 Oct. 1846, ibid., pp. 133–4.
21 *Nation*, 8 Aug. 1846.
22 ibid., 12 Sept. 1846.
23 ibid., 15 Aug. 1846.
24 ibid., 5 Sept. 1846.
25 Smith O'Brien Papers, NLI MS 3444, quoted in Gwynn, *Young Ireland and 1848*, op. cit., p. 86. This particular MS does not appear to be among the Smith O'Brien papers any longer.

26 Address of Loyal National Repeal Association to the People of Ireland, *Freeman's Journal*, 3 Oct. 1846.

27 Thomas Arkins to O'Connell, 26 Sept. 1845, O'Connell, *Correspondence*, vol. viii, p. 101.

28 T. M. Ray to O'Connell, 10 Oct. 1846, ibid., p. 119.

29 C. G. Duffy, *Four Years of Irish History* (London, 1883), p. 338.

30 Smith O'Brien Papers, NLI MS 437, item 1691.

31 Rev. Michael Comyn to O'Connell, 26 Nov. 1846, O'Connell, *Correspondence*, vol. viii, p. 145.

32 21 Nov. 1846, ibid., pp. 141–2.

33 ibid., p. 142.

34 Bishop Michael Blake to Repeal Association, 22 Nov. 1846, *Nation*, 28 Nov. 1846.

35 10 Dec. 1846, O'Connell, *Correspondence*, vol. viii, pp. 152–3.

36 12 Dec. 1846, Fitzpatrick, *Correspondence*, vol. ii, p. 394.

37 17 Dec. 1846, ibid., p. 397.

38 John Mitchel to William Smith O'Brien, 30 Dec. 1846, Smith O'Brien Papers, NLI MS 437, item 1747.

39 C. G. Duffy to William Smith O'Brien, 26 Dec. 1846, Smith O'Brien Papers, NLI MS 434, item 1303.

40 O'Connell to T. M. Ray, 13 Feb. 1847, Fitzpatrick, *Correspondence*, vol. ii, p. 407.

41 22 Jan. 1847, O'Connell, *Correspondence*, vol. viii, p. 161.

42 19 Aug. 1846, ibid., p. 86.

43 5 Nov. 1846, ibid., p. 137.

44 16 Nov. 1846, ibid., p. 140.

45 21 Nov. 1846, ibid., p. 143.

46 Maurice O'Connell to Pierce Mahony, 17 Dec. 1848, Rathcon Papers, quoted in M. R. O'Connell, 'O'Connell: Income, Expenditure and Despair', *Irish Historical Studies*, vol. xvii, Sept. 1970, p. 219 n. 3.

47 27 Aug. 1846, O'Connell, *Correspondence*, vol. viii, p. 87.

48 18 Nov. 1846, ibid., pp. 140–1.

49 Maurice O'Connell to O'Connell, 18 Nov. 1846, O'Connell to Maurice O'Connell, 21 Nov. 1846, ibid., pp. 140, 143.

50 5 Nov. 1846, ibid., p. 138.

51 16 Oct. 1846, ibid., p. 129.

52 5 Dec. 1846, ibid., p. 149.

53 10 Dec. 1846, ibid., p. 154.

54 Memo of Fitzpatrick, 11 Jan. 1847, Fitzpatrick, *Correspondence*, vol. ii, p. 399.

55 6 Feb. 1847, ibid., pp. 401–2.

56 8 Feb. 1847, O'Connell, *Correspondence*, vol. viii, p. 162.

57 8 Feb. 1847, *Hansard*, 3rd series, vol. lxxxix, cols 944–5.

58 Memo of Fitzpatrick, 11 Jan. 1847, Fitzpatrick, *Correspondence*, vol. ii, p. 399.

59 11 Feb. 1847, O'Connell, *Correspondence*, vol. viii, pp. 163–4.

60 Certified copy of O'Connell's will, O'Connell MS, University College, Dublin..

61 1 March 1847, O'Connell, *Correspondence*, vol. viii, p. 165.

62 3 March 1847, ibid., p. 165.

63 12 Feb. 1847, ibid., p. 164.

64 16 Feb. 1847, ibid.

65 Rev. John Miley to P. V. Fitzpatrick, 22 Feb. 1847, Fitzpatrick, *Correspondence*, vol. ii, p. 408.

66 19 March 1847, ibid., p. 410.

67 P. V. Fitzpatrick to his sister, 22 March 1847, ibid., p. 411.

68 Remigius Sheehan, quoted in ibid., p. 404.

69 P. V. Fitzpatrick to his sister, 22 March 1847, ibid., pp. 410–11.

70 MacDonagh, *Life of O'Connell*, op. cit., pp. 404–5.

71 8 April 1847, Fitzpatrick, *Correspondence*, vol. ii, p. 412.

72 Rev. John Miley to P. V. Fitzpatrick, 16 April 1847, ibid., p. 413.

73 April/May 1847, ibid., p. 414.

74 Duggan's diary, 11 May 1847, ibid., p. 415 n. 8.

75 Rev. John Miley to Morgan O'Connell, 15 May 1847, W. B. MacCabe, *The Last Days of O'Connell* (Dublin, 1847), p. 87.

76 James Shirley, 'The Contention of Ajax and Ulysses for the Armour of Achilles', scene iii, *The Dramatic Works and Poems of James Shirley*, (ed.) William Gifford (London, 1833), vol. vi, p. 397.

77 Rev. John Miley to P. V. Fitzpatrick, 14 May 1847, Fitzpatrick, *Correspondence*, vol. ii, p. 416.

Select Bibliography

I PRIMARY SOURCES

1 MANUSCRIPTS
Diocesan Archives, Kildare and Leighlin, Carlow.

Dublin Diocesan Archives. Drumcondra, Dublin.

Graham Papers (Brighton, Sussex, Harvest Press Microform Publications).

Monteagle Papers. National Library of Ireland.

O'Connell Papers. National Library of Ireland.

O'Connell Papers, University College, Dublin, Archives.

Peel Papers, British Library.

Annals, Sisters of Mercy, St Leo's, Carlow.

Records of Home Office relating to Ireland, H.O.100, Public Record Office.

Records of the National Bank of Ireland, in the possession of the Royal Bank of Scotland.

Scully Papers (in the possession of Mr B. MacDermot).

2 PARLIAMENTARY PAPERS
Parliamentary Reports. First report from the Select Committee on the State of Ireland, vol. xxxv, no. 129, 1825.

Parliamentary Reports. Select Committee of the House of Lords, Appointed to inquire into the State of Ireland, vol. xxxvi, no. 181, 1825.

Report of the Select Committee on the Carlow Election Petition, 11 March 1836, *House of Commons Papers*, vol. xl, 1836.

3 PARLIAMENTARY DEBATES
Cobbett's *Parliamentary Debates*.

Hansard, T.C., *Parliamentary Debates*, 1st, 2nd, new and 3rd series.

4 PUBLISHED SELECT DOCUMENTS AND LETTERS
Aspinall, A. (ed.), *The Letters of George IV, 1812–30*, 3 vols (Cambridge, 1938).

Aspinall, A. (ed.), *Three Early Nineteenth Century Diaries* (London, 1952).

A Collection of Speeches by D. O'Connell and Richard Sheil, on subjects connected with the Catholic Question (Dublin, 1828).

Cusack, M.F. (ed.), *The Speeches and Public Letters of the Liberator*, 2 vols (Dublin, 1875).

Fitzpatrick, W.J. (ed.), *Correspondence of Daniel O'Connell the Liberator*, 2 vols (London, 1888).

Gooch, G.P. (ed.), *The later correspondence of Lord John Russell, 1840–78*, 2 vols (London, 1925).

Houston, A., *Daniel O'Connell: His Early Life and Journal, 1795–1802* (London, 1906).

Hudson, D. (ed.), *The Diary of Henry Crabb Robinson, An Abridgement* (London, 1967).

MacHale, J., *Letters of the Most Reverend John MacHale, 1820–34* (Dublin, 1893).

O'Connell, J. (ed.), *The Life and Speeches of Daniel O'Connell*, 2 vols (Dublin, 1846).

O'Connell, J. (ed.), *The Select Speeches of Daniel O'Connell*, 2 vols (Dublin, 1854).

O'Connell, M.R. (ed.), *The*

Correspondence of Daniel O'Connell, 8 vols (Dublin, 1972–80).

Russell, R. (ed.), *The early correspondence of Lord John Russell, 1805–40*, 2 vols (London, 1913).

Wellington, A. (ed.), *Despatches, Correspondence and Memoranda of Arthur Duke of Wellington*, 8 vols (London, 1867–80).

5 NEWSPAPERS

Dublin Evening Post
Freeman's Journal (Dublin)
Morning Register
Nation
Pilot
The Times

6 CONTEMPORARY PRINTED SOURCES

Anon., *A Historical Sketch of the Condition of the Irish People before the commencement of Mr O'Connell's career; a History of the Catholic Association; and Memoirs of Mr O'Connell* (2nd edn, Edinburgh, 1835).

Barrington, (Sir) J., *Historical Anecdotes of Ireland*, 2 vols (London, 1833).

Barrington, (Sir) J., *Rise and Fall of the Irish Nation* (Paris, 1833).

The Charitable Bequests Act. A letter to the most Reverend Doctor Murray – By a lay Roman Catholic (Dublin, 1844).

Civis (pseud.), *The Important Discovery; or, a reply from Civis, to a letter addressed by Daniel O'Connell, Esq. to the Marquis Wellesley* (Dublin, 1822).

Cloncurry, Lord Valentine Browne (Lawless), *Personal recollections of the Life and Times, with Extracts from the Correspondence of Valentine Lord Cloncurry* (Dublin, 1849).

Courtenay, Ellen, *A Narrative of the Most Extraordinary Cruelty, Perfidy and Depravity Perpetrated against Her by Daniel O'Connell Esq.* (London, 1837).

Curran, W. H., *Sketches of the Irish Bar*, 2 vols (London, 1855).

Cusack, M. F., *The Liberator: his Life and Times, Political and Social*, 2 vols (Kenmare, n.d.).

Daunt, W. J. O'N., *Personal Recollections of the late Daniel O'Connell, M.P.*, 2 vols (London, 1848).

Daunt, W. J. O'N., *Eighty-Five Years of Irish History, 1800–1885*, 2 vols (London, 1886).

Daunt, W. J. O'N., *Ireland and her Agitators* (Dublin, 1867).

Daunt, W. J. O'N., *A Life Spent for Ireland. Being Selections from the Journals of the late W.J. O'Neill Daunt*, (ed.) A.I.O'N. Daunt (London, 1896).

de Beaumont, G. (trans. W.C. Taylor), *L'Irlande, Sociale, Politique et Religeuse*, 2 vols (London, 1839).

Doyle, J. W., *Letters on the State of Ireland* (1825).

Doyle, J. W., *An Essay on the Catholic Claims* (Dublin, 1826).

Duffy, C. G., *Four Years of Irish History 1845–1849* (London, 1883).

Duffy, C. G., *Thomas Davis. The Memoirs of an Irish Patriot 1840–1846* (London, 1890).

Duffy, C. G., *Young Ireland. A Fragment of Irish History 1840–45*, 2 vols (London, 1896).

Fagan, W., *The Life and Times of Daniel O'Connell*, 2 vols (Cork, 1847–8).

Graeme, J., *O'Connell, His Contemporaries and Career* (Dublin, 1842)

Gregory, (Lady) Isabella Augusta (ed.), *Mr Gregory's Letter-box 1813–1830* (London, 1898).

Greville, C., *The Greville Memoirs:*

a Journal of the reigns of King George IV and King William IV, (ed.) H. Reeve, 3 vols (London, 1875).

Greville, C., *The Greville Memoirs (second part) a Journal of the Reign of Queen Victoria from 1837 to 1852,* (ed.) H. Reeve, 3 vols (London, 1885).

Hobhouse, J. (Lord Broughton), *Recollections of a Long Life, with Additional Extracts from His Private Diaries,* (ed.) Lady Dorchester, 6 vols (London, 1909–11).

Huish, R., *Memoirs Private and Political of Daniel O'Connell, Esq., M.P., His Times and Contemporaries* (London, 1836).

Levy, J. (ed.), *A Full and Revised Report of the Three Days' Discussion in the Corporation of Dublin on the Repeal of the Union* (Dublin, 1843).

Luby, T. C., *The Life, Opinions, Conversations and Eloquence of Daniel O'Connell* (New York, 1872).

MacCabe, W. B., *The Last Days of O'Connell* (Dublin, 1847).

MacGee, T. D., *Historical Sketches of O'Connell and his Friends* (Boston, 1845).

Madden, D. O., *Ireland and its Rulers since 1829* (London, 1844).

A Munster Farmer, *A Letter to Daniel O'Connell ... occasioned by the petition adopted at the late aggregate meeting of the Catholics of Ireland* (Dublin, 1824).

[O'Connell, D.], *Historical Account of the Laws Against the Roman Catholics of England* (London, 1811).

Mr O'Connell's Letter to the Lord Lieutenant [concerning the sentence passed on the Rev. Mr Houlton] [Dublin, 1823].

[O'Connell, D.] *Letter to the Members of the House of Commons ... on the Legal Right of Roman Catholics to sit in Parliament, to which is added a reply to E. B. Sugden* (London, 1829).

O'Connell, D., *A Letter to the Duke of Wellington* (London, 1835).

O'Connell, D., *Speech on Justice to Ireland* (1836).

O'Connell, D. (ed.), *A Full report of the Proceedings of the Great Meeting of the Catholics of London. With an Address to the English People, and the Letters to the Wesleyan Methodists* (London, 1839).

O'Connell, D., *Liberty and Intolerance. An Address to the Weslyan Methodists, being a Reply to the Manifesto, lately published by the Methodists of Manchester, on national education* (Sheffield, 1839).

O'Connell, D., *Instructions for the Appointments of Repeal Wardens and Collectors of the Repeal Fund, their Duties &c.* (Dublin, 1843).

O'Connell, D., *A Memoir on Ireland, Native and Saxon, 1172–1660,* vol. i [no more published], (Dublin, 1843).

O'Connell, D., *Daniel O'Connell upon American Slavery* (New York, 1860).

O'Connell, D., *Liberty or Slavery. Daniel O'Connell on American Slavery. Reply to O'Connell by S. P. Chase* [Cincinnati?, 1864].

O'Connell, J., *Recollections and Experiences from a Parliamentary Career from 1833 to 1848,* 2 vols (London, 1849).

O'Connell, M. J., *The Last Colonel of the Irish Brigade, Count O'Connell, and old Irish life at home and abroad, 1745–1833,* 2 vols (London, 1892).

Pearce, R. R., *Memoirs and*

Correspondence of the Most Noble Richard Marquess Wellesley, 3 vols (London, 1846).

Peel, (Sir) R., *Memoirs by Sir Robert Peel*, (eds.) Earl Stanhope and E. Cardwell, 2 vols (London, 1857–8).

Plowden, F., *History of Ireland from its Union with Great Britain, 1801 to 1810*, 3 vols (Dublin, 1811).

Shaw, H., *Authenticated Report of the Irish State Trials 1844* (Dublin, 1844).

The Speeches of the Right Honourable Richard Lalor Sheil, M.P., with memoir by Thomas MacNevin (Dublin, 1845).

Sheil, R. L., *Sketches, Legal and Political*, (ed.) M. W. Savage, 2 vols (London, 1855).

A Special Report of the Proceedings in the Case of the Queen against Daniel O'Connell, J. O'Connell in the Court of Queen's Bench, Ireland, 1843 and 1844, on an indictment for conspiracy and misdemeanours, (ed.) J. Flanedy (Dublin, 1844).

Stokes, W., *William Stokes: his life and journal* (London, 1898).

Taylor, W. F., *A Munster Farmer's reminiscences of Daniel O'Connell* (London, 1847).

Thackeray, W. M., *The Irish Sketch Book* (Collins edn, London and Glasgow, n.d.).

Venedey, J. (trans. W. B. MacCabe), *Ireland and the Irish during the Repeal Year 1843* (Dublin, 1844).

Wakefield, E., *An Account of Ireland, Statistical and Political*, 2 vols (London, 1866).

Whately, E. J., *Life and correspondence of Richard Whately*, 2 vols (London, 1866).

Wyse, T., *Historical Sketch of the late Catholic Association of Ireland*, 2 vols (London, 1829).

Wyse, T., *The Political Catechism, explanatory of the Constitutional*

Rights and Civil Disabilities of the Catholics of Ireland (London, 1829).

II SECONDARY SOURCES

1 BOOKS AND ARTICLES

Anglesey, Marquess of, *One-Leg, The life and letters of William Henry Paget, first Marquess of Anglesey, KG, 1768–1854* (London, 1961).

Aspinall, A., *Lord Brougham and the Whig Party* (Manchester, 1927).

Aspinall, A., *Politics and the Press c. 1780–1850* (London, 1949).

Atkins, J. B., *The Life of Sir William Howard Russell*, 2 vols (London, 1911).

Auchmuty, J. J., *Sir Thomas Wyse, 1791–1862: the life and career of an educator and diplomat* (London, 1939).

Aydelotte, W. O., 'The House of Commons in the 1840s', *History*, 1954.

Best, G. F. A., 'The Protestant Constitution and its Supporters, 1800–1829', *Transactions of the Royal Historical Society*, fifth series, vol. 8, 1958.

Bowen, D., *The Protestant Crusade in Ireland, 1800–70: a study of Protestant-Catholic relations between the Act of Union and Disestablishment* (Dublin, 1978).

Brock, W. R., *Lord Liverpool and Liberal Toryism, 1820 to 1827* (Cambridge, 1941).

Broderick, J. F., *The Holy See and the Irish Repeal Movement, 1829–47* (Rome, 1951).

Bryce, J., *Two Centuries of Irish History, 1691–1870* (London, 1888).

Chart, D. A., *Ireland from the Union to Catholic Emancipation* (London, 1910).

Clarke, R., 'The Relations between O'Connell and the Young

Irelanders', *Irish Historical Studies*, vol. iii, 1942.

Connolly, S. J., *Priests and People in Pre-Famine Ireland, 1780–1845* (Dublin, 1982).

Corcoran, T., 'O'Connell and Popular Education', 'O'Connell and University Education', *Studies*, vol. 18, Sept. 1929.

Curran, Constantine P., 'Religious Aspects of O'Connell's Early Life. I – His Deistic Tendencies', *Studies*, vol. 18, March 1929.

D'Arcy, F. A., 'The Artisans of Dublin and Daniel O'Connell, 1830–47', *Irish Historical Studies*, vol. xvii, 1970.

Davis, R. W., 'The Tories, the Whigs, and Catholic Emancipation, 1827–1829', *English Historical Review*, vol. xcvii, no. 382, Jan. 1982.

Dunlop, R., *Daniel O'Connell and the Revival of National Life in Ireland* (London, 1900).

Edwards, R. D., 'The contribution of Young Ireland to the development of the Irish National idea', in S. Pender (ed.), *Tórna Féilscríbhinn* (Cork, 1947).

Edwards, R. D. and Williams, T. D., *The Great Famine* (Dublin, 1956).

Edwards, R. D., *Daniel O'Connell and his World* (London, 1975).

Farrell, B., *The Irish Parliamentary Tradition* (Dublin, 1973).

Fitzpatrick, W. J., *The Life, Times and Correspondence of the Right Rev. Dr Doyle*, 2 vols (Dublin, 1880).

Gash, N., *Mr. Secretary Peel: the Life of Sir Robert Peel to 1830* (London, 1961).

Gash, N., *Sir Robert Peel, The Life of Sir Robert Peel after 1830* (London, 1972).

Gladstone, W. E., 'Daniel O'Connell', *Nineteenth Century*, vol. 25, no. 143, Jan. 1889.

Good, W. J., 'O'Connell and Repeal', *Dublin Review*, vol. 184, 1929.

Graham, A. H., 'The Lichfield House Compact, 1835', *Irish Historical Studies*, vol. xii, 1961.

Gwynn, D., *The Struggle for Catholic Emancipation, 1750–1829* (London, 1928).

Gwynn, D. 'Bishop Doyle and Catholic Emancipation', 'Religious Aspects of O'Connell's Early Life. II – The Catholic Democrat, 1790–1815', 'Daniel O'Connell and his Lieutenants', Studies, vols 18 and 19, 1928–29.

Gwynn, D., *Daniel O'Connell and Ellen Courtenay* (Oxford, 1930).

Gwynn, D., *Daniel O'Connell* (rev. edn, Oxford, 1947).

Gwynn, D., *O'Connell, Davis and the Colleges Bill* (Oxford, 1948).

Gwynn, D., *Young Ireland and 1848* (Cork, 1949).

Hall, F. G., *The Bank of Ireland, 1783–1946* (Dublin, 1949).

Hamilton, J. A., *Life of Daniel O'Connell* (London, 1888).

Hill, J., 'Nationalism and the Catholic Church in the 1840s: Views of the Dublin Repealers', *Irish Historical Studies*, vol. xix, 1975.

Hill, J., 'The Protestant response to Repeal: the case of the Dublin working class', in F. S. L. Lyons and R. A. J. Hawkins (eds.), *Ireland under the Union: Varieties of Tension* (Oxford, 1980).

Hill, J., 'The Politics of Privilege: Dublin Corporation and the Catholic Question, 1792–1823', *The Maynooth Review*, vol. 7, Dec. 1982.

Hoppen, K. T., *Elections, Politics, and Society in Ireland* (Oxford, 1984).

Horgan, J. J., *Great Catholic Laymen* (Dublin, 1907).

Inglis, B. 'O'Connell and the Irish

Press, 1800–42', *Irish Historical Studies*, vol. viii, 1952.

Inglis, B., *The Freedom of the Press in Ireland, 1784–1841* (London, 1954).

Kelleher, D. L., *Great Days with O'Connell* (Dublin, 1929).

Kennedy, B. A., 'Sharman Crawford on the repeal question, 1847', *Irish Historical Studies*, vol. vi, 1949.

Kerr, D., *Peel, Priests and Politics* (Oxford, 1982).

LaFaye, J. De, *O'Connell* (Paris, 1896).

Lecky, W. E. H., *Leaders of Public Opinion in Ireland*, 2 vols. (New York, 1912).

Lefevre, G. S., *Peel and O'Connell. A Review of the Irish Policy of the Parliament from the Act of Union to the Death of Sir Robert Peel* (London, 1887).

Luby, T. C., *The Life and Times of Daniel O'Connell* (Glasgow, [187?]).

Lynch, P. and Vaizey, J., *Guinness's Brewery in the Irish Economy 1759–1876* (Cambridge, 1960).

Lyne, G. J., 'Daniel O'Connell, Intimidation and the Kerry Elections of 1835', *Kerry Archaeological and Historical Society*, vol. iv, 1974.

MacCaffrey, L. J., *Daniel O'Connell and the Repeal Year* ([Lexington, 1966]).

MacCartney, D., 'The Writing of History in Ireland 1800–30', *Irish Historical Studies*, vol. x, no. 40, Sept. 1957.

McCartney, D. (ed.)., *The World of Daniel O'Connell* (Dublin, 1980).

MacCullagh, W. T., *Pro-Consul and Tribune. Wellesley and O'Connell* (London, 1880).

MacDonagh, M., *Bishop Doyle* (London, 1896).

MacDonagh, M., *The Life of Daniel O'Connell* (London, 1903).

MacDonagh, M., *Daniel O'Connell and the Story of Catholic Emancipation* (Dublin, 1929).

MacDonagh, O., 'The Contribution of O'Connell', in B. Farrell (ed.), *The Irish Parliamentary Tradition* (Dublin, 1973).

MacDonagh, O., 'The Politicization of the Irish Catholic Bishops 1800–50', *Historical Journal*, vol. 18, no. 1, 1975.

MacDonagh, O., 'Ambiguity in Nationalism – the case of Ireland', *Historical Studies*, vol. 19, no. 76, 1981.

MacDonagh, O., 'O'Connell and Repeal, 1840–1845', in M. Bentley and J. Stevenson (eds.), *High and Low Politics in Modern Britain* (Oxford, 1983).

MacDonagh, O., 'The Victorian Bank, 1824–1914', in F. S. L. Lyons (ed.), *Bicentenary Essays. Bank of Ireland 1783–1983* (Dublin, 1983).

MacDonagh, O., *States of Mind: a Study of Anglo-Irish Conflict 1780–1980* (London, 1983).

McDowell, R. B., *Public Opinion and Government Policy in Ireland 1801–1846* (London, 1952).

McDowell, R. B., *The Irish Administration, 1801–1914* (London, 1964).

Machin, G. I. T., *The Catholic Question in English Politics 1820 to 1830* (Oxford, 1964).

Macintyre, A., *The Liberator: Daniel O'Connell and the Irish Party, 1930–47* (London, 1965).

Macken, U., *The Story of Daniel O'Connell* (Cork, 1975).

MacManus, M. J. (ed.), *Thomas Davis and Young Ireland* (Dublin, 1945).

Mansergh, P. N. S., *The Irish Question 1840–1921: a commentary on Anglo-Irish relations and on social and political forces in Ireland in the age of reform and revolution* (3rd edn, London, 1975).

Moley, R., *Daniel O'Connell, Nationalism Without Violence: an essay* (New York, 1974).

Monypenny, W. F. and Buckle, G. E., *The Life of Benjamin Disraeli, Earl of Beaconsfield*, 6 vols (London, 1910–20).

Mulvey, H. F., 'The Correspondence of Daniel and Mary O'Connell', in M. R. O'Connell (ed.), *The Correspondence of Daniel O'Connell* (Shannon and Dublin, 1972–80), vol. i.

Murphy, M., 'Repeal, Popular Politics and the Clergy of Cork', *Journal of the Cork Historical and Archaeological Society*, vol. lxxxii, 1977.

Nemours, G., *Daniel O'Connell* (Paris, 1893).

Nowlan, K. B., 'The Meaning of Repeal in Irish History', *Historical Studies IV* (Dublin, 1963).

Nowlan, K. B., *The Politics of Repeal: a study of the relations between Great Britain and Ireland, 1842–50* (London, 1965).

Nowlan, K. B. and O'Connell, M. R (eds.), *Daniel O'Connell: Portrait of a Radical* (Belfast, 1984).

O'Brien, G., 'O'Connell and the Ireland in which he lived', *Dublin Review*, vol. 184, 1929.

O'Brien, J., *The Catholic Middle Classes in pre-Famine Cork* (O'Donnell Lecture, NUI, 1979).

O'Brien, M. C., 'The Gaelic Background', *Irish Times*, 6 Aug. 1975.

O'Brien, R. B., *Fifty years of concessions to Ireland, 1831–1881* (London, n.d.).

O'Brien, R. B., *Thomas Drummond, under-secretary in Ireland, 1835–40: Life and Letters* (London, 1889).

O'Connell, B. M., *O'Connell Family Tracts*, nos. 1–3 (Dublin, 1947–51).

O'Connell, M. R., 'Daniel O'Connell: Income, Expenditure and Despair', *Irish Historical Studies*, vol. xvii, 1970.

O'Connell, M. R., 'Daniel O'Connell and Religious Freedom', *Thought*, vol. 50, no. 197, June 1975.

O'Connell, M. R., 'O'Connell as Lawyer and Landlord', Thomas Davis Lecture for Radio-Telefis Eireainn, spring 1975.

O'Connell, M. R., 'Daniel O'Connell and his family', *Irish Times*, 6 Aug. 1975.

O'Connell, M. R., 'O'Connell Reconsidered', *Studies*, vol. lxiv, 1975.

O'Connell, M. R., 'O'Connell, Young Ireland and Violence', *Thought*, vol. 52, 1977.

O'Connell Centenary Record 1875 (Dublin, 1878).

Ó Faoláin, S., *King of the Beggars: A Life of Daniel O'Connell* (London, 1938).

O'Ferrall, F., 'The Growth of Political Consciousness in Ireland', *Irish Economic and Social History*, vol. i, 1979.

O'Ferrall, F., *Daniel O'Connell* (Dublin, 1981).

O'Ferrall, F., 'The Only Lever ... ? The Catholic Priest in Irish Politics, 1823–29', *Studies*, vol. 70, winter 1981.

O'Ferrall, F., *Catholic Emancipation: Daniel O'Connell and the Birth of Irish Democracy* (Dublin, 1985).

O'Ferrall, F., 'Daniel O'Connell and Henry Cooke: the conflict of civil and religious liberty in Modern Ireland', *Irish Review*, vol. i, 1986.

O'Flanagan, J. R., *Bar Life of O'Connell* (London, 1875).

O'Flanagan, J. R., *Life and Times of Daniel O'Connell* (Dublin, 1875).

O'Higgins, R., 'Irish Trade Unions and Politics', *Historical Review*, vol. iv, 1961.

O'Rourke, J., *The Life of O'Connell* (Dublin, [1875]).

Osofsky, G., 'Abolitionists, Irish Immigrants, and the Dilemmas of Romantic Nationalism', *American Historical Review*, vol. 80, no. 4, Oct. 1975.

Ó Tuathaigh, G., *Ireland before the Famine, 1798–1848* (Dublin, 1972).

Ó Tuathaigh, G., 'Gaelic Ireland, Popular Politics and Daniel O'Connell', *Journal of the Galway Archaeological and Historical Society*, vol. xxxv, 1975.

Ó Tuathaigh, M. A. G., *Thomas Drummond and the Government of Ireland 1935–41* (O'Donnell Lecture, NUI, 1977).

Parker, C. S., *Sir Robert Peel from his private papers*, 3 vols. (London, 1899).

Parker, C. S., *Life and letters of Sir James Graham, second baronet of Netherby, 1792–1861*, 2 vols. (London, 1907).

Patterson, M. W., *Sir Francis Burdett and His Times (1770–1844)*, 2 vols (London, 1931).

Plunket, D., *The Life, Letters, and Speeches of Lord Plunket*, 2 vols (London, 1867).

Reynolds, J. A., *The Catholic Emancipation Crisis in Ireland 1823–1829* (New Haven, 1954).

Riach, D. C., 'Daniel O'Connell and American anti-slavery', *Irish Historical Studies*, vol. xx, 1976.

Roberts, M., *The Whig Party, 1807–12* (London, 1939).

Senior, H., *Orangeism in Ireland and Britain 1795–1836* (London, 1966).

Slattery, M., *The National Bank 1835–1970* (London, n.d.).

Tierney, M. 'Politics and Culture: Daniel O'Connell and the Gaelic Past', *Studies*, vol. 27, Sept. 1938.

Tierney, M. (ed.), *Daniel O'Connell. Nine Centenary Essays* (Dublin, 1949).

Torrens, W. T. MacC., *Memoirs of Sir Richard Lalor Sheil*, 2 vols (London, 1855).

Trench, C. C., *The Great Dan. A Biography of Daniel O'Connell* (London, 1984).

Tyrrell, A., *Joseph Sturge and the Moral Radical Party in Early Victorian Britain* (London, 1987).

Walpole, S., *The Life of Lord John Russell*, 2 vols (London, 1889).

Walsh, W. J., 'The Board of Charitable Donations and Bequests', *Irish Ecclesiastical record*, 3rd series, vol. xiv.

Walsh, W. J., *O'Connell, Archbishop Murray and the Board of Charitable Bequests* (Dublin, 1916).

Ward, B., *The Eve of Catholic Emancipation, 1803–1829*, 3 vols (New York, 1911–12).

Whelan, B., 'Behind the Scenes of Catholic Emancipation', *Dublin Review*, vol. 184, 1929.

Whyte, J. H., 'Daniel O'Connell and the repeal party', *Irish Historical Studies*, vol. xi, no. 44, Sept. 1959.

Whyte, J. H., 'The Influence of the Catholic Clergy on Elections in Nineteenth Century Ireland', *English Historical Review*, vol. lxxv, 1960.

Woodham-Smith, C., *The Great Hunger: Ireland 1845–9* (London, 1962).

Wyse, W., *Memoirs of Sir Thomas Wyse* (Waterford, 1901).

2 THESES

Coldrick, Sister H., 'Daniel O'Connell and Religious Freedom', PhD thesis, Fordham University, 1974.

O'Ferrall, F., 'The Growth of Political Consciousness in Ireland 1829–1847: a Study of O'Connellite Politics and Political Education', PhD thesis, Trinity College, Dublin, 1978.

Bibliographical Note

MISE-EN-SCÈNE

M. R. O'Connell's Preface in volume i of his edition of the *Correspondence* includes a brief description of the O'Connell locale and an outline of the O'Connell genealogy; the latter is set out in detail in B. M. O'Connell's *Family Tracts*.

CHAPTER 1

'The Gaelic Background' by Gerard Murphy, in Tierney, ed., *Daniel O'Connell: Nine Centenary Essays*, is a penetrating and imaginative short survey of its subject. An article of the same title by M. C. O'Brien (*Irish Times*, 6 Aug. 1975) and Gearóid Ó Tuathaigh's 'The Folk-hero and Tradition', in McCartney, ed., *World of Daniel O'Connell*, and J. A. Murphy's 'O'Connell and the Gaelic World', in Nowlan and O'Connell, eds, *O'Connell: Portrait of a Radical,* are also important considerations of O'Connell's place in his native cultural inheritance. For O'Connell's sojourn at Fr Harrington's school, see P. Thompson, 'Reddington's Academy on the Great Island' (*Cork Examiner*, 22 July 1972).

Thomas Wall's 'Louvain, St. Omer and Douai', in Tierney, ed., *Daniel O'Connell: Nine Centenary Essays,* is an excellent study of O'Connell's Continental education.

CHAPTER 2

For a general account of late-eighteenth-century British radical organization and thought, see S. Maccoby, *English Radicalism 1786–1832* (London, 1955); for the French Revolutionary period, H. T. Dickinson, *British Radicalism and the French Revolution* (London, 1985); and for Godwin, in particular, M. Butler, *Burke, Paine, Godwin and the Revolution Controversy* (Cambridge, 1984). The main source for the life and career of General Count Daniel O'Connell is Mrs M. J. O'Connell's *Last Colonel of the Irish Brigade.*

CHAPTER 3

C. Maxwell, *Dublin under the Georges: 1714–1830* (London, 1936) and M. Craig, *Dublin, 1660–1860* (London, 1952) provide useful descriptions of the late-eighteenth-century city.

'The Volunteers and Parliament, 1779–84' by P. D. H. Smyth, in T. Bartlett and D. W. Hayton, eds, *Penal Era and Golden Age: Essays in Irish History, 1690–1800* (Belfast, 1979) illuminates the reality of the early Volunteering movement which O'Connell persistently idealized.

W. E. H. Lecky, *A History of Ireland in the Eighteenth Century* (new impression, London, 1913), vols iii and iv, remains the best detailed survey of Irish politics in the 1790s; T. Pakenham, *The Year of Liberty: the Story of the Great Irish Rebellion of 1798* (London, 1969) is the most up-to-date general account of the 1798 rebellion and its aftermath.

CHAPTER 4

Mulvey's 'Correspondence of Daniel and Mary O'Connell' (O'Connell, ed., *Correspondence*, vol. i, pp. xix–xxx) is a sensitive and perceptive analysis of

O'Connell's marriage as revealed by the letters between him and his wife, and M. R. O'Connell's 'Daniel O'Connell: income, expenditure and despair' is the authoritative source for O'Connell's personal finances.

The widespread tradition that O'Connell was unfaithful to his wife and fathered many bastards deserves some special consideration. I have found only two pieces of evidence which lend any colour whatever to such assertions. The first is the charge by Ellen Courtenay in her *Narrative*, published in 1832, that O'Connell had violated her in his house in Dublin fifteen years before and that she bore him an illegitimate son in November 1818. Denis Gwynn devoted a monograph, *Daniel O'Connell and Ellen Courtenay*, to an investigation of the case and concluded, convincingly, that the story was baseless. O'Connell himself claimed (in a letter of 14 January 1832) to have ascertained, through inquiries, that Courtenay was acting with a company in Gosport and the Isle of Wight during 1817, the year in which he was meant to have raped her in Dublin, and also that she was in fact childless. Earlier (in a letter of 30 November 1831), he made the point that such a 'calumny . . . would have been worth any money in Ireland at any time during the last twenty years, that is, if it had the least face of probability' (O'Connell, *Correspondence*, vol. iv, p. 367). Furthermore, it is suggestive that her pamphlet was published by Barnard Gregory, editor of the *Satirist* (London). Gregory was notorious as a blackmailer of prominent public men, occasionally obtaining large sums of money for refraining from publishing highly derogatory material: he was fined heavily and gaoled briefly for his part in the attempted blackmail of the Duke of Cumberland in 1839. Courtenay's (or Gregory's) style in the pamphlet is typical of the language used in this blackmailing trade, common in the 1820s and 1830s – 'Vain were all my struggles, all my prayers, all my cries for assistance; he sunk the man in the brutality of the monster, and desisted not from his prey'. (For this subject generally, see I. McCalman, *Radical Underworld: Prophets, Revolutionaries and Pornographers in London, 1795–1840*, Oxford, 1987). Taking the evidence as a whole, I conclude that O'Connell was almost certainly innocent of the charge. Certainly, he paid Courtenay nothing – though payment would not have necessarily implied guilt, as these blackmailers were sometimes bought off merely to avoid trouble.

The second possible shadow on O'Connell's reputation arises from Mary O'Connell's objection in 1823 to his visiting Miss Gaghran, who had been their children's governess up to the preceding year. O'Connell agreed not to visit her in future without Mary's express agreement, adding, 'Surely I said enough on that subject – at least I think I did – to set your mind at ease. But why should it be otherwise, I confess I am at a loss to understand. I never in my life showed the slightest tinge of preference to any being above you' (O'Connell, *Correspondence*, vol. ii, p. 522). Mary had long disliked Miss Gaghran, and perhaps also been jealous of her capabilities; and this is probably the explanation of her objection to O'Connell's calling on her. Mulvey rightly concludes that 'Subsequent letters [in one of which O'Connell was given a commission by Mary to get Miss Gaghran to execute some embroidery for her] . . . strengthen the impression that Mary was accusing her husband of conduct inconsiderate to her feelings but not sexually immoral' (ibid., vol. i, p. xxix).

The question remains: why has O'Connell gone down in Irish popular tradition as a tireless womanizer? Why have innumerable legends of immense virility gathered about him? Diarmaid Ó Muirithe, the leading authority on the folklore of O'Connell, has suggested a possible answer, that O'Connell acquired legendary status in the countryside even in his own time: 'All these stories are the product of the folk-mind. The heroes of old, on whom the O'Connell of folklore is to a great degree modelled, were ever famous for their sexual energy.' (D. Ó Muirithe, 'O'Connell in Irish Folk Tradition', in Nowlan and O'Connell, eds. *O'Connell: Portrait of a Radical*, pp. 59–60.)

CHAPTERS 5 AND 6

Ward's *Eve of Catholic Emancipation* presents the full background of the Catholic question (especially in its British bearings) in the early nineteenth century; and R. Dudley Edwards' essay 'O'Connell and Rome' in McCartney, ed., *World of Daniel O'Connell*, usefully places O'Connell in this general context.

McDowell's *Public Opinion and Government Policy in Ireland* and Ó Tuathaigh's *Ireland before the Famine* are recommended as surveys of Ireland in the first half of the nineteenth century. McDowell's main emphasis is on political and constitutional matters; Ó Tuathaigh's, on social and economic.

Roberts, *The Whig Party, 1807–12*, remains a valuable authority on whig attitudes and ideology, not just for the years dealt with specifically but also for the early nineteenth century as a whole. Gash's *Mr Secretary Peel* is the standard work on Peel's early career.

CHAPTER 7

O'Connell's income from the bar may have been underestimated by earlier scholars, who generally assumed that his fee-books tell the whole story. In fact, the information from this source is not consistent. For instance, *two* fee-books cover the same eight years, 1798–1805: the one which has usually been drawn upon (P/12/5/152, UCD Archives) lists fewer fees and produces smaller annual totals (roughly one-third less in most cases) than the other (NLI MS 130). Secondly, it is unlikely that the fee-books listed all O'Connell's professional income; in particular, returns from election, registry and arbitration work may have been omitted. This would help to account for such discrepancies as his telling his wife on 4 December 1827 that his income (the context suggests that the reference is to his *bar* income) is 'upwards of £7,000' per annum, whereas his fee-books gives annual totals of £3893, £4497 and £4868 for 1825, 1826 and 1827, respectively (Reynolds, *Catholic Emancipation Crisis*, p. 38 n.2) or his claim 'to have earned professional emoluments [which] exceeded £8,000' in 1828 (Cusack, *Speeches and Letters*, vol. ii, pp. 259–69), whereas his fee-book gives a total of £5178 for that year. O'Connell was apparently making a more or less precise calculation when he reported earnings of over £8000 in 1828, for he went on to say that it was 'an amount never before realised in Ireland in the same space of time by an outer barrister'. Wherever there is a clear and specific choice, I have preferred the higher figure.

CHAPTER 8

P. J. Jupp, 'Irish Parliamentary Elections and the Influence of the Catholic Vote, 1801–20' (*Historical Journal*, vol. x, 1967) provides a good description and analysis of the general election of 1818 in Ireland. Brock, *Lord Liverpool and Liberal Toryism, 1820–7* is recommended for an understanding of tory policies and approaches to Irish and Catholic, as well as more general, issues. See also N. Thompson, *Wellington after Waterloo* (London, 1987).

CHAPTER 9

For further information on O'Connell's children and landed property, see M. R. O'Connell, 'O'Connell and his family', in McCartney, ed., *World of Daniel O'Connell*, 'Daniel O'Connell and his family' (*Irish Times*, 6 August 1975) and 'O'Connell: Lawyer and Landlord', in Nowlan and O'Connell, eds, *O'Connell: Portrait of a Radical*.

CHAPTERS 10–12

O'Ferrall, *Catholic Emancipation* is an excellent study of contemporary political organization and two other authoritative books, Machin, *Catholic Question in English Politics*, and Reynolds, *Catholic Emancipation Crisis*, provide further information on various aspects of Irish and Anglo-Irish politics, 1823–9. Wyse, *Catholic Association of Ireland*, is the best primary source for the same subjects, and Sheil's essays, 'The Catholic Deputation' and 'The Clare Election', in his *Sketches, Legal and Political* (vol. ii, pp. 19–54 and 121–42), are especially important eye-witness accounts of important happenings in O'Connell's campaign for Emancipation.

CHAPTERS 13–24

Much the most important contemporary biographical sources for O'Connell's life after 1829 are Fagan's *Life and Times,* O'Neill Daunt's *Personal Reminiscences* and *Life Spent in Ireland,* and the detailed annotations in W. J. Fitzpatrick's collection of the *Correspondence.* Fagan was close to

O'Connell and his Cork 'manager' during the 1830s; O'Neill Daunt was his personal secretary for several years: and W. J. Fitzpatrick was the nephew of P. V. Fitzpatrick, O'Connell's friend and agent. M. MacDonagh's *Life* includes some contemporary comment on O'Connell in the 1840s not otherwise extant, and Gavan Duffy in *Four Years of Irish History* provides some first-hand accounts of the 'traversers'' sojourn in Richmond prison.

Two excellent studies, MacIntyre's *The Liberator* and McDowell's *Public Opinion and Government Policy*, cover the entire post-Emancipation period. With Nowlan's *Politics of Repeal*, they provide, between them, a thorough background to the relevant politics and political organizations of the years 1830–47. Ó Tuathaigh's *Drummond and the Government of Ireland* and Broderick's *Holy See and the Irish Repeal Movement* are particularly useful monographs on the Irish Administration, 1835–41, and the political attitudes of the Catholic hierarchy, respectively. Although O'Ferrall's *Catholic Emancipation* lies outside the period under consideration, it illuminates a political methodology which O'Connell was to repeat and perfect in later years.

A number of articles in learned journals or volumes of collected essays give authoritative accounts of various facets of O'Connell's conduct or situation during his last seventeen years. Chief among them are D'Arcy's 'Artisans of Dublin and O'Connell' (Chap. 18), Graham's 'Lichfield House Compact' (Chap. 17), J. Hennig, 'Continental Opinion' in Tierney (ed.), *O'Connell: Nine Centenary Essays*, Inglis's 'O'Connell and the Irish press' (Chap. 16), M. R. O'Connell's 'O'Connell: Income, Expenditure and Despair' (Chaps 13, 20), 'O'Connell and

his family' (Chaps 18, 20) and
'O'Connell and Religious Freedom'
(Chap. 13), Osofsky's 'Abolitionists,
Irish Immigrants, and the Dilemmas of
Romantic Nationalism' (Chap. 13),
Riach's 'O'Connell and American anti-
slavery' (Chap. 13), K. F. Roche's
'Revolution and Counter-Revolution'
in Tierney (ed.), *O'Connell: Nine
Centenary Essays* (Chap. 13), H.
Rollet's 'The Influence of O'Connell's
Example on French Liberal
Catholicism' in McCartney (ed.), *The
World of O'Connell* (Chap. 24),
Walsh's 'Board of Charitable
Donations and Bequests' (Chap. 22) and
Whyte's 'O'Connell and the repeal
party' (Chaps 15–19).

GENERAL

Among earlier biographies of
O'Connell, Dunlop's *Daniel O'Connell
and the Revival of National Life*, Ó
Faoláin's *King of the Beggars* and
O'Ferrall's *O'Connell* are outstanding,
the first for its immediately post-
Parnellite perspective, the second for its
remarkable psychological insight and
empathy, and the third as a very well-
balanced brief biographical essay.
Lecky's analysis of O'Connell's career
and personality in *Leaders of Public
Opinion* is full and fair, and Gladstone's
1889 review article extraordinarily
perceptive.

Biographical Notes

James ABERCROMBY (1776–1858)
MP for Midhurst 1807–12, for
Calne 1812–30, for Edinburgh
1832–9.
Judge advocate general 1827–8.
Chief baron of the exchequer
(Scotland) 1830–2. Master of the
mint in 1834. Speaker of the House
of Commons 1835–9. Created
Baron Dumfermline in 1839.

Rev. William ABRAHAM (1792–1837)
Bishop of Waterford and Lismore
1830–7.

John Charles (Spencer) styled
Viscount ALTHORP (1782–1845)
MP for Oakhampton 1804–6, for
St Albans 1806, for
Northamptonshire 1806–34. A lord
of the treasury 1806–7. Chancellor
of the exchequer and leader of the
House of Commons 1830–4.
Succeeded as third Earl Spencer in
1834.

William (Arden), second baron
ALVANLEY (1789–1849)
Officer in the Coldstream Guards,
later Capt. 50th Reg. of Foot.
Succeeded as second baronet in
1804.

Henry William (Paget) first Marquess
of ANGLESEY (1768–1854)
Army officer, MP 1790–6, 1802–4,
1806, 1807–10. 1812 became Earl
of Uxbridge. 1815 created first
Marquess of Anglesey. Master-
general of the ordnance 1827–8,
1846–52. Lord lieutenant of Ireland
1828–9, and again 1830–3.

Lord ANNALY (John Gore) (1718–
1784)
1764 he became chief justice of the
King's Bench. 1766 he was made
an Irish peer.

Thomas ARKINS
Repeal warden. Merchant tailor in
Dublin.

Anthony Ashley Cooper, Lord
ASHLEY, seventh earl of
Shaftesbury (1801–1885)
MP 1826–46, 1847–51. 1828
commissioner of the board of
control, 1834 board of the
admiralty. Refused later offer of
cabinet positions. A philanthropist
concerned with the treatment of
lunatics, of workers in factories and
mines, and of chimney sweep
apprentices; and with the education
of the poor, working class
dwellings and religious societies.

Thomas ATTWOOD (1783–1856)
A Birmingham banker and political
reformer. MP for Birmingham
1832–40.

Dr Herbert BALDWIN
First cousin of O'Connell. From a
landowning family, Clohina, co.
Cork. 1832–7 MP for Cork City.

Walter J. BALDWIN J.P. (1774–1835)
Eldest son of James Baldwin,
Clohina, co. Cork, and first cousin
of O'Connell. Author of pamphlet,
*An Appeal to Common Sense and
to Religion on the Catholic
Question . . .* (1823).

Nicholas BALL (1791–1865)
1836 admitted as a bencher of the
King's Inns; 1836 MP for Clonmel;
1837 attorney general; 1838 privy
councillor in Ireland; 1839 till his
death judge of the common pleas.
He was the second Catholic
promoted to a judgeship after the
Relief Act.

John BANIM (1798–1842)
Irish novelist, dramatist and poet.

He wrote the O'Hara Tales with his brother Michael. His other works include 'The Celt's Paradise', 'Damon and Pythias' and *Boyne Water*.

Michael BANIM (1796–1874)
He wrote the O'Hara Tales with his brother John, and organized the family's business affairs. He worked hard for Catholic Emancipation. In 1852 he was appointed postmaster in Kilkenny.

Richard BARRETT (d. 1854)
Editor and proprietor of the *Pilot* newspaper which he established in 1827 to support O'Connell.

Sir Edward BELLEW (d. 1827)
Sixth baronet, Barmeath, co. Louth.

Richard Newton BENNETT (1769–1836)
Called to the Irish bar in 1796. Married Sophia Hart. 1832 appointed chief justice of Tobago. 1833 suspended from his post because of alcoholism.

William George Frederick Cavendish BENTINCK (1802–1848)
Officer in 10th hussars. 1822–5 private secretary to Canning, his uncle. 1825 joined the 2nd life guards. 1828–48 MP for Lynn. Leading defender of the corn laws. In 1846 he organized the protectionists as a third political party.

Lord George Thomas BERESFORD (1781–1839)
Third son of the Marquess of Waterford. 1830–1 MP for co. Waterford.

Ralph BERNAL (d. 1854)
Whig MP 1818–52. Chairman of committees 1833–41, 1847–52. Well-known art collector.

John William (Ponsonby) Earl of BESSBOROUGH see Duncannon, Lord

Rev. Thomas BETACH S.J. (1739–1811)
With other members of the Society of Jesus (after its suppression) he carried on a school in Dublin where he became a curate. He was subsequently appointed parish priest in Dublin and vicar-general of that archdiocese.

Charles BIANCONI (1786–1875)
Promoter of passenger and mail car system in Ireland from 1815. Mayor of Clonmel 1845 and 1846. 1863 appointed deputy lieutenant.

James BIRCH
Journalist. Proprietor of *World* newspaper, founded in Dublin in 1840. After it had become a Dublin Castle organ, he took an action against the Irish chief secretary for insufficient payment for his services.

Francis BLACKBURNE (1782–1867)
Attorney-general for Ireland 1831–5, 1841–2. Master of the rolls 1842–6.
Chief justice of queen's bench 1846–52. Lord chancellor of Ireland 1852.
Lord justice of appeal in Ireland 1856.

Maxwell BLACKER (born c. 1774)
Called to the bar 1795. He was appointed chairman of the Dublin quarter sessions in 1826.

Anthony BLAKE (1786–1849)
Though a Catholic he was a member of the Irish Administration of Marquess Wellesley who appointed him chief remembrancer in 1823.
His *Thoughts upon the Catholic Question* was published in 1828.

Mark BLAKE
MP for co. Mayo 1840–6.

Rev. Michael BLAKE (1775–1860)
Parish priest of Townshend Street 1831–3. Catholic bishop of Dromore 1833–60.

Edward BLOUNT (1769–1843)
Secretary of the English Catholic Board from 1822 and later of the British Catholic Association. 1830–2 MP for Steyning.

Simon BOLIVAR (1783–1830)
Leader of revolutionary armies which gained independence for most of South America from Spanish rule.

Rev. Charles BOYTON (1799–1844)
Church of Ireland rector of Conwall, co. Donegal from 1833.

Maziere BRADY (1796–1871)
Solicitor-general 1837–9. Attorney-general 1839–40. Chief baron of the exchequer 1840–6. Judge of the court of chancery 1846–66. Lord chancellor of Ireland 1846–52, 1853–8, 1859–66. Created a baronet 1869.

Maurice BRENAN
New Street, Killarney. Son of John Brenan and Ellen, youngest daughter of Charles Sugrue. A close relative of O'Connell.

John BRIC (1793–1826)
Clerk to O'Connell in 1815; admitted to King's Inns in 1816 and to Middle temple, London, in 1819. He was called to the bar in Dublin in 1824 and killed in a duel in Dublin in December 1826.

Admiral Pedro Lius BRION (1782–1821)
A wealthy Jewish merchant from Curacao. Admiral of Bolivar's naval forces 1816–19.

Henry Peter BROUGHAM (1778–1868)
Barrister and whig-radical MP. In 1830–4 while lord chancellor he carried through significant law reform. In 1830 he was created Baron Brougham and Vaux. He was also an advocate of the abolition of slavery and of educational and parliamentary reform.

Rev. George Joseph Plunket BROWNE (c. 1790–1858)
Bishop of Galway 1831–44. Bishop of Elphin 1844–58.

Col. Samuel BROWNE
Colonel of York Light Infantry and deputy quarter-master general, c. 1814.

Henry BRUEN (d. 1852)
MP for co. Carlow 1812–31, 1835–7, Dec. 1840–52. Colonel in Carlow militia.

Major George BRYAN (1770–1843)
1837–43 MP for co. Kilkenny.

Charles BULLER (1806–1848)
Liberal politician and pamphleteer. MP for West Looe, Cornwall 1830–1, for Liskeard 1832–48. Secretary to governor-general of Canada in 1838. Chief poor law commissioner in 1847.

Sir Francis BURDETT (1770–1844)
Fifth baronet. Entered Parliament in 1796 and was MP for most of the period until 1844. Political and radical reformer.

Rev. Patrick BURKE (c. 1776–1843)
Coadjutor of Elphin 1819–27, bishop of Elphin 1827–43.

Charles BURTON (1760–1847)
Born in Northamptonshire. Called to the Irish bar in 1792. Became a justice of the King's Bench in 1820. As a judge in the state trials of 1844 he passed sentence on O'Connell.

Charles BUTLER (1750–1832)
Secretary to the English Catholics 1782–91; member of the English Catholic Board from 1808. He was called to the English bar in 1791, the first Catholic to qualify since 1688, but he scarcely ever appeared in court. In 1831 he was made a bencher of Lincoln's inn.

James BUTLER (1780–1863)
From Waterville, co. Kerry.

Lt. Col. Hon. Pierce BUTLER D.L. (1774–1846)
MP for co. Kilkenny 1832–46.

Colonel in co. Kilkenny militia.

Captain Whitwell BUTLER
Of the Irish Revenue Force.
Formerly a naval officer.

Isaac BUTT (1813–1879)
Chair of political economy TCD
1836–41. Called to the Irish bar in
1838. Elected alderman of the new
Dublin corporation, as a
conservative, in 1841. Established
Protestant Guardian newspaper in
Dublin. 1844 called to the inner bar.
Defended Smith O'Brien and
others in the state trials of 1848.
MP for Harwich 1852, liberal-
conservative MP for Youghal
1852–65. Called to the English bar
in 1859. 1865–9 defence counsel for
Fenian prisoners. President of the
Amnesty Association in 1869. MP
for Limerick city and leader of the
Home Rule party 1871–9.

George Gordon BYRON (1788–1824)
Poet. He succeeded as sixth lord in
1798. he spoke in the House of
Lords three times 1812–13, but any
political ambition was
extinguished by his literary success.
His works include *Childe Harold,
Don Juan, The Waltz, the Giaour,*
the *Bride of Abydos,* and *The
Corsair.* Despite his aristocratic
vanity, he was critical of the cant
and immorality of the ruling classes
at home and abroad. He started
a journal called the *Liberal* in
1822, but it only lasted four
numbers.

John CAMPBELL (1779–1861)
Solicitor-general of England 1832–
4. Knighted 1832. Attorney-general
of England 1834, 1835–41. Lord
chancellor of Ireland June–Oct.
1841. Chief Justice 1850–9.
Chancellor of England 1859–61.
Legal biographer.

Robert CANE (1807–1858)
Surgeon. Mayor of Kilkenny 1845
and 1849. Chief promoter of

Repeal in Kilkenny. He did not take
part in the 1848 insurrection but
was arrested and imprisoned for a
time. In 1853 he originated the
Celtic Union, a semi-political and
semi-literary society.

George CANNING (1770–1827)
Canning's toryism was founded on
the maintenance of the royal
prerogative, but he also advocated
the repeal of Catholic disabilities
and the gradual removal of
restrictions on trade and commerce.
He held a number of cabinet posts
including the foreign office in 1807
and 1822. In April 1827 he became
prime minister in an alliance with
the whigs.

Rev. John CANTWELL (1792–1866)
Catholic bishop of Meath 1830–66.

John CARTWRIGHT (1740–1824)
English radical. From 1775 he
advocated universal suffrage,
annual parliaments and the ballot.

Robert Stewart, Viscount
CASTLEREAGH (1769–1822)
1797–8 acting chief secretary in
Ireland. 1798–1801 chief secretary.
He was in favour of the Union and
repeal of Catholic disabilities. He
resigned in 1801 following the
king's refusal to grant
Emancipation. In 1802 he became
president of the (East India) board
of control. 1805–6, 1807–9
secretary of state for war. 1812–22
foreign secretary.

Hon. Henry CAULFIELD D.L. (1779–
1862)
Younger son of first earl of
Charlemont. MP for co. Armagh
1802–7, 1815–18 and 1820–30.

James Caulfield, fourth viscount and
first earl of CHARLEMONT (1728–
1799)
He was involved with the Octennial
Bill of 1768, the Volunteer
movement and measures for Irish
independence in 1782. He was in

favour of a regency during the king's indisposition, but opposed both Catholic Emancipation and the Union.

Valentine Browne (Lawless), second baron CLONCURRY (1773–1853) United Irishman 1795–8. He was imprisoned 1798, 1799–1801 on suspicion of treason. He wrote many pamphlets against the Union and was a warm advocate of Catholic Emancipation, but differed from O'Connell in the early 1830s because he did not want to hamper Lord Anglesey's second administration (1830–3). He was created Baron Cloncurry (UK) 1831.

William COBBETT (1762–1835) Journalist and political radical. 1802–35 proprietor and editor of the weekly *Political Register*. 1803–12 he produced the *Parliamentary Debates*.

Richard COBDEN (1804–1865) 1838–46 he was a key figure in the Anti-Corn Law League. MP for Stockport 1841–7, for West Riding 1847–57, for Rochdale 1859–65. He negotiated a commercial treaty with France 1859–60. In 1861 he returned to Paris as chief commissioner for working out the scale of duties on particular articles.

Rev. William COCKBURN He married Robert Peel's sister, Elizabeth, in December 1805. In 1822 he became Dean of York.

Rev. Thomas COEN (d. 1847) Coadjutor bishop of Clonfert 1816–31, bishop of Clonfert 1831–47.

Rev. John COGHLAN (d. 1863) Parish priest, Kilmovee, Ballaghaderreen from 1846.

Rev. Patrick COLEMAN (d. 1838) Curate of Townshend Street Catholic chapel for many years. PP

of St Paul's, Dublin 1825–8; St Michan's, Dublin, 1828–38. Sometime vicar-general of the Dublin archdiocese.

Sir Nathaniel CONANT (1745–1822) Chief Magistrate at Bow Street 1810–20.

Elizabeth (Betsey) CONNOR (1777–1815) Sister of Mary O'Connell and wife of James Connor of Tralee.

James CONNOR (c. 1763–1819) Clerk of the peace for co. Kerry. Husband of Mary O'Connell's sister Betsey. He conformed to the Church of Ireland in order to qualify as an attorney but reverted to Catholicism before his death.

Thomas [O'] CONNOR Merchant in Dublin.

Frederick William CONWAY (1782–1853) Editor *Freeman's Journal* 1806–12, editor Dublin weekly *Messenger* 1808–12. Editor and proprietor of the *Dublin Evening Post* 1814–53.

Sir John Singleton COPLEY *see* Lyndhurst, Baron

Stephen COPPINGER (1795–1858) Called to the Irish bar in 1818.

Rev. William COPPINGER (1753–1830) Catholic Bishop of Cloyne and Ross 1791–1830.

Marcus COSTELLO (born c. 1801) First president of the National Trades Political Union 1831–c. 1833. Attorney-general of Gibraltar 1842–68. A Protestant.

Patrick COSTELLO (d. 1858) Solicitor. Engaged in Catholic agitation and anti-tithe campaign. MP for Waterford city 1848–52.

Walter ('Watty') COX Editor of a Dublin monthly periodical, the *Irish Magazine* 1807–15.

Philip Cecil CRAMPTON (1782–1862) Professor of law TCD 1816–34. MP for Milborne 1831–2. Solicitor-general for Ireland Dec. 1830–4. Judge of the court of king's bench 1834–59.

William Sharman CRAWFORD (1781–1861)
1811 sheriff of Down. MP for Dundalk 1835–7, Rochdale 1841–52. Strong advocate of tenant-right, Catholic Emancipation and radical parliamentary reform.

Martin CREAN (c. 1802–1867)
Acting-secretary of the Repeal Association for part of 1846. Associated with the glass manufacturing industry.

Rev. Paul CULLEN (1803–1878)
Rector of the Irish College, Rome 1832–48; of the Propaganda College, Rome 1848–9. Archbishop of Armagh 1849–52, of Dublin 1852–78. Cardinal in 1866. He may be regarded as the founder of the Catholic University in Ireland.

John Philpot CURRAN (1750–1817)
In 1782 he became a king's counsel, and was elected to the Irish House of Commons in the following year. 1806–14 master of the rolls. A strong supporter of Catholic Emancipation. On retirement in 1814 he received an address from the Catholic Board.

William Henry CURRAN (1789–1858)
Called to the Irish bar 1816. Insolvency commissioner in Ireland. Bencher of King's Inns, Dublin 1848. Author of Life of John Philpot Curran (his father), and Sketches of the Irish Bar.

Rev. Patrick CURTIS (1740–1832)
Catholic Archbishop of Armagh and primate of all Ireland 1819–32.

James DALY (d. 1847)
1805–11 MP for Galway borough, 1812–30, 1832–5 for co. Galway. In 1845 he was created Baron Dunsandle.

Col. Hon. George Lionel Dawson DAMER (1788–1856)
Third son of the first earl of Portarlington. MP for Portarlington 1835–47. Comptroller of the household 1841–7.

John (Bligh), fourth earl of DARNLEY (1767–1831)
Succeeded in 1781. He took his seat in the Irish House of Lords in 1789. A whig.

William Joseph O'Neill DAUNT (1807–1894)
Convert to Roman Catholicism. Returned for Mallow, in the general election of 1832 but unseated on the petition of the tory candidate. 1841–2 secretary to O'Connell, as lord mayor of Dublin. Daunt was the Repeal director for Leinster, and head Repeal warden for Scotland, and much involved in Repeal Association proceedings in 1845–6.

Thomas Osborne DAVIS (1814–1845)
Poet and journalist. Called to the bar in 1838. 1839 he joined the Repeal Association. In 1841 he was joint editor of the Dublin Morning Register with John Dillon. July 1842 he, Dillon and Duffy founded the Nation, to which he was a leading contributor, 1842–5.

George Robert DAWSON ((1790–1856)
Private secretary to Rober Peel. MP for co. Londonderry 1815–30, for Harwich 1830–2. Under-secretary of state for the home department 1822–7. Financial secretary to the treasurer 1828–30. In 1830 he was made a privy councillor.

Robert DAY
In 1798 he became an Irish judge.

Arthur (French), Baron DE FREYNE (1786–1856)
Whig MP for co. Roscommon 1821–32. 1839 created Baron de

Freyne of Artagh. Having no male issue, he was in 1851 created Baron de Freyne of Coolavin, with a special remainder, failing direct heirs, to his brothers. Lieutenant of co. Roscommon 1854–6.

John (French), Baron DE FREYNE (1788–1863)
Rector of Grange Sylvae, co. Kilkenny. Succeeded as Baron de Freyne of Coolavin in 1856.

Thomas Philip DE GREY, second earl De Grey (1781–1859)
He became the second earl De Grey in 1833. First lord of the admiralty 1834–5; lord lieutenant of Ireland 1841–4.

James DELAHUNTY (1808–1885)
Waterford merchant. Alderman of Waterford 1842–5. Coroner of co. Waterford 1850–67. MP for Waterford City 1868–74; for co. Waterford 1877–80.

Thomas DENMAN (1779–1854)
MP 1818–26, 1830–2; chief justice of the king's bench 1832–50; knighted 1830; created Baron Denman of Dovedale 1834.

Sir Edward DENNY (d. 1831)
Third baronet. High sheriff of Tralee 1794. Commanding officer of the Yeomanry Corps 1802–3. 1828–9 MP for Tralee.

Rev. Cornelius DENVIR (1791–1866)
Professor of mathematics and natural philosophy at Maynooth 1813–26. Parish priest of Downpatrick 1826–35. Bishop of Down and Connor 1835–65.

John Norcot D'ESTERRE (d. 1815)
Provision merchant to Dublin Castle. Member of the Trinity guild of the common council. Captain on half-pay in the Royal Marines since 1810.

John DEVEREUX (1778–1860)
He took part in the 1798 rebellion, was hidden by Fr William L'Estrange and then went into voluntary exile in the USA. Bolivar accepted his offer to raise a volunteer force in Ireland for service in Venezuela. His legion reached there in the second half of 1819, but he did not arrive until June 1820 by which time the legion had mutinied and the greater part had been sent to Jamaica. In 1824 he returned to England having, on his own admission, made a considerable fortune.

William George Spencer (Cavendish), sixth duke of DEVONSHIRE (1790–1858)
Succeeded in 1811. A whig.

John Blake DILLON (1816–1866)
A member of the Young Ireland movement. With Davis and Duffy he founded the *Nation* in 1842. He took part in the 1848 rebellion, escaped to the US and returned to Ireland in 1855 after the amnesty. He helped to found the National Association and became its first secretary. MP for co. Tipperary 1865–6.

Benjamin DISRAELI (1804–1881)
Man of letters and statesman. Became an MP in 1837, and in 1848 leader of the conservative party in the House of Commons. Chancellor of the Exchequer 1852, 1858–9, 1866–8. Prime minister 1868, 1874–80. In 1876 he was created earl of Beaconsfield.

Michael DOHENY (1805–1862)
A leading member of the Repeal Association. Contributed prose and verse to the *Nation*. After the 1848 insurrection he escaped to New York, where he was admitted to the bar. Became a colonel of the 9th New York State militia regiment, and wrote *The History of the American Revolution* and *The Felon's Track: a Narrative of '48*.

John DOHERTY (1783–1850)
Solicitor-general 1827–30. Lord

chief justice of the common pleas 1830–50.

Richard (Hely-Hutchinson), 1st earl DONOUGHMORE (1756–1825)
MP from 1777; from 1788 in the Irish upper house as Baron Donoughmore. He voted for the Union, hoping thereby to secure Catholic Emancipation. In 1800 he was created Earl of Donoughmore and elected as one of the twenty-eight representative peers of England.

Richard DOWDEN
Merchant at Cork. Mayor of Cork 1845.

William DOWNES, first Baron Downes (1752–1826)
He became an MP in 1790 and two years later a justice of the king's bench; 1803–22 lord chief justice of the king's bench; 1806–18 vice chancellor of the University of Dublin; 1822 an Irish peer.

Rev. James Warren DOYLE O.S.A. (1786–1834)
Catholic Bishop of Kildare and Leighlin 1819–34. Author of numerous works under his episcopal initials J.K.L. He gave evidence to parliamentary committees in 1825, 1830 and 1832.

William DRENNAN (1754–1820)
Belfast physician, United Irishman, poet. In 1791 he wrote the original prospectus of the Society of United Irishmen. He was tried for sedition and acquitted in 1794. In 1808 he founded the *Belfast Magazine*.

Thomas DRUMMOND (1797–1840)
Engineer. He invented the lime-light or Drummond light, and a form of heliostat. Head of the boundary commission for the great Reform bill. In 1833 he became secretary to Lord Althorp. Under-secretary for Ireland 1835-40.

Charles Gavan DUFFY (1816–1903)
Joined the *Morning Register*, Dublin in 1836. 1839–41 first editor of the Belfast *Vindicator*. With Davis and Dillon he founded the *Nation* and edited it 1842–9. MP for New Ross 1852–5. Emigrated to Australia in 1855 and settled in Melbourne. In 1856 he stood for the first Victorian parliament under responsible government. Minister for Lands 1858–9, 1861–3. In 1868 he helped to found the Melbourne *Advocate*. 1871–2 premier of Victoria. Became Speaker in 1877. 1880 returned to Europe.

John William Ponsonby, styled Lord DUNCANNON (1781–1847)
Styled Lord Duncannon until 1844. Created Baron Duncannon (UK) in 1834. Succeeded as fourth earl of Bessborough in 1844. MP for various English constituencies 1805–26, 1832–4, for co. Kilkenny 1826–32. Home secretary July–Dec. 1834. Lord lieutenant of Ireland July 1846–May 1847.

Edward DWYER (1767–1837)
Permanent secretary of the Catholic Association 1825–9. From 1829 until his death O'Connell paid him £300 per annum privately out of his own pocket.

Hugh Fortescue, styled Viscount EBRINGTON (1783–1861)
MP almost continuously 1804–39. Went to the House of Lords in 1839 in his father's barony of Fortescue. Succeeded as second earl Fortescue in 1841. Lord lieutenant of Ireland 1839–41. Lord steward of the household 1846–50.

Maria EDGEWORTH (1767–1849)
Novelist. Her works include *Castle Rackrent, Belinda, Essay on Irish Bulls* (with her father), *Tales of a Fashionable Life, Patronage, Harrington* and *Ormond*. She finished and published her father's *Memoirs*.

John Scott, first baron ELDON (1751–1838)
In 1788 he became solicitor-general; created Baron Eldon in 1799. 1799–1801 lord chief justice of the common pleas, and in 1801–6 and 1807–27 lord chancellor. Created earl of Eldon in 1821. He was strongly opposed to the Catholic claims throughout his career.

Edward Granville (Eliot) styled Lord ELIOT (1798–1877)
MP for Liskeard 1824–32, for East Cornwall 1837–45. Chief secretary for Ireland 1841–5, postmaster general 1845–6, lord lieutenant of Ireland 1853–5. Styled Lord Eliot 1823–45, succeeded as third earl of St Germans in 1845.

Edward Law, second baron ELLENBOROUGH (1790–1871)
Tory MP for St Michael's 1813–18. Chief clerk of Pleas, King's Bench, 1812–38. Privy councillor 1828. Privy seal 1828–9. President of the board of control 1828–30, 1834–5, 1841, 1858. Governor general of India 1841–4. Created Viscount Southam and Earl of Ellenborough in 1844. First lord of the admiralty 1846.

Edward ELLICE (1781–1863)
MP for Coventry almost continually 1818–63. Secretary to the treasury and liberal whip 1830–3. Secretary at war 1833–4.

John Richard ELMORE MD (d. 1860)
A member of the London Board of Directors of the National Bank. Friend and physician of O'Connell.

Robert EMMET (1778–1803)
A United Irishman who organized a rising in July 1803. The rioters were easily dispersed. He was tried and hanged.

Thomas ERSKINE (1750–1823)
A whig, a very successful barrister, first Baron Erskine. In 1792 he defended Paine when he was prosecuted for *The Rights of Man*. Paine was found guilty and Erskine was dismissed aas the Prince's attorney-general. In 1802 he became chancellor of the duchy of Cornwall.

Sir Thomas ESMONDE (1786–1868)
Ninth baronet, succeeded in 1803.

George Hampden EVANS
MP for co. Dublin 1832–41.

Chevalier Christopher FAGAN (1733–1816)
A kinsman and friend of the O'Connell family. Formerly a captain in the French army. He ran a school from his house in London.

William Trant FAGAN (1801–1859)
Merchant at Cork. Alderman in Cork, mayor in 1844. MP for city of Cork 1847–51, 1852–9. Author of *The Life and Times of Daniel O'Connell*.

Hugh FALVEY
Still a Catholic in 1768 when he tried to save his own lands through the intervention of a Protestant friend. Conformed later to the established church, saved his land and was called to the Irish bar. He frequently acted as trustee for Hunting Cap and Morgan O'Connell, as nominal purchaser of their property, and for other purposes.

Rev. Thomas FEENY (d. 1873)
1839 appointed administrator of the diocese of Killala, as Bishop of Ptolemais. 1848–73 bishop of Killala.

Robert Cutlar FERGUSON (1768–1838)
Barrister. MP for Kirkcudbright Stewartry 1826–38. Judge advocate-general 1834–8. Fined and imprisoned in 1799 for his alleged part in the attempted rescue of Arthur O'Connor at Maidstone in 1798.

Elizabeth (Betsy) FFRENCH *see*
O'Connell, Elizabeth Betsey

Nicholas FFRENCH (d.1842)
In 1831 he married O'Connell's
youngest daughter, Betsey. He was
appointed a stipendiary magistrate
in Oughterard, co. Galway in 1836.

Lord Thomas FFRENCH (1765–1814)
A Catholic and strenuous
supporter of complete
Emancipation. Succeeded in the
baronetcy in 1784.

Arthur James (Plunkett), 8th earl of
FINGALL (1759–1836)
Lord Killeen until 1793, then eighth
earl of Fingall. One of the leaders
of the Catholics in their agitation
for relief. At the head of a corps of
yeomen, mainly Catholics, he took
an active part in suppressing the
1798 rebellion. He was one of the
six extraordinary knights made at
the coronation of George IV,
becoming a knight in ordinary in
1829. In 1831 he was created a
baron (UK).

John FINLAY (1780–1856)
Called to the bar in 1809.

William Francis FINN (1784–1862)
MP for co. Kilkenny 1832–7. Son
of a rich Carlow merchant who
owned Finn's *Leinster Journal*,
Kilkenny. Married O'Connell's
sister Alicia in 1812.

Edward Michael FITZGERALD
Secretary of Carlow liberal club.

William Vesey FITZGERALD (1783–
1843)
Chancellor of the exchequer (Ire.)
1812–16, lord of the treasury (UK)
1812–17, envoy to the court of
Sweden 1820–3. 1808–12, 1813–18
and 1831–2 MP for Ennis; 1818–28
MP for Clare; 1829 MP for
Newport; 1830 MP for Lostwithiel.
He was made an Irish peer in 1832,
and an English peer in 1835. Lord
president of the board of control
1841–3.

John FITZGIBBON (1749–1802)
Earl of Clare, lord chancellor
of Ireland from 1789. He
consistently used his influence to
resist reform and was totally
opposed to Catholic
Emancipation.

Hugh FITZPATRICK (d. 1818)
Bookseller. He published Denys
Scully's *Statement of the Penal
Laws* in 1812 and was prosecuted
for libel for so doing. He was fined
£200 with eighteen months'
imprisonment.

James Coleman FITZPATRICK (c.
1818–1880)
Called to the Irish bar in 1842.
Chief justice of the Gold Coast
1857–61. Judge of British Kaffraria
1861–72. Judge of Supreme Court
of Cape of Good Hope 1872–9.
Author of *The pope, his rights and
duties* (1860).

Patrick Vincent FITZPATRICK (1792–
1865)
Educated at St Patrick's College,
Maynooth, and called to the Irish
bar. He became O'Connell's close
friend, confidant and political
'manager' and was largely
responsible for the collection of the
'O'Connell Rent' from 1830. He
was assistant-registrar of deeds
from 1847 to 1865.

Christopher FITZ-SIMON (1793–
1856)
Landowner and barrister (1821).
Married O'Connell's daughter,
Ellen. 1832–7 MP for co. Dublin;
clerk of the crown and hanaper
1837–56.

Nicholas FITZ-SIMON (b. 1806)
MP King's co. 1832–41; knighted
1841; a magistrate in Dublin Castle
from 1841.

William (Wentworth Fitzwilliam),
second Earl FITZWILLIAM (1748–
1833)
1794, 1806 president of the council,

655

Dec. 1794–March 1795 lord
lieutenant of Ireland.

Henry FLOOD (1732–1791)
A prominent leader of the popular
party. It was through him that a
powerful opposition was organized
in the Irish House of Commons.
His main objects were to shorten
the duration of parliament, reduce
pensions, create a constitutional
militia, and secure the
independence of the Irish
legislature. 1775–81 vice-treasurer
of Ireland, but removed from office
because of his hostility to the
government. In 1783 he entered the
English House of Commons. He
opposed the extension of the
franchise to Catholics.

Nicholas FORAN (d. 1855)
Ordained 1808. President St John's
College, Waterford, 1814–18.
Parish priest, Lismore 1824–9,
Dungarvan 1829–37. Bishop of
Waterford and Lismore 1837–55.

Thomas Campbell FOSTER (1813–
1882)
Barrister and legal writer.
Parliamentary reporter for the
Times.

Charles James FOX (1749–1806)
Foreign secretary in 1782, 1783 and
1806, and leader of the opposition
for many years. An advanced
liberal.

Sir Philip FRANCIS (1740–1818)
Reputed author of *Junius' Letters*.

Matthew FRANKS
Deputy guardian and keeper of the
rolls. O'Connell's memorial for
admission as a student of King's
Inns was signed by a Mr Franks,
barrister, and a Mr Franks,
attorney.

Arthur FRENCH (born c. 1802)
Secretary of the General
Association. First cousin to Arthur
French, created Baron de Freyne in
1839.

Edmund FRENCH O.P. (d. 1852)
Bishop of Kilmacduagh and
Kilfenora 1824–52.

Mary Jane GAGHRAN (c. 1787–
1854)
Sister of John Gaghran, physician.
She married William Ford, town
clerk of Dublin city. Governess for
O'Connell's children.

John Matthew GALWEY (c. 1790–
1842)
Merchant, shipowner and
landowner. 1832–5 MP co.
Waterford. J.P., grand juror, co.
Waterford.

Frederick John Robinson, Viscount
GODERICH (1782–1859)
MP from 1806. He held a variety of
cabinet posts 1810–13. 1823–7
chancellor of the exchequer. 1827
he was created Viscount Goderich
and appointed secretary of state for
war and the colonies and leader in
the House of Lords. Aug. 1827–Jan.
1828 prime minister. He held office
again in the 1830s. In 1833 he was
created Earl of Ripon. He was
opposed to Catholic Emancipation
early in his career but supported
Grattan's motion for a committee
on Catholic claims in March 1813.
He denounced the Catholic
Association in 1825 but did
support the Roman Catholic Relief
Bill in 1829.

William GODWIN (1756–1836)
At first a Nonconformist minister.
Political Justice published in 1793.
In 1833 he was made Yeoman of
the Usher of the Exchequer, and
was allowed to retain this sinecure
for life, though it was abolished
soon after his appointment. He
married Mary Wollstonecraft.

Isaac GOLDSMID (1778–1859)
A wealthy financier and
philanthropist, and the political
leader of the British Jews. He was
active in the foundation of

University College, London.
Created a baronet in 1841.

Thomas GOOLD (1766?–1846)
Called to the Irish bar in 1791. MP
in the last session of the Irish
Parliament. 1823 third serjeant;
1830 king's serjeant; 1832 master
in chancery.

William GOSSETT (d. 1848)
Private secretary to the lord
lieutenant. MP for Truro 1820–6.
Under-secretary for Ireland 1830–
5. Knighted in 1831.

Henry GOULBURN (1784–1856)
Chief secretary for Ireland 1821–7;
chancellor of the exchequer 1828–
30, 1841–6; home secretary 1834–5.
Resisted the Catholic
Emancipation bill in 1821.

Sir James Robert George GRAHAM
(1792–1861)
MP almost continually 1818–21,
1826–61. First lord of the admiralty
1830–4, 1852–5. Home secretary
1841–6.

Henry GRATTAN (1746–1820)
He espoused free trade, Irish
parliamentary independence (for
which the House of Commons
voted him £50,000 for land to show
the nation's gratitude), the
disbanding of the volunteers in
1783, tithe commutation, and
Catholic Emancipation. Founded
the Whig Club. He entered the
British House of Commons in
1805.

Henry GRATTAN jnr (1789–1859)
Biographer of his father Henry
Grattan. J.P., barrister, landowner
and owner-editor of the *Freeman's
Journal* until 1830. MP for Dublin
City 1826–30, for co. Meath 1831–
52.

Charles GREVILLE (1794–1865)
1821–59 clerk to the privy council.
He had close relations with the
Duke of Wellington, the Duke of
Bedford, Lord Palmerston and

Lord Clarendon and was
sometimes used as a negotiator
during ministerial changes.

Charles (Grey), second earl GREY
(1764–1845)
He opposed the Union in 1800, and
supported the Catholic claims
1800–29. Prime minister 1830–4.

Gerald GRIFFIN (1803–1840)
Dramatist, novelist and poet. He
was a law student at the University
of London for a time. In the late
1830s he joined the congregation
of the Irish Christian Brothers.

Arthur GUINNESS J.P. (1768–1855)
He became the head of Guinness'
brewing firm in 1803. Director of
the Bank of Ireland 1808–39;
governor 1820–2. Supporter of
Catholic Emancipation.

Rev. Francis HALY (1781–1855)
Administrator of Mountrath 1813–
22. Parish priest of Kilcock 1822.
Bishop of Kildare and Leighlin
from 1838.

Sir Henry HARDINGE (1785–1856)
Secretary at war 1828–30, 1841–4;
Irish secretary July–Nov. 1830,
Dec. 1834–April 1835; governor-
general of India 1844–8. In 1846 he
was created Viscount Hardinge of
Lahore and of Durham. His army
career culminated in his becoming
field marshal in 1855.

John HARDY (1773/4–1855)
Barrister. Bencher 1840, reader
1850. Recorder of Leeds 1806–33.
MP for Bradford 1832–7, 1841–7.

Thomas HARDY (1752–1832)
In January 1792, Hardy, with a few
friends, founded 'The London
Corresponding Society' with the
object of promoting parliamentary
reform. On 12 May 1794 he was
arrested on a charge of high
treason, but in November found
'not guilty'.

William HARE (1801–56)
1826–30 MP for co. Kerry; 1841–6

657

for St Albans. He was styled Viscount Ennismore 1827–37, succeeding to the earldom of Listowel in 1837.

Rev. James HARRINGTON S.J. He ran an 'academy' at Reddington, near Cove, co. Cork, which was said to have been the first school opened in Ireland by a Catholic priest after the relaxation of the penal laws.

Sir Anthony HART (c. 1754–1831) In 1816 he was appointed solicitor-general to Queen Charlotte. He was vice-chancellor of England April–Nov. 1827; lord chancellor of Ireland from 1827 to 1830; knighted in 1827.

Benjamin HAWES (1797–1862) MP for Lambeth 1832–47, for Kinsale 1848–52. Under-secretary for the colonies 1846–51. 1851–7 deputy secretary for the war department. Knighted 1856. 1857–62 permanent under-secretary for war.

Edward HAY (1761?–1826) He acted as secretary to various associations for the Emancipation of Irish Catholics, but was superseded as secretary to the Catholic Board in 1819, supposedly for having opened communications with a cabinet minister without authority. He died in penury.

Joseph HAYES Merchant at Cork. Alderman of Cork.

Rev. Richard HAYES O.F.M. (d. 1824) of the Franciscan College, Wexford. Expelled from the papal states, 1816.

John HELY-HUTCHINSON 1826–30 and 1831–2 MP for co. Tipperary.

William A'Court, first baron HEYTESBURY (1779–1860) Succeeded his father as second baronet in 1817. Ambassador to Portugal 1824–8, to Russia 1828–32. In 1828 he was created Baron Heytesbury of Heytesbury, Wiltshire. Lord lieutenant of Ireland 1844–6. Governor of the Isle of Wight until 1857.

Robert HICKSON (d. 1816) 36 College Green, Dublin.

Robin HICKSON of the Square, Tralee. In 1809 or 1810 he became a Roman Catholic 'publicly'.

Francis HIGGINS (1746–1802) When he owned the *Freeman's Journal* he placed it, and his own services, at the disposal of the government in Dublin. In 1788 he was appointed a magistrate, but was dismissed by Fitzgibbon three years later. In 1794 he was struck off the roll of attorneys. In 1795 he warned the government of the projected attack on the lord lieutenant, Lord Camden, and acted as informer on the revolutionary movement before and during 1798.

Sir John Cam HOBHOUSE, second baronet (1786–1869) MP for Westminster 1820–33, for Nottingham 1834–47, for Harwich 1848–52. Succeeded as second baronet in 1831. 1832 became a privy councillor. Secretary of war 1832–3, chief secretary for Ireland March–April 1833, first commissioner of woods and forests 1834, president of the board of control 1835–41, 1846–52. Friend and executor of Byron. Created Baron Broughton in 1851.

Prince Alexander Leopold Franz Emerich von HOHENLOHE Waldenburg Schillingfurst (1794–1850). Ordained a Catholic priest in 1815. He was renowned for the miraculous cures attributed to him.

Henry Richard (Vassall Fox) third baron HOLLAND (1773–1840)
Lord privy seal 1806–7, chancellor of duchy of Lancaster 1830–4, 1835–40.

Robert HOLMES (1765–1859)
Called to the Irish bar in 1795. Opposed the enactment of the Union. Married Robert Emmet's sister Mary and was imprisoned on suspicion during Emmet's rebellion. He declined to receive any favours from the government, refusing various offers of legal offices.

Joseph HUME (1777–1855)
A Radical. MP in 1812 and almost continuously 1818 to 1855. Leading advocate of Catholic Emancipation and economical reform.

Henry HUNT (1773–1835)
Radical, reformer and orator who spoke at St Peter's Fields (Peterloo) in 1819; imprisoned 1820–2; 1830–3 MP for Preston.

Peter Bodkin HUSSEY (1778–1838)
From Farrinakilla, co. Kerry. Barrister.

Robert HUTTON
Presbyterian coachbuilder and merchant. MP for Dublin city 1837–41. Member of the Council of University College, London and of the British Association. Elected a fellow of the Geographical Society in 1813.

Sir John Kingston JAMES (1784–1869)
Created a baronet in 1823. Lord mayor of Dublin in 1822 and 1841.

Edward JONES MD
Physician to the lunatic asylum, Waterford. Appointed a magistrate for Waterford city 1837.

Leslie Grove JONES (1779–1839)
He served in the army throughout the Peninsular War, becoming captain and lieutenant-colonel in 1813. His pamphlet, 'Principles of Legitimacy' was published in 1827. During the reform agitation he wrote strong letters to the *Times* signed 'Radical'.

Sir Richard KEANE bt
MP for co. Waterford 1832–5.

Rev. James KEATINGE (1783–1849)
Appointed provincial coadjutor with right of succession 6 Dec. 1818; bishop of Ferns, 1819–49.

Richard KEATINGE (1793–1876)
K.C. in 1835. Appointed Queen's serjeant in 1842, judge of the prerogative court 1843. Judge of the probate court 1858–68.

George Bourke [O'] KELLY (1760–1843)
Acton, Middlesex. Married in 1799 Mary, second daughter of Peter Pentheny MD, Tara, co. Meath.

Charles KEMBLE (1775–1854)
His early performances on the stage were unsuccessful mainly because of his ungainly figure, but he was said to have improved steadily over thirty years. His 'affectations of speech were the subject of much satire'. He managed Convent Garden from 1822–3.

John Philip KEMBLE (1757–1823)
1788–96, 1800–2 manager of Drury Lane Theatre. In 1802 he bought a sixth share of Convent Garden.

Valentine (Browne), second earl of KENMARE (1788–1853)
Styled Viscount Castlerosse 1801–12. Became second earl of Kenmare in 1812.

Rev. Patrick KENNEDY (d. 1850)
Coadjutor 1835–6, bishop of Killaloe 1836–50.

Rev. Peter KENNEY S.J. (1779–1841)
In 1812 he was appointed vice-president of Maynooth College, where he stayed for about a year. He was the Superior of the Jesuit mission in Ireland for many years, and later its vice-provincial.

Opened Clongowes Wood College, co. Kildare, in May 1814, and later helped in the establishment of St Stanislaus College, Tullabeg, and of the Jesuit residence of St Francis Xavier in Dublin.

Rev. John KENNY (1792–1879)
Parish priest, Kilrush, co. Clare 1828–48. Parish priest, Ennis and dean of Killaloe 1848–79.

John KEOGH (1740–1817)
Dublin merchant. Led the Irish Catholics 1791–1808. He had sympathy with the objects of the United Irishmen but refused to allow Catholic claims to be compromised by connection with them.

Maurice Fitzgerald, Knight of KERRY (1774–1849)
Hereditary Knight of Kerry. He represented Kerry for thirty-six years. 1799–1801 commissioner of customs in Ireland. He was in favour of the Union. 1801–7 at the board of the Irish treasury. 1827 lord of the English treasury. 1830 vice-treasurer of Ireland. Dec. 1834–Mar. 1835 lord of the admiralty.

Charles William (Fitzgerald), marquess of KILDARE (1819–1887)
Styled marquess of Kildare till 1874 when he succeeded as fifth duke of Leinster. A Commissioner of National Education 1841 until his death. High sheriff for co. Kildare 1843. Liberal MP for co. Kildare 1847–52. Chancellor of the Queen's University of Ireland 1870–81. President of the Royal Dublin Society 1874 till his death.

Abraham Bradley KING (1773–1838)
Alderman and king's stationer. Lord mayor of Dublin in 1813 and in 1821. Former deputy grand master of the Orange order. 1821 created a baronet.

Thomas KIRWAN.
Merchant, Abbey Street, Dublin.

Henry LABOUCHERE (1798–1869)
Liberal MP from 1826. 1832–41 he held a number of ministerial posts. Chief secretary for Ireland 1846–7. 1847–52 president of the board of trade. 1855–8 secretary of state for the colonies. Created Baron Taunton in 1859.

(Jean-Baptiste-) Henri LACORDAIRE (1802–1861)
Leading ecclesiastic in the Catholic revival in France following the 1789 revolution. Ordained as a priest in 1827. Co-founder of L'Avenir, a journal advocating separation of church and state. Joined the Dominican order at Raine in 1838. Reestablished the Dominican order in France in 1843. Head of French Dominicans 1850–4. In favour of a Republican France. Elected to the French Academy in 1860.

Patrick LALOR (d. 1856)
1832–5 Repeal MP for Queen's County. Prominent in anti-tithe movement as a Catholic farmer with a large estate. Father of James Fintan Lalor, the young Irelander.

Hon. George LAMB (1784–1834)
Brother of Lord Melbourne. Author of many essays and articles. MP for Westminster 1819–20, for Dungarvan 1826–34; under-secretary of the home department 1830–4.

Henry LAMBERT J.P., D.L. (1786–1861)
MP for co. Wexford 1831–5.

(Hughes-) Félicité (-Robert de) LAMENNAIS (1782–1854)
Priest and liberal Catholic philosophical and political writer. Co-founder of the newspaper L'Avenir in 1830. Publication was suspended in Nov. 1831, and after a vain appeal to the pope, its

principles were condemned in the encyclical, *Mirari Vos*. Lamennais then attacked the papacy, which led to his severance from the church. He served in the Constituent Assembly after the 1848 revolution.

Henry Petty (-Fitzmaurice), third marquess of LANSDOWNE (1780–1863)
Chancellor of the exchequer 1806–7. In 1809 he succeeded as third marquess of Lansdowne. In 1818 he became the earl of Kerry, viscount Clanmaurice and the twenty-third baron Kerry and Lixnaw, and in the same year reverted to the family name of Petty-Fitzmaurice. 1827–8 home secretary; 1830–4, 1835–41, 1846–52 lord president of the council; 1852–8 in cabinet but without office. He was lord lieutenant of Wiltshire from 1829 till his death. Above all else Catholic Emancipation caught his attention.

David LA TOUCHE (1772–1838)
Banker. Third son of Rt Hon. David La Touche MP, Marlay, co. Dublin.

Patrick M. LAVELLE (c. 1802–1837)
Proprietor and editor of the *Freeman's Journal* from 1830 till his death.

Cecil John LAWLESS (1820–1853)
Second son of second baron Cloncurry. MP for Clonmel 1846–53.

John LAWLESS (1773–1837)
He was refused admission to the bar by Lord Clare because of his closeness to leaders of the United Irish movement. From 1817 to 1819 he was the editor of the *Ulster Register*, and subsequently of the *Belfast Magazine*. In 1831 he was briefly under arrest.

Nicholas Philpot LEADER (c. 1773–1836)
1830–2 MP for Kilkenny City.

Rev. Sir Harcourt LEES (1776–1852)
Anglican clergyman 1800–6. He published several pamphlets, chiefly in support of the Protestant Ascendancy.

Augustus Frederick (Fitzgerald), third duke of LEINSTER (1791–1874)
Succeeded to the title in 1804. A whig. Lord lieutenant of co. Kildare from 1831 till his death. Commissioner of National Education in Ireland 1836–41.

Denis LE MARCHANT (1795–1874)
Secretary to Lord Brougham in 1830. Appointed clerk to the crown in chancery in 1834. Secretary to the board of trade 1836–41. He was also joint secretary to the treasury in 1841. Created a baronet in 1841. MP for Worcester 1846–7; under-secretary for the home department 1847; secretary of the board of trade 1848; chief clerk to the House of Commons 1850–71.

Rev. William L'ESTRANGE O.D.C. (d. 1833)
Educated and ordained on the Continent. He was provincial of the Irish Carmelites and prior of St Teresa's, Clarendon St, Dublin.

Francis LEVESON-GOWER (1800–1857)
Second son of first duke of Sutherland. MP almost continuously 1822–46. A lord of the treasury 1827, under-secretary of state for the colonies 1828, chief secretary for Ireland 1828–30, secretary to war 1830. Created Earl of Ellesmere in 1846. Assumed the surname Egerton in 1833.

George LIDWILL (Lidwell) (d. 1839)
Landlord and litterateur. High sheriff of co. Tipperary 1807.

Edward John LITTLETON, first baron Hatherton (1791–1863)
MP for Staffordshire 1812–32, for South Staffordshire 1832–5. Chief secretary for Ireland 1833–4. He

became a member of the privy council in 1833. Created Baron Hatherton of Hatherton in 1835. Lord lieutenant of Staffordshire 1854–63.

Robert Banks (Jenkinson), second earl of LIVERPOOL (1770–1828) 1812–27 prime minister. Though opposed to Catholic Emancipation himself, he had to treat the question as open in order to include pro-Catholic tories in his administration. He was prepared to confer the elective franchise on *English* Roman Catholics and to open the magistracy to Catholic gentlemen.

Edward LUCAS (1787–1871) MP for co. Monaghan 1834–41. Under-secretary to the lord lieutenant 1841–5.

John Singleton (Copley), Lord LYNDHURST (1772–1863) Attorney-general 1824–6; master of the rolls 1826–7; in 1827 he was created Baron Lyndhurst; lord chancellor 1827–30, 1834–5 and 1841–6; chief baron of the exchequer 1831–4.

Thomas Babington MACAULAY (1800–1859) Historian. Commissioner in bankruptcy 1828–31. MP for Calne 1830–3, for Edinburgh 1839–47, 1852–6. Commissioner for the board of control 1832. On the supreme council of India Dec. 1833–Jan. 1838. Secretary of war 1839–41. He became lord rector of the university of Glasgow in 1848. Raised to peerage 1856.

William Bernard MACCABE (1801–1891) Author and historian. Journalist in Ireland 1823–35. Published a 3 volume Catholic History of England 1847–54.

Eneas MACDONNELL (1783–1858) Called to the Irish bar 1810. Editor and proprietor of *Dublin Chronicle* 1815–17; editor of *Cork Mercantile Chronicle*. Fined £100 and sentenced to six months' imprisonment in 1816 for publishing a 'libel' written by Denys Scully.

Joseph Myles MACDONNELL (1796–187?) Sometime J.P. for co. Mayo 1846–7.

Richard Graves MACDONNELL (1814–1881) Called to the Irish bar in 1838, to the English bar in 1841. Chief justice of Gambia 1843–7. 1847–72 colonial governor in Gambia, St Lucia, St Vincent, South Australia, Novia Scotia and Hong Kong.

Rose MCDOWELL (c. 1821–1902) Eldest daughter of Robert McDowell, merchant, of Belfast.

Rev. Nicholas MCEVOY (1800–1860) Curate 1830–40, administrator 1841–5 and parish priest of Kells 1845–60. Active in support of tenant rights in co. Meath.

Rev. John MACHALE (1791–1881) Lecturer in theology at St Patrick's College, Maynooth 1814–25; titular bishop of Moronia and coadjutor bishop of Killala 1825–34; archbishop of Tuam 1834–81.

Thomas MCKENNY (1770–1849) Alderman from 1811, lord mayor of Dublin 1819, created baronet 1831.

Rev. Peter MACLAUGHLIN (c. 1760–1840) Catholic bishop of Raphoe 1802–19; administrator of Derry 1819–24; bishop of Derry 1824–40.

Cornelius MACLOGHLIN (1761–1851) Catholic merchant. A member of the United Irishmen. He was a trustee and treasurer of the O'Connell testimonial in 1829 and of the O'Connell Tribute in succeeding years.

Rev. Charles McNALLY (d. 1864)
Coadjutor 1843–4, bishop of
Clogher 1844–64.

Major William Nugent
MacNAMARA (1775–1856)
1830–52 MP for co. Clare.
Landowner. High Sheriff, Clare, in
1798

William James McNEVIN (1763–
1841)
A United Irishman, who was
imprisoned 1798–1803. Active in
Irish-American politics thereafter.

Rev. Patrick MacNICHOLAS (c.
1781–1852)
Bishop of Achonry 1818–52.

Myles McSWINEY
c. 1804 he married O'Connell's
sister, Bridget. He acted as land
agent to O'Connell from about
1812 to 1822.

Daniel Owen MADDEN (1815–1859)
Worked for the *Press* newspaper.
Author of many works including
Ireland and its Rulers since 1829,
The age of Pitt and Fox and a
memoir of H. Grattan.

John MAGEE
Proprietor and editor of the *Dublin*
Evening Post, which he inherited
from his father, also a journalist. In
1813 he was prosecuted by the
government for publishing an
alleged libel on the duke of
Richmond's administration. A
Protestant.

Rev. Francis MAGENNIS (d. 1847)
Parish priest of Clones 1842–7.

Rev. Edward MAGINN D.D. (1802–
1849)
Curate in Moville, co. Donegal
1825–9. Parish priest of united
parishes of Fahan and Deysertegny
1829–45. He was appointed
coadjutor to the bishop of Derry in
1845. Bishop of Ortosia 1846–9. An
enthusiastic nationalist politician.

Maurice (Mark) MAGRATH (born c.
1765)

Educated Trinity College, Dublin
1784–8. 1796 called to the bar.
Assistant barrister for co. Wicklow
from 1815.

Rev. Thomas MAGUIRE D.D. (1792–
1847)
Parish priest of various parishes in
the diocese of Kilmore from 1818
until his death. Also dean of
Kilmore.

Rev. James MAHER (1793–1874)
Parish priest of Killeshin, co.
Carlow from Jan. 1841. An uncle
of Cardinal Cullen and one of the
most distinguished Irish priests of
his time.

James Patrick O'Gorman MAHON
(1800/1803–1891)
1830–1, 1879–85 MP for co. Clare;
1847–52 for Ennis; 1887–91 for co.
Carlow.

Nicholas MAHON (c. 1746–1841)
Wealthy woollen merchant, in
business in Dublin for over seventy
years. A delegate to the Catholic
convention of 1792.

James Mountain MAHONY
Lieutenant, Kerry Militia, 1796–c.
1811.

Pierce MAHONY (1792–1853)
Attorney, Woodlawn, Killarney.
Parliamentary agent to the
Catholic Association 1828–9.
1837–8 MP for Kinsale.

Charles MANNERS-SUTTON, first
viscount Canterbury (1780–1845)
Speaker of the House of Commons
1817–35; judge advocate general
1809–17. He was created Baron
Bottesford and Viscount
Canterbury in 1835.

Thomas MANNERS-SUTTON, 1st
baron Manners (1756–1842)
Created Baron Manners of Foston
in 1807. 1807–27 he was lord
chancellor of Ireland. He voted
against the second reading
of the Catholic Relief Bill in
1829.

Ralph MARSHALL (1773–1809)
From Callinapfercy, Milltown, co. Kerry. He helped to keep Kerry free of turmoil in 1798 and was concerned about the welfare of his tenants. He was high sheriff in 1799. He joined the Spanish Army in 1808, and was killed at the siege of Gerona.

Richard MARTIN (1754–1834)
In 1782 he was high sheriff for co. Galway. A member of the Irish Parliament 1776–83, 1798–1800, and represented co. Galway in the British Parliament 1801–26. A firm supporter of Catholic Emancipation.

Rev. Theobald MATHEW (1790–1856)
Ordained in 1814 as a Capuchin priest and worked in Cork at the 'Little Friary'. In 1838 he began his campaign for total abstinence, travelling throughout Ireland. In 1843 he went to London and travelled in the USA 1849–51. In 1848 he was named by the clergy of the diocese for the vacant bishopric of Cork but the choice was not ratified by the Vatican. A pension was granted to him through the influence of Lord John Russell.

Edward MAYNE (c. 1756–1829)
Justice of the Common Pleas 1806–17; justice of the King's Bench 1817–20.

Thomas Francis MEAGHER (1823–1867)
Young Irelander, and a founder of the Irish Confederation in 1847. Transported to Van Dieman's Land in 1849 for his part in the 1848 insurrection. In 1852 he escaped to USA and lectured and worked as a journalist there 1852–4. Admitted to the bar in 1855. In the US federal army from 1861. 1862 became a brigadier general.

Enrolled as a Fenian in 1863. Temporary governor of Montana 1866 until his death.

John Chambre (Brabazon), tenth earl of MEATH (1772–1851)
Lord lieutenant of co. Dublin 1831–51. Created Baron Chaworth (UK) 1831.

William (Lamb), second viscount MELBOURNE (1779–1848)
Succeeded as the second Viscount Melbourne in 1828. He was chief secretary for Ireland 1827–8, home secretary 1830–4, prime minister July–Nov. 1834, 1835–41.

Rev. John MILEY D.D. (1805–1861)
Curate Marlborough St, Dublin 1835–49. Rector of the Irish College, Paris 1849–59. Parish priest, Bray 1859–61. Historian.

Joseph (Leeson), fourth earl of MILLTOWN (1799–1866)
He was styled Viscount Russborough 1801–7. Succeeded to the earldom in 1807.

Rev. John MILNER D.D. (1752–1826)
Vicar apostolic of midland district, England, from 1803. At first he accepted the royal veto but later became an uncompromising opponent. This led to his expulsion from the English Catholic Board and his exclusion from the meeting of vicars-apostolic in Durham in October 1813. In 1814 the Irish bishops sent him with Dr Murray to act as their agent in Rome to secure the recall of the Quarantotti rescript.

John MITCHEL (1815–1875)
Young Irelander. Admitted as a solicitor in 1840. Assisted in editing the *Nation* 1845–7. Founded the *United Irishman* in 1848. Transported to Van Dieman's Land for sedition in 1848. In 1853 he escaped to San Francisco where he was editor of various journals

and papers. He was imprisoned for five months because of his articles in defence of the southern cause in the American Civil War. Elected MP for co. Tipperary in 1875, but his election was disallowed after his death.

James Henry MONAHAN (1804–1878)
Solicitor-general for Ireland 1846–7. Attorney-general 1847. Chief justice of the common pleas 1850–76. 1867 he presided at the special commission for the trial of the Fenian prisoners at Cork and Limerick.

Charles MONTALEMBERT (1810–1870)
Orator, politician and historian who was a leader in the struggle against absolutism in church and state in France in the nineteenth century. He began his political career with the newspaper *L'Avenir*. He helped found a Catholic school in 1831 for which he was prosecuted. Wrote for *L'Univers Religieux*. After the 1848 revolution he swung the Catholic party behind Louis Napoleon, an act which he later regretted. He came into conflict with the Church for his insistence that it encourage civil and religious liberties.

George Henry MOORE J.P. (1811–1870)
MP for co. Mayo 1847–57, 1868–70. Father of George Moore, the novelist.

George Ogle MOORE (born c. 1779)
Called to the bar 1800. MP for Dublin city 1826–31. Deputy registrar of deeds 1802–31, registrar of deeds 1831–46.

Louisa MOORE
A Catholic. Daughter of Hon. John Browne and grand-daughter of the first earl of Attamont.

Thomas MOORE (1779–1852)
Both his parents were Catholics.

Through his 'Irish Melodies' he became known as the 'national lyrist' of Ireland. He wrote biographies of Lord Byron and Lord Edward Fitzgerald and 'The History of Ireland' for Lardner's *Cabinet Cyclopedia*. His 'Lalla Rookh' was published in 1817.

George William Frederick (Howard) styled Lord MORPETH (1802–1864)
1825–48 known as Lord Morpeth. Succeeded as seventh earl of Carlisle in 1848. MP 1826–41, 1846–8. Chief secretary of Ireland 1835–41. Chief commissioner of woods and forests 1846–50. Lord lieutenant of East Riding 1847–64. Chancellor of the duchy of Lancaster 1850–2. Lord lieutenant of Ireland 1855–8, 1859–64.

Lucretia MOTT (1793–1880)
Quaker preacher and reformer, advocate of anti-slavery and women's rights.

Rev. Francis MOYLAN D.D. (1735–1815)
In 1775 he became Catholic bishop of Kerry; was translated to Cork in 1786. He was in favour of the Union, but eventually opposed the veto.

Constantine Henry (Phipps), second earl of MULGRAVE (1797–1863)
MP almost continually 1818–30. In 1831 he succeeded as earl of Mulgrave. Governor of Jamaica 1832–4. Lord privy seal July–Dec. 1834. Lord lieutenant of Ireland 1835–9. Created marquess of Normanby in 1838. Secretary of state for war and the colonies 1839. Secretary of state for the home department 1839–41. Ambassador to Paris 1846–52. 1854–8 minister at the court of Tuscany.

Joseph Denis MULLEN
Trimming manufacturer. Sometime governor of the Four

Courts Marshalsea. A prominent member of the Catholic Association. A director of the Royal Canal Co. from c. 1821.

Frederick W. MULLINS (1804–1854)
MP for co. Kerry 1831–7.

Philip Henry MUNTZ (1811–1888)
Merchant in Birmingham. Chief promoter of incorporation of the borough in 1837, mayor 1839 and 1840. MP for Birmingham 1868–85.

John Joseph MURPHY
Attorney of Murphy and Ruthven, solicitors, 13 College Green.

William MURPHY (d. 1849)
A rich Dublin salesmaster, who had taken part in the 1798 rebellion.

Rev. Daniel MURRAY (1768–1852)
President of St Patrick's College, Maynooth; archbishop of Dublin from 1823. He opposed the veto.

Thomas Lamie MURRAY
Managing director of the National bank.

Rev. Francis Joseph NICHOLSON (1803–1855)
He joined the Discalced Carmelites in 1825. Consecrated coadjutor archbishop of Corfu in 1846, succeeding in 1852.

John Toler, first earl of NORBURY (1745–1831)
In 1776 he became an MP, in 1789 solicitor general, in 1798 attorney general. He supported the Union and in 1800 became chief justice of the court of common pleas in Ireland and was created Baron Norbury. In 1825 O'Connell drew up a petition to Parliament calling for his removal on the ground that he had fallen asleep during a trial for murder and was unable to give any account of the evidence. Peel said it would be enquired into but Norbury was not induced to resign until 1827.

Bernard Edward (Howard), twelfth duke of NORFOLK (1765–1842)
He was empowered by an Act of Parliament in 1824 to exercise the office of Earl Marshal notwithstanding his adhesion to Catholicism. He was admitted to the House of Lords in 1829.

John NUGENT M.B. (1806–1899)
Travelling physician to O'Connell. An original member of the Reform Club, London. Inspector of commissioners of control of lunacy, Ireland 1846–90. Knighted 1890.

Cornelius O'BRIEN (1782–1860)
He became an attorney in 1811. MP for co. Clare 1832–47, 1852–7.

William Smith O'BRIEN (1803–1864)
MP for Ennis as tory Emancipationist 1828–31. MP for co. Limerick as liberal and Repealer 1835–49. A leader of the Young Ireland movement and of the 1848 rising, for his part in which he was transported to Tasmania in 1849. Returned to Ireland 1856.

Catherine O'CONNELL (née O'Mullane) (1752–1817)
O'Connell's mother. She had ten children.

Catherine (Kate) O'CONNELL (daughter) (1807–1891)
O'Connell's second daughter. In 1832 she married her distant cousin Charles O'Connell.

Charles O'CONNELL (1805–1877)
Cousin of O'Connell. He married Kate, O'Connell's second daughter. MP for co. Kerry 1832–4. Appointed resident magistrate in April 1847.

Daniel O'CONNELL (son) (1816–1897)
Youngest son of O'Connell. 1846–7 MP for Dundalk; 1847–8 for Waterford city; 1853–63 for Tralee. In 1863 he was appointed commissioner of income tax. In 1866 he married Ellen Mary Foster.

General (Count) Daniel O'CONNELL (1745–1833)
Son of Donal Mór and Máire O'Connell, Derrynane. In 1783 he was created count of France. He was Commander of the Order of St Louis, lieutenant-general in the French army, colonel in the British army.

Daniel O'CONNELL (Splinter) (d. 1814)
Son of Edward O'Connell, first cousin of Mary O'Connell. Married in 1803 to Ellen, O'Connell's sister.

Daniel Stephen O'CONNELL (29 Dec. 1812–c. 10 Feb. 1814)
Son of O'Connell.

Donal Mór (Big Daniel) O'CONNELL (d. 1770)
Father of Maurice (Hunting Cap), Daniel (General), and Morgan (O'Connell's father). Married Máire Ní Duibh (Mary) O'Donoghue.

Elizabeth Mary (Betsey) O'CONNELL (daughter) (1810–1893)
O'Connell's youngest daughter. In 1831 married Nicholas Joseph Ffrench.

Ellen O'CONNELL (sister) (born 1777)
Sister of O'Connell. In 1803 she married Daniel O'Connell (Splinter).

Ellen O'CONNELL (daughter) (1805–1883)
O'Connell's eldest daughter. In 1825 she married Christopher Fitz-Simon.

James O'CONNELL (brother) (1786–1872)
Youngest brother of O'Connell. In 1818 married Jane O'Donoghue. He lived in Killarney. He was created a baronet in 1869.

John O'CONNELL (brother) (1778–1853)
Second brother of O'Connell. In 1806 married Elizabeth (Bess) Coppinger. Lived at Grenagh, near Killarney. High sheriff of Kerry 1838.

Lieutenant John O'CONNELL (d. 1826)
He was referred to as Captain O'Connell in a letter from Mary O'Connell. He was in the 67th Regiment, going on half pay in 1816. He joined the 7th Veteran Battalion in 1820.

John O'CONNELL (son) (1810–1858)
O'Connell's third surviving son. Barrister. 1832–7 MP for Youghal; 1837–41 Athlone; 1841–7 Kilkenny City; 1847–51 Limerick City; 1853–7 Clonmel; clerk of the crown and hanaper, 1857–8. Married Elizabeth Ryan in 1838.

Máire ní Duibh (Mary) O'CONNELL (née O'Donoghue)
Her soubriquet indicated her branch of the O'Donaghue family. She had 22 children, one of whom was Morgan, Daniel O'Connell's father.

Mary O'CONNELL (wife) (1778–1836)
Daughter of Thomas O'Connell, a Tralee physician. She married O'Connell on 24 July 1802.

Maurice O'CONNELL (Hunting Cap) (uncle) (1728–1825)
Eldest surviving son of Donal Mór and Máire O'Connell, Derrynane. Married in 1758. No children. Known as Hunting Cap because he wore a cap to avoid paying the tax on a conventional gentleman's hat. He was a landowner, grazier, merchant and smuggler.

Maurice Daniel O'CONNELL (son) (1803–1853)
O'Connell's eldest child. Called to the bar 1827. 1831–2 MP for Clare; 1832–7, 1838–53 for Tralee. In 1832 he married Mary Frances Scott. Director of National Bank.

Maurice Morgan O'CONNELL
(brother) (1776–1797)
O'Connell's eldest brother.
Lieutenant in Count Walshe de
Serranti's regiment in British army
as part of 'Pitt's Irish Brigade'. He
died on active service in San
Domingo.

Morgan O'CONNELL (father) (1739–
1809)
O'Connell's father.

Morgan O'CONNELL (son) (1804–
1885)
O'Connell's second son. In June
1819 he purchased a commission in
the Irish South American Legion
under Devereux. He served in the
Austrian army and returned to
Ireland c. 1830. In 1840 he married
Kate Balfe. 1832–40 MP for Meath.
1840–6 assistant registrar of deeds;
1846–69 registrar. He fought one
duel and was challenged to another
on his father's behalf.

Morgan John O'CONNELL (1811–
1875)
Eldest son of O'Connell's brother
John. MP for co. Kerry 1835–52.
In 1865 he married Mary Anne,
daughter of Charles Bianconi.

Peter O'CONNELL (d. 1824)
From Clare. A considerable scholar
in literary Irish and a master of the
spoken tongue.

Rickard (Rick) O'CONNELL (d.
1832)
Married Betsey Tuohy of Tralee in
1801. Brother of Mary O'Connell.
Lieutenant, 89th Regiment, 1796–
1804. Adjutant, Kerry Militia.

Thomas O'CONNELL (c. 1735–1785)
Physician, Tralee. Third cousin of
O'Connell. They had a common
ancestor in Geoffrey O'Connell (c.
1569–1635).

Fergus Edward O'CONNOR (1794–
1855)
Chartist leader. Son of Roger
O'Connor, a United Irishman. MP

for co. Cork 1832–5, for
Nottingham borough 1847–52. He
founded the central committee of
radical unions in 1836, and the
London Democratic Association in
1837. Established the *Northern
Star*, a weekly radical paper in
1837. In 1840 he was found guilty
of seditious libel and imprisoned
for eighteen months. In 1846 he
inaugurated the 'Chartist Co-
operative Land Company', and in
1847 a journal called *The Labourer*.

Hugh O'CONNOR
Merchant, Mountjoy Square,
Dublin.

Denis O'CONOR (1794–1847)
O'Conor Don from 1831. MP for
co. Roscommon 1831–47. A lord
of the treasury 1846–7.

Owen O'CONOR (1763–1831)
Succeeded to the title of The
O'Conor Don in 1820. 1830–1 MP
for co. Roscommon.

Eugene O'CURRY (1796–1862)
A pioneering Gaelic scholar of
distinction. In 1849 and 1855 he
examined the Irish manuscripts in
the British Museum and wrote the
catalogue. He became the first
professor of Irish history and
archaeology in the Catholic
University of Ireland.

Laurence O'DONNELL (d. 1855)
Bishop of Galway 1844–55.

William O'DONNELL
Retired merchant. The Cottage,
Carrick-on-Suir, co. Tipperary.

Andrew Carew O'DWYER (1800–
1877)
MP for Drogheda 1832–5, reelected
1835 but unseated on petition. 1837
appointed filacer of the exchequer.

Richard More O'FERRALL (1797–
1880)
MP for co. Kildare 1830–47, 1859–
65; for co. Longford 1851–2. A lord
of the treasury 1835–9. Secretary of
the admiralty 1839–41. A secretary

of the treasury in 1841. Governor of Malta 1847–51.

Nicholas Purcell O'GORMAN (1778–1857)
Imprisoned in Ennis in 1798. Called to the bar 1803. Member of the Catholic Board. c. 1815 became secretary to the Catholics of Ireland and was the first secretary of the Catholic Association. In 1834 appointed assistant barrister.

Richard O'GORMAN (d. 1867)
Junior partner in his uncle's woollen business.

Thomas O'HAGAN (1812–1885)
Called to the Irish bar 1836. Edited the *Newry Examiner* 1836–40. He defended Gavan Duffy in 1842 and 1843–4. Assistant barrister of co. Longford 1847–57, of co. Dublin 1857–9, 1859 third serjeant, 1861 solicitor-general, 1862 attorney-general, 1863 MP for Tralee, 1865 judge of the court of common pleas in Ireland. Lord chancellor of Ireland 1868–74. Created Baron O'Hagan in 1870.

James O'HEA (1809–1882)
Called to the Irish bar 1838. One of the defending counsel in state trial of 1844. Crown prosecutor in co. Limerick 1860–82 and the county and city of Cork 1849–82.

Patrick O'HIGGINS (d. 1854)
Merchant in Dublin. Became known as 'the Irish Chartist'.

Rev. William O'HIGGINS (1793–1853)
Bishop of Ardagh and Clonmacnoise 1829–53. An especially active supporter of Repeal.

Arthur (Art) O'LEARY
Served in the Austrian Army. O'Leary challenged and struck Mr Morris, a rich Protestant, for offering him only £5 for a famous race mare (no Papist was allowed by law to own a horse of greater value than £5). Morris refused to fight a Papist and got O'Leary outlawed. O'Leary was shot by soldiers on 4 May 1773.

Eileen Dubh O'LEARY (*née* O'Connell)
'Dark Eileen', sister of Hunting Cap. She married Mr O'Connor of Fines at fourteen. He died within six months. She married Arthur O'Leary, later outlawed, in 1768.

James O'LEARY
Woollen merchant and shopkeeper, Killarney.

Colman Michael O'LOGHLEN (1819–1877)
Second baronet. Called to the bar 1840. 1856–9 chairman of Carlow quarter sessions. 1859–61 chairman of Mayo quarter sessions. 1863–77 MP for Clare. 1865 third serjeant-at-law for Ireland, 1866 second serjeant-at-law for Ireland. 1868–70 judge advocate general. Subsequently emigrated to Australia.

Michael O'LOGHLEN (1789–1842)
Called to the bar in 1811. K.C. in 1830. MP for Dungarvan 1835–7. Solicitor-general Oct. 1834–Jan. 1835, April-Sept. 1835. Attorney-general Aug. 1835–Nov. 1836. Baron of the court of exchequer Nov. 1836–Jan. 1837. Master of the rolls 1837–42. Created a baronet in 1838. He was the first Catholic law officer and the first Catholic judge since the reign of James II.

Margaret O'MARA (d. 1874)
Daughter of Thomas O'Mara and Margaret (née Callan) formerly Mrs T. Fitz-Simon. Half sister of Christopher Fitz-Simon. In 1845 she married James Netterville Blake M.D. (d. 1847). In 1854 she married William Bowman.

Dowell O'REILLY (1795–1855)
Called to the bar about 1824.

Attorney-general of Jamaica 1831–55.

Rev. Terence O'SHAUGHNESSY (1763–1848)
Parish priest of Ennis and Dean of Killaloe, 1820–48.

Lord OXMANTOWN (William Parsons) (1800–1867)
1821–35 MP for King's co. A moderate whig – he voted for Catholic Emancipation and the Reform Bill. He was styled Lord Oxmantown 1807–41; in 1841 he became the Earl of Rosse. He was lord lieutenant of King's county 1831–67 and a representative peer from Ireland 1845–67.

Wray PALLISER (1789–1862)
Kilcomragh Lodge, near Kilmacthomas, co. Waterford. Lieutenant-colonel in the Waterford Malitia, 1810–62. Son of John Palliser, Derrylusken, co. Tipperary.

Henry John (Temple), third viscount PALMERSTON (1784–1865)
A lord of the admiralty 1807–9. Secretary at war 1809–28. Secretary for foreign affairs 1830–4, 1835–41, 1846–51. Home secretary 1852–5. Prime minister 1855–8, 1859–65.

Sir Henry PARNELL (1776–1842)
He held a number of ministerial appointments. He voted against the Union and consistently supported claims for Catholic Emancipation. He had a high reputation as a political economist and writer on finance. In 1812 he succeeded to the baronetcy, and was created Baron Congleton in 1841.

Rev. Robert PARSONS S.J. (1546–1610)
The aim of his public life was to restore England, by persuasion or force, to the Roman church. He was a zealous promoter of the Spanish invasion of England. In 1581–2 he founded a grammar school for English boys at Eu. He later established a similar one on a more solid basis at St Omer with an annual pension from King Philip of Spain in 1592–3. He also established St Alban's and St Gregory's in Spain.

Joseph PEASE (1772–1846)
A rich Yorkshire woollen merchant. A Quaker who strongly supported the anti-slavery cause.

Sir Robert PEEL (1788–1850)
1812–18 chief secretary for Ireland; 1822–7 home secretary. In April 1827 he resigned from the cabinet because he was opposed to Canning on Catholic Emancipation. 1828–30 home secretary again, he now agreed on the need for Catholic Emancipation, and prepared the three bills relating to it. 1834–5, 1841–6, prime minister.

Richard PENNEFATHER (1773–1859)
Chief baron of the Irish exchequer 1821–59.

Spencer PERCEVAL (1762–1812)
He successively held the posts of solicitor to the board of ordnance and solicitor general to the queen, solicitor general, attorney general. Under Pitt he insisted on his freedom to oppose Catholic Emancipation. In 1807 he became the chancellor of the exchequer. 1809–12 prime minister. In May 1812 he was assassinated.

Louis PERRIN (1782–1864)
Called to the Irish bar 1806. MP for Dublin city May-Aug. 1831, for co. Monaghan 1832–5, for Cashel Jan.-Aug. 1835. Third serjeant-at-law 1832–5; first serjeant Feb.-April 1835. Attorney-general April-Aug. 1835. Justice of the King's Bench 1835–60.

David Richard PIGOT (1797–1873)
Called to the bar in 1826, created
K.C. in 1835. MP for Clonmel
1839–46. Solicitor-general 1839–40.
Attorney-general 1840–1. Chief
baron of the exchequer 1846–73.

William PITT (1759–1806)
Prime minister 1783–1801, 1804–6.
During the 1790s he supported
Catholic relief bills. When he
brought forward the proposals for
Union he held out the prospect that
the recognition of Catholic claims
would follow. In 1801 he resigned
because of the king's opposition to
measures for Catholic relief.

William Conyngham PLUNKET
(1764–1854)
Attorney-general 1805–7, 1822–7;
chief justice of the common pleas,
1827–30; created Baron Plunket in
1827; lord chancellor of Ireland
1830–4, 1835–41. He opposed the
Union as an Irish MP. In 1807 he
entered the English House of
Commons briefly, then again in
1812. He was in favour of Catholic
Emancipation but supported the
bill for suppression of the Catholic
Association, 1825.

Hon. Frederick George Brabazon
PONSONBY (1815–1895)
Called to the bar in 1840. Succeeded
in 1880 as sixth earl of
Bessborough. A liberal in politics.
A member of the commission to
inquire into the land system in
Ireland 1880–1 (known as the
Bessborough commission).

George PONSONBY (1755–1817)
MP in Ireland from 1776 until the
Union, in England 1801–17. He
supported the Catholic claims. He
acted as counsel for Henry Sheares
and Oliver Band and led the
opposition to the Union in the Irish
House of Commons. 1806–7 lord
chancellor of Ireland. 1808–17 the
official leader of the opposition.

John William PONSONBY, fourth earl
of Bessborough (1781–1847)
Lord Duncannon until 1844.
Member of Commons 1805–34
almost continuously. 1834 Baron
Duncannon of Bessborough. In
1844 succeeded to earldom of
Bessborough. 1831–4, 1835–9 first
commissioner of woods and forest;
1834–5 home office; 1846–7 lord
lieutenant of Ireland. Supporter of
Catholic Emancipation and
parliamentary reform. He
acted as chief whip of the whig
party.

William Francis Spencer PONSONBY
(1787–1855)
Son of the third earl of
Bessborough. He was married to
Lady Barbara Ashley-Cooper.

Caleb POWELL J.P. (1793–1881)
Called to the Irish bar 1817. MP for
co.Limerick 1841–7. Sheriff of
Limerick in 1858.

John PRIMROSE (d. 1840)
From Hillgrove, Cahirciveen, co.
Kerry. Married Honoria
O'Connell, cousin of O'Connell.

John PRIMROSE jr J.P. (c. 1796–1865)
Cousin of O'Connell and land
agent to him from 1822. He
married Rickarda Connor,
daughter of James Connor, niece of
Mary O'Connell, in 1830.

Francis Aldborough PRITTIE (1779–
1853)
1801 MP for Carlow; 1806–18,
1819–31 for co. Tipperary.

Peter PURCELL (d. 1846)
Founded the *Monitor*, a Dublin
liberal journal in 1838.

Thomas Rodney PURDON
Governor of the Richmond
Bridewell, South Circular Road,
Dublin at the time of O'Connell's
imprisonment in 1844.

Michael QUIN (1796–1843)
Editor of *Monthly Review* 1825–
32, *Catholic Journal* 1828–9, first

editor of *Dublin Review* 1836.
Barrister.

Alexander RAPHAEL (1775–1850)
English merchant born in India.
Converted to Roman Catholicism
from Judaism. Sheriff of London in
1834. He was elected MP for
Carlow 1835, but was unseated on
petition. MP for St Albans 1847–
50. He opposed Jewish
emancipation.

Thomas Mathew RAY (1801–1881)
Secretary of the National Trades
Political Union in Dublin.
Secretary of the Precursor Society
1838–40. Secretary of the Repeal
Association from April 1840. Tried
and sentenced with O'Connell in
1844 state trials. Assistant registrar
of deeds in Ireland 1865–80.

Thomas Nicholas REDINGTON
(1815–62)
MP for Dundalk 1837–46. Under-
secretary for Ireland 1846–52.
Later knighted.

Thomas Devin REILLY (1824–1854)
Wrote for the *Nation* and *United
Irishman*. He escaped to New York
in 1848 and contributed to Irish-
American newspapers. He edited
the *Democratic Review* and later
the *Washington Union*.

John REYNOLDS (1794–1868)
Secretary in Ireland of National
Bank 1834–41. Appointed
managing director of the Land
Investment Co. of Ireland in 1841.
MP for Dublin city 1847–52. Lord
mayor of Dublin 1850.

Thomas REYNOLDS
Merchant. Vice-president of the
National Trades Political Union.

Dominick RICE (1785–1864)
Of Bushmount, co. Kerry.

Stephen Henry RICE
Of Day Place, Tralee. Called to the
Irish bar in 1792.

John RICHARDS (1790–1872)
K.C. in 1830. Solicitor-general

1835–6. Attorney-general Nov.
1836–Feb. 1837. Baron of the
exchequer 1837–49.

Charles (Lennox) fourth Duke of
RICHMOND (1764–1819)
1790–1806 MP for Sussex; lord
lieutenant of Ireland 1807–13;
governor general of British North
America 1818–19.

David ROCHE (1791–1865)
MP for Limerick city 1832–44.
Created a baronet in 1838. Agent
to Edward Bouchier Hartapp.

James ROCHE (1770–1853)
A wine merchant in Bordeaux, who
favoured the revolutionary
movement originally. In 1793 he
was arrested as a British subject
and imprisoned for six months. In
1800 he established a bank in Cork
with his brother Stephen. It
flourished till 1819. He spent the
next seven years in London as
parliamentary and commercial
agent for Youghal and the counties
of Cork and Limerick. From 1833
he was local director of the bank of
Ireland in Cork.

David C. ROOSE (d. 1836)
Stockbroker and state lottery office
keeper. Knighted in 1830.

David Robert ROSS J.P., D.L. (1797–
1851)
High sheriff of co. Down in 1837.
MP for Belfast 1842–7. Lieutenant
governor of Tobago in 1851.

Werner William (Westenra) second
baron ROSSMORE (1765–1842)
1800–1 MP for co. Monaghan;
created Baron Rossmore in Ireland
in 1801, Baron Rossmore of
Monaghan (UK) in 1838; lord
lieutenant of co. Monaghan 1831
until his death.

Lord John RUSSELL (1792–1868)
Home secretary 1835–9; colonial
secretary 1839–41; prime minister
1846–52, 1865–6. Created Earl
Russell in 1861.

Thomas RUSSELL (1767–1803)
A United Irishman. A soldier. In
gaol 1796–9. In exile in Scotland
1799–1802. When freed, he went to
Europe. In 1803 he returned to
Ireland and was involved in
Emmet's plans. He was arrested in
September 1803 and executed in
October.

William Henry RUSSELL (1820–1907)
Reporter in Ireland for the *Times*
during part of the Repeal
campaign. Celebrated Crimean
war correspondent. Knighted in
1895.

Edward Southwell RUTHVEN (1772–
1836)
He assumed the name Ruthven,
instead of Trotter, in 1800. MP for
Downpatrick 1806–7, 1830–2; for
Dublin City 1832–6 when he was
unseated on petition, after his
death.

William SAURIN (1757?–1839)
In 1796 the Irish bar elected him
captain commandant of their corps
of yeomanry. In 1798 he was
granted a patent of precedence
after the prime serjeant, attorney
general and solicitor general. He
served the government in some of
the trials arising out of the
rebellion. His opposition to the
Union was based on professional
interest and hostility to the Roman
Catholics. From 1807–22 he was
attorney general for Ireland and at
the centre of opposition to the
Catholic claims. In 1828 he was an
active promoter of the formation
of the Brunswick Club.

Sir Charles SAXTON, second baronet
(1773–1838)
Under secretary for Ireland 1808–
12. 1812–18 MP for Cashel.

Sir James SCARLETT (1769–1844)
Knighted in 1827. Attorney general
1827–Jan. 1828, 1829–30, chief
baron of the exchequer 1834–44.

He was created Baron Abinger in
1835.

Joshua SCHOLEFIELD (1775–1844)
Radical MP for Birmingham 1832–
44. Banker, merchant and
manufacturer. Vice president of the
Political Union during the reform
agitation 1830–2. Director of the
National Provincial Bank of
England and the London Joint-
Stock Bank.

Bindon SCOTT
Cahircon, Kildysert, co. Clare.
Married Frances Percy in 1810.
Their daughter Mary married
O'Connell's son, Maurice, in 1832.

Sir Walter SCOTT (1771–1832)
Scottish poet, novelist, historian,
antiquarian, editor and
biographer. His works include *The
Lay of the Last Minstrel,
Marmion, The Lady of the Lake,*
the *Waverley* novels, *The Bride of
Lammermoor, Ivanhoe* and the *Life
of Napoleon.* In 1805 he became a
secret partner in the Bardu Press
with James and John Ballantyne.
This company failed in 1825,
leaving him enormously in debt.

William SCOTT
Sheriff of Dublin in 1830.

Denys SCULLY (1773–1830)
Barrister. In 1803 he published a
pamphlet against the Union – 'An
Irish Catholic's Advice to his
Brethren, how to estimate their
Present Situation, and repel French
Invasion, Civil Wars and Slavery'.
In 1812 his *Statement on the Penal
Laws* appeared. It resulted in the
prosecution of the printer, Hugh
Fitzpatrick.

Alice SEGERSON (*née* O'Connell)
One of Hunting Cap's older sisters.
Married John Segerson/Sigerson,
Ballinskelligs Manor, about 1750.

John SEGERSON (Sigerson) (d. 1825)
From Westcove, Caherdaniel, co.
Kerry.

Frederick SHAW (1799–1876)
MP for Dublin city 1830–2; for
Dublin University 1832–48.
Recorder of Dundalk 1826–8.
Recorder of Dublin 1828–76.
Succeeded his brother as third
baronet in 1869.

John SHEARES (1766–1798) and
Henry SHEARES (1753–1798)
They became imbued with the
political principles of the
Revolution when visiting France in
1792. Both were lawyers. The
younger brother John governed
their political actions. In 1798 they
were elected to the directory of the
United Irishmen. After the 1798
uprising, they were charged with
high treason and publicly executed.

Rev. John SHEEHAN (d. 1854)
Parish priest, St Patrick's,
Waterford 1828–54.

Remigius SHEEHAN (d. 1847)
Cork attorney. Converted from
Catholicism to Church of Ireland.
1824 became editor of the *Dublin
Evening Mail*. Proprietor of the
Star of Brunswick which he
established about 1828 to combat
the Emancipation movement.
Made a freeman of the city of
Dublin in 1828.

Richard Lalor SHEIL (1791–1851)
Barrister and dramatist. Favoured
the veto but joined O'Connell in
forming the Catholic Association.
In 1827 he was indicted for
seditious libel but a change of prime
minister led to the dropping of the
prosecution. In 1830 admitted to
the inner bar. In 1831 MP for
Milborne Port, 1831–2 co. Louth,
1832–41 co. Tipperary, 1841–51
Dungarvan. He reluctantly took
the pledge to support Repeal. In
1838–9 Commissioner of
Greenwich Hospital; 1839–41 vice-
president of board of trade; 1841
judge advocate-general. At the

trials of the 'traversers' in 1844 he
acted for John O'Connell. From
1846–50 master of the mint. 1850–
1 minister at the court of Tuscany.

Dr Edward SHERIDAN
Dominick Street and 39 Usher's
Quay.

Richard Brinsley SHERIDAN (1751–
1816)
Statesman and dramatist. He
opposed the war with America in
1782. 1782 under-secretary for
foreign affairs. 1783 secretary to
the treasury. He was conspicuous
in the proceedings against Warren
Hastings. He opposed the Union
between Great Britain and Ireland.

John (Talbot) earl of SHREWSBURY,
also earl of Waterford (1791–1852)
Admitted to take his seat in the
House of Lords under the Roman
Catholic Relief Act in 1829. 1841
Commissioner for inquiring into
the best mode of promoting the
Fine Arts in the UK. Hon. Member
of the Pontifical Academy of St
Luke's, Rome.

Mrs Sarah SIDDONS (1755–1831)
Very highly regarded as an actress
after her first few years. Married in
1773. Had five children.

Henry Addington, first viscount
SIDMOUTH (1757–1844)
In favour of the Union. Opposed
Catholic Emancipation. From
1789–1801 speaker of the House of
Commons; 1801–4 first lord of the
treasury and chancellor of the
exchequer; president of the council
several times; 1806–9 lord privy
council; 1812–21 secretary of the
home department.

Major Henry Charles SIRR (1764–
1841)
1778–91 in army. From 1791
onwards he was a wine merchant.
In 1796 on the formation of the
yeomanry in Dublin he was
appointed town-major or head of

police. He retired in 1826. In 1808
he was appointed a police
magistrate for the city of Dublin.

Rev. Michael SLATTERY (1785–1857)
Professor of philosophy at Carlow
College, 1809–15. Parish priest of
Cashel 1815–33. President of St
Patrick's College, Maynooth 1833–
4. Archbishop of Cashel 1834–57.

Edmond SMITHWICK (1800–1876)
Brewer. Alderman of Kilkenny
1843, mayor of Kilkenny 1844,
1864, 1865.

Charles SMYTH (1715?–1762)
Apothecary. Irish county
historian – published histories of
counties Down, Waterford, Cork
and Kerry.

Thomas SPRING-RICE (1790–1866)
MP 1820–39; under-secretary to the
home office 1827–8; secretary to
the treasury 1830–4; chancellor of
the exchequer 1835–9; created
Baron Monteagle in 1839.

Charles STANHOPE, third earl (1753–
1816)
Politician and man of science. He
supported the French Revolution
and opposed the Union in 1800.

Sir Edward STANLEY (d.c. 1852)
Deputy barrack master to the city
of Dublin, sheriff's peer. Wine and
provision supplier to Dublin
Castle.

Edward George Geoffrey Smith
STANLEY (1799–1869)
Lord Stanley from 1834, succeeded
as fourteenth earl of Derby in 1851.
MP from 1822. Under-secretary for
the colonies 1827–8; chief secretary
for Ireland 1830–3, secretary of
state for the colonies 1833–4, 1841–
5; prime minister 1852, 1858–9,
1866–8.

Rev. Gregory STAPYLTON D.D.
(1748–1802)
He was Procurator of the English
college at Douai for twelve years.
In 1787 he was appointed President

of the English College at St Omer.
For a time he and his students were
imprisoned. He later converted a
school at Old Hall Green in
Hertfordshire into a Catholic
college. In 1800 he accompanied
Rev. John Nassau to Rome on an
important secret mission, and was
raised to the episcopate and made
vicar apostolic of the Midland
district.

Michael STAUNTON (1788–1870)
Editor of *Freeman's Journal* 1813–
24; proprietor of the *Dublin
Evening Herald* 1821–3; editor and
proprietor of the *Morning Register*
1824–43; lord mayor of Dublin
1847.

Thomas STEELE (1788–1848)
Raised money for and joined revolt
against Ferdinand VII of Spain
1823–4. Enthusiastic supporter and
admirer of O'Connell. His position
as a Protestant landlord increased
his value to O'Connell. He was
appointed 'head pacificator' by
O'Connell.

William STOKES (1804–1878)
Physician. In 1837 he published a
treatise on *Diseases of the Chest*
and in 1854 *Diseases of the Heart
and Aorta*. In 1861 he was elected
FRS and appointed physician in-
ordinary to Queen Victoria. 1874
President RIA.

Henry Villiers STUART (1803–1874)
1826–30 MP for co. Waterford;
1830–1 for Banbury. In 1839 he was
created Baron Stuart de Decies of
Dromana.

Thomas (Howard) earl of SUFFOLK
(1776–1851)
1802–6 MP for Arundel. Colonel of
Wilts. Regiment of the Militia. He
succeeded to the earldom in 1820.

Sir Edward Burtenshaw SUGDEN
(1781–1875)
Solicitor-general of England 1829–
30; lord chancellor for Ireland Dec.

1834–April 1835, 1841–6; lord chancellor of England 1852. In 1852 created Baron St Leonards. Author of legal textbooks.

James SUGRUE
Cousin and friend of O'Connell, for whom he acted as informal financial agent before 1830.

Richard SULLIVAN (c. 1795–1855)
Merchant at Kilkenny, engaged in brewing, malting and milling. MP for Kilkenny city 1832–6. Resigned his seat in favour of O'Connell. Mayor of Kilkenny 1837–8.

Napper TANDY (1740–1803)
He was elected as the first secretary of the United Irish society in late 1791. In 1792 he tried to revive the Volunteer movement. In 1793 he left Ireland before his trial related to a pamphlet he wrote called 'Common Sense'. In 1799 he was returned to England and convicted for the part he played in the invasion of Rutland Island.

Arthur THISTLEWOOD (1770–1820)
He planned a number of risings and assassinations. His final plan, which was to be launched from a loft in Cato St, was to assassinate cabinet ministers, attack Coutt's or Child's Bank, set fire to public buildings and seize the Tower and Mansion House where a provisional government was to be set up. After its failure Thistlewood was hanged.

Sir John Courtenay THROCKMORTON (1753–1819)
Fifth baronet; member of the English Catholic Board from 1808.

Theobald Wolfe TONE (1763–1798)
In 1792 he became assistant secretary to the general committee of Catholics. Before ending its existence the Catholic convention voted him £1500 and a gold medal as thanks. Founder of the United Irish Society. In 1798 he was captured with a French expedition to Ireland. He cut his throat the night before he was to be executed.

Dominic TRANT (d. 1790)
K.C. Member for Dingle in the Irish parliament.

William Le Poer TRENCH (1771–1846)
Third son of the first earl of Clancarty. Member of the board of customs (Ire.).

John Thomas (Barnewall), baron TRIMLESTON (1773–1839)
He succeeded in 1813.

Rev. John Thomas TROY D.D. (1739–1823)
1776–84 Catholic bishop of Ossory. From 1784 archbishop of Dublin. He was on terms of friendly cooperation with Dublin Castle. He believed that Catholic Emancipation would never be granted by the Irish Parliament so supported the proposal for Union in 1799.

John Ormsby VANDELEUR (c. 1766–1828)
From Kilrush, co. Clare. Commissioner of customs for Ireland 1799–1801, 1809–10, 1814–22.

Nicholas Aylward VIGORS (1785–1840)
MP for Carlow borough 1832–4, for co. Carlow 1837–40. Protestant landowner. Army officer.

Thomas WALLACE K.C. (born c. 1766)
Called to the Irish bar 1798. MP for Yarmouth 1826–30; Drogheda 1831–2; co. Carlow 1832–5.

Henry WARBURTON (1784–1858)
Radical politician. MP for Bridport 1826–41, for Kendal 1843–7.

Richard Colley (Marquess) WELLESLEY (1760–1842)
1797–1805 governor general of India. 1820–8 lord lieutenant of Ireland. He was in favour of

676

removing the disabilities of Catholics and resigned when Wellington (his brother) became prime minister pledged to the Protestant Ascendancy. From 1832–4 again lord lieutenant of Ireland.

William WELLESLEY-POLE (1763–1845)
Chief secretary for Ireland 1809–12; created Baron Maryborough in UK in 1821; succeeded as third earl of Mornington in peerage of Ireland in 1842. He was Perceval's chief supporter in his resistance to the concession of the Catholic claims, but in May 1812 he formally acquiesced in his brother's (Marquess Wellesley) more liberal views on the Catholic question.

Arthur (Wellesley) duke of WELLINGTON (1769–1852)
Chief secretary for Ireland 1807–9. Commander-in-chief of the army 1809–27. Prime minister 1828–30, Nov.–Dec. 1834. Foreign secretary Dec. 1834–April 1835. 1842 reappointed commander-in-chief by patent for life.

Richard WHATELY (1787–1863)
He became principal of St Alban Hall, Oxford in 1825. 1829–31 professor of political economy. In 1831 he was apppointed archbishop of Dublin, and took his seat in the House of Lords in 1833. Head of the commission to administer the new system of 'united national education' 1831–53. He presided over the royal commission on the condition of the Irish poor 1833–6.

WILLIAM IV (1765–1837)
In 1779 he joined the navy. In 1789 he was created Earl of Munster and Duke of Clarence and St Andrew's. In 1811 he became admiral of the fleet, in 1827 lord high admiral. In 1830 he succeeded as William IV.

Mary WOLLSTONECRAFT (1759–1797)
Writer and feminist. Married William Godwin.

Alexander WOOD
Irish journalist for the *Traveller* in London.

Sir Matthew WOOD (1768–1843)
In 1807 he became alderman of the ward of Cripplegate Without and in 1809 was appointed sheriff of London and Middlesex. Lord mayor 1815–17. 1817–43 MP for city of London. A consistent radical and supporter of all the whig ministries. He was one of the chief friends and advisers of Queen Caroline.

William WOODLOCK (b. 1801)
Attorney in Dublin, employed by O'Connell.

Stephen WOULFE (1787–1840)
1830 crown counsel for Munster; May 1835 third serjeant; 1835–8 MP for Cashel; 1836 solicitor general for Ireland; 1837 attorney general for Ireland; 1838 chief baron of Irish exchequer, first Catholic so appointed.

Sir Thomas WYSE (1791–1862)
Chairman of the co. Waterford election committee in 1826. In 1829 he recommended dissolution of the Catholic Association and published *A Historical Sketch of the Catholic Association*. At the 1830 election he withdrew from co. Waterford in favour of O'Connell but he was elected for co. Tipperary. He retired from Tipperary in 1832 and was MP for Waterford city from 1835 to 1847. Lord of the treasury 1839–41. He favoured a subordinate parliament for Ireland but declined to join the Repeal Association. In 1847 he was defeated at Waterford because of Young Ireland opposition. 1846–9 Secretary for board of control for

India. 1849 British minister at
Athens.

John Ashton YATES (1782–1863)
MP for co. Carlow 1837–41.

Frederick Augustus, duke of YORK
and Albany (1763–1827)
Second son of George III and close
companion of George IV.

Apart from using such conventional
sources as the *Dictionary of National
Biography*, the *Handbook of British
Chronology*, Dod's *Parliamentary
Companion*, and *The Complete
Peerage of England, Scotland,
Ireland, Great Britain and the United
Kingdom* (ed. Hon. Vicary Gibbs,
London, 1910), I have drawn largely
on the annotations in M. R.
O'Connell, ed., *Correspondence*, as
well as those in Macintyre, *The
Liberator*, and *Parliamentary Results
in Ireland*, 1801–1922 (ed. B. M.
Walker, Dublin, 1978), in compiling
these Notes.

Index

Details of O'Connell's relationships are indexed under the names of the people involved, e.g. his relationship with his eldest son, Maurice, is indexed under O'Connell, Maurice.
Noblemen appear under their titles.
Titles of books are listed under the name of the author.
The method of alphabetical arrangement is letter-by-letter.
Sub-headings are arranged in chronological order where possible.

biographical note, 677; attitude to
Emancipation, 217, 230, 247, 257, 264;
O'Connell's opinion of, 233, 237, 247, 255,
261, 330, 416; as prime minister, 247, 248,
255, 257, 259, 264, 271; franked letter from
O'Connell to, 256; opinion of Lord
Anglesey, 259; attitude to Irish legislation,
437, 440; alarmist reaction to Repeal, 518,
520
Westmeath, co., election in 1826, 225
Westmoreland, 10th earl (John Fane), 119
Whateley, Richard, archbishop of Dublin
(Church of Ireland), 448, 677
White, Dr, 430
Whiteboys, 189, 190, 206
William III, statue of, 488
William IV, king of Great Britain and Ireland,
398; inimical to O'Connell, 388, 391, 404;
death, 440, 452
William, 4th duke of Clarence, later William
IV, 232, 321, 677
Wollstonecraft, Mary, 82, 677; *A Vindication
of the Rights of Women*, 42
Wolverhampton Political Union, 346
Wood, Alexander, 172, 677
Wood, Alderman Matthew, 172, 677
Woodlock, William, 455, 677
Woulfe, Stephen, 114, 677
Wyse, Thomas, 114; biographical note, 677–8;
his summation of Catholic politics 1821–2,

181; and the election in Waterford 1826, 223–
4, 226; plan for Liberal clubs, 242, 243, 260;
on changes in the nature of the Catholic
Association, 243–5; *Political Catechism*,
246–7; on situation at Ballybay 1828, 258;
believed Protestant support for
Emancipation important, 263; election in
Waterford 1830, 319; relationship with
O'Connell, 319, 400, 531–2; motion on state
trials, 531–2; mentioned in O'Connell's
dying delirium, 599

Yates, John Ashton, 477, 480, 678
Yeomanry, Irish, 345
York, 12th duke (Frederick Augustus), 678;
against Catholic Emancipation, 219, 232
Young Ireland, 3, 557, 561, 580, 587;
O'Connell's opinion of, 584; criticisms of
O'Connell, 308, 574; different philosophical
approach from O'Connell, 310, 506, 547,
549; views on use of force, 562–3, 573, 577;
strengthened O'Connell 1842–3, 506, 508;
early use of the term, 551; and academical
institutions (Ireland) bill, 543, 550–1; against
alliance with whigs, 559, 571; and Smith
O'Brien's imprisonment, 569, 572;
Catholic's clergy attitude to, 572–3, 577–8;
and slavery, 302; secession from Repeal
Association, 577–8; attempted reconciliation
with O'Connell, 585–8, 589–90